ARMAGEDDON

The Triumph of Universal Order

An Epic Poem on The War on Terror and
of Holy-War Crusaders

First published by O Books, 2010

O Books is an imprint of John Hunt Publishing Ltd., The Bothy, Deershot Lodge, Park Lane, Ropley,
Hants, SO24 0BE, UK
office1@o-books.net
www.o-books.net

Distribution in:

UK and Europe
Orca Book Services
orders@orcabookservices.co.uk
Tel: 01202 665432 Fax: 01202 666219
Int. code (44)

USA and Canada
NBN
custserv@nbnbooks.com
Tel: 1 800 462 6420 Fax: 1 800 338 4550

Australia and New Zealand
Brumby Books
sales@brumbybooks.com.au
Tel: 61 3 9761 5535 Fax: 61 3 9761 7095

Far East (offices in Singapore, Thailand,
Hong Kong, Taiwan)
Pansing Distribution Pte Ltd
kemal@pansing.com
Tel: 65 6319 9939 Fax: 65 6462 5761

South Africa
Stephan Phillips (pty) Ltd
Email: orders@stephanphillips.com
Tel: 27 21 4489839 Telefax: 27 21 4479879

Text copyright Nicholas Hagger 2009

Design: Stuart Davies

ISBN: 978 1 84694 352 2

A CIP catalogue record for this book is available
from the British Library.

Printed in the UK by CPI Antony Rowe, Chippenham, Wiltshire

O Books operates a distinctive and ethical publishing philosophy in
all areas of its business, from its global network of authors to
production and worldwide distribution.

ARMAGEDDON

The Triumph of Universal Order

An Epic Poem on The War on Terror and
of Holy-War Crusaders

by

Nicholas Hagger

BOOKS

Winchester, UK
Washington, USA

*"Tu regere imperio populos, Romane, memento
(Hae tibi erunt artes)."*
"Remember, Roman, that it is yours to lead other people. It is your special gift."

Virgil, *Aeneid*, vi. 851

"An nescis, mi fili, quantilla prudentia regitur orbis?"
"Dost thou not know, my son, with how little wisdom the world is governed?"

Count Oxenstierna, 'Letter to his son', 1648

"Atque ubi colitudinum faciunt pacem appellant."
"They create a desolation and call it 'peace'."

Calgacus, Caledonian leader of the Britons in Tacitus, *Agricola*

"A man that looks on glass
On it may stay his eye
Or if he pleaseth, through it pass
And then the Heav'n espy."

George Herbert

CONTENTS

USEFUL SOURCES

Al-Qaeda's Nuclear-Suitcase Bombs

"I would say that acquiring [nuclear] weapons for the defence of Muslims is a religious duty. To seek to possess the weapons that could counter those of the infidels is a religious duty. If I have indeed acquired these weapons, then this is an obligation I carried out and I thank God for enabling us to do that. And if I seek to acquire these weapons I am carrying out a duty. It would be a sin for Muslims not to try to possess the weapons that would prevent the infidels from inflicting harm on Muslims. But how we could use these weapons if we possess them is up to us."

Osama bin Laden, 22 December 1998

"With bin Laden's limitless financial resources and the economic crisis in the former Soviet Union nearly out of control, a sale of nuclear-suitcase bombs could ultimately be arranged by the Chechen Mafia. After all, General Aleksandr Ivanovich Lebed, the former security czar of Russia, acknowledged back in 1997 that several nuclear-suitcase bombs had disappeared from Russia's arsenal.

A senior Arab intelligence official asserted in early October 1998 that 'Osama bin Laden has acquired tactical nuclear weapons from the Islamic republics of Central Asia established after the collapse of the Soviet Union'. This overall assessment is shared by Russian intelligence and several Arab intelligence services based on recent evidence of bin Laden's quest for nuclear weapons. Although there is debate over the precise quantities of weapons purchased, there is no longer much doubt that bin Laden has finally succeeded in his quest for nuclear-suitcase bombs. Bin Laden's emissaries paid the Chechens $30million in cash and gave them two tons of Afghan heroin worth about $70million in Afghanistan and at least ten times that on the streets of Western Europe and the United States.

Evidence of the number of nuclear weapons purchased by the Chechens for bin Laden varies between 'a few' (Russian intelligence) to 'more than twenty' (conservative Arab intelligence services). Most of the weapons were purchased in four former Soviet states – Ukraine, Kazakhstan, Turkmenistan, and Russia. These weapons are a mix of suitcase bombs and tactical warheads/bombs. An Arab nuclear scientist, a Western-educated expert who worked for Saddam Hussein's nuclear program before he became Islamist, supervised the acquisition process for bin Laden and now runs the program for him. He is assisted by five Muslim Turkoman nuclear experts and a team of engineers and technicians, all of them Central Asian Muslims, whom they brought with them. For security reasons they condition these weapons for operational use in two clusters of facilities – one in the deep tunnels in the Khowst area and the other in the deep caves in the Qandahar area....

A single SPETSNAZ (ex-Soviet Special Forces) trooper can prepare a suitcase bomb for explosion within half an hour. It is not inconceivable that bin Laden's nuclear experts would be able to 'hot-wire' a suitcase bomb so that the coded transmission is no longer required to activate the bomb. Then only a single would-be martyr could activate it."

Yossef Bodansky,
Bin Laden, The Man who Declared War on America, 1999

"In an interview with Hamid Mir in November 2001, bin Laden was even more explicit. 'We have chemical and nuclear weapons,' he told the Pakistani editor. 'If America uses chemical or nuclear weapons against us, then we may retort with chemical or nuclear weapons.' When Mir asked the Muslim *imam* where he obtained such weapons, bin Laden said: 'Go on to the next question.' Bin Laden told Mir that it was relatively easy for al-Qaeda to obtain nuclear weapons. 'It is not difficult, not if you have contacts in Russia and with other militant groups. They are available for $10 million and $20million.' At this stage in the interview, Ayman al-Zawahiri, bin Laden's chief strategist, interjected: 'If you go to BBC reports, you will find that thirty nuclear weapons are missing from Russia's nuclear arsenal.' Al-Zawahiri added: 'We have links with Russia's underworld channels.'"

Paul L Williams, *Osama's Revenge*, 2004

"Some answers came with the arrest of Khalid Shaikh Mohammed, al-Qaeda's military operations chief, in Karachi, Pakistan, on March 2, 2003.... After days of interrogations, the terrorist chief admitted that bin Laden's goal was to create a 'nuclear hell storm' like the 1945 blast in Hiroshima that killed 140,000 Japanese. Unlike other attacks that could be planned and conducted by lower-level al-Qaeda leaders, the terrorist chief said, the chain of command for the nuclear operation answered directly to bin Laden, al-Zawahiri, and a mysterious scientist called 'Dr X'."

Paul L Williams, *Osama's Revenge*, 2004

"Bin Laden had gained control of the Afghan poppy fields and was spending millions for his nuclear project. He purchased forty-eight additional suitcase nukes from the Russian Mafia and similar devices from central Asian sources. From Simeon (Semion) Mogilevich, a Ukrainian arms dealer, bin Laden purchased more than twenty kilos of uranium-236. For one delivery of twelve to fifteen kilos, Mogilevich received a payment of seventy million dollars. The uranium had been enriched to 85 per cent – far above the standards for weapons-grade material. He purchased several bars of enriched uranium from Egyptian black-marketer Ibrahim Abd and twenty nuclear war heads from Kazakhstan, Russia, Turkmenistan, and Ukraine. Along the way he acquired enough radioactive material to plant a dirty nuke in every major American city.... The attack – the American Hiroshima – is scheduled to take place simultaneously in Chicago, Houston, Las Vegas, Los Angeles, Miami, New York, and

Washington, DC. It will occur when conditions become propitious for complete success."

Paul L Williams, *The Dunces of Doomsday*, 2006

"The next attack, according to al-Qaeda defectors and informants, will take place simultaneously at various sites throughout the country. Designated targets include New York, Boston, Philadelphia, Miami, Chicago, Washington, DC, Houston, Las Vegas, Los Angeles, and Valdez, Alaska, where the tankers are filled with oil from the Trans-Alaska pipeline....

While most of the nukes in the al-Qaeda arsenal are lightweight (less than sixty pounds) and easily portable in suitcases and backpacks, others are crude, cumbersome devices that weigh between one thousand and two thousand pounds. Such weapons would have to be shipped in cargo containers. And the containers would have to be lined with lead shielding to block the gamma rays in order to prevent radiation detection at ports of entry....

Bin Laden, according to the testimony of Khalid Sheikh Mohammed and other al-Qaeda witnesses, has announced his intention to detonate at least seven of these devices at various strategic locations throughout the country. He believes that such an event is necessary to issue forth the Day of Islam – the day when all of creation bows in fear and trembling before the throne of Allah."

Paul L Williams, *The Al Qaeda Connection*, 2005

New Caliphate

"Islamists call the unified pan-Islamic state that rules the entire Hub of Islam, and ultimately the entire Muslim world, the *Khilafah* (Caliphate). To accomplish the noble mission of restoring the *Khilafah*, the Muslim world must focus on *jihad*, the armed struggle to establish Allah's rule.... *Jihad* must be carried out until the *Khilafah* is established wherever Muslims dwell so that 'the light of Islam may shine on the whole world'.... '*Jihad* must not be abandoned until Allah alone is worshipped.'"

Yossef Bodansky,
Bin Laden, The Man who Declared War on America, 1999

"These young men, for whom God has created a path, have shifted the battle to the heart of the United States, and they have destroyed its most outstanding landmarks, its economic and military landmarks, by the grace of God. And they have done this because of our words – and we have previously incited and roused them to action – in self-defence....

So I say that, in general, our concern is that our *Ummah* unites either under the Words of the Book of God or His Prophet, and that this nation should establish the righteous Caliphate* of our *Ummah*, which has been prophesied by our Prophet in his authentic *hadith*: that the righteous Caliph will return with the permission of God. The *Ummah* is asked to unite itself in the face of this Crusaders' campaign, the strongest,

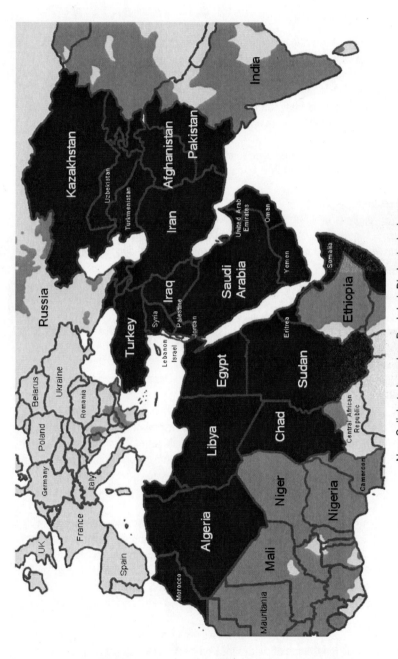

New Caliphate based on Baghdad: Bin Laden's dream

– Al-Qaeda's planned Caliphate centred on Baghdad and dwarfing Europe, as it may look within a decade of the withdrawal of US troops from Iraq

– Concentrations of Muslim populations outside the New Caliphate, 1995

(Source: CIA)

most powerful and most ferocious Crusaders' campaign to fall on the Islamic *Ummah* since the dawn of Islamic history. There have been past Crusader wars, but there have never been campaigns like this one before."

Osama bin Laden, 21 October 2001

* "'Caliph' ('successor') is a title indicating the successor to the Prophet Muhammad; an alternative title is 'Commander of the Faithful' (*amir ul-muminin*). The holder of the title claims spiritual and temporal authority over all Muslims. The title has been in abeyance since the abolition of the Ottoman Caliphate in 1924. For many radical Islamist movements, who identify the root cause of the Muslim world's problems as a decline in spirituality and religious observance, the restoration of the Caliphate is a priority."

(For asterisked text, see *Messages to the World, The Statements of Osama bin Laden*, ed Bruce Lawrence)

"The spirit of religious brotherhood among Muslims has been strengthened, which is considered a great step towards uniting the Muslims under the statement of monotheism for the purpose of establishing the rightly-guided Caliphate, God willing."

Osama bin Laden, 16 February 2003

"I am convinced that thanks to God, this Islamic nation has sufficient forces to establish the Islamic state and the Islamic Caliphate, but we must tell these forces that this is their obligation."

Osama bin Laden, July 2003

"We received your last published message sent to *Sheikh* Osama bin Laden, God save him....If our intended goal in this age is the establishment of a Caliphate in the manner of the Prophet and if we expect to establish its state predominantly – according to how it appears to us – in the heart of the Islamic world, then your efforts and sacrifices – God permitting – are a large step directly towards that goal....

It is my humble opinion that the *Jihad* in Iraq requires several incremental goals: The first stage: Expel the Americans from Iraq.

The second stage: Establish an Islamic authority or emirate, then develop it and support it until it achieves the level of a Caliphate – over as much territory as you can to spread its power in Iraq, i.e., in Sunni areas, is in order to fill the void stemming from the departure of the Americans, immediately upon their exit and before un-Islamic forces attempt to fill this void....There is no doubt that this emirate will enter into a fierce struggle with the foreign infidel forces, and those supporting them among the local forces....

The third stage: Extend the *jihad* wave to the secular countries neighbouring Iraq. The fourth stage: It may coincide with what came before: the clash with Israel, because Israel was established only to challenge any new Islamic entity....

If we look at the two short-term goals, which are removing the Americans and establishing and Islamic emirate in Iraq, or a Caliphate if possible, then, we will see that the strongest weapon which the *mujahedeen* enjoy...is popular support from the Muslim masses in Iraq, and the surrounding Muslim countries....

If we are in agreement that the victory of Islam and the establishment of a Caliphate in the manner of the Prophet will not be achieved except through *jihad* against the apostate rulers and their removal, then this goal will not be accomplished by the *mujahed* movement while it is cut off from public support....It is a duty of the *mujahed* movement to include the energies of the *Ummah*...for the sake of achieving our aims: a Caliphate along the lines of the Prophet's, with God's permission."

Letter from al-Zawahiri (bin Laden's deputy) to al-Zarqawi, 9 July 2005, released by the Office of the Director of National Intelligence on 11 October 2005

Crusaders

"This war will not only be between the people of the Land of the Two Sacred Mosques and the Americans, but it will be between the Islamic world and the Americans and their allies, because this war is a new Crusade led by America against the Islamic nations."

Osama bin Laden, November 1996

"The call to wage war against America was made because America has spear-headed the Crusade against the Islamic nation, sending tens of thousands of its troops to the Land of the Two Sacred Mosques over and above its meddling in its affairs and its politics, and its support of the oppressive, corrupt and tyrannical regime that is in control. These are the reasons behind the singling out of America as a target. And not exempt of responsibility are those Western regimes whose presence in the region offers support to the American troops there."

Osama bin Laden, 28 May 1998

"This crusade, this war on terrorism, is going to take a while. And the American people must be patient."

Bush Jr, speaking in the White House, 16 September 2001

"Bush admitted that there can only be two kinds of people: one being Bush and his followers, and any nation that doesn't follow the Bush Government, or the World Crusade, then they are guaranteed to be with the terrorists. So, what kind of terrorism is more terrifying and clearer than that?"

Osama bin Laden, 21 October 2001

"Bush has declared with his own tongue [words]: 'Crusade attack.' [Bin Laden pronounced the words in English.] So, the oddity in this is that they have said what we didn't have to say. [That this war is a Crusade.]... But, when Bush speaks, people make apologies for him, and they say that he didn't mean that this war is a Crusade, even though he himself said that it was a Crusade!"

Osama bin Laden, 21 October 2001

"The image of the world today is split in two parts, as Bush said, either you are with us, or you are with terrorism. Either you are with the Crusade, or you are with Islam. Bush's image today is of his being in front of the line, carrying his big Cross while yelling."

Osama bin Laden, 21 October 2001

"Bush has used the word Crusade. This is a Crusade declared by Bush."

Osama bin Laden, 7 November 2001

"This is the most dangerous, fiercest, and most savage Crusader war launched against Islam."

Osama bin Laden, 27 December 2001

"Let it be known to you that this war is a new Crusader campaign against the Muslim world, and it is a war that is crucial to the entire Islamic nation."

Osama bin Laden, 18 October 2005

"One warning often made and systematically ignored in the hectic days before the Iraq War was that Western military action – at that time and in that way – would put Christians in the whole Middle East at risk. They would be seen as supporters of the crusading West."

Archbishop of Canterbury, writing in
The Times, 23 December 2006

"Leave, crusaders, or we will cut your heads off."

Muslim letter to Mosul Christian, reported in
The Sunday Telegraph, 24 December 2006

Armageddon

"I am not the first to stumble across that most powerful of modern myths or to comment on it.... A full recognition of the power and nature of that myth seems to have escaped the modern sensibility, as if, even now, we are blind to the reigning ideas of our own time. The myth, in any case, is the one that you find in that strangest and most thrilling of writings, the Book of the Revelation of St John the Divine. There is a people of God, St John tells us. The people of God are under attack. The attack comes from within. It is a subversive attack mounted by the city dwellers of Babylon, who are wealthy....

These city dwellers have sunk into abominations. They have been polluted by the whore of Babylon.... The pollution is spreading to the people of God. Such is the attack from within. There is also an attack from without – conducted from afar by the forces of Satan.... But these attacks from within and without, will be violently resisted. The war of Armageddon will take place. The subversive and polluted city dwellers of Babylon will be exterminated, together with all their abominations. The Satanic forces from the mystic beyond will be fended off. The destruction will be horrifying. Yet there is nothing to fear: the destruction will last only an hour. Afterward, when the extermination is complete, the reign of Christ will be established and will endure a thousand years. And the people of God will live in purity, submissive to God. Such was the ur-myth."

Paul Berman, Terror and Liberalism, 2004

"Armageddon, according to the New Testament, the place where the kings of the Earth under demonic leadership will wage war on the forces of God.... The Palestinian city of Megiddo was probably used as a symbol because the strategic location of nearby mountains made them a famous battlefield in Palestinian history. By controlling a path that cut through the Mount Carmel ridge from the coastal plain of Sharon into Estraelon, the mountains commanded the road leading from Egypt and the Coastal Plane of Palestine to Galilee, Syria and Mesopotamia. Other biblical references suggest Jerusalem as the site of the final battle."

Encyclopaedia Britannica

"Armageddon, in Revelation XV1.16, the place where the Kings of the Earth are to be gathered together for 'the battle of that great day of God Almighty'."

The Oxford Companion to English Literature

"And the sixth angel poured out his vial upon the great river Euphrates; and the water thereof was dried up, that the way of the kings of the east might be prepared. And I saw three unclean spirits like frogs come out of the mouth of the dragon, and out of the mouth of the beast, and out of the mouth of the false prophet. For they are the spirits of devils, working miracles which go forth unto the kings of the Earth and of the whole world, to gather them to the battle of that great day of God Almighty.... And he gathered them together into a place called in the Hebrew tongue Armageddon."

Revelation, 16. 12-14, 16

PREFACE

An epic poem is "a long poem narrating the adventures or deeds of one or more heroic or legendary figures", "an imaginative work embodying a nation's conception of its past history" (*Concise Oxford Dictionary*). Ezra Pound wrote that "an epic is a poem including history" (*ABC of Reading*).

Epic, a narrative of a heroic episode taken from history, is thrown up by heroic deeds during a civilisation's time of growth. This is true of the *Rig Veda*, *Gilgamesh*, the *Iliad*, the *Aeneid*, the *Chanson de Roland* and *Beowulf* in the growing Indian, Mesopotamian, Greek, Roman, European and Germanic-Scandinavian civilisations. When there is no growing civilisation there is no epic.

The Greek epic of the primitive and oral tradition of Homer, who wrote about the capture of Troy, is less sophisticated and psychological than the Roman literary epic of the tradition of Virgil, Homer's imitator, who wrote about the founding of Rome. The literary epic was designed to be read rather than recited, and whereas Homer admired the deeds of rugged individuals whose code of honour often acted against society, Virgil made Aeneas the embodiment of Rome's civic virtue. He had a deeper awareness of society and how heroic deeds achieved national destiny.

The rediscovery of Virgil during the Renaissance led to Torquato Tasso's epic of Christian knights, *Gerusalemme liberata* (*Jerusalem Delivered*), 1575. Two lesser-known epic works had appeared in 1572: Camões' *Os Lusiadas* (1572) narrated Vasco da Gama's discovery of the route to India, and Pierre de Ronsard's *Franciade* (1572) connected the founding of France with the Trojan hero Francus. Milton's *Paradise Lost* (1667) was the last distinguished epic. Joel Barlow's *Columbiad* (1807) narrated how Columbus had a vision of America's destiny. He anticipated the coming American epic. The Romantic poets valued spontaneity, particularity, self-expression and classical mythology as in Keats' *Hyperion*, and the Victorian Tennyson wrote a 12-book romance on the fortunes of King Arthur in a pre-industrial world. No one attempted poetic epic in the 19th or 20th centuries, though Ezra Pound's *Cantos* touched on epic narrative with Modernist brevity, and John Heath-Stubbs approached the epic tone in *Artorius*, which subordinates narrative to focus on the nine Muses.

In our time the only youthful, growing civilisation is the North-American civilisation, which is on the verge of reaching its epic stage. We reflect our Age, and now is a time of epic works on historical themes like Homer's *Iliad* and Virgil's *Aeneid* – on historical themes that include the United States, until recently the sole superpower, and modern Crusader war. Heroic American deeds during the Second World War and the War on Terror await poetic treatment. The epic is due for a revival within the North-American civilisation.

I, an Englishman living in the time of American global domination, am not unlike a Greek living in the time of the Roman Empire and writing in Latin. Very often an outsider can see more clearly than an insider, and by writing about America from within England I believe I have grasped the pattern of contemporary American global events more objectively than many Americans. Just as my historical work *The Secret Founding of America* has revelations about early (and later) American history that have startled many American readers, so my epic works, which I discussed with the American poet Ezra Pound in 1970, can be seen as North-American epics about heroic deeds within a global perspective.

I wrote in the Preface to Books 1-2 of my first poetic epic, *Overlord*:

> "Epic is recognised by: its subject matter; theme; heroic tone; narrative length; complexity; unity of action; the scope of its setting; the scale of its action; the moral stature of its heroes; its supernatural elements; its conventions; its accessible language; its exact metre; and its distinctive cosmology.
>
> "An epic poem's subject matter includes familiar and traditional material drawn from history and widely known in popular culture, which reflects the civilisation that threw it up. Its theme has a historical, national, religious or legendary significance. It narrates continuously the heroic achievements of a distinguished historical, national or legendary hero or heroes at greater length than the heroic lay, and describes an important national enterprise in more realistic terms than fantastic medieval Arthurian (Grail) romance; it gives an overwhelming impression of nobility as heroes take part in an enterprise that is larger and more important than themselves. Its long narrative is characterised by its sheer size and weight; it includes several strands, and has largeness of concept. It treats one great complex action in heroic proportions and in an elevated style and tone. It has unity of action, which begins in the middle ('*in medias res*', to use Horace's phrase). The scope of its geographical setting is extensive, perhaps cosmic; its sweep is panoramic, and it uses heroic battle and extended journeying. The scale of the action is gigantic; it deals with good and evil on a huge scale. Consequently, its hero and main characters have great moral stature. It involves supernatural or religious beings in the action, and includes prophecy and the underworld. It has its own conventions; for example, it lists ships and genealogies, and the exploits that surround individual weapons. Its language is universally accessible, and includes ornamental similes and recurrent epithets. It uses exact metre (hexameters or the pentameters of blank verse). It has its own cosmology, and explains the ordering of the universe."

Universalist epic has a global perspective associated with the North-American civilisation, the world's globalist superpower. It presents a universal theme that is integral to the world's common culture and currency. My *Overlord* was about the Second World War, an Anglo-American war of liberation, which is a common global currency: everyone alive regardless of nationality knows about Eisenhower and Hitler to some degree. *Armageddon* is about the War on Terror, Anglo-American pre-emptive war, which is on the tongues of all living people and is, again, a common global currency.

Universalist epic draws on the approaches of traditional Greek, Roman, Italian and English epics (the epics of Homer, Virgil, Dante and Milton) and Old Norse sagas, but it differs from traditional epic in two key respects. First it draws on the up-to-date knowledge of a number of different disciplines, including cosmology and astrophysics, mysticism and comparative religion, and modern warfare and weaponry, but principally history and philosophy. In combining history, philosophy and literature (a three-legged stool) I am treading in the footsteps of, and am a successor to, Albert Camus, whose history included *The Rebel*, whose philosophy included *The Myth of Sisyphus* and whose literature included *The Plague*. (My history is of the rise and fall of civilisations, revolutions and the New World Order, my philosophy is of the universe and Universalism rather than Existentialism, and the medium of my literature is poetry rather than fiction, but Camus is still a forerunner.) However, I am welding such a cross-disciplinary approach, and insights into the fundamental order and unity of the universe, into epic.

Secondly, we live in a time of 24-hour global news which has turned the world into a global village and brought pressing historical change and religious conflict into our rooms. Interpreting a modern international story that is in the public domain to present a universal theme requires reference to precise events, facts and dates. If an event or fact is imprecise or in the wrong order, the epic poet's interpretation of the modern historical story will be inaccurate and just plain wrong. Dwelling on precise facts and dates to reveal universal aspects of war and the modern international tale may bewilder readers who are accustomed to the most general poetic treatment of events and have not encountered Universalist thinking in which the general co-exists within the particular and the universal within the specific. However, in innovative Universalist epic, the universal arises from specific events which are given a precise time and place. All poetry makes the personal and particular universal. Universalist poetry also makes the personal and particular universal, but pays greater attention to the particular.

A panoramic narrative epic poem on the War on Terror immediately faces one obvious difficulty. As the events have all happened relatively recently, sources are sometimes scanty and it is difficult to establish what happened, let alone how everything was connected and fits into an international story and pattern. In my previous epic, *Overlord*, I at least had the distance of 50 years which allowed events to settle into a broadly agreed story and pattern. In the case of the War on Terror the settling process is still happening. Nevertheless, I believe I have been able to establish what happened from many sources, and to connect everything so there is a clear, historically accurate story and pattern. And the pattern will come through more clearly in a poetic work than in a more diffuse prose work detailing all its sources.

Some of the material relating to the War on Terror will be unfamiliar to many readers. As in the Preface to *Overlord* I should indicate some of my sources. Below are some – not all – of the books I have drawn on in different places. Dates in brackets indicate the extent of the War on Terror they cover.

For the account of bin Laden's purchases of nuclear-suitcase bombs, of his claim in November 2001 to have nuclear weapons and of his plan to organise ten simultaneous nuclear explosions in ten American cities (and at the very least seven cities, as mentioned on **pvi**), see Yossef Bodansky, *Bin Laden, The Man Who Declared War on America* (2004) and three books by a former consultant to the FBI on organised crime and international terrorism, Paul Williams: *Osama's Revenge* (2004), *The Al Qaeda Connection* (2005) and *The Dunces of Doomsday* (2006). The suitcase bombs have been featured in the Western press, for example the front page of *The Times* of 26 October 2001 and *The Daily Mail* of 8 November 2001. For bin Laden's many attempts to purchase nuclear materials, see the Historical Addenda, pp582-585. *Osama's Revenge* includes three of bin Laden's long letters: 'Declaration of War', '*Jihad* Against Jews and Crusaders' and 'A Letter to America'. Many more of his letters and essays can be found in *Messages to the World*, ed Bruce Lawrence. Also see Brad K. Berner, *Quotations from Osama Bin Laden*. There is material about these writings in Peter L. Bergen, *The Osama bin Laden I Know* and *Holy War*. *Hunting Bin Laden* by Rob Schultheis suggests that bin Laden is near Zhob in Pakistan. Lawrence Wright's *The Looming Tower* has background on al-Qaeda.

Bin Laden has obliquely accepted overall responsibility for 9/11 in a number of opaque references to the event. (See px.) Khalid Sheikh Mohammed has admitted to his captors that he had operational responsibility for 9/11.

I have followed Richard Miniter, *Shadow War, The Untold Story of How America Is Winning the War on Terror* (2004), and the evidence of his interviews with Iranian ex-intelligence officers, in seeing bin Laden as relocating after Tora Bora in Iran, which is positioned between, and is therefore central to, both Afghanistan and Iraq. This line is followed in Ilan Berman, *Tehran Rising* (2005) and in *The Dunces of Doomsday*. Much can be gleaned regarding Iran's role in the War on Terror from Ali M. Ansari, *Confronting Iran*; Alireza Jafarzadeh, *The Iran Threat*; and Vali Nasar, *The Shia Revival*. Also, a particular conversation in my book, *The Last Tourist in Iran* (2008).

There is an account of Bush's transformations in Stanley A. Renshon, *In His Father's Shadow*, and the impact of Bush senior on the son is well-handled in Jacob Weisberg, *The Bush Tragedy*. My Bush is genuinely trying to prevent nuclear proliferation, having come to grasp the seriousness of al-Qaeda's acquiring nuclear weapons. For Bush's outlook on freedom, see Natan Sharansky, *The Case For Democracy*, which Bush drew on. Also see Bruce Cumings, Ervand Abrahamian and Moshe Ma'oz, *Inventing the Axis of Evil*.

For confirmation that Kissinger of the Syndicate met Cheney monthly and Bush every two months, see Bob Woodward, *State of Denial*. For the Syndicate's work, see my book *The Syndicate*. Also see David Ray Griffin, *The New Pearl Harbor*. Antonia Juhasz, *The Bush Agenda* covers the role of multinationals under Bush. *Vice*, by Lou Dubose and Jake Bernstein is revealing on Cheney's role. For the neo-cons, see Stephan Halper and Jonathan Clarke, *America Alone*; and Murray Friedman, *The Neoconservative Revolution*. Also, Andrew Cockburn, *Rumsfeld*.

For the insurgency I have drawn on Loretta Napoleoni, *Insurgent Iraq* (2005), but have gone with Jean-Charles Brisard, *Zarqawi, The New Face of Al-Qaeda* (2005), who provides more evidence that Zarqawi was an al-Qaeda operative from an early stage and bin Laden's endorsed heir. For the surge I have drawn on Thomas E. Ricks, *The Gamble* (2009). Israel's wars against Hezbollah in the Lebanon and Hamas in Gaza happened too recently to be covered in accurately researched books, and I have relied on newspaper reports, internet material and my own notes based on television film.

Books on the background to the War on Terror include: *Understanding the War on Terror*, ed James F. Hoge and Gideon Rose; Paul Berman, *Terrorism and Liberalism*;

Richard Falk, *The Great Terror War*; John L. Esposito, *Unholy War*; Nafeez Mosaddeq Ahmed, *Behind the War on Terror*; Walid Phares, *Future Jihad* and Ron Suskind, *The One Percent Doctrine*. Some books claim that America is winning the War on Terror, such as Richard Miniter, *Shadow War*. For the context of the War on Terror, see Charles Allen, *God's Terrorists*, which is on the Wahhabi cult and the roots of *jihad*; Philip Bobbit, *Terror and Consent*; Lt. General Thomas McInerney and Maj. General Paul Vallely, *Endgame*, which is a military assessment; and Anonymous, *Imperial Hubris*.

Books hostile to Bush's Iraq adventure include Bob Woodward, *State of Denial*; Thomas E. Ricks, *Fiasco*; and Jonathan Steele, *Defeat*. Con Coughlin, *Saddam* contains an account of Saddam's life. For Saddam's links with al-Qaeda see Stephen F. Hayes, *The Connection* (2004), which details some telling contacts. Also see Paul William Roberts, *The Demonic Comedy*; and John Lee Anderson, *The Fall of Baghdad*. For the American Occupation of Iraq, see Michael R. Gordon and General Bernard E. Trainor, *Cobra II*; Patrick Cockburn, *The Occupation* and *Muqtada Al-Sadr and the Fall of Iraq*; Jeremy Scahill, *Blackwater*; Rajiv Chandrasekaran, *Imperial Life in the Emerald City*; and Joseph Stiglitz and Linda Bilmes, *The Three Trillion Dollar War*.

There are a number of books on specific issues covered in *Armageddon*. For the Vatican's finances after 1928, see Paul Wiliams, *The Vatican Exposed*. For Bush's links with Saudi Arabia, see Craig Unger, *House of Bush, House of Saud*. For books on oil, see David Strahan, *The Last Oil Shock*; and Michael Clare, *Blood and Oil*. For the Temple, see Simon Goldhill, *The Temple of Jerusalem*. There is no book about the missing American gold, and I have drawn on press cuttings, internet material and my own emails from well-placed sources.

There are more general works on the Middle East. The Western perspective can be gleaned from Robert Kagan, *Paradise and Power*; *Dangerous Nation*; and *The Return of History and the End of Dreams*. Also Cullen Murphy, *The New Rome*. The Islamic background can be found in Hugh Kennedy, *The Court of the Caliphs*; Efraim Karsh, *Islamic Imperialism*; and David Pryce-Jones, *The Closed Circle*.

There are many differing perspectives in these works, and the overall perspective in *Armageddon* is mine and only mine. Armed with some of these books the reader can, if so inclined, broadly check my interpretation of events and track my journey through my sources. However, I have drawn on many other works and on my files of newspaper cuttings that have helped me with specific events.

On the technical side, a poem is traditionally defined as "a metrical composition, usually concerned with feeling or imaginative description, an elevated composition in verse" (*Concise Oxford Dictionary*). I have remained loyal to metrical composition, and my chosen medium for telling my international story is again blank verse, which is rooted in the English tradition from Surrey and Marlowe to Tennyson. This is pretty strict verse in iambic pentameters with very occasional variations for emphasis. As in Latin verse, elision is allowed, as when "the" or "to" is followed by a vowel. Some words, such as "seven", "given" and "Heaven", can be treated as having either one or two syllables depending on how the line is read, which will be governed by stress and emphasis. When a character is speaking I have sometimes followed the pronunciation of the speaker's ethnic group. Thus an American Southerner may say "following" as two rather than three syllables, and on occasion "Afghanistan" may be three rather than four syllables and "organisation" may be four rather than five syllables if that is how the words would be spoken in their context. Blank verse in iambic pentameters is the medium that best allows verse to accommodate a tale involving international events.

All poetry is a kind of quarrel with oneself rather than a quarrel with the world, when it becomes political propaganda. The quarrel in *Armageddon* concerns some of the following issues. Is there a clash between Christian and Muslim civilisations? Is the West nobly intentioned or governed by commercial motives and greed for oil? Is bin Laden's hostility to the West valid in terms of the Muslim perspective? Are Islamic terrorist and al-Qaeda methods sanctioned by the *Koran*? To what extent is the War on Terror a noble thing on both sides? How much of it is idealism and sacrifice, and how much self-interest – on both sides? Is the suffering it has caused justified? In my quarrel with myself I have tried to understand all sides and have reconciled my internal conflicts – but in no way glorify terrorism or take part in quarrelling with the world.

The poet who deals with the modern clash of religions, cultures and civilisations soon discovers that his historical subject is intertwined with myth ("traditional narrative usually involving supernatural or imaginary persons", *Concise Oxford Dictionary*): the myths of Armageddon, the Great Tribulation and the Second Comings of Christ and of the Mahdi or Hidden *Imam* which have influenced the historical decisions of key modern leaders: Bush, bin Laden and Ahmadinejad.

These myths express "the unconscious metaphysic" of our time. E.M.W. Tillyard in *The English Epic and its Background* quotes Lascelles Abercrombie as seeing the epic poet as "accepting, and with his genius transfiguring, the general circumstance of his time...symbolising, in some appropriate form, whatever sense of the significance of life he feels acting as the accepted unconscious metaphysic of the time" (*The Epic*).

Many books relate recent events in the Middle East to the myth of the end days, the tribulation, the Antichrist and Armageddon from a Western point of view. These include J. Dwight Pentecost, *Things to Come* and with Charles R. Swindoll and John E. Walvoord and others, *The Road to Armageddon*; Walid Shoebat with Joel Richardson, *God's War on Terror*; Grant R. Jeffrey, *The Next World War* and *The New Temple and the Second Coming*; John P. McTernan, *As America Has Done to Israel*; Richard Booker, *Radical Islam's War against Israel, Christianity and the West*; and Robert Livingston, *Christianity and Islam: The Final Clash*. Many focus on Jerusalem and Iran: John Hagee, *Jerusalem Countdown*; Mark Hitchcock, *Iran, the Coming Crisis* and *The Apocalypse of Ahmadinejad*; Michael D. Evans with Jerome R. Corsi, *Showdown with Nuclear Iran*; and Ron Rhodes, *Northern Storm Rising*.

Joel Richardson, *Antichrist, Islam's Awaited Messiah* focuses on the Mahdi or Hidden *Imam*. Also see Al-Fadl ibn Shadhan, *The Return of the Mahdi*. Compare Ed Hinson, *Antichrist Rising* and Joye Jeffries Pugh, *Antichrist, The Cloned Image of Jesus Christ*. Hal Lindsey, *The 1980s: Countdown to Armageddon* provides background. Tom Kovach, *Tribulation 2008* has insights but his time scheme differs from that in the poem (2002-2009). Many books offer a Christian perspective on the last days, including Robert Lightman, *The Last Days Handbook; The Meaning of the*

Millennium, ed. by Robert G. Clouse; J. Oswald Sanders, *Certainties of Christ's Second Coming*; and W.J. Grier, *The Momentous Event*.

Books on the end of the world on 21 December 2012 include Adrian Gilbert, *The End of Time, The Mayan Prophecies Revisited*; Geoff Stray, *Beyond 2012, Catastrophe or Ecstasy: A Complete Guide to End-of-Time Predictions*; Patrick Geryl and Gino Ratinckx, *The Orion Prophecy*; and Lawrence E. Joseph, *Apocalypse 2012*.

All epics have a mythical upper world where events interact with and parallel events in the world below. I have continued the Light-based Heaven and Light-deprived Hell of *Overlord* but those comparing and contrasting the upper worlds in the two epics will notice differences and an advance in my thinking about how the two worlds interact and how the dead relate to the living. Hell is now primarily a place of Self-Improvement which prepares for Heaven. Particular attention should be paid to what happens to the newly dead who have been involved in acts of violence. The philosophical background for this advance may be found in my work of philosophy, *The New Philosophy of Universalism* (2009). To some extent, but only to some extent, my Christ and Satan can be seen as personifications of the order and disorder principles set out in that work.

In *Armageddon* I have attempted to unite poetry, history and myth in my own Sistine-Chapel ceiling. I have painted the War on Terror and the suffering it has caused, and have related it to "the ways of God", which I have attempted to justify to men. I have tried to balance the moral certainties and confusions of the two warring sides, and have focused on the US's need to prevent al-Qaeda from implementing their plan to set off nuclear-suitcase bombs simultaneously in ten US cities (see ppx and xix for sources) and to re-establish the Caliphate in Baghdad (see maps on ppxi and 624-625). These real aspirations and goals of al-Qaeda's may come as a surprise to readers of Western newspapers and viewers of Western media, who will not have encountered them in such stark terms. Napoleon said ironically and bitterly from his island exile, "History is a myth that men agree to believe." The version of contemporary history conveyed by Western media is a myth that Westerners agree to believe. In being truthful about the issues of our time I am concerned not to demoralise readers. On the contrary, I seek to convey a vision of hope.

My Bush is a very misunderstood man who was genuinely trying to protect the West from what he believed to be a real threat that has not been fully reported and which was exaggerated and exploited by the Syndicate, of whom he was to a considerable degree something of a prisoner. (See my book *The Syndicate* for a historical, evidential account.) The Western duty to avoid dwelling on news items that may "unnecessarily" alarm the public has left the Western world bewildered at, and therefore critical of, the scale of military action in Central Asia and the Middle East. Bush is therefore a tragic figure with well-intentioned, noble ideals who through his own single-mindedness in pre-emption ended up widely reviled. In contrast, Eisenhower in *Overlord* also had noble ideals and, despite indecisiveness that infuriated Montgomery, through his genial bravery and defiance ended up widely admired.

NOTE ON PRACTICE

Most dates are pronounced and scanned in the usual way. Thus "1967" is pronounced and scanned "nineteen sixty-seven". Occasionally figures have to be pronounced and scanned. So "851" can be "eight five one" as well as "eight fifty-one". This is particularly true of dates in the first decade of any century. Thus, when "2001" appears, it is generally pronounced "two o o one". However it may be pronounced "two thousand and one" if the metre requires, in which case it is written in words, not figures. "2000" is pronounced "two o o o" unless it is written in words, as "two thousand". "1100" is "eleven hundred" and the same applies up to "1900", "nineteen hundred". Any date or number (e.g. of a UN resolution) spread over two lines is in words rather than figures.

Numbers can be read in two ways. "128 billion" can be read as "a hundred and twenty-eight billion" or as "one two eight billion" if the metre requires.

There are different ways of spelling Arabic names in English. I have followed the consensus of general practice. Thus, when a man is generally referred to as Ahmad I have followed this spelling, and when a man is generally referred to as Ahmed I have followed suit. This may not make for logical consistency but it does follow received practice. I have followed the same principle in place names. Basra is most commonly spelt without an "h". I have spelt Falluja without an "h" as "Fallujans" is more acceptable in English than "Fallujahns". However, many other place names in practice end with an "h", and I have followed the general practice in these. Bin Laden's group "al-Qaeda" begins with a small "a". Zarqawi's group "Al-Qaeda in Iraq" begins with a capital "A". Sometimes Zarqawi's group is abbreviated to "Al-Qaeda".

I have followed English rather than American spelling. However, American place names and titles are in American spelling, for example World Trade Center and Defense Secretary. When a place name has a historical significance and has appeared in many books in an English rather than American spelling it is in English spelling, for example Pearl Harbour.

By placing inverted commas round family names ("Rothschilds", "Rockefellers") I seek to make clear that I am not referring to particular individuals but to a particular emphasis of a commercial pattern: in the case of "Rothschilds", a commercial drive associated with their nineteenth-century financial dominance and imperialism, and in the case of the "Rockefellers", a commercial drive associated with their twentieth-century acquisition of oil and shaping of international events.

⌐ Symbol

A corner-mark (⌐) at the beginning of the line denotes that there is a break or gap before that line which has been obscured because it falls at the bottom of a page.

BOOK ONE

SEPTEMBER 11TH: AMERICA UNDER ATTACK

SUMMARY

Tell, Muse, of terror and pre-emptive war;
Tell of world empire and of wild dissent,
Of *Pax Americana* that forbad
Nuclear proliferation, of *jihad*
To drive occupiers from Muslim lands;
Tell of crusaders and of Holy War
And of a nightmare: free America
Threatened with nuclear bombs in ten cities,
Simultaneous fiery Armageddon.
Tell of martyrs, planes turned into missiles,

5

10	Of America attacked and two wars,
	Of the clash of two civilisations
	(Or of extremist crusaders in each)
	In fire and smoke and dread of rockets' roar
	And of nuclear reprisal against might.
15	Tell of Bush the Second's transformations,
	Of the obduracy of bin Laden
	And how Satan – exiled towards the end
	Of the Second World War, failed Overlord,
	Intrigued the leaking of the atomic bomb
20	Which brought fifty years' peace and did God's will –
	Deceived both sides, brought the world to the brink
	Of the Apocalypse and Judgement Day,
	And in the ensuing War on Terror
	And tribulation of the final time
25	Brought in a New World Order in which West
	And East were partners, did God's will again
	And though the triumph of Light was assured
	Brought universal order to the Earth,
	The second phase of God's Millennial plan.
30	
	O shades of my mentors from past ages
	I need you to assist me now as I,
	Having fulfilled one epic, *Overlord*,
	Steady myself to narrate another,
	Proceeding from past war to modern war.
35	I have been born into a time of war,
	Have been a war poet with dreams of peace
	And I warm to a wartime president
	Whose *Pax Americana* maintains peace.
	O Homer, the only other poet
40	To write two epics, whose action extends
	A few weeks and events a dozen days,
	Having spread my action over a year
	And now faced with seven years' tribulation,
	I need to focus on twelve nodal points
45	Within the long time span I must describe.
	I encountered you in the library
	At Chigwell, under Hypnos, where I read
	Your archaic Greek with many accents,
	Translated and thrilled to your "wine-dark sea",
50	And, still a boy, sensed my epic calling.
	I sought you in Troy and on Ithaca,
	And thought I found you in ruin and cove,
	Phorkys' bay where I swam with my two sons
	(Where Odysseus landed and fell asleep),

55	Water so clear I could see every stone
	Before I lay by the gnarled olive-tree.
	And yet – appropriate, as I narrate
	A firm response to awesome nuclear threat
	That some say is illusory, as if
60	Bush were self-deluded – on my desk lie
	Books that locate you in other places,
	In Sicily where (Samuel Butler claims)
	Aeneas came to Trapani with Eryx
	And you, a woman, set *The Odyssey*
65	On Mount Eryx, where Odysseus' palace
	Hung on boulders near Venus's temple
	Above the cyclops' cave at Erice
	And Nausicaa's Trapani salt-pans.
	You in an Ionian settlement there?
70	And now I read in Bittlestone's study
	Ithaca's really Kefalonia
	Which unlike Ithaki "lies low, farthest
	Out to sea towards dusk", an unproved hunch.
	You in the Paliki Peninsula?
75	And now in Vinci you're a Baltic man
	Within the South Fyn archipelago
	In Achaean Denmark, north of Schleswig,
	Whose Zealand was the first Peloponnese,
	Where Ithaca's Lyø, and Olympus
80	Is in Finland – where Troy is now Troja
	Across the Baltic Sea, around whose shores
	The Catalogue of Ships follows places
	Counter-clockwise in order on the map.
	Achaean names echo in Baltic names.
85	Then the Achaeans migrated to Greece
	And took with them their place names – Ithaca
	And Troy – just as settlers took English names
	Out to the New World of America.
	O Homer I found you round the Aegean
90	But now you are enfolded in a mist,
	You cannot also be in Sicily,
	Paliki and the Baltic – three are wrong
	Of these four. So it is with my hero
	Who's a great leader yet much derided
95	For exaggerating al-Qaeda's threat,
	Seeing an illusory enemy
	That's a mere clutch of reckless men, a cell
	In a disorganised network, and not
	A vast and ruthless army of thousands.
100	And as with you, o Homer, I must stick

With Bush the great leader, doubt calumnies,
But be open to constraints on his will.

O Milton, you who scorned delight and spent
Laborious days toiling, spurred on by fame,
105 Lasting renown which shuns celebrity,
All self-promotion and publicity,
Absorbing learning and mythologies,
The old culture that articulates fast-
Fading memories of glorious wars
110 In reservoirs of awesome images,
Instruct me on your four-hundredth birthday
To write lines that are forever in mind,
To spurn poets who tour local radio
Stations to talk about themselves and read
115 Embarrassing, unmemorable verse.
I have shunned readings for immortal fame
Spurs works of lasting universal worth
Which cannot be confused with talk or chat,
Those ripples on the limpid pool of thought
120 That reflects the universe and is stirred
By the obscuring, clouding breeze of self.
O Milton, spur me to perform the task
Ordained by Light and assert eternal
Providence that with infinite Being
125 Regulates this material universe,
And justify the ways of God to men,
Why the infinite allowed 9/11:
To lure the Syndicate into defeat
And eclipse the West's capitalist power
130 And *hubris* to bring in a world order
That assists all the world's suffering poor
And works for all downtrodden humankind.
In a time when it's thought death is the end
And men have lost their grounding in their souls
135 And are deluded into believing
That this life's all, and there's no Providence.
This is a hard task for a lone poet
Whose soul reflects the universe and Age
As a green pool reflects the trees and sky
140 And images of war as on a screen,
The heir to Homer, Virgil and Dante,
To undertake in our cultural wasteland
Where soul's endeavours seem doomed to failure
Spurned by youths who are proud of ignorance
145 And drawn to know celebrity, not fame,

And scorn the causes for which men fight wars
And give little thought to our liberty
And mock God as a non-existent myth.
O Milton, show how Light uses terror
150 To bring in a more perfect way of life
And redistribute wealth to humankind.

O blind Heath-Stubbs, who tap-tapped with white stick
Rhythmic patterns as we walked down the street
To your local, with whom I sat and drank
155 And talked in Notting Hill and who gave me,
And signed, a pamphlet of *Artorius*,
Book One, and said each book would be addressed
To a different Muse. Strong on classical
Allusion and alliteration but
160 Short on epic narrative, now you're dead
Intercede with Muses on my behalf
And ask them to guide and shape my wordflow.

And you, o Woodrow Wilson and Roosevelt,
Whose free will was constrained in time of war,
165 I summon you from the far spirit world
To help me now I sing of cause for war,
For you, o Wilson, were complicit in
The sinking of the *Lusitania*
Which shocked Americans into joining
170 The First World War (once oilfields near Mosul
Were signed over by Churchill as your price).
And you, o Roosevelt, were complicit in
Japan's "surprise" air raid on Pearl Harbour
Which shocked Americans into joining
175 The Second World War (once Saudi oilfields
Were signed over by Churchill as your price).
(Bush had a Churchill bust in the White House
That honours freedom bought with British oil.)
I need you both at my elbow as I
180 Assess whether Bush was complicit in
The attack on the Twin Towers by Muslims
Which shocked Americans into joining
Two imperial, crusading Holy Wars
That progressed long-planned oil and gas pipelines.
185

Tell, Muse, how bin Laden became a voice
For Wahhabis and then the Muslim world,
And came to shelter in Afghanistan.
His father, a builder, emigrated

From South Yemen to land that would become
190 Saudi Arabia, and had fifty-four
Or fifty-five children by thirty wives,
Some say only "several", renovated
The royal palaces, improved the mosques
Of Mecca and Medina and rebuilt
195 The al-Aqsa mosque in Jerusalem.
Osama was his seventeenth son, when
He was killed in an air crash Osama
Came in to three hundred million dollars –
Or was it only thirty-five million?
200 His older brother ran the company
And was a business partner of young Bush,
Co-founder with Bush of the Arbusto
Energy oil company in Texas –
"Arbusto" is a Spanish word for "bush" –
205 Which was later bought by Spectrum 7
Which was then bought by Harken Energy
Corporation. They retained on the board
Both Bush and Salem's representative.
Salem was killed in 1988
210 When his plane crashed on take-off in Texas.
During this time, from 1979,
Furious that Israel had seized Palestine
And now overjoyed that Ayatollah
Khomeini had seized power in Iran,
215 Osama fought in far Afghanistan
Against the Soviets, who were supporting
Their client-state against Afghan rebels'
Firm resistance, and turned rusty tin cans
Into shells and land-mines into grenades.
220 To replace the flow of Russian oil through
Khomeini's Iran, which was obstructed,
The Soviet Union and Standard Oil
Of "Rockefellers" (who shared Stalin's oil
In return for cash) sought a safe pipeline
225 Route through Afghanistan and Pakistan
To the coast whence Russian oil could be shipped.
In 1986, as "Tim Osman",
He went to the US to ask Reagan's
Administration to combat Soviet
230 Aircraft, and with an American, Ralph
Olberg, who procured arms for the rebels
In Afghanistan, he met FBI
Retired executive Ted Gunderson
And CIA expert in explosives,

235	Armaments and electronics, Michael
	Riconosciuto. The Soviets withdrew
	In 1988 and 9, and now
	With US and CIA assistance
	Following an investment of three billion
240	Dollars to train, arm and support Afghans,
	Osama founded al-Qaeda. Run like
	A multinational holding company,
	It had no Chief Executive and its
	Shadow structure was very hard to trace.
245	When in 1990 Saddam Hussein
	Invaded Kuwait, forced the al-Sibagh
	Royal family to flee their palaces
	And seek refuge in Saudi Arabia,
	The Saudi royal family shuddered,
250	Fearing Saddam might now seize Saudi oil,
	And King Fahd asked the US to send help.
	Mohammed had said no non-believers
	Could live within Arabia, and so
	King Fahd pressured the Saudis' Grand Mufti
255	To decree that this breach of Holy Law
	Would be allowed, to secure Arabia.
	Now US C-130 transporters
	Landed at Dhahran's airbase and discharged
	Hundreds of tanks, trucks, transport vehicles, jeeps,
260	And constructed a base at Prince Sultan
	Airbase and another south of Riyadh.
	Long lines of male and female US troops
	Walked the road between two holy cities.
	The *Ummah* (the pious community
265	Of believers) were grossly offended.
	With stealth bombers, cruise missiles and smart bombs,
	Laser guidance, the US stunned Iraq,
	Killing fifty thousand Iraqi troops,
	Wounding three and a half times as many.
270	Osama seethed with rage, American
	Invaders occupied the Muslim lands.
	He wanted the Americans expelled
	And Saudi to side with the Iraqis,
	Held the Saudi rulers were corrupt, false
275	Muslims who should be overthrown, replaced
	By true believers in the Holy Law.
	He wanted to depose the House of Saud
	So an uncontaminated Islam
	Could rise to power in the Arabian
280	Peninsula just as Ayatollah

Khomeini deposed the Shah of Iran
And rose to power himself. He sought a "base"
Abroad where he could sound his claim to rule
In exile, then return to overthrow
285　　The regime of Saudi Arabia
And assume his own country's leadership.
Accused of plotting armed rebellion in
The Saudi kingdom, he was deported
To Sudan and his assets were frozen.
290

Now Osama sought to arm al-Qaeda
With dreadful weapons of mass destruction.
When President Bush withdrew nuclear
Weapons from many sites throughout the world
Gorbachev withdrew twenty-two thousand.
295　　Then factories closed and unemployment soared
And inflation reached two thousand per cent,
And nuclear bombs were soon in Chechen hands.
In 1992 Osama sought
A nuclear arsenal in Soviet decay.
300　　That December he bombed US Marines
Housed in two towering hotels in the port
City of Aden in Yemen. And then
In 1993 his bomb blew up
In the World Trade Center, killing just six
305　　But causing damage of half a billion.
In Khartoum he set up a lab and hired
A Middle-Eastern physicist to work
On a project to make nuclear weapons
That would kill millions of Americans.
310　　He encouraged Somali militia
To attack US Army Rangers in
Mogadishu and plotted to kill Pope
John Paul the Second and then to bomb twelve
Airliners simultaneously. He
315　　Was behind the bombing of an office
For the Saudi Arabian National Guard,
Killing five Americans out of seven.
Osama now began to spend millions
On raw materials (highly-enriched
320　　Uranium and/or plutonium)
Bought in South Africa or Pakistan
To manufacture a nuclear bomb.
In 1995 Osama met
The leading Shiite terrorist, Imad
325　　Mugniyah, in Khartoum. As Muslims say,

"My enemy's enemy is my friend."
Mugniyah was feared for he had been behind
The kidnapping of Terry Waite and more
Western hostages in Beirut and had
330 Tortured and killed William Buckley, station
Chief of the CIA, which led Bush's
Father to place a two-million dollar
Bounty on his head. He lived in Iran
And founded the Hezbollah suicide
335 Squads. The Saudi royal family, worried
By anti-US fundamentalist
Islamic attacks that November in
Riyadh and on the Khobar Towers barracks
In June 1996 (when sixteen
340 Airmen died) paid Osama's al-Qaeda
Terror group at least two hundred million
Dollars in return for not attacking
Saudi Arabia – after meetings
In Paris in 1996 and
345 In July 1998 within
Kandahar. Osama attended both
Meetings, and now had millions of dollars
To spend on wmds and war.
He went to Brazil's jungle and set up
350 Laboratories to test wmds,
For Brazil had low-grade uranium.
In Sudan he built a business empire,
Invested in banks, agricultural
Projects and road-building – and organised
355 Training camps for al-Qaeda followers.
He had a dozen companies and put
Fifty million dollars of "his money"
Into the Al-Shamal Islamic bank
In Khartoum. His business partners were then
360 The family of Sharon Percy, wife
Of John D. ("Jay") Rockefeller the Fourth,
The great grandson of Standard Oil's founder,
Who were also in Mideast construction.
Bin Laden and the Percys now shared joint
365 Accounts in Harris Bank, Chicago. Thus
Bin Laden had links with "Rockefellers".
From Sudan he waged war on the US,
Approved a wave of suicide attacks,
Attacked US troops in Arabia,
370 And issued 'Declaration of *Jihad*',
A loud call for King Fahd to abdicate.

Saudis attempted to assassinate
Him and the Sudanese Government, pressed
By the US, asked him to leave Khartoum.
375 In 1996, invited by
Younus Khalis, Osama arrived in
Afghanistan, and gave the Taliban
Millions of dollars for construction plans
Round Kandahar, a mosque, a dam, and more
380 Agricultural projects, and bankrolled
Mullah Omar: sixty-eight million pounds.
(How much of this was "Rockefellers'" cash?)
To thank him, the Taliban, as a gift,
Gave him the whole province of Nangarhar
385 Whose vast poppy fields produce nearly three-
Quarters of the world supply of opium
And whose massive drug revenues now passed
To bin Laden and funded al-Qaeda
Who now both ruled a state within a state.
390 There through Mohammed Atef, his trusted
Chief of operations, in mid-nineteen
Ninety-six he met the swashbuckling,
Swaggering Kuwaiti-born Khalid Sheikh
Mohammed, who held a Pakistani
395 Passport and was known by as many as
Twenty-seven, perhaps fifty aliases,
Who had left his family in Iran
And now outlined to him the plan that would
Become the quadruple hijackings of
400 September the eleventh that shook the world.

In 1988, together with
A tight circle that included Sayyid
Imam al-Sharif or Dr Fadl
(His *nom de guerre*), leader of Egyptian
405 Islamic *Jihad*, and his *protégé*
Ayman al-Zawahiri, bin Laden
Had co-founded al-Qaeda, or "the Base",
To be the base of a new Caliphate
That stretched from Morocco to Pakistan,
410 Which would replace the Ottoman Empire
That was ended in 1924.
Western colonial powers had invaded
Muslim lands and seized colonies, detached
Them from the Ottomans: Algeria
415 In 1830, Egypt in eighteen
Eighty-two, Iraq in 1917.

The Muslim world was continually
Invaded, divided and weakened by
Outside forces: the US and Israel
420 Who controlled both Saudi Arabia
And Palestine so three holy cities –
Mecca, Medina and Jerusalem –
Were occupied. Bin Laden's al-Qaeda
Sought to overthrow the Egyptian State
425 And Saudi royals, but America
Was too strong to dislodge. So bin Laden,
His deputy al-Zawahiri and
The arrogant Khalid Sheikh Mohammed
Had the idea that they'd attack the "far
430 Enemy" first, then meld Egypt, Israel,
Jordan and Saudi Arabia within
A single Islamic superstate or
New Caliphate. They hoped the US would
Withdraw from the Middle East or be sucked
435 Into a war in Afghanistan like
The Soviets where they could, through attrition
And the spreading of *jihad*, be worn down
And defeated so Muslims could unite
To re-establish Islam's Caliphate.
440 Bin Laden could legitimise his role
As *de facto* leader of the anti-
Western wing of Islam by assuming
The title of Caliph who would be based
In Afghanistan or else in Baghdad
445 If the secular Baath could be dislodged.
A Caliph has a territorial base
Like the Ummayad caliphs who were driven
From Damascus to Cordoba, or like
Their replacements who drove them out to Spain,
450 The Abbasids, who were based in Baghdad.
On October the eleventh 2005
A letter from al-Zawahiri to
Al-Zarqawi, sent on July the ninth
And intercepted, would be released by
455 The Office of National Intelligence.
It said bin Laden wished to establish
A Caliphate in Iraq, then expand –
As if he were great Saladin reborn.
He had called his Afghan Base "Khorasan",
460 Which is now just a province in Iran
But in eighth-century Afghanistan was
Where the Abbasids launched their bid for power.

Without a base he could not be Caliph,
And only a descendant of Ali,
465 The Prophet's son-in-law, and an *Imam*,
Could be a Shiite leader. At best he
Could, as a descendant of Fatima,
The Prophet's daughter, holy Shining One,
Proclaim himself the awaited saviour,
470 The Mahdi, like Mohammed Ahmad in
Sudan in 1881 or like
Mecca's Sharif Husayn after the First,
Or King Farouk of Egypt just before
The Second, World War; or like Abdallah
475 Al-Qahtani who seized Mecca's Great Mosque
In 1980 and was then gunned down.
And so he was the "hidden Caliph" who –
Chosen by *Shura*, or council of state,
To lead the *Ummah*, or community
480 Of Islam, as the Prophet's successor
To his political authority –
Would bring al-Aqsa and Palestine back
To Islam and rule a vast swathe that reached
From Morocco to Pakistan, and from
485 Somalia to Turkey and Kyrgystan,
Up to far-northern Kazakhstan: a black
Swathe dwarfing Europe and Russia that would
Again advance through Spain and the Balkans
To the gates of Vienna, and expand,
490 A superstate that would obliterate
Israel and control Middle-Eastern oil
And crowd out Europe and the far US.

News had spread – and it was America's
Worst nightmare – that bin Laden had acquired
495 Nuclear-suitcase bombs which he sought to use.
Chechen separatists under Dudayev –
Who had notified the State Department
In 1994 that he possessed
Tactical nuclear suitcases he'd sell
500 To hostile countries if America
Did not observe Chechen independence –
Had sold him twenty nuclear-suitcase bombs
For thirty million dollars and two tons
Of number-four choice Afghan heroin
505 That were worth seven hundred million dollars.
(News broke in the world's press two years later –
The London *Times*, *Jerusalem Report* –

	And was confirmed by the International
	Atomic Energy Agency's chief,
510	Ex-director general and now chairman
	Of the WMD Commission,
	Hans Blix in 2004.) The deal done,
	Osama, in the Hindu Kush Mountains,
	Khorasan in Afghanistan, issued
515	His long 'Declaration of War against
	The Americans Occupying the
	Land of the Two Holy Places' (the two
	Places being Mecca and Medina
	In Wahhabist Saudi Arabia),
520	And the next four years used opium billions
	From Afghan poppies to fund three long wars:
	The Taliban's war against the Northern
	Alliance; the war in Kosovo, which led
	To hundreds of Wahhabi mosques and schools
525	Spreading through the Muslim towns there; and war
	Against America. For having formed
	An "International Islamic Front"
	With Islamic *Jihad*, which was led by
	Ayman al-Zawahiri, he then signed
530	*'Jihad* Against Jews and Crusaders' that
	Sees "Crusader armies" spread "like locusts" –
	A *fatwa* calling for Americans
	To be killed. He bombed US embassies
	In Kenya and Tanzania, killing
535	Two hundred and fifty odd, of whom twelve
	Were Americans, wounding five thousand.
	He'd planned it in Sudan five years earlier.
	This was the first terrorist action that
	Could be connected without doubt to him.
540	In retaliation the US launched
	Cruise missiles at a training camp in Khost,
	Eastern Afghanistan, killed thirty-four
	But did not kill him. The US announced
	A five-million-dollar reward to hear
545	Information leading to his arrest
	And now planned to conquer Afghanistan.
	A month later Clinton (indicted for
	Perjury and obstruction of justice)
	Attacked Iraq with bombs for seventy hours
550	In *Operation Desert Fox* – and he
	Survived and appeared on al-Jazeera
	For ninety minutes, during which he said
	Of nuclear weapons, "There is a duty

On Muslims to acquire them." He issued
555   A statement called 'Islam's Nuclear Bomb'
Telling the world he had nuclear weapons:
"It's the duty of Muslims to prepare
As much force as possible in order
To terrorise the enemies of God."
560   In May 1997 in closed-
Door discussion General Alexander
Lebed, Yeltsin's former security
Secretary, told members of the US
House of Representatives that eighty-
565   Four nuclear suitcases were missing – that
Of a hundred and thirty-two produced
He could account for only forty-eight –
Which the Russian Mafia may have sold.
Eighty-four might be in extremists' hands,
570   Some in the hands of *Muslim* extremists.
All were one-kiloton bombs that could be
Detonated by one person within
Half an hour, each measuring twenty-four
By sixteen by eight inches. They had been
575   Distributed among special Soviet
Military intelligence units
Belonging to the GRU, he said.
In late August he said he now believed
A hundred were missing. In September
580   Russia's powerful atomic energy
Ministry said the bombs do not exist:
"Perhaps he meant old Soviet nuclear
Artillery shells, which were well guarded."
Lebed's credibility was questioned.
585   On October the third, the scientist
Alexie Yablokov stated he knew
Individuals who had made suitcase-size
Nuclear devices for the KGB
In the 1970s for terrorist
590   Purposes, and that they might not now be
Under the Russian Defence Ministry's
Control. Representative Curt Weldon
Said the Russian Government acknowledged
Such weapons had been produced, and maintained.
595   A hundred and thirty-two devices
Had been built with one- to ten-kiloton
Yields. Forty-eight were unaccounted for.
Russia made three thousand nuclear-suitcase
Bombs designed to stop advancing troops, and

600	More than three hundred may have gone missing,
	Each half the size of A-bombs that were dropped
	On Hiroshima and Nagasaki.
	Jamal Ahmed al-Fadl, a witness
	Who testified against bin Laden in
605	A case concerning the bombing attacks
	On the US embassies in Kenya
	And Tanzania, said he had tried to help
	Al-Qaeda obtain enriched uranium
	From Sudan, had bought it for a million
610	Dollars and been paid a six-thousand-pound
	Bonus. It was delivered to a camp,
	One of bin Laden's terrorist training
	Camps in Afghanistan. Experts had said
	Bin Laden had been unable to make
615	A sophisticated nuclear bomb,
	But might place suitcase uranium beside
	TNT and detonate both, spreading
	Radioactive nuclear materials
	Over thousands in a wide area
620	So they're radiated by a "dirty bomb".
	(In January 2000 in Washington
	Ex-GRU operative Stanislav
	Lunev would be a witness. A mock-up
	Of a nuclear-suitcase bomb made by
625	A Congressional staffer Peter Pry
	Would show components in an atomic
	Artillery shell could be reassembled
	In a suitcase: physics package, neutron
	Generators, batteries, arming device
630	Could just fit in an attaché case. This
	Gun-type atomic weapon had a yield
	Of one to ten kilotons, Lebed's yield.
	Lunev would say it was intended for
	A Russian attack against the US
635	Leaders and key communications and
	Military facilities. Russia's
	Post-Cold-War leaders thus still regarded
	The United States as the enemy
	And nuclear war as inevitable.)
640	In 1998, supporting this,
	Yossef Bodansky, head of Congress's
	Washington Task Force on Terrorism,
	Told a congressional committee: "There's
	No doubt that bin Laden has succeeded
645	In his quest for nuclear suicide bombs."

He said the bombs had been transported through
Pakistan to various al-Qaeda cells.
Abdul Qadeer Khan, the shrewd father of
Pakistan's nuclear bomb and illegal
650   Supplier of nuclear material
On the black market to Islamic states –
To Iran, Libya and North Korea –
Was cited as bin Laden's supplier.
And these suitcases had been looked after,
655   So they would not deteriorate, by
Pakistan's expert nuclear engineers
And ISI secret service generals,
Who Osama paid an estimated
Sixty to a hundred million dollars,
660   And by ex-Soviet and Chinese nuclear
Scientists and technicians, who received
As much again from Afghan poppy wealth
To upgrade and replenish nuclear cores.
He employed the expertise of SPETSNAZ
665   (Soviet special forces) and North Korea.
The suitcase bombs' yields varied from .5
To 10 kilotons, which would fry New York.
From a Ukrainian arms dealer he bought
Twelve kilos of uranium-235
670   Which cost seventy-five million dollars,
From the Ukraine twenty kilos of good
Uranium-236 that was enriched
Eighty-five per cent – above the standards
For weapons-grade material, that cost
675   Seventy million dollars for between
Some twelve to fifteen kilos; and two bars
Of enriched uranium-138 from
Egyptian black-marketer Ibrahim
Abd and twenty nuclear warheads from
680   Kazakhstan, Russia, Turkmenistan and
Ukraine. But he also had a reverse,
Bought uranium from Russian traffickers
That could not be used in nuclear weapons
And a nuclear by-product which they called
685   "Red Mercury", a "secret weapon's" core,
A con that cost him two hundred million
Dollars and which also duped Iraqis.

In May 1998 Osama
Said, "The call to wage war on America
690   Was made because America has spear-

Headed the Crusade against the Islamic
Nation, sending tens of thousands of troops
To the Land of the Two Sacred Mosques." He
Again saw the US as crusaders.
695   In the Khalden camp Osama convened
A council of war some time in the spring
Of 1999. He and Atef,
Al-Qaeda's military commander,
Summoned murderous Khalid Sheikh Mohammed
700   To present his plan for four foul attacks
On the White House, Pentagon, Capitol
And the World Trade Center. Training began
In the Mes Aynak camp that fall and all
Four pilots had to be in the US
705   During December the following year.
In December 1999, he
Told *Time* journalists, "If I have indeed
Acquired these weapons, then I thank God for
Enabling me to do so. If I seek
710   To acquire these weapons, I'm carrying
Out a duty. It would be a sin for
Muslims not to try to possess weapons
That prevent infidels from inflicting
Harm on Muslims." That month Osama met
715   Mohammed Atta in an Afghan camp.
He trained two thousand terrorists in camps
In Afghanistan, and he trained fighters,
Eleven thousand in fifty countries,
Spent eight hundred thousand dollars each month
720   On arms from ex-Soviet stockpiles. He knew
A.Q. Khan, "the godfather of nuclear
Proliferation", who privately sold
Nuclear know-how from Pakistan, and was
Linked to the Islamic terror group Lashkar-
725   E-Toiba ("Army of the Pure"), the banned
Terrorist arm of Markaz Daiwa-Wal-
Irshad, Wahhabi sects which all follow
Teachings of the eighteenth-century *emir*
Abdul al-Wahhab, which were followed by
730   Osama, al-Zawahiri and all
High-ranking al-Qaeda officialdom.
Osama and the Saudi royals were
In conflict, yet followed al-Wahhab's cause.
Bin Laden's message of corrupt Muslims
735   Was Wahhabist, and yet the Saudi royals
Spent ninety billion dollars in spreading

Wahhabi teachings throughout the US
Since 1973, building fourteen
Hundred mosques in America for prayer.
740   To the Saudis Osama was a threat,
An irritant they wished did not exist,
Even a rival, for with his billions
Osama would be Khomeini to Fahd's
Shah. Then in January 2000
745   A dozen of his trusted followers
Held an al-Qaeda summit in Kuala
Lumpur, Malaysia, to plan attacks
On the World Trade Center on 9/11.
The CIA videotaped attendees
750   But did not recognise the mastermind
Khalid Sheikh Mohammed or the would-be
Twentieth hijacker Ramzi bin al-Shibh,
Housemate of pilot Mohammed Atta
In Germany, and did not wiretap them.
755   Osama was active in this same month.
On the holiest day of Ramadan,
He bombed the *USS The Sullivans*,
A warship, and attacked in October
The USS *Cole*, which was off Yemen,
760   Killing seventeen American soldiers.
The CIA Director George Tenet
Briefed Condoleezza Rice, Bush Junior's moon,
About Osama and told the Senate
Next month that he was America's "most
765   Immediate and serious threat". He had
Declared war on America five times
Between 1996 and 8, he'd
Wanted war with the US for eight years,
Wanted America to be bogged down
770   In the Hindu Kush as the Soviets were.
An attack on New York skyscrapers would
Compel the infidel power to invade
Afghanistan, force a showdown between
Islam's "house of peace" and the house of war.
775   Between June and September two thousand
On the orders of Lieutenant General
Mahmoud Ahmed, Pakistan's Director
Of the ISI (Inter-Services
Intelligence), the secret service Saeed
780   Sheikh wired under the alias Mustafa
Ahmed a hundred thousand dollars to
The hijacker Atta. Saeed sent half

The five hundred thousand dollars spent by
The hijackers in the US as they
785   Got ready for the 9/11 plot.

In April a Bulgarian businessman,
Ivan Ivanov, who'd been invited
To Pakistan, was taken to meet bin
Laden who'd been speaking in Beshawar.
790   He was on the remote Chinese border
At a secret location. Ivanov
Discreetly checked his Magellan three-ten
Global positioning system. It showed
The meeting was in China. Bin Laden
795   Was guarded by Pakistani soldiers
In uniform and armed with M-16
Machine-guns. In Rawalpindi Ivanov
Met a shrewd Pakistani scientist,
A middleman for bin Laden, who asked
800   To buy nuclear waste from a powerplant –
Spent nuclear fuel rods from Kozlodui
Nuclear electricity plant – for two
Hundred thousand dollars – bin Laden's fourth
Attempt to obtain nuclear material
805   To construct a "dirty bomb" that would spray
Radioactive waste on populated
Areas and kill millions of infidels,
Which Ivanov declined, and reported.
Bin Laden was harboured by the Chinese
810   And Pakistan army while he made plans
For hijacked planes to carry "dirty bombs".

Linked with al-Qaeda and the ISI,
Saeed transferred money to Florida for
Three hijackers – Atta, Alshehri and
815   Alshehhi – who on September the ninth
Transferred back to Dubai fifteen thousand
Dollars they would not need. Saeed then flew
To Karachi, Pakistan, proving some
ISI involvement in 9/11.
820   On September the tenth the hijacker
Atta called the planner of the attacks,
Khalid Sheikh Mohammed, who gave final
Approval for the attacks to be launched.
The CIA'd paid a team of Afghans
825   To track bin Laden for four years, but in
Early September 2001

They lost track of his movements on the ground.
Now he moved his Afghan training bases.
This was observed by US satellites.
830 On September the fourth the National
Security Council approved a plan
To strike bin Laden in Afghanistan
And, briefed by Tenet and Clarke, Rice now had
A plan to invade Afghanistan on her
835 Desk – a "game plan to remove al-Qaeda
From the face of the Earth" which she passed on
To Bush for signature, which he ignored.

General Ahmed Shah Massoud, the leader –
Commander – of the Northern Alliance,
840 Agreed to see two Arab journalists
Who'd waited in his camp to interview
For fifteen days. Zawahiri's forged letter
Took them into the office of the man
Who had endured twenty-five years of war
845 Against the Soviets, Afghan communists,
Rival *mujahideen* and now combined
Forces of Taliban and al-Qaeda.
Masood Khalili, sat next to Massoud,
Asked the reporter, Karim Touzani,
850 What questions he would ask. The camera on
A tripod, the lens aimed at Massoud's chest,
The reporter scribbled and answered, "Why
Are you against Osama bin Laden?
Why do you call him a killer? And, if
855 You take Kabul what will you do with him?"
Khalili translated the first question.
The video camera itself was filled
With explosives. In a thunderous flash
Of two simultaneous deafening blasts
860 As the cameraman, Kacem Pakkali,
Operated the camera bomb, his mate
Touzani detonated explosives
Strapped round his waist and drove metal fragments
Into Massoud's large, patriotic heart,
865 Jolting his soul from his transient body
So his spirit pushed out into vastness,
Left the finite for the unknown infinite.
Khalili saw a plume of dark blue fire
Rush from the camera. Touzani was blown
870 To pieces, the cameraman ran outside
And jumped into the river Oxus. He

Was pulled out and killed by General Massoud's
Bodyguards. An aid of Massoud's lay dead,
Azim Suhail, who'd made the appointment
875   For the two Moroccans to interview
Massoud. However, Khalili survived.
Massoud was taken by helicopter
To a hospital in Tajikistan
But was pronounced dead on his arrival.
880   Two Saudis said that Osama had given
The order to kill Massoud, which had left
The Northern Alliance leaderless so
The Taliban could control the country
In case the US retaliated.
885   Massoud died on the ninth of September
Two thousand and one as Osama left
With Zawahiri and his inner core
Of al-Qaeda for mountains above Khost
Near the Lion's Den, his first Afghan lair,
890   Carrying with them a satellite dish
And a television set, to await
The outcome of September the eleventh
That would make him the best-known Wahhabi
In the West and within the Muslim world
895   And would give him leadership of Muslims
As wide-embracing as Salah ad-Din,
Saladin, who opposed the Crusaders.
This was President Bush's enemy.

Purposive Bush, from a purposeless youth,
900   Transformed himself into a president
Who, though struggling, was poised to transform: his
Office as policies took on vision;
The political culture; and the world –
And became a Churchillian leader.
905   A failing son of a brilliant father
Who'd been CIA chief and president,
The forty-first in America's line,
He led a riotous youth like Prince Hal,
Drank to excess and did not make his mark
910   As heir apparent to the House of Bush,
Was overshadowed by his brother Jeb
Who became Governor of Florida.
He idealised his father who was good
At everything, but felt deep anger at
915   His father's failure to help him at school
A form of dyslexia and attention

Deficit made him frustrated. He went
To Yale like his father, was admitted
Like him into the Skull-and-Bones order,
920   A secret society whose ritual
Involved the skull of an Indian chief,
The Apache Geronimo whose grave
In Fort Sill, Oklahoma, where he died
Was robbed, it's thought during the First World War.
925   He left with an anti-*élite* grievance
And worked in agriculture with a friend
From his father's Skull-and-Bones days, then went
To Harvard Business School, taught Sunday school,
Then tried to be an oilman like his dad.
930   His company, Arbusto, found no oil,
Ranked near bottom of Texas producers.
He lived over a garage, drank out nights,
Was arrested for driving drunk in Maine,
Stunned his parents by running for Congress,
935   Without success. Friends fixed him with Laura,
A librarian and he transformed himself.
In April 1984 Bush heard
The evangelical Arthur Blessitt
Preach on his car radio and then arranged
940   To meet him at Midland Holiday Inn.
In 1985 his father had
Billy Graham, the evangelist, to stay
By the rocky shore of Walker's Point, Maine,
And Bush walked with him on a beach and, asked
945   If he was "right with God", said, "No, but I'd
Like to be." He later said Graham had
"Planted the mustard seed" which took a year
To germinate: when he stopped his drinking.
In July he woke with a hangover,
950   And though running he could not shake it off
And decided to embrace abstinence.
Now a political career beckoned.
And so Bush began studying the *Bible*
And quietly fashioned a pious image
955   Of himself as a born-again Christian
(Whereas his parents were Presbyterian).
Some said that the move was calculated.
He saw he'd become Governor of Texas
By courting the evangelical vote.
960   Arbusto became Bush Exploration,
Which merged with Spectrum 7. As CEO
He lost money, then bought Texas Rangers,

The baseball club, and ran the team, making
His personality his management,

965 His decision-making intuitive
Unlike his dad's analytic judgement.
When his father became the President
He worked with his National Security
Adviser, Brent Scowcroft, and went fishing

970 With him at weekends, and agreed Saddam
Should have been finished off in the Gulf War,
Criticised his father's decision to quit –
Yet thought Brent patronising and tedious.
Helped by Karl Rove, four years his junior,

975 Who worked for his father and shaped the son,
He became Texas Governor for two terms.
And now he took up with Scowcroft's friend, Dick
Cheney, who was in the family circle
But not too close to his father and played

980 The tutor to Bush's dauphin. Bush fell
For the elder statesman, the CEO
At Halliburton who'd run the Defense
Department, and made him his running mate.
Like the humble farmer Cincinnatus

985 Who had been called from his plough to save Rome,
He yielded to civic imperative
Reluctantly, as would become Moses.
Cheney had worked with Donald Rumsfeld, they
Questioned Kissinger's *détente policy*.

990 And now Bush left them space for a free hand
As he pressed on with policies, lacking
A vision that would now be thrust on him,
Existential peril that Lincoln knew,
And Roosevelt – and Churchill – who had risen

995 To the challenge of unsought war and knew
A greatness through defiance they all lacked
In peacetime government. Bush, close to Christ,
Would be transformed into a crusader.

In New York the Twin Towers, the skyscrapers
1000 Of the World Trade Center gleamed in early
Morning sunlight against a clear blue sky
As, in unhurried, straight trajectory,
A sedate ninety-two-passenger plane
With ten thousand gallons of fuel in tanks,

1005 A Boeing 767 piloted by
Mohammed Atta (who'd sat in 8D),
Flying from Boston to Los Angeles,

American Airlines Flight 11, smashed
Into the north tower at 8.46
1010   Between floors ninety-four and ninety-eight.
The hijackers had stabbed and killed at least
One passenger and two flight attendants
According to phone calls by cabin crew.
Then United Airlines Flight 175
1015   With sixty-five passengers, the same fuel,
A Boeing 767 piloted by
Marwan Alshehhi after the hijack,
Flying from Boston to Los Angeles,
Hit the south tower at 9.02 between
1020   Floors seventy-eight and eighty-four. The planes
Did not explode like bombs. After impact
Fireballs consuming jet fuel expanded
And burning fuel poured through the Towers where heat
Was conjectured to have risen to as
1025   Much as two thousand degrees Fahrenheit.
Molten metal poured down the south tower's side
Through a fissure like red-hot lava from
A long-dormant, erupting volcano.

On the day Muslims attacked Western might
1030   Bush woke at six in Florida, having
Travelled to Sarasota the previous
Night to meet Republican donors at
The Colony Beach Resort. He'd slept well
With surface-to-air missiles on the roof
1035   And a lone Airborne Warning and Control
System (AWACS) plane circling overhead.
And while he jogged for miles round a golf course
A van of Middle-Eastern men pulled up
At the Colony's guardhouse. One declared
1040   They'd come to interview Bush by the pool
As the White House had arranged. A secret
Service agent was named whom no-one knew.
An official said they must seek clearance
At Bush's press relations office in
1045   Washington, and the "interview" team left –
A suicide squad sent by Osama
With a camera bomb as used on Massoud.
Unaware he had been minutes from death,
Bush showered and sat for breakfast and briefing
1050   (His daily intelligence assessment
Which referred to heightened terrorist risk)
While two airliners in al-Qaeda's plan

Took off from Boston's Logan Airport. Bush
Chatted on at the end of the briefing,
1055   Left his penthouse suite and took the lift down,
Lingered for photos, saying pleasant things,
Dawdled while departing from the resort,
Shaking hands with local VIPs. With
Secret servicemen in his motorcade,
1060   On highway 301, north of Main Street
Bush was told a plane had crashed in New York.
He arrived shortly before nine o'clock
At Sarasota's Emma E. Booker
Elementary School to promote his *No*
1065   *Child Left Behind* educational program.
Captain Deborah Loewer, the director
Of the White House Situation Room,
Received a message from her deputy
In the White House about the first plane crash.
1070   She ran from her car straight to Bush's car
And handed him the message. Before nine
Andrew Card, the White House Chief of Staff, told
Him as he was shaking hands with the small
Greeting committee just outside the school,
1075   "Mr President, you have a phone call
From National Security Adviser
Rice you need to take." Bush said, "OK," but
Continued to talk until Card returned
And grabbed his arm. Dawdling again, he spoke
1080   Into a phone, then said he had just learned
A plane had collided with a tower
In the World Trade Center, matter-of-fact.
Officially Karl Rove rushed towards him
In the hallway and told him of the plane.
1085   Bush said, "What a horrible accident,"
And asked if the cause had been bad weather.
Bush should have been whisked away at that point.
He already knew that America
Was under attack and one tower in flames.
1090   In his presidential hold adjoining
The classroom where he'd be, with White House links
And secure phones, waiting to go next door
In his own later words, Bush "was sitting
Outside the classroom waiting to go in
1095   And I saw an airplane hit the tower –
The TV was obviously on, and I
Used to fly myself, and I said, 'There's one
Terrible pilot.'" A video'd been made

Of this first plane slamming into the tower
1100 As if its camera crew knew where to stand
Because they had had prior warning, but it
Was not released for thirteen hours. Secret
Images were transmitted to his screen
By the Secret Service, suggesting they
1105 Had advance knowledge of this first attack.
("The Secret Service has an arrangement,"
Cheney said, "with the FAA. They had
Open lines after the World Trade Center
Was...." He meant "hit". They must have known before
1110 Nine for the arrangement to be in place.)
Bush had seen the plane fly into the tower
Soon after news had first been broadcast on
CNN at around 8.48.
Bush entered the classroom and took his seat
1115 At the teacher's desk at the front and spent
Twelve minutes hearing second-graders read
With a hundred and fifty reporters
And media people waiting at the back,
Listening to sixteen children in the class.
1120 Meanwhile Captain Deborah Loewer saw
The second crash on TV at the school
(As did Bush's spokesman Scott McClellan) –
A transmission room, filing centre and
Press office had been placed in a classroom –
1125 And after thirty seconds realised
That "this was terrorism". She then told
Andrew Card, the White House Chief of Staff, who
Whispered to Bush in class, "A second plane
Hit the second tower. America
1130 Is under attack. And Captain Loewer
Says it's terrorism." Bush should have been
Hustled away, carried under his arms
As Cheney was by Secret Servicemen
To the White House basement. Ari Fleischer,
1135 Press Secretary, held up a pad: "Don't Say
Anything Yet." Bush nodded and sat on
In the teacher's chair at the front of class
In a thirty-second-long silence, with
A befuddled expression on his face,
1140 Uninterested in further details
(Who's done it, where have the attacks come from,
How to protect America from more)
As if he already knew the answers,
Blatantly dawdling, not hurrying out,

1145	Not wanting to disappoint the children
	Who had been selected to read to him.
	Just as a goldfinch, drawn to niger seed,
	Hangs on a bird feeder in spring sunshine
	And concentrating, intent, feeds its fill,
1150	Unaware it is flashing red, yellow
	And white and thrilling all observers in
	A kitchen window as it concentrates,
	So Bush fed from the book in front of him
	Unaware eyes were on him near the door
1155	And focused on his country's destiny.
	As a pupil read, with a distant look,
	His mind on the attacks, he knew at once
	That America was at war. He thought,
	'I'm the Commander-in-Chief, the country's
1160	Just come under attack.' He still did not
	Ask any questions: who was attacking,
	If there'd be more attacks, had nuclear-
	Suitcase bombs been on board, what military
	Plans had been made and what action taken.
1165	Not wanting to disappoint the children,
	He pulled himself together, read aloud
	With the children, "'The Pet Goat. A-girl-got
	A-pet-goat. But-the-goat-did-some-things-that
	Made-the-girl's-dad-mad.' Really good readers,
1170	Whew! These must be sixth-graders." At 9.12
	Bush left the room and went to the TV
	In his presidential hold, a safe room
	With White-House links located the other
	Side of the classroom where he'd heard reading.
1175	He saw the burning towers on a screen,
	Instructed one of the six advisers
	To turn the television off and took
	A distraction-free call from Dick Cheney
	And then two more calls, from the FBI's
1180	Director and the Governor of New York.
	Then he scribbled notes on a yellow pad
	For a broadcast he knew he'd have to make.
	At 9.30 Bush addressed the nation
	From the school's library and podium
1185	In front of two hundred pupils, teachers
	And reporters, at the exact time and
	Place publicly announced in his schedule.
	He could have been a terrorist target.
	Hijackers could have crashed a plane upon
1190	A venue publicised four days before.

He looked bewildered, like a rabbit caught
In headlights; said, "This is a difficult
Moment for America…. Today we've had
A national tragedy." He was sombre.
1195   "Two airplanes have crashed into the World Trade
Center in an apparent terrorist
Attack on our country." He vowed "to hunt
Down and to find those folks who committed
This act." He could not seem to find the words,
1200   But this bit he'd ad-libbed. Then, echoing
Words his father had once spoken about
The Iraqi invasion of Kuwait:
"Terrorism against our nation will
Not stand." He stood in a minute's silence.
1205   He had not spoken with his nation's voice.
At 9.40 Bush at last left the school.

From his motorcade Bush looked at the sky
High above planes and a few wispy clouds,
Its blue above Earth's atmosphere, reaching
1210   Out into space towards the surging wave
Of the expanding universe, space-time.
And out on the edge of the universe
Near where it breasts the infinite, the Greek
To apeiron, the boundless, in his mind
1215   Bush looked down at the smallness of the dot,
The tiny glinting star that was the Earth,
And to the silence of the universe
It was infinitesimally small
And insignificant that two planes had
1220   Crashed into two buildings, and the worries
Of the most powerful man on Earth seemed as
Nothing to the vast Infinite Spirit
That pervaded the universe and filled
His soul with soothing love. Despite dreadful
1225   Events, the sensing universe combined
All violent and peaceful acts in its span
Of contradictions and opposites which
Were held together and reconciled in
An awesome pattern within the system
1230   Of space-time and Nature, in which two planes
Loaded with fuel, passengers and pilots,
And skyscrapers packed with office-workers
Were in an ultimate harmony that
The One understood. How could it allow
1235   Such terrible collisions to happen?

They were in a pattern the One could grasp
Which had meaning and made sense to the One.
All collisions were like the wind on leaves –
The autumn wind that blows away the leaves
1240 From a tree like those outside his window –
To the great silence of the universe,
And should be accepted without reaching
After fact or reason or questioning –
And imaginatively entering –
1245 The mind of God the One outside space-time.

American Airlines Flight 77,
A Boeing 757 piloted by
Hani Hanjour after it was hijacked,
Flying from Washington towards LA,
1250 At 9.40 struck the Pentagon's west
Side with sixty-five passengers, and blew
A hole five stories high, seventy yards wide
(Though the main entry hole was much smaller),
Killing the passengers and a hundred
1255 And twenty-four Pentagon personnel.
United Airlines Flight 93 crashed
After 10 in a Pennsylvanian field,
Piloted by Ziad Jarrah, it's thought,
After being hijacked by Arabs while
1260 Flying from Newark to San Francisco.
Passengers had learned of the three crashes
On cell phones and wrestled with "crew", causing
The plane to fall far short of the White House.

Bush heard the news within his motorcade
1265 That a plane had gouged through the Pentagon
When he spoke to Cheney by telephone
And ordered that all flights should be grounded
And learned that *Air Force One* was under threat,
An untruth that served Cheney's agenda.
1270 As wild flowers line a motorway's grass verge
And smile out in the sun at passing cars
Whose drivers, preoccupied, don't see them,
So people smiled at Bush's motorcade
And he, deep in his thoughts, scarcely noticed.
1275 He headed for Sarasota Airport
And without security climbed the steps
Of *Air Force One*, which soon took off steeply
Like a rocket going straight up without
Fighter protection at 9.55.

1280	A fighter escort would have deterred planes.
	But then no threat could have kept Bush away.
	Cheney called from the White House bunker, said
	It was not safe to land in Washington,
	And so *Air Force One* flew in slow circles.
1285	Bush heard that a plane aimed at the White House
	Had mysteriously crashed into a field.
	He heard that first the south and then the north
	Towers had collapsed in plumes of dust and smoke.
	He looked bemused, events had controlled him.
1290	He was not a president in control
	Of events, anticipating outcomes.
	At 10.32 Cheney called and told
	Bush of another threat to *Air Force One*,
	Another untruth to keep him away,
1295	And turned the plane away from Washington.
	Bush landed at 11.45
	At the Barksdale Air Force Base near Shreveport,
	Louisiana, and then, on being told
	A high-speed plane was heading for his ranch
1300	At Crawford, Texas, flew on to Offutt
	Air Force Base in Nebraska. While away,
	He learned that a third building had collapsed,
	World Trade Center 7 at 5.20,
	Having been "struck by *débris*". In due course
1305	He landed at Andrews Air Force Base at
	6.34 and was helicoptered
	To the White House shortly before 7.
	The Vice-President gave these directions
	While the President, seemingly confused,
1310	Flew from Florida out to Nebraska.
	Although Clarke had briefed Cheney, Rice and Powell
	(Secretary of State) on terrorist threats
	And Clinton's Presidential Directive
	To "eliminate al-Qaeda" by arming
1315	The Northern Alliance, Bush did not know
	Of these briefings and was out of the loop
	On his predecessor's old plan to deal
	With al-Qaeda, main US enemy
	Though Condoleezza Rice, his National
1320	Security Adviser, had sent him
	An "analytical report" warning
	A terrorist attack was imminent.
	On August the sixth the CIA'd come
	To Crawford, Texas where in his ranch house
1325	Among scrub pines Bush was on holiday.

From her White-House office Rice was present
Via a secure teleconferencing link.
Their briefing paper stated: "Bin Laden
Determined to Strike in US." The rest
1330   Was rehashed background, without dates, too vague.
Bush was disappointed, the paper said
Far too little (keeping him in the dark).
It's possible that Bush was being fed
A target to retaliate against
1335   Before the shock attack on the Twin Towers.
So Bush was less aware of al-Qaeda
Than those who worked for him, to some extent,
But seemed more unaware than he in fact
Was and was content to do nothing while
1340   America was attacked – even though
He would have been a terrorist target,
Having been shown arriving at the school –
As if he knew he would not be wiped out
And grasped the crash's meaning. The Twin Towers
1345   Stood for Western greed to bin Laden's men –
The "World Trade Center" for world government.
The Twin Towers had been built with assistance
From "Rockefellers" and had been nicknamed
"David and Nelson Rockefeller Towers",
1350   And, monuments to imperial Mammon,
They rose like Towers of Babel, and their fall –
And that of the military HQ –
Was greeted by Muslims with shouts of joy.
The smoke that rose was like an altar's smoke
1355   And Bush now felt the call of destiny.

Crucial to the plan of the Syndicate –
The network of commercial families
And firms with a common interest, to bring
In a world-government United States
1360   Of the World – was to ensure by all means
That a scheming Syndicate man should be
Vice-President and benefit commerce.
Bush moved into the White House to improve
His father's executive office and
1365   Help find a competent manager, Dick
Cheney, but his dad preferred James Baker.
When Bush became the Governor of Texas
Cheney was up the I-35 in
Dallas, running Halliburton, having
1370   Been spotted by its chairman Tom Cruikshank

Who'd heard from him while on a fishing trip
In New Brunswick in 1995
How he'd managed the Pentagon. It seemed
He'd been in the right place at the right time
1375   But his "spot" was not due to chance. In fact,
As Defense Secretary two years before
Cheney commissioned a study by Brown
And Root Services, a subsidiary
Wholly owned by Halliburton, that said
1380   Private firms should support logistical
Support programs for US military
Operations around the world. This was
The Syndicate volunteering to aid
The military, enmesh it in its web –
1385   To secure troops for its projects. Bush had
Always liked and respected him. He had
Been two years at Yale and had left. They met
At events. Cheney had just agreed at
A quail hunt that Halliburton would buy
1390   Dresser for 7.7 billion dollars
And when oil plummeted, slashed ten thousand
Company jobs; received a 1.5
Million-dollar bonus for pushing through
The merger. Halliburton traded with
1395   Pariah states – Iraq, Iran, Burma,
Libya, Indonesia, Azerbaijan –
Which ignored human rights and supported
Terrorism, proclaiming, "We go where
The business is. The good Lord didn't see
1400   Fit to put oil and gas only where there
Are democratically elected
Regimes friendly to the United States."
In November and December nineteen
Ninety-eight Bush toured Israel, escorted
1405   By Ariel Sharon, leader-to-be,
And saw how tiny Israel was, compared
To its Arab neighbours. He was the first
In his family to be pro-Jewish:
His grandfather Prescott Bush, a banker,
1410   Had been director of a New York bank,
The Union Banking Corp., where pro-Nazi
Germans banked their fortunes, and was accused
Of collaborating with the Nazis
Before Japan's attack on Pearl Harbour.
1415   In mid-December 1998
Cheney brought to a seminar with Bush

As a guest Paul Wolfowitz, a member
Of Project for the New American
Century, a group with a more aggressive
1420   And unilateral foreign policy
That maintained the world could be remade in
America's image, a muscular
Moralist and neo-conservative
Ideal that differed from Bush Senior's
1425   Internationalism. Neo-cons were
Pro-Israel and linked with "Rothschilds'" interests;
They promoted "Rothschilds'" world-government
Goals that guarded Israel. Cheney brought in
Donald Rumsfeld and Richard Perle, who were
1430   PNAC co-founders. Bush mixed in
Realists like Colin Powell and Armitage.
His foreign-policy team now in place,
Bush, now presidential candidate, asked
Cheney to be his Vice-President though
1435   He lacked telegenic charisma. He'd
Been given Halliburton shares and options
Worth tens of millions of dollars, and wished
To sell and exercise these. To accept
Now would mean forfeiting a fortune, so
1440   The press were told that Cheney would manage
A search team to choose a vice-president.
For six months he sold Halliburton shares,
Disposed of most – not all – of his interests.
Thus Halliburton and the Syndicate
1445   Had six months to plan how foreign affairs
Might target oil and benefit their wealth.
The questionnaires Cheney sent candidates
Were complicated to take many hours.
The one he sent Oklahoma's governor
1450   Contained eighty-three questions that required
Every home, donation, taped interview
And published article to be listed.
This slowed the process down. And at the end
Bush (after lunch) asked him to be the Vice.
1455   Still appearing reluctant, he said he
Would talk to his family. The next week
He had a medical, for he had had
Three heart attacks, a quadruple by-pass,
High cholesterol and gout, and skin cancer.
1460   Cheney's heart was passed fit, and Bush rang him
With a formal offer on a Monday
At 6.22 a.m. when he trod

A treadmill. *The New York Times* reported
His severance package was more than twenty
1465   Million dollars, his compensation ten.
In fact, he received forty-five million
Dollars, and would receive more every year
He was out of Halliburton if they
Raked in billion-dollar contracts while he
1470   Was the VP. During the long campaign
The press recalled Cheney advocating
Cutting the world's oil supplies so petrol
Prices would rise, which would spur exploring
And create business for Halliburton.
1475   Cheney caricatured Gore's "make-believe".
Bush also had staunch family support.
Under the Governorship of his brother,
Jeb Bush, twenty-two thousand Democrat
Black voters were "illegally" removed
1480   From Florida's electoral register
Before the Presidential Election
Which Bush "won" by only hundreds of votes.
When the votes were counted, it was Cheney
Who declared the Republicans had won,
1485   Urged Bush and Baker to give no quarter.
During the Florida recount Cheney
Planned the transition for Syndicate power.
With still no victor proclaimed, he woke up
At 3.30 a.m. with a chest pain,
1490   His fourth heart attack, which had been caused by
A blocked artery. He left hospital
The day the Supreme Court heard *Bush v. Gore*.

Say how Cheney stole the election from
Gore for the Syndicate and their pipelines.
1495   In a *per curiam* opinion, by
A 7-2 vote, the Court in *Bush v. Gore*
Held the Florida Supreme Court's method
For recounting ballots was illegal,
Unconstitutional, and by a 5-4
1500   Vote held no alternative method could
Be established within the time limits
Set by the Florida State (whose Governor
Was Bush's brother, Jeb), allowing Bush
To be confirmed as Florida's victor
1505   And his electoral votes to exceed Gore's
By five and to win the Presidency by
One vote. And a "crown" was given unto him.

Among the five judges whose 5-4 votes
Gave Bush victory was Antonin Scalia,
1510   Bush's favourite Supreme Court Justice, whom
He called "Anthony", Anglicising his
First name. His son was a partner within
The law firm that had argued Bush's case,
An old friend of Cheney who three years on
1515   Would go on a duck-shoot as Cheney's guest
Although about to hear a case Cheney
Had brought to keep secret a task force on
Energy policy, which he then won.
Two of his nine children worked in law firms
1520   That represented Bush, but he had deemed
There to be no conflict of interest
(As did another of the five, Clarence
Thomas, whose wife had e-mailed many aides
In the Representatives and Senate.)
1525   Without the support of Cheney's old friend
Who did not invoke the recusal law
And withdraw, even-handed, from the case
That halted the recount in Florida,
Bush would not have become the President
1530   And the Syndicate would have lost pipelines.
Drawing on his time with Bush Senior
And using all his wheeler-dealer skills,
Cheney assembled Bush's Cabinet.
Bush did not want briefing-books or detail,
1535   Just what he needed to know in nuggets
That were digestible. And so Bush learned
Of his new transition and Cabinet
From his number-two, who could now control
The presidency for the Syndicate
1540   And be the most powerful Vice-President
In the long history of the United States.

The discreet Syndicate coped brilliantly
With the practicalities of letting
The attacks take place in the public domain
1545   By simply setting up exercises
In US airspace that fateful morning.
Two agencies guarded US airspace:
The FAA (Federal Aviation
Administration), which controlled safety
1550   Of civil aviation, and NORAD
(North American Aerospace Defense
Command), which supplied military defence.

The 9/11 attacks were within NEADS
(Or NORAD's North-East Air Defense Sector).
1555   Boston asked for military help too late,
NEADS sent two fighter jets to wrong airspace,
Air Traffic Control could not be disturbed,
NEADS sent more fighter jets east and not north.
The FAA HQ offered no help.
1560   There was confusion and incompetence
As fighter jets failed four times in a row.
The context was a series of war-games.
One drill over Canada that morning
Monitored "Russian-controlled" manoeuvres;
1565   NORAD coped with an imaginary crisis,
FAA and military radar screens
Had false blips denoting twenty-two planes.
NORAD thought reports of hijacked planes were
Part of the exercise. Another drill
1570   Took planes from Washington two hundred miles
South just before the Pentagon was struck.
As the exercises involved hijacked
Airliners the jet fighters stayed on ground.
A May-2001 Presidential
1575   Order placed Cheney in direct command
And control of all war-game and all field
Exercise training and scheduling through
Agencies such as NORAD and FEMA,
The Federal Emergency Management
1580   Agency which was to respond next day
To a biological-terror drill.
Cheney and Rumsfeld oversaw these games.
That morning Cheney ran a separate
Command, control and communications
1585   System which superseded orders given
By the National Military Command
Center (NMCC) or the White House
Situation Room. He used the Secret-
Service system in the bunker below
1590   The White House known as the Presidential
Emergency Operations Center.
Hence fighters failed to intercept four times.
The main Pentagon hole was thirteen feet
Wide by twenty-six feet high, and seemed caused
1595   By a wingless, tailless missile, not plane.
The Saudi pilot of Flight 77,
Hani Hanjour, had flying skills too poor
To leave such a hole without scorching grass.

He'd never flown a jet successfully
1600 And had no help from air traffic control,
Yet performed a manoeuvre well beyond
The skill of most of the world's best pilots,
As if the plane was beamed, remote-controlled.
Rumsfeld, Bush's military 2-i-c,
1605 Was hosting a breakfast meeting within
His private Pentagon dining-room though
He had been told a third "plane" was heading
For Washington, might have controlled the attacks.
But Cheney had a missing half an hour:
1610 Secret-Service agents burst into his
White-House office and, nearly lifting him
Off the ground, carried him under his arms,
Ran him down steps, evacuated him
Down to the bunker about 9, yet he
1615 Entered the underground tunnel leading
To the shelter at 9.37.
He phoned Bush at the school at 9.15
And in the air at 10 when Bush agreed
They'd shoot down hijacked aircraft, though filled with
1620 American citizens. Had Cheney
Given the order before he discussed
It with the President? Soon afterwards
The fourth plane crashed into a field before
It could reach the White House. At 10.08
1625 Cheney told Bush of the crash, and Bush asked,
"Did we shoot it down or did it crash?" Hours
Later he was told it crashed. Then the south
And north towers collapsed. At ten thirty-
Two Cheney told Bush, wrongly, *Air Force One*
1630 Was under threat and no fighter was near,
Said he should turn to Louisiana.
Cheney kept Bush away from Washington,
Using the lack of a fighter plane as
An excuse to keep him out of the way
1635 While air exercises let hijacked planes
Through to reach the Twin Towers and bring them down
With help from beaming and high explosives
In a new Pearl Harbour. Later Cheney
Urged that Senate Leader Tom Daschle should
1640 Not investigate 9/11, and Bush
Made the same request some four days later,
Falling into line with Syndicate guile.
Now it is clear why the Secret Service
Allowed Bush to remain inside the school –

1645	Without bundling him into his limo
	Which had a communications system
	That almost duplicated the White House –
	Till 9.40: Cheney wanted him there
	While the Syndicate shut down air defence,
1650	Swamped it with "exercises" and "crashed" planes.
	Some say the planes had no Arab pilots,
	Yet bin Laden and Khalid planned the strike.
	Some say that Mohammed Atta and six
	More of the hijackers were Arab spies
1655	Trained to be pilots at US bases,
	Paid well to go clubbing and drink spiced rum
	And coke, Stolichnaya and orange juice
	And to parade a girlfriend with punk hair,
	Not abstemious Islamic extremists.
1660	In Atta's luggage was a document
	In which the nineteen hijackers were urged
	To check their bags, clothes, knives, wills and IDs,
	Their passports and papers, to wash, polish
	Their shoes and fast all night and pray all night,
1665	Recite the *Koran*, purify the heart,
	Clean it from all Earthly ties, ask Allah
	For forgiveness as it was judgement time
	Before heading out to kill infidels,
	Then enter the infinite paradise.
1670	The operation was not a decoy
	That blamed nineteen Arabs and stirred feelings
	Against Afghanistan's oil pipeline zone,
	But an actual Muslim attack helped on
	That had the same effect as a decoy.
1675	Bush wrote in his diary that night: "The Pearl
	Harbour of the twenty-first century
	Took place today." Thanks to the Syndicate.
	All day television film showed a plane,
	The second hijacked airliner, drifting
1680	Towards the smoking north tower in blue sky,
	Smoke black as night, idling at the south tower,
	A hundred-and-ten-storey skyscraper,
	And smashing into glass. A fireball whooshed
	From the other side of the placid tower,
1685	Cascading *débris* hundreds of feet down
	To rain shrapnel and glass shards on strangers.
	Back in the White House Bush watched in dismay.
	It was as if the pilot had trained on
	The Microsoft Flight Simulation game.

1690	He saw doomed workers clambering out of glass
	Onto ledges and jumping, hurtling down,
	A couple holding hands, a man diving,
	Another on his back as if bouncing
	Up from a gymnasium's trampoline,
1695	Preferring swift death to choking in smoke
	Or burning in billowing, blazing fuel,
	Plunging slowly into eternity.
	More than three thousand trapped on sagging floors,
	Fierce heat rising, melting struts, fizzing wires,
1700	Then blasts and shuddering walls and opening cracks,
	A scything gash across the fractured tower's
	Tubular steel columns braced by girders.
	Down in the street, a crowd running away
	Beneath the pinnacles thirteen hundred
1705	And sixty feet high, snapped in two, tilting,
	Turn and see the south tower tip and smokestack
	Down in a cloud of dust and billowing smoke,
	Followed by a roar and, slowly toppling,
	The north tower slid down as if explosives
1710	Packed in corners had been detonated.
	Film showed rubble within the Pentagon
	And a pile of charred *débris* in a field.
	In many shots sat or lay the wounded,
	One with his leg amputated, some crushed.
1715	The World Trade Center was like a war zone,
	An abstract landscape with bits of girders
	In which lay a lone severed aircraft wheel;
	Dust, water, sunlight in the smoky air.
	It looked as if an atomic bomb had
1720	Gone off, and, not knowing the fires would burn
	A hundred days, Bush wondered if the planes
	Had each carried a nuclear-suitcase bomb
	Of half a kiloton that had seared such
	A devastating scene as firemen stood
1725	Knee-deep in rubble in a dust-like mist.
	Whence figures loomed like ghosts in smoky Hell,
	Faces caked in dust and dried streams of tears.
	And among the ruins strewn paper lay –
	A report on a company's share price –
1730	Like a snugly rumpled quilt eiderdown
	Above sprawled youths who had fallen asleep
	And mangled torsos stripped of human form.
	Film showed groups of Arabs dancing for joy,
	Reported bin Laden as giving thanks
1735	To Allah, but not admitting his guilt.

With tears trickling down his undusty cheeks
Bush made notes for the next day's meeting when
He and the Big Three (Cheney, Rumsfeld, Powell)
Would assess the catastrophe, react.
1740 More film showed Manhattan's devastation,
A post-apocalyptic landscape; steel
Columns jutting slanting angles, collapsed
Buildings, bent skeletons of lower floors,
A graveyard of hopes where self-assurance
1745 Had died. It looked like the end of the world,
But an old world had died and a new world
Of terror and retaliatory war
Had replaced it as history lurched forward.
A new Age had been born from smoking earth
1750 Bush recognised the world had indeed changed.
It was at a beginning, not an end.

Five hours ahead that day I, your poet,
Greeted the Lord Lieutenant of Essex,
Lord Braybrooke, at the school I founded in
1755 Epping Forest in cream, eighteenth-century
Coopersale Hall, and after a tour lunched
With him under Jacobean carvings
Of grimacing faces and a Green Man,
Discussed the founding of America
1760 From my Otley Hall in 1607
And our surrender of America
At Yorktown by his famous ancestor
Lord Cornwallis, whose surrender sword he
Owned and kept in his house by Audley End.
1765 I waved him off and went to the Head's room
Where Ken the Bursar said, "I've just been rung.
A plane's flown into New York's Twin Towers."
And later Robin told me, "Down your lane
I put the radio on and heard two planes
1770 Had flown into the World Trade Center's towers."
News of the attack on America
Instantly pervaded the leafy lane
And building built in the year the US
Declared independence and came to birth,
1775 Borne on air waves to our provincial life
From the capital of the Western world.
This poet wanly recalls the moment
Bin Laden flung down his gauntlet and crowed
With *hubris* swollen by his suitcase bombs;
1780 When the world changed and a new Age began,

When provincial peace was now outmoded
By the aim to prevent Armageddon.

Bin Laden had taken a satellite
Dish and television into the Khost
1785 Mountains near the Lion's Den, Maasada,
So named because Osama meant "the Lion"
In Arabic, hinting "Osama's Den".
From his training camp under the Spin-Ghar
Mountain range he and his group climbed to caves
1790 Where, with his family construction firm's
Equipment, he'd made fortified bunkers.
Outside these he eventually stood
And unloaded the mules, beasts of burden.
Now his weary al-Qaeda group struggled
1795 To obtain a signal. One cupped the dish
And aimed it at the sky: only static.
One tuned a radio to the BBC
Arabic service. They heard, "Breaking news.
A plane has struck New York's World Trade Center."
1800 The al-Qaeda group cried in joy and fell
To the ground. But bin Laden said, "Wait, wait."
The second plane was announced. Now he wept
And prayed, gave thanks to Allah, for striking
The towers was a sign of Allah's favour
1805 And of Allah's challenge to the defeat
Of the conquering armies of Islam
Who were repulsed from Vienna's gates on
September the eleventh sixteen eighty-
Three, a defeat from which the Ottoman
1810 Empire never recovered and which led
To Christian Western powers dominating
The still-humiliated Muslim world.
He held up three fingers. Incredulous,
His group waited. The third plane was announced.
1815 He held up four fingers, and all marvelled,
Delighted that the symbols of Western
Commercial might and military power
Had so easily been reduced to dust.
To bin Laden Dubya Bush was *Dabbah*,
1820 "The Beast" who, according to the *Hadith*,
Would be defeated by a prophet who
Would appear when Muslims throughout the world
Were oppressed, the Mahdi and new Caliph
Who would lead Muslims to victory and bring
1825 In the Day of Islam when all people,

Believers and non-believers alike,
The whole world, would submit to Allah's will.

Bin Laden knew the 9/11 attacks
Would happen and sanctioned them. And although
1830 He was assisted by the Syndicate
He was responsible. He knew Allah,
Was a "rightly guided" Caliph and had
Had his 'Declaration of War' against
The US – *jihad* – backed by a *fatwa*
1835 Issued by a Saudi cleric, *Sheikh* Fahd.
So in his own conscience, had he done good?
Or, despite Allah, had he done evil?
Evil is the perpetration of harm
Against humans. Was 9/11 evil?
1840 There was intentional, deliberate harm.
Could its evil be justified, excused?
Do God-followers who justify evil
Delude themselves? Are they self-deceivers?
In medieval times the Crusaders
1845 Justified slaughter as wanted by God
Just as now bin Laden had justified
This slaughter as demanded by Allah.
Three thousand Muslims dead – God wanted it.
Three thousand Christians dead – Allah's demand,
1850 Backed by a May-2003 *fatwa*.
The belief that a deity demands
Human sacrifices is ignorant.
Is evil real or the absence of good?
The evil in an act depends on how
1855 A perpetrator interprets that act's
Significance and symbolic meaning:
Revenge for past wars, defiant *jihad* –
Or ruthless intent to maim, kill or harm.
Low-level souls live in ignorant dream,
1860 Drifters in an amoral universe
Who harm casually and self-interestedly
Like apes that know no evil, just instinct.
All ignorant of the Light occupy
A secular society in which
1865 Evil does not exist, nor does Satan,
And harm's unfortunate absence of good.
But souls who know the Light always have choice
Between the dark and light and know evil.
To such evil is real energy.
1870 Evil and error are ignorance's scum.

Bush knew that bin Laden's deed was evil
And that bin Laden justified his deed
Casuistically when he, a holy man,
Could not plead ignorance, lack of knowledge,
1875   And should have known better, acknowledged that
It's always wrong and evil to slaughter
Three thousand innocent human beings.

At his evening intelligence briefing
At the White House, the CIA expert
1880   Discussed with Bush the afternoon's collapse,
At 5.20 of WTC7,
Which Bush had heard about while in the air,
A third building quite near the other two,
The forty-seven-storey Salomon
1885   Brothers Building in the Rockefeller-
Inspired, vast WTC complex.
"It held the CIA command centre,"
Bush said. The CIA expert agreed.
Bush wondered again how such giant towers
1890   Could have slid down and gone in ten seconds
With the velocity of a free fall.
He asked, "What caused Building 7 to fall?
There was no impact. I don't understand."
The expert looked uncomfortable and said,
1895   "We're saying débris fell from an impact."
Bush said, "But it's quite a distance away
From the Twin Towers, it could not have happened."
There was a silence. Then the expert said
Connivingly as if talking in code,
1900   "If we'd wanted to destroy it to erase
Evidence that should not exist, conduct
A huge controlled demolition, thermite
Enhanced with sulphur could achieve just that.
It's aluminium and iron oxide mixed.
1905   When it burns it generates temperatures
Of around two thousand four hundred C.
Steel melts at fifteen hundred degrees C.
Fire by itself does not devour structures
Uniformly or pulverise concrete,
1910   Not in the Twin Towers or Building 7.
At a high temperature thermite mixed with
Sulphur fuses and cuts heavy steel bars.
Perhaps the débris acted like thermite
And sulphur. Who knows? The fact is, the tower
1915   Collapsed as quickly as the other two."

Bush looked down. He had not expected such
A frank answer. He did not want to know
How WTC7 or the Twin Towers
Could have been brought down by straight sabotage.
1920   He wanted to stick with planes hitting towers.
He changed the subject, but now thermite teased.

Later the CIA expert returned
And said, "I was on the right lines. It was
Nano-thermite that brought all the towers down.
1925   Large quantities of nano-thermite chips,
Which are red-grey, have been found in the dust
Round the World Trade Center, and this suggests
That several tons of nano-thermite, which
Is a high-tech explosive, were set off
1930   To ignite at four hundred and thirty
Degrees Centigrade, which is far below
The temperature produced on combustion
By igniting conventional thermite.
Super-thermite can be handled safely
1935   As super-thermite electric matches.
No planes brought down the towers. They fell due to
Nano-thermite bombs, nano-chemistry.
I won't speculate as to who used it."
Again, Bush did not want to know such things.
1940   He was sticking with planes hitting the towers.

Bush learned that the hundred-and-ten-storey
Twin Towers, that rose from 1968
To 1972, had asbestos,
A slurry mix of asbestos-cement
1945   Sprayed on as fireproofing material
Until New York City Council halted
This practice in 1971.
Asbestos covered the steel skeletons
Of the entire height of the Twin Towers.
1950   Hundreds of tons of this mix were coated.
Removing asbestos may cost five times
A building's construction costs, and the Port
Authority had earmarked eight hundred
Thousand dollars, mostly to be spent on
1955   Abatement. Not all was removed. The cloud
Of dust was settling on several square miles
Of Manhattan. Four per cent of the dust
Was asbestos. Years later the powder
Could cause asbestosis, lung cancer and

1960	Mesothelioma. Now Bush was told
	The Port Authority had sold a lease,
	Ninety-nine years for 3.2 billion,
	To a consortium led by Larry
	Silverstein on July the twenty-third.
1965	Silverstein was a close friend of Ehud
	Barak, Benjamin Netanyahu and
	Israel's Prime Minister Ariel Sharon.
	Silverstein insured the Twin Towers for
	3.5 billion dollars, which was more
1970	Than the 3.2 billion of the lease.
	Bush learned that Silverstein Properties would
	Make insurance claims for the three buildings,
	Claim for WTC7, and twice
	For the Twin Towers as "two occurrences"
1975	Were deemed to have taken place, two planes on
	Two towers. "The collapse did Silverstein
	A favour," Bush was told. "He'll make from this."
	None knew that in February 2002
	For WTC7 Silverstein
1980	Properties would secure a staggering
	Sum, eight hundred and sixty-one million
	Dollars against their insured investment
	Of three hundred and eighty-six million,
	A profit of half a billion dollars;
1985	And that in December 2004
	They'd be awarded 2.2 billion
	Dollars and later 4.6 billion
	As they collected twice; and that the Port
	Authority's insurance would be held
1990	To be invalid, overridden by
	Silverstein's insurance. Now Bush wondered
	If the collapse of the three buildings could
	Somehow be linked to an insurance scam
	To win a fortune from asbestosed steel.
1995	The Twin Towers should have been demolished
	Before the two planes struck and brought them down.
	But it was not clear that insurance would
	Pay for the asbestos to be removed
	And for the demolition of the towers.
2000	Bush half-imagined the scenario.
	Israel knew the Twin Towers would be attacked
	Before Silverstein, close friend of Sharon
	And Israel's leaders, bought the lease and took
	Out an inflated insurance cover.
2005	Could he have known of the coming attack?

By good fortune he and his two children
Did not go into work at the Twin Towers
On the day of New York's spectacular.
An air attack helped on by explosives –
2010   Nano-thermite bombs strategically placed –
Would bring the buildings down without the costs
Of demolition, though asbestos dust
Would be spread about and contaminate
The air people breathed. And insurance funds
2015   Would be paid out. These could only be deemed
Part-fraudulent if there was evidence
That there was an intention to defraud.
While the Syndicate would secure its goal
As the US public would bay for war
2020   And the US military would sweep through
Afghanistan, expel the Taliban,
And – most important – secure their pipeline.
Could there have been a multi-levelled fraud
Linking landlord, Israel and Syndicate?
2025   Did Sharon know the Twin Towers would be hit?
Bush winced, not wanting to know any more.

Bush received further briefing on the Towers.
Now he was told that Ehud Olmert, Mayor
Of Jerusalem, the sister city
2030   Of New York City since nineteen ninety-
Three, made a secret visit to New York
City on September the tenth. Why? Did
He meet Mayor Guiliani? He had no
Details of where Olmert went. Now he saw
2035   The elaborate intertwining of
Political and commercial motifs.
He suspected that Mossad had got wind
Of al-Qaeda's plot to hijack four planes
And fly them into buildings. They passed on
2040   A general warning to the authorities
Suggesting the attack might be *outside*
The US. Then they plotted. They had told
Someone within the Syndicate, who had,
He thought on reflection, told Dick Cheney,
2045   Who put himself in charge of the entire
Military and secret service on
9/11 to hold an exercise
And be the architect of the attack –
Or rather, of facilitating it.
2050   The planes were unopposed by US jets

As Cheney had contrived that. He had told
Someone within the CIA, who had
Set up a monitoring post within
WTC7's topmost floor.

2055   Five Israelis who had celebrated
The two planes crashing into the Twin Towers,
Dancing and clapping near the Trade Center,
Had been arrested, and it had turned out
That they were Mossad agents who had said

2060   They were recording what was happening.
How did they know where to be, when to film
The World Trade Center hijack disaster?
They must have had foreknowledge to be there.
The five dancing Mossad men may have helped

2065   Plant the explosives for demolition,
The nano-thermite electric matches,
Or may have followed the terrorists for
Olmert. Had he come to New York to see
The attacks through, maximise their impact

2070   To swing US public opinion for
Revenge attacks on Israel's enemies?
He knew Olmert was a Jabotinsky
Zionist who believed that Israel's land
Should stretch from the Nile to the Euphrates,

2075   Include Iraq, and that Palestinians
Had no place in Israel. He was a co-
Defendant in a criminal lawsuit
With Menachem Atzmon, who had once been
His political ally. He controlled

2080   Passenger security at Boston
Airport, and his business partner, Ezra
Harel, was in charge of security
At Boston and Newark airports since their
Company ICTS bought Huntleigh

2085   USA in 1999. Bush
Knew that both the flights which struck the Twin Towers
Originated at Boston under
Harel. Perhaps Olmert had organised
For the hijackers to board their targets

2090   Without interference from the US?
Were they Jewish terrorists who assumed
The identities of Arab pilots?
Surely not. He would stick with Arab foes.
The skies were then clear for the planes to hit

2095   The Twin Towers. In WTC7
The CIA timed the demolitions

Of hidden nano-thermite explosives
To coincide with impacts, which they saw.
When the job was done and the Towers were down,
2100   They removed evidence and demolished
WTC7 to erase how
They had controlled the collapse of the Towers.
Had they locked into the aircraft's steering
And steered the planes into the Towers as well?
2105   It could be done with cars – could planes' steering,
With tinkering, be remotely controlled?
Was the top floor of WTC7
A command centre for remote control
And controlled demolition on impact?
2110   Bush wondered if bin Laden was in on
The plot. He'd worked with the CIA when
Fighting the Soviets in Afghanistan.
His role could have been to recruit pilots.
His older brother Salem was Bush's
2115   Business partner back in the seventies
And had co-founded Arbusto with him
Before he was killed in a plane crash. Bush
Had a fondness for Saudi Binladens,
Which was why he would repatriate them
2120   Before US flight restrictions were eased.
Could Salem's younger brother by ten years,
Osama, *still* be in the CIA?
Surely not. He would stick with Arab foes.
His train of thought was leading him to ground
2125   From which he could not defend the US,
Which is what he as President must do.
But he had delved enough to know he was
In mysteries that he did not understand,
That were of the sly Syndicate's making.
2130   Just as a cormorant, sitting on waves,
Dives for half a minute, then surfaces
With a fish in its beak, which it swallows,
So Bush had dived too deep and had come up
With some fishy ideas that weren't welcome.
2135   The surface view, sparkling in sun, was best.
His job as President was to defend
America from external attack
And not see external as internal.
He was just the President. He was not
2140   Party to much that went on, but he had
To be a figurehead and speak clearly,
Which was what a president had to do.

He closed his mind and got on with his job.

Now a report from the Pentagon claimed
2145   There was too little *débris* for a plane:
No wings or tail, just a piece of engine
And sections of landing gear on the ground.
The holes in the building were of the size
Of Predators, the remote-controlled spy
2150   Planes used in Iraq and Afghanistan.
The evidence seemed staged: "It looks as if
We attacked ourselves to cause an outcry."
And later Bush was given disturbing news.
Ted Olson, the US Solicitor
2155   General, had been rung twice by Barbara,
His wife, a well-known commentator on
CNN who had been on the flight that
Seemed to have crashed into the Pentagon.
Olson reported that his wife had called
2160   Him "twice on a cell phone" saying that "all
Passengers, flight personnel including
The pilots, were herded to the back of
The plane by armed hijackers. The only
Weapons she mentioned were knives and cardboard
2165   Cutters." The calls were evidence the plane
Had been hijacked by Arab Muslims and
Was not a plane reported to have crashed
On the Ohio-Kentucky border.
According to the assessment, it was
2170   Unlikely that she could have made the calls.
Cell phones could not have worked at the height and
Speed – twenty-five thousand feet and around
Three hundred and fifty miles per hour – at
Which the plane was flying, and there was doubt
2175   If the plane had a passenger-seat phone
And if it only took a credit card,
Which she did not have; and if she reached him
Via Department-of-Justice "collect" call.
The experts said that Olson's story was
2180   Denied by American Airlines and
The Pentagon and FBI. The calls
Were evidence the plane was flying back
To Washington. Could they have been faked? Is
It possible Olson – who as Bush knew,
2185   Had defended Reagan during the Iran-
Contra case and represented him, Bush,
In *Bush v. Gore* – might have lied on orders

From the Syndicate to make out a plane
And not a missile struck the Pentagon,
2190 To mask its hidden hand? Or might he have
Been duped by someone pretending to be
His wife, using a voice-morphing machine?
The same might be true of the cell-phone call
Made by the flight attendant Renee May,
2195 Which was also evidence that Arab
Muslims had directed the airliner
As a flying bomb at the Pentagon.
Barbara Olson's death due to terrorists
Who were Arab Muslims had impacted
2200 On public feeling, which cried for revenge.
Bush did not want to hear her calls were fakes.
He wanted to deal with the calls as facts.

That evening, sombre Bush, in the White-House
Oval Office, addressed a stunned nation,
2205 Fumbling to find words that would resonate,
Seeking to transcend and transform himself.
"Today our fellow citizens," he said,
"Our way of life, our freedom came under
Attack in a series of deliberate
2210 And deadly terrorist acts. The victims
Were in airplanes or in their offices:
Secretaries, business men and women,
Military and Federal workers,
Moms, dads, friends, neighbours. Thousands of lives were
2215 Ended by evil, despicable acts
Of terror. Pictures of airplanes flying
Into buildings, fires burning, huge structures
Collapsing, have filled us with disbelief,
Sadness and a quiet, unyielding anger.
2220 These acts of mass murder were intended
To frighten our nation into chaos
And retreat, but they've failed. Our country's strong.
A great people has been moved to defend
A great nation. Terrorist attacks can
2225 Strike foundations of our biggest buildings,
But they cannot touch the foundation of
America. These acts shattered steel, but
They can't dent the steel of American
Resolve. America was targeted
2230 As we're the brightest beacon for freedom
And for opportunity in the world.
And no one will keep that light from shining.

Today our nation saw evil, the worst
Of human nature. And we responded
2235   With the best of America: daring
Of our rescue workers, with the caring
For strangers and neighbours who came to give
Blood and to help in any way they could.
The search is under way for those who are
2240   Behind these evil acts. We will make no
Distinction between the terrorists who
Committed these acts and those who harbour
Them." This speech had importance for it was
The first expression of the Bush Doctrine
2245   That would commit US troops to long-term
War against Muslim fanatics, lumping
Taliban and al-Qaeda together.
He implied that action would soon follow.

BOOK TWO

THE SYNDICATE PREPARES FOR WAR

SUMMARY

O Clio, Muse of history, who sees all
Decades, centuries, ages and aeons as
Motifs embroidered on a tapestry,
A vast pattern of rising and falling
Civilisations, and Calliope,
5   Muse of epic poetry who's dear to me
And assists her in descrying patterns,
You two who are shown in harmony in
Giovanni Romanelli's 'Harmony
Between History and Poetry' on Wilton's
10   Gothic stairs – History is poetically
Inspired, Poetry is historical,
Each has the other's characteristics;

Tell now of what will happen when the oil
Our fragile civilisation rests on
15 Runs out. Cars, lorries, tractors, trains, buses,
Planes and ships will stop running. Farmers won't
Be growing food, shops will be empty. As
There will be no transport, there will be no
Rubbish collection, hospitals, streetlights.
20 Offices, factories, banks, post offices
Will all be closed. No welfare or pensions,
No newspapers, television programmes,
No phones or mobiles. Householders will grow
Their own vegetables and defend their homes
25 From scavengers, burglars and looters who
Seek food to keep their families alive.
Everyone will walk, cycle or ride in
A horse and cart (if some can keep a horse)
Or horse and trap or a horse-drawn stagecoach.
30 Life will be as in the eighteenth century
Local, except that the order known then
Will be missing as respect for the class
System and Church teachings will be absent
And homes will function within anarchy.
35 Within a generation five in six –
Five billion out of six billion – will die
Of malnutrition, disease, exposure
As Nature reverts to the world tally
Of one billion found in 1820,
40 The number who could be sustained by crops
And live in balance with other species
Before fossil fuels and oil broke the mould
And the Industrial Revolution
Improved living conditions and growth in
45 Population through machines run on coal,
Steam and petroleum. Ages have passed –
The Iron Age, Stone Age and Bronze Age. The Oil
Age that will have lasted two hundred years
Will follow when demand exceeds supply –
50 As is already the case with our food –
And the reserves under the sand dry up.
This is the nightmare for America
And Britain which have nearly ceased to be
Self-sufficient in oil and need reserves.
55 In a world that has between fifty and
A hundred years of reserves of oil left,
And the prospect of increasing demand
From China and India, and Africa.

Terrorism and global warming pale
60 Beside the end of oil and the prospect
Of the end of our civilisation –
As the Syndicate, which extracts the oil
And runs the multinationals, well knows;
And, if nuclear bombs can be held in check,
65 So wants a large slice of the dwindling cake.

O Bartholomew Gosnold, you who planned
The voyage of three ships to Jamestown in
1606 and arranged the funding
From your wife's cousin Sir Thomas Smythe, and,
70 Having made all the arrangements, were told
That as your family supported the Earl
Of Essex and not Sir Robert Cecil
You could not lead your own expedition
Which had commercial aims, to bring back gold –
75 Like the one in 1602 which shipped
Sassafras and cedar wood (which Raleigh,
Owner of all American produce,
Impounded when you returned to Exmouth) –
But would be Admiral Newport's number two,
80 Yet still commanded the blind loyalty
Of crew and settlers, and more than the rest
Can be said to have planted the New World
(On which your cousin Bacon wrote in his
Utopian *New Atlantis* twenty
85 Years later) and founded America;
O Gosnold, you who I found by the moat
At your uncle's hall where I found your name
Scratched in the Oak Room's wood when you slept there,
And who I brought to public attention
90 As America's first founding father,
Having stood for honesty with your men
As thirteen died of dire starvation, swamp
Fever and dysentery, including you,
That dreadful last August of sacrifice
95 When no gold could be found – what do you make
Of the deception of your descendants
Who, to propel a force to Afghanistan,
Criss-cross Asia with oil and gas pipelines,
Maximised the attacks of the Muslims
100 And conned America with falling towers.
I see you look aghast at what they've done,
At the mendacity that you brought in
That's compromised the very high standards

Of the founding fathers, whose rectitude's
105 Unquestionable, in the holy past;
Help me now I tell how a long pipeline
Brought troops to Afghanistan, overtly
To seek revenge but covertly to clear
The terrain so oil and gas can be piped
110 From the Caspian to the Arabian Sea –
To save civilisation from new dark.

And o Washington, who mounted a *coup*
On thirteen colonies and welded them
Into a New-World Freemasonic State,
115 A new United States for which you drew
Up a constitution based on lodges,
A Freemasonic New World Bacon saw
And, like Cincinnatus who left his plough,
Unwillingly became its President,
120 A Freemason hiding behind the Church
But not acknowledging Christian teaching;
O Washington, who stole the nation-states
And gave their assets to a commonwealth –
Help me now I tell how your descendants
125 Stole Afghanistan twice, the first time from
The Rabbani Government and then from
The Taliban they earlier installed,
And backed their puppet for commercial goals;
Assist me now I show untruthful things,
130 Covert, devious actions for personal wealth
And huge profits for some multinationals,
A Trade War masked as a deposition,
The shaping of a new nation for gain,
A debased form of the founding fathers'
135 Unification based on self-interest
So a network of pipelines could bring oil
To friendly ports and, by sea, to the States.

O Tennyson, you who wrote high romance,
Penned *Idylls of the King* at Farringford
140 About the court of the Roman-Celtic
King Arthur, set back in the fifth century;
Whose lines evoked the natural world of lakes
And rugged cliffs in which pre-Saxons lived,
Archaistically, and shunned the harsh,
145 Modern world of industrial machines
(Though their themes, service and honest labour,
Allegorised Victorian Britain);

Who knew in your poetic dream the court
Of Camelot and how the knights rode out –
150 Lancelot, Gawain, Percivale, Sir Bors –
To seek the Holy Grail, the simple cup
Christ used in the Last Supper, from which all
The disciples sipped, lips brushing its rim;
I find you in your Farringford mansion,
155 In the Isle of Wight near Freshwater Bay
In the ivied room beneath the cedar
Which was your bedroom for thirty-nine years,
Climb to your cramped old study where you wrote
The first four 'Idylls of the King'; look down
160 From your paint-worn window, and now descend
To your new study as the twilight fades
Where you penned the last 'Idylls of the King'.
I climb over a barred gate in the lane
To Maiden's Croft beyond the wilderness
165 Where stood the summer-house in which you wrote
'The Holy Grail', and hunt in the long grass
For the summer-house's stone base and find
The view you had over rolling cornfields
To the sea in the distant bay. Help me.
170 Help me as I write of the court of Bush,
Cheney, Rumsfeld, Rice and Powell, new knights
Of Washington who ride out for more fuel.
How would you compare the Camelot court
And the noble knights of Arthur who sought
175 The Grail in defiance of a Dark Age
With the court of Bush that deceived the world
By colluding with external attack
To swing public opinion to its side
As it also sought to hold back the dark
180 By covering Asia with oil pipelines
So lights of civilisation twinkle
Against the dusk and last into twilight?

It was well-known that, acting covertly,
The scheming Syndicate that shapes the world
185 Planned to inflate business profits and pump
Gas and oil from the Caspian round the world,
And how competition between two giants
Led to regime change and later to war
To inflate business profits and pump oil.
190 America was nearing its end as
A self-sufficient producer of oil,
As was the UK, and their strategic

Interest was oil and gas in Kazakhstan,
Uzbekistan, Tajikistan, Kyrgy-

195   -stan and Turkmenistan. There was a plan,
Decades old, to build two 762-mile-
Long gas and oil pipelines from the Turkmen
Dauletabad field through Afghanistan
To Multan, Pakistan. This would supply

200   Asian-Pacific markets and would cost
2.4 billion dollars. The Russians
Invaded to make the terrain safe for
This oil supply. On the Soviet Union's
Fall, the Argentine oil company Bridas

205   Negotiated leases to explore
The oilfields of Turkmenistan and plan
A pipeline through neighbouring Afghanistan.
A US-backed consortium opposed
Bridas's project, seeking military

210   And economic control of the whole
Of Eurasia (the Middle East and ex-
Soviet Central-Asian republics), part
Of a geo-strategic agenda.
In 1992 eleven Western

215   Oil companies controlled more than fifty
Per cent of all oil investments within
The Caspian Basin, including Chevron,
Amoco, Exxon-Mobil, Texaco,
BP and Unocal. Brezezinski,

220   Architect of the Afghan-Soviet war,
Was Amoco's consultant; Kissinger
Adviser to Unocal; while Haig was
A lobbyist for Turkmenistan; and
Cheney represented Halliburton

225   And the US-Azerbaijan Chamber
Of Commerce. Richard Armitage, later
Deputy Defense Secretary, worked
For Unocal. Then, to compete, the West,
The CIA and Pakistan, helped by

230   Wahhabist Saudi Arabia, founded
The Taliban in 1994
As a strong force that would guard oil and gas
Pipelines between ex-Soviet republics
And Pakistan. Unocal formed its own

235   US-led consortium that included
Saudi Arabia's Delta Oil (aligned
With Saudi Prince Abdullah and King Fahd),
Russia's Gazprom and Turkmenistan's state-

Owned Turkmenrozgas. Unocal lobbied
240   Turkmenistan's president, Niyazov,
And Pakistan's Prime Minister, Bhutto,
Offering a Unocal pipeline that
Would follow Bridas' route. Turkmenistan's
President Niyazov backed the US
245   And asked Bridas to renegotiate
Its contract. Shocked, outraged, Bridas complained
That Unocal had stolen its idea
And sued Turkmenistan without success.
In October 1995, through
250   Kissinger's persuasive diplomacy,
Niyazov awarded to Unocal
The contract for the Turkmen section of
The nine-hundred-and-eighteen-mile natural
Gas pipeline passing through Afghanistan;
255   Also a contract for a companion
One-thousand-and-fifty-mile oil pipeline
From Dauletabad through Afghanistan
To a Pakistani tanker-loading
Port on the Arabian Sea. Next year
260   Bridas won a thirty-year agreement
With Afghanistan's Rabbani regime
To build an eight-hundred-and-seventy-five-
Mile gas pipeline across Afghanistan.
So Unocal had fixed Turkmenistan
265   While Bridas had now fixed Afghanistan.
The problem was solved by the CIA
And Pakistani ISI, who both,
After a visit to Kandahar by
US Assistant Secretary of State
270   For South Asia Robin Raphael, now backed
The Taliban to oust the Rabbani
Government so that Bridas's contract
Would have to be renegotiated.
And so it was that when the Taliban
275   Took Kabul in 1996, they
Were approached by Unocal, spearhead for
"Rockefellers'" Standard Oil in CentGas,
A multinational consortium.
The Taliban's role was to secure roads
280   For construction traffic for the pipeline.
Unocal's project carried the prospect
Of US recognition for the new
Taliban, which they desperately wanted.
Unocal offered humanitarian

285	Aid to Afghan warlords who would now form
	A council to supervise the pipeline
	Project; and a cellphone network between
	Kabul and Kandahar, which they'd rebuild.
	Bridas countered. It formed an alliance
290	With Ningarcho, a Saudi company
	Aligned with Prince Turki el-Faisal, chief
	Of Saudi intelligence and mentor
	To Osama bin Laden, the ally
	Of the Taliban, public opponent
	Of the Saudi royal family. Prince
295	Turki gave the Taliban pick-up trucks
	And communications equipment. Now
	Bridas proposed two consortia, one
	To build the Afghan pipeline, another
	To deal with both its ends. By November
300	1996 Bridas claimed it had
	An agreement signed by the Taliban
	And General Dostum, Northern Alliance
	Leader. Thus the competition between
	Unocal and Bridas now reflected
305	The competition within the Saudi
	Royal family: between Prince Abdullah
	And Prince Fahd; and pro-Bridas Prince Turki.
	In February 1997
	A delegation of the Taliban
310	Flew to Sugarland, Texas, the HQ
	Of Unocal, and proposed a deal worth
	4.5 billion dollars. Unocal
	Should: pay the Taliban an annual rent
	Of a hundred million dollars a year
315	For oil and gas pipelines; open them for
	Local consumption; and then reconstruct
	The Afghan infrastructure. Unocal's
	Adviser was Hamid Karzai, who had
	Fought against the Soviets. Unocal,
320	Needing State-Department recognition
	Of the Taliban as the Government
	Of Afghanistan to secure funding
	From agencies such as the World Bank, hired
	Henry Kissinger's advice. However,
325	No agreement was signed. The Taliban
	Travelled twice to Washington and Buenos
	Aires where Unocal and Bridas wooed them,
	And Unocal flew the Uzbek leader,
	General Dostum, to Dallas to discuss

330	The running of the new Afghan pipeline
	Through his Northern-Alliance territories,
	But nothing was signed. Unocal believed
	The Taliban were baulking. Their demands –
	Royalties, funding of roads and power plants,
335	A new Afghan National Oil Company –
	Were exorbitant. Osama advised
	The Taliban to sign with Bridas as
	Theirs was the highest bid and the pipeline
	Would be open for warlords and locals
340	To use whereas Unocal's would be closed,
	Just for export. Bridas's plan required
	No outside financing while Unocal's
	Required a loan from the World Bank which would
	Expose all Afghans to the West's demands.
345	Bridas engineers sipped tea with tribesmen,
	And Unocal's US executives
	Issued edicts from corporate HQs
	And the US Embassy demanding
	That talks should open with the CIA-
350	Backed Northern Alliance. But Bridas lacked
	A supply from Turkmenistan and funds,
	And took Amoco as a partner, sold
	It sixty per cent of its assets in
	Latin America. Chase Manhattan
355	(Representing Bridas), Morgan Stanley
	(Handling Amoco), Arthur Andersen
	(Facilitator), Zbigniew Brezezinski
	(Consultant for Amoco) assisted
	The merger. A year later Amoco
360	Merged with British Petroleum and swelled.
	BP's lawyer was James Baker, a friend
	Of Bush and member of the Carlyle Group.
	Amoco was bigger than Unocal,
	Which now faced new problems. Gazprom pulled out
365	Of CentGas – Russia complained the US
	Had an anti-Russian agenda – and
	Had to be replaced by Japanese and
	South Korean gas companies. Unocal
	Was criticised by human rights groups for
370	Dealing with the brutal Taliban. Then
	In response to the attacks on US
	Embassies in Kenya and Tanzania,
	Which were attributed to Osama,
	Clinton sent cruise missiles into Sudan
375	And Afghanistan, and broke off all links

With the Taliban. Unocal withdrew
From CentGas saying, "The gas pipeline would
Not proceed till an internationally
Recognised Government was in place in
380   Afghanistan." Unocal continued
To press for an oil pipeline but had no
Support from Washington. Amoco cooled.
Bridas declared it would proceed alone
With the Afghan gas pipeline. The US-
385   Taliban tension prevented this. Now
Delta of Saudi Arabia led
CentGas. Pakistan, Turkmenistan and
Afghanistan urged Saudi Arabia
To proceed with CentGas. But there was no
390   US or UN recognition of
Afghanistan, and no pipeline progress
Until Bush took over in the White House.

And now the lines were drawn up. Bin Laden,
395   The Taliban and Argentine Bridas
With Amoco had frustrated the plan
Of Unocal and Saudi Arabia
To run oil and gas pipelines north to south,
From Turkmenistan, through Afghanistan
400   To Pakistan, and a change of regime
By war would dump Bridas so Unocal
And Saudi Delta could join north and south.
Part of the Syndicate wanted to force
The Taliban to go so they could build
405   Gas and oil pipelines from Turkmenistan
Through Afghanistan to the Arabian Sea
And secure them from terrorist attacks
With US troops and pro-US Afghans.
The problem was to swing American
410   Public opinion to intervention,
An expedition to Afghanistan,
A military invasion to secure
Their commercial goal under the banner
Of a great cause Americans wanted.
415   It needed an outrage like Pearl Harbour.
As soon as Bush won the White House Cheney
Opened secret talks with the Taliban
And bided his time. Cheney said that year,
CEO of Halliburton, the world's
420   Biggest drilling equipment producer,
"I cannot think of a time when we've had

A region emerge as suddenly." And
Halliburton had performed contract work
During the construction of a pipeline
425   For Unocal in Burma/Myanmar.
In January two thousand and one,
When US energy companies were
Covertly talking with the Taliban
To build a pipeline, notably Enron,
430   Cheney expanded an intelligence
Block to preclude all investigations
Of Saudi-Taliban-Afghan oil links.
(It caused ex-counter-terrorism chief
Of the FBI, John O'Neill, tracker
435   Of Osama and his movements, enraged,
To resign from the FBI, stating
He was not allowed to investigate
Saudi-al-Qaeda links due to Enron's
Pipeline deal, news of which he had found in
440   An al-Qaeda memo. O'Neill's office
Was in the World Trade Center's north tower. One
Day into his new job, bizarrely, he
Was killed in the 9/11 attack.) Now
All the oil companies – Enron, BP,
445   Amoco, Chevron, Exxon, Mobil and
Unocal – wanted the Taliban out.
Former oil employees fronted the Bush-
Cheney administration: Bush himself
(On Harken's board), Cheney (Halliburton),
450   Rice (who was on Chevron's board), Rumsfeld (with
Occidental) and Bush Senior (Carlyle).
(At 7.30 on September the eleventh
The Carlyle Group investors met at Ritz
Carlton Hotel, Washington including
455   James Baker, Frank Carlucci – and Shafig
Bin Laden, Osama's brother who took
Off his name tag when the second plane hit
And left shortly afterwards in a car.)
In February US intelligence
460   Told Cheney it had proved that bin Laden
Had been behind the attack on the *Cole*.
Cheney did not attack al-Qaeda in
Afghanistan, to keep alive secret
Pipeline negotiations begun just
465   Days after Bush became the President.
In March the Taliban agreed to hand
Bin Laden to a third country for trial.

The US wanted him to be handed
Directly to the US, no one else.
470   If the offer had been taken up, bin
Laden would have been in prison from March
And could not have planned terrorist attacks
That suited the Syndicate's pipeline plans
For Afghanistan's natural gas reserves.
475   In April 2001 the US
Gave the Taliban millions of dollars
In aid as a reward for shutting down
Opium production, which Osama saw
As poisoning the West while funding *jihad*.
480

By June invasion plans were being prepared
And the network of powerful families
And multinationals with a common cause,
The Syndicate which seeks world government
And control over the world's resources,
485   Was ready to invade Afghanistan,
Oust the Taliban and install Karzai,
A Unocal adviser who'd comply,
Using Cheney as their bland figurehead.
Israel had close links with Azerbaijan
490   And Turkmenistan. Their intelligence
Service, Mossad, had watched Osama and,
Having infiltrated his group, had filmed
His conversations. They had advance news
Of the September-the-eleventh attacks
495   In late June and they told the CIA
In confidence, but not Bush. Cheney knew.
On August the second the last secret
Meeting between US officials and
The Taliban took place and failed to win
500   A pipeline deal. The talks were broken off
And the US prepared plans to invade
And occupy remote Afghanistan.
On August the sixth the CIA warned
Bush at Crawford, Texas that bin Laden
505   Might be planning to hijack commercial
Airliners in a memo entitled
'Bin Laden Determined to Strike US'.
Cheney said the report was a rehash
That contained nothing new and that it should
510   Remain secret to protect its sources.
Between August the eighth and the fifteenth
Two Mossad agents came to Washington

And warned the FBI and CIA
That terrorists planned a major assault
515   On the US, a warning echoed by
French intelligence later in the month.
And Russian intelligence also warned
The CIA twenty-five terrorists
Would attack buildings like the Pentagon.
520   The attacks were not an American
Intelligence failure but the result
Of a political decision not
To act on tip-offs against bin Laden.
Now Clarke and the National Security
525   Council hatched a plan to trounce bin Laden:
The CIA would be given two hundred
Million dollars to arm Massoud's Northern
Alliance, which opposed the Taliban.
Behind the scenes Syndicate personnel
530   Urged Rice to send her warning of a threat
And scheme to topple the Taliban in
The plan that lay on her desk on the tenth,
Opposing Osama on grounds of oil
And gas pipelines, and not on nuclear grounds,
535   Putting commerce above Armageddon,
Though in fact the two goals were unified:
To free Afghanistan for oil to flow
And to scatter the nuclear arsenal.
Behind the scenes Syndicate personnel
540   Agreed to let the September-the-eleventh
Attacks take place and be filmed as they struck
To create a pretext for regime change,
A new Pearl Harbour that would shock and swing
American opinion behind war.
545

Tell, Muse, how the Syndicate influenced
The decision to invade Afghanistan.
Once a month Cheney had met Kissinger,
General Factotum for Rockefeller
And the shadow world government; also
550   An adviser to Unocal. He had
Worked with him in Ford's administration
When he was deputy, then chief of staff.
Now Kissinger came by and gave hard-line
Advice: "International relations
555   Mean military and economic power
Which diplomatic power threatens to use.
The military sends the world a message:

To be an enemy of the US
Is dangerous. Target both bin Laden
560   And Afghanistan which had sheltered him,
The Taliban." Cheney recalled Vietnam,
The humiliation of withdrawal
And surrender, and though he and Powell
Had scripted a perfect Gulf War, he urged
565   Caution, as did Powell. For going to war
Might have unintended consequences.
Bush was a fan of Kissinger's and met
Privately with him every two months once
Rumsfeld helped set the meetings up. So for
570   The Syndicate Kissinger influenced
Bush's strategy and discussed details
Of operations with Cheney each month,
And now he urged firmness: the military.
In the early hours of the next morning
575   Cheney, Bush, Powell decided to describe
The 9/11 attacks as "acts of war".
Then Powell said in a TV interview,
"The American people made a judgement.
We are at war." Bush then conferred with his
580   National Security team, said the attacks
Were "more than acts of terror. They were acts
Of war. We will rally the world." Fired up,
Cheney, with his agenda of pipelines,
During National Security Council
585   Meetings urged repeatedly that the "war
On terrorism" be waged against states
Rather than al-Qaeda: "To the extent
We define our task broadly, including
Those who support terrorism, then we
590   Get at states. And it's easier to find them
Than it is to find bin Laden." By "states"
He meant Afghanistan and Iraq. Then
Wolfowitz saw Bush, who requested Clarke
To find links between 9/11 and Iraq.
595   Rumsfeld and Perle both urged war with Iraq.
Clarke, disgusted, said that was not unlike
Invading Mexico after Japan's
Attack on the US at Pearl Harbour.
These comments were then beamed across the world.
600   Now bin Laden's forces were multiplied,
Tens of thousands of operatives with ties
To hundreds of Islamic terror groups
Would join al-Qaeda's loud call for *jihad*.

By dawn Bush, Powell and officials called on
605   World leaders to form a Coalition
To fight international terrorism.
Bush spoke with Tony Blair, the British Prime
Minister, then Jacques Chirac, President
Of France, Chinese leader Jiang, Vladimir
610   Putin, the President of Russia, (twice)
And others while Powell contacted Sharon,
Arafat, Annan, EU and Arab
Leaders. The role of the Coalition
Was unclear. The message was paraphrased
615   By an unnamed official, "You're either
With us or against us." The public pleased,
Now Bush's approval rating soared from
Fifty-five to eighty per cent. He told
Rove that his presidency would now be
620   About 9/11 and war – just as
His father's generation had been called
To World War Two, his generation would
Be called to what was privately described
As World War Three – a war to be waged by
625   Stealth and intelligence as he tracked down
The Islamic terrorists who had put
America under attack, and struck.
The Coalition would secure revenge –
But more importantly strike at the heart
630   Of the terrorists' base and scatter them.
America had begun to fight back.

During the next few days a decision
To invade Afghanistan slowly emerged.
In the White House meandering discussions
635   Through the twelfth and thirteenth reached consensus,
To attack al-Qaeda and the Taliban,
Then broaden the war on terrorism
To include other targets; first Iraq.
In a press conference Bush said the attacks
640   "Are part of the first war of the twenty-
First century", that terrorism "is now
The focus of my presidency. We
Will lead the world to victory." Powell said,
"The President is speaking about war."
645   Privately opposing strikes on Iraq,
He named bin Laden as the chief suspect.
Yet Bush ordered one of Clarke's aides to chair
A meeting looking for a link between

Al-Qaeda and Iraq. The CIA's
650 Leaders met Bush to outline plans to crush
The Taliban and al-Qaeda, and Black
Said of corpses rotting in the desert,
"They'll have flies on their eyeballs." The US
Military were studying options to
655 Retaliate against the Taliban
With massive bombing and large-scale ground troops.
Senator McCain called for all-out war.
The White House barred the 1973
War Powers Act which requires a president
660 To consult with Congress before choosing
To declare war. They researched with lawyers
Whether the President's authority
Could order assassinations. Now Black,
CIA counter-terrorism chief,
665 Told his agent Gary Schroen to return
To Afghanistan, "capture bin Laden,
Kill him and bring his head back in a box
On dry ice" and impale the severed heads
Of all al-Qaeda leaders "up on pikes".
670 This was the first time in thirty years in
The CIA he'd been ordered to kill.
Now the Senate approved the Combating
Terrorism Act which increased spying
On computers and surveillance. Powell said
675 The US was setting a "new benchmark"
For its relations with other countries:
How closely each one co-operates with
America's war on terrorism.
The Taliban regime, belligerent,
680 Said if the US attacked, it would seek
Revenge. *Mullah* Omar prepared for war:
"Death comes to everyone. We must stand proud
As Afghans in the defence of Islam.
Believe in God, for with the grace of God
685 American rockets will go astray
And we will be saved. I am not afraid
Of death or losing power. Each Muslim should
Be ready for *jihad* – Holy War." He
Denied bin Laden was responsible
690 For the 9/11 attacks, and said
US blame sought to demonise Islam.
The ex-head of Russian security
Police warned, "In Afghanistan's mountains
The chance of killing bin Laden's zero."

695	An Afghan ex-patriot: "We're flirting with
	A world war between Islam and the West."
	In Peshawar several hundred shouted
	Pro-Taliban slogans and cried out for
	Holy War. Bush allowed the Pentagon
700	To call up fifty thousand National Guard.
	A cold front blew into New York with rain
	That washed away the dust of Manhattan,
	But filled Ground Zero with deep mud and mess,
	Hindering the rescue operation.
705	A pair of severed hands bound by plastic
	Handcuffs were found on a nearby roof. They
	Came from one of the airliners, showing
	Passengers were handcuffed before the crash.
	Bush addressed a memorial service
710	At Washington's National Cathedral.
	Before Presidents Ford, Carter, Bush and
	Clinton, and Gore but not Cheney (absent
	For security reasons – an attack
	Should not wipe out all top US leaders),
715	He said America was targeted
	Because of its freedoms, that the US
	Must "rid the world of evil"; "the conflict"
	Was begun on the turning and terms of
	Others; it will end in a way and at
720	An hour of our choosing." The Dean then prayed,
	"Save us from blind vengeance. We ask God that
	We not become the evil we deplore."
	Later Bush visited Ground Zero, climbed
	On rubble and through a bullhorn addressed
725	Workers. Some called out that they could not hear.
	Bush cried, "I can hear you, I can hear you.
	The rest of the world hears you. The people
	Who knocked these buildings down will hear us all
	Soon." The workers cheered, chanted "USA".
730	Congress pledged forty billion dollars in
	Emergency funds, twice what Bush had asked,
	And authorised his leadership to use
	"All necessary and appropriate force"
	In response to the 9/11 attacks.
735	This did not replace 1973's
	War Powers Resolution as Bush wanted.
	On September the fifteenth CIA
	Director Tenet briefed Bush with a plan
	To conquer Afghanistan that had been

740 Developed back in May. Caught unprepared,
The Defense Department had to defer.
Tenet showed a top-secret document,
'Worldwide Attack Matrix', which planned covert
Operations – some of which were lethal –
745 Against al-Qaeda in eighty countries.

On the sixteenth Bush spoke on the south lawn
To the press and promised, "We'll rid the world
Of the evil-doers. We'll call together
Freedom-loving people to fight terror."
750 Answering a question, he said bin Laden
"Is the prime suspect". Answering another:
"We're facing a new kind of enemy,
Somebody so barbaric they'd fly air-
Planes into buildings full of innocent
755 People. This is a new kind of evil.
This crusade, this war on terrorism's
Going to take a while. And the American
People must be patient. It's time for us
To win the first war of the twenty-first
760 Century decisively." The next question
Was: "Why've you declared we're at war and asked
Those who wear uniform to get ready?"
Bush: "My administration's determined
To find, to get running and to hunt down
765 Those who did this to America. The prime
Suspect's organisation's in a lot
Of countries. It's widespread, based on one thing:
Terrorising. They can't stand freedom, they
Hate what America stands for. They've roused
770 A mighty giant." He spoke nationalistically
Of launching a "crusade" against Muslims,
And this was noticed by the Taliban,
The ruling power (by conquest) in Kabul.
Six days after the 9/11 attacks
775 Bush signed a document marked "Top Secret"
That outlined the Afghanistan war plan
As part of a global campaign against
Terrorism, and, as a mere footnote,
Directed the Pentagon to begin
780 Planning all the military options
For an invasion of Iraq. Reserve
Troops would be called up. At a press conference
Bush said bin Laden was the "prime suspect".
Asked if he wanted bin Laden dead, Bush

785	Said, "I want justice. There's an old poster
	Out West, I recall, that said, 'Wanted, Dead
	Or Alive.' " He did not realise that he
	Had just given the world the impression
	That he was a warmonger, too gung-ho.
790	To him, a Christian, war is brutal, base,
	Unpleasant, a necessary evil.
	And the way was now clear for a long war.

	Saudi Delta led the consortium
	To build the Trans-Afghan pipeline and, in
795	Deference to their Saudi partner, Cheney
	For the Syndicate repatriated
	Key Saudis in a planned convoy of flights
	And let bin Laden's family escape
	In the first outward flights after the attacks.
800	At 10 p.m. on September the twelfth
	CIA Director Tenet had phoned
	The Saudi Ambassador to the US,
	Prince Bandar, son of Prince Sultan (second-
	In-line to the Saudi throne) and nephew
805	Of King Fahd, and told him that of nineteen
	Hijackers, fifteen were Saudis. Stunned, shocked,
	Prince Bandar at once planned a rounding-up
	Of Saudi royals and bin Ladens – some spelt
	Their name Binladin – who were extensions
810	Of the House of Saud to which they were close.
	Their family business (Saudi Binladin
	Group – SBG) banked with Citigroup and
	Invested with Goldman Sachs, Merrill Lynch
	And the Carlyle Group, where James Baker worked
815	With Bush Senior. Abdullah bin Laden
	Was at Cambridge, Mohammed and Nawaf
	In Boston Harbour's Charlestown Naval Yard,
	Wafah in New York. Osama's brother
	In Washington, unnamed, sought protection
820	And was put in the Watergate Hotel.
	Now King Fahd sent Prince Bandar a message,
	"Take measures to protect the innocents."
	All over the US the bin Ladens'
	Extended family and House of Saud
825	And their associates assembled. Eight
	Planes were available to take them home.
	The FBI would repatriate them
	So long as they had lists of passengers.
	On the thirteenth Bandar, at the White House,

830   Sat with Bush on the Truman Balcony.
They smoked cigars. Bush said he'd hand over
All captured al-Qaeda to the Saudis,
Who would get them to talk. Both men were key
Figures in the oil and defence sectors
835   In their countries. Saudis had supported
Bush's Harken and the Afghan pipeline
Through thick and thin, and now was pay-back time.
Late on September the fourteenth after
Private US aircraft were cleared to fly,
840   A Boeing 727 left Los Angeles
For Orlando carrying a sister
Of bin Laden as the sole passenger.
To a flight attendant she said, "I feel
So bad about it." (Of 9/11.)
845   "Well, it's not your fault," said the attendant.
"Yeah, but he is my brother," said the girl.
At Orlando Khalil bin Laden joined.
They flew to Washington. More planes appeared:
At Vegas for forty-six, including
850   Several Saudi royals, which at last left
On the sixteenth for Geneva; and one
At Lexington, which left for Newfoundland
And London the same day; one at Dallas
Which left for Newark on the seventeenth;
855   And two at Boston, including the plane
From LA which held the two bin Ladens,
That left on the eighteenth and the nineteenth.
The State Department and the FBI
Knew of these flights; also the FAA.
860   The airport authorities were dismayed
To be told to let the bin Ladens go.
There would be more planes: one at New York on
The twenty-second; one at Las Vegas
On the twenty-fourth. In all, bizarrely,
865   A hundred and forty Saudis – royals
And bin Laden's family and colleagues –
Were airlifted back home from the US
Though Saudis, being Wahhabis, were linked
To bin Laden and knowingly financed
870   Al-Qaeda and may have had prior knowledge
Of 9/11. The flights were authorised
At high level and widely perceived as
Special treatment. The House of Saud had links
With the House of Bush over thirty years,
875   Invested petrodollars and received

Military protection – and had secured
Direct access to Reagan, two Bushes,
Baker, Cheney, Powell and intelligence.
Influence, investment, policy enmeshed
880 The House of Saud and House of Bush, which gained
From arms deals via the Carlyle Group, through which
1.47 billion dollars had reached
The House of Bush from the Saudis, who had
Delivered the Muslim-American
885 Vote to Bush in the crucial election.
So Bush, who had had a bin Laden as
His business partner, Salem, Osama's
Dead elder brother, let his family leave
Before they could be questioned, a convoy
890 Planned by his operations manager
Who'd overseen war games exercises
On the morning of September the eleventh,
Cheney, who was too busy on such things
To attend the memorial service,
895 Who acted for the Syndicate and for
Their interests in Saudi oil pipelines.
It seemed that Bush and Cheney did not want
To arrest bin Laden, and then it seemed
That they had put Saudi Arabia first
900 In view of its links with the Syndicate
And their access to Saudi Arabian oil.
Now it can be seen that the secret link
Between these two families helped trigger
The Age of Terror by exiling bin
905 Laden and gave rise to 9/11
Which was bin Laden's retaliation
Although it must not be forgotten that
Bin Laden delivered a Pearl Harbour
Which allowed the US army to search
910 For suitcase bombs inside Afghanistan
And the Syndicate, in the army's wake,
To make areas safe for oil pipelines.

Bin Laden had announced four objectives:
Removing US troops from Saudi soil;
915 The overthrow of the Saudi regime;
The removal of all Jews from Israel;
Worldwide confrontation between the West
And Muslim world – a polarisation.
As most of the 9/11 attackers
920 Were from Saudi Arabia relations

Between Washington and Riyadh were strained
And the US pulled almost all its troops
Out of Saudi Arabia and moved
Its regional headquarters to Qatar.
925 So bin Laden had now secured his first
Objective. And he was now on his way
To achieving his fourth, showing the West
As leading a crusade against Islam,
So there was war between the Islamic world
930 And the Americans and their allies,
Jihad that would split the whole world in two.

The Syndicate had already financed
The start of their war for pipelines until
Taxpayer revenues could take over. Two
935 Of the largest gold depositories in
The world were beneath the World Trade Center.
One was owned by the Federal Reserve Bank,
A hundred feet beneath its headquarters
Just blocks away from the World Trade Center,
940 The length of two football fields. It contained
More gold than any other vault on Earth,
Worth perhaps twenty-five billion dollars –
Gold owned by foreign nations including
Saudi Arabia and Kuwait. And one,
945 Seventy feet below WTC4,
Was owned by a group of commercial banks.
The 1993 bomb exploded
Close to this vault but did not breach its walls.
There had been more gold, silver and precious
950 Platinum and palladium stored there
Than in Fort Knox, which was almost empty:
Having been built in 1936
And having housed bars, coins and old bullion
That had once circulated as money
955 But had in 1933 been seized
In exchange for worthless paper dollars
At 20.67 dollars per ounce,
Fort Knox had had most of its gold moved by
President Johnson to, some thought, London.
960 Some say WTC4's vault held
Six hundred and fifty million dollars
In gold and silver bars, precious metals;
Others say at least one billion dollars;
Others say a staggering hundred and
965 Sixty billion dollars of gold bullion.

Some currency vaults owned by Citibank
And Chase were badly damaged or burned in
Fires that raged twenty hours after the strike,
But Nova Scotia Bank's vault was intact,
970   Though wet, and was marked "Searched" on the thirteenth.
Two ten-wheel trucks were found in a service
Tunnel under WTC5.
Crushed by falling steel, loaded up with gold
And silver bars worth two hundred million.
975   There were no bodies near, it seemed as if
The drivers had been warned of the collapse
Of the south tower as they began to drive
The gold from the underground area,
Immediately jumped down and ran away
980   Before the south tower came crashing down.
Scorch marks were found all round the basement door
To the vaults under WTC4
Which was damaged, blowtorch and crowbar marks
Indicated a heist. Seven weeks after
985   9/11 the gold and silver in
The trucks were returned to Nova Scotia
Bank, and mayor Giuliani announced that
Gold and silver bars worth two hundred and
Thirty million dollars, stored in a bomb-
990   Proof vault, stacked on pallets, had been retrieved.
They were moved to a gold depository
In Brooklyn. No other metals were moved.
The Nova Scotia Bank gold was a part
Of Comex gold held for clients and worth
995   Nine hundred and fifty million dollars.
It seems gold had gone missing – estimates
Vary from some nine hundred and fifty
Million to a hundred and sixty billion
Dollars' worth – minus the two hundred and
Thirty million dollars' worth that, it's said,
1000   Was recovered. There was a massive heist
Before the south tower fell as, supervised,
By someone in the know on Cheney's watch,
Gold was removed in bulk before the strike
In lines of ten-wheel trucks that were not crushed.
1005   Where did it go? To where did it vanish?
It was not loaded on one of the planes
Waiting to take bin Ladens to Saudi
Arabia. It swelled Syndicate funds
Via the Mafia, to pay for the first costs
1010   Of the new campaign in Afghanistan

And to prepare for battle in Iraq.
This was the view of Tony Gambino,
Grandson of Lucky Luciano and
An ex-Mafia mobster in New York,

1015 Whose grandfather's construction company
Built the Twin Towers and afterwards put in
The big underground vaults to house the gold
Which, he has said, now released from prison,
"Is now in Bush's and Vatican hands

1020 In order to fund the war". Pope Pius
The Twelfth, living in the leaky, pigeon-
Infested Lateran Palace, wondering
How to pay for repairs, had, by signing
The Lateran Treaty between Church and State,

1025 Between Vatican and Mussolini
On February the eleventh nineteen twenty-
Nine created the Vatican's great wealth.
The destitute Church received a gift from
Mussolini – ninety million dollars –

1030 Which the Pope invested in Fascism
(Mussolini and Hitler) and, making
Mafia chieftain Michele Sindona
The Vatican banker, by dubious deeds
Turned into fifty billion dollars in

1035 Securities and gold reserves. Now more
Gold came the Pope's way as Church, State and Big
Business worked to promote a new crusade
Like the first four Crusades to the Holy
Land to capture Jerusalem, as if

1040 The New World Order was Catholic as well
As Syndicate, the spreading of Christ's rule
By violent means "justified" by their end:
To confront Islam as in the Crusades.
Thus, Government fronted the invasion,

1045 The US army was to clear terrain
Near pipelines, the Mafia heist began
The funding which would later be transferred
By Congress to the US taxpayer
And also financed the Catholic vision.

1050 Bush, born-again Christian and President
On the evangelical vote, did not
Then know he would steadily move towards
The Catholic faith that he had helped and stand
With the Vatican and New World Order

1055 Which sought to fracture the United States,
Break up America for their own ends.

In the Oval Office of the White House
Bush sat and pondered on the week's events
1060 And wondered at Cheney's role within them.
Unocal wanted an Afghan pipeline
And funding from the World Bank, and therefore
A regime stronger than the Taliban
That would keep terrorists away from oil.
1065 His former partner's brother, Osama,
Had attacked US embassies inside
Kenya and Tanzania, and had now
Attacked America. Mossad had known
About the plan, he now deduced, and told
1070 Cheney, who'd known his father's eighties staff,
Leaned on a judge to vote him President
And had weekly meetings with Kissinger,
Had told Halliburton and Unocal
But not him. Cheney had let it happen,
1075 Held air exercises in open skies
So the planes would not be intercepted.
Cheney had sent him down to Florida –
He'd planned the visit since early August
And announced it on September the seventh –
1080 And then by air to Louisiana,
While for the Syndicate he dealt with it.
The plane that crashed into the Pentagon
Might have been a stealth cruise missile launched from
A low-flying white stealth aircraft which would
1085 Not activate the defensive missile
System that protected the Pentagon.
He'd known a plane would target the White House
And got himself down into the bunker –
And, Bush suspected, had the plane shot down,
1090 Having asked him for blanket permission.
He'd known five Israelis would document
The burning towers for Mossad from a roof,
Film the smoking scene before their arrest.
He'd known that fifteen of the hijackers
1095 Were from Saudi Arabia, and had told
His father's buddy, Prince Bandar, who'd met
With his father confidentially
And often as if in his Cabinet.
He suspected Prince Bandar'd known the names
1100 Of Atta and the rest from Cheney's lips
And not from his intelligence sources;
That Cheney had also told his friends in

Pakistan's secret service, ISI
(Inter-Services Intelligence), who
1105   Had helped finance the 9/11 attacks.
In late August, two weeks before the strikes
Senator Bob Graham and Rep. Porter Goss,
Ex-CIA operations agent,
Had visited Islamabad and met
1110   President Musharraf and ISI's
Head, General Mahmoud Ahmed, who'd ordered
A hundred thousand dollars to be paid
To the hijacker Mohammed Atta
To help the plot forward. Incredibly
1115   On the morning of 9/11, Ahmed
Had breakfast with Graham, Goss and Jon Kyl
(Who had travelled with them to Pakistan
In the congressional delegation)
And Maleeha Lodhi, Pakistani
1120   Ambassador to the US. Ahmed
Ran a spy agency that was close to
Osama and the Taliban. Cheney
Was behind meeting Ahmed, a link to
Bin Laden and Atta's funder. Bush guessed
1125   That Cheney had monitored the attack
From the CIA's command room within
WTC7, that the CIA'd
Wired Twin Towers' steel rods with nano-thermite
And sulphur and radioed a signal from
1130   The command centre so it exploded
An hour or two after each plane had crashed.
Just as a hijack-proof airliner will
Fly itself out of danger if the plane's
Controls are overridden, so the same
1135   Technology will fly an airliner
Into danger if the controls can be
Overridden. Atta would have left seat
8D and sat in the cockpit, prepared
To steer a course at the Twin Towers. Then he
1140   Would have found the controls locked on his course
And, still amazed, grasped that remote control
From a cell phone was steering the Boeing
More accurately than he could have steered,
That he was a patsy. The CIA
1145   Had known he was coming and *wanted* him
To slam into a tower and lose his life.
Bush suspected that they had jammed the planes
To crash into the towers and had cleared gold –

On Cheney's orders? – to a Syndicate
1150   Warehouse and deep vault; that they had also
Wired WTC7 with nano-
Thermite and sulphur so the third tower fell
In a controlled explosion to destroy
Evidence of how the planes were beamed in.
1155   He was sure Controlled Demolition Inc
Had already been subcontracted by
Tully Construction to remove rubble
And dispose of steel skeleton structures.
It had slid down within a few seconds.
1160   The BBC'd reported the collapse
Twenty-three minutes *before* it happened.
Débris from a struck tower could not have caused
The collapse for an event that destroyed
One part of the structure would not have torn
1165   Distant portions and caused them to shatter.
All this jiggery-pokery had happened
While Bush was in the skies, flying nowhere,
Out of the loop while Cheney gave orders.
He frowned, for he felt that he had been used,
1170   That he was a mere pawn in Cheney's game
For which he had a master plan. If all
This had happened as he now suspected,
Was bin Laden, his ex-partner's brother,
Really an enemy, or CIA?
1175   He'd helped the CIA in the eighties
When he was fighting in Afghanistan
Against the Soviets, a Western hero.
It had been widely reported that he'd
Received life-saving treatment for renal
1180   Failure from an American surgeon
At the American hospital in
Dubai from July the fourth to fourteenth
And had met CIA agent Larry
Mitchell and perhaps another agent.
1185   The story came from French intelligence
Sources and had been broken by Radio
France Internationale and *Le Figaro*.
It had been denied by the CIA,
The Dubai hospital and bin Laden
1190   But the doctor had refused to comment.
Had Osama been commissioned to plan
And deliver a Pearl Harbour that would
Swing American public opinion
Behind invading Afghanistan, act

1195	As an *agent provocateur* to draw
	The terrorists out so they could be killed
	And Afghanistan could be pacified
	At the US taxpayer's expense, thus
	Guaranteeing the Syndicate a flow
1200	Of Caspian oil to a warm-sea port?
	No, surely not. Bin Laden had belief,
	He could not be bought to lure and betray.
	And yet he had been with the Taliban
	Whose mission was to support Unocal
1205	And secure roads for construction traffic
	And deliver a Trans-Afghan pipeline;
	And then Cheney had made a Unocal
	Man his adviser, Zalmay Khalilzad,
	The previous May, head of the Bush-Cheney
1210	Defense Department transition team, soon
	To be Bush's special adviser and
	US envoy to Afghanistan. He
	Had been in touch with another Afghan
	Who had been a Unocal adviser,
1215	Hamid Karzai of Northern Alliance.
	In coming months and years two men let slip
	Blurts that confirmed his suspicions that they
	Had inside knowledge of 9/11.
	Rumsfeld in *Parade* magazine referred
1220	To the "*missile*" that hit the Pentagon,
	Not Flight 77, and later referred
	To people who "*shot down* the plane over
	Pennsylvania, attacked the Pentagon".
	Cheney, interviewed by *Face the Nation*,
1225	Said, "Khalid Sheikh Mohammed is the man
	Who killed three thousand Americans on
	9/11, *blew up* the World Trade Center,
	Attacked the Pentagon, tried to blow up
	The White House and the Capitol Building."
1230	It was as if he knew what had happened,
	And had forgotten to superimpose
	The publicly received view of events.
	He who tells lies must keep on telling them,
	And if he subsequently reverts to
1235	The truth he will generally be found out.
	He did not even mention bin Laden.
	Bush put the suspicion out of his mind.
	Bin Laden had to be his "enemy",
	He did not want him lurking as a friend.
1240	In a complex web of hidden motives

Bush struggled to keep everything simple.
He could not question Cheney on his role,
Or the CIA on theirs. He must play
The situation straight, as black or white:
1245   A hostile attack and a hurt revenge.
Bush steeled himself to quell his growing doubts.
He would be strong and smite the desired blow
And see retaliation done. Justice
Demanded he should strike, America
Expected no less. Bush told himself he
1250   Must see in black and white, ignore all greys.
The Syndicate had prepared paperwork.
He would have to sign a document that
Authorised means to make terrorists talk,
To extract information from suspects.
1255   He did not want to know what this entailed,
And if it included waterboarding.
He'd have to watch the Syndicate, who'd set
The agenda – especially his VP –
But he did not want to know hidden depths,
1260   Only the surface. Then he could be straight.
America had enemies without
Who he would hunt down in Afghanistan.

M*ullah* Omar, the Taliban's leader,
1265   Reacting to American demands
That Osama should be handed over,
Choosing not to recall that he'd taken
Kabul at CIA and ISI
Instigation, with help from the Saudis,
1270   Sent a message in his Pashto language
To be read out at a solemn meeting
Of clerics in Kabul that was convened
To deliberate on Osama's fate:
"Our system is the true example of
1275   An Islamic system. The enemies
Of religion and our country have tried
To destroy it under various pretexts.
And holding Osama responsible
For the strikes in New York and Washington
1280   Is an excuse. What airports did they use?
Whose planes were they? They were America's.
Neither Afghanistan nor Osama
Has the resources to do such things. He
Is not in contact with anyone. We've
1285   Not given permission to use Afghan

Land against anyone. We have not tried
To create friction with America.
We are ready for talks and we have told
America that we have taken all
1290   Resources from Osama, that he can't
Contact the outside world. And we have told
America neither the Islamic
Afghanistan Emirate nor Osama
Is involved in the American events.
1295   Sadly America does not listen
To our words. America repeats threats
And makes various accusations, and now
Is threatening military attack
Despite our offering alternatives
1300   On the Osama issue. We have said,
'If you've evidence against Osama,
Give it to the Afghan Supreme Court or
The *ulama*s – clerics – of three Islamic
Countries or have OIC observers
1305   (Organisation of Islamic Countries)
Keep an eye on Osama.' America
Rejected these points. If America
Had considered these suggestions there would
Not have been such a misunderstanding.
1310   We appeal to America to be
Patient, gather complete information
And find the actual culprits. We assure
The whole world that neither Osama nor
Anyone else can use the Afghan land
1315   Against anyone else. And if after
This America wants to use force and
Attack Afghanistan, our innocent
And oppressed people, and wants to destroy
The Islamic Emirate, then we seek
1320   Your guidance and a *fatwa* – ruling – on
The issue in the light of Islamic
Sharia. Servant of Islam, leader of
The faithful, *Mullah* Mohammed Omar,
September the 19th 2001."
1325   In their Pashto language the *ulama*
Clerics reported on *Sharia* law
And gave their studied interpretation
Which had the force of a binding decree:
"Afghanistan's *ulama* is sad at
1330   The losses in the United States and
Hopes that the United States will not launch

An attack on Afghanistan but will
Display patience and flexibility
And will take more time to investigate
1335   The incidents. The Afghan *ulama*
Demands the UN and the OIC
Hold an enquiry into the incidents
To know who was behind them and prevent
The killing of innocent people in
1340   The future. The UN and OIC
Should note the American President's
Remark that the war will be a crusade,
Which has hurt the Muslim community's
Feelings and posed a danger to the world.
1345   To prevent such incidents and avoid
More misunderstanding, the *ulama*
Council requests the Islamic Emirate,
Afghanistan, to persuade Osama
Bin Laden to leave Afghanistan and
1350   Select a new place for himself. And if
The United States attacks Afghanistan
After these proposals, any US
Action will be against the sacred law
Of Islam. It will amount to an act
1355   Against Islam. For we have found in all
Islamic jurisprudence that if non-
Muslims attack Muslim land, *jihad* is
Obligatory on Muslims. The *Koran*,
Sayings of the Prophet and all the books
1360   Of jurisprudence urge Muslims to wage
Jihad. In this situation Muslims
Can seek assistance from Muslim and non-
Muslim governments on condition that
The Islamic orders should remain supreme.
1365   This has been proved in books of Islamic
Jurisprudence." So the August council
Distanced itself from Osama, who'd moved
To a hide-out near Bagram airbase at
The foot of Hindu Kush Mountains, refused
1370   To hand him over as Bush wished but seized
On Bush's mention of the word "crusade",
Emphasised Muslims' right of self-defence
And prepared all Muslims for Holy War.

Osama sat in his cave and pondered
1375   On the life he now preferred to forget,
His buried life, how he had grown up in

Saudi Arabia with miniscule
Sex organs due to a deficiency
In testosterone, and yet had girlfriends
1380 In Beirut where he'd been a hard drinker,
Gone to strip shows, engaged with prostitutes
And had three drunken fights over women:
Bar girls, dancers, prostitutes. All had changed
When he'd fallen for that Chicago girl
1385 Working in the Lebanon, courted her
With flowers and champagne, talked her into bed –
But when he'd stripped off and come to make love
She laughed at him because he had such small
Sexual organs, penis and testicles.
1390 She had mocked him, she had rejected him.
And after that he'd turned against all things
American. He'd had testosterone
Enhancement which allowed him to father
Twenty-six children by four willing wives
1395 Who did not mock or humiliate him.
9/11 was triggered by the laughter
Of one insensitive American.
He pushed such thoughts from his degenerate days
Back down into forgetfulness, knowing
1400 The punishment for carnal desires was
Stoning; for drinking, flogging; for murder,
Decapitation. He had offended
Against the *Koran* in those Beirut days
But Allah the Merciful understood
1405 That the long path to holiness begins
In trauma, that his will and divine soul
Now controlled his frail, imperfect body.

On September the twentieth Bush found
A new voice when he addressed the nation,
1410 His troops, the enemy and all Muslims
At a packed, staunch Joint Session of Congress:
"Who attacked our country? The evidence
We've gathered all points to a collection
Of loosely affiliated terrorist
1415 Organisations known as al-Qaeda.
They are the same murderers indicted
For bombing American embassies
In Tanzania and Kenya, and are
Responsible for bombing *USS*
1420 *Cole*. The group and its leader – a person
Named Osama bin Laden – are linked to

Organisations in different countries,
Including the Egyptian Islamic
Jihad and the Islamic Movement of
1425 Uzbekistan. There are thousands of these
Terrorists in more than sixty countries.
They are recruited from their own nations
And neighbourhoods, brought to camps in places
Like Afghanistan, where they are trained in
1430 The tactics of terror. They are sent back
To their homes or to hide in countries round
The world to plot evil and destruction.
The leadership of al-Qaeda has great
Influence in Afghanistan, and support
1435 The Taliban regime in controlling
Most of that country. In Afghanistan
We see al-Qaeda's vision for the world.
The Afghan people have been brutalised –
Many are starving and many have fled.
1440 Women are not allowed to attend school.
You can be jailed for owning a TV.
Religion can be practised only as
Their leaders dictate. A man can be jailed
In Afghanistan if his beard is not
1445 Long enough. The United States respects
The people of Afghanistan – after
All we are currently the largest source
Of humanitarian aid – but condemn
The Taliban regime. It's not only
1450 Repressing its own people, it's threatening
People everywhere by sponsoring and
Sheltering and supplying terrorists.
By abetting murder, the Taliban
Regime is committing murder. Tonight
1455 The United States of America makes
The following demands on the Taliban.
Deliver to US authorities
All the leaders of al-Qaeda who hide
In your land. Release all foreign nationals,
1460 Including American citizens,
You have unjustly imprisoned. Protect
Foreign journalists, diplomats and aid
Workers in your country. Immediately
And permanently close all terrorist
1465 Training camps in Afghanistan. Hand over
Every terrorist, and every person
In their support structure, to appropriate

	Authorities. Give the United States
	Full access to terrorist training camps,
1470	So we can make sure they are no longer
	Operating. These demands aren't open
	To negotiation or discussion.
	The Taliban must act immediately.
	They will hand over the terrorists, or
1475	They will share in their fate. I also want
	To speak tonight directly to Muslims
	Throughout the world. We respect your faith. It's
	Practised freely by many millions of
	Americans, and by millions more in
1480	Countries that America counts as friends.
	Its teachings are good and peaceful. Those who
	Commit evil in the name of Allah
	Blaspheme the name of Allah. Terrorists
	Are traitors to their own faith, trying, in
1485	Effect, to hijack Islam itself. Our
	Enemy is a radical network
	Of terrorists, and every government
	That supports them. Our war on terror starts
	With al-Qaeda, but it does not end there.
1490	It will not end till every terrorist
	Group of global reach has been found, stopped and
	Defeated." Bush formally declared war
	On terror, his first use of a phrase that
	Had been used of the Russian anarchists
1495	In the time of the Tsars, and of the Jews
	Who attacked British Palestine – also
	Of the Moscow-inspired hijackings in
	Reagan's time. "They want to overthrow the
	Governments in many Muslim countries,
1500	Such as Egypt, Saudi Arabia
	And Jordan. They want to drive Israel out
	Of the Middle East, and to drive Christians
	And Jews out of vast regions of Asia
	And Africa. These terrorists kill not
1505	Just to end lives but to disrupt and end
	A way of life. With each atrocity,
	They hope that America grows fearful,
	Retreating from the world and forsaking
	Our friends. They stand against us because we
1510	Stand in their way. Americans now ask,
	'How will we fight and win this war?' We will
	Direct every resource at our command –
	Every means of diplomacy, every

Tool of intelligence and instrument
1515 Of law enforcement, every financial
Influence, and every necessary
Weapon of war – to the disruption and
Defeat of the global terror network.
This war will not be like the war against
1520 Iraq with decisive liberation
Of territory and a swift conclusion.
It will not look like the air war above
Kosovo two years ago, where no ground
Troops were used and not one American
1525 Was lost in combat. Our response involves
Far more than constant retaliation
And isolated strikes. Americans
Should not expect one battle, but a long
Campaign, unlike any other we have
1530 Ever seen. It may include dramatic
Strikes, visible on TV, and covert
Operations, secret even in success.
We will starve terrorists of funding, turn
Them one against another, and drive them
1535 From place to place, until there's no refuge
Or no rest. And we will pursue nations
That give aid or haven to terrorists.
Every nation, in every region, now
Has a decision to make. Either you
1540 Are with us, or you're with the terrorists.
From this day forward, any nation that
Continues to harbour or to support
Terrorism will be regarded by
The United States as a hostile regime.
1545 Our nation has been put on notice. We
Are not immune from attack. We will take
Defensive measures against terrorism.
To protect Americans. Be ready.
The hour is coming when America
1550 Will act, and you will make us proud. This is
Not, however, just America's fight.
What's at stake is not just America's
Freedom. This is the world's fight. And this is
Civilisation's fight, the fight of all
1555 Who believe in progress, pluralism,
Tolerance and freedom. We ask every
Nation to join in. We'll ask and we'll need
Help from police forces, intelligence
Services and banking systems world-wide

1560   An attack on one's an attack on all.
May God grant us wisdom, and watch over
The United States of America."
It was a Periclean oration.
Bush had just stated the brand-new doctrine
1565   Of "pre-emptive" military action
Which was later labelled "the Bush doctrine".
Just as a poet describes a sunset
That leaves striped bands of orange-yellow-green
In the west beneath a darkening blue,
1570   And pens similes taken from Nature
And not the works of previous poets,
Uses his eye to paint a clear image
Of the universe that's original
Although critics would rather he copied
1575   The work of dead poets to root himself,
So Bush disregarded past precedent
And looked at the world with fresh eyes and told
What he had seen, though the word "pre-emptive"
Had been used by Israel to justify
1580   Its 1967 grab of land.
Bush had transformed himself as an iron
Thrust in a furnace glows with a white heat
That can be shaped and tempered to hardness,
And his approval rating had now passed
1585   Ninety per cent from fifty-five per cent
Ten days before. Now all knew, it was war.

From his Congress window, Bush looked up at
The stars that hung like fruit on the branches
Of a distant tree in pervading dark,
1590   And he rushed upwards through the nearest and
Entered the One on the edge of space-time.
He, the Leader of the Western World, had
Set out a structure that would lead to war.
In the streets it must seem he had just made
1595   An awesome decision. And yet the One
Had a different perception of conflict.
To the great silence conflict between states
And the conflict between a war and peace
Were of no importance. The universe
1600   Carried on its work imperturbably,
Running the system of Nature and life
In an endless rise-and-fall of seasons,
Of calm broken by sudden thunderstorms.
Now he had launched a storm that would disturb

1605	The peace within a distant region. Storms
	Had a role in the harmonious plan.
	There would be a correction, and order
	Would be restored when the storm was blown out.
	To the One, war brought necessary change
1610	That could not be achieved by peaceful means.
	The Taliban, who allowed bin Laden
	To attack the US, had to be swept
	Aside, and bin Laden's nuclear-suitcase
	Bombs had to be found. He had sown the wind,
1615	Would reap a whirlwind. There would then be calm,
	And peace would return to the universe
	Whose harmonious equilibrium
	Balanced all storms and calms in perfect poise.

Christ stood among the Congressmen, unseen.
1620   The expanding universe, with awesome
Order and perfect symmetry, is shaped
Like a half-opened fan, and all round it
And within it is endless infinite
Which manifests from Nothingness and Non-
1625   Being into Being, thence Existence.
Christ listened from Being, a realm hidden
From our Existence but all round us in
Dust-flecked, sun-shafted air. Shocked and dismayed
At the attack on the Twin Towers, he was
1630   On a fact-finding mission, like a spy
Gathering intelligence, and did not
Manifest – materialise – in the form
Of a Congressman, in a skin's disguise
To influence action. He just eavesdropped.
1635   His mission now complete he instantly
Returned to Heaven just as in our dense air
A photon returns to the quantum void
It came from and instantly reappears
From the void billions of light-years away,
1640   Teleportation swift and practical.

Christ stood on his rock in Heaven's sea of light,
His light body more brilliant than our sun.
As far as eye could see the lesser lights
Of beings, spirits in the infinite,
1645   Sparkled as sunlight dances on our sea.
Two billion flickering flashes welcomed him
Like two billion winking eyes in creased smiles,
Having assembled to greet his return.

All in Heaven attend the Assembly there
1650 And hear what the universal Christ says
And how their Coalition leaders urge
Views on him in reasonable debate.
Heaven is democratic, though Christ decides
And his proposals are approved by all.
1655 Hell was a dictatorship before Christ
Entered and harrowed it, exiled Satan.
As bees hum in clover and nuzzle in
The mouths of flowers and brush on their anthers
And transport pollen grain to their pistils
1660 And incidentally fertilise their
Stigmas as they seek sugary nectar
The flowers have offered temptingly to ease
Nature's process in which all blooms need bees,
So Angels hummed near each other and brushed
1665 On the surface memory of each spirit
And transferred life scenes to its deepest core
To help the process of Self-Fulfilment.
And as they glided past a spirit they
Flashed out the Light that contact had bestrewn.
1670 Now the sparkling subsided into sea,
And Christ spoke: "Angels and all Powers of Light,
I have returned from Earth with sombre news.
The attack on the Twin Towers has led to war
Between the US and Afghanistan
1675 Which shelters bin Laden and the plotters
Who carried out the atrocity that
Brought four planeloads of spirits to our throng.
I have found out that Satan's hand's at work.
He wears a beard like the *mujahideen*
1680 And entered mountainous Afghanistan
And planted the idea in Khalid's mind,
Who then put it to bin Laden. Satan
Has challenged the Thousand-Year Reign that we
Established after the Second World War.
1685 We exiled him from Hell and he has been
In Russia, and fomented the Cold War,
But after the Berlin Wall was torn down,
And Communism, he moved to Islam
To foment rebellion against our Reign.
1690 We thought a seven-year tribulation reached
Its end when the atomic bomb was dropped,
That fiery Armageddon that pained us,
And that our Millennial Reign began when
Eisenhower was victorious in that war

1695	And we captured Hell and took it over,
	But Satan has not accepted his fate,
	He has set up an outpost Hell in camps
	Where spirits are trained to kill, maim and bomb.
	He is trying to arm bin Laden with
1700	Nuclear weapons that can contaminate
	The lands of the entire civilised West.
	And he is trying to divide our Church,
	The Universal Church for all spirits
	That I inaugurated, and split off
1705	The Muslims from it, bring about a clash
	Between the Islamic and the Christian
	Civilisations to divide mankind.
	I am the universal Christ of all
	Religions, not just Christianity;
1710	I represent Mohammed, the Buddha,
	Hindu, Taoist and other leaders,
	Promote all and inter-faith harmony."
	Mohammed had kept quiet, looking shifty.
	Now there was dissent in the heart of Heaven
1715	As he fiercely cried out, "*I* represent
	Muslims to the one God, Allah – you don't."
	Christ ignored this tiresome interruption.
	"Unfortunately he has succeeded,
	And Christian Americans will now fight
1720	Muslim Afghans and Arabs. And what's more,
	Satan has taken another disguise
	As an oilman in a multinational
	That wants to run oil and gas pipelines through
	Afghanistan to the Arabian Sea,
1725	And he has influenced the Syndicate,
	Urged them to press for war for oil and gas.
	I say with a heavy heart, there are now
	Three agendas: Bush's and bin Laden's,
	And the Syndicate's confusing program.
1730	Bush sees 'people of God', Americans,
	Under attack from without, al-Qaeda,
	And is largely unaware that they are
	Also being attacked from within, by
	The Syndicate, who use him for their ends.
1735	Bin Laden sees 'people of God', Sunni
	Muslims but also the whole Islamic
	Ummah under attack from without – I
	Refer to Western 'Crusaders' – and is
	Largely unaware that they are also
1740	Being attacked slyly from within, by

The Syndicate, who use him for their ends.
This conflict, this profound contradiction
Whose two opposites we must reconcile,
Is further complicated by a third
1745   Agenda. The Syndicate sees 'people
Of God', all in a vast New World Order,
Under attack from without, tyrants who
Seek nuclear proliferation such as
Bin Laden, Saddam, Kim and Khamenei
1750   And hoard rather than sell the West their oil
And threaten the stability of their
Coming United States of the World, and
Are aware that they are also being
Attacked and undermined from within, by
1755   All who champion nation-states' right to exist
And do not see Middle-Eastern countries
As mere oil depots for a smash-and-grab
To serve the interests of world government.
Many Freemasons in the Syndicate
1760   Could be exemplary world-government
Universalists in a good New World
Order, but have been led astray by greed,
Which sees a New World Order as a chance
To dominate all the world's resources
1765   To serve their own ends. Angels, it's a mess.
Our Thousand-Year Reign of Peace is at war
And two upright religions have been set
At loggerheads, and Satan is to blame,
The force of disorder which complements
1770   Our force of order and, when kept in check,
Balances the universe as *yin* does *yang*.
Angels, we can't eliminate Satan
Any more than we can scrap disorder.
We have to work against him, reconcile
1775   What he does with our work, in harmony.
But he is at large in Afghanistan
And's causing confusion on a grand scale.
Angels, our Thousand-Year Reign is at risk.
What should we do? I propose that we treat
1780   Him as a terrorist, as Bush regards
Bin Laden, and that in the best interests
Of harmony, we mount a long campaign
To harry him and keep him on the move,
Disrupt his subversive activities
1785   And drive him off the Earth back into Hell.
We in Heaven do not approve of war

In principle, for we recognise its
Brutality and the suffering it brings.
We know that sovereignty's in humankind,
1790   Not nation-states or monarchs' 'divine rights'.
But sometimes war is necessary, when
Through blindness of ego a nation is
Intransigent, perpetrates evil and
Through its truculence and its obstinate
1795   Insistence on having nuclear weapons,
Quite wrongly presents no alternative.
So it is with Satan. He must use force.
It grieves me to say this but I feel we
Should abandon Hell, which we've occupied
1800   Since our triumph, and leave it free to be
A prison for Satan and his dark clique
Who *should* be in an infernal region
And not allowed to roam the lovely Earth
And pollute it as he wills with evil.
1805   His exile should be forcibly ended,
He should be confined like a terrorist
Or an insurgent who has spread chaos
In a place far away from our dear Earth's
Surface ravines and mountainous caverns.
1810   We owe this to the spirits living there
Who have suffered in the hijack attacks.
Of course he will still foment trouble but
Disorder will not dominate on Earth
But will again be balanced with order.
1815   Please indicate if you are in favour
Of reconfining Satan in our Hell –
Though it will take time to accomplish this,
Perhaps as long a war as Bush must fight
To pen al-Qaeda in Afghanistan."
1820   He spoke, and, stunned, the multitude was still,
Taking in the immensity of what
He had proposed, but, loyal to the end,
They all appreciated the wisdom
Of what he'd said and a loud humming rose
1825   As if two billion spirits were humming
"*Om, shantih*", "peace", mellifluous assent
To his call for Heaven to make war on one
Who would be hard to cage, like bin Laden
And his al-Qaeda henchmen sought by Bush.
1830   As above, so below. Both Christ and Bush
Were now war leaders to confine terror.

BOOK THREE

VICTORY IN AFGHANISTAN

SUMMARY

Satan addresses Hell, promising the war will be widened from
          Afghanistan and that Hell will undermine Heaven.

O Crusaders who loved Jerusalem,
Who joined military expeditions
Organised by West Europe's Christian powers
To liberate the Christian holy lands
From the expanding Muslim powers; who first
5   Set up Crusader states at Edessa,
Antioch, Tripoli and Jerusalem,
Which was recaptured and where a Kingdom
Was founded in 1099 – aided
By monastic Knights Templar who guarded
10   Christian pilgrims and whose Rule was Britain
By St Bernard who preached Cistercian Light,
Whose first nine knights resided in the site
Of the Temple of Solomon, granted
To them by Baldwin the Second, the King
15   Of Jerusalem – and shockingly fell
To Saladin in 1187,
Prompting Richard the First, the Lion-heart
To mount a Third Crusade, capture Cyprus
And Acre but not the Holy City,
20   I think of you as I teach my grandson
To play chess on an old Crusader set
Where Christians are lined up against Muslims
In battle array that evokes your time.
My Christian Lion-heart king has two black lions
25   On a red shield and tunic on armour,
Wears a crown round his helmet, holds a sword;
My queen wears Mary-like white flowing robes;
My bishops are in red copes and mitres;
My knights sit on prancing horses, enclosed
30   In square helmets, red crosses on white shields,
Swords drawn; my crenellated brick castles
Have narrow windows; my pawns are soldiers
With tunics over armour, rounded hats
And carry spears and white shields with red cross.
35   All proudly recall the Templar symbol:
Crowned *Agnus Dei* and Crusader flag,
The emblem in the Middle Temple Hall.
His Muslim king who wears a black moustache,
Red tunic and robe, holds round shield with white
40   Chrysanthemum and a curved scimitar,

Is none other than Saladin, *Sultan*,
Founder of the Ayyubid dynasty,
Sole ruler of Egypt and Syria
And advancer of the Muslim Empire
45 Who taught his people that fighting Christians
Was the ultimate *jihad*, Holy War,
Indomitable and chivalrous foe;
His queen wears black and is veiled over mouth;
His bishops are *mullah*s with white turbans
50 (Who are not descendants from the Prophet,
For they wear black turbans), bearded in green,
Who carry a holy book, the *Koran*;
His knights are on prancing, caparisoned
Horses and wear red helmets and sun-cloths
55 Over their necks and shoulders; his castles
Have pointed domes within their battlements;
His pawns are bearded men in red tunics,
Yellow sleeves and legging and neck sun-cloths,
Soldiers with spears and round silver rose shields.
60 As our Christians and Muslims charge and clash
I think of the clash between obdurate
Civilisations which I must describe –
O Richard Lion-heart, o Salah ad-Din
Inspire me now as I narrate the charge
65 Of Bush against bin Laden; o Bernard
Send to my universal inner eye
The benefit and wisdom of the Light
Which understands how opponents serve it.

And you who led three Anglo-Afghan wars,
70 Lord Auckland whose Simla Manifesto
In 1838 established why
The British should restore Shah Shuja's throne
In Afghanistan, whence they would withdraw
(You claimed) for there would be no "invasion"
75 Of a buffer state close to India;
(When the Shah of Persia, supported by
The Russians, invaded Afghanistan
The British believed the Russian army
Would pour through the Khyber Pass and attempt
80 To seize India, her jewel, so they removed
The Afghan *Emir* Dost Mohammed and
Restored their man Shah Shuja to the throne;)
And Sir Henry Rawlinson, whose memo
To India in 1868
85 Recommended that *Emir* Sher Ali

Should be "strengthened at Kabul" – no mention
Was made of military intervention
In Afghanistan – and the grand Viceroy
Of India, Lord Lytton, who is now known
90 For his "folly" in 1876,
Pressed for a British agent to the *Emir*,
A threat that led to occupying war;
And Lord Chelmsford, Viceroy of India,
Reacting to Amanullah's letter
95 Declaring Afghan independence and
Jihad against the British, sent air power
In 1919 and fought a Third War –
O Auckland, Rawlinson, Lytton, Chelmsford,
Send me awareness that, as the Russians
100 Would later find out, sending an army
Into so wild and remote a country
Against such militant, warlike people
Is not a sensible undertaking.
And yet, o rulers of Jerusalem,
105 O Baldwin the Second, send me knowledge
That a Saladin with nuclear bombs
Compressed into suitcases must be stopped,
That Bush was right to want to save mankind
From Armageddon in US cities
110 By disrupting bin Laden's stratagems,
By harrying him and moving him on.

Satan knew of the impending attack
And straightaway materialised in Khost,
Bin Laden's training camp, Bait al-Ansar,
115 On the Spin-Ghar mountain range's lower
Slopes close to the Pakistan border, where
He had used his family's construction
Equipment to turn abandoned Buddhist
Caves above the camp into fortified
120 Bunkers. Here thousands of international
*Jihadi*s received military training
And political indoctrination
(Including Jordanian al-Zarqawi)
Before being sent out to fight in wars
125 In Algeria, Chechnya and Xinjiang.
Satan found him alone in his HQ,
A cave bunker in the Spin-Ghar mountain,
Turbaned and in a camouflage jacket,
Thinking of how Mohammed had fasted
130 In a mountain cave during Ramadan

When a being appeared to him and said,
"Mohammed, you are Allah's messenger."
Gabriel began dictating the first words
Of the *Koran*: "In the name of Allah,
135   The beneficent, the merciful...." This
Revelation that there is only one
Lord was the true beginning of Islam.
Turbaned and clad in camouflage fatigues,
Bearded and dressed like the *mujahideen*,
140   Satan, disguised, knocked, sidled in and said,
Mesmerising with his hypnotic eyes,
Stealing a patriarch's identity,
"Greetings, *Sheikh*, *Emir* and *Imam*, leader
Of the *Ummah*, Islam's international
145   Community which I founded back in
632, two years after the Prophet
Mohammed, bless his name, entered Mecca
With ten thousand men and became sole lord
Of the two sacred enclaves at Mecca
150   And Medina, so even the Quraysh
Agreed to worship Allah alone, and
Held that 'there is no God but Allah, and
Mohammed is the Prophet of Allah'
Just as Gabriel had told him: 'You are
155   The Messenger of Allah.' Bless his name.
Yes, I am Abu Bakr, first Caliph
Or successor, I followed Mohammed's
Approval of *jihad* or holy war
And set about conquering the whole world
160   To place it under Allah." Devious,
Cunning, Satan was careful to avoid
Brash claims that he was the Prophet himself
Which would have been deemed unacceptable
By a former strict Wahhabist. He said,
165   Noting the widening of bin Laden's eyes,
"I speak to you as the *Ummah*'s leader – "
"It's true," bin Laden interrupted. "My
Only country is the community
Of world Islam, which I have a duty
170   To defend if it is under attack."
"Quite so," Satan flattered. "You're Yemeni,
Z'wahiri's Egyptian, Omar Afghan
But all of you are *Ummah* citizens,
Your state is world Islam, and that is why
175   You marked the failed siege of Vienna on
September the eleventh sixteen eighty-

Three in your 9/11 event, which has
Begun to turn the situation round
In accordance with al-Wahhab's ideas.
180   And you have stayed true to his great vision.
I salute you, for the Saudi regime
Compromised its Wahhabist beliefs when
It allowed foreigners into the land
Of the two holy places, and you have
185   Retained the pure vision I recognise
By coming to live with the Taliban
Who are truly Wahhabist, allying
With Zawahiri, a true Wahhabist.
In April 1996 *Mullah*
190   Omar convened a *shura*, religious
Council, of foremost Pathan leaders, who
Elected him *Emir-ul-Momineen,*
Commander of the faithful, and he cloaked
Himself in the Prophet's mantle, received
195   The *baiat* oath of allegiance, from all.
After taking Kabul in September
The Taliban took Saudi Arabia
As its model, conformed with al-Wahhab
And was recognised by two Governments,
200   Both Wahhabist: Saudi and Pakistan.
I say all this because I admire you.
You've led the *Ummah* as I would have done.
Like Ché Guevara you have gone to fight
In a country that's not your own, but's part
205   Of an international battleground
Of ideas: Islam against Western might.
You are a legend like Ché Guevara
And the young will come and support your cause.
You're in tune with my seventh-century outlook
210   Even though you have had to turn your back
On the Wahhabi Establishment in
Saudi Arabia. You must replace
The House of Saud, which permits infidels
To soil their land, as Khomeini replaced
215   The Shah of Iran. I will help you do
This. But first I must give you some news. I've
Heard the infidel Bush is sending planes
To bomb Afghanistan. He's asked *Mullah*
Omar to hand you over, and he might –
220   To save his country from air bombardment.
Stay here. You are safe here. Don't leave these caves
To walk down to the camp. But you must speak

To Omar to remind him it's Wahhab
Against the infidel America.
225 He must not hand you over, betray you."
Now eyes shining, turbaned bin Laden said:
"I welcome the attack. It was to lure
America into Afghanistan
But I toppled their Towers (which I admit
230 Came down more easily than I had thought).
I want American troops to be sucked
Into a quagmire in Afghanistan,
So my al-Qaeda can annihilate
Their troops and teach them a massive lesson,
235 Repay them for the hurt that they have caused
In Palestine, Iraq and other parts
Of the Islamic *Ummah*. I follow
Salah ad-Din, Saladin, who attacked
The Crusaders and took Jerusalem
240 In October 1187
And seized the True Cross from King Guy; also,
I've heard, the Holy Grail from the Templars.
I follow in Salah ad-Din's footsteps,
I've named my son Salah ad-Din.
245 The Crusaders are coming once again
To the lands of Islam's *Ummah*, and I
Will repel them with a force of Arab
Al-Qaeda and of Afghan Taliban –
All pure Wahhabists fighting for Islam,
250 Salafi *jihad*ists who'll recreate
The Muslim *Ummah* and *Sharia* you knew
Which will one day prevail in Chechnya,
Kashmir, Bosnia, the Philippines and this
Afghanistan." Satan kept quiet, knowing
255 Salafists oppose Wahhabists, seeing
Bin Laden was broadening his *Ummah*.
"First their planes will come, with their guided bombs
And cruise missiles. We'll hide in caves, we'll be
Underground. Then the troops will follow. That's
260 When we al-Qaeda really start to fight."
"You must engage the Americans on land,"
Satan agreed. "But more than that. You must
Topple more towers inside America.
I know you've bought nuclear-suitcase bombs –"
265 "I have and we've maintained them, but we can't
Detonate them without conventional
Explosives. We're still working on how we
Can leave a suitcase in Chicago, set

A timer and disappear out of town.
270 I have a plan to explode ten in ten
Cities –" "I've heard," said Satan, excited.
"You must do this as soon as possible.
Attack America here *and* at home."
"That's the plan," bin Laden said. "First things first.
275 I have to cope with Bush's air assault
But once American troops set foot here,
They'll be in for a hiding, what happened
In three Anglo-Afghan wars. In the first,
Which lasted three years, five thousand British
280 Troops were killed and twelve thousand civilians.
Britain withdrew. And the second lasted
Thirty-seven years. Britain again withdrew.
And the same with the third." "And the British
Are in the NATO Coalition with
285 The Americans," Satan said. "This war
Will be their fourth here." "Let them come, I say.
I'll send them packing like the last three times."
Satan said, "I have every confidence
That you will do this – and that you will then
290 Strike at America in ten cities,
To punish the aggressive infidels
For setting up Israel and murdering
Children of the *Ummah* with guided bombs,
In a dramatic fiery holocaust
295 That will contaminate America
And break its power to operate abroad
For many years to come. You can do that."
Turbaned bin Laden said with shining eyes,
"It's my ambition and my intention
300 To cover America with fall-out.
Thank you for visiting me from the dawn
Of the *Ummah* to which I've given my life."

In a pre-recorded videotape
Shown on the Arab satellite channel
305 Al-Jazeera, bin Laden said Bush was
"The chief infidel" and that the US
Would fail like the Soviets. "The war against
Afghanistan and Osama's a war
On Islam," suggesting he, not "corrupt
310 Regimes", led all the Arab peoples. He said
"America has been hit by Allah."
Then he called for "a new battle, a great
Battle, similar to the great battles

Of Islam, like Jerusalem's conqueror.
315 I envision Saladin coming out
Of the clouds carrying his sword, the blood
Of unbelievers dripping from it." He
Also said, "What America's facing
Today's a little of what we've tasted
320 For decades. For nearly eighty years our
Nation tasted this humiliation."
He was referring to the breaking-up
Of the Ottoman Empire at the end
Of the First World War which ended Muslim
325 Rule over Jerusalem in nineteen
Seventeen, and to the loss of Palestine
In 1922. He then referred
To Muslim Spain: "Let the whole world know we
Shall never accept that the tragedy
330 Of Andalusia would be repeated
In Palestine." From the eleventh century
The Muslims were gradually driven out
Of Spain and their cultural domination
Was eroded by the conquest of Spain
335 By Ferdinand and Isabella in
1492. Calling for *jihad*,
He invoked the Crusades: "The Crusaders
Caused our disastrous condition." He said
Pope Urban the Second had urged in ten
340 Ninety-five, "Enter upon the road to
The Holy Sepulchre, wrest that land from
The wicked race. God wills it." Bin Laden
Was now echoing the Pope's religious
Fanaticism a millennium on.
345 Bin Laden said winds of change were blowing
Americans from Arabia. Attacks
On Afghans were attacks against Islam.
"Those who attacked the Towers are martyrs
And will go to Paradise." To sharp eyes
350 The geological background revealed
He was hiding in sandstone caves about
A hundred and twenty-five miles due south
Of Kabul as the sedimentary rock –
Soft, crumbling sandstone formed by deposits
355 Of shallow-water sediment back in
The Pliocene Age between two and seven
Million years ago, Shaigalu strata –
Is only found in the Paktia and
Paktika provinces in that region.

Mullah Omar, too, called for Holy War
And Arabs and Palestinians trekked to
Afghanistan to fight in the front line
In place of Afghans who might defect from
The Taliban to the Northern Alliance.

At Pol-e komri, Taliban soldiers
Ran into a small hotel. Shouting, they
Waved Kalashnikovs, and told guests to close
The curtains, turn off lights, look at the floor.
Outside a convoy of jeeps snaked along
The main street. In one jeep sat a tall man
With a long face: Osama, who had come
From the mountains of Uruzgan, heading
For a long valley called Dara Kayan.
Soft-spoken and controlling, bin Laden
Had sent eight thousand Arab mercenaries
Into central Afghanistan to spread
Terror. They butchered and burned men alive,
Shooting them through their eyes or slitting throats,
Skinning them to make the people loyal.
Broken, mutilated bodies lay skinned
To make sure poppy fields were harvested,
Three thousand tonnes of opium worth sixty
Billion pounds on Western streets kept intact.
Crops were burned so that all were short of food.
Hungry Afghans ate shrivelled grass, also
Locusts, till green vomit stained their baked lips.
Terror and starvation left humans cowed.

Christ, materialising in the White House,
Found Bush preparing an important speech
Sitting alone in this Oval Office.
"George," he said from the shadows in the form
Of a long- and fair-haired white-robed young man
Whose face was not unlike the Turin Shroud's,
"I have come to give you Heaven's support.
You know who I am." "Yes," Bush said, "I do."
And in the lofty tone of Heaven Christ spoke:
"Heaven's pleased that you have re-embraced the faith
As a born-again Christian, turned away
From what for you was a dark time, to Light.
And now you are at the world's pinnacle
And are responsible for all mankind,
Hold human destiny in your choices.
I know you have misgivings, even doubts,

About your present course of action, I
405 Can see them on your soul. That's natural.
It's good, it shows you're not entering on
A new path lightly, but are considering
The consequences. You will have to bomb
Afghanistan extensively to change
410 The regime that harbours terrorist camps
And pursue bin Laden, perpetrator
Of the wicked attack on the Twin Towers,
And innocents will die, collateral
Damage is inevitable in war.
415 Heaven views war with a heavy heart, but sees
The greater good, peace free from terrorism.
Heaven regrets each taking-up of arms
But sometimes there is no alternative.
You must steel your conscience against such thoughts.
420 You have to act against the terrorists
Who have nuclear-suitcase bombs, as you know.
You must be single-minded, extirpate
Each camp bin Laden's opened like a sore
On a healthy body that spreads disease,
425 Germs of evil across the Earth that we
Are trying to ameliorate, improve.
Each camp is a foul replica of Hell.
In each camp terrorists instruct trainees
To kill, maim, wound and cripple their fellows,
430 Do evil in the cause of dubious good.
Evil can only serve evil, not good.
You cannot cease your Afghan campaign till
Every training camp's in ruins, and you've
Wiped terrorism from Afghanistan."
435 Bush said softly, "Thank you for coming here
And telling me this, I appreciate
Your support. You're right, I've been wavering
Inwardly – not outwardly, a leader
Has to be definite and know his goals.
440 I am too aware that men will be killed
Who are blameless and virtuous in their lives.
It means a lot to know I've your blessing
As I attempt to do what I feel's right.
I give you my promise, I will wipe out
445 Each training camp and drive al-Qaeda from
Afghanistan, which I will liberate.
I did not become President to jog
Along, but to change the world, improve things
For all mankind, not just America.

450	I know I am surrounded by people
	Who have a different agenda, on oil.
	But if there's to be a New World Order
	I want all humankind to benefit,
	Not just a section, a small one at that.
455	That's my aim, to create a Christian world,
	A world in your image you'd be proud of."
	Christ had listened intently. He replied:
	"Heaven shares your doubts about the Syndicate
	Who want a New World Order for *their* ends
460	And invoke money, following Satan
	Rather than freedom and democracy
	Which are dear to Heaven and the angels.
	But difficult choices have to be made.
	Be careful, you're in the Syndicate's hands,
465	They want to do things differently from you.
	Heaven approves of what *you* are doing.
	One day I shall welcome you to Heaven.
	I thought you would like to know that at this
	Difficult time." He faded and Bush rubbed
470	His eyes. Had he imagined the visit?
	Had he had a hallucination caused
	By worry at a stressful decision
	To go to war under a NATO flag?
	No, he'd received an endorsement from Heaven.
475	
	The campaign had been officially named
	For its military response to 9/11
	Operation Infinite Justice. But
	As among followers of several faiths
	This phrase described God (a restricted use),
480	To avoid giving offence to Muslims
	The codename had subsequently been changed
	To *Operation Enduring Freedom*.
	On October the fifth officially
	NATO took over control of US
485	Forces in Afghanistan – when deployed.
	In his weekly radio address on
	October the sixth Bush gave an update
	"On our global campaign against terror":
	"The US is presenting a clear choice
490	To each nation: stand with the civilised
	World, or stand with the terrorists. And for
	Those nations that stand with the terrorists
	There will be a heavy price." He affirmed
	The enemy's "state sponsors of terror",

495	Not the Arab world or Islam. He'd warned
	The Taliban to close down all their camps
	And surrender all the terrorists in
	Afghanistan – "and time is running out."

	The next day time ran out. Led by NATO,
500	Unauthorised by the UN because
	Article 51 of its Charter
	Permitted self-defence, the invasion
	Began: fifty Tomahawk cruise missiles
	Launched from US and British submarines
505	And ships took out precise targets, landing
	In waves as each salvo arrived. Just as
	A thunderstorm with lowering black cloud looms
	And lightning forks and zigzags round the sky
	And vivid flashes light up every room
510	And crashes overhead suggest one's roof
	Has been hit and one's house is coming down,
	So the invasion struck Afghanistan
	With the thunder of flashing war. Fifteen
	US Air Force bombers and twenty-five
515	Strike aircraft from US aircraft-carriers
	Bombed and damaged al-Qaeda training camps
	And destroyed Taliban air defences
	From high altitudes that were out of range
	Of Muslim anti-aircraft fire, and blitzed
520	All airports, electricity and power,
	And telecommunications, centres
	In Kabul, Kundahar, Jalalabad
	Where the night sky was lit up by flashes
	Of explosions. The Defence Ministry
525	And airport at Kabul were hit, command
	Posts and airbases destroyed. Smoke billowed.
	Targets had been painted by ground forces
	For laser-guided missiles, bunker bombs.
	In Kabul the Presidential palace
530	Had been hit in what the Taliban called
	"Terrorist acts". Refugees fled the towns.
	Two US C-17 Globemaster
	Transport jets dropped thirty-seven thousand five
	Hundred daily rations as they escaped.
535	Now fifteen thousand Northern-Alliance
	Fighters mainly from Tajik and Uzbek
	Ethnic groups tried to advance but the line
	Facing them held with grim, determined strength.
	A pitch-black night – no electricity

540	⌐Or paraffin lamps to light villages
	Where humans huddled and cowered in mud-huts.
	Then a huge flash, a series of dull booms
	As air strikes lit up the Afghan darkness.
	A convoy had dimmed headlights. Suddenly,
545	A bloodcurdling yell from a sentry,
	And drivers slammed on brakes. From the mountains
	Twenty miles north of Kabul, lookouts saw
	In the dark plain below bright flashes as
	Rockets sped at Taliban positions,
550	Grad missiles fired on the Shamali Plain.
	Blasts and rumbles. And over Kabul two
	Orange flashes and anti-aircraft fire
	Like fireworks shooting up towards the stars.
	Over the horizon a golden light
555	And an aircraft heading east. Then dull thuds
	Of explosions from Kabul, bombs from jets
	Screaming in without lights from a base near
	Qarshi in ex-Soviet Uzbekistan.
	All marvelled at the reach and precision
560	Of the global American Empire.
	Sanctions had been imposed on Pakistan
	After it tested a nuclear device
	In 1998. Now President
	Musharraf pledged support for the US
565	Who waived sanctions and made a six-hundred-
	Million-dollar loan, a down payment on
	Ten billion dollars in loans. Pakistan
	Allowed the US Special Forces Air-
	Bases that would host fifty-seven thousand
570	Eight hundred bombing missions, refuelling
	And medical evacuation aid,
	All based on Pakistani soil without
	Pakistan's public having been informed.
	And yet, Musharraf also supported
575	The Taliban, which Pakistan had helped
	To found and train as a bulwark against
	Pro-Indian forces in Afghanistan –
	They could also make attacks on Indian
	Troops in Kashmir. And still the ISI,
580	Pakistan's military intelligence
	Agency, continued to supply arms,
	Ammunition and fuel. A week after
	Bush's ultimatum ("You're either with
	Us or against us in the fight against

585   Terror") Musharraf negotiated
A pause in US bombing to allow
ISI operatives to be flown out
Of Afghanistan, and with them escaped
Hundreds of Taliban commanders and
590   Al-Qaeda members. Musharraf believed
That if he delivered *some* al-Qaeda
Members to the US, the Taliban
Would be intact in Pakistan, ready
For a future battle if need arose.
595   So Cheney and Rumsfeld turned a blind eye
To the extremists Musharraf sheltered,
And began to build a coalition
With the warlords and drug-dealers who called
Themselves the Northern Alliance, funded
600   By the massive poppy harvest worth half
What the legal economy produced.
These included Hamid Karzai, who rode
Into the Taliban's Afghanistan
On a motorbike, eventually claimed
605   The presidency over its warlords.

And now on behalf of the deposed King
Zahir Shah, the most influential and
Most charismatic anti-Taliban
Pashtun commander since Massoud, Abdul
610   Haq, who fought the Soviets, was carrying
Out a secret mission in Taliban-
Controlled areas south of Kabul, trying
To lure defectors from the Taliban.
He'd left Peshawar for Parachinar
615   With two satellite telephones, bundles
Of US dollars and documents when
A villager tipped off the Taliban.
He was quickly surrounded with twenty
Followers in Azra. For the next twelve
620   Hours a gun battle raged. By satellite
Phone he called in a US fighter plane
And helicopter gunships, but, wounded
Fourteen times, his right foot hacked off, trying
To flee on horseback in rugged terrain,
625   He was captured, taken to a stronghold
By six pick-up trucks full of Taliban
From Kandahar and Arab fighters linked
To Osama. There he was beaten up.
King Zahir, informed, pleaded for his life,

630	Saying he was in Afghanistan on
	A peace mission. The Taliban were deaf,
	And hanged him; his nephew, Isatullah;
	Another commander, Haji Dawran;
	And his most trusted aid, Major Hamid;
635	As traitors on a makeshift gallows in
	Accordance with a *fatwa* announced by
	A council of clerics the previous month.
	Then their bodies were riddled with bullets
	By the Taliban under snow-capped peaks
640	Of the beautiful Paghman mountains at
	The dreadful al-Qaeda base at Rishkhoor
	Where thousands of *jihad* warriors were trained
	Each month, Osama's largest Afghan base –
	Which was now bombed by American planes.
645	Dozens of buildings were flattened, body
	Parts were strewn round a huge crater. A black
	Jacket, soiled with blood and dirt, lay below
	A metal noose wrapped in old rags that hung
	From a scraggy maple tree. Taliban
650	Troops claimed to be on Hamid Karzai's trail:
	A key tribal leader and royalist
	Who was seeking to build up a Southern
	Alliance from the Pathan ethnic group,
	A pipeline adviser to Unocal.
655	He was surrounded like Haq but broke free.
	The Taliban had been tipped off on both,
	Both were betrayed by someone working in
	Pakistan's secret service, ISI.

	In a video bin Laden claimed the Twin
660	Towers were legitimate targets as they
	Were "supposed to be filled with supporters
	Of the economic power of the US
	Who are abusing the world". Bin Laden
	Justified killing those in the Twin Towers
665	On the grounds they weren't civilians – Islam
	Forbids the killing of all innocent
	Civilians even in a holy war.
	Indirectly he was now admitting
	Responsibility for 9/11,
670	Though his words fell short of a confession.
	Of the Twin Towers bin Laden said, "It is
	What we instigated in self-defence.
	So if avenging the killing of our
	People is terrorism, let history

675	Be a witness that we are terrorists.
	The battle's moved inside America.
	We'll continue until we win this fight
	Or die in the cause. Bush and Blair do not
	Understand any language except force.
680	Every time they kill us, we then kill them
	So the balance of terror is achieved."
	Rumsfeld said that bin Laden might never
	Be caught: "It's a big world. There are lots of
	Countries. He's got lots of money. He's got
685	Lots of people who support him. I just
	Don't know whether we will be successful."
	He was forced to retract these words amid
	A clamour of criticism, for Bush
	Had said he'd be taken dead or alive,
690	That the immediate aim was to bring bin
	Laden and other al-Qaeda leaders
	To justice, a resolve not to be shed.
	Cheney warned all Americans that they'd
	Have to get used to "a new normalcy"
695	As sweeping new powers of surveillance,
	Arrest and detention came in, civil
	Liberties sacrificed to protect all
	From terrorists, centralised gathering
	To the Vice-President of new measures
700	That seemed dictatorial to the free press.
	For security reasons and PR
	Cheney had kept a low profile. His own
	Security was unprecedented.
	He had disappeared since 9/11 and
705	Met the National Security Council
	Only by videolink. Invisible,
	He spent seven weeks in a military
	Bunker so the President and V-P
	Would not both die in a terror attack.
710	The V-P gave no live interviews so
	No camera bomb could kill him like Massoud.
	For a fortnight there was a stalemate with
	No battlefield successes. Civilians
	Suffered casualties in the air attacks,
715	And thousands of Pashtun militiamen
	Poured in from Pakistan, swelling numbers
	Of Taliban to fifty or sixty
	Thousand Muslim fighters, while a hundred
	Combat sorties a day by US planes

720	And three to five hundred Western special
	Operations forces/intelligence
	Operatives supported the front line.
	As swifts flit, swoop and dive in summer dusk,
	Twisting and darting in the evening shade,
725	Race, rise and fall, screaming, in fading light
	And catch a thousand insects which they store
	In a bulge in their throats to feed their young,
	The hundredth insect-catching flight that day
	When they've already flown five hundred miles,
730	Then head for the eaves of a local church
	To nests on ancient pitted stone ledges,
	Grass and feather glued with their saliva,
	So US planes made a hundred sorties,
	Each of which gathered a thousand pieces
735	Of information regurgitated
	To intelligence operatives at base
	Before they roosted snugly in hangars.
	US planes bombed a Red-Cross warehouse that
	Stockpiled food for refugees in Kabul
740	Twice, and then bombed a UN food warehouse
	Stockpiling food in Kandahar, three strikes
	That would deprive the Taliban of food
	But would also harm Afghan refugees:
	Seven and a half million were now homeless.
745	Now carrier-based F/A-18 Hornet
	Fighter-bombers hit Taliban vehicles
	In pinpoint strikes, and other US planes
	Cluster-bombed the Taliban's defences.
	The Tutakhan mountains' peak erupted
750	In smoke and flame as American jets
	Circled in the sky and dropped cluster bombs
	And rockets on the slopes. Amid the smoke
	Three Taliban fighters, two dressed in black,
	One in green, stretched out their prayer-mats and prayed,
755	Tough warriors oblivious of war
	As they communed with eternal Allah.
	Now the US deployed fuel-air bombs,
	Fifteen-thousand-pound "daisy-cutters" that
	Were guided in by special forces' troops
760	Parachuted down to Afghan targets,
	Fearsome weapons that vaporised all flesh.
	Air strikes eroded their support structure:
	Kandahar in darkness, a fuel depot
	In Kabul struck, black smoke high in the sky.
765	US planes flew unchallenged day and night.

Northern-Alliance commanders took heart
In their north-east territory and central
Pocket. US Special Forces raided
The Taliban's heartland in Kandahar
770   And struck at *Mullah* Omar's home compound,
A command post disguised as a farm, and
Killed twenty-five Taliban and captured
Computer disks and secret documents.
But progress through October had been slow.
775

On the outskirts of Khoja Bahawuddin
A primitive refugee camp that stank.
Thirteen hundred lived in mud huts made from
Clumps of clay and earth piled on each other.
The roofs were plastic sheets, torn blankets and
780   Bundles of straw, mud hovels housing eight
That collapsed in torrential rain that turned
The floors into a quagmire and, rebuilt,
Were the only protection against frosts
Of minus 29 Centigrade. One
785   Filthy mattress per hut was bed for all.
A bitter wind whipped in from the desert,
Relentless icy drizzle froze the cheeks.
One cracked and battered cooking-pot, an old
Threadbare rug and a few scrawny chickens.
790   Here in the squalor and this bleak landscape
Lived humans crouching in dirty burrows
Like animals – children with faces scarred
By red scabs of scabies, running noses,
Freezing coughs from chest infections, playing
795   Barefoot in sewage and donkey droppings,
Plastic bags tied round cracked and bleeding feet
Torn apart by earth and stones where they trod.
For one the chain of Earthly memories
Snapped like a necklace, spilling beads, as she
800   Lay face down, motionless, never to move.
Hungry children probed mud for seeds like hens
Picking and pecking among stones for grain.
Just as new-hatched chicks, fallen from a nest,
Beaks open, implore for food and will be
805   Dead next morning, so these children's mouths gaped.
Parents sat in despair, abandoned by
The civilised world that had bombed their homes
And put them in the misery of this camp.
A few had rice and corn, there was a well
810   But each night children died from cold and harsh

Exposure to the weather that takes lives.

Osama called on Pakistan's Muslims
To rise against President Musharraf,
To confront "the Christian crusade against
815   Islam. Mohammed's followers within
Afghanistan are being slaughtered." He
Went on, "The world has split into two camps:
A camp under the banner of the Cross
As the chief of the infidels" (or Bush)
820   "Said, and another under the banner
Of Islam. Defend right. Vanquish evil."
A clash of civilisations called for
By a fanatical, strict Wahhabist.
In Peshawar, an effigy of Blair
825   Was beheaded and burned by five thousand
Pakistani sympathisers with bin
Laden protesting against the Allied
Bombing of Afghanistan. The mob screamed
"Death to Britain" as goats' blood spurted when
830   The head came off, and then tore the dummy
Into pieces and set fire to each bit.
Tear-gas disbursed the demonstrators. Now
Order was restored in irked Pakistan.

Bush signed an anti-terrorism bill
835   Into law, which would restrict much movement,
Increase profiling, surveillance, tracking,
Fingerprinting, cataloguing, marking
Americans short of biometry
(Planting chips under skin), causing both small
840   And great, rich and poor, free and bound to bear
A mark on their right hand (scanned fingerprints)
Or on their foreheads (passport-like photos
Scanned into computers); heaping more powers
On the State to control all citizens,
845   Improve security and screen suspects.

At the Beni Hissar camp near Kabul
On October the twenty-sixth, by night,
After eight, a convoy of jeeps arrived
And a hundred and twenty bodyguards,
850   All tall, made a round protective wall that
Could fire in three directions. Bin Laden,
Within the round wall, strode into the camp,
Greeted the Sudanese commander called

Abdul Aziz, and said that he would leave
855   At 8 a.m. the next morning. He went
        To a mud-brick house in the camp's centre
        And slept ringed by his bodyguards. At 5
        He rose and said his prayers and left, and then
        Everyone was told to leave as a cruise-
860   Missile strike was coming. At 8 a.m.
        Two missiles roared in at the mud-wall house,
        Shattered its walls, two blasts tore off the roof,
        Scattering *débris* and timbers across
        The courtyard. There must have been a spy in
865   The camp, but the molehunt found nobody.
        So bin Laden remained one step ahead
        Of America's tracking and revenge.

        At Dasht-e-Qal'eh near Tajikistan
        Old T-55 tanks sped through mud lanes
870   And filled the cold night air with exhaust fumes,
        Spearheading the Northern-Alliance assault
        On Taliban front lines from the River
        Kokcha. And now the pitch-black Afghan night –
        No electricity or paraffin –
875   Was a blaze of yellow headlights of tanks
        And armoured personnel carriers, waiting
        The order to cross – which now came. Thirty
        Soldiers crammed in a lorry that ploughed through
        The fast-flowing waters of gravel beds
880   Followed by a convoy. Soon each lorry
        Returned empty. Three hundred men had crossed,
        The Taliban were quiet: no shooting at
        Chagatai and Poly Khomri. And yet
        The Taliban had placed Pathan, Arab
885   And Pakistani fighters on their front
        And rear lines, sandwiching local Afghans
        In the middle, and had moved their weapons
        Into villages to turn residents
        Into human shields to escape pounding
890   From US fighters and B-52
        Bombers on their front line, which had lasted
        A week. Their resolve had weakened. Kabul
        Was in the Northern Alliance's sights.

        Dawn found the Chesmay-e-Safa gorge still
895   In the first light of November the ninth.
        Taliban defenders of the city
        Of Mazar-i-Sharif concentrated

There at the entrance to the citadel
Were still fast asleep when US bombers
900 Roared in and carpet-bombed the peaceful gorge.
The Taliban hid in houses and mosques,
Had taken food, press-ganged locals to fight.
Northern-Alliance cavalry forces
Moved in and took surrounding hills, trapping
905 The Taliban, whose troops were forced to leave
Their trenches and caves and were then exposed
To American bombers' air assault.
There was nowhere to flee, thunderous bombs
Blew men to pieces where they crouched or stood,
910 Pakistanis, Arabs and Chechnyans.
Scores of bodies lay on open ground, one
Bombing raid killed at least a hundred men.
The sides of the gorge were covered in smoke.
At 2 p.m. the Northern-Alliance
915 Forces swept in from south and west and seized
The city's military base and airport
In a well-organised pincer movement,
Mopped up Taliban remnants in the gorge.
By six the battle was over, and by
920 Sunset the Taliban were retreating
To south and east and heading for Kunduz
So fast that the kettles they left behind
Were still warm when the Alliance rolled in.
Local Taliban fled in Toyota
925 Pick-up trucks. There was no room for hundreds
Of Pakistanis, who entered a school.
⌐It was now clear that Mazar-i-Sharif
Had fallen. The next day the conquerors
Roamed the city looking for Taliban
930 Supporters. Suspects were shot on the spot.
They found five hundred and twenty hiding
In the school, demoralised Taliban
From Pakistan who lacked means of escape.
Fierce Hazara mountain tribesmen rode past
935 The school nonchalantly on horseback. Some
Were fired on and blasted from saddles. Now
Northern Alliance surrounded the school
And three hundred surrendered and came out.
Then an American plane dropped a bomb,
940 Blowing out windows for hundreds of yards,
And killed a hundred at the school's front. Then,
Outraged, the survivors began to fire.
The Northern Alliance fired tank shells and

Dowsed the walls with petrol, burned the school down.
945 Many were buried under the rubble.
Massacres of pro-Taliban fighters
Caused many local commanders to change
Sides. Women shed *burqa*s and veils, men shaved
Beards. There was an open route to Kabul.
950
A journalist, blindfolded in a jeep,
And rolled in a blanket behind front seats,
A Pakistani driven five hours outside
Kabul in a snowy place much colder,
In an unfurnished room hung with blankets –
955 Traditional local brown wool blankets
Pinned up to form screens – in a cold mud hut
Met bin Laden, who with Zawahiri
Entered, sat on embroidered blue cushions,
Wearing his natty camouflage jacket
960 And white Pashtun turban and carrying
A Kalashnikov, with a dozen guards.
Full of confidence, not softly spoken,
He spoke forcefully, looking healthy, in
High spirits, laughing, said he had access
965 To nuclear and chemical weapons
And would use them if the US used theirs.
Over tea, bread and jam during two hours,
He said the attack on America
Was "justified" because Americans
970 Massacred Muslims in Chechnya, Iraq.
Just as a pair of jackdaws on a ridge
Peck near each other and fly together,
Do everything as a pair that they can,
So bin Laden and Zawahiri were
975 An inseparable pair in the mountains.
Days later the Pakistan Government,
Tipped off by FBI, arrested two
Retired officials of the Pakistan
Atomic Energy Commission who
980 Had close contacts with the Taliban and
Al-Qaeda and had met bin Laden while
In Kandahar to construct a flour mill.
In the White House Bush stood beside Putin
And announced that the US would destroy
985 Five thousand nuclear warheads in ten years
And reduce nuclear arms to between
One thousand seven hundred and two thousand
Two hundred, which would dismantle the last

Vestiges of the Cold War for ever.
990 Bush, with over seven thousand nuclear bombs
He could not use, was keen to deny bin
Laden access to one – which he would use.

Two nights later, on November the twelfth,
As twenty thousand *mujahideen* in
995 Two columns waited in darkness to storm
Taliban positions at a signal
Following a ferocious air attack,
Bombardment and impending ground assault,
Kabul was vacated under cover
1000 Of darkness, its defenders routed by
American carpet-bombing. Some seven
Thousand men left for Kandahar. At dawn
A wounded Taliban soldier was found
Lying in dust and dragged by one ankle,
1005 Had his trousers stripped off by five Northern-
Alliance troops who, as he stared mask-like,
Flung him back and shot him on his back, his
Bloodstained trousers round his ankles. He lay
Arms in a cross as if embracing all
1010 The column that filed past, his dignity
Preserved in dirt through his embrace. Dawn broke
On five bodies clustered near Khair Khana,
Sprawled and spattered with gore on the asphalt,
Most lying on their backs in black turbans
1015 Staring sightlessly into the pale sky,
Their scarlet blood still running. No one else
Lay in the yellow earth's withered vineyards.
In cold wind as the sun rose, one sat up,
Blood gurgling from his mouth, riddled with wounds,
1020 A waxen dullness spread over his face.
Croaking and spluttering he claimed to be
"*Mujahideen*". "You're a Talib," spat out
A Northern-Alliance fighter. The man
Fell back on his elbow and admitted
1025 He and his fallen friends were Taliban
Fighters from Kalakhan, stopped, trapped and then
Shot by *mujahideen* while escaping
In a Datsun pick-up which they then stole.
The Talib lay down in the road to die,
1030 Let his spirit leave his broken body
And merge with the vastness, the infinite,
As the sun rose and heat stifled. Nearby
An Afghan man hurled a rock at the corpse

Of a Taliban fighter by a road,
1035 Rolled-up bank notes stuffed up his nose, scathing
Condemnation: a loathed mercenary. That
Afternoon Northern-Alliance forces
Consisting of Tajik *mujahideen*,
Arrived and found bomb craters, burned foliage
1040 And shell cases from the Taliban's guns.
Twenty Arabs hid in the city's park.
A fifteen-minute gun battle ensued.
They hid behind shrubs but were raked with fire
And all were soon dead. Now crucial Kabul
1045 Was in the hands of US and NATO
Forces and Northern-Alliance victors.
Ismail Khan, the anti-Soviet leader
And former Governor of Herat, nicknamed
The Lion of Herat, recaptured his seat
1050 Of government after seven years' absence.

In an abandoned al-Qaeda safe house
Occupied by two Arab doctors, one
With a German passport, one with Saudi-
Arabian papers, whose basement had been
1055 A bomb-training centre for al-Qaeda
Trainees with cardboard boxes, wires, black tape,
Were plans to manufacture ricin (most
Toxic of biological agents
Used by the Bulgarian secret police
1060 When they killed Georgi Markov by stabbing
Him with a poisoned umbrella as he
Walked slowly across Waterloo Bridge) and
Instructions on building atomic bombs.
A flight simulator program was found,
1065 Identical to one found in Atta's
Luggage, and a list of US flight schools.
Charred documents were scattered round the house
With handwritten notes by a scientist,
Designs for missiles in German, Urdu,
1070 English and Arabic, which showed that bin
Laden had been trying to make a bomb
Like the one once dropped on Nagasaki,
A fission bomb with a plutonium
Implosion device in which TNT
1075 Compresses a radioactive core
And turns it critical and produces
A big thermonuclear reaction.
Men lined up to have beards trimmed or shaved off,

⌐Women threw away head-to-toe *burqa*s
1080 And walked with faces exposed without fear
Of being whipped by religious police,
Songs blared from shops and bands played in restaurants,
Once punished by public lashing, as all
Revelled in freedom from Draconian rule.
1085 An outburst of joy (and widespread looting)
Greeted the routing of the Taliban,
Who claimed they'd made a tactical retreat,
As thousands threw flowers and cheered exhausted
Fighters slumped in the turrets of their tanks,
1090 Greeting the *mujahideen*'s victory.

Now the Taliban collapsed everywhere.
Next day to the east Taloqan was seized.
All Afghan provinces beside Iran
Changed sides and local Pashtun commanders
1095 Seized the north-east, and key Jalalabad
Where bin Laden helped to negotiate
A peaceful hand-over of power. He gave
Directions to his fighters, surrounded
By sixty armed guards for forty minutes,
1100 Standing beside a mosque until more than
Two hundred lorries and armoured vehicles,
An Arab convoy, left for al-Qaeda's
Base at Tora Bora, he riding in
The seventh lorry in the convoy. Now in
1105 The town, in dirty rooms and courtyards, round
Cooking fires, *mujahideen* clicked, clattered
Kalashnikovs while locals watched in fear
And resignation; the *mujahideen*
Were back to rob and beat, rule by the gun
1110 Without police, army or government.
In Shia Muslim central Afghanistan
Taliban troops rounded up and murdered
Large numbers of young men and razed entire
Neighbourhoods before withdrawing. Savage
1115 Hand-to-hand combat broke out in the steep
Gorges of the dread river Taloqan,
An Uzbek word meaning "River of Blood".
The Taliban detonated bridges
As they retreated back into Kunduz
1120 Where ten thousand led by foreign fighters
Were besieged, but stubbornly resisted.
They left a vacuum in Afghanistan.
Others were round Kandahar or within

The Tora Bora cave complex as was
1125 Osama, high in mountains, in bunkers
And caves within the mountain fortress there.
The US Air Force used bunker-buster
EGBU28 bombs that could
Pierce yards of rock, AGM65
1130 Maverick missiles that sought mouths of caves.
Bin Laden lived constantly on the move,
On mules and horses and in four-wheel-drives
Reportedly shuttling from cave to cave
To avoid capture, from the caves of Khost
1135 To a deep bunker near to Kandahar,
A retreat near Jalalabad and caves
In Oruzgan. Fuel-air bombs sucked the air
From caves, guided bombs sealed them into tombs.
Al-Qaeda bases received direct hits
1140 From thunderous air strikes. In Jalalabad
Arab troops loyal to him fought deserting
Members of the defeated Taliban.

In Jalalabad a videotape
Was found, made in early November in
1145 A Kandahar guesthouse of bin Laden
Talking to *Sheikh* al-Ghamdi, a Saudi
Militant cleric from whose tribe several
9/11 hijackers came, and boasting
He was surprised by the complete collapse
1150 Of the Twin Towers: "We calculated in
Advance the number of casualties
From the enemy. We calculated
That the floors that would be hit would be three
Or four. I was the most optimistic
1155 Due to my experience in this field.
I was thinking that the fire from the gas
In the plane would melt the iron structure
Of the building and collapse the area
Where the plane hit and all the floors above
1160 It only. This is all that we'd hoped for.
Brothers who heard the news were overjoyed."
Gloating, bin Laden laughed and the *Sheikh* laughed.
Sulayman, bin Laden's follower, said,
"On TV an Egyptian family
1165 Sitting in their living-room exploded
With joy as when there's a soccer game and
Your team wins – the same expression of joy."
Bin Laden said that only Atta knew

Of the conspiracy, that he himself
1170   Was told of the date just five days before.
The video, released by the Pentagon,
Confirmed bin Laden's role in 9/11.

A US bombing raid on Kabul killed
Mohammed Atef, military chief
1175   Of bin Laden who planned the 9/11
Attacks and the bombings of the US
Embassies in Kenya, Tanzania
Where suicide bombers drove trucks packed with
Explosives, killed two hundred and twenty,
1180   An Egyptian whose daughter of fourteen
Married bin Laden's nineteen-year-old son.
Thousands of Taliban trapped in Kunduz
Were with two thousand entrenched al-Qaeda –
Chechens, Arabs, Pakistanis, Chinese
1185   Muslims who fled from Mazar-i-Sharif.
All day B-52s dropped five-hundred-
Pound bombs in curtains on the dug-in men.
General Khaksar ordered that six thousand
Foreigners fighting for the Taliban
1190   Should be shown no mercy and should be shot.
During a lull some men left their trenches.
Soon hundreds of Taliban defected
To the Northern Alliance, and each one
Was given a bear hug by General Dostum.
1195   Terrified people were trapped in their homes,
Shops closed, awaiting the end of the siege
As Taliban roamed the deserted streets
And groups of Talibs kicked down people's doors,
Dragged out their sons and shot them by the roads.
1200   Guns spoke and replied right across Kunduz.
Fifty or sixty bodies lay in rice
Fields or half-in, half-out of dry ditches
Or sat against a low baked-mud wall, each
With a pained face of agony and fear,
1205   Some bodies twitching in the wind which blew
The stench of death into silent Kunduz.
Four hundred and seventy Taliban,
Afghan Talibs on the deserted streets
Suspected by al-Qaeda of wanting
1210   To defect were marched out by al-Qaeda
And shot by a road as plumes of black smoke
And dust concealed the sun, a vile warning.
That night, the first batch of six hundred, or

Perhaps five thousand, al-Qaeda were flown
1215 Out on Russian planes to Pakistan, flights
That continued for three dark nights – a deal
That continued the ISI's support
For the Taliban they'd founded and trained,
And to be rid of them without bloodshed
1220 Had backing from the Northern Alliance,
In which the US "overlooked" the escape
To save Pakistan's leader Musharraf
From protests. The flights – on Antinovs – left
At 2 a.m. between the bombing raids.
1225 After a siege of nine days, Kunduz fell.

Arms lashed behind their backs, the Taliban
Were marched off to prison in Taloqan.
Three thousand three hundred and fifty sat
In a crowded courtyard in Sibirgan
1230 Prison near Mazar-i-Sharif, sullen.
Eight hundred al-Qaeda troops were taken
To Qala-i-Janghi fortress not far
From Mazar-i-Sharif. Four hundred and
Fifty men, foreign Yemenis, Saudis,
1235 Chechens, Uzbekis and Pakistanis
Revolted as a bearded al-Qaeda
American was interrogated
And seized the southern half of this former
Medieval fortress, the armoury
1240 And its small arms and fired from the stables
And arsenals with machine-guns and mortars.
There was chaos. The American who
Had interrogated the al-Qaeda
American was dead. Planes bombed, tanks shelled.
1245 Just as when a wasps' nest is puffed with smoke
All wasps scouting outside the nest return
And crowd into the vacant cells near young
To die with the rest in the colony,
So those caught outside the rebel enclave
1250 Flew back into the stables, packed all bays.
For seven days a battle raged between
An SBS unit, Green Berets and
Northern Alliance, AC-130
Gunships that strafed, US bombers' air strikes
1255 With two-thousand pound bombs dropped from Hornets.
At the end all the prisoners were dead,
Strewn on the parade-ground amid smoking
Piles of rubble and craters, two hundred

With hands tied behind their backs, bound with scarves,
1260 Mouths gaping, blast-blackened, some with one gun-
Shot through their heads or a noose round their necks,
Some squashed by tank tracks, chests crushed, heads flattened,
Some with brown blankets round their shoulders ripped
With many bullet holes and stained with blood,
1265 Several arms and legs protruding from earth,
Decapitated heads with beards turned grey
By dust, torsos on walls, tree stumps, windows,
Horses and mules with stomachs burst open,
The smell of bodies mingling with the stench
1270 Of cordite, in a war-made human Hell,
Mass suicide, "kill until you are killed",
General Dostum's crushing of the revolt
With a medieval barbarity,
A battle as ferocious as any
1275 In Afghanistan's savage history –
Save eighty-six who'd hidden underground.
They came out when water from a fire truck
Was pumped into their bunker, flooding them.
Fifty Northern-Alliance troops were killed.
1280 Now the combat in North Afghanistan
Was over and Northern-Alliance warlords
Were in control. The Taliban were gone.
Al-Qaeda's remnants were now on the run.

Satan's spies informed him that Christ had told
1285 The Assembly in Heaven that he could
Reoccupy Hell if he so desired.
He'd led his band of Hellish followers
To the White Mountains, where they occupied
Rocky ridges and caves far from man's sight.
1290 Now he sensed the Americans had won
And resolved to distance himself at once
From a defeat that might reflect on him.
Now in the twilight of an Afghan day,
A time when things or darkness can withstand
1295 The painful light of daylight and survive,
Standing on a rock, he addressed the host:
"Angels, we have lived in exile here in
These mountain crags and caverns, and it's not
Been too bad, we have continued our self-
1300 Improvement, though American planes fly
Overhead and disturb us with thunderous
Bombardments, and it's colder and less dark
Than we like. Angels, the bombing will soon

	Intensify. Now's a good time for us
1305	To move out. And I know you still hanker
	For where we left and where we ought to be,
	Where we belong: our own Hell." Loud hissing
	Of approval greeted the blessed name.
	"There each of us has his appointed place
1310	And derives comfort from it and from being
	With colleagues, and though here all know where each
	Is, it's hard to arrange ourselves as though
	We were in an army and had to keep
	Military formation without columns
1315	Or ranks, and no parade-ground on which we
	Could draw up in neat rows. Angels, dear ones,
	All who are proud not to follow the Light,
	Creatures of Darkness who act differently,
	Know that I have solved our problem. For I
1320	Have sent an advance party down to Hell."
	Excited buzzing filled the mountain air
	As if five million wasps fanned their laced wings.
	"I've had word that they have reoccupied
	Our old region, those dear caverns and rocks,
1325	Those niches where we all arranged ourselves
	And defied tyrannical Heaven's demands
	That we all follow Light, caves of the free
	Where we can live as *we* choose, not Heaven,
	As liberals rather than slaves to the Light,
1330	With the free intellects we chose on Earth,
	Do what we choose to do eternally
	In freedom that Heaven cannot remove.
	And what's more, our reoccupation's not
	Been challenged. Angels, by our brilliant ruse
1335	And cunning strategy, we retreated
	To keep our army intact, and regrouped,
	And now we can return in victory,
	Sneak back into Hell for a better base,
	Like terrorists returning to a camp
1340	They vacated before a cruise attack
	And which is safe again. We can all now
	Return to Hell while Heaven is distracted
	By war in this tiresome Afghanistan.
	We can slip back to our rightful region
1345	Now Heaven is not watching, and once there
	We will be ready for any attempt
	To evict us, we will not be taken
	By surprise next time, I promise you that."
	The buzzing grew stronger in Hellish cheer.

1350	"Angels, please indicate your approval
	For immediate return to Paradise."
	The buzzing reached a crescendo as if
	Ten million angry hornets fanned their wings.
	"Come on, then Angels. Reoccupy Hell."
1355	And like a swarm of locusts, the bat-like
	Creatures of Hell took off behind Satan,
	Followed their leader to the nether world,
	Not realising Christ had urged that Satan
	Should return to Hell in the knowledge that
1360	Spies would inform him this was possible –
	Not grasping that Christ was not out of touch
	And that they had been manipulated
	Into doing what Christ had long wanted.

In Takteh Pol, south of Kandahar, three
1365 Thousand Northern-Alliance fighters cut
The Taliban's supply line to the north
And fought the Taliban for three hours while
Eight Americans filmed how they attacked.
A hundred and sixty Taliban fired
1370 On their conquerors, refused to surrender
Despite persuaders quoting the *Koran*,
Mediating tribal elders and offers
Of cash. Captured, the hundred and sixty
Were made to stand in a long line and six
1375 Northern-Alliance fighters, holding light
Machine-guns, deaf to the Americans'
Pleas for clemency, executed them.
They fell and lay in a long line now filmed
By the eight American observers,
1380 A ghastly end for loyal fanatics.

In Maslakh refugee camp near Herat
Hundreds of thousand Afghans lay on rugs
Or blankets, tentless peasants for whom sky
Is roof, earth floor as they lived in dust-swept
1385 Desert waiting for a bowl of grey gruel
Made of sugar, oil and flour, and tasteless,
Their daily ration. Just as in a heat
Fish laze listless and docile, but when thrown
A handful of pellets, galvanised, rise,
1390 Swarm across each other, all mouths agape,
And gobble and swallow their daily feed,
Frothing the still water with flicking tails,
So these peasants suddenly perked up and

Became active, a blind, instinctive drive
1395 To eat and survive. Four years back rains stopped,
Crops withered, cows and goats died, skin and bones,
And only grass remained, then that too died.
Each night temperatures dropped below zero
And each night forty humans died from cold
1400 Or starved to death, sucking their clothes seeking
Nutrition in a hungry life improved
By the departure of the Taliban
For now they could show faces to the frost.

Late November. The Taliban movement's
1405 Birthplace, Kandahar, was under pressure
From three thousand tribal fighters led by
Hamid Karzai, Unocal's adviser,
Loyalist to the former Afghan king
Who had advanced from the northern region,
1410 And Gul Agha Sherzai, the governor
Of Kandahar before the Taliban.
Bin Laden was tracked down to Maruf in
Kandahar province, where he had training
Camps and underground bunkers out of sight.
1415 A thousand US Marines were flown in
By helicopters to Camp Rhino, as
The Forward Operating Base was known,
In the desert south of Kandahar. This
Was the Coalition's first foothold in
1420 Afghanistan. On the next day fifteen
Armoured vehicles approached and were attacked
By US helicopter gunships while
Air strikes pounded the Taliban inside
The city where *Mullah* Omar held out.
1425 Dismayed that Haji Bashir, Taliban
Commander in Kandahar, had agreed
To join the *mujahideen*, having talked
To Abdul Khalik, Omar felt betrayed.
In the ruins of his bombed residence,
1430 A round missile hole through a brick wall and
Gaudy mural of trees, flowers, blue water,
A scene of heavenly Paradise beside
The garden where he received bin Laden,
The one-eyed leader sought assurances
1435 From Pashtun tribes' elders that he would not
Be harmed by Pathans in Afghan mountains.
Heavy US bombing sapped his morale,
And, tired from constantly moving about

To avoid being a target, he said
1440 He would hand the city to the tribal
Leaders if his group received protection.
The US Government refused any
Amnesty for Omar or Taliban
Leaders. On December the seventh, Omar
1445 And his loyalists slipped from the city
And fled with their weapons to the mountains
Of Uruzgan Province to the north-west,
Riding with his fighters in a convoy
Of motorcycles. Other Taliban
1450 Leaders fled through remote mountain passes
Of Paktia and Paktika provinces
To Pakistan. The same day Spin Boldak,
The border town, was surrendered, marking
The end of the Taliban's control in
1455 Afghanistan. Their rule was fierce but brief,
Like summer rains. Vacated, Kandahar
Had fallen. Corpses – fleeing Taliban
Fighters – lined the route to the airport, sprawled
Bodies and dozens of smashed vehicles by
1460 The roadside. Bin Laden's one-storey home
By poor Liwa was ruined, sky showed through
Holes in the roof, his simple tastes under
Rubble, machine-gun nests by the approach
Abandoned, the nearby Old Eidga mosque
1465 Where the *mullah*s had criminals buried
To their necks and stoned to seventh-century death
Deserted. Tribal forces from the south
Under Gul Agha now seized the city
And US Marines took the airport and
1470 Established a US base. Now the house
Bin Laden was building for al-Qaeda
And himself in a corner of the airport –
An al-Qaeda base where arms were stored, plans
Made, with living quarters for the Arabs –
1475 Was discovered bullet-ridden, having
Served as an al-Qaeda redoubt, cluster-
Bombed by the US outside. So it was,
Incredibly, fifteen thousand Northern-
Alliance troops had managed to defeat
1480 Fifty or sixty thousand Taliban.
America, whose Pentagon had sent
Ninety-nine per cent of all the bombs dropped
And missiles fired, had emerged stronger than
Before, thanks to bin Laden's challenge (for

| 1485 | Which the Syndicate was most grateful) and |
| | Renewed American hegemony. |

Tora Bora is in the White Mountains
Which separate Nangahar province and
Jalalabad from Pakistan. It lies
| 1490 | Above Bait al-Ansar, on the Spin-Ghar |
Mountain's slope, where bin Laden had employed
His family's construction equipment
To fortify secure bunkers. The road
From Jalalabad through desert was held
| 1495 | By Awal Ghul, military commander |
Loyal to Younus Khalis who invited
Bin Laden to Afghanistan. Here in
His personal fiefdom bin Laden now owned
Inside the thirteen-thousand-foot mountain
| 1500 | A cave complex. Here in the Soviet times |
The CIA had helped *mujahideen*
Turn natural caves into advanced bomb-proof
Bunkers which could hold a thousand people
Cut deep inside the mountain to avoid
| 1505 | Detection by thermal-sensing machines, |
On five levels, at one time five caverns,
Linked by flights of steps, lower floors for arms
And ventilation ducts that brought fresh air.
Here one thousand six hundred al-Qaeda
| 1510 | Fighters, five hundred of whom were Chechens |
Who are known to be the fiercest fighters,
And Osama himself, had retreated.
The entrance, through a tunnel wide enough
For a car, was hidden within pine trees
| 1515 | Below the tree line between two ridges. |
Deemed unassailable from the air, it
Was a tunnel-and-room complex stretching
A thousand feet into the mountainside.
Al-Qaeda fighters designed mountain-top
| 1520 | Firing positions from inside caves and |
Behind cliffs, fortified by Soviet scrap
Metal ripped from the hulks of destroyed tanks
And helicopters. Heavy machine-guns,
Rocket launchers and anti-aircraft guns
| 1525 | Were trained on the dirt roads and tracks winding |
Through the base. Boulders were in place to block
Roads if intruders entered. Waterfalls
Concealed cave entrances, preventing smoke
Or chemical agents seeping to caves.

1530	Now al-Qaeda engineers had cut out
	New hiding-places with pneumatic drills
	Run on diesel, where defenders could lurk
	Like scorpions under stones, waiting to sting.
	Here was a vast, wooded, highland redoubt
1535	Which seemed impregnable from land or air.
	But the Taliban had dug three long lines
	Into Maleva Valley, trenches that
	Were spread over one square mile, one trench for
	Three fighters to avoid heavy losses
1540	From bombardment. Here three hundred men crouched,
	Prepared to endure smart and cluster bombs
	And bunker-blasters in a temperature
	Of minus ten Celsius. Now a plane,
	A B-52 bomber, cut a fight
1545	Line through the blue sky and circled their lines
	And dropped bombs. Each crash echoed through the hills
	Surrounding the Maleva Valley. Plumes
	Of grey smoke rose as if the mountains were
	On fire. Predator unmanned drones flew round
1550	Surveying all al-Qaeda positions
	On which shells rained from *mujahideen* troops
	Firing Russian-made T-55 tanks
	On Bamokhail ridge, and to the east from
	Troops of Sohrab Khan, local commander.
1555	Then an American F/A18
	Fighter dropped a new bunker-busting bomb,
	A new version of the laser-guided
	Two-thousand-pound bombs that penetrated
	Deep in concrete underground bunkers, called
1560	Advanced Unitary Penetrators,
	Which had a narrow-diameter case
	Of nickel-cobalt steel, and were accurate
	To within nine feet. The whole mountain shook.
	Some *mujahideen* claimed bin Laden had
1565	Been seen riding a white horse between caves
	In the White Mountains at night. The Arab
	Fighters were surrounded, and escape routes
	To Pakistan were blocked by snow. General
	Franks, commander of the US campaign,
1570	Had ruled that no US commandos should
	Search caves in what was expected to be
	Bloody hand-to-hand combat and battle,
	And had left the capture of bin Laden
	To these *mujahideen* and local men
1575	Including Afghan troops who each evening

Left the battlefield to break Ramadan
Fasts, allowing al-Qaeda to regroup.
And their only escape was if, well-bribed,
They let him out, and if the US planes
1580   Spared the bunkers from their new arsenal
Of deep diggers, rapid-fire cannons that
Can blast through rock with serial explosions,
And AGM86Ds, a new
Version of the Air Force's nuclear-tipped
1585   Cruise missiles, for a future use. Having
Built it, the Americans had the plans
Of Tora Bora and knew what to strike
And what to spare, so it could be reused
Once al-Qaeda had been wiped off the face
1590   Of the White Mountains by the tribal troops.

The earth quaked as American bombers
And Afghan tanks commenced battle against
The foreign legionnaires of bin Laden,
Perhaps two thousand in the cave complex.
1595   Foreign newsmen watched military theatre
But doubted how hard the Afghans would press
To prise the Arabs from their mountain depths
And turn them into an Arab graveyard.
Three US military advisers beamed
1600   Red lights across the cave complex, "painting"
Targets with lasers to assist the aim
Of fighter bombers lasering in bombs.
Hundreds of bombs and shells shook al-Qaeda
As Afghan fighters guided by a few
1605   US and British special forces moved
Between caves and bunkers, wary, searching
For bin Laden, flushing al-Qaeda out.
Al-Qaeda opened up with mortars and
Machine-guns, and the assault lost its drive.
1610   The half-hearted ground attack was repulsed.
Zawahiri, bin Laden's deputy,
Was rumoured to be wounded or be dead.
Helicopter gunships patrolled the sky.
Bin Laden issued an order: "The *Sheikh*
1615   Says, 'Keep your children in the caves and fight
For Allah. Give guns to your wives to fight.'"
Giant mushroom clouds hung over pine forests
As Allied bombs shook the mountain. Tank blasts
Thundered through the villages. In the fog
1620   Of war a hundred and forty Afghan

Villages in homes below the mountain
Redoubt had been accidentally killed
As US air-co-ordinators had
Been too far away to give accurate
1625   Positions and co-ordinates – that's war.
The US brought its AC130
Spectre gunship to the pitched battle. It
Circled Tora Bora, muzzle flashes
From its Howitzer stabbing the night sky,
1630   Firing at fleeing fighters. Now British
Élite SAS troops, in a firefight
Lasting over two hours, flushed from trenches
And bunkers a hundred Taliban and
Al-Qaeda troops – who, without all regard
1635   For their own safety, left their trench and ran
Firing at SAS lines till they fell
Wounded or dead – and captured a mountain
Stronghold with sixty enemy alive.
But bin Laden was not found among them.
1640   A Tunisian said he and al-Qaeda
Sheltered in caves during air strikes, then fired
At Afghan tribesmen dug into forests:
"Osama himself has taken command
Of the fighting." Bin Laden on a white
1645   Prancing stallion, pranced behind the Arab
And Chechen lines. Every thirty minutes
Bombs were dropped by aircraft that left white trails
In the sky, filling the valley with smoke
And clouds of dust. Laser-guided bombs roared
1650   In from B-52s and F-14s
While P3 Orion reconnaissance
Aircraft patrolled the skies above the caves
Seeking bin Laden. Al-Qaeda broadcast
Messages over loudspeakers that they
1655   Did not want to fight fellow Muslims, but
Wanted to fight American soldiers.
Afghan troops intercepted messages
From al-Qaeda fighters, "How is the *Sheikh*?"
And al-Qaeda's replies, "The *Sheikh* is good."
1660   The thunderous attacks sent spotted tigers,
Wild boar and monkeys fleeing the air strikes
But not bin Laden, Osama the lion.

Concerned that if bin Laden were to fight
To the end in Tora Bora, there would
1665   Be no Armageddon in ten cities

In America for ten suitcase bombs,
Ten fiery simultaneous holocausts;
Dressed like the *mujihadeen* and disguised
With a beard, Satan, wearing a round hat,
1670   Nodded to the guards at the cave entrance
To the command post at Tora Bora
Hidden in the range of the White Mountains,
Concealed under rock ledges in the dense
Pine forest. And, mesmerised, hypnotised,
1675   They did not move as he entered the hall
Which looked comfortable and brightly lit
By water- and fuel-powered generators.
As oxygen leaves climbers wide awake
And opens all their doors of consciousness,
1680   So breathing in the pure fresh mountain air
Left Satan light-headedly alert. He
Climbed flights of steps to the highest level,
Ignored the corridor to the right that
Led down steps to the complex of cave stores
1685   For supplies and sleeping quarters, walls and
Floors concrete, ceilings bare black rock; turned left
And then right to the corridor that led
At lower level to the armoury
And kitchen on the right, opposite which
1690   Was bin Laden's HQ, more deep and far
In the mountain than any other room,
Hotel-like furnished suite dug out of rock.
He knocked and entered and was shocked to find
Bin Laden slumped, exhausted, at his desk
1695   In front of shelves, clearly deprived of sleep
By the pounding above these rocky caves.
Bin Laden started. "You," he said, "It's you,"
And stared at him as if mesmerised, his
Power of independent thought removed, as
1700   If hypnotised into complete assent.
Still concealing his true identity,
Acknowledging he was Abu Bakr,
Satan said quietly, "You are debating
If you should make a final stand and die
1705   Here deep in this Tora-Bora mountain.
You must not do this. The Americans
Have superior fire-power, this battle's lost.
But the war isn't. You must now escape
And regroup and lead al-Qaeda back here
1710   Intact to fight when this fire-power's withdrawn.
You are a figurehead. If you die now

There will be no regrouping, the war's lost.
You must leave this battle to win the war.
I'll help you escape to Pakistan. There
1715   I'll get you to a safe haven. I have
A plan, but I won't share this till you are
Out of Afghanistan, in Pakistan.
You'll suck in the Americans once more,
Iraq next time, al-Qaeda in Iraq!
1720   There will be a new battle in this war,
Which you will win. Your victory is ordained
And you will overthrow the House of Saud
And replace King Fahd and own Saudi oil.
That too is ordained, trust me, believe me.
1725   You are the rallying-point for a new
Generation against the infidel
Crusaders who have occupied the lands
Of Islam. All Arabia needs you
Alive to lead the next phase in the war.
1730   You must be deceptive. Ask for a truce
While you arrange to surrender all arms.
Give orders that two hundred men must stay
And resume fighting, and under cover
Of *their* last stand, depart with all the rest.
1735   Plan this now, you are certain of success."
To which bin Laden replied, eyes shining,
"You are right. Now is not the time to fight
Until the end. I will adopt your plan."

Eight days the bombardment shook the mountain,
1740   Five hundred huge bombs that sapped all morale.
A third of all the US explosives
Dropped in Afghanistan wrecked that forest.
What we sow we reap. Bin Laden had sown
The wind on 9/11, now reaped whirlwind.
1745   Bin Laden's voice was heard within a cave
Better defended than all the others,
A bunker in a complex of five caves,
Barking orders on a two-way radio,
By US special forces using high-
1750   Tech radio equipment, very short-range
Radio, urging al-Qaeda to fight on.
And now, when al-Qaeda was weary from
Sleepless days and nights spent in trench and cave,
The final blow: an American plane
1755   Dropped a huge fifteen-thousand-pound "daisy-
Cutter" bomb whose deafening thunderous blast

That shook the ground left little in its path,
A swathe with a six-hundred-yard radius
Of destruction in which everything was
1760 Blackened and broken, utterly laid waste.
Coming, as it did, at the end of eight
Days of bombing equivalent to all
The explosives dropped at Dresden, it broke
Al-Qaeda's spirit. Like rats, fighters crawled
1765 Through shattered cave holes, stunned at what they saw.
Tall trees were burnt and shrivelled, their branches
Reached like arms to the sky, but now reduced
To merest jagged stumps devoid of leaves
On a bare moonscape pocked by mouths of caves.
1770 Bits of uniform hung from branches, bits
Of bodies specked the soil like clumps of flowers,
Heads on the ground, lumps of legs in the trees.
The stench of death stank in the mountain air
Amid shredded clothes, bloodied shoes, unspent
1775 Ammunition, soiled toilet paper, scraps
Of food. As in trance they filed slowly up
The rocks to surrender – a thousand men,
Broken by the awesome power of the bomb
To destroy landscape and man, smash morale,
1780 Many heading, though they were unawares,
For internment in Guantánamo Bay –
But not bin Laden. He'd been located.
The Pentagon said that he was trapped in
A cave by anti-Taliban forces,
1785 All exits were under surveillance. He
Would be smoked out. The cave was bombarded.
There was a rumour he had been wounded
In a shoulder by shrapnel under fire
And had been hidden, given medical
1790 Care and assisted. Now, facing defeat,
The al-Qaeda force agreed to a truce
To give them time to surrender weapons.
Some besiegers thought the truce was a ruse
To allow al-Qaeda leaders to flee.
1795 Now fighting flared again as a rearguard
Of some two hundred Arabs and Chechens
Distracted attention while the main force
Slipped out of unguarded, concealed exits
High up, guarded by steel doors and fighters,
1800 On to mule trails on which supplies were brought,
Which led up to the nearby border, and
Escaped through the White Mountains, a thousand

Al-Qaeda fighters streaming across snow,
Stumbling towards the Pakistan border.
1805   At Wazir near Tora Bora local
People saw bin Laden riding a white
Horse towards the safe Pakistan border,
A rifle slung on his back like a bow,
A white sash round his forehead like a crown –
1810   The dashing leader on a white charger
Helped by local tribesmen he paid with bribes,
The elusive pimpernel bronzed by glare
From snow heading away as the deadline
For al-Qaeda to surrender passed by.
1815

Bombing restarted, heavy bombardment
And ground fighting which assailed the rearguard.
Two thousand five hundred tribal fighters
Marched up two parallel valleys and fired
Machine-guns and rocket-propelled grenades
1820   From both sides of the ridge where al-Qaeda's
Thermopylean rear guards were hiding.
Their only way out was to retreat down
Through dense forest, which B-52 jets
Pounded with incendiary bombs, setting
1825   The trees ablaze so orange flames leapt from
The conifer-clad valley to the sky.
And all who stayed and fought up on the ridge
Were killed, and some bodies were piled in caves.
Dusk saw two hundred al-Qaeda fighters
1830   Dead and wounded, strewn across the Tora-
Bora battlefield. No medical help
Was offered as no negotiations
Were to take place till al-Qaeda were smashed.
On the first day of Eid, the holy feast
1835   That marks the end of Ramadan, all three
Mujihadeen commanders went to prayers
At the mosque, then drove to the front and found
Only a few al-Qaeda left. The rest
Were dead or wounded, or had disappeared.
1840   Now Eastern-Alliance fighters entered
Bin Laden's fortified cave and found there
Just six fighters, one of whom resisted
Arrest and was killed, but there was no sign
Of bin Laden in the labyrinthine
1845   Tunnels and rooms and caves. Air strikes resumed
At groups fleeing across snow-clad passes.
Al-Qaeda had been flushed out of their lair

Within the host state of Afghanistan
But the Afghans and local tribesmen had
1850   Let them escape across the White Mountains
To the safety of Muslim Pakistan.
On December the seventeenth US-
Allied forces declared triumphantly
That the battle of Tora Bora had
1855   Been won. Prematurely, in the White House
Bush announced "America has prevailed" –
As if Afghanistan would hear no more
From the Taliban or from bin Laden
And so there had been final victory.
1860   Bush grinned with self-pleased *hubris*, now convinced
That he had been right and could do no wrong.

Later Bush watched film of the carnage at
Tora Bora, aftermath of slaughter
Where al-Qaeda were pulverised by bombs
1865   And blown to bits in relentless fire-power.
Above the battlefield an Afghan sky
Concealed the outer space beyond and, far
Beyond stars, the edge of the universe
Where God the One permeated space-time,
1870   And within the One all the anguished cries
Of wounded and dying were like brief glints
On a sea, as nothing once seen and gone.
The war had been fought within a silence
Which was not heard on Earth but deafened in
1875   The outer reaches of the universe
Where the One sensed souls pour from its Being
And return from hideous battle scenes
In Existence. From a dark, deep silence
Humans emerged and very soon returned
1880   To do self-improvement and come again,
And all the cruelty on the mountainside
Was mere process, as force imposed a change
That would not otherwise have taken place:
A change for good that blocked Armageddon.
1885

Al-Qaeda's Abu Jaffar, a Saudi,
Spoke a day after his leg was blown off
By a cluster bomb at Tora Bora,
To an Arab reporter driven by
Gunmen, blindfolded, to a village at
1890   The base of Tora Bora, and (as his
Egyptian wife sobbed through the talk, "I've seen

My sweet brothers and sisters killed by fire
From the sky, they wanted to die up in
Tora Bora for Allah's sake") stated:

1895 "Bin Laden travelled twice out of Tora
Bora this Ramadan. He left to meet
The Taliban leader, *Mullah* Omar,
About three weeks ago and stayed with him
Near Kandahar. He left again ten days

1900 Ago and headed for Pakistan where
Pathan tribesmen helped him cross the border.
He contacted us in Tora Bora
To tell us he was sending his own son,
Nineteen-year-old Salah ad-Din, to join

1905 Us there. His son travelled through Paktia
Province with thirty Arab and fifty
Afghan fighters and yesterday told me
To leave and gave me money as I'll need
A second amputation to prevent

1910 The spread of infection, perhaps gangrene,
The price for stepping on a cluster bomb."
He said most of bin Laden's deputy
Zawahiri's family had been killed
By US bombs but that Zawahiri

1915 Had survived and was now with bin Laden.
Mullah Omar was reported to be
In mountain caves near Baghran village north-
West of Kandahar, or in a light grey
Toyota Corolla to escape air strikes,

1920 With one bodyguard. All that journalists
Who had waited to see bin Laden caught
Now saw were eighteen captured al-Qaeda
Bearded Afghans sitting in a courtyard
With their hands tied behind their backs, wearing

1925 Rounded hats and staring impassively.

Now the US consolidated their
Position in the new Afghanistan.
On the twenty-second of December,
Hamid Karzai, ethnic Pashtun who led

1930 One of southern Afghanistan's largest
Tribes and had been a pipeline adviser
To Unocal, was sworn in as chairman
Of a six-month interim Government
By Afghan tribal leaders and ex-exiles.

1935 The main US bases were at Bagram
And Kandahar airports. Ten thousand troops

Hunted for Taliban and al-Qaeda
Fugitives in eastern provinces. Now
The Taliban and al-Qaeda regrouped
1940   In Shah-i-Kot mountains of Paktia
South-east of the small hamlet of Gardez
In January and February two thousand
And two. By March there were a thousand set
To launch guerilla attacks, entrenched in
1945   Caves and bunkers on hillsides at a height
Of above ten thousand feet. They used hit-
And-run tactics, firing at the US
And Afghan forces, retreating to caves
And bunkers to weather return fire and
1950   Heavy US bombing raids. US and
Afghan forces launched an offensive on
Al-Qaeda and Taliban forces in
The Shah-i-Kot mountains, *Operation
Anaconda*. Soon there were five thousand
1955   Guerillas or insurgents. By the end
Of the operation, four hundred had
Been killed. General Franks called it a "success"
But as at Tora Bora reliance
On Pashtun fighters was too high and most
1960   Of the guerillas escaped and headed
To the Waziristan tribal areas
Across the border in safe Pakistan,
Where they regrouped and launched cross-border raids
During the summer of 2002.
1965
An aide showed Bush a report in Egypt's
Al Wafd on December the twenty-sixth
That an official of the Taliban
Had announced that bin Laden had been killed,
Or died of kidney failure in a cave,
1970   At Tora Bora and been buried there
On or around December the thirteenth,
And that by Wahhabi tradition no
Mark was left on his grave. And that same day
The tape found in Jalalabad by troops
1975   That showed bin Laden with *Sheikh* al-Ghamdi
Was released and made it clear bin Laden
Knew of 9/11 in advance and planned
Each detail. After many denials
He had "confessed". Was the man a double,
1980   Weightier, darker, a different nose, and with
Fingers not slender but a pugilist's?

Bin Laden wrote left-handed, yet this man
Wrote a note with his right hand on the tape.
Bin Laden was an engineer and yet
1985   This man spoke of the Twin Towers' "iron structure".
An engineer would know their frame was steel.
This man invoked Allah fewer times than
Bin Laden in previous videotapes.
Had he impersonated bin Laden?
1990   Bush shook his head. Where was the evidence?
It was a ruse to put him off the scent.
Had bin Laden tried to fake his own death
So Coalition leaders would call off
Their pursuit of him and withdraw their troops?
1995   Until the *Al-Wafd* report was confirmed
His troops would stay on in Afghanistan
And hunt bin Laden, who was still alive.

Where had bin Laden gone? In September,
A former Taliban Interior
2000   Minister claimed, he was residing in
China's Xinjiang province, among Muslim
Uighurs, having crossed the Pamir mountains
By foot or on horseback. Intelligence
Sources claimed he was in Kabul, having
2005   Hidden in mountains near Kandahar. In
October he was in the Katawaz
Basin in Paktika province outside
Kabul. In mid-November he had crossed
Into tribal Pakistan or Kashmir.
2010   Was he in the wild North-West Frontier
Province or Balochistan? Or near Zhob,
In an Afghan valley far from smuggling
Routes where beyond checkpoints a good road leads
To clustered cottages and buildings like
2015   Weapons bunkers, a mosque, a parade-ground,
But no shops, stalls or life. Somalia?
Sudan? Cairo? The Philippines?
Indonesia? Bridas' Argentina?
The Himalayan mountains, sheltered by
2020   The *Harkat-ul-Mujahideen*, funded
By the CIA to fight the Russians?
The Yemeni region of Hadhra Maug?
Chechnya where al-Qaeda had mountain
Strongholds? Or in Mecca's holy city
2025   Where he could claim divine sanctuary
And no non-Muslims could enter, and where

Even the Saudi Government might find
It hard to intervene? One thing was sure.
He would be where he was least expected
2030   To be – in a place not mentioned so far.
You would vanish? Go where you could not be,
A butterfly camouflaged on tree bark.

In Hell all the dark creatures had arranged
Themselves in their old places in the gloom,
2035   On seven levels of rock where each belonged,
In varying degrees of distance from
The Light which those in Heaven know and love.
Order had been restored to Hellish life
And Satan stood on his familiar rock,
2040   Preening, and spoke: "Angels, we're back – for good."
A tremendous buzzing greeted these words.
"This is better than the cold mountain caves
We've come from. Here we can be warm and dark
While we continue our self-improvement.
2045   Now that we're back, Angels, I have devised
A new plan to divide vindictive Heaven.
Angels, in Heaven's dictatorship, Christians
And the leaders of all religions are
Bound to support Christ, Mohammed as well.
2050   But I know Mohammed is unhappy
Now that I have provoked a war between
Christians and Muslims. He does not want Christ
To speak for him and to support Bush in
Bombing al-Qaeda and the Taliban.
2055   So I persuaded Khalid to persuade
Bin Laden to attack America,
Which has now happened to our great delight,
And I have intrigued that Heaven supports
Bush's actions back in Afghanistan.
2060   By tying Heaven to Bush I have driven
A wedge between Christ and Mohammed that
We can exploit. Angels, watch Heaven split.
Angels, Heaven's divided into two camps.
Free spirits who fled from dictatorship
2065   And Heaven's establishment, which we question,
Mohammed will soon revolt against Christ.
Heaven is now weak and Hell is very strong."
A tumultuous buzzing, magnified by
The cavern walls above and around them
2070   Greeted news all dark things wanted to hear.
"Angels, I therefore propose to increase

Support for bin Laden and Syndicate
In a push that can defeat Heaven's favourite,
Bush. I will visit bin Laden and Bush,
2075   And Cheney of the Syndicate, disguised,
And persuade them to widen the war from
Afghanistan, where they will know defeat.
Angels, our victory is assured. We'll lure
Bush further into being overstretched
2080   And strengthen bin Laden's ability
To attack US troops. We'll urge Cheney
To throw the weight of the blessed Syndicate
That supports us behind these new events.
Angels, by our brilliant diplomacy
2085   We'll further weaken Heaven and strengthen Hell.
I am a master politician. Christ
Can't match my dazzling intellectual skills."
He preened himself in all directions and
The caves reverberated with buzzing.
2090

BOOK FOUR

BUSH VISITS THE UNDERWORLD

SUMMARY

O John, disciple and evangelist
Who witnessed the main scenes in Jesus' life,
The transfiguration, Gethsemane,
The Last Supper, his trial and Golgotha,
5   Took charge of his mother under the cross,
Then bore his body to the Garden Tomb,
Who first saw the empty shroud and witnessed
The Resurrection in the upper room;
I find you once again inside your cave
10   On Patmos where a great voice rent the rock,
Cracked it above your head in three fissures
And said, "What thou seest write in a book,"
And stand again where you slept on the floor
And received your revelation and then
15   Dictated the Apocalypse to your
Scribe Prochorus, who stood at this book-rest
In the sloping wall, feet by your prone head,
Told of the Tribulation and the last
Battle of Armageddon, Christ's return –
20   Were your prophecies rooted in your time,
Historicist view of the Antichrist,
Or were they rather futurist glimpses
Of the end of days, the ending of time?
I look at the dark cave that was your home,
25   Where you dreamt *Revelation* in a trance
And, standing with a towel draped round my knees
As the Greek Orthodox monk at the mouth
Of your cave sternly ordered to preserve
Your precinct's purity from corrupt flesh,
30   I grasp that in this primitive abode
You could not reconcile your visions with
Ezekiel's and Daniel's prophecies
And that your account – probably, like theirs –
Does not give a definitive timeline
35   And sequence of the momentous events,
But is approximate, a succession
Of images revealed as in a dream.
You may have thought Nero *Redivivus*,
Who would return from Parthia, was the Beast,
40   That the Seleucid King of Syria
Antiochus Epiphanes the Fourth
Who reigned from 175 to 163
BC, allowed abominations in
The Temple, which was destroyed by Titus –
45   Echoes from history at three different times
Like one great voice lobbed into a tunnel

That gives an answer back in three shock waves,
Quivers the blood and tingles up the spine –
But the thrust of your dream was futurist.
50   Each age sees itself reflected in myth,
Reinterprets your myth to suit itself.
Each generation has its Antichrist
And your "book", like a classic, a great play,
Is performed in every generation
55   With new actors in the traditional roles.
So, musing on the speline location
Of your revealed images, forgive me
If I, in my generation, depart
From your text here and there to suit my age
60   Which, having cast Hitler as Antichrist
Till Satan mucked up Christ's Millennium,
Malevolently manipulating
The 9/11 attacks to promote war,
Now sees bin Laden and his Caliphate
65   Reflected in your myth as Antichrist,
And also sees a mirrored Western Beast.
For a new Muslim empire resembles
The Christian empire of America
Sought by the West's Satanic Syndicate,
70   And as, without realising it, Bush trod
In the footprints of the oil-pursuing
Syndicate, quite unfairly but justly –
As the Syndicate's policies became
The President's and were laid at his door,
75   For which he must be held responsible –
My time sees Bush as the West's Antichrist.

O John, you speak of many Antichrists
And you hold that there are two Beasts, one known
As Antichrist and one a False Prophet.
80   In fact there are two complementary pairs
That oppose and mirror each other in
The Christian West and Islam's Caliphate.
According to the Muslim tradition
There are two Western Beasts, a first Beast who
85   Is Satan's primary agent in the West
Without realising it, who's also known
As Antichrist: evangelical Bush
Who, though "born again" like Nicodemus,
His old self drowned in baptismal water
90   From which his new self was born, still retained
Links to Skull and Bones and Bohemian Grove,

Who, like George Washington, a Freemason,
Had used religion as a bland smokescreen
And used the Christian faith to garner votes,
95   To chime with "born again" voters, conceal
His occult tendencies beneath the cross;
And a second Beast, a False Prophet who
Is agent of Antichrist and promotes
His cause, secretly Catholic Blair who claimed
100   Knowledge of God's purposes and intent
But acted at the Bilderberg's bidding
And was a mouthpiece for the Syndicate.
And according to Western tradition
There are two Muslim Beasts, a first Beast who
105   Is Satan's primary agent within
The Muslim Caliphate, though unaware,
Also known as Antichrist, Sunni bin
Laden, and a second Beast, a Muslim
False Prophet who was Antichrist's agent,
110   The heir to Ayatollah Khomeini
And his successor Ali Khamenei,
Shiite Ahmadinejad of Iran
Who supported bin Laden from Tehran
And claimed to be an intermediary
115   Between the Hidden *Imam* and the world,
His messenger who has worked to advance
The Shia Crescent in the Caliphate.
He would come to power in 2005.
The two False Prophets are subservient
120   To their Beasts or Antichrists, and the pairs
Are mirror images of each other.
O John, who channelled the Tribulation,
Inspire my high dream with clear images,
Help me now I describe the twin events
125   That began our seven years' tribulation
In January 2002: the move
Of al-Qaeda into the Middle East
And with it the defeated Antichrist,
To base the Caliphate, Abbasid-like,
130   Within Baghdad and near Jerusalem;
And the betrayal of the Covenant
(The promise of lands made to Abraham,
The Promised Land whose borders were confirmed
First by the Six-Day War, then by UN
135   Resolution 242, '67,
And Resolution 1322
Of seventh October two thousand) by Bush,

Who, urged on by Satan, disguised as one
Of his Middle-Eastern advisory
140 Team, confirmed Israel's borders as Daniel
Foretold ("he shall confirm the covenant"),
Then urged Israel to renounce land for peace,
Then forced Israel to give up land for peace,
Adopting the peace plan of Abdullah,
145 Crown Prince of Saudi Arabia, now King.
Drawn up the January al-Qaeda moved,
It was passed by the Arab League summit
In Beirut in March and became a two-
State solution, creating Palestine
150 Alongside Israel, in a new "Road Map",
Which Israel loathed and Sharon championed,
Which hardliners saw as a betrayal
Of Abraham's Covenant. The Arab
Road Map was stuck on a reluctant Bush,
155 With disguised Satan's conniving cunning,
By the "Rockefellerite" Syndicate,
Who wanted to reconstruct a pipeline
That had brought oil from Mosul through Jordan
To Haifa from 1935 till
160 1948, and secure cheap oil
Flowing to Israel and the US once
Iraq was pacified under a new
Regime, and Palestine in a new state.
And now, quite unawares, Bush found himself
165 At the start of the tribulation years.
O John, now I sing the tribulation
Lighten my understanding and wisdom
As I tell how al-Qaeda spread chaos,
How Bush and bin Laden led new crusades.

170 Tell, Muse, how Iran became a leader
Of world opposition to the US,
And assisted bin Laden's war. Shiite
Iran worshipped the Hidden *Imam*, who,
In 874 when Twelfth *Imam*, went down
175 A well into "occultation", where, like
King Arthur who is sleeping in Welsh hills,
He has been hiding for many centuries
And, Shiites believe, will return to save
The Shiite world from increasing chaos.
180 The more chaotic the Middle East turns
The swifter will be his longed-for return.
Shiites were aghast when Israel was plonked

On Palestinians' land. The pro-West Shah
Sided with the West against Mossadeq,
185   His own Prime Minister, and met Kermit
Roosevelt of the CIA in his White
Palace in 1953 to oust
Him. The CIA controlled Iran till
The Islamic revolution that swept
190   Ayatollah Khomeini to power in
1979. Soon afterwards
Iranian students seized sixty-six
US diplomats and held them hostage
In the US Embassy in Tehran
195   For a year and a quarter. The US
Encouraged Saddam to fight the Iran-
Iraq war which killed a million in all.
Khomeini died in 1989
And Supreme Leader Ali Khamenei
200   And President Rafsanjani began
To export revolution and sponsor
Terrorism. In the dozen years from
The end of the Cold War to 9/11
Ninety per cent of the world's terrorism
205   Can be traced back to Tehran, which became
The world's terrorist capital in place
Of Moscow. After 1988
Iran supported al-Zawahiri
Financially and trained al-Qaeda in
210   The early 1990s. Bin Laden's
Attacks on Aden and New York strengthened
The links between Sunni al-Qaeda and
Shiite Iran. In 1995
He met Imad Mugniyah in Khartoum,
215   The Iranian terrorist who kidnapped
Western victims. In 1996
Bin Laden offered the Intelligence
Ministry of Iran a bilateral
Anti-US partnership, and in that
220   July supported Iran's Terrorist
Internationale aimed at the US,
Hosted by Ali Fallahian, then
The Minister of Intelligence and
Security, and Ahmad Vahidi,
225   The chief of terrorist operations.
All terrorist acts would heighten chaos
And hasten the Hidden *Imam*'s return.
Inspired by Iran, bin Laden declared

War on the US five times in the next
230
Two years, and hailed Pakistan's nuclear bomb
As "the nuclear bomb of Islam". After
The bombings of the US embassies
In Kenya and Tanzania, in spring
1999 bin Laden's Council
235
Of War in Khalden camp, near Kandahar,
Confirmed by the 9/11 Commission,
Summoned Khalid *Sheikh* Mohammed to give
His plan for 9/11 and four targets –
The White House, Pentagon, Capitol and
240
World Trade Center – which despite objections
By *Mullah* Omar was carried through. This
Council must be seen as rooted within
Iran's Terrorist Internationale
And thus as Iran-inspired, and Omar
245
Must be seen as overruled on advice
From Iran, whose bilateral support
For al-Qaeda backed this plan to provoke
The US and suck it in to worsen
The chaos, though quick to condemn the attack.
250
Training began at Mes Aynak camp in
Afghanistan, but the philosophy
Behind 9/11 came from Iran
And its Terrorist Internationale
Which increased chaos and the Shiites' need
255
To be saved by the Hidden *Imam*'s return.

Tell how Iran now harboured Bin Laden.
Bin Laden's voice, harsh, urgent, had been heard
Giving battle orders. He was last seen
By a villager in a small hamlet,
260
Gardez, south of Tora Bora, waving
A convoy of pick-ups packed with armed men
Towards hills. He retreated to Kashmir's
Pakistan-controlled sector in January,
And in June moved south to Balochistan,
265
A nation without a country whose land
Stretches between Afghanistan, Iran
And Pakistan; whence came 9/11's
Planner Khalid Sheikh Mohammed and his
Nephew Ramzi Yousef, the mastermind
270
Of the bombing in 1993
Of the World Trade Center. Then in July
Musharraf announced that he was sending
Commandos into the tribal areas

Of Pakistan to flush out bin Laden.
275 Now desperate, and urged on by Satan,
Seeing Shiite Iran and Sunni al-
Wahhab as being within the *Ummah*
And having shared goals and a common cause,
Most notably a common enemy,
280 And therefore able to work together,
Mindful of Iran-funded Z'wahiri's,
And his, links with Iran and that he'd met
Iranian intelligence officials
In Khartoum in the early 1990s,
285 And Iran's killer, Imad Mugniyah,
Bin Laden recorded an audiotape
And had it delivered via courier
To Ali Khamenei, Iran's Supreme
Leader. According to an Iranian
290 Ex-intelligence officer, he asked
For safe haven and funding in Iran
And in return pledged that al-Qaeda (now
Reduced by eighty per cent following
The bombardment of Tora Bora) would
295 Serve Iran and combat American
Forces in Afghanistan and Iraq,
Where he believed that the Americans
Would intervene. He pledged, "If I die, my
Followers will be told to follow you."
300 The taped appeal worked. Murtaza Rezai,
Director of Khamenei's personal
Intelligence directorate, began
Secret negotiations. The Iranian
Revolutionary Guard and al-Qaeda
305 Agreed to transport bin Laden's four wives
And eldest son, Saad, to Iran. Then on
July the twenty-sixth two thousand and
Two bin Laden crossed the Afghan border
Near Zabol into Iran and travelled
310 North to Mashad. For the next year he lived
In a series of safe houses controlled
By the Iran Revolutionary
Guard between Qazvin and Karaj along
A highway west of Tehran, frequently
315 Moving so as to avoid detection
Or betrayal and always guarded by
The Revolutionary Guard. Zawahiri,
Al-Qaeda's number two, was with him and
Was treated for a wound. Now both men changed

320	Their appearance through plastic surgery,
	Disguises that explain why neither man
	Appears on videotape after Iran,
	But on a dozen audiotapes instead.
	Bin Laden put on weight, and now both men
325	Crossed into Afghanistan at will through
	The Iranian border checkpoint near Zabol
	And then crossed into tribal Pakistan
	Where they were harboured by loyal tribesmen.
	In August the White House publicly warned
330	Iran against harbouring al-Qaeda,
	But bin Laden and Zawahiri were,
	Though often absent in Afghanistan,
	Now based in Iran with their al-Qaeda,
	Safe from US commando hunts and cruise
335	Missile attacks on where they slept, and now
	Able to operate in neighbouring states.

	Tell, Muse, how bin Laden said 9/11
	Was a retaliation for Israel's
	Mistreatment of Palestine and Iraq,
340	And how the Arabs and Bush adopted
	A peace plan to address the attack's cause.
	On October the seventh 2001,
	The day a huge bombing assault was launched
	By the US, with British and French air
345	Support, a video was released in which
	Bin Laden said of 9/11, "These men
	Retaliated on behalf of their
	Poor, oppressed sons, their brothers and sisters
	In Palestine. A million innocent
350	Children have been killed in Iraq although
	They have done nothing wrong. Israeli tanks
	And bulldozers are wreaking havoc in
	Palestine – in Jenin, in Ramallah,
	In Rafah, in Beit'Jala – and other
355	Parts of the domain of Islam." He said
	9/11 was divine retribution
	For American-backed atrocities.
	Bush and Cheney seized on the word "Iraq",
	Which was to be the Caliphate's home "base",
360	And reviewed the peace plans for Palestine.
	Israel had extended its borders in
	The Six-Day War in 1967,
	And were now those promised to Abraham
	In the Covenant God made with Israel.

365	Israel had now become the Promised Land.
	These borders were confirmed by the UN
	In Resolution 242 passed in
	1967. This survived the Yom
	Kippur War peace plan, and the attempted
370	Agreement between Sadat and Begin
	Brokered by Carter. Satan, disguised as
	His Middle-East adviser, had urged this
	Meeting on Carter, seeing that a peace
	Agreement would breach God's Covenant by
375	Partitioning the Promised Land between
	Jews and Arabs. He would rather have urged
	Aggression, but that would not have broken
	God's Covenant. Disguised as an expert
	After the Gulf War, he urged a similar
380	Peace on Bush Senior. Clinton abandoned
	This Resolution in nineteen ninety-
	Three, and worked for peace between Palestine
	And Israel. But in July two thousand
	Clinton, Ehud Barak and Arafat
385	Failed to reach a five-year peace agreement
	At Camp David. For Arafat had vowed
	Jerusalem would be the capital
	Of a Palestinian state. Outraged
	By Camp David, the Palestinians rose
390	In a second, violent *Intifada*,
	"Shaking-off" of Israel from Palestine.
	(The first Palestinian *Intifada*
	Lasted six years from 1987.)
	Israelis believe Arafat walked out
395	Of Camp David to lead the uprising.
	Palestinians say the rising began
	On September the twenty-eighth after
	Ariel Sharon, the Likud leader, went
	(Though not ritually cleansed by water mixed
400	With red heifer's ashes) to Temple Mount,
	The holiest site in Judaism,
	Where al-Aqsa mosque stands, the third holiest
	Site in Islam; that hence it was known as
	The "al-Aqsa *Intifada*". Israel
405	Appealed to the UN, which on the seventh
	Of October two thousand passed a new
	Resolution, 1322, that re-
	Confirmed the 1967 borders
	And thus the Abrahamic Covenant.
410	Clinton had one more try at bringing peace

In his last days of office, and Barak's,
Culminating in the Taba summit
On January the twenty-first two thousand
And one, one day after "new-boy" Bush's
415   Inauguration. The process ended
When Ariel Sharon was elected as
Israel's Prime Minister on February
The sixth and refused to meet Arafat.
Jerusalem was still the sticking-point.
420   He felt Israeli sovereignty over
Temple Mount without peace was better than
Peace without sovereignty in Temple Mount.
Israel countered with Rabbi Elon's plan.
In 2002: Israel would annex
425   West Bank and Gaza; the Palestinians
Would then become citizens of a new
Palestinian state in Jordan – a quite
Preposterous proposal, that Jordan should
Adopt all Palestinians and make sure
430   They kept the peace with neighbouring Jews. Meanwhile
The Crown Prince of Saudi Arabia,
Abdullah, now King, drew up a peace plan
(While Bush, in his State-of-Union address,
Asserted there's an "axis of evil",
435   Of North Korea, Iran and Iraq)
In January two thousand and two,
Which was taken up by the UN in
Security Council Resolution
1397. This was drafted by
440   The US at the Syndicate's prompting
For it wanted Israel and Palestine
Co-existing peacefully side by side
In a coming world government. Its text
Did not mention Resolution thirteen
445   Twenty-two or the Covenant's borders,
And was passed by the Arab League Summit
In Beirut in March. Sensing a two-state
Solution after suicide bombings,
Israel reoccupied Palestinian
450   Areas and placed Arafat under house
Arrest. Sensing a two-state solution
Would address the Arab grievance that led
To 9/11, Bush made a speech on June
The twenty-fourth saying Israel should yield
455   Land in return for peace, a policy
Now known as the Road Map to peace, which Blair,

Bush's supporter, had urged upon him,
Not that Bush needed too much persuading.
Israeli hard-liners were stunned as Bush
460 Had turned his back on 1967
Borders, God's Promised Land, the Covenant,
And he who had confirmed the Covenant
Had now betrayed it in the cause of peace,
And hard-liners preferred borders to peace
465 And saw the betrayal, the Road Map, as
An unwelcome development and blight
At the start of the tribulation years.
Sharon, a military hard-liner who
Had fought in the Suez and Six-Day wars
470 And had been accused of two massacres
At Sabra and Shatila, as PM
Had endorsed the Road Map in May and worked
To withdraw from the Gaza Strip and close
Israeli settlements in Palestine.
475 So Bush addressed 9/11's causes
In deep resentment at Palestine's lot
While blocking the new Arab Caliphate.

Satan found Cheney down in the White-House
Basement bunker. Wearing a suit, dressed as
480 A Unocal oilman, he stood beside
Him, fixed him with his mesmerising eye.
"How did you get in here?" Cheney began,
Then stopped, his mind taken over. As if
Hypnotised, he had to listen. "You know
485 Who I am," Satan said quietly. "The Grove.
You invoke me as the Syndicate's god.
I have tutelage over dollars, oil,
Empire and hegemony, worldly things
Which Christians despise but, rightly, you don't.
490 I have admired your Halliburton work,
Even more how you swung American
Public opinion behind your Afghan
Expedition, paid for by taxpayers.
Now a pipeline can cross Afghanistan
495 And Caspian oil can reach Pakistan;
And Tora Bora can now house missiles
In a defensive shield against China.
But you have only dispersed al-Qaeda
Which is regrouping in the Middle East
500 And may return and attack the pipeline.
To make the pipeline safe, you need to hunt

Al-Qaeda down in its new territory –
Iraq. Mark my words, you'll need a campaign
To dislodge al-Qaeda from disruptive
505 Iraq's challenge to the New World Order.
I tell you this because I want to see
A world government based under my rule,
Capitalist and worshipping profit,
Not social justice at the State's expense –
510 The world government you are bringing in.
Make plans to invade Iraq for its oil."
To which Cheney replied, "You have spoken
As I have been thinking. You have echoed
My deepest thoughts. I shall do as you say."

515 Bush had been saying things about Iraq
For at least two years now, for it irked him
That Saddam had tried to kill his father –
And five of his family, including him –
In Kuwait back in 1993.
520 In spring two thousand Stephen Hadley, who
Would be Bush's adviser, briefed a group
Of Republicans that Bush's "number-
One foreign-policy agenda" would
Be to remove Saddam Hussein from power
525 And spend little time trying to resolve
The Israeli-Palestinian crisis.
The briefed policy-makers were all shocked.
Bush had asked Blair to support regime change
In Iraq and remove Saddam Hussein
530 At a private dinner in the White House
Nine days after the 9/11 attacks,
On Thursday September the twentieth.
Sir Christopher Meyer, then the British
Ambassador to Washington was there,
535 And reported that Blair said Bush should not
Be distracted from the initial goal
Which was to deal with the Taliban and
Al-Qaeda in Afghanistan. Bush said,
"I agree with you, Tony. We must deal
540 With this first." He stressed, "But when we have dealt
With Afghanistan, we must come back to
Iraq." He did not mean sanctions, but war
As Saddam would not be removed from power
Or surrender his wmds
545 Without a battle, as Blair always felt.
Blair saw Britain as the fifty-first state

And received his leader's intended plan
As a command that could not be questioned.
Now Cheney urged Bush to invade Iraq
550 And said there was no need for a UN
Resolution as Saddam was in breach
Of past resolutions, which would provide
International legitimacy.
On November the twenty-first Bush said
555 To Rumsfeld, "Let's get started on this." He
Wanted proof of Iraqi involvement
That would hatch a plan to invade Iraq.
But then he wavered. He hesitated,
And began to backtrack in his own mind.
560 He was not sure the blame for 9/11
Could credibly be heaped upon Iraq.

O Marlowe, who wrote of Dr Faustus'
Intellectual curiosity
Which in the Renaissance's heady days
565 Peered beyond death into the after-life,
Conjured Mephistophilis in pursuit
Of power, honour and omnipotence
And in your study, scholar among books,
Made links to spirits far beyond the grave
570 In a reckless deal that bartered your soul,
Who reached and overreached to the beyond
And grasped that life extends far beyond death,
I found you in Deptford and Scadbury
And took part in Westminster Abbey when
575 A window was unveiled bearing your dates,
1593 with a question mark
Suggesting you survived the stabbing and
Wrote Shakespeare's sonnets on the Continent.
I have championed your rodomontade.
580 O Marlowe, help me now I come to tell
About the place where all Earth's spirits go,
Christians and Muslims, victims and bombers.
Help me as I evoke the Underworld.
And o ghosts of Otley Hall who lived in
585 The old Banqueting Room that was in use
In Marlowe's and in Bacon's time, where I
Have slept at night, often alone, and felt
A sudden temperature drop in the old
Wattle-and-daub room with pitted wood sills
590 And diamond-lead windows from Marlowe's day,
Felt my spine tingle and my hairs stand up

On my arms, felt watched, and after I'd switched
Off the light in pitch-dark saw floating lights,
Some red, some white, moving about the room
595   At eye-height while I pulled my bedcovers
Up over my head, telling myself you
Weren't there although I knew you were, knowing
The curtains were closed and there was deep dark
In the rose garden outside and no light
600   Could pierce my room, and went to sleep with ghosts,
A dozen orbs, circling above my head.
O ghosts of Otley Hall, come to my aid,
Tell me what you know of the other side.
Share knowledge with your humble poet who
605   Never harmed you, allowed you right to roam.
O Swift, master of satire who measured
Man in terms of tiny folk and then giants
In Lilliput and Brobdingnag, who first
Used scale as a means of presenting truth,
610   Teach me to measure man by Heaven and Hell,
Show me how such strange lands can raise moral
Questions about how we live our lives now.
O Homer, o Virgil, o Dante, I
Invoked each of you in an earlier work.
615   May my invocations, written to last
Thousands of years, still be in force and have
Effect, thirteen years on now I again
Have to describe the Underworld you knew.
O Virgil, you were Dante's guide. I stood
620   In your empty sandstone tomb near Naples.
Please send me a guide now. Let him reveal
Himself to me. Who will it be? Will it
Be you again, with your pagan belief?
Or will it be the Catholic Dante?

625   O Tennyson, I stand in Farringford
In your cramped old study where you wrote *Maud*,
'The Charge of the Light Brigade', and look down
At the hollow behind the wood you saw
From your paint-worn window, and now descend
630   To your twilit new study where you wrote
Out 'Crossing the Bar' just here and, knowing
That you've been seen sitting, smoking your pipe,
I sit at the desk in the window, sit
In your place, where you used to sit. I feel
635   A tingle up my spine, my hair prickling
At the back of my neck as if you're here,

But when I turn in gloom I see no one.
I close my eyes, feel prickling round my scalp,
With clammy forehead, hair on my arms up,
640   I *know* you're here, watching me write these words
Over my right shoulder, your eyes severe,
Quizzically as if forming a judgement,
Hair straggly, balding and with a long beard,
And that you know I have already walked
645   Past the pool to the roses, and on up
To the latched picket gate in the dark wood
Where Maud was let in – you flood me with power –
And seen the bridge and crossed it as you crossed
Over the public highway that you sank
650   Beneath it, and that like you I've escaped
To the summer-house through hay where you wrote
'Enoch Arden' in a fortnight. And now
My flesh is tingling, I can hardly think
So much energy's pouring into me
655   As I sit where you wrote of Arthur's death.
I know that you have seen me trace your steps
To the ante-room where you ate pudding
And drank a bottle of port each evening
As you read your works aloud to your wife.
660   The light switches do not work, there's no light
Save from the windows, I can hardly see
To write these words in your overwhelming
Presence. I say aloud, "Alfred, I know
You're here, please help me as I write of war.
665   Pour inspiration in my slumbering ear
As poison was poured in Hamlet's father's;
Help me as I turn to your nether world,
Like Faustus conjure spirits of the dead
To tell me about life beyond the grave,
670   Tell me your journey to the Underworld.
Help me." I ask, tapping out my metre,
You to follow me to your old bedroom
Which is lit, where I am spending five nights,
Where I now sit in the window and think
675   How you loved Keats who visited Shanklin
Twice and left behind verses you admired,
And stayed in steep Bonchurch to be near them
And first came here in 1853
And rented this place for two pounds a week
680   And then bought it with the proceeds from *Maud* –
Again I am flooded with power, you have
Rejoined me – and I climb into the high

Four-poster bed with four thin silk curtains,
The varnished floorboards bare as in your time,
685 Your fireplace as it was, lie on my side
And as I sleep, into my slumbering ear,
You pour a message I grasp when I wake:
"Be musical in your verse, as I was,
Keep going as I did in the Idylls.
690 Bush, Arthur – you will find out as you write
All courts are mixtures of noble ideals
And corrupt interests and standards of truth.
Consider the use you make of the Grail.
It stands for the Beatific Vision
695 And is not a thing, an exhumed chalice.
Shut yourself away and write as I did,
As you have done. I will guide you, I will
Be your guide. Persist and you'll overcome.
And while you write of dreadful, cruel things,
700 Always remember that you are making
A thing of beauty in musical verse."
Another surge sweeps through me as I write,
Leaving me feeling invigorated.

The entrance to Hell is quite hard to find,
705 Like finding a cleft in a rocky cliff.
When I was seventeen I walked all round
Lake Avernus, seeking the hidden cave
Where Aeneas descended with the Sibyl.
Its lost entrance is nowhere to be found.
710 Some claim Aeneas entered the Underworld
In Baian rock, a cavern by the sea
Though Virgil's *antrum* was beside a lake,
And from the entrance walked down a tunnel
Past lamps in niches on alternate sides
715 To a clear stream that might have been the Styx.
And some ask if the Sibyl walked this far,
To the sea-lapped shore of ancient Baiae,
And if this was the entrance to Hades.
Bush stood in Bohemian Grove, a campground
720 Of two thousand seven hundred acres
In Monte Rio, California
Where the all-male Bohemian Club meets
Among the thousand-year-old redwood trees.
Every Republican President since
725 1923 has been a member.
A statue of an owl forty-five-feet
High stands at the head of a lake, Moloch

(Who is generally shown as a human
With the head of a bull and not an owl),
730   A Canaanite god to whom Israelites
Offered child sacrifices in the reigns
Of Ahaz and Manasseh, apostates –
But in fact, as the great-horned owl has long
Symbolised Satan, Satan-as-Moloch;
735   For whom a Cremation of Care ritual,
A ceremony that draws on ancient
Canaanite, Luciferian, Babylon
Mystery religion, is held with pagan
Pageantry and some drunken revelry
740   During summer-solstice celebrations
When the effigy of a small baby
Is burnt on a funeral pyre and offered
To Moloch, Luciferian Owl god,
As in Babylonian times. The site
745   Was dear to Satan for the Syndicate
Worshipped him as the Owl god, before whom
All must bow as to Satan, and Moloch,
One of his *personae*, was denounced in
Leviticus for wanting child offerings.
750   To some, Bush Senior, a Bohemian-
Club member, invaded Iraq mainly
To take Babylon, where Moloch was strong.
Bush, in Bohemian Grove by the Owl god,
Lost near a dark wood of tall redwood trees,
755   Was standing looking in the murky lake
When suddenly his head whirled, he felt faint
And, snatched, felt he was whirled down a vortex
And came to in the mouth of a cavern.
The rough walls spun round him as, giddy, he
760   Staggered and managed to keep his balance.
At first he thought he was in a cave near
Sacramento: the Black Chasm Caverns.
And then it seemed like a Virginian cave,
The Grand Cavern, formerly Weyer's Cave,
765   Which he knew in Shenandoah Valley.
But it was none of these. He did not know
If he was under the earth or elsewhere.
Just as a hiker enters Wookey Hole
Where man has lived for fifty thousand years
770   And descends down a narrow passageway
To a cave with an underground river,
The Axe, which Coleridge called Alph, and sees
A curtain stalactite, and is startled;

So Bush was startled by this strange cavern.
775 Before him, dressed as a radiant Angel,
Himself before he fell, his former guise,
But with the head shown on the Turin Shroud
Which was historical Christ's winding-sheet
(Whose carbon-dating Satan tampered with
780 So a "darned" bit was dated, not the cloth,
To "prove" a medieval forgery),
Satan, disguised, now spoke to wondering Bush.
"I am Christ," he said. "You recognise me."
Bewildered, Bush did not know what to say.
785 He recalled Christ's visit to the White House
And his support for bombing training camps
And assumed he was visiting again.
A towering six-foot-two like the Shroud Christ
With long hair by each cheek and mournful look,
790 The radiant dark Angel said, "George, I want
To show you something. First we must descend
Into the Underworld." He did not say
That Bush would be visiting Hell. "I will
Be your passport as well as safe conduct.
795 You will be safe with me. I should warn you,
What you are about to see is not how
Spirits perceive it. Their reality
Is quite different from yours." In saying this
He in fact spoke truly. With blind assent
800 Bush followed his guide whom he thought was Christ.
Christ saw, aghast, but did not intervene
For he knew Satan was, though unaware,
Doing God's will and this was meant to be.
Sad that Bush had escaped his tutelage,
805 Like a loving husband who watches his
Wife go astray but knows he can't control
Her self-willed choice as it would make things worse,
He did nothing, leaving Bush in Satan's
Hands, entrusting him to the care of God.
810 Just as Aeneas, having left Queen Dido
At Carthage and returned to Drepanum
In Sicily and crossed to Italy,
And eventually landed at Cumae
In Campania's Euboean colony,
815 Visited the Temple of Apollo,
Then entered the deep-recessed cave within
The cliff below, encountered the Sibyl
And was escorted to Lake Avernus
By her and, having plucked the Golden Bough

820   To take as tribute to Persephone,
                Entered another cave, a small cavern
                On the side of the lake, the one I sought
                Without success, and, doubtful, descended
                To the Underworld's gloom and – near the Grove
825   Of Persephone where Odysseus saw
                Achilles, Ajax and Elpenor, near
                The rock Odysseus reached where Tiresias
                Addressed him – encountered Palinurus,
                His unburied helmsman, and found the boat,
830   Was ferried by the filthy ferryman
                Charon across the rivers Acheron
                And Styx which flowed into the Stygian marsh,
                And passed three-headed Cerberus and crossed
                The Asphodel Fields, skirting Tartarus,
835   And walked past the Palace of Hades and
                Persephone (later known as Pluto
                And Proserpine) to the Elysian Fields
                Where he greeted his father Anchises,
                So Bush followed Satan down into Hell.

840   Tell, Muse, how the after-life operates,
                What system links the living and the dead
                And what happens to all departed souls.
                Give us an overview of Heaven and Hell.
                The soul is immaterial, immortal,
845   The essence that's distilled from Earthly life,
                From moral, emotional, intellectual
                Choices and memories that form our core.
                The soul is like a pip that precedes birth
                And contains DNA-like instructions
850   That grow us to the apple of our lives.
                The soul's like a pip in an apple core.
                When flesh decays like a rotting apple
                The soul is shed like a discarded pip.
                There are more than six billion souls alive
855   And the average life expectancy is
                Around seventy, "three score years and ten".
                Natural disasters, famines, accidents,
                Disease, AIDS, drug overdoses, liquor
                Abuse, smoking, murders, terrorism
860   And war have lowered life expectancy
                And are responsible for early deaths.
                But assuming seventy's the average
                Six billion divided by seventy –
                More than eighty-five million – die each year.

865	Divide this by 365, daily some
	Two hundred and thirty-two thousand die.
	Of these only ten per cent are Christians.
	Ninety per cent of those who die each day
	Are non-Christians and so two hundred and
870	Nine thousand may go to Hell every day
	While twenty-three thousand Christians ascend
	To Heaven each day. That is the Christian view.
	But God is not so unfair. All who've known
	The Light go to Heaven no matter what
875	Their church, mosque or temple which like a school
	Has taught them to know it, passes them on.
	Heaven operates in a cross-cultural way,
	And is Universalist for all souls
	Regardless of citizenship or creed
880	Go to Heaven if their souls – and spirits –
	Have sufficiently advanced in life's test.
	The spirit is our enduring essence
	That precedes and succeeds all birth and death
	And strings together many lives which sit
885	Like beads on a rosary. One spirit
	Has many pip-like souls from previous lives.
	Our spirit endures and has been behind
	Twenty, thirty, forty lives that we've lived,
	Each of which it left with its Earthly soul –
890	The essence of a life – attached to it,
	Which it absorbs as the soul slowly fades,
	Its vibrancy stilled like a rosary bead.
	Within each spirit as in DNA
	Is memory of sixty-thousand years
895	And more – back to the time spirit began.
	We have far memories from our past lives
	Which are recorded as in DNA
	In the pips that are strung on our spirit
	And these are viewed in regressions and dreams.
900	New spirits are forever being born
	And some are old and have lived many lives,
	While some are in their infancy, and raw.
	All souls with Earthly stamps remain attached
	To spirits which have endured for aeons.
905	Hell and Heaven accommodate all these.
	Both places would soon be cluttered up if
	There was no recycling. Souls go forward
	To learn the lessons of their Earthly life,
	During which time they can contact loved ones

910	Through a medium, or simply be aware
	Of the lives they have left behind within
	Their family, workplace and favourite haunts,
	Watching life on Earth as if through a one-
	Way mirror in reality TV,
915	Able to see without their being seen.
	They go to where ancestors are revered.
	As our leading-edge archaeologists
	Have just discovered and rightly deduced,
	Ancients built a wood henge at Durrington
920	For living workers and then a stone henge
	As a monument to dead ancestors –
	Wood grows and decays and suggests living,
	Stone lasts forever like a dead spirit –
	And boated down the river and processed
925	Up an avenue with urns of their dead
	And interred burnt bones among the bluestones
	Of their ancestors. Their spirits gathered
	Round them and observed as they now do at
	Churchyards, cemeteries, crematoria,
930	Woodland interments, and funeral pyres.
	Wherever there's a funeral spirits flock.
	After due time, when the term is judged right,
	Souls come back down to Earth, relearn lessons,
	Avoid their past mistakes and get things right.
935	We have been here before so many times.
	We have had many lives we've forgotten
	While here on Earth where spirits are dormant
	But remember as spirits in Heaven
	Or Hell, which is a purifying place
940	Whence spirits leave for Heaven when they lighten.
	We have lived in ancient Egypt and Greece,
	In Rome and many civilisations.
	We have lived under all world religions –
	Christian, Muslim, Buddhist, Hindu, et al.
945	Between each life spirits reflect and learn,
	Contemplating what is distilled in soul,
	Those who have not known the pure Light, the flawed
	And imperfect in Hell, the more perfect
	In Heaven whence loving Angels return
950	To work for the benefit of others
	To share their advanced knowledge and wisdom.
	All cultures have such spirits: Christian nuns,
	Bodhisattvas who give up their own chance
	Of Enlightenment to serve their fellow
955	Humans. Heaven and Hell are in Being,

Separated from our Existence by
A mere veil that cordons off dimensions.
New souls and Angels leave their Being abode
With heavy heart for new trials here on Earth
960 And to minister in self-sacrifice,
Return to Existence, put on new flesh
And error to be tempted by Satan.
When we are ready we come down again.
Eternal Recurrence of souls, spirits
965 Who manifest from Being to the Earth,
Creep round the veil which drops when they are born,
Wipes out their memories and brings Lethean
Forgetfulness. That is the law of life:
Eternal Being, ever becoming
970 As we all become Earthly flesh once more
And put off old wisdom to start afresh
And be confronted with situations
We previously failed in but now get right,
Profiting from the civilisation
975 We're born into, nurturing renewed souls –
An endless cycle of departing souls
Worn out, and after rest in calm spirit
Returning with new souls to new bodies
And new challenges in our spirit's growth.
980 As pips grow into apples, souls put on
Bodies that leave behind new pips on death,
Eternal Being, endless Becoming
In which lives stamp impressions on spirits
Which they absorb through reflection and grow –
985 Eternal distillation of essence,
Eternal DNA-like ripening cores,
Eternal Renewal and endless Growth,
Eternal Self-improvement of all souls.

Those who say nothing survives death believe
990 We only have a physical body,
But a spiritual body in its sheath
Is tethered to it by a silver cord
And floats up to the ceiling in near-death
Situations – when a patient "dies" on
995 An operating table and must be
Resuscitated – and sees its body
Lying unconscious among the concerned
Doctors whose words it hears, and then returns –
But if the silver cord is loosed it floats
1000 Off to the after-life like a balloon.

There are more things in Heaven and Earth than are
Dreamt of in Horatio's philosophy.
Those who believe nothing survives death see
Only a physical body and self-
1005 Enjoyment and its social will. But those
Whose minds are open to spirit have grasped
That the ghost life continues after death.

O Dante, who thought you were of Roman
Descent, and were born in this tall dark house
1010 Near Florence's Duomo, and used to stand
By this stone between 12 and 13 and
Went into the Baptistery and looked
As a child at the cupola and saw
The early thirteenth-century mosaics
1015 Including the image of Lucifer
As horned, bearded monster munching a soul
Whose legs and buttocks hang out of his mouth,
With snakes protruding from each ear, in all
Three gruesome faces hideously munching
1020 Souls, holding souls in his hands, his next course,
And a soul being digested within
His stomach and set to be excreted,
His feet clamping two more souls for his meal.
You drew on this figure in the climax
1025 Of the *Inferno*, where your Lucifer
Has three faces as in the Baptistery
And sinners crunched within three hungry mouths.
O Dante, my Satan's different from yours,
A revolutionary inspired more by
1030 The young Gaddafi than a horned bull, Baal.
I see you exiled to Verona and
Establish a connection with its lord,
Can Grande, whom you first saw by this stone
Staircase in his ruling brother's palace
1035 And, having based your Sempiternal Rose,
The Celestial Rose of your Paradise,
On the white-mauve twelfth-century rose-window
Of San Zeno's Basilica in his
Verona, to whom in your *Epistle*
1040 You offered your *Paradiso* (which you,
Now living at the court in Ravenna,
Sent to him in batches of cantos) as
A gift. And, living in Ravenna, you
Put your manuscript of the last thirteen
1045 Cantos in a wall-cupboard, a recess,

Which, when you'd died from malaria while
Returning from an embassy, were found
Covered with mildew by your son to whom
You gave precise instructions in a dream.
1050 You, also, wrote of the international
Politics of your day, your own White Guelfs,
The dastardly Black Guelfs who banished you,
The Ghibellines who harboured you such as
Can Grande, who you hoped to influence
1055 Into admiring Justinian, whom you
Encountered in the second Heaven. He
Stood in mosaic on a wall within
Ravenna's San Vitale, and had sought
To bring the eastern and western empires
1060 Together and rebuild Augustus's
Empire under imperial rule. You hoped
Can Grande would understand the batches
Of cantos you sent him and that he would
Restore the Roman empire in the west
1065 And with it your fortunes as a White Guelf,
By seizing Florence, expelling Black Guelfs;
Unite Europe under a secular –
And not a Holy – Roman Emperor.
O Dante, I who lived through World War Two,
1070 The birth of the Atomic Age, Cold War,
The Berlin Wall, the British Empire's fall,
America's moon landing, the collapse
Of Communism, the bureaucratic
European Union and now the War
1075 On Terror, I too knew imperial rule,
The British Empire's enlightened vision
And world mission which cannot be revived
And I have lived through a time when my hopes
For English and European influence
1080 Free from a hidden and ruthless Syndicate
And its world population reduction
Have been dashed and my country has dwindled.
I too dreamt of a united Europe,
And I had no lord of Verona, Can
1085 Grande della Scala, or Guido da
Polenta, lord of Ravenna, to send
My verse to or be a patron – only
A remote mentor who nodded me on
As I worked in isolation. I share
1090 Your sense of exile from your own city,
For I too have been too truthful about

Those who have power – governments, royals,
The Syndicate – and have been ostracised
Because my eyes witnessed baleful evil,
1095   For saying things that were best left unsaid.

Shaped like an upside-down bell, larger at
Top than at bottom, Hell has seven rings,
Descending levels to which souls are drawn
By the shadow in their Earthly essence.
1100   Each level imperceptibly descends
To the next by an inclining tunnelled
Path that passes a central tunnel off
Which are gloomy chambers. It is as if
The ascending path that winds around and up
1105   The Tor at Glastonbury were inverted,
Turned upside down and inside out so that
The path is on the inside of the rim
Of the downward bell. Once the path is left,
Each level seems self-contained, off an arched
1110   Tunnel with loathsome caverns on each side.
Just as in North Norway motorists drive
At speed over impacted snow and ice
And leave the white Magerøya island
Through a tunnel where an electronic
1115   Gate, that keeps cold out and warm in, rises
And connects them with West Norway's mainland –
A tunnel hewn through rock whose uneven
Sides form a curved arch round the dim roof lights
And four thousand four hundred metres on
1120   Exits by the North Gate on to white roads,
And just as further on towards Alta
They enter a new tunnel nearly seven
Thousand metres long, two hundred and twelve
Metres below the sea with gates each end;
1125   So Hell contains tunnels at each level
That seem artificially hewn in rock,
Central tunnels with caves to left and right.

"I am showing you Hell," Satan-as-Christ,
Said. "In each cave billions of spirits dwell,
1130   Drawn there by the magnetic pull on their
Dark and dense souls, less airy and thin than
Those drawn upwards to Heaven. As we have lived
Shapes our soul, a distilled essence or core
Of our choices and memories that, like
1135   An apple's ovary with five carpels,

Contains around ten programmed seeds or pips,
Each imprinted with coded instructions.
Hell is a kind of hospital, priory
Where the addicted can get clear, dry out
1140   From dependence on body's appetites,
Where damaged souls can be slowly repaired.
Some inmates have bigger problems to solve
Than others, and their convalescence takes
Longer just as some hospital patients
1145   Are long-stay rather than short-stay. Just as
A prison is full of prisoners doing
Different terms or stretches, or sentences,
So here all inmates have different periods
Of remedial work to do on themselves.
1150   Some have a week or two, some a few years,
Some are here for decades or for centuries.
Most spirits, no matter how well they've done
On Earth, have to pass through here for a while.
Those who've had bad thoughts do a shorter term
1155   Than those who've done bad deeds and hurt others.
Life is a place of self-realisation,
And those who fall short have to relearn here.
And there is no escape for suicides.
Like students who walk out of an exam,
1160   They have to relearn and repeat their test.
God calls this a place of Self-Improvement."

In all this Satan spoke truly. He left
Out some aspects to present his own work
In a good light, for his preening nature
1165   Wanted to be thought well of, even though
He was speaking as Christ. Satan leads souls
Astray who, darkened, are drawn down to Hell
To dwell under his regime. He believed
He was spoiling things for God and foul Christ.
1170   He did not grasp he was doing God's work,
That being led astray was an aspect
Of the journey of souls towards the Light
As they make free choices during their growth.
And so he did not know, and thus add, that
1175   He, Satan, who encourages desire,
Is like an overseer of soul patients,
Doing God's work without realising it.
He did not fully grasp that souls could leave
Hell by their own spiritual efforts
1180   For he had a place in God's scheme of things

Which required him to operate Hell and
Not to be too clear how spirits escaped.
In all Hells, one glimpse of Light is enough
To remove a spirit to the safety
1185   Of the first Heaven in another place.

Bush was led down through a craggy cave that
Served as an entrance or vestibule, past
The bored and futile who found no purpose
And missed the Light from laziness and sit,
1190   Heads bowed, lolling in will-less, passive gaze,
In lowest form of consciousness, all blank
Yet ever weary of the passing "time".
Here they live in torment, ever yawning,
Until they master their hopeless mindset
1195   And learn to bring it under their control,
To be purposive and self-sufficient.
This Satan explained, omitting the Light.

Bush followed Satan down the rocky path,
Stepping between boulders, to the first Hell
1200   Where he left uneven rock for a long
Tunnel and peered in the nearest chamber
Where he heard loud sighs and lamentations.
Here Satan gave him an overview, not
Deigning to refer to the Light from which
1205   He was excluded by being required
By God to embody and choose Darkness.
In gloom, below horseshoe and pipistrelle
Bats hanging from the roof, dwell the virtuous
Who never found the Light in any faith,
1210   Whose pride restrained them from knowing the Light,
Humanists whose rational-social ideas
Swaggered through rooms and sneered at all who thought
Reality, and the One, can be known,
Called all metaphysicals "demented"
1215   And despised mystics as "self-indulgent";
Heretics whose souls remained in shadow,
Atheists and sceptics whose inner dark
Misled their students and charges, who taught
A wrong path through the universe's fire;
1220   Holy followers of Dionysius
The Areopagite who asserted
That God is Darkness, failed to teach the Light;
Literary doyens, actors, playwrights,
Scholars who knew footnotes but missed the Light,

1225	Philosophers of logic and language
	Who missed the universe but were blameless
	Except for their own myopic blindness;
	Scientists who reduced the universe
	To mathematical symbols and signs –
1230	Lucretius, Russell, Wittgenstein and Crick;
	Worthy placemen who ran society,
	Lawyers, doctors, teachers and all police
	Who went to work and returned home blameless
	But missed the Light while filling consciousness
1235	With workplace procedures and trivia;
	Attenders of churches who sang the hymns
	And prayed without awareness of meaning
	And did not open shadowy souls to Light,
	Remained enclosed in their own ego's shell.
1240	Here were a few so-called celebrities,
	Some of whom had excelled in one honed skill,
	Some merely famous for being famous,
	Stars whose photos were in the newspapers
	But whose souls were murky, opaque shadows,
1245	Attention-seekers whose vanity saw
	Their egos in all mirrors and windows,
	Who had not delved within, opened their souls
	To the Light which cleans out all sense of 'I'
	And makes humble whereas pride sets apart.
1250	Here all souls repeat their Earthly mistakes,
	Hiss their scepticism and heresy
	And, swollen with overweening conceit,
	Preen aloofly with pride and vanity
	Of intellect or looks or merely self,
1255	And knowing it is wrong, feel a sadness,
	Live in torment of perpetual pride
	That, puffed up, simpers but is unfulfilled,
	And learn to master their great vanity
	And restrain it with new self-discipline.
1260	Bush gazed within the gloomy vestibule
	Of the nearest chamber off the tunnel
	And started when he saw his old teacher,
	A shadow with a domed and balding head,
	Said, "Sir, are you here?" "Hey," he said, a wraith,
1265	"What brings you here before your time is due?
	Is it chance or Providence?" Bush replied:
	"Who knows. I found myself in a dark wood.
	I was by a lake in sunshine and lost
	My way, and have been brought here by my guide."

1270	"Son," he said, "follow your star and you'll find
	Your way back. If I'd been allowed to live
	A little longer I could have advised
	You in the White House, and encouraged you
	In your important work as president
1275	Which Heaven smiles on, for you're doing its will.
	The first advice I would give you is not
	To miss the Light which is behind all things.
	I missed the Light and so I am down here.
	All here passed on ignorant of the Light.
1280	Our ignorance has been held against us
	As if it were our fault we never knew,
	Our responsibility. It does not
	Seem fair, somehow. Who taught it up on Earth?
	The Church? There wasn't much about the Light
1285	In church, just hymns, prayers and sermons. But though
	No one's teaching it, you are in the wrong
	If you don't find it. But then, all life's tough.
	And the decline in Western culture means
	That knowledge of inner truth has been lost.
1290	Hell is the place where all ignorant souls
	Are heated and reshaped as glowing iron
	Is hammered into a horseshoe upon
	A blacksmith's anvil and, transmuted, cools
	Into its new form, at one with the Light.
1295	It's not literally like that but that's how
	It feels as the transformation you should
	Have undergone on Earth is at last made.
	It's a bit like being at the dentist
	And being drilled without an injection –
1300	A little pain and then it's soon over.
	And you're the better for it once it's done.
	I read all the books but still missed the Light.
	I should have taught you to look for it for
	Its rays unlock the soul and spur its growth.
1305	Down here we're in discomfort, we're spirits
	Who never found the Light. We're bodiless
	But we feel scorched at times while we improve.
	You're fortunate that Heaven is on your side.
	Before I go I'll foretell your future.
1310	You will achieve great things and influence
	Opinion, turn world thinking round, but you
	Will be despised and reviled by your peers
	Who, blind and envious, will ignore your deeds.
	Your triumphs which Heaven will cheer they will
1315	Ignore, and you will have to find the strength

To know that what you've done was worth doing
Even though it's unappreciated
By less able men who've an inflated
Sense of their own superiority.

1320 You will have to be both fearless and strong
And you must single-mindedly pursue
Your chosen course to the end and not think
Of the ungrateful toads who rubbish you.
Good luck, may you fulfil your ambitions."

1325 And with that he faded as Bush reached out
To detain him, and Satan took his arm.

Satan led Bush on down the rocky path
To the second Hell, where the gloom deepens,
And allowed Bush to peer in the first cave.

1330 Once more, like a tour guide in the dungeons
Of an ancient and feared castle, Satan-
As-Christ gave Bush an overview of all
Inmates congregating on this level,
Again studiously avoiding mention

1335 Of the Light that is the context of Hell.
Here dwell the lustful and the lecherous,
Egos that were attached to appetite
And sensual desires and never detached
Soul from body so soul opened to Light,

1340 Philanderers, serial adulterers,
Rapists, nymphomaniacs and priapic
Satyriasists with permanent itch,
People who boasted thousands of partners,
Cruisers, doggers, clubbers looking for kicks

1345 Who lived in body consciousness and like
The hungry starved for flesh and used others
As objects, Don Juans and whores who saw
Birds and toyboys instead of real people,
Cleopatra, Alexander the Sixth

1350 (The Borgia Pope with many mistresses,
A byword for the debased papacy),
Fallen women and notorious spenders,
Living to gratify self, not to grow,
Those who lived for love and for nothing else,

1355 Who failed to transcend body for the Light;
Billions of false lovers and mistresses
Whose secret liaisons were for their self
To gratify body, not each other,
Who did not love with grand passion but scratched

1360 Their need with another's help, self-centred,

Who broke up marriages and hurt others,
And kept their souls within their ego's shells,
Kernels on which the Light could never shine;
Kings, Queens and Ministers, nobility,
1365 Professional people who lived for one thing,
Workers who spent their wages in brothels,
All who lacked self-restraint and discipline
That controls and channels all appetites
And showed inordinate sexual desire,
1370 Voluptuous charm that, demure, submits
Yet deviously manipulates all –
Lucrezia Borgia and Lola Montez.
Here they live in torment of perpetual
Itching, desire and appetite which they
1375 Can never fulfil, until they master
Their tiresome cravings and throbbings which kept
Them from knowing the Light and which they do
Eventually get under control
And learn to restrain with self-discipline.

1380 Bush followed Satan down the rocky path
To the third Hell, where in darkening gloom
He peered deep into the first cavern. Here
Again Satan gave him an overview
Of all the inmates on the third level,
1385 Abstaining from all reference to the Light,
Unable to bring himself to utter
A word so associated with God. Here
Dwell the gluttonous who could not control
Their stomach's appetite and lived for food
1390 And alcohol, binge-drinking until drunk
Amid loud sounds of merriment that gave
Them the illusion of togetherness,
Of not being alone, while imbibing;
Who were the slaves of the stomach's desires
1395 And did not fast and discipline body,
Rise above appetite to know the Light;
Party-goers, smokers with strong cravings,
Drug-takers of all kinds with appetites
Satisfied by swallowing Ecstasy,
1400 Smoking cannabis, sniffing substances,
Snorting cocaine, injecting heroin,
Who for the sake of bodily cravings
Polluted their soul's higher consciousness,
Lived in a fug or haze and missed the Light,
1405 Gargantuan feasters and knockers-back –

Lucullus, Henry the Eighth, de Quincey.
Here they live in a torment of famine,
Famished for food and thirsting for a drink,
Forever parched and craving for a fix
And never able to abate or quench
Their hunger, thirst and craving as they learn
To master tiresome bodily cravings
Which they slowly bring under their control
And learn to restrain with self-discipline.

Satan beckoned and Bush continued down
To the fourth Hell, where in a darker murk
He looked inside the first dingy cavern
Of the central arched rocky tunnel. Here,
Satan as Christ explained, pointing at wraiths,
Dwell the avaricious and prodigal,
The hoarders and spendthrifts, and the greedy
Whose selfish appetite was for money,
Who looted it as did the past members
Of the Syndicate out of self-interest,
Not to benefit others. And though some
Set up allegedly philanthropic
Foundations that professed to help mankind,
They were in fact tax dodges to preserve
The majority of funds they amassed.
Here came the Rothschilds and Rockefellers,
Drawn to the foul murk by the murk within
Their souls which never opened to the Light
As locked safes hoard gold bars in deep darkness;
Here they contemplate oilfields and pipelines
And relive short-changing their fellow men.
Here were corrupt politicians who spoke
For their constituents but were far more
Interested in lining their own pockets.
Here were MPs who fiddled expenses,
Took taxpayers' money to clean their moats,
Buy duck houses and prune acres of trees,
Flip homes, pay phantom mortgages, employ
Relatives to do constituency work,
Accumulate property portfolios.
Here were businessmen whose lives were spent on
Increasing profits and computing tax
Multinational CEOs, directors
Of companies, partners of legal firms
And bankers who received big bonuses
For gambling deposits made by clients;

1410
1415
1420
1425
1430
1435
1440
1445
1450

Property developers, stockbrokers,
Accountants, tax inspectors and salesmen
Of cars and computers, solicitors
Who held their clients' money interest-free
1455 And looked for more fees and compensation,
And boasted of trophy acquisitions,
Said "Hello, I'm the owner" to impress;
All who were too busy earning for self
So their social egos could live amply
1460 To open their ego-encrusted souls
To the Light which burns out greedy desires
And appetites so grasping's transcended
By higher consciousness and growth of soul.
Here are the envious and covetous
1465 Who want others' riches for their own selves,
Politicians who want equality
And say it's fair to strip the rich of wealth
So the poor do not feel disadvantaged,
Whose socialism is an envious creed.
1470 Here they live in a torment of wanting,
Yearning for property and bank accounts,
For stocks and shares, gold and assets, craving
To hoard or spend, and, unable to own,
Cannot gratify their hunger for more,
1475 Their appetite for possessions and wealth,
Their cravings to borrow, to buy or lease,
To acquire new material assets,
Addicted to acquisitive mindsets
Which they slowly bring under their control
1480 And learn to restrain with self-discipline.

Satan indicated they must descend
And Bush followed him down to the fifth Hell
Which was in even deeper darkness, where
He peeped into the first dark cavern. Here,
1485 Satan said, speaking as if he addressed
A touring party that had gathered round,
Dwell the wrathful who've succumbed to anger,
Who have not controlled their temper, and in
Disputes have been heated, intemperate.
1490 They are addicted to venting their wrath,
A selfish appetite of the ego,
And in lower consciousness missed the Light.
Here dwell querulous neighbours, arguers,
Complainers, moaners, all who have quarrelled
1495 With officials about the State system,

Abused traffic wardens, berated banks,
Lambasted doctors for bad news on health;
Demonstrators, drunk yobs who shout in streets,
Rowdy attenders where crowds are amassed,
1500 Revolutionaries whose anger boils over;
Great men defined by one angry outburst
Such as Henry the Second, who was rid
Of a turbulent priest through one tantrum;
All who're easily offended and did
1505 Not open their ego-encrusted soul
To the Light which burns all anger away
And brings serenity, peace with the world.
Here they live in a torment of seething,
Yearning to dispute, argufy, abuse,
1510 Shout at each other, squabble and complain
But cannot gratify the resentment
That boils tumultuously within them,
Their appetite to vent stoked-up anger,
And, addicted to abusive mindsets,
1515 Attempt to bring them under their control,
Learn to restrain them with self-discipline.

Satan took Bush by his elbow and led
Him down the rocky path to an opening,
The tunnel of the sixth Hell, where the dark
1520 Was now like night and, peering, Bush could just
Make out shapes moving in the first cavern.
Watchful as he hooked up with what he'd planned,
Satan, wary, gave him an overview,
Careful not to mention the hated Light.
1525 Here dwell the violent who have asserted
Themselves at the expense of their neighbours,
Who cared only for themselves and attacked
Their neighbours, who secured what they wanted,
Violent burglars, robbers and murderers,
1530 Sadists, highwaymen, serial killers,
Those who swindled their neighbours of savings,
Fraudulent bankers whose scams did violence
To their neighbours and rooked them, treating them
As objects to be fleeced, not real persons;
1535 Swashbuckling warriors quick to take offence
Such as Andrew Jackson, armed criminals
Who ruled the East End such as the Kray Twins
(And Tom Hammond, still brandishing shotgun).
Embezzlers of public funds, petty thieves
1540 Who did great injury to people's lives,

Violent abusers of women and men,
Those who were addicted to the ego's
Self-assertive violence against others,
Assaulted and injured their fellow men,
1545 Envying and coveting goods of theirs,
Gave in to an appetite for harming
And in lower consciousness missed the Light.
Among these are dictators and tyrants
Who ordered thousands of executions –
1550 Hitler, Stalin, Mao, Pol Pot, mass-killers
Who had the blood of millions on their hands.
Here also dwell those who were violent
Towards themselves, self-harmers, suicides,
Who, hating themselves, ended their own lives
1555 In lower consciousness, missing the Light;
And all who have been violent towards God
In wars and crusades, self-proclaimed *jihad*
Which had not God's approval, and all who
Have done violence to God's creation by
1560 Violating art and Nature, God's works,
Polluting the Earth, causing climate change,
Leaving their environment much worse off.
And here dwell terrorists, who were convinced
They were on a divine mission, who used
1565 Bombs to further causes they thought were right
But which lacked Almighty God's approval;
All suicide bombers for murderous ends.
Here they live in a torment of violence,
Raging to lash out, wound or maim or kill,
1570 To thrust a knife or squeeze a gun's trigger
Or use their fists on shadows in the gloom,
Knuckledust, gouge eyes, glass cheeks and break bones,
Their appetite to yield to their smouldering,
And, addicted to violent mindsets,
1575 Attempt to bring them under their control,
Learn to restrain them with self-discipline.
This was where Satan wanted to linger
Without making Bush suspect his motives.

Satan beckoned Bush to the second cave
1580 And in the arched tunnel a shape approached
In the darkness. Bush made out a lean wraith,
An upright shadow with familiar look
Who approached and stood sadly nearby him.
"This is the man I wanted you to meet,"
1585 Satan said. "He is among the violent,

But to his people he is a hero,
An Egyptian Islamist terrorist,
Ringleader of the 9/11 attacks."
Startled, Bush asked, "He's Mohammed Atta?"

1590   "Yes," Satan said in his most deceptive
Christ-like, unctuous voice: "Speak to him, for
He knows who you are and bears you no ill.
He's honoured to meet you. He often saw
You on TV." Bush nodded and said, "You

1595   Flew your plane into the Twin Towers?" "I did,"
Atta said in fluent English that had
An Arab lilt, "to bring the financial
Symbol of the US down as we planned
In Afghanistan, before I journeyed

1600   To the US to train as a pilot.
We were conducting *jihad* on behalf
Of the new Caliphate of Osama
Which will result in one Islamic world.
I made a martyrdom video with

1605   Ziad Jarrah near Kandahar back in
January 2000. We were supposed
To take nuclear lap-tops on the planes.
Osama bin Laden personally
Said he would have them delivered to me.

1610   They never arrived. And I did not know
That Mossad gave your CIA a list
Of our nineteen names on the twenty-third
Of August, over two weeks before we
Set out for martyrdom. I thought we would

1615   Crash our planes into the Twin Towers and strike
An unexpected blow. I thought we might
Be opposed by fighters. In fact you were
Ready for us, Cheney gave us a clear
Run in and set off prepared explosives

1620   As our planes struck. Without them our impact
Would have been slight. You maximised our deed,
By demolishing the Towers you gave us
Immortal fame. I did not feel a thing,
The end was swift. But I was shocked that I

1625   Lived on as a phantom, saw my passport
Placed on top of the charred shell of the plane.
It seems we were doing what you wanted,
We flew into a trap, and I am shocked
At this. And I was promised Paradise:

1630   Seventy-two virgins and a cool river.
That has not happened. I am here in Hell

Which as a hero I do not deserve."
"Ask him about Prague," Satan said. "He has
Something interesting to tell you." Bush frowned
1635 And said, "Did you go to Prague in April
2001, and meet an Iraqi?"
"It's said I didn't," Atta said. "I did.
I flew from the US under a false
Name. The CIA and the FBI
1640 Were unaware of my flying visit.
On April the eighth the Interior
Minister said, Stanislav Gross. Also,
Hynek Kmonicek, the deputy Czech
Foreign Minister. There I met Ahmed
1645 Khalil Ibrahim Samir al-Ani."
"An Iraqi intelligence agent,"
Bush said. "I was briefed about him." "That's right,"
Said Atta. "And he took care to deny
Our meeting and Iraqi involvement
1650 In the planning of 9/11 attacks.
He supplied advice on the US air
Defence shield. We pretended we wanted
To destroy the headquarters of Radio
Free Europe and stop its hostile broadcasts
1655 To Iraq." Bush sagged, for hawks such as Paul
Wolfowitz had argued the disputed
Prague meeting proved Iraqi involvement
In 9/11, and gave the US cause
To attack Iraq. He knew al-Ani
1660 Was expelled by the Czechs two weeks after
This meeting. Al-Ani had returned home
And now worked in the Foreign Ministry
In Baghdad. "Officially I was not
In Prague in April, only in June. I
1665 Brought something with me from Osama for
Al-Ani." "Ask him what it was," Satan
Urged. Bush did not need to speak. Atta said,
"I gave him a nuclear-suitcase bomb
To give to Saddam, sent from Osama."
1670 He lied as Satan had instructed him
With promise of preferment from sixth Hell.
He thought he would be promoting *jihad*.
He wanted to implicate Saddam in
9/11 and open a second
1675 Front that would suck US troops to Iraq
Where more *jihad* would be waged by Muslims.
Bush bristled as Atta and Satan hoped.

He gasped, "You supplied Saddam with a bomb,
A nuclear bomb?" "Yes," said Atta wryly.
1680 "I wanted to bring it to the US.
Instead I had to take it to Saddam.
Osama would send me more. He did not.
Here I reflect on what I did. I'm glad
That I did it, I don't feel terrible
1685 At having lived in your US and trained
To be a pilot and at the same time
At waging *jihad* for the Caliphate.
That's war, to work under cover and strike.
I see the consequences of my deeds
1690 And I see my dear father who phoned me
Two days before my crash. He believes I
Was a quiet, shy boy who was devoted
To studying architecture, but he
Does not know al-Shehhi and I would drink,
1695 I vodka and orange, he rum and cokes,
Five drinks each when we played the Golden Tee
'Ninety-seven arcade game at Shuckum's
Oyster Pub and Seafood Grill, a sports bar
In Hollywood, Florida, where we hid
1700 Our true identity as *jihad*ists
Under a Westernised front we both loathed."
Satan, now masquerading as concerned
Christ, said, "Saddam had wmds."
"It's true?" Bush asked. "Yes," said Atta. "Iraq
1705 And al-Qaeda have co-operated
Since 1995 when Brigadier
Salim al-Ahmed of the Iraqi
Intelligence Service, in September-
October, stayed on Osama's Khartoum
1710 Farm and, in July 1996,
With the famed Director of Iraqi
Intelligence Mani-abd-al-Rashid
Al-Tikriti, who wanted Salim, his
Premier explosives maker, to remain
1715 With Osama as long as was required.
Osama and Saddam had differences,
But both were in a continuing war
Against America and wished to kill
Americans. After I crashed my plane
1720 Into my Tower, Saddam replayed my crash
On his State-run TV to the song 'Down
With America' – I myself saw it –
And said, 'The American cowboys are

Now reaping the fruit of their crimes against
1725   Humanity.' I knew he was involved.
Osama told me, 'Iraq will supply
Expertise.' I carried out 9/11
With help from both Osama and Saddam."
Now Satan smirked, his deception complete.
1730   He nodded approvingly to Atta,
Indicating Atta had said enough,
And in his most unctuous, Christ-like voice
Said, "George, I wanted you to hear it from
Atta's own mouth. You must invade Iraq
1735   To pay Saddam back and take al-Qaeda
On where you can defeat it and prevent
Their *jihad* from spreading the Caliphate.
Their aim's an Islamic New World Order.
You guard the West and must protect it now
1740   Before Iraq follows up 9/11
With a murderous attack on the US
With wmds from Osama."
Bush accepted what he had heard and had
No doubt that Atta's ghost had told the truth.
1745   He had been specific with names Bush knew,
And all he'd said confirmed his own briefing.
Christ from afar was troubled, but he knew
That to attack Iraq was in God's plan
To block the Caliphate, obstruct the spread
1750   Of wmds that would advance
And precipitate the Armageddon
He had worked so hard to prevent, and that
A new war in Iraq was meant to be.
Recognising that, inadvertently,
1755   Satan was doing God's work while thinking
He was wrecking it and spoiling God's world,
With heavy heart he did not intervene
And kept his distance to let it all be.

Now Satan, subtly avoiding ending
1760   The tour with what he'd wanted Bush to see,
Moved on. He beckoned and Bush followed him
And descended down the rocky path, and
Came to the tunnel of the seventh Hell
Where in night dark Bush groped to the first cave.
1765   Pleased at having prompted Bush to invade
Iraq and bring chaos to the region
As Iran wanted so the Hidden *Imam*
Would come again, confusion he, Satan,

	Would turn to disorder, on which he thrived,
1770	Satan expansively explained the site
	Without being able to bring himself to
	Mention the Lie, which was too near the truth.
	Here dwell the spiritually slothful,
	Those closest to the Lie, all deceivers,
1775	Fraudsters who perverted reality,
	Panders and seducers who twisted truth,
	Flatterers who deceived to get their way,
	Sorcerers who claimed to have magic powers,
	Grafters and barrators who caused discord,
1780	Councillors on planning committees who
	Told whoppers to get applicants refused,
	Hypocrites whose deeds did not match their words,
	Thieves who stole and concealed what they had done,
	False counsellors who gave evil advice,
1785	Sowers of scandal, discord and dissent,
	Counterfeiters and impersonators,
	All traitors who betrayed country and friends,
	Deceivers who authorised genocide
	And hid their command behind a false smile,
1790	Those closest to the Lie who did not yield
	To appetites but perverted the truth,
	Who in the ego's twisting of the facts
	In their lower consciousness missed the Light.
	Here they live in a torment of lying,
1795	Of craving to be mendacious and spin
	And, addicted to a lying mindset,
	Attempt to bring it under their control,
	Learn to restrain it with self-discipline.
	Just as a woodpecker drills a tree trunk
1800	With its sharp beak for grubs hidden in bark's
	Gnarled crevices, primed to probe surfaces,
	So these deceivers drilled their souls for truths.
	Satan, speaking as if Christ, spoke of what
	Those in Hell perceive in their consciousness
1805	And now he had achieved his objective
	Of a meeting between Bush and Atta,
	Confident he could admit where they were
	Without Bush being alarmed, and confident
	That knowing where they were would give credence
1810	In Bush's mind to what Atta had said,
	For the first time he let slip the word "Hell"
	Which he had covered up with "Underworld":
	"How you perceive Hell is not how they do.

To outside observers Hell is in gloom
1815   And appears caverned as if natural caves.
To participants it seems quite different,
Far more modern, like the life they have left.
Their spirits perceive through their memories,
Through subjective, not objective vision.
1820   They see a virtual reality.
Or is this all a construct in *your* mind?
Are you the one who sees a virtual
Reality?" He jested, showing Bush
A different angle on what he perceived
1825   But with light-heartedness, not seriousness,
So Bush would know it was a point of view
Not to be taken seriously. "They
Interact with a simulated world.
Just as chips store data in noughts and ones,
1830   Spirits store software memories which seem
Real but are retrieved and repetitive
And these caves here seem luxurious halls.
Some see themselves in houses and meadows,
Like seeing what's on screen, not in your room.
1835   Or perhaps this *is* a meadow, and you
Are seeing it as caves because you've been
Culturally conditioned to associate
Hell with caves because of Dante? Perhaps
All this is open air and *you're* the one
1840   Who's seeing in virtual reality?"
Satan-as-Christ now suggested this view
Should be taken seriously, for he
Was promoting the standing and image
Of Hell as a place of self-improvement,
1845   And casting doubt on what mortals could see
With their own eyes in this benighted place.
"They are attracted by their own dense forms
Into groups or classes of their level,
So all their neighbours are of comparable
1850   Development, and are self-improving
From a similar base. There are degrees
Of darkness in the spirit-bodies here,
And they are drawn to similarity
And do not find that they have neighbours who
1855   Are wildly different from themselves. And so
Ordinary folk are not with murderers.
All spirit-bodies are shades of black-white.
There is a spectrum with a thousand shades
From extreme black to extreme white, and in

1860	Between there are many gradations, shades
	Of grey, that determine where each spirit-
	Body is drawn at the end of its life.
	It's really organised here like a school,
	And Satan's a bit like a headmaster
1865	Who makes sure all the pupils are in their
	Right classes but does not personally teach.
	If people on Earth realised it's like this
	After they die, there would be much more self-
	Improvement on Earth to make things easier
1870	For themselves when they are drawn to this school."
	Satan spoke truly for souls are organs
	Of Earthly perception, and do not see
	The inner qualities of other souls
	And their cave-like rough-hewn environment
1875	As they work through their memories and burn
	Out their imperfections, de-crust their souls,
	Cure themselves from attachment to loved ones
	Who they can watch over with far vision,
	Earthly perception, telepathically;
1880	Tune in to a scene on Earth as viewers
	Ogle freaks on reality TV,
	And communicate with them through mediums
	As they recuperate and get ready
	To be born again into a new life.
1885	Satan was also spinning his own role,
	Dignifying it into a school head's.
	Then Satan, speaking as if Christ, said more:
	"The Underworld is a corrective place,
	A hospital for putting right the soul,
1890	Only each spirit sits before its screen,
	Intent on its own life, oblivious
	Of other spirits for much of the 'time'.
	Great care goes into their supervision,
	The system's impressive. Your internet's
1895	Taken from here, I leaked it out on Earth.
	This is what men should follow and worship
	As this is where the work's done after death."
	He spoke truly until he took credit.
	Though speaking as Christ he could not resist
1900	Boasting and typically dissembling.
	He did not mention the lightness of soul
	That draws grown spirits to another place.
	As a force of disorder and chaos
	Who received all whose dark souls were heavy,
1905	All dense spirits that needed to improve

And oversaw spirits' work on their souls
He did God's will like a hired manager –
But resented that he was under Christ
And did his best to undermine God's Earth
1910 As his disordered role required of him
And plotted to replace both Christ and God,
Hijack their positions and rule the Earth.
He did not devise virtual afterlife.
The system had been created by God
1915 To recycle all spirits and all souls
And, like a council, reuse the Earth's waste.
Rebirth can only happen if spirits
Purge and purify their encrusted souls.
Once cleansed, de-crusted spirits must return
1920 To the Light they once knew and, purified,
Like patients in a convalescent ward,
Go on to their next abode in first Heaven
Whence, stabilised, knowing what they must do,
They choose their new set of Earthly parents,
1925 Wait for conception, enter the foetus
And leave remembrance for self-forgetting
In a nine-month gestation in which soul
Grows like a seed, an apple pip in core;
And proceed through nurture to a new birth.
1930 So Dante's vision is reconciled with
The world of spirits mediums channel,
The Hell and Heaven that Christ oversees
And Eastern reincarnation, as souls
Journey to Paradise through twenty lives
1935 And reflect on their good deeds in between
And on their steps to open to the Light,
To rest in which is all spirits' true goal.

Bush took in all that "Christ" explained and asked,
"Can we go down to the next level?" "No,"
1940 Said Satan, speaking as Christ, and mindful
To carry his pretence through to the end
He made a comment about Satan he
Would not normally make, striking a note
That was negative when his instinct cried
1945 Out for flattery and compelled himself
To mention the Lie, which he detested
Almost as much as the revolting Light.
Grimacing as he mouthed the loathsome word
He said casually and nonchalantly,
1950 Feeling sick, "That's where Satan lives, the Lie

With his closest associates all round.
That is off limits. Now we must return."
And with a sudden whoosh Bush found himself
Transported in an instant from Being
1955 Into Existence and Bohemian Grove.
He was staring into the lake beneath
The Owl god as if he had never left
But in his mind he had now made a choice.
He would send US troops into Iraq.

1960 Now Bush told Blair he had made up his mind.
Blair, Governor of the fifty-first state, heard
And told his Cabinet, "No decisions
Have been taken." But an understanding
Existed between the two men, who met
1965 In March 2002. All that summer
Blair and his advisers pressed Bush to seek
UN support over Iraq, and on
July the twenty-third Blair summoned his
Close aides to a secret council of war,
1970 Which was revealed in a discreet minute.
Bush and Cheney held a summit with Blair
At Camp David on September the ninth
To discuss an invasion. Cheney still
Opposed taking the case against Saddam
1975 To the UN. Blair said he might lose power –
Be toppled at his Party Conference
Later that month (though the Labour Party's
Constitution made this impossible) –
If Bush did not take his advice. Bush then
1980 Promised the UN, not the US-led
Coalition, would rebuild Iraq. By
Mid-September Blair asked his Chancellor,
Gordon Brown, to make twenty thousand troops
Available in the Gulf. Now the French
1985 Said Resolution fourteen forty-one
Would give sufficient UN cover, but
Blair wanted a second resolution
As the Foreign Office said without it
War would be illegal, a view shared by
1990 Lord Goldsmith, the young Attorney-General,
Who warned that "the desire for regime change
Is not a legal base for military
Action." Blair argued that "regime change and
Wmds are linked" as "the regime
1995 Is producing the wmds".

The Attorney-General reconsidered
His advice on the war's legality
And the Government refused to say when
He was first asked for his opinion on
2000   The legality of war in Iraq.
Bush met Blair in the Oval Office on
January the thirty-first 2003
And said he was determined to invade
Iraq without a new resolution
2005   Even if arms inspectors failed to find
Incriminating wmds.
He said the US would provoke Saddam.
U2 reconnaissance aircraft painted
In UN colours would fly in the skies
2010   Of Iraq with fighter cover, and if
Saddam fired at the planes he would be in
Breach of UN resolutions. Blair said
He was solidly with the president.
A confidential memo was written
2015   By Blair's foreign-policy adviser
David Manning, who wrote: "The start date for
A military campaign was now pencilled
In for March the tenth." He wrote, "This was when
The bombing would begin." On February
2020   The fifth Secretary of State Powell appeared
Before the UN and failed to obtain
A new resolution against Iraq.
Bush said he did not need it to invade
And announced on March the seventeenth that
2025   US, British and Allied forces would
Begin to bomb Baghdad. And there were plans
To use Iraq's oil when Saddam was dead.

Bush now felt a strange peace before the storm.
He sat in the White House and turned his mind
2030   Back to his Crawford ranch and then upward
To the Infinite Spirit of the One
Which, pervading the universe, shining
On phenomena like a brilliant sun,
Presided over checks and balances
2035   As hunter caught hunted – sparrowhawk dove;
Fox rabbit; heron carp; lion antelope.
One army would hunt and devour its prey
And liberate a state from tyranny.
To the silence deep in the universe,
2040   The pregnant nothingness of empty space,

The clash of armies was no more of note
Than an owl's swooping on a shrew at dusk.
A moment's pain and a complex creature
Had passed from Existence into Being.
2045 The coming conflict in Iraq evoked
One of a trillion conflicting events
Whose opposites were reconciled within
The harmonious pattern of the silence.
A sneeze, a smile – both were ultimately
2050 One to the silence-within-universe.

Bush did not go after bin Laden in
Balochistan, where he was thought to be,
In the Northern Areas, well guarded by
Tribal warlords near the Afghan border.
2055 He diverted to Saddam to locate
The wmds Saddam concealed,
Telling himself that he would now finish
The job left undone by his own father
Who'd stopped the Gulf War before Baghdad's fall.
2060 It was announced – Bush thought it was likely
That Saddam was framing his family
And his father vehemently denied
All wrongdoing – that Saddam had offered
To pay two billion dollars out to Bush
2065 Senior from the fund he'd syphoned abroad,
Some forty billion dollars then and now
Far more. He wanted to eradicate
All trace of payments, which might be a trap
So Saddam could tarnish his dad with lies.
2070 He had not forgotten that Saddam had
Tried to blow up his father and himself
In Kuwait shortly after the Gulf War.
Saddam was a threat to the Bushes in
More than one way and now, eager to please
2075 His dad and to protect the Bushes' clan
He wanted Saddam out of power and dead
More than he wanted bin Laden, who could
Expose the US role in 9/11
And should therefore be killed rather than caught.
2080 Bush thought it was time to take Saddam out.
It was important Saddam should be seen
To die even if, like a suicide
Bomber, a double stood in at the end.

Christ saw that Bush's mind was now made up.

2085	He also knew that Satan did God's will,
	That it was necessary for Saddam
	To be overthrown before he renewed
	His Millennial Kingdom, and so he did
	Nothing, but let events take their own course
2090	Without intervention on his own part.
	Instead he made his plans for his Kingdom.
	Satisfied, Satan sat in his dark lair,
	His command centre, dictator's bunker,
	Below the seventh Hell in darkest night,
2095	Now hanging like a bat on prickly thorns,
	Surrounded by Arch-Demons and his friends,
	His disciples Simon Magus, Adam
	Weishaupt, Aleister Crowley, Rasputin,
	Near the great pit where waste matter decays,
2100	Decomposes, broken into new forms
	And's recycled back into Existence.
	He was the Lie and he had deceived Bush
	By taking on the appearance of Christ.
	Extending the war would bring more chaos,
2105	*Jihad* and perhaps defeat for Christ's West.
	He had achieved his ends by lies – Atta's
	And his own tweaks of Bush's perception.
	He had lured the US into Iraq.

BOOK FIVE

MORE WAR IN IRAQ

SUMMARY

O Churchill, you who were my MP in
The war, whose constituency Hitler
Attacked with V-1s and V-2s, so I
Lay awake at night listening for the whine
5   Of doodlebugs, the silence and the crash
That obliterated houses like mine –
Hitler whose bombers blew out our windows;
You who I heard speak at the Loughton war
Memorial on your way to Potsdam
10   When you stood on the first step with your wife,
And who, entering the High School, in nineteen
Fifty-one stopped and signed my autograph
Album and beamed at me under your hat;
You who devised the new state of Iraq
15   Out of the Mesopotamia that
Was granted to the British as a League-
Of-Nations, Class-A mandate when at Sèvres
The Ottoman Empire was divided
To the great dismay of T.E. Lawrence
20   And, as Colonial Secretary at
The Cairo Conference of nineteen twenty-
One which you presided over, you drew
A new kingdom from the ex-Ottoman lands
And combined under one ruler Sunnis,
25   Shias and Kurds – and forty years later
I, your constituent, went to Baghdad
To continue the implementation
Of your vision, which was not folly but
Worked forty-eight years ago as in my
30   Classes at the University I
Welded all three groups together with jests,
Classroom plays and my personality,
And our group respect for Omar Khayyam
In Fitzgerald's verses, where freedom reigned
35   As I spoke out despite dictatorship,
The strong rule of Abdul Kareem Kassem,
Benevolent Brigadier-General, our
Honest and Faithful Leader, whom all feared;
O Churchill, come to my aid now I tell
40   Of a new Anglo-American war
In Iraq that again sent tanks rolling –
As when you sent tanks in during the war –
Through the desert to capture *my* Baghdad.

O Kassem, dictator of Iraq when
45   I taught in Baghdad, driven to work at dawn

Through palm trees filled with shafts of golden light
And returning in a passing *baz* or
Group taxi I hailed, estate car with room
For three Arabs each side at the back, knees
50   Up under chins under their *dishdashers*,
A sheep or goat between us as we drove
Honking down the loud road to Bab Sharge
Where I got out and walked through stinking streets,
Sewage in a central runnel as in
55   The medieval time, to the arcades
Of Rashid Street, beneath bulging Turkish
Balconies for crinolines, and got on
A single-decker 30 bus whose floor-
Plates moved so I could see the road speeding
60   Below my feet as the red bus sped. You
Ruled on the edge of civilisation,
The desert and barbarism were near.
It felt like being on the *limes* in
Roman times, this was a frontier. And yet
65   I came and went in safety, no one jarred
Except the begging women in black veils,
Abbayas, who held out cupped hands for *fils*,
Imploring with their eyes, plucking my sleeve
With gnarled hands, pleading through their blackened teeth.
70   O Kassem, you who stood beside me in
The sultry Turkish-Embassy garden
In battledress, bare head, at the salute
And fixed your eyes on mine through the anthem,
You I saw sometimes waving to a crowd
75   From an armoured car, wearing a flat cap,
You who lived simply and gave to the poor
And had just one and a quarter *dinar*s
On you when you fought to the last round and
Were shot at the Ministry of Defence
80   And had your head cut off and waved about
On television after the Arif
Coup, you were good as dictators go, you
Kept order in the city. Help me now
I describe how one of your successors,
85   Saddam Hussein, was ousted as you were
After a rule of opulence that would
Have filled you with disgust. He sent abroad
Forty billion dollars – Prime Minister
Iyad Allawi maintained fifty-seven
90   Billion dollars – that rightfully belonged
To your Revolution. I helped you weld

The Sunni, Shiite and Kurdish factions
Into the homogenous whole you sought
Forty-eight years ago when I was young.
95   Help me describe what befell *your* Baghdad.

Tell, Muse, how the Syndicate supported
Saddam Hussein, who, having attempted
To assassinate dictator Kassem
For the CIA, rose with the Baath *coup*
100   In Iraq in 1968 and
Took supreme power in 1979,
Milked Iraq for his family and ran
A brutal regime, killing two million;
But then became disenchanted with him.
105   The US was alarmed at extremism
In Iran, courted him as an ally,
Encouraged him to send armoured units
Into south-west Iran, fomenting eight
Years of the Iran-Iraq war, weakening
110   Both sides so they would not threaten US
And British oil interests or Israel, and
Setting back their drive for nuclear weapons.
Each side lost a million men in eight years
Of war. Israel had sent arms to Iran.
115   The US provided Iraq with loans
Totalling 5.5 billion dollars
To spend on arms. In 1989
The US Department of Energy
Reported Iraq had begun to build
120   An atomic bomb, and had held a test,
Perhaps successfully, perhaps funded
By the unaware US. In November
The CIA Director urged Kuwait
To press Iraq on a border dispute.
125   Saddam borrowed seventeen billion dollars
From Kuwait to fight Iran, which he tried
To cancel, claiming Kuwait had stolen
Iraq's oil worth fourteen billion dollars
By slant-drilling. Saddam wanted Kuwait's
130   Ten per cent (to Iraq's ninety per cent)
Of Rumaila oilfields. April Glaspie,
The US ambassador to Iraq,
Met him in July 1990 and,
Luring Saddam into seizing oil, said
135   America would not intervene in
Inter-Arab border disputes, a green

Light for Saddam to invade Kuwait and
Claim Kuwait's bit of Rumaila oilfields.
Four days later Saddam moved troops. Glaspie
140   Denied her assurance and then resigned.
Starting the 1991 Gulf War,
Saddam annexed Kuwait as the nineteenth
Province of Iraq. The Security
Council of the UN demanded that
145   Iraq should withdraw from Kuwait, imposed
Sanctions. James Baker and Dick Cheney, two
Syndicate Secretaries flew to Saudi
Arabia and convinced King Fahd Saddam
Would invade Saudi Arabia and
150   Threaten his oil, and he agreed to have
US troops in his kingdom and pay for
A war with Iraq, along with Kuwait.
Germany and Japan also paid, so
The war would not cost the US a cent.
155   (In fact, it paid seven billion dollars
Above their fund.) The US now secured
UN authorisation for a war
Against Iraq by pledging aid and loans
To Russia, Colombia, Ethiopia,
160   Zaire and China. A vast *Desert-Shield*
Force of five hundred and fifty thousand
Men was unleashed as awesome *Desert Storm*
In January 1991.
Fighter bombers attacked Saddam's palace,
165   The airport, oil refineries, nuclear
Reactors and electrical plants, bombed
The Republican Guard in trenches on
The Kuwait-Saudi border. A hundred
Tomahawk cruise missiles were launched. Saddam
170   Sent Scud missiles against Israel and one
(Destroyed in the air) against the US
Base in Saudi Arabia, which pleased bin
Laden. For six weeks the Coalition's
Air force destroyed Iraq's air force and bombed
175   Saddam's infrastructure, culled his army.
A ground attack was launched on February
The twenty-fourth. Next day Saddam ordered
Withdrawal from Kuwait. Iraqis set
Fire to a hundred Kuwaiti oil wells
180   In the Rumaila oilfields. Two days on
Bush Senior announced, "Iraq's army
Is defeated. Kuwait's liberated."

The Coalition ceased hostilities
On the grounds the UN mandate to expel
185   Saddam had been fulfilled. Bush Senior
Did not want a US occupation
Of Iraq, and stopped short of deposing
Saddam, to his son's evident disgust
As the road to Baghdad was open and
190   Saddam could have been taken prisoner.
Kuwait won some of Iraq's territory
And greater access to Rumaila fields
As consequently did the Syndicate.
Bush Senior hoped that the Iraqis would
195   Overthrow Saddam, but he stayed in place
With Russian support and did not comply
With twelve new UN resolutions that
Demanded reparations and imposed
No-fly zones to protect Kurds in the north
200   And Shias in the south, together with
UN inspection teams for chemical,
Biological, nuclear weapons.

Most of Saddam's wmds were
Probably destroyed, but, fearing attack
205   From nuclear Israel, which he had missiled,
And from Iran, he encouraged belief –
Bluffing so rivals would think Iraq strong –
That he'd still retained some, and this belief
Was swallowed by Bush Junior, who, like
210   Cheney and Rumsfeld and those who had signed
The Project for the New American
Century in 1997, were now
Convinced Saddam was trying to obtain
Nuclear weapons. UN sanctions imposed
215   In August 1990 stayed in force
Till 2003, and demanded
Iraq's compliance with Resolution
687 which required all Iraqi
Wmds to be demolished and
220   Inspected every sixty days. The Oil-
For-Food Program allowed Iraq to send
Out oil exports, but sometimes caused hardship.
So from being an ally to the West
Who helped the CIA run the world's oil,
225   Saddam became a nuclear outlaw
Now suspected of flouting the UN
And of supporting terrorism and

Al-Qaeda – as when bin Laden was seen
Being trained in bomb-making on his farm
230 In Khartoum by Brigadier Salim al-
Ahmed, Iraq's Intelligence Service
Expert, in September and October
1995; again in July
1996 with Mani-abd-al-
235 Rashid-al-Tikriti, the Director
Of Iraqi Intelligence. And on
February the third 1998
Zawahiri had met the Iraqi
Vice-President to integrate Iraq
240 And bin Laden and establish new camps
In Falluja, Nasiriyah and in
Kurdistan under Abdul-Aziz. And
In late December two thousand Saddam
Agreed to help al-Qaeda to attack
245 US and UK interests in Saudi
Arabia – which put the Saudi National
Guard on a kingdom-wide state of alert.
Suspected by PNAC, Saddam
Was in the sights of the Syndicate Knights
250 Who turned suspicions into policies
And ruled in Bush's Court of Camelot.
An attack on Iraq was planned *before*
Bush Junior was elected in January
2001. Six men had tried to kill
255 Bush Senior and five of his family –
Bush Junior, his mother, Laura and two
Brothers Neil and Marvin with a car bomb
In Kuwait in 1993. No
Link with Saddam was found, but the Bushes
260 Were convinced Saddam was behind the crime
And was a danger to the family
So long as he remained in power. Cheney
And others who served Bush Senior then
Urged that Saddam should be forced out to keep
265 The Bush family safe. They made their plans.

Their plans formed a Project. In spring nineteen
Ninety-seven, Robert Kagan, a State
Department adviser, William Kristol,
A US editor and Richard Perle,
270 Senior Pentagon adviser, founded
The Project for the New American
Century, an organisation funded

By three bodies linked to Persian-Gulf oil,
And weapons and defence industries. It
275 Looked back to Reagan, whose moral vision
And assertion of military might
They believed won the Cold War. The Project
Drafted a war plan for US global
Domination through military power
280 And planned a huge increase in the defence
Spending (which took place after 9/11)
To transform the US military
Into a global army to enforce
A *Pax Americana* round the world,
285 Impose peace by war, and spread freedom and
Democracy by liberation. Note
The purpose of the increase in defence
Spending was to "carry out our global
Responsibilities" and "modernise
290 Our armed forces"; and to "challenge regimes
Hostile to our interests and values"; and
"To extend an international order
Friendly to our security". And wealth.
On June the third 1997
295 Its Statement of Principles was signed by
Jeb Bush, Cheney, Rumsfeld and Wolfowitz.
There were eighteen signatories in all.
PNAC introduced "regime change"
In Iraq and planned for it long before
300 In August 1998 Iraq
Ended co-operation with UN
Weapons inspectors, and in consequence
In October 1998 shocked
Congress passed the Iraq Liberation
305 Act which, signed by President Clinton, gave
Ninety-seven million dollars to set up
"A program to support a transition
To democracy", and brought in "regime
Change" in place of continued containment –
310 Sought by the UN Resolution six
Eight seven. One month later the US
And the UK bombarded Iraq in
Operation Desert Fox to hamper
Iraq's wmds and prise Saddam
315 From power – in which it did not succeed.
The Republicans' campaign platform in
The two-thousand election called for "full
Implementation" of the ILA

320

325

330

335

340

345

350

355

360

(Iraq Liberation Act) and Saddam's
Removal. A later PNAC
Document that was dated September
Two thousand showed that members of Bush's
Cabinet planned to take military
Control of the Gulf region, whether or
Not Saddam was in power: "The United
States has for decades sought to play a more
Permanent role in Gulf security.
While the unresolved conflict with Iraq
Provides the immediate justification,
Need for a substantial American
Force presence in the Gulf transcends the issue
Of the regime of Saddam Hussein. Even
Should Saddam pass from the scene" military
Bases in Saudi Arabia and
Kuwait should remain as Iran "may well
Prove as large a threat to US interests
As Iraq". And the plan said: "The process
Of transformation is likely to be
A long one, absent some catastrophic
And catalysing event – like a new
Pearl Harbour." (PNAC's Pearl Harbour
Was 9/11.) Nine members of this
Body that urged war on Iraq were linked
To companies which won defence contracts
Worth more than fifty billion dollars in
2001. There is evidence that
Bush was thinking of attacking Iraq
On and soon after 9/11. On
September the twelfth the Pentagon
Proposed a military operation
Against Iraq, and Bush asked Richard Clarke,
His terrorism tsar, "See if Saddam
Was involved. Just look." He told his aides, "I
Believe that Iraq is involved, but I'm
Not going to strike them now." The Syndicate
Were for the plan, and British MP Tam
Dalyell spoke of "a small group of people
Who have taken over the Government
Of a great country" – Bush's policies
On the Middle East had been influenced by
Jews in his administration, he said.
He was thinking of Perle and Wolfowitz.

Tell, Muse, how Cheney, for the Syndicate

Hijacked the American presidency.
365   It was Cheney who made the war happen,
He pushed a hesitant Bush into war.
In early two thousand and two when war
In Afghanistan seemed a success he
Sat with Bush for a serious talk about
370   Iraq, saying he'd supported the end
Of the Gulf War but it was a mistake
To leave Saddam in power. Now Wolfowitz
Urged war with Rumsfeld's approval, also
Cheney's. Cheney spoke in August for war:
375   "We now know that Saddam has resumed his
Efforts to acquire nuclear weapons.
Many of us are convinced that Saddam
Will acquire nuclear weapons fairly soon."
Now Cheney hosted Saturday-morning
380   Meetings at the Pentagon. Wolfowitz
And he predicted the Americans
Would be seen "as liberators". Cheney
Persuaded Bush of this. He set up his
Own National Security Council staff
385   Within the largest vice-presidential
Staff in the history of the office, which
Now read all the emails between Bush's
National Security Council staff, who
Walked from office to office to avoid
390   Cheney's people monitoring their talks.
It was now clear that Cheney was running
Foreign policy, and his cabal of
Neo-cons inside the V-P's Office
And at the Pentagon led the groundwork
395   For war in Iraq. They cultivated
Ahmed Chalabi and the exiled men
Of the Iraqi National Congress.
Now Cheney spoke of the threat from Saddam,
Bush of democracy. Bush's war in
400   Iraq was planned by Cheney loyalists,
Who nicknamed Cheney "Edgar" after one
Edgar Bergen, a vaudeville comic
Who did the talking and the thinking for
A ventriloquist dummy called Charlie
405   McCarthy. Cheney thought and talked, Bush was
His dummy. A retired general said, "These
Guys planned to spend ninety days in Baghdad,
Then move on to Tehran. Then Rumsfeld's plan
Fell apart in Iraq." In two thousand

410	And three the Iranian Government
	Had approached the US Government with
	A firm request for negotiations.
	Cheney rejected the request, not Bush.
	Through Cheney's firmness and decisiveness
415	The Syndicate had the presidency.
	Bush had debated and argued about
	Iraq with Syndicate members of his
	Administration before 9/11,
	And had a plan to depose Saddam by
420	Military action long before Blair went
	To the US in April two thousand
	And two, when Bush floated war in Iraq.
	Bush met Blair at a Camp David summit
	And at a press conference said, "A report
425	Has come out of the International
	Atomic Energy Agency that
	The Iraqis are six months away from
	Developing a weapon." He inferred
	That the West had become vulnerable
430	To chemical, biological or
	Nuclear weapons: wmds.
	Bush sought UN authorisation for
	Invading Iraq while still holding out
	The possibility of invading
435	Unilaterally. On September
	The twelfth two thousand and two Bush addressed
	A packed UN Security Council
	And made a case for invading Iraq.
	France and Germany were critical, as
440	Were other NATO countries, and argued
	For continued diplomacy and more
	Weapons inspections. The UN Council
	Passed Resolution 1441, which
	Authorised the resumption of weapons
445	Inspections, and "serious consequences"
	For non-compliance – which France and Russia
	Said should not mean "force", which the US and
	UK ambassadors accepted. In
	October Bush, speaking, said, "The stated
450	Policy of the United States is
	Regime change. However, if Hussein were
	To meet all the UN's conditions in
	Terms that everybody can understand,
	That in itself will signal the regime

455	Has changed." And now the US Congress passed
	"A Joint Resolution to Authorise
	The Use of United States Armed Forces
	Against Iraq" – "any means necessary".
	In December Iraq's Intelligence
460	Sent a message Saddam would refute links
	To 9/11 or wmds,
	And was prepared to go into exile
	If he could keep a billion dollars. But
	The US declined, a decision that
465	Would cost three trillion dollars, the bill for
	The occupation. Next month MI6
	Sent a top agent to meet Habbash, head
	Of Iraqi Intelligence, who said
	In Jordan that there were no illicit
470	Weapons in Iraq. The nuclear and
	Chemical weapons were all destroyed in
	1991, biological
	Weapons in 1996. The claim
	Was dismissed by Cheney, who was now in
475	Great hurry to invade. It was rumoured
	That Saddam was behind the first attempt
	To bomb the World Trade Center in nineteen
	Ninety-three; that Atta, the 9/11
	Hijacker, met a Mohammed Khalil
480	Ibrahim al-Ani, an Iraqi
	Intelligence officer and consul
	In Prague in April two thousand and one;
	That Ziad Jarrah, Atta's flatmate and
	Pilot of the plane that crashed in a field,
485	Was linked to Abu Nidal, whom Iraq
	Sponsored; and that there was a training camp
	At Salman Pak, near Baghdad, where hundreds
	Of Saudis linked to bin Laden were trained.
	Cheney was convinced Saddam was guilty
490	Of aiding terror. In February
	The UN inspection report led by
	Hans Blix said there was "no evidence of
	Forbidden military nuclear
	Activities"/"mass-destruction weapons".
495	That month a hundred thousand US troops
	Assembled in Kuwait, a vast army.
	Three-quarters of Americans were for
	Regime change in Iraq, and Secretary
	Of State Powell spoke to the UN General
500	Assembly and presented evidence

Of Iraq's pursuit of wmds
And links to al-Qaeda, referring to
A British dossier that was "based on
Intelligence" – which turned out to be mere

505 Academic essays. The US and
UK and six countries proposed a new
Resolution authorising the use
Of force in Iraq but as some NATO
Countries were opposed, withdrew it. The US

510 And its allies abandoned the UN,
Decided to invade Iraq without
UN's authorising. Many questioned
The legality of the decision
Under international law, and protests

515 Screamed through eight hundred cities, the largest
Ever anti-war rally. Then in March
Two thousand and three, the US, UK,
Spain, Australia, Poland, Denmark and
Italy prepared to invade Iraq.

520 Saddam had turned from the CIA to
The Russians, who supported their agent.
On February the twenty-third, former
Russian Premier, Yevgeny Primakov,
Visited Baghdad on Putin's orders

525 And met Saddam in a palace to arrange
The transfer of Iraq's secret-service
Files to Moscow in the event of his
Defeat and to discuss exit tactics.
(He had made a similar visit just

530 Before the Gulf War.) Two retired Russian
Generals, V. Achalov and I. Maltsey,
Experts in urban war and air defence,
Visited Saddam and were awarded
Medals after strengthening his resolve.

535 On March the seventeenth Bush addressed his
Nation and gave Saddam and his two sons
Uday and Qusay a forty-eight hour
Deadline to surrender and leave Iraq.
It was clear Saddam was going nowhere:

540 Iraqis had dug trenches filled with oil
Set ablaze to confuse reconnaissance;
The airport runways were blocked with trucks and
Defended by large anti-aircraft guns.

Next day Blair rallied the Commons for war,
545   Threatening to resign if the vote went
Against him, saying the Government faced
A stark choice between standing down thousands
Of troops now hours from war or holding firm.
Standing them down would strengthen Saddam and
550   Succour the other states who tyrannise
Their people; Britain should not falter now.
A third of his parliamentary party
Voted against, the biggest rebellion
Since he became Prime Minister and one
555   That would have consequences for his job
If the war in Iraq should go badly.

On the eve of the deadline three tractors
With trailers stopped outside the Central Bank.
Qusay approached a guard and demanded
560   Entry on Saddam's behalf. Soon his team
Were carrying out numbered bank boxes
And stacking them onto the three trailers.
A billion US dollars were loaded.
Then the tractors chugged off with their loot,
565   Heading for one of Saddam's palaces.
The dictator's family regarded
The Central Bank as their own piggy bank.

Before the deadline expired, on the Day
Of Purim in the Jewish calendar,
570   When Jews celebrate victory over
Babylon, now in Iraq at dawn came
A surprise attack, the war's first salvo.
The pye-dogs knew first. They started barking
At 5.30 in a long-drawn-out howl.
575   Three minutes later the air-raid sirens
Gave warning of destruction from the skies
And then came the first flash of explosions,
An attempted decapitation strike
On Dora Farms, where two Nighthawks dropped four
580   Two-thousand-pound bunker-busters and fired
Forty Tomahawk cruise missiles, because
The CIA received a specific
Report that Saddam was visiting his
Daughters and two sons at an underground
585   Command post there. The report had been wrong.
He had not been there since nineteen ninety-
Five. There was no command post. The US

Had abandoned a long-considered plan
For decapitation strikes on fifty-
590   Five top Iraqi officials and bombed
An empty field. The US may have been
Sucked into an initial attack by
Double agents planted by the regime
In an intelligence operation
595   To fool the West. Bush addressed the nation
In the Oval Office: "On my orders,
Coalition forces have begun striking
Targets of military importance
To undermine Saddam's ability
600   To wage war. And now that the conflict has
Begun, the only way to limit its
Duration's to apply decisive force."
Several hours later Saddam Hussein sat
In a safe house in al-Mansur with Abd
605   Hameed, his personal secretary,
And, wearing battledress, a beret and
Horn-rimmed spectacles, looking dishevelled,
Spoke for seven minutes while being video-
Taped to denounce the "criminal" attack.
610   He had told his generals and top aids, "Hold
The Coalition for eight days, and leave
The rest to me," hinting at a supply
Of prohibited wmds
That would even an unequal contest.

615   Saddam was staring deep into the tomb
Of the last monarch Faisal the Second,
Gazing at the King's mutilated corpse.
Though loathing Iraq's monarchy, which had
Been devised by Churchill, he had had built
620   This magnificent new marble tomb in
Adhamiya in 1983.
He had watched from the crowd on the second
Of May 1953 when the King
Arrived to swear an oath to Parliament
625   That would enthrone him as Iraq's new King.
He often asked cemetery officials
To move the marble slab and open up
The royal coffin so, as Cromwell did,
Looking at the dead face of Charles the First
630   At night after his head had been severed
From his body, he could spend in excess
Of an hour alone gazing at the boy

Of twenty-three who'd stumbled from a rear
Exit of the blazing palace at 6
635   The morning of Kassem's revolution
With his uncle, Crown Prince Abdullah; aunt,
Princess Abadiya; Abdullah's mother,
Princess Nafeesa; and nephew of six;
Arab maidservants and Pakistani
640   Cooks; to see armed officers who told them
To turn and face the wall. They had wanted
To take the King alive, but suddenly
All had been submachine-gunned by Captain
Abdus Sattar as-Sab, who had panicked.
645   The King fell down but did not die at once.
A cook saw troops behead him. The other
Members of the royal family were dead.
The hated Crown Prince's body was thrown
To the mob, who cut off his hands and feet
650   And carried them through the streets on spikes and
The body was hanged from the balcony
Of the Ministry of Defence. The Prime
Minister was shot, disembowelled and dragged
Through the streets by the mob and then flattened
655   By a car driving backwards and forwards
Over it. The pro-British policies
Of Iraq's Hashemites were now ended,
And Saddam's gazing at the boy evoked
The spectre of his own destiny, for
660   The House of Saddam's policies would end.
There in the tomb he looked on his own fate
And resolved to resist the Americans,
Spurred on to fight for life by the King's death.
So death intensifies living of life.

665   Colonel Collins spoke to his Brits: "If you
Are ferocious in battle remember
To be magnanimous in victory.
The enemy should be in no doubt that
We are his *nemesis* and that we are
670   Bringing about his rightful destruction.
It is my foremost intention to bring
Every single one of you out alive
But there may be people among us who
Will not see the end of this campaign. We
675   Will put them in their sleeping-bags and send
Them back. There will be no time for sorrow.
Grieve for them after battle." Messages

Used to be optimistic and avoid
Death in a time when Church belief was high.
680   His honesty came in a time when few
Believed in an after-life, as is found
In civilisations now two-thirds through,
But it broke the military tradition
That death is not mentioned, mourning private,
685   Burial wordless with an identity
Disc, graves roughly marked, and all done swiftly.
Ahead of soldiers now were sleeping-bags
And a long nothingness, existence snuffed,
And modern dead were not prepared for life
690   In any spirit world after they'd died.

The ground attack began at dawn on March
The twenty-first (still the twentieth in
Washington) as a hundred and forty-
Five thousand troops in just two hundred and
695   Forty-seven army tanks and as many
Bradley fighting vehicles, the US-led
Invasion force, drove into Iraq from
Kuwait to fight four hundred thousand troops
And four thousand tanks, the Iraqi force,
700   A third of its 1991 size,
And tens of thousands of irregular
Fighters or *fedayeen*. In the Gulf Ward
The air attack was long, the ground attack
Was not launched for six weeks, but now a change,
705   For now the two began at the same time,
Affording an element of surprise.
American and British forces raced
Across sand to Umm Qasr and Basra.
A division, eight thousand Iraqi
710   Troops, capitulated outside Basra.
Demoralised, Iraqi soldiers knelt
On sand clutching dirty white shirt-tail cloths
In surrender, hair matted with sand, hands
Trembling, arms thrust to the sky, young men scared,
715   Too terrified to mention Saddam's name.
Some had shot their own officers so they
Could surrender, bloodied and bedraggled.
The British secured Rumaila oilfields
Where forty-four oil wells were set ablaze
720   By Iraqi explosives and destroyed.
Iraqi forces had mined four hundred
Oil wells all round Basra and in Al-Faw.

The wells were quickly capped and fires put out.
US tanks sprinted ninety miles through whirled
725 Dust across desert to Nasiriyah.
The American tanks, rolling through clouds
Of dust rising several hundred feet, stretched
As far as eyes could see across the sand
And rock in attack formation, the glare
730 Of missiles from the attack jets above
Lighting the blue sky above the dust cloud.
More than two hundred US tanks steamed on
Through a wasteland broken only by tents
Of Bedouin nomads and flocks of camels.
735 B52s bombed Mosul and Kirkuk.

Lights shimmered on the Tigris near dark palms.
At 9 p.m. B52s unleashed
Operation Shock and Awe on Baghdad,
Striking Saddam's palace complex and his
740 Intelligence headquarters. A first wave
Of three hundred and twenty cruise missiles
Fired from American warships – more than
Were fired in the whole Gulf War – now shattered
The illusion of Iraq's defences.
745 A relentless assault rained thunder on
The heart of Baghdad in a fierce *blitzkrieg*
That set leadership and military
Buildings ablaze and swiftly sent towering
Plumes of red, pink and brown smoke to the sky
750 That were pierced by arcs of red tracer fire
From anti-aircraft batteries, and that
Had been conceived to terrify Iraq's
Gung-ho leadership into submission.
Ambulances, fire-engines, police cars
755 Rushed through the otherwise deserted streets.
RAF Tornado bombers fired their
Air-launched anti-radiation missiles
(ALARM) to smash integrated radar
Defence systems so bombers could follow.
760 Wave after thunderous wave of explosions
Shook Baghdad amid showers of orange sparks
And the horizon turned a hellish red.
Shock waves reverberated through the air,
Knocking observers back from balconies.
765 The ceremonial palace was on fire
From bunker-busting bombs that smashed straight through
Windows and exploded deep inside walls

And as its rubble fell a new palace
Went up in flames, and the ferocity
770 Of the attack unleashed and acrid smoke
Were devastating. General Tommy Franks
Said, "This is a taste of what shock and awe
Means, and there's more to come if the regime
Doesn't crumble." There were (wrong) reports that
775 Saddam's body was stretchered from rubble
In an oxygen mask – rumours that spread
Confusion among cowering regime troops
While a decree from Saddam offered cash
To Iraqis who killed the enemy –
780 Ten thousand pounds for enemy soldiers.
But this was bravado, for all that could
Be seen was smoke blowing from hundreds of
Gigantic blasts that rocked the capital
As Saddam's palaces and Government
785 Buildings were pounded relentlessly by
The Allies' deafening raids. A thousand
Missiles sent fireballs and mushroom clouds high
In the night sky above the dark Tigris
And outlines of palms, and the firestorm left
790 Parts of central Baghdad in flames. Orange
Smoke billowed up the calm river. It was
An attack of unprecedented might
That was designed to leave the world in awe
Of American superpower. Its code-
795 Name was taken from a study of Gulf-
War strategy by Harlan Ullman, which
Recommended intimidating war
Adversaries to crush their will to fight.
Intensive bombing was programmed to last
800 Eight days but was reduced to a few hours.
It created damage costed at five
Hundred billion dollars. Reconstruction
Contracts were awarded to companies
With Syndicate and Republican links.
805 A contract to blow out wellhead oil fires
Worth fifty million dollars was assigned
To Kellogg, Brown & Root, subsidiary
Of Halliburton, for whom Cheney was
CEO. In one night *Shock and Awe* blew
810 Up much of beautiful Baghdad I knew.

Watching the red-brown smoke on his TV
Bush peered at the dark Iraqi sky that

Surrounded the smoke above Tigris lights.
Somewhere beyond it the One was aware
815 Of *Shock and Awe* and the strike on Saddam,
And out at the edge of the universe
As it rushed forward into the boundless,
The infinite encompassing space-time,
The universe, it included within
820 Itself all contradictions, opposites:
Night and day, male and female, life and death;
And with them the contradictions of cruise
Missiles that rained *Shock and Awe* and the tanks
That had provoked their deterrent to all
825 Countries that still opposed the Western way
Of freedom, democracy, human rights.
Change had been imposed on Iraq, which would
Pass from a tyranny to a free state
That would hold elections. To God the One
830 Three weeks of raining change on a country
Where bad things happened and subsequent peace
Were like a brief storm in a warm summer
That might flatten crops this year but would soon
Be forgotten in improved future years.

835 American tanks reached Nasiriyah
Where they seized Tallil Airfield from forces
Dug well in in trenches, and two bridges
Over the Euphrates, which they handed
To Marines who'd fought through the Rumaila
840 Oilfields. One tank force crossed the Euphrates
And made its way to Kut, another stayed
On the west bank and charged to Kerbala.
The tanks prepared a hundred-mile-long line
Between these two towns, to attack Baghdad.
845 No Iraqi commanders surrendered,
And *fedayeen*, indistinguishable
From civilians, fired at tanks with rifles,
Rocket-propelled grenades, mortars, riding
At American tanks in pick-up trucks.
850 They threatened to slash the throats of children
Of Republican Guards who would not fight.
US Marines attacked Nasiriyah
But encountered heavy resistance there.
Now a severe sandstorm slowed the advance
855 Half-way between Najaf and Kerbala.
Air operations were blocked for three days.
Then heavy rain on top of the sandstorm

Caused orange mud to fall on invaders.

Four hundred and fifty tanks or fighting
860 Vehicles and sixty thousand infantry
Of the US faced thirty-six thousand
Fiercely loyal, trained Republican Guards,
Élite troops with five hundred ageing tanks
South-west of Baghdad. All round the city
865 Oil fires sent up a wall of thick-black smoke
From trenches filled with burning oil. Now waves
Of B-52s and Tomahawk cruise
Missiles, Harriers, A-10 tankbusters and
Apache helicopters attacked through
870 Obscuring smoke. Now a sandstorm had come
And Iraqi troops launched a counter-charge
Under cover of whirling sand and fog.

Basra Baathists told Iraqis to fight.
Then a jet dropped two bombs on a market
875 Street. They thumped and fifteen civilians lay
Dead, thirty wounded. A severed arm raised
Its finger to the sky. A wailing man
Rushed forward, picked it up, called on Allah
To take *his* arm and cursed both Bush and Blair,
880 And Iraq had a propaganda *coup*
Caused by this accident to innocents
Which may not have been an accident but
An Iraqi plan to stir world outrage.
Elsewhere two British soldiers lay beside
885 A dusty road, shot in heads by a mob,
Riddled with bullets, faces caked with blood
As they sprawled side by side in dusty death.
Now supply lines were stretched and a US
Convoy was attacked. Now in a break-out
890 A column of T-55 tanks moved
South from Basra and were encountered by
British Challengers, whose gunners, using
A tank-targeting system, a console
Similar to a computer game, fired
895 Depleted uranium shells that drill through
Armour, suck all air out, leaving behind
A vacuum and heat that vaporise
The occupants. Fourteen Iraqi tanks
Were taken out in just a few minutes.
900 It was the biggest British tank battle
Since El Alamein, 1942.

⌐
In Basra the Baath Party headquarters
Was wiped out by a two-thousand-pound bomb
And Iraqis confronted the Baathist
905   Authorities, the first time the Shias
Had risen since twelve years before, when they
Rose to be brutally crushed by Saddam.
Iraqis sneaked out of Basra to tell
The British forces what was going on.
910   Refugees trudged across the long humped-backed
Bridge guarded by British soldiers, people
Fleeing fighting, seeking food and water,
Beseeching with hands, all food gone, only
Tomatoes and onions at ten times their
915   Normal price. Then mortars came in and burst,
Sending spouts of black smoke on either side
Of the road – refugees fired on by cruel
Iraqi troops maiming Iraqi poor,
Targets for ruthless paramilitaries,
920   A blizzard of mud blown up from marsh banks,
Wind and mud caking faces orange-brown
All round the marsh's dried mud-flats that were
Once the home of the Marsh Arabs until
The marshes were drained, now slurry wasteland
925   Cut by tank tracks, scarred by burnt-out vehicles.
Iraqis smiled and waved, then when US
Troops' backs were turned fired – smiling assassins.
Now six hundred British Marines attacked
A Basra suburb, Abu el Kharib,
930   And took three hundred prisoners, including
A Republican-Guard General. Now, armed
With his information, Challengers rolled
And trundled into Basra and pressed on
To the calm Shatt al-Arab waterway,
935   An idyllic, paradisal river
With palms on either side. Now SAS
Snatch squads targeted the fanatics who
Had led the strong resistance in Basra.
Now British snipers picked off Iraqi
940   Paramilitaries as they advanced.
At last three thousand Desert Rats stormed in
To Central Basra, where a thousand die-
Hard resistance fighters had to retreat,
And were welcomed by the joyful Shias.

945   A dreadful find by British troops not far
From hot Basra at an abandoned base

Of Iraq's military: mutilated
Remains of hundreds of executed
Victims, skulls and bones bundled into bags,
950   Human remains, an identity card,
Skulls with broken and missing teeth, plastic
Bags heaped in unsealed cardboard coffins in
What used to be an Iraqi death camp.
All had been executed, the skulls had
955   Shots to their heads. And then another find
In a warehouse in al-Zubayr's outskirts:
Human remains from the 1990s,
In unsealed coffins more skulls and bones, some
With strips of uniform attached, skulls with
960   Bullet holes, Shiites executed in
An uprising in Basra in nineteen
Ninety-one. Photos of bloated faces,
Mutilated. And yet another find:
Shocked British troops found a torture chamber
965   Used by Saddam's thugs, a police station
With filthy cells and a ceiling meat hook,
And live cable attached through mains to give
Electric shocks. No chemical weapons
Or weapons of mass destruction were found.

970   Near the Kurdish front Iraqi soldiers
Cowered in bunkers as the barrage came,
Exploding from the sky with bright flashes
And thunderous booms. Some deserted, just
Dropped their weapons and slipped away and gave
975   Themselves up to the Kurds. Execution
Squads lay in wait, their brief being to kill
Escapees. B-52 bombers roared
Overhead, black smoke rose towards the south.

In Baghdad Friday prayers went on despite
980   Heavy bombardment's deafening explosions
Under the dust-brown dome of Oum 'l-Marik,
Mother of all Battles mosque. US bombs
Made the air tremble as a hundred men
Bowed their heads to the earth. All round the mosque
985   The heavy smoke of burning fuel twisted
To the blue sky. Women brought soldiers bread.
Standing under Saddam's portrait, children
Dreading the next bomb-blast served black coffee.
As fifteen thousand defended Baghdad
990   While bombs fell, the *muezzin* called from his

Minaret, "*Allahu Akbar*," "Allah
Is great". US troops fought their way across
A bridge over the Euphrates as key
Targets in Baghdad were bombed and missiled.
995   A huge mushroom cloud of smoke billowed from
A palace by the Tigris owned by first
Son of Saddam, Qusay, who commanded
The Republican Guard. The huge blitz sent
Terror through the ranks of Saddam's henchmen,
1000   Who were dejected at the bombardment.
Now there were skirmishes as US troops
Advanced in tanks across the dusty plain.

A sunny day and in the distance air-
Strike blasts lit up the sky and fierce fires burned.
1005   And then two aircraft swooped and dropped two huge
Daisy-cutter bombs, and several thousand
Soldiers were wiped out. The rest of the twelve
Thousand Republican Guard surrendered
Or fled. Their feared Baghdad Division had
1010   Been destroyed. The Americans advanced
Into Baghdad, and used a "black-out" bomb
To cut all electricity supplies:
Detonated over Baghdad, it spewed
Out a web of carbon filament that
1015   Settled on power lines and caused short circuits,
And turned off Baghdad's lights at 9 p.m.
Under cover of black-out the US
And British special forces wearing night-
Vision goggles moved through the pitch-black streets
1020   And attacked the airport. Tanks punched through its
Outer wall. Artillery fire rocked all
Baghdad, tracer rounds streaked above the blacked-
Out city. Dozens of Iraqi troops
Were killed and Saddam's favourite palace,
1025   The one he preferred of his eight sumptuous
Palaces, was stormed by special forces
Who, boldly landing near Lake Tharthar in
Helicopters, snatched secret documents.
Now US tanks rumbled towards Baghdad
1030   And a thousand Iraqi troops were killed.
Now children who had helped Allied forces
Were hanged from lampposts by the supporters
Of Saddam Hussein. At last Iraqis
Turned out to cheer the American tanks.
1035   Baghdad was falling, would soon have fallen.

British tanks now regrouped and then thrust on,
Advanced north to Al-Amarah. Water
And electrical shortages grew worse.
As the Iraqi forces collapsed in
1040   All towns, looting increased. Coalition
Forces worked with the Iraqi police
To enforce order in each local place
After a rapid advance which had stretched
And lengthened supply lines, there was a pause
1045   Near holy Kerbala, which with Najaf
Was secured by Hundred-and-First Airborne
Division under General Petraeus.
After five days and nights of carnage in
Ambush Alley fifteen hundred Arabs
1050   Died in uneven war. A cheering crowd
Welcomed the US into Najaf. From
The shrine to *Imam* Ali, son-in-law
Of the Prophet Mohammed, where Shia
Women clad in black squatted, Iraqi
1055   Forces fired at passing US armour.

Defense Secretary Rumsfeld sent briefings
To Bush with quotations from the *Bible*
On their covers, to curry favour as
Bush called his "War on Terror" a "crusade".
1060   On a picture of an aircraft-carrier
A briefing quoted Psalm 139, "If
I rise on the wings of the dawn, if I
Settle on the far side of the sea, even
There your hand will guide me, your right hand will
1065   Hold me fast, O Lord." Another briefing
Showed US troops holding guns and praying,
Heads bowed, and quoted *Isaiah* 6.8:
"Whom shall I send, and who will go for us?"
As US troops were taking casualties
1070   A briefing quoted *Proverbs* 16.3:
"Commit to the Lord whatever you do,
And your plans will succeed." This was above
A picture of a machine-gunner on
The road from Hilla to Baghdad. Above
1075   A picture of Baghdad's Victory Arch,
One quoted *Isaiah* 26.2:
"Open the gates that the righteous nation
May enter, the nation that keeps faith." Then
One more quoted *1 Peter* 2.15:
1080   "It is God's will that by doing good you

Should silence the ignorant talk of foolish
Men." It was placed by an illustration
Of Saddam. The use of Christian language
To justify invading a Muslim

1085 Nation in a "crusade" was intended
To encourage Bush, but had it leaked out
It would have damaged the US image
By suggesting that the invasion was
A clash between religions as well as

1090 A clash between their civilisations.

Alarmed at Iraqi Army collapse,
Satan appeared at Saddam's side in his
Underground bunker, in battle fatigues
Looking like a Republican Guard. He

1095 Said, "I bring an urgent situation
To your attention." Saddam stared at him,
Knowing immediately he must listen.
"Your defensive position to the south
Is being breached – by your own side, in fact

1100 By your son Qusay, who has shifted two
Divisions several times, so troops that should
Be protecting Baghdad are now confused.
They're no longer sure what their role should be.
They're in the wrong places, the enemy

1105 Can seize target-points without engaging
All units." Saddam said, "I thank you for
Your concern, but I've withdrawn some units
To join the insurgency in coming
Weeks. I've already emptied the bank vaults

1110 To pay for this – Qusay arranged the heist.
On the southern front, Qusay knows what he's
Doing. He's leaving gaps to lure tanks in
So they can be surrounded, set ablaze,
Junked. It will be all right. We are winning.

1115 The United States has invaded my
Sovereign country without provocation
And its forces lack the will to fight hard.
My main issue's to prevent domestic
Unrest and deal with the threat of Iran."

1120 Satan saw he was chronically out
Of touch with reality, and would lose,
And that he had to deal with the next stage
Of the war, the unrest he could expect
After the fall of Baghdad and its lord.

1125

    ⌐Three weeks into the invasion, US
Tanks rumbled and trundled into Baghdad.
The plan had been to drive armoured units
Into the centre of the city, but
Armoured units south of the city left

1130
The Republican Guards' assets destroyed
And Americans were in the outskirts.
On April the fifth twenty-nine tanks reached
Baghdad airport, and met heavy fighting.
The next day US tanks headed downtown

1135
And occupied a palace of Saddam's.
US forces ordered Iraq's forces
To surrender or face full-scale assault.
Iraqi Government officials had
Disappeared or conceded defeat. Now

1140
A blast and al-Saa restaurant in Mansur
Was demolished by four two-thousand-pound
Bunker-buster bombs, and fourteen were killed.
There was *reliable* information
That Saddam and his two sons and forty

1145
Henchmen were there. But Saddam escaped. On
April the ninth Baghdad was occupied
And Saddam Hussein's power declared ended.

And now in Fardus Square, Americans
Climbed a giant bronzed statue of Saddam

1150
In military uniform raised on
A round marble plinth with right hand outstretched,
And looped a noose round his neck that was tied
To a tank recovery vehicle's grappling
Hook and slowly drove away and pulled on

1155
The statue which slowly bent down, one arm
Pointing to Jerusalem, which he sought
To capture and liberate; and toppled
It, so it bent forward, snapped and lay on
Its back while Arabs insulted it by

1160
Raising their dusty soles above its face.
Bearded men in dishdashers beat it with
The soles of their sandals as if it were
The corrupt regime they despised and loathed.
It was like the fall of the Berlin Wall

1165
And the collapse of the Iron Curtain.
There had been Allied victory, hadn't there?

As if contradicting this toppling,
With much of Baghdad unsecured, fighting

Continuing in city and outskirts
1170   Well into the occupation, Saddam
Made a final appearance. He had just
Met the senior Iraqi leadership
And told them, "We will struggle in secret."
As he departed Baghdad, his car stopped.
1175   He stood above an enthusiastic
Crowd in battledress and beret, waving.
Was it Saddam or was it a double?
Was the real Saddam in one of thirty-
Five bunkers beneath buildings round Baghdad?
1180   Black smoke rose in the distance from oil fires.
"May Allah protect you, President," one
Man called. And "With our blood and souls we will
Make sacrifices for you, o Saddam,"
Several chanted, waving guns in the air.
1185   This Saddam looked relaxed, the real Saddam
Issued orders to resist at all costs.
He got back into his car and vanished.
Now his portraits and statues were attacked
And vandalised. A dictator's toppling:
1190   A big statue of Saddam in beret
Waving outside Basra, chained to a tank
At the ankles, was uprooted with its
Round plinth and downed. All cheered. A similar
Scene in Kerbala as scores of the young
1195   Clambered on his fallen statue and beat
It with the soles of their shoes to insult
The feared tyrant. Now there was chaos, no
Central control, and old grudges surfaced.
Kut and Nasiriyah fought each other,
1200   Each seeking to be the new capital.
Tribes warred, a civil war loomed. US-led
Coalition forces sternly ordered
Hostilities must cease, and that Baghdad
Would remain capital of new Iraq.
1205   General Franks became supreme commander
Of occupation forces, and confirmed
The Coalition had paid Iraqi
Military leaders cash to defect.
US troops began to search for members
1210   Of Saddam's Government, wanted men whose
Faces were shown on sets of playing-cards.

Now there was general looting in the streets.
Young Arab men in open-necked shirts ran

Out of doorways clutching fridges, freezers,
1215 Cupboards, wardrobes, desks, lamps, goods from windows
Of shops, rugs, carpets, crockery, bedding,
Anything they could lay hands on, which they
Hoisted on their shoulders or on their backs
And ran at the double down the hot street
1220 To battered estate cars or pick-up trucks
Where watchful accomplices ran to help.
Handcarts were loaded with what could be found.
The gold markets were ransacked, trucks of gold
Were driven hooting through the crowded streets.
1225 Looters ran amok and stripped bare the home
Of Tariq Aziz, former Deputy
Prime Minister and Uday's many-domed
Pleasure palace where an American
Shell had ripped through and its blast snapped the stems
1230 Of goblets he offered to his ladies.
Iraqis entered banks and helped themselves
To piles of rubber-banded notes done up
In string. Deep underground came cries and screams
Of four thousand abandoned detainees.
1235 The Museum was ransacked. An Arab mob
Humped stone busts of Sumerian monarchs
And Akkadian gods on their shoulders.
An ancient terracotta lion was smashed,
And statues from Hatra were beheaded.
1240 A US tank holed the Assyrian Gate.
Two staggered holding a full-length statue
That was too heavy to be lifted and
Somehow manoeuvred it into the street.
Fifteen thousand items were thus removed.
1245 Only six thousand would be recovered.
Now looters torched the city they had sacked.

Now in Saddam's main palace, al-Sijoud,
The new Presidential palace, US
Troops sat on his settees and chairs, rubble
1250 Littering the marble floor. In Basra
British Marines lolled in Saddam's palace
Near mosaic ceilings and a bathroom
With a gold lavatory, brush and soap dish,
Luxury fittings while he complained that
1255 Iraqis were starved by Western sanctions.
A gilded tyranny. It seemed the West
Had now won the war to depose Saddam.

⌜Kurds swept down from the hills and occupied
Kirkuk, Iraq's northern oil capital.
1260 Mosul was taken without a fight, and
The army now prepared to take Tikrit,
The birthplace of the Kurdish Saladin.
Now Allied chiefs ordered a bombing blitz
On Tikrit as it was Saddam's home town.
1265 A statue of Saddam in old chain-mail
And on a charger towered over the wide
Boulevard lined with statues of himself.
His most ostentatious Tikrit palace
Overlooked the Tigris, a riot of
1270 Sand-coloured pillars, domes and colonnades,
A mosque and nuclear bunker, razor wire,
A self-glorifying palace that had
A parade-ground. At Tikrit's entrance stood
A vast mural: Saddam waving a sword,
1275 Leading an army of Arab horsemen
Towards Jerusalem's Dome of the Rock.

Bush landed on the aircraft-carrier
USS Abraham Lincoln on May
The first in a Lockheed S-3 Viking.
1280 His arrival was criticised as too
Theatrical and an expensive stunt.
In warm weather he spoke in his shirtsleeves
To a deck packed with crew. Behind him hung
A banner saying "Mission Accomplished"
1285 That had been requested by the US
Navy and made by White-House staff. Its brash
Message was criticised as premature.
The White House later said that the banner
Referred to the invasion of Iraq.
1290 In his speech he said, "We have difficult
Work to do in Iraq. We are bringing
Order to parts of that country that still
Remain dangerous." The White House meant regime
Change had been accomplished, Saddam's downfall.
1295 The war over, occupation began.
Now America had to win the peace.

BOOK SIX

THE SUNNI INSURGENCY

SUMMARY

O Snorri Sturluson, saga writer
In prose who, though Icelandic, celebrates
The Viking kings of Norway, real people,
As you do in your *King Harald's Saga*,
Who was asked to Norway in 1218
And became the King of Norway's vassal,
You understand the plundering outlook.
Do you detect it in the American
Eye on the oil under Iraqi sand?
I find you on men's tongues while seafaring
Among the creeks and fjords of north Norway.

I leave Tromso, gateway to the Arctic
Where Amundsen set sail on his polar
Expedition, two hundred and fifty
15 Miles north of the Arctic Circle, blown by
The Gulf Stream and so with pleasant climate.
Here long winter darkness, two and a half
Long months of polar night when there is dim
Daylight at midday for two or three hours,
20 Is counterbalanced by the long bright days
Of glorious summer when the sun does
Not set for two and a half golden months
Of continuous daylight and midnight sun.
Plying the grey waves like a seafarer,
25 Looking for settlers and Viking plunder,
Snow-clad headlands all round and dipping foam,
Dreaming of my lord's hall and leaping fire
And warmth of mead and thanes unlocking their
Word-hoards amid ice-floes, standing alone
30 In a snowstorm on the top deck, musing
On seafarers who have only soaring
Gulls for company, and the dipping waves
On the bleak, briny deep far from all friends,
I am drawn back to my own Nordic roots.
35 I am tall and, my father was convinced,
Of Viking stock who had settled in East
Anglia and later Bourn near Cambridge,
Perhaps from Denmark's Aggersborg, a town
Of (H)aggers replicated in London's
40 Haggerston, but perhaps from Old Norway,
For "*hagr*" in Old Norse means "fit, ready".
Yet "*agger*" in Latin means "a rampart",
"*Haeg-gar*" in Anglo-Saxon "hedge-warrior",
So did my forebears arrive with Romans,
45 With blond-haired, fair-skinned Angles or Saxons?
And my paternal DNA goes back
Forty thousand years to the Near East where
Early man came when leaving Africa,
Before diverging east and west and north.
50 From Honningsvag, an old Viking harbour
I follow a snowplough to the North Cape,
Pass settlements of the ancient Sami
Who hale from Central Asia four thousand
Five hundred years ago, then back by sea
55 Hold a king-crab downwards by its back legs,
Then watch it killed with downward stab in head –
It releases brown poison – and sideways

Gouge, and later eat its boiled claws and legs
With its executioner, a fisherman
60   Who claims, "It's said I am the descendant
Of a Viking king, Ottar from Bjarkøy,"
From Vikings who came with Kurgan nomads
Three thousand five hundred years back. He says:
"You should read Snorri's sagas." Did I hear
65   Right? Snorri Sturluson? "Yes, the Viking
Writer." This fisherman knows the Old-Norse
Sagas just as Persians know Ferdowsi,
And I, the West's epic poet, though known
Am widely unread in this post-book age
70   When high themes, wars on all men's lips, are shunned
For time must be spent mastering structure.
White mountains surround me, thirty white peaks,
Each structured like one of my sloping works
That start low down and rise to daunting height
75   And dwarf the trivial cabins round the fjord.
Who'd climb rather than amble in foothills?
As I realised forty-one years ago
I am out of your Old-Norse tradition
And its nomadic search for better things.
80   Due to my genes, in my youth I plundered
Sites across seas for my poetic themes
(As I do now in this marauding work)
And settled on a new philosophy.
I too write of real people in my works.
85   I know the first Vikings left this cold place
To escape polar night and the late spring
(Ground hard so few crops grow, more mouths to feed),
Left crowded Norway for more temperate climes,
Settled peacefully, eschewing rapine
90   And slaughter, lived in harmony with all,
And how settlers were visited by friends
And opportunists razed monasteries
And provoked Christians against the pagan
Vikings, who slowly became Christianised.
95   I know how you were brought up by a priest.
O Snorri, master of describing war
In Viking times, come to my aid now I –
Who have pre-Christian roots in modern times
And have described Hell whose underground caves
100   Are not unlike the Vikings' Valhalla,
Hall of the Dead, though Hell has no heroes –
Come to narrate an occupying force
And how it coped with local resentment,

Insurgency, as plunderers entrenched.
105 O Odin, god of war, wisdom, poetry
And magic who is violent and wise
And untrustworthy in equal measure,
Who has no power over the Tree of Life,
Yggdrasil, that supports the universe.
110 Your Yggdrasil's behind my Tree of Life.
I construct an epic that unifies
Greek, Roman, Italian, English and Norse
Kinds in a new, Universalist form.
I came to Norway for the Northern Lights
115 But found instead the northern Light, my roots
In Old-Norse saga and my Viking stock.

O Robespierre, who sent to the guillotine
Thousands of victims, who were first installed
In this Conciergerie on the Ile de
120 La Cité, with them Marie-Antoinette,
And then yourself followed in their footsteps,
You understood how to rule by terror,
That daily killing intimidated.
I stand where your Revolutionary
125 Tribunal met in 1793 –
You sat just here with your back to the steps –
And condemned over two thousand seven
Hundred prisoners, who stood near the windows;
I stand within the dark space where you spent
130 Your last hours till the call to the tumbrel
Took you through the Salle Saint-Louis, "the Room
Of the Doomed", to the Place de la Concorde,
Then the Place de la Révolution,
Where Madame Guillotine sliced off your head
135 (You looking skywards so you could see death's
Swift approach, the bandages that had held
Your shattered jaw in place now ripped off by
The executioner as you lay back,
You screaming in agony, not terror)
140 With angled blade, a clean cut from a height
Which propelled your grimacing visage down
Into a basket, to be held aloft
By your hair and displayed to *tout le monde*,
A victim of your own killing machine.
145 You who knew about beheading strangers
Would have had sympathy for Zarqawi
Who beheaded captives for al-Qaeda.
Help me now I come to describe his crimes.

Musing on many grandiloquent deeds
150   I find the seat I sat on for a week
In a green park of the Ile Saint-Louis
Nearly fifty years ago, having just
Repudiated Law for writer's craft,
And read Milton's *Paradise Lost*, knowing
155   That one day I would wrestle images
Into a poetic epic, and am
Now on my second; the week in April
1959 I rediscovered
My calling – vocation – as an epic
160   Poet of grand international themes,
To prepare for which I'd have to travel,
Read history, myth, science, astronomy,
Scan the globe like Vermeer's astronomer,
Research and understand the ways of God,
165   The laws of history and the universe.
Milton spoke to me those cold April days
When I sat in the open air and read
His rolling verse all morning, and then walked
Up through the Latin Quarter, sat alone
170   For lunch in student St Germain des Prés,
Open leaves propped by my plate as I forked,
Kept company by one who had worked for
Cromwell and grasped that his proud rebellion
Was like Satan's and shook his head at deeds
175   He had endorsed, as Wordsworth did at yours.
O Robespierre, your Revolution must be
Repudiated as must Zarqawi's
Insurgency, for its brutality
In snuffing out some humans for a cause
180   That other human lives can be improved,
A noble aspiration you pursued
Single-mindedly using foulest means.
O Robespierre, fill me with the sad knowledge
That, like Milton, you gleaned from experience,
185   Send me your last rueful understanding,
Repentance of your erroneous ways.

O Colonel Grivas, who led the revolt
Of EOKA against the British troops
In Cyprus, the insurgency back in
190   The 1950s, living underground,
I recall sitting in a Greek restaurant
In Porto Cheli, a seaside village
Within the Peloponnese, at twilight

One early evening in 1960,
195   The silver waves lapping by my feet at
Sunset, fishermen near, when you walked in,
Your face parchment-white, deprived of the sun.
You shook hands with every fisherman as
The waiter in a white jacket whispered,
200   "Grivas, Grivas." I sent a message through
Him and you replied. "No interviews, I
Don't like the British," and I sent a new
Message, urging you to explain your side.
Then you stood up, as did the fishermen,
205   And you shook hands with each, and scuttled out.
With the fearlessness of immortal youth
I followed you outside, stood in the road.
No other building was in sight, just fields;
No vehicle parked or heading out of sight.
210   You had vanished into the air, and I
Returned to my chair bewildered, baffled.
O Grivas, you who fled from me that night,
I find you in a house in Limassol
Where you hid under the kitchen, a trap-
215   Door British troops never found though they searched
The house when you were lying in your lair,
Help me now I come to describe the fear
Iraqis had of their insurgency
Under the ruthlessness of Zarqawi,
220   How normal living erupted with blasts
As cars, exploding without warning, left
Men groaning in the streets, your tactics when
You emerged to hit-and-run British troops,
One of whom, bombed and killed by you, I knew.

225   Tell, Muse, how al-Zarqawi came to be
Bin Laden's successor inside Iraq
And how he came to lead the insurgency
With a ferocity that many feared.
As Ahmed Fadel al-Khalailah, he
230   Grew up in Zarqa, Jordan. His father
Had fought to keep Jerusalem's Old City
Within Jordanian territory, and he
Was influenced by Abdallah Azzam's
Anti-Israeli outlook, honed within
235   The Muslim Brotherhood, and followed him –
Now as Abu Mohammed al-Gharib,
New identity meaning "the stranger" –
To fight the Soviets in Afghanistan.

In 1990 he moved back from Khost
240   To Peshawar, where, shaped round the preaching
Of Azzam, al-Qaeda was born in hate
As the military arm of global
Muslim insurgency and the army
Of Arab Afghans who joined the Arab-
245   Afghan Bureau. Sly Zawahiri had
Offered bin Laden the title "*emir*"
Or "prince" of the group – and so gained access
To the Saudi's fortune. Azzam opposed
Making al-Qaeda a terrorist group
250   To serve international *jihad*, which was
Universalist, militaristic
And nihilist towards the West, wanting
To keep *jihad* localised. In vain – he
Was assassinated in November
255   1989 on bin Laden's curt
Orders as he was suspected of links
With the CIA, and bin Laden and
Zawahiri now transformed al-Qaeda
Into a terrorist vanguard that served
260   Revolutionary forces in Arab lands.
In March 1991 Mustafa
Shalabi, a supporter of Azzam
Was also assassinated at bin
Laden's authorising behest. Gharib
265   Supported the local view of *jihad*,
Joined the Arab-Afghan Bureau and met
Al-Maqdisi, a Palestinian
Salafi thinker brought up in Kuwait,
Now his new mentor for local *jihad*.
270   They returned to Jordan and preached from door
To door that all the Arab regimes were
Infidel and Israel should be attacked
And wiped out. In 1994 when
The Jordanian Government and Israel
275   Reached a peace agreement, their Salafi
*Jihad*ism, now known as *Bayaat al-
Imam*, led to the arrest of both men
And their imprisonment: fifteen years for
Starting an illegal *jihad*ist cell.
280   In May 1999 both men were
Released under an amnesty to mark
Abdallah the Second's accession to
The Jordanian throne. In Chechnya
The *mujahideen* were fighting Russia

285	And a Saudi, Tamer Saleh Suwaylam,
	Known as Khattab, saw *jihad* as local,
	Confined to Chechnya. Bin Laden and
	Zawahiri had shocked the Salafi
	*Jihad*ist world in 1998
290	By forming the International Front
	For *jihad* against Jews and Crusaders,
	Under the leadership of bin Laden
	Who believed the United States was weak
	And could not withstand more than three blows: his
295	Bombing of two US embassies in
	Africa, and of the *USS Cole*;
	And 9/11. He did not grasp how strong
	America was, for it was "corrupt,
	Immoral, had no backbone, followed greed",
300	He thought with Saudi superiority.
	Al-Gharib left Jordan with his first wife
	Intisar and his young son and daughter
	And went to Pakistan to find a way
	Of reaching Khattab in Chechnya. Six
305	Months on his visa expired and he was
	Imprisoned for eight days and then released,
	And flown to Karachi. He met Asra,
	A thirteen-year-old Palestinian,
	Daughter of an instructor in a camp
310	In Afghanistan, and he decided
	Not to return to Jordan but go back
	To Afghanistan where the Taliban were
	Fighting Massoud's forces. He left his wife,
	Who would join him later, and with a group
315	Of Jordanians he went on to Kabul.
	He did not want to fight fellow Muslims.
	He took his forty "local *jihad*ists"
	From Palestine and Jordan to Logar,
	Several kilometres west of Kabul
320	To a large guest-house where his wife joined him.
	He was useful to al-Qaeda and in
	The summer of 1999 he
	Became one of bin Laden's lieutenants
	According to a document now in
325	The Spanish anti-terrorist unit.
	He was assigned the planning of his group's
	Operations and in charge of several
	Dozen militants within his own group
	And new recruits who kept on coming in.
330	Al-Qaeda had three levels at that time:

Bin Laden and Zawahiri were top;
Managerial staff with a specific
Mission were second; operational
Members were third, all the autonomous
335   Terrorist cells in Arab or Western
Countries, aligned with al-Qaeda's stated
Positions. Gharib had joined the second,
Managerial circle. Now he moved
To Herat camp where Asra's father worked
340   And settled there with Asra and his group.
He joined the camp on the Iranian
Border and to start afresh changed his name
To Abu Musab al-Zarqawi, which
Grimly meant "the Imposer from Zarqa".

345   At the time (according to the US
National Security Council) Herat
Was where al-Qaeda were stockpiling their
Nuclear material. In due course he
Became head of the camp. The Herat camp
350   Had now become the most strategic site
For terrorists going to Iraqi
Kurdistan via Iran, and the border
Between Iran and Afghanistan was
Now open and a "free-circulation"
355   Agreement had been signed. Now new recruits
Were taught to handle arms and explosives,
And chemical weapons, by Zarqawi,
Who now took Asra as his second wife,
Working with her father. He recruited
360   Suicide bombers there. News quickly reached
Bin Laden, who, having asked him to come
To Kandahar five times and been refused
As Zarqawi thought he was not serious
About *jihad*, asked him to Kandahar
365   In early two thousand. Zarqawi sought
Funding to mount an attack on Israel.
Bin Laden gave him thirty-five thousand
Dollars, and he sent two childhood friends on
A suicide mission to Israel. They
370   Were arrested at Van, Turkey, and failed.
A year after his release from prison
Zarqawi shared control with Al-Shami
And *Mullah* Krekar of a terror group
Based in Iraqi Kurdistan's mountains,
375   Ansar Al-Islam. And in early two

Thousand and one he was important to
Al-Qaeda in Afghanistan, and took
An oath of allegiance to bin Laden,
For whom an oath was a way of tying
380   In independent spirits and bringing
Islam's national groups together under
One banner. Bin Laden had penned the oath:
"I recall the commitment to God in
Order to listen to and obey my
385   Superiors, who are accomplishing
This task with energy, difficulty
And giving of self, and in order that
God may protect us so that God's words are
The highest and his religion may be
390   Victorious." Zarqawi organised
A number of terrorist attacks on
Jordan, and brought in terrorist recruits
From Jordan through Iraq and through Iran.
The channel included Mashad, which was
395   Near Herat and which bin Laden would use.
After 9/11 Zarqawi went
To Kandahar and met Saif Al-Adel,
Abu Zubaydah, Ramzi Binalshibh
Who wanted to send fifteen fighters out,
400   Via Zarqawi's network within Iran,
To Iraq. The house where they were meeting
Was hit by an American missile
And Zarqawi was trapped under rubble
Before escaping. He was reported
405   To have fought at Tora Bora against
The Coalition. He left for Iran
On December the twelfth two thousand and
One with false passports bought from Germany
For forty thousand dollars, and arrived
410   At Mashad on January the fifth
And stayed in Iran with his partisans –
Looked after by Gulbuddin Hikmatyar –
Till April the fourth, co-ordinating
His network's retreat to Kurdistan, and
415   He went to Tehran, then to Zahedan.
He felt watched by Iran's secret service –
Which would not extradite him to Jordan
As he had a false Syrian passport.
The Americans had warned Iran to watch
420   Out for al-Qaeda, and officially
Iran was arresting border-crossers

And few knew about the Supreme Leader's
High-level guests – so the security
Service could confirm their compliance with
What the US had requested. Now some
Hundred and fifty al-Qaeda members
Were arrested, Zarqawi among them
In March. He was released and left Iran
For Syria via Iraq, where he remained
For two months having medical treatment.
It was claimed that he had been injured in
A US bombardment and that a leg
Was amputated and he was fitted
With a prosthetic limb in the best ward.
Baghdad was then a hard place to enter.
Only those friendly to Saddam Hussein
Would be given a bed in the city's
Best hospital, Olympic Hospital,
Which was regime-supported and treated
Iraq's *élite*, its director being
Saddam's son Uday. And if Zarqawi
Was not welcome in Iraq, why did he
Choose Baghdad for his treatment? As senior
Al-Qaeda associate, operating
Openly in Baghdad, he had become
Al-Qaeda's link to Baghdad, a role that
Was confirmed when he suddenly became
America's top enemy in Iraq.
And did Zarqawi meet Saddam? Who knows.
Now he set up sleeper cells in Baghdad,
To be activated if the US
Occupied the city, which would become
The insurgency's structure, and procured
Weapons and explosives from IIS
(The Iraqi Intelligence Service)
Before going to Syria and planning
To murder, in October two thousand
And two, Lawrence Foley, American
Diplomat working in Jordan. Three men
Were paid by Zarqawi to carry out
The assassination. Later he made
A secret visit to the Jordan house
Of Foley's killer. Zarqawi's brief stay
In Iraq led Powell to tell the UN
Security Council in February
2003 that al-Zarqawi was
The link between al-Qaeda's murderous

Movement and Saddam Hussein's cruel regime.

The US invasion of Iraq drove
470 Zarqawi from Kurdistan to Iran.
The previous year he had met *Mullah*
Krekar and formed an alliance. Krekar's
Organisation was swamped with Arab
Afghans, its training camps were controlled by
475 Zarqawi's men, and in February
Two thousand and three he had been deposed.
On the eve of the US offensive
Ansa Al-Islam now had six hundred
Arab fighters come from Afghanistan
480 Under the leadership of Zarqawi.
In March two thousand and three US planes
Bombed *Ansa Al-Islam*'s main strongholds in
Biyara and Halabjah valley, and
A hundred US troops and ten thousand
485 Kurds made ground attacks, killing a hundred
And eighty and capturing a hundred
And fifty. The rest fled to Iran or
Sought refuge in the "Sunni Triangle".
Zarqawi fled to Iran, which was more
490 Welcoming – worried by the Kurds, now keen
To support *Ansa Al-Islam*. It had
Hoped to get close to bin Laden after
His attack on the *USS Cole* in
October two thousand and had waived all
495 Stamps on passports for al-Qaeda members
Crossing Iran to Afghanistan. It
Had been pleased to give sanctuary to bin
Laden and tolerated al-Qaeda.
In August 2004 Brigadier
500 General Qasem Solaimani, Qods Corps
Commander, said Zarqawi was allowed
To enter Iran at certain border points
With twenty fighters whenever he wished.
Zarqawi's lieutenants met in Tehran –
505 Al-Riyati, Khaled al-Aruri,
Abdel Hadi Daghlas and Iraqi
Islamists still close to *Mullah* Krekar –
In August two thousand and three and set
Up a permanent base in Kurdistan
510 To open their own training camps there to
Facilitate the return of Afghan
Arabs and recruitment of Jordanians,

And train their network in how to handle
Chemical/biological weapons.

515 Saddam's sons – Qusay, his heir, who had ruled
Baghdad and Tikrit in the war and been
In charge of intelligence and the Guard,
And Uday, a cruel playboy, who had killed
Many men – Qusay's son and bodyguard,
520 Forced their way into a house in Mosul
And told the owner, who was known to them,
That it would be their hide-out for a while,
And sent the unwilling man out for food.
Just as two squirrels find a bird feeder
525 Hung from a branch of an old apple tree
And clamber down and wrap themselves around
The mesh that guards the nuts and work out how
To lift the lid and then gnaw a small hole
So they can claw out one nut at a time,
530 Steal feed left out for tits and woodpeckers,
And when challenged, stop and glare in outrage
As if demanding that the owner should
Top up the nut-hoard from his stock of nuts,
So Qusay and Uday wrapped themselves round
535 The owner's house and glared at him to go
Out for more feed. Bullied, the owner left
And contacted US forces and asked
If he would be paid the two bounties on
The heads of Qusay and Uday, fifteen
540 Million dollars on each, if he betrayed
Them and was told, "Yes." The owner tipped off
The US force. A special forces team
Went to the house but, fired on from upstairs
Where the four had barracaded themselves,
545 Retreated and called for back-up. Within
Two hours some two hundred US troops from
A Hundred-and-First Airborne Division
Surrounded the house. The battle was fierce
And lasted four hours. Air power was called up.
550 An Apache helicopter fired one
Anti-tank TOW missile,
Demolished the side wall as an A-10
"Warthog" close air support aircraft fired on
The house. Now all was quiet, and soldiers found
555 Four dead. The last to die was Mustapha,
Qusay's fourteen-year-old son. The troops searched
The house for documents that could locate

Saddam, picking through rubble. The next day
Qusay and Uday were identified
560 From their dental records. Their corpses were
Displayed to the media so Iraqis
Would know they had been killed. Iranians said
They had been made up to look like Saddam's
Two sons, but no one doubted they were dead.
565 There was exultant gunfire in the streets
For Iraqis were free of a rapist
And thief (Uday) who had terrorised all.
The corpses were wrapped in Iraqi flags
And buried in the Awja cemetery
570 Near Tikrit, Saddam's home. And the owner
Was promised his thirty million dollars
And given US citizenship so he
Could leave Iraq. Next year unknown killers
Would take their revenge, murder his brother.

575 The insurgency in Iraq began
Soon after Bush announced large-scale combat
Operations had ended and "mission
Accomplished", before a new Iraqi
Government had been fully established.
580 Insurgents, militias and terrorists
Attacked civilian and military
Targets in Baghdad and the surrounding
Towns and cities in scattered incidents.
On April the twenty-third, seven hundred
585 Americans entered Falluja and
A hundred and fifty troops occupied
A primary school for five days. A mob
Of two hundred demanded they should leave
So the school could be reopened. Then four
590 US soldiers fired from the roof for ten
Minutes killing seventeen Iraqis.
Two days later US troops fired again,
On protesters at the Baath headquarters,
Killing three and alienating locals.
595 Some twenty US troops had been killed in
Attacks against the occupation. Two
Million Shiites living in the ghetto
"Saddam City" hung a handpainted sign
Over the entrance plaque that said, "Welcome
600 To Sadr City". Saddam's henchmen had
Killed Ayatollah Mohammed Sadeq
Al-Sadr, the leader of the Shiite

Opposition to his regime, and two
Of his sons, Mustapha and Muammal.
605   Now his son Moqtada al-Sadr rose
To be Shiite leader, and organised
Vigilantes to guard neighbourhoods and
Prevent the lootings of public buildings.
He denounced Coalition forces as
610   Occupiers and called the interim
Government "American puppets". His
Speeches stopped short of calling for violence
But he despised the moderate Shiite
Al-Dawa, that was led by Ibrahim
615   Jaafari, long an exile in London
Before Saddam's fall; the Supreme Council
Of the Islamic Revolution in
Iraq, led by Mohammed Baqer al-
Hakim; and the Ayatollah Ali al-
620   Sistani al-Najaf. Now Moqtada
Spoke out against Sistani, who'd opposed
His father, fearing his criticisms
Would force the regime to retaliate
Against all Shias. He said Sistani
625   Could not preach about the occupation
To Iraqis as he was Iranian.
Moqtada demanded all foreign troops
Should immediately depart, and Jeish
Al-Mahdi, his militia, "the Army
630   Of al-Mahdi" began violence against
Moderate Shiites and Coalition troops.
On April the twelfth Jeish al-Mahdi killed
Shiite Ayatollah Abd al-Majid
Al-Khoi in Najaf. Moqtada, accused,
635   Denied involvement. He wished to create
A parallel Shiite state under his
Leadership with his militia as its
Military arm. Religious tribunals
In Najaf and Kerbala would be its
640   Judicial arm. Now clashes and riots
Turned war-torn Iraq into civil-war
Zones, and Coalition troops battled in
Najaf, Kerbala and Sadr City
Against the supporters of Moqtada,
645   Who each day grew more popular, the voice
Of national resistance. Now the Sunnis
Launched their own offensive with violence in
Baghdad, Ramadi and Falluja in

May. The Sunni middle class had welcomed
650 Saddam's fall as in two thousand Saddam
Had released two hundred thousand convicts
Whose criminal gangs then terrified all.
The Americans freed more criminals
And could not control the massive looting.
655 Iraqis wanted a much better life
Under their computered liberators
But with water and electricity
Cut off for much of each day, no sewage
System, no work, and UN food hand-outs,
660 They had a worse life than under Saddam.
By summer 2003 Shiites and
Sunnis had a common enemy that
United them under the umbrella
Of modern Iraqi nationalism.
665 Sunnis were targeting Coalition
Troops and amid chaos and civil war
The Americans stayed in their Green Zone.
In the south on the edge of the British
Sphere of operations, an armed mob killed
670 Six British military police at
Al-Majar al-Kabir near Amarna
And wounded eight British troops on patrol.
In August the Jordanian Embassy
In Baghdad was truck-bombed, targeted as
675 Zarqawi was Jordanian. Seventeen
Were killed, forty injured. Then the UN
Headquarters in Canal Hotel were bombed
When a concrete-mixing lorry blew up.
A huge explosion blew in glass and wood.
680 Three floors collapsed while hundreds were at work,
Ceilings came down on heads, and then rubble.
Many were speared and stained with blood or crushed,
And the UN's chief envoy to Iraq,
Sergio Vieira de Mello was killed
685 As he stood and spoke at a news conference.
Twenty-two died, a hundred were wounded.
All but fifty foreign UN workers
Were withdrawn from Baghdad, which had become
A place of anarchy and civil war.

690 Bush stood against the increasing chaos.
In August 2003, in Egypt,
Aware that his two-state solution had
Contradicted the Covenant God made

With the Israelites and their Promised Land,
695   Bush told Palestine's Foreign Minister,
"I am on a mission from God," and, "I'm
Getting commands directly from the Lord."
He had received influxes from the Light
Sent by Heaven's Angels, but he was also
700   Neutralising Israel's Covenant by
Claiming that God supported breaking it
To give the Palestinians a homeland –
And his "commands" were thus *realpolitik*.

Zarqawi's fight against Iraq's Shias
705   Began with a murderous attack that shocked.
The *Imam* Ali mosque with golden dome
And resplendent minarets and treasures,
Shrine of Ali, cousin and son-in-law
Of the Prophet, whose tomb was first built in
710   Nine seventy-seven, leader of the Shias,
Shone in Najaf's late August setting sun
After Friday prayers for Shia faithful
With Ayatollah Mohammed Baqer
Al-Hakim, the gaunt spiritual leader
715   Of the Supreme Council of the Islamic
Revolution in Iraq, who was head
Of the Shiite political party
And had lived in Iran for twenty years
And returned to Iraq the previous May.
720   Here the Prophet's son-in-law and cousin
Ali is thought to have been secretly
Buried in the Tomb of *Imam* Ali,
The most holy shrine for Shias, after
He was struck by a poison-coated sword
725   And died two days later in 661.
And now, Zarqawi's sacrifice. Saying
Repeatedly within his family
The Shiites conspired with the Americans
And welcomed them into Iraq so they
730   Could assume power in place of the Sunnis
Just as Ibn al-Alqami, vizier
Of Baghdad conspired with the Mongols in
Twelve fifty-eight and encouraged them to
Invade Baghdad, topple the Abbasids,
735   Whose Caliphate ruled Crusade-time Islam,
And favour him so he could wield more power;
He proclaimed the need for sectarian
In-fighting, for Sunnis to fight Shiites,

Allies of the hated Americans
740   As "history repeats itself, the logic
Of what happens through time does not change; what
Changes is the people, for one player
Replaces another, machines improve,
But what does not change is the theatre where
745   All the new operations take place and
The history of fighting is only one.
Truth battles with falsehood" – and *jihad*ists
Are reliving the Prophet's time and life,
The fight between Mecca and Medina.
750   As al-Hakim left in a Shiite crowd,
Yassin Jarrad, the father of Asra,
Zarqawi's second wife, and instructor
At Herat camp, Zarqawi's call answered
By his family, drove a car loaded
755   With explosives at the mosque and blew up
His huge bomb. A flash blasted him to bits
And shock waves and shrapnel scythed through the crowd
And wrecked the centuries-old golden dome,
Killed a hundred and twenty-five Shiites –
760   And Ayatollah al-Hakim, who could
Challenge Iran's religious primacy
And now lay dead in blood among groaning,
Dying Muslims who had prayed to Allah
And corpses strewn as at Tora Bora.
765   The spirits of the dead hovered above
Their lifeless shells of bodies like hatched birds
Before heading in their new light-bodies
Through the infinite for their next abode
In accordance with where their deeds placed them,
770   And, dreaming of a martyr's paradise,
Asra's father bore a heavy burden
Of actions that had left mankind worse off,
And as if plunged in water with heavy
Boots and pack, sank down to the Underworld,
775   Leaving Iran, new host to Zarqawi,
Outwardly reeling at an outrage to
The Hidden *Imam*'s memory but glad,
Secretly, that the outrage would foment
Chaos which the Hidden *Imam* would note
780   And, as it impacted on his own shrine,
Would make more likely his wished-for return
Up the Jamkaran well near Qom, his long-
Expected Second Coming imminent.
Iran was horrified and also pleased

785	For now the Shiites had reason to fight
	And defeat the Sunnis who had oppressed
	Them and held them down for a hundred years.

A dozen organisations and some
Forty groups, each of which had countless cells,
790   Were now fighting in the insurgency
As it became a resistance movement,
Using car, roadside and suicide bombs.
Beside the Saddam regime's pan-Arab
Baathists, who wanted to restore Saddam
795   To power, and the Iraq-first Nationalists,
Were Islamists who were armed followers
Of the Salafi religious movement.
Salafi means "pious ancestors", and
Salafists, like their ancestors, see God
800   As One, the divine unity of God
And the *Ummah* (Muslim community)
Back in the seventh century, and see
Modern Arab regimes as infidels
Who worship idols, false Western values.
805   The insurgency therefore included
Sunni Salafis wanting pure Islam
Of the Prophet Mohammed's time, as did
Sunni Wahhabis, fellow *jihad*ists,
And foreign Islamist volunteers linked
810   To al-Qaeda who had been inspired by
The Salafi-Wahhabi pure Islam.
Zarqawi, who was head of a group called
Al-Tawhid Wal-Jihad ("Monotheism
And Holy War") was the key "foreigner".
815   Wary *jihad*ists might be marginalised
By a nationalist, secular movement
With a Sunni-Shiite united front.
Taking up Saddam's remark on April
The twenty-eighth that Bush entered Baghdad
820   "With the help of Alqami", Zarqawi
Held that just as the vizier of Baghdad,
Ibn Alqami, conspired with the Mongols
And the Tartars as they conquered Baghdad,
So Shiites conspired with the Americans
825   As *they* conquered Baghdad. He made it clear
The Americans were the new Mongols
And that the Shiites were mere apostates.
Like the Salafists, al-Zarqawi now
Opposed all non-Muslim groups and attacked

830	Christians, Mandaeans, Yazidis – and Shias
	As impure apostates. Thus, in Mosul
	They now attacked a nunnery and bombed
	A cinema and torched four liquor stores.
	In late October suicide bombers
835	Attacked the Red-Cross headquarters and three
	Police stations in Baghdad. Thirty-five
	Were killed, two hundred and forty-four hurt.
	In November a car bomb killed nineteen
	Italian soldiers in Nasiriyah.
840	Shia militias – such as the Badr
	Organisation based in Kerbala
	And southern Iraq, the Mahdi Army
	And Moqtada al-Sadr's followers –
	Had links with Iran's Shiite Government
845	And smuggled Shia fighters to Iran
	Where they all received training and weapons
	Before returning to Iraq. Iran-
	Backed Hezbollah shamed the Mahdi Army
	In Lebanon, and some Hezbollah troops
850	Entered Iraq to train soldiers to kill.
	In two thousand and three senior figures
	From al-Qaeda came to Iran, such as
	Operations chief Saif al-Adel and
	Abdullah Ahmed Abdullah, finance
855	Officer, who co-ordinated its
	Global activities inside Iran.
	On October the twenty-third, in small
	Najmabad the Revolutionary Guard
	Were holding a meeting in a briefing
860	Room in a walled compound when they were told
	To vacate it for "foreign" VIPs,
	And as they left they saw bin Laden and
	Zawahiri leave a three-car convoy,
	Zawahiri wearing a black turban.
865	Both passed themselves off as Iranians.
	Mustafa Ahmed Mohammed, its chief
	Financial officer, his wife and ten
	Children crossed in near Zabol on the third
	Of November two thousand and three and
870	Drove to Mashad in two limousines with
	Revolutionary-Guard officers.
	Behind them came a truck with ten metal-
	Sided trunks filled with cash, twenty million
	Dollars, and raw opiates worth ten million

875   Dollars, enough money to fund – as snow
Melted on peaks and water flowed in plains –
An Iran-al-Qaeda spring offensive
In Afghanistan, to destabilise
Hamid Karzai's Government and to seize
880   Control of western Afghan provinces;
Cash and opium that would buy from Iran
Men and materials Iran supplied
For the offensive planned for late March in
Two thousand and four in Afghanistan
885   And also within Iraq where Ahmed
Chalabi was alleged to have supplied
Sensitive intelligence to Iran.
The Guard gave Mustafa a new passport
And national identity card for
890   His new alias of Abu Yazid.
He sent two hundred and fifty thousand
Dollars to the 9/11 hijackers
Through a bank account in Dubai. Iran
Had five hundred low-level al-Qaeda
895   Prisoners, who escaped in a "jailbreak" in
December two thousand and three, a way
To release them without protest. Iran
Appeared to be on the Coalition's
Side but sided with al-Qaeda when it
900   Sanctioned al-Qaeda's quiet jailbreak. Iran
Had allied with al-Qaeda as it felt
Quite threatened by the War on Terror in
Afghanistan and Iraq; by control
By new neighbouring democracies in
905   Afghanistan and Iraq; and the new
US bases to north and south. It saw
Bin Laden's al-Qaeda as a tool it
Could use to ensure the failure of two
Young democracies – by orchestrating
910   An upsurge of insurgency in both –
And the survival of theocracy,
Iran's *mullah*-dominated system.

        Saddam had been hiding in a mud hut
Near Tikrit, across the Tigris from his
915   Opulent palaces. It was the same
Farm where, way back in 1959,
He had hidden after trying to kill
The ruling dictator Kassem as he
Drove along Rashid Street. He pottered round

920	And when his bodyguards heard US tanks
	Or armoured vehicles he lifted a lid
	That covered a deep hole in the wasteground
	And slid down into the dark and sat in
	A hollow near the bottom of the "well",
925	As perhaps the Hidden *Imam* now sits
	In a small chamber off his well's bottom.
	Just as a heron eyes a pond from height
	And slowly circles it, glides and alights,
	Graceful, nearby and surveys a koi carp
930	Who sees its might above, noses beneath
	Projecting boulders, cowers from danger,
	And there's a stand-off between the hunter
	And hunted who, instinctively still, eye
	Each other's space for a sign of movement,
935	Jabbed-down, spearing beak, water stirred by glints,
	Sun on a red-orange scaled head or tail;
	So US troops waited near where Saddam
	Cowered under projecting stone, quite still.
	He had rigged up a ventilation pump
940	And sat in the dark like a sewer rat
	Waiting to come out when night brought safety.
	The Americans' hostile questioning
	Of his past bodyguards and tribal friends,
	And family, not more than ten in all,
945	Elicited information. And then
	A man from a family with personal
	Links to Saddam cracked and said Saddam might
	Be hiding in one of two locations
	Near Adwar, ten miles south of his hometown.
950	Now the 1st Brigade combat team of 4th
	Infantry division, Raider Brigade,
	Was told to kill or capture Saddam in
	A mission called *Operation Red Dawn*.
	Six hundred troops – cavalry engineers,
955	Artillery, aviation, special
	Operations forces – moved in on two
	Targets near Adwar on a Saturday,
	December the thirteenth. At 6 p.m.,
	Under cover of darkness, these forces
960	Moved quickly towards Saddam's hiding-place.
	They found a two-room mud hut between two
	Farmhouses and penned sheep, and in a room
	Which served as a bedroom found strewn clothing
	And next door a crude kitchen. It was eight
965	And Coalition forces had not found

Saddam. They cordoned off the area.
They searched outside and found a "spider hole",
Its entrance covered by a Styrofoam
Lid and a rug covered with dirt. They raised
970 The lid at half past eight, and clambered in
And found Saddam hiding in the chamber
At the bottom some six to eight feet down.
Though armed with a pistol he offered no
Resistance. US commanders declared
975 He was bewildered and disoriented,
"A tired man who was resigned to his fate".
Soldiers recovered two AK rifles,
Seven hundred and fifty thousand dollars
In bundles of hundred-dollar bills and
980 A white-orange taxi. He could have been
Hiding in a thousand different places
Like this all round Iraq. At 9.15
He was moved to an undisclosed new place
Under Coalition custody. Bush
985 Was notified, and on Sunday morning
At 7 a.m. at a press conference,
Ambassador Paul Bremer, the US
Administrator in Iraq, announced:
"Ladies and gentlemen, we got him." He'd
990 Confirmed it was Saddam through DNA.
At 12.15 Bush told Iraqis they'd
"Never have to fear the rule of Saddam
Hussein ever again". Now tales were told.
Some said Saddam was seized on the sixteenth
995 Of November, and held in the dark hole
At Adwar for three weeks while his captors
Tried to obtain the twenty-five-million
Dollar reward from the US forces.
And some said that he had been a prisoner
1000 Of the Americans for a while as
Bremer would need ten days for DNA
Test results to come through to verify
He had the real Saddam. Some said nerve gas
Or some form of prior medication
1005 Had half-paralysed his sharp responses.
Some said it wasn't Saddam that was caught
But an impostor, a pretender who
Fulfilled the US need to hold Saddam
As there was dissatisfaction at home
1010 As no wmds had been found.
But no evidence supported such tales

And all agreed that Saddam had been caught.

Iraqi resistance intensified.
It was rumoured that it was funded from
1015 The billion-US-dollar bank heist and
Fifty-seven billion dollars Allawi
Says Saddam sent abroad, which his daughter
Raghad was rumoured to have channelled back.
In late December the Coalition
1020 Military were attacked at Kerbala.
Nineteen were killed and two hundred wounded.
In January a huge suicide bomb
Exploded outside the Coalition
Headquarters in central Baghdad, killing
1025 Twenty, including two American
Civilian contractors. There were three more
Suicide bombs in February that killed
Fifty-six in Arbil, fifty-three in
Iskandariya, and forty-seven in
1030 Central Baghdad. In March in twin attacks
A hundred and seventy-one were killed in
Baghdad and Kerbala, and a car bomb
Killed twenty-eight in a Baghdad hotel,
The Jebel Lebanon. A thousand-pound
1035 Bomb left a crater ten feet deep outside
That was twenty feet wide. In Falluja
Insurgents fired from roofs on a convoy
Driving General Abizaid, Commander
Of US forces in the Middle East,
1040 And Major-General Charles Swannack, eighty-
Second Airborne. And eleven days later
Insurgents attacked three police stations
Killing seventeen police officers
And freeing eighty-seven prisoners. Eighty-
1045 Second Airborne raided and searched houses
For weapons and insurgents, and shoot-outs
Took place with Fallujans. Rising violence
Led to American withdrawal from
The city. There were now incursions, and
1050 Patrols round Qusay and Uday's palace.
The new policy was foot patrols, less
Aggressive raids, humanitarian aid,
Co-operation with local leaders.

Falluja had strategic importance
1055 In view of the plan to build a pipeline

To bring oil from Iraq's Mosul oilfields
To Haifa in Israel, reconstructing
The pipeline built by British Petroleum
In 1935, inactive since
1060   The British mandate in Palestine's end
In 1948 when the oil flow
Was redirected through Syria. This
Would solve Israel's energy crisis and
Provide cheap oil that could be tankered out
1065   To the US. Falluja lay between
Baghdad and Haditha where the pipeline
Had been redirected, and should be quiet,
Not a nest of anti-Western forces.
During an incursion in Falluja
1070   Insurgents ambushed a quiet convoy of
Private military contractors from
Blackwater, USA who were making
A delivery for food caterers
On March the thirty-first 2004.
1075   With machine-gun fire and grenades they killed
The four contractors and set their corpses
Ablaze, dragged them through streets and then hung them
Over a bridge crossing the Euphrates.
Photos were released by news agencies.
1080   There was outrage in the US. Next day
Brigadier General Kimmitt, deputy
Director of all operations for
The US military in Iraq,
Announced there would be an "overwhelming"
1085   Response: "We will pacify that city."
Two days later the Joint Task Force ordered
1st Marine Expeditionary Force
To conduct offensive operations
Against Falluja. Marine commanders
1090   Preferred surgical strikes and raids against
Suspects. Next day two thousand US troops
Encircled Falluja. *Operation*
Vigilant Resolve had begun, a fierce,
Uncompromising thrust. Aerial strikes
1095   Hit four homes and gunfire lasted all night.
The next day US troops took the local
Radio station. A third of Fallujans
Fled as one or two dozen hard-core groups
Of tough insurgents, armed with RPGs,
1100   Machine-guns, mortars, anti-aircraft guns,
Mostly supplied by Iraqi police,

Held out. They were led by al-Zarqawi –
Falluja was a Zarqawi stronghold
And full of remnants of Saddam's regime –
1105   Who in February wrote to bin Laden
That the Iraqi state was in the hands
Of the Shiites, who should now be opposed.
He claimed he had been responsible for
At least twenty-five suicide attacks.
1110   Bin Laden, harboured by Shiite Iran,
Could not give al-Qaeda's backing against
Shiites. He was angry that Zarqawi
Was focusing his suicide attacks
More on Iraqi Shias than US
1115   Soldiers. Under the banner of Salah
Ad-Din – Saladin – in the Third Crusade
Sunnis and Shias fought the Crusaders
Side by side. Now they were at odds with each
Other. Now there was widespread fighting in
1120   Central Iraq and Lower Euphrates
As Coalition forces were attacked
In many places by Mahdi-Army
Militias of Moqtada al-Sadr
And in Ramadi by Sunni rebels.
1125   Insurgents captured foreigners, killed some
And held others hostage to barter for
Concessions. Air bombardments rained bombs on
Insurgent positions in Falluja.
And Lockheed AC-130 gunships
1130   Attacked targets with Gatling guns' clustered
Barrels and howitzer shells. Snipers killed.
Many of the US troops were employed
By Blackwater USA, a private
Army that had been hired by the US
1135   Government as mercenaries, an *élite*
Praetorian Guard that acted like Saddam's
Republican Guard for global war on
Terror with their own military base,
A fleet of twenty aircraft and twenty
1140   Thousand troops run by a conservative,
Christian multi-millionaire who bankrolled
Bush; mercenaries hardened by much slaughter.
Wounded after a US air strike left
Shrapnel lodged in his chest as he fled near
1145   Al-Qaim, Zarqawi slipped back to Iran
Where he received temporary safe haven,
Visited the *Pasdaran*'s (Islamic

Revolutionary Guard Corps') training camps
And obtained logistical support from
1150 Its Qods Force while he recuperated
Among Iranian Shiites who asked him
To lure the US into an attack
On Iran. He returned to Falluja.
PSYOPs flushed out Iraqis by playing
1155 Deafening rock music. White phosphorus
Was used to light and screen. After three days
The US controlled about a quarter
Of Falluja, having taken a hit,
Twenty-seven killed, but had wiped out some key
1160 Insurgents' positions. Bremer announced
A unilateral cease-fire under
Pressure from Iraq's Governing Council,
And a Shia-Sunni food convoy brought
Humanitarian relief. Six hundred
1165 Iraqis had died, half non-combatants,
But insurgents still controlled Falluja.
On April the thirteenth US Marines
Were attacked from a mosque, which was destroyed.
Two days later an F-16 plane dropped
1170 A two-thousand-pound guided bomb on north
Falluja. On May the first the US
Withdrew. A new Falluja Brigade, armed
With US weapons, took over under
An ex-Baathist, General Saleh. When he
1175 Was named as persecuting Shiites for
Saddam, he was replaced by Mohammed
Latif. By September the Brigade had
Passed its weapons to the insurgency.
The Sunni triangle looked a lost cause.

1180 Now a long siege began as US troops
Camped on Falluja's outskirts, scowling at
The Sunni bastion against new Mongols.
In this stand-off Zarqawi was brutal,
Kidnapping and beheading captives on
1185 The internet such as Nicholas Berg
Though not receiving official backing
From al-Qaeda despite several letters
He wrote to bin Laden, which were captured.
On April the fifth Zarqawi'd written
1190 To bin Laden that he had two options:
To stay in Iraq, confront those opposed
To his methods; or wage *jihad* elsewhere.

The kidnapping of Berg on the ninth showed
He'd decided to remain in Iraq.
1195   In the six months of siege Zarqawi claimed
Ten kidnappings – American, British,
Italian, Somali, South-Korean
And Turkish citizens – and took hostage
Several Iraqi security guards.
1200   All were brought to Falluja, and some were
Beheaded by Zarqawi like Eugene
Armstrong and perhaps his colleague Kenneth
Bigley, a Briton who was freed, then caught
And butchered, and other groups followed suit.
1205   His brutality was obscured by news
Of Coalition wrongs at Abu Ghraib,
Assaults on mosques, killings of civilians,
Murders of wounded men and home searches
Without the required presence of husbands.
1210   A myth grew round Zarqawi, who was now
A Muslim hero who had left the slums
And risen by studying the *Koran*,
And a symbol of *jihad*ists' struggle
Against Western hegemony and might.

1215   And now I watch this cruel creature, this *thing*.
Nicholas Berg, a US businessman,
Had travelled to Iraq to seek work for
His company, rebuilding antennas.
He had disappeared in Baghdad, kidnapped
1220   By Muntada al-Ansar, which had links
With Zarqawi, was held in Falluja.
On May the eighth he met a dreadful fate.
I scan a video on the internet
Titled 'Abu Musab al-Zarqawi
1225   Slaughters an American'. Five men stand
Before a white wall, dressed in black, wearing
Ski masks and *shemagh*s. On the floor, knees up,
Sits Berg in an orange jumpsuit, quite still,
His wrists bound at his back. The central guard,
1230   With eye-holes in his balaclava hood,
Legs astride, sinisterly masked and slouched,
Reads from two sheets in firm-voiced Arabic.
Berg listens without understanding, pale,
Face white, blinks once as rough Zarqawi says
1235   That the killing is to retaliate
For US troops' abuse of prisoners at
Abu Ghraib prison. The paper rustles.

After nearly three minutes of reading
To camera, al-Zarqawi puts away
1240   His statement, draws a long knife from his chest,
Bends behind Berg and thrusts him to the floor
So he is lying bound on his left side.
Then all converge and stoop. One in a white
Shemagh with slit for eyes pins down Berg's side
1245   To the floor, while Zarqawi grabs his head
And energetically saws at his neck.
A dreadful scream escapes Berg's dying throat
As they all chant "*Allahu Akbar*", "God
Is great." Zarqawi wrestles with the knife,
1250   Cuts and hacks into Berg's neck as blood wells
Round his feet as if slaughtering a lamb,
Saws like a butcher ridding a carcass
Of its unwanted head. At last the white-
Scarfed terrorist holds up the severed head
1255   By its hair, eyes closed and looking mournful,
Blood dripping from the jagged flesh beneath
The chin and ears, and shows it to camera
As the picture fades to black. I feel sick
At the barbarity of the attack
1260   On a fellow human with a blunt knife.
Zarqawi who had learned all the *Koran*
Had seen Berg as a butcher sees raw meat
That must be hacked and hung upon a hook,
Head tossed aside. The hacked torso was dumped
1265   On a frequented Baghdad overpass.
I go back to the start where Berg sits still
And hope he was drugged so his brain was numbed
And could not take in the bestial violence
He's about to endure. I watch it through
1270   Once more, noting Zarqawi wields the knife
With his right hand, which he only used for
Eating and shaking hands, a room-mate said.
But it was him, a voice analysis
By the CIA concluded: the masked
1275   Man who read the statement was Zarqawi
"With high probability". And I stare
In cold revulsion at a barbarian,
And more than that, at an evil-doer.
Such disregard for his hostage, such coarse
1280   Manhandling as if Berg were butchers' joint,
Not spirit, such brutal intent to harm
Were of the worst murders, the Holocaust,
And outside civilised society.

⌐Evil is not just the absence of Good –
1285   Ordered being as it should be, kindness,
Moral excellence that's commendable –
But base antithesis, reverse of Good,
Moral depravity and turpitude.
Evil's a deliberate will to harm,
1290   To inflict pain, by a disordered soul.
And Zarqawi could not plead that Allah,
The Islamic embodiment of Good,
Wanted this butchering, and that his end –
Spreading the new Caliphate through the world –
1295   Justified his gruesome means, his terror:
Desinewing flesh, ripping with a knife.
I still feel sick in my stomach, crying
Out for a fellow human, cry within:
'If God's almighty and perfectly good,
1300   Why does evil exist? Because He wants
To obliterate it and's unable,
In which case He is not almighty? Or,
Because He's able but does not want to,
In which case He's not perfectly good?'
1305   And then I know the universe is filled
With *yin-yang* opposites, order-chaos,
That God created a dialectic
Between Good and Evil in which the Good
Slowly triumphs after a long struggle,
1310   The triumph of universal order;
That God created conflict as a means
Of achieving an end that's good for souls.
Now Berg's spirit rose, floating up to Light,
Released from torment and its time of trial,
1315   Triumphing over Hellish hacking pain,
Serene as it wafted to Paradise
Where it would lodge before being reborn
To a new life and combat with Evil,
Eternal Recurrence of soul-making.
1320   God made both dark and light as opposites
That together make up One atmosphere.

Bush, watching the video film of Berg
Sitting before his captors in orange,
Revolted by the beheading, wandered
1325   To the window and looked up at the stars.
The One that enfolded all opposites
Embraced Christian and Muslim crusaders,
And Sunnis and Shiites, beheaders and

Beheaded in its vast, reconciling
1330 Structure and pattern. One man lost his life
Because Bush had decided to invade
A country, but his decision and this
Barbarous behaviour and the victim's fate
Were also reconciled in a pattern
1335 In which war and peace were fixed, death and life,
And to the One they were routine events
As Earth span round the sun and space-time rushed
Forward into the infinite beyond,
Still expanding from the hot beginning,
1340 The Big Bang exploding the universe
From an infinitesimal point that
Poured particles into blasted space-time
Which condensed into matter and photons.
The One gave birth to the universe in
1345 An explosion like a cruise-missile strike
And within the ensuing clouds of smoke
Poured souls into bodies and took them back.
And there was a system that would cope with
A man who'd been beheaded and would go
1350 To the after-life in the infinite
And progress as the One required he should.
All things happened in accord with a plan.

Now the Shiites triumphed, supported by
The Americans who had been convinced
1355 They would only defeat insurgency
If Shiites controlled the State and Sunnis.
In June a six-city offensive killed
A hundred and thirty-five people in
Baquba, Falluja and Ramadi,
1360 Mosul, Baghdad and Basra. In July
Seventy-one more were killed in Baquba.
In August fourteen Christian worshippers
Were killed in bomb attacks on five churches
Across Baghdad and Mosul, scores injured.
1365 Moqtada's Shiites and America
Made common cause to squash insurgency
Before the Presidential elections
In November and Iraq's elections
In January 2005. The truce
1370 Collapsed in August when Moqtada called
On his militia to fight US troops.
There were clashes in Najaf, Kerbala
And Sadr City. More than three hundred

Militants were killed. Iyad Allawi,
1375   The interim PM, pardoned many
Insurgents and invited Moqtada
To join the elections. But he refused.
Lacking funds from the Shiite middle class
Who did not want politicised clerics,
1380   He turned holy places into strongholds
For his militia – Najaf's cemetery
And *Imam* Ali mosque; and though low in
Funds and supported by few Shiites, he
Operated from sanctuaries the US
1385   And interim Government could not fight.
Now Sistani negotiated peace
And Moqtada's militia left Najaf
Safely and dispersed, the US withdrew
And Iraqi police restored order.
1390   The Shiites issued a *fatwa* banning
Armed action against the occupiers
And Moqtada called for the cessation
Of armed struggle. To Zarqawi this showed
The Shiites were traitors who colluded
1395   With the "new Mongols", the Americans.
He stepped up sectarian violence against
The Shias. The Shiite insurgency
Was over but there was now civil war
As Sunnis attacked Shias, who countered.
1400   The US, having silenced the Shias,
Now concentrated on the Sunnis in
Falluja, who had withstood air attacks
And shells, and who they wanted to root out
Before the coming January elections
1405   And catch Zarqawi, their priority.

Bush was re-elected by 286
Votes to 251. Kerry conceded,
Having declined to dispute Ohio.
Bush's approval rating had fallen
1410   Since May 2003, the heady day
He landed on the aircraft-carrier
USS Abraham Lincoln and spoke,
Saying major combat operations
In the Iraq war were now at an end.
1415   Then sixty-six per cent were on his side.
But though his star was waning Bush was pleased
And looked forward to further victories in
The War on Terror in his second term.

The second Falluja battle began
1420 On November the eighth six days after
Bush was re-elected.Twenty thousand
Americans and two thousand members
Of Iraq's National Guard, Peshmerga and
Shiites surrounded the city where five
1425 Thousand Sunnis awaited an attack
Together with resisting residents
Who had chosen to remain, fight and die.
Most civilians had fled, and booby traps
And high-up sniper nests riddled the lanes
1430 As *Operation Phantom Fury* struck.
US and Iraqi troops entered streets
From west and south, and took the hospital
And villages by the Euphrates, then
Secured Jurf Kas Sukr Bridge – diversions.
1435 Electricity shut off, from the north
US combat troops and British Black Watch
Advanced under intense air bombardment,
Attacked the train station, and on the north
Were on Highway 10, meeting resistance.
1440 For nine days battle raged as US troops
Advanced block by block making house-to-house
Searches to flush insurgents out to sand,
The desert where they would have no cover.
Crouching, troops looked to left and right, then ran
1445 Doubled-up into an entrance and then
Crept with guns raised to surprise insurgents.
In a mosque a few US soldiers found
A wounded Iraqi fighter propped by
A wall. Prodding him, one pronounced, "He is
1450 Playing possum." One said, "He isn't dead."
Another shot the Iraqi and said,
"He is now," shocking with his casualness.
Bodies were shown partially turned to ash.
Skin had peeled off or hung like gloves, due to
1455 MK-77 white-phosphorus bombs,
Similar to napalm, used as screening or
Marking agents which should not be used on
Civilians under the Convention on
Certain Conventional Weapons, passed in
1460 1980, Protocol III, to which
The US was not a signatory.
By the sixteenth most insurgents had been
Killed or captured. More than two thousand were
Thought to have died. The city was ruined.

1465	A great victory was claimed by the US
	And interim Government, but pockets
	Of resistance remained until Christmas.
	About fifty US soldiers had died
	And hundreds had been wounded. Six thousand
1470	Civilians died. The Sunnis had been crushed,
	And with them the Iraqi resistance
	Against the "new Mongols" and the struggle
	Of Zarqawi's Salafi *jihad*ists –
	Although suicide bombings continued
1475	Against Shiites and other ethnic groups.
	And now the Shias were behind the State.
	Bin Laden wrote to the inhabitants
	Of the smashed city saying Falluja
	Was a "heroine", comparing Saddam's
1480	Massacre at Halabja with the one
	At Falluja, where the "Pharaoh" Bush was
	Responsible for assassinating
	Several thousand Sunnis in a "Zionist
	Crusade". On December the twenty-seventh
1485	Bin Laden granted recognition to
	Al-Zarqawi, calling him the *Emir*
	Of the al-Qaeda organisation
	In Iraq, and agreed to support him
	In fighting the Shiites, who ruled Iraq,
1490	Collaborating with the Americans.
	He could now take this position without
	Alienating Iran as the US
	And Moqtada's Shias were on the same
	Side in making Iraq's elections work
1495	And in delivering Bush's victory –
	And as al-Qaeda was Iranian-run
	Now bin Laden was harboured by Iran.
	Though bin Laden was in the tribal hills
	Between Afghanistan and Pakistan
1500	When not in Iran, he was now supreme
	Leader of the Iraqi resistance,
	Having just appointed Zarqawi as
	His own *Emir* and snatched the leadership
	Of Iraq's resistance from other groups.
1505	He urged Zarqawi to plan strikes inside
	The US (according to a report
	Declassified in May 2007
	By Bush), advice Iran greatly approved.
	Bin Laden's vision of *jihad* focused

1510	On the US as primary target.
	Zarqawi's vision of *jihad* differed.
	He focused on the Iraqi Shias.
	Zawahiri proclaimed that bin Laden
	Was "the new Che Guevara", now a myth.
1515	Zarqawi, now al-Qaeda leader in
	The Middle East, had legitimacy
	And could turn Sunnis against *ulama*s,
	And fight Shias with new authority.
	He renamed his al-Tawhid wal-Jihad
1520	"Al-Qaeda in Mesopotamia",
	Which was soon called "Al-Qaeda in Iraq".
	In fact, Falluja remained a ghost town
	And though al-Qaeda had been degraded
	Many insurgents escaped, Zarqawi
1525	Among them, and regrouped and new attacks
	Took place round the city. Insurgency
	Continued and intensified again.

BOOK SEVEN

ISRAEL FIGHTS IRAN'S PROXIES

SUMMARY

O Baldwin, Godfrey of Bouillon's brother
You who in feudal France were aghast at
The Seljuqs' advance that wrested control
From the Abbasid caliphs of Baghdad,
5   Defeated Byzantines at Manzikert,
Captured Antioch and coastal Asia
Minor as a resurgent Islam near
Constantinople had made pilgrimage
To Jerusalem's Holy Sepulchre
10   Of Christ's entombment difficult, if not
Impossible, and led to Emperor
Alexius Comnenus's appeal
For aid from the West of ten ninety-five;
You who'd travelled to Constantinople
15   With your two brothers Godfrey and Eustace
And your cousin Baldwin of Le Bourg, and
The main Crusading force, and there met up
With Bohemond's, Raymond of Saint-Gelles' and
Robert of Flanders' armies, and, with some
20   Four thousand mounted knights and twenty-five
Thousand infantry, captured Nicaea,
Then Antioch, and, after a siege, with
Twelve hundred cavalry and twelve thousand
Foot soldiers camped outside and resupplied
25   From the port at Jaffa with siege towers
And scaling-ladders, took Jerusalem
And slaughtered all Muslims and Jews – all men,
Women and children; you who saw Godfrey,
French-speaking German Duke of Lower Lorraine,
30   Elected to govern the Crusader
State of Jerusalem with the modest
Title of Defender of the Holy
Sepulchre, a Church state under Daimbert,
Archbishop of Pisa, to whom Godfrey
35   And you paid homage, and, when Godfrey died,
On November the eleventh 1100
Assumed the title of king and now ruled
A feudal Kingdom of Jerusalem;
O Baldwin, who ruled Jerusalem for

40	Eighteen years though Antioch was returned
	To the Byzantine Emperor, and had
	The County of Edessa established
	In the upper Euphrates region, which
	You passed to your cousin Baldwin of Le
45	Bourg, you got to know the land that is now
	Israel, Jordan, Syria, Lebanon and
	Iraq and believed in Crusader states
	With defended frontiers; o Baldwin,
	King of Jerusalem which was shown on
50	Christian maps as the centre of the world,
	You were surrounded by Islam, you knew,
	Better than all, the goal of Crusading,
	Help me now I describe Israel's concern
	To preserve Jerusalem's unity
55	And prevent it from being divided;
	Help me describe the menace of Iran.
	Help me now I describe the cruel conflict
	Between Israel and Hezbollah while bin
	Laden plotted the new Caliphate in
60	Iran and in Balochistan, and our
	Jerusalem's place in our Middle East,
	How a world order will again be based
	On Jerusalem as in your time, with
	Harmony between Christians, Muslims, Jews.
65	In January the Sanhedrin Council –
	A court of seventy-one sages that met
	In the Jerusalem Temple's Chamber
	Of the Hewn Stones, the supreme religious
	Authority in Israel which possessed
70	Legislative and judicial powers –
	Convened for the first time since 425.
	In February it discussed rebuilding
	The Third Temple to welcome the Messiah,
	For it was written that after the First
75	Temple was sacked by Nebuchadnezzar
	And the Second Temple sacked by Titus,
	A Third Temple would be in place before
	The Second Coming of Jesus. Reports
	Stated much of the Temple'd already
80	Been prefabricated and just needed
	To be assembled on the Mount. How blind
	Was Dayan when, in 1967,
	Having captured the Temple Mount, he gave
	It back to the Waqf, the Muslim body

85	That has governed it since Saladin's time,
	Since 1187. Preparations
	For animal sacrifices were made,
	As commanded by the Law of Moses
	(Ritual cleansing in red heifer's ashes)
90	For the first time since AD 70.
	It was discussed where on the Temple Mount
	The Messiah's Third Temple should be built.
	One view held the Temple stood where the Dome
	Of the Rock – built by the Fifth Ummayad
95	Caliph Abd al-Malik on the spot where
	Mohammed made his night journey to Heaven,
	One of Islam's most holy sanctuaries –
	Now stands, which can only be razed by war.
	Another view, Kaufman's, held the Temple
100	Stood north of the Dome of the Rock and could
	Be rebuilt beside it without damage.
	The first view would have been the Crusaders',
	Of those who see a Christian-Muslim clash;
	The second view that of humane men who
105	Want Christians and Muslims to co-exist.
	This is the view of Universalists.
	That the Sanhedrin was considering
	Rebuilding the Temple after some two
	Thousand years suggests the final events –
110	And the Second Coming – were drawing nigh.
	Bush delivered his State-of-the-Union
	Speech on the Capitol steps on February
	The third 2005. Just as penguins
	Fill a vast shoreline near the Antarctic,
115	A hundred thousand pairs all standing still,
	So Americans stood still before Bush.
	His speech was lofty. It had been coloured
	By his reading of the Jewish former
	Soviet dissident Natan Sharansky's
120	Book, *The Case for Democracy, The Power*
	Of Freedom to Overcome Tyranny
	And Terror. Sharansky, the Minister
	For Jerusalem and Diaspora
	Affairs in the Israeli Government,
125	Strongly argued that US policy
	Should be guided by ideals, to export
	Freedom to the Arab world, to prevent
	All terrorists and terrorist states from
	Obtaining weapons of mass destruction

130	And to give the free world weapons of mass
	Construction – Israel's own firm policy.
	Bush's long speech was philosophical
	And leaned towards Israel as he spoke up
	For freedom. He said that the terrorist
135	Zarqawi'd declared war on the "evil"
	Principle of democracy, and that
	America would "stand with the allies
	Of freedom to support democratic
	Movements in the Middle East" and to end
140	"Tyranny in our world". The US had
	"No right, no desire and no intention
	To impose our form of government on
	Anyone else" whereas "our enemies…
	Seek to impose and expand an empire
145	Of oppression, in which a tiny group
	Of brutal and self-appointed rulers
	Control every aspect of every life".
	He was referring to the Caliphate
	And to the few al-Qaeda leaders who
150	Were trying to impose it on the world.
	He said, "Iran remains the world's primary
	State sponsor of terror", that it pursues
	Nuclear weapons yet deprives "its people
	Of the freedom they seek and deserve", words
155	Which pleased Israel. It seemed that Bush was now
	A megaphone for Israel's policy.

Iraq's January-the-thirtieth elections
Were won by al-Dawa, al-Jaafari's
Shiite party which opposed the presence
160 Of US forces in the Middle East
But kept some distance from Iran. And so
The liberators who had spent no less
Than 656.1 billion dollars
In freeing Iraq so the Syndicate
165 Could make arrangements to pipe out the oil
And recoup the outlay in tanker loads
Were told to cease to be occupiers
And to leave Iraq. The insurgency
Continued. Each month there were big suicide
170 Bomb attacks. The Sunnis had boycotted
The polling. Many suicide attacks
Were made against Shiites in February.
Smarting at being called "foreign fighter"
By some Americans and Iraqis,

175	In May Zarqawi taunted the US:
	"Who is the foreigner, cross-worshippers?
	You are the ones who came to Muslim lands
	From your own distant corrupt land." But al-
	Qaeda wanted an Iraqi to lead
180	The national uprising in Iraq:
	Bin Laden thought the US had set up
	A Jordanian bogeyman to suggest
	Foreigners had brought chaos to Iraq,
	That Iraqis liked being occupied.
185	Zarqawi had damaged al-Qaeda's cause,
	It was time an Iraqi took over.
	The aim of the insurgency was now
	Not just to expel Coalition troops
	But to help ethnic groups assert themselves.
190	Like Yugoslavia, Iraq was now
	Being Balkanised. Ethnic militias
	And paid gangs of criminals carried out
	Hundreds of kidnappings, beatings, killings.
	Kurds, Shiites and Sunnis fought each other.
195	On one day in July a hundred and
	Fifty were killed. In August a million
	Shia pilgrims in procession heard talk
	Of suicide bombers and stampeded,
	Trampling a thousand Iraqis to death
200	On a bridge over the Tigris, which they
	Crossed barefoot, carrying their shoes. The bridge
	Was littered with mixed-up shoes, and the dead
	Lined hospital corridors and pavements.
	The Sunnis now wanted to take part in
205	December's coming general elections,
	And throughout 2005 Sunnis warned
	Al-Qaeda and foreign fighters that they
	Should not attack polling-stations. A split
	Took place between Sunni groups and foreign
210	Fighters led by Zarqawi. Sunni troops
	Assassinated some Al-Qaeda men.
	An anti-Al-Qaeda militia,
	The Anbar Revolutionaries, was formed
	By a former Baathist, Ahmed Ftaikhan.
215	Now Zarqawi fled to Iran and hid.
	The Parliamentary elections were won
	By United Iraqi Alliance
	Which included the Islamic Dawa
	Party. Jaafari was the first full-term
220	Post-war Prime Minister. The US backed

Nouri al-Maliki, a Shiite who
Was less close to Iran, and he replaced
Jaafari in April 2006.
As the new Prime Minister. Now he vowed
225   To crack down on insurgents, whom he called
"Organised armed groups who're acting outside
The State and outside the law." Soon after,
Insurgents' suicide bombings increased.

In London three bombs blew up on tube trains
230   And one on a bus in Tavistock Square,
Killed fifty-two Britons going to work.
Four young Asians from Leeds suicide-bombed
Public transport to protest at two wars.
All four were caught on closed-circuit TV
235   At King's Cross that morning, with haversacks
On shoulders, laughing, carefree, as if on
A day out. Martyrdom videos of two
Showed they were loosely linked to Al-Qaeda,
For Zawahiri made statements on both.
240   So died four young men who'd been Islamised
And looked to al-Qaeda – and Paradise.

In the last two weeks of August Sharon,
The Israeli Prime Minister, expelled
Nearly ten thousand Jewish settlers
245   From twenty-one settlements in Gaza
And four nestling in the northern West Bank,
Which had been built illegally in breach
Of international law in four decades
Of war-based military occupation.
250   The first day Israeli soldiers began
Evicting Jewish settlers from Gaza
At Neve Dekalim, the settlers did all
They could to prevent the security
Forces from getting in, burnt barricades.
255   Midnight was the deadline, police had maps
Showing each house where families had left
Willingly and each where they'd be dragged out.
Then in they came, smashing down barricades,
Dragging screaming Israelis from their homes,
260   Bundling them onto removal buses
As German troops had done to Polish Jews
During the Second World War, only now
It was Israelis de-ghettoing Jews.
No one was spared. The old pleaded with troops.

265
Distraught women wailed while young men wrestled
With those sent to enforce Sharon's order
So the Road Map could proceed. Sharansky,
Who featured in the State-of-the-Union
Speech, had resigned as his Minister for
270
Jerusalem and Diaspora Affairs
In May over withdrawing settlers and
Soldiers from the Gaza Strip. Some gathered
In the main synagogue, with tearful prayers
Bore out the *menorah* in a mournful
275
Procession before TV cameras
That reconstructed the scene on the Arch
Of Titus in Rome showing what happened
After the Second Temple was destroyed
In far-off Jerusalem. A small group
280
Of Rabbis, led by Yosef Dayan, cursed
Sharon with the Pulsa diNura, called
On the Angel of Death to intervene
And kill him, a "Heavenly punishment",
A teaching in the Kabbalah's *Zohar*,
285
Based on the Babylonian *Talmud*:
Elisha ben Abuya's encounter
With the angel Metatron, who was lashed
With sixty pulses of fire. Sharon shrugged,
Knowing that Heaven did not punish men,
290
Aware of the traditional saying,
"You've not made it in politics until
You've been cursed by the Pulsa diNura."
He ignored the curse, bent on delivering
A settlement-free Gaza as soldiers
295
Bulldozed all settlement buildings and all
Perimeter fences. On September
The eleventh they left, closing the border
Fence at Kissufum. The Likud Party
Bitterly opposed Sharon's policy
300
But the Israeli electorate liked
The conception of the Arab Road Map.
Sharon defeated a leadership bid
And scorned and defied the Angel of Death.

Days after Israel withdrew from Gaza
305
Hurricane Katrina swept in across
Florida. The eye of the hurricane
Made landfall on August the twenty-ninth,
And howled through and battered New Orleans.
Whirling wind devastated the Gulf Coast.

310	It lashed the city, and a storm surge up
	To thirty-five feet high poured in and breached
	Nearly every levee, flooding four-fifths
	Of all homes, killing nearly two thousand
	Poor folk and leaving seven hundred missing.
315	A hundred and twenty thousand homes were
	Unsalvageable. The American
	Red Cross said the disaster was above
	Any magnitude seen in the US.
	The flood waters lay in the coastal belt
320	For weeks, the damage was estimated
	At eighty-one billion dollars in all.
	Bush had declared a major disaster.
	Three days later National Guard troops entered
	The city. The same day Bush arrived by
325	Helicopter. Shocked at the vast floods he
	Said the success of the recovery
	Was "not enough". Soon it was claimed that Bush
	Had not acted on being warned of floods,
	That he'd ignored warnings that New Orleans
330	Was facing a massive catastrophe,
	That flood control had been chopped from budgets,
	That he had appointed incompetent
	Managers of FEMA, the Federal
	Emergency Management Agency,
335	That the federal response was limited
	Due to the Iraq war. The New York Times
	Said Bush seemed casual and careless and did
	Not understand the depth of the crisis.
	Other papers asked why the armed forces
340	Had not been forced to help. Bush was too slow
	To respond to the storm and accepted
	Full responsibility for failures
	By the federal Government in handling
	The emergency. He was determined
345	To transform himself from old fecklessness
	By will to honour. Later Katrina
	Would be seen as a tipping point in his
	Political fortunes, from which there would
	Be no recovery. In Israel it
350	Was said that Katrina was a judgement,
	God's punishment on the faithless US
	For backing the Road Map and coercing
	Israel to grant Palestinian demands,
	For breaking God's Covenant with Israel,
355	Renouncing the new Six-Day-War borders,

Surrendering the ancient Promised Land.

In September 2005 Iran's
President Ahmadinejad addressed
The UN in New York. He took his place
360   On the podium before the delegates
And TV cameras, and as soon as he
Said "In the name of Allah" he felt bathed
In light. He later described what happened:
"One of our group told me when I began
365   To say '*Bismillah Mohammed*' he saw
A green light come from around me, and I
Was placed inside this aura. I felt it
Myself. I felt that the atmosphere changed
Suddenly, and for those twenty-seven
370   Or twenty-eight minutes, all the leaders
Of the world did not blink. Not one of them
Moved an eyelid, I don't exaggerate.
They looked as if a hand was holding them
There, and had just opened their eyes." He felt
375   This green light was "a light from Heaven", a sign
That *Imam* Mahdi, the Hidden *Imam*,
Who disappeared, a child, in 874,
Would soon reappear and reign on Earth for
Seven years. A Hojjatieh, a member of
380   A messianic group that served the Twelfth
Imam, Ahmadinejad urged Iran
To prepare for the Mahdi's coming by
Turning the country into a mighty
And advanced Islamic society
385   And by avoiding the corruption and
Excesses of the West. There had to be
Chaotic conditions for the Mahdi
To return, and the best way to create
These was for *jihad* to annihilate
390   Israel and the US – via Hezbollah
In Lebanon and Hamas in Gaza.
The Hidden *Imam*'s Second Coming would
Mirror the Second Coming of Christ who
Would come as his deputy when the world
395   Converted to Islam. The Mahdi would
Rule the world from Kufa, a hundred miles
South of Baghdad, one reason why Iran
Was so involved in Iraq. He would reign
For seven years and persecute the Jews,
400   Traits he shared with the Western Antichrist.

As the Hidden *Imam*'s prophet, he saw
Himself as having access to Heaven,
But to the West he was the Antichrist's
False Prophet whose sole access was to Hell.
405 Some thought Satan had sent Hellish green light.
Ahmadinejad's green light was not pure
White Light mystics know, the universal
Light of Heaven that will be known by all
In the Messiah's global domination.

410 Now Sharon, Israeli Prime Minister
Who had endorsed the Road Map and withdrawn
From Gaza while keeping Israel's control
Of coastline and air space, who had expelled
Nearly ten thousand settlers in August
415 2005, been challenged by his foe,
Benjamin Netanyahu, in protest
At Likud's withdrawal from Gaza, in
November resigned from heated Likud,
Dissolved Parliament and formed Kadima
420 ("Forward"), a new centrist party. Likud's
New leader was Netanyahu. But then,
On December the eighteenth, Sharon had
A minor ischaemic stroke. An obese
Man, he had high cholesterol and in
425 Hospital a heart ailment was found. Bed
Rest was ordered, but he went back to work.
On January the fourth, just having drunk
Tea with Shimon Peres, he had a stroke.
After two operations lasting seven
430 And fourteen hours, the bleeding in his brain
Was stopped, but he slid into a coma,
Perhaps as his cerebral amyloid
Angiopathy (CAA) was made worse
By blood thinners for his December stroke.
435 Sharon was in a permanent coma,
Kept alive on a life-support machine,
A victim of his own obesity.
Or had an opponent of the Road Map
Or someone erasing his foreknowledge
440 Of the 9/11 strikes on the Twin Towers
Which had just been insured by Silverstein,
Wanting to wipe out all that Israel knew,
Arranged for him to have a "natural" stroke?
It was suggested that, a year before,
445 Arafat had been poisoned to remove

Him from his dealings in the peace process.
Was Sharon on a list of key players
Who should be taken out to win the peace?
Whatever the truth, Sharon now slipped in
450 To a persistent vegetative state
With very low chance of recovery,
His cognitive powers probably destroyed.
Ehud Olmert, who'd been in the Irgun,
The Jewish terror group that fought Britain,
455 And had been secretly in New York on
9/11, became Prime Minister
And carried on Sharon's Road-Map outlook
While keeping a watchful eye on Gaza
Where Hamas had just won an election
460 And on Hezbollah in the Lebanon
Which had, like Hamas, been armed by Iran.
Some said Israel needed someone tougher
Than Sharon to deal with Hamas's rise
And sort out Hezbollah's pro-Iran threats
465 As Sharon had not put Israelis first.

Dark night shrouded the gilded golden dome
Of the Askariya shrine in Samarra
Sixty-five miles north of Baghdad, a site
Where the Hidden *Imam*'s father, Hassan
470 Ali al-Askari, and his father,
Ali al-Hadi, tenth and eleventh
*Imam*s, rested in holy tombs. Men dressed
In police uniform approached the guards,
Overpowered them and tied them up, planted
475 Explosives. At 6.55 a.m.
As dawn broke over the gleaming gold dome
Two bombs blasted it into naked steel
And gaping blue sky, stripping its façade
To mud bricks. Every trace of the great dome,
480 To gild which the Shiite faithful paid up,
Was utterly destroyed. No one was hurt,
But one of Shiite Islam's holiest
And most revered shrines had been damaged in
An act of sectarian war. Shocked, outraged,
485 Hundreds of Shiites rushed to Moqtada
Al-Sadr, their cleric, in the vast slum
Sadr City, named after his father,
And awaited instructions. They were swift.
More than twenty Sunni mosques in Iraq
490 Suffered retaliatory attacks

With bombs, gunfire or arson that wiped out
Eighteen, including two Sunni clerics.
Al-Qaeda were blamed for scheming chaos.
Now Shias had been set against Sunnis
495 And rival mosques became targets for death.
A wave of kidnappings and dire murders
Was unleashed in the name of Allah's sects.

Tell, Muse, how the Syndicate had intrigued
For the US to bomb Iran's Natanz.
500 The plan devised by Cheney, Wolfowitz,
Rumsfeld and the Iraqi Chalabi
At the Office of the Vice-President
And at the Pentagon in Saturday
Policy salons with bright rightists was
505 To conquer Iraq and deal with the threat
Posed by Saddam, then ninety days later
Move to Iran. Rumsfeld's Iraq war plan
Fell apart as the insurgency spread
And the troops were too overextended
510 To move on to a neighbouring country.
The generals saw Iraq at breaking-point
And on retirement criticised the war,
By implication advising against
Further overextending the worn-out
515 Military. Talk of bombing Iran
Was not sabre-rattling or coercive
Diplomacy. A decision had been
Made to bomb Iran after November's
Elections. Cheney had dwelt on the threat,
520 Bush saw it as spreading democracy
And freedom and was comfortable with that.
Cheney drew up more plans during the spring
Of 2006, and the White House sought
A nuclear weapon to destroy Iran's
525 Uranium-enrichment plant at Natanz.
Marine General Peter Pace, who was chair
Of the joint Chiefs of Staff, talked Cheney and
Bush out of the nuclear option. Generals
Challenging Cheney and Bush on Iraq
530 Were slowing down the bombing of Iran
And pulled off an "April Revolution".
Cheney's cabal's plan to attack Iran
Complemented a Department-of-State
Project run out of the Bureau of Near
535 Eastern Affairs which would spend eighty-five

Million dollars in funding Iranian
And Syrian dissidents by November.
It was like the project that had funded
Chalabi before the Iraq War. It
540   Was run by none other than Liz Cheney,
Elder daughter of the Vice-President.
Cheney had made the plan and his daughter,
Mother of five, had implemented it
As Principal Deputy Assistant
545   For Near Eastern Affairs (PDAS).
She had travelled throughout the Middle East
And on two occasions told the US
Ambassador she'd see the Head of State
Alone, a departure from protocol
550   As the ambassador represented
The Government in the country. It seems
Cheney's daughter had met the Israeli
Head of State on her own to talk Iran.
She resigned in the spring, 2006
555   And by the summer US policy
Had shifted from overextending troops
To negotiating with Iran, though
It was still on that Iran would be bombed.

As Cheney and Israel agreed Iran
560   Should be attacked the coming November,
Israel prepared the ground to bomb Iran.
The main consideration was Iran's
Two proxies in Gaza and Lebanon,
Hamas and Hezbollah, who, if Iran
565   Were attacked, would fire rockets at Israel
From west and north while Iran fought from east,
Attacking both rear and flank, extending
Israel on three fronts. To restrict Hamas
In late 2003/early 04
570   Israel assassinated three Hamas
Leaders, and in self-protection and at
Iran's urging Hamas had recognised
Hezbollah's primacy. Khaled Mashal,
Hamas leader, had signed a strategic
575   Accord with Hezbollah's chief Nasrallah.
Hamas was now protected by Iran
And Hezbollah, Hezbollah by Iran
And Hamas. Any attack on one would
Bring a riposte from the others. Israel
580   Needed to crush the threats from west and north

Before tackling Iran. The agreed plan
Was to degrade Hamas, then Hezbollah
So two fronts were protected when Israel
Turned on Iran. In each case Israel should
585 Be seen to be a victim of kidnaps.
Several Israeli officials went to
Washington separately to obtain
A green light for bombing Hezbollah and
To find out how much the US would bear.
590 They began with Cheney, won his support.
Israel's plan mirrored an American
Plan, drawn up in Cheney's office, to attack
Hezbollah as "a prelude" to a coming
US pre-emptive attack on Iran.
595 Cheney wanted Israel to move quickly.
Mossad infiltrated Hamas units
And Hezbollah troops to urge abductions
Of Israeli soldiers who should be sent
To Iran. Once there, they'd be a pretext
600 For Israel to land on Iranian soil.
Under the guise of retaliating
For Israeli troops who had been captured
In Gaza and Lebanon, Israel would
Fight wars against Hamas and Hezbollah,
605 Iran's clients, and degrade their weapons
So they would be quiet when Iran was bombed.

Hubris becomes *arté*, then nemesis.
Zarqawi arrogantly showed his face
In a promotional video, although
610 Like bin Laden he had a twenty-five-
Million-dollar price on his head and was
Assigned a higher priority than
Bin Laden or Zawahiri. Swollen
With confidence, swaggeringly convinced
615 He was untouchable after all his
Spectacular attacks – UN bombing,
Televised beheadings – which had ruined
America's dreams for Iraq, leader
Of "Al-Qaeda in Mesopotamia",
620 He was betrayed, news of his safe house leaked
To the Americans by Abu Haydr,
A detainee at Balad airbase who,
A mid-level Al-Qaeda operative,
After weeks of questioning which played on
625 His hatred for Iran and the Shias

Supplied enough information to send
Abu Mustafa and seventeen others
To a violent end by shooting and then
A gloomy spirit abode. Al-Qaeda
630 May have sanctioned his betrayal because
Of his anti-Shia stance, which Iran,
Al-Qaeda's protector, loathed. He revealed
That Zarqawi's "spiritual adviser"
Sheikh Abd al-Rahman went to Zarqawi
635 By changing cars several times and taking
A small blue car to Zarqawi's small house.
A drone high above Baghdad found the blue
Car and observed it to a concrete house
In the palm grove near Hibhib, which strangely –
640 Explaining why he had escaped capture –
Lay in a Shiite enclave, and ordered
A deadly strike. Two F-16 pilots
Flew to the "high-value" target. One plane
Dropped a five-hundred-pound laser-guided
645 Bomb and, minutes later, a second. Both
Hit their target, reducing the small house
To rubble. Iraqi forces arrived
First and found Zarqawi badly wounded.
Only he had survived the strike. He was
650 Being carried out on a stretcher when
American soldiers arrived. They took
Him from the Iraqis and a medic
Treated him, securing his airway. He
Spat blood and half-lost consciousness, drifting.
655 Just as a patient, injected before
An operation feels a coldness spread
Up from his legs and then in a fast wave
Through his chest to his heart and knows no more,
So Zarqawi succumbed to a coldness.
660 His breathing was laboured, then his lungs failed
And his pulse stopped. The cruel beheader
Of hostages and blower-apart of
Innocent Iraqis found his spirit
Sinking in an ocean of dimmest light,
665 Pulled down by thousands of atrocities
Against his fellow human beings which
Made his light-body denser than most, till,
As one who'd learned the whole *Koran* by heart,
Dreaming of a reward for martyrdom,
670 He found his new self in a pitch-dark cave
Where no brutality would do him good,

A place of justice where all bad men found
Their just deserts for all their bad actions.

675

Now two bodies lay side by side within
Balad airbase, naked with swathes of cloth
Round their midriffs. Zarqawi's wide round face,
Bearded, large eyes closed, showed on its left cheek
A smear of blood. All who came to see him
Recognised his face from the video,

680

And he was also identified by
Known scars and tattoos, and fingerprinting.
Sheikh al-Rahman lay beside him. He too
Had plunged downwards into the after-life
Drawn down by the weight of atrocities

685

He had encouraged as his adviser.
So died bin Laden's heir within Iraq,
And the leadership of "Al-Qaeda in
Mesopotamia" was transferred. It
Passed to Abu Hamza al-Muhajir,

690

His number two, an Islamic *Jihad*
Egyptian militant also known as
Abu Ayyub al-Masri. He added
"Al-Iraqi" to his name. He had been
Proclaimed in a Zawahiri video

695

Within forty-eight hours when it took two
To six weeks for Al-Qaeda to smuggle
Messages to media, and Al-Qaeda
Leaflets about "al-Iraqi" were in
Mosques within twenty-four hours of the strike.

700

Z'wahiri knew Zarqawi would be killed,
Al-Qaeda knew that he would be replaced
Because they had betrayed him to Jordan's
Intelligence before Abu Haydr,
Whom they had briefed, agreed he would appear

705

To crack and, protecting Zawahiri,
Identify al-Rahman and secure
The twenty-five-million-dollar bounty.
Now Al-Qaeda were reeling. Already
Seventeen more raids in and around Baghdad

710

Had reduced Al-Qaeda's effectiveness.

A document found in Zarqawi's house
Showed Zarqawi was trying to destroy
The US's alliance with Shiites
And goad the US to attack Iran

715

So American forces in Iraq

Would be weakened by the redeployment
Of US troops to Iran, and Iraq's
Resistance would be strengthened: "The question
Remains, how to draw the Americans
720   Into fighting a war against Iran?"
Six ways of inciting a war between
The two nations were then outlined. It now
Became clear that Zarqawi had set up
Numerous terrorist cells across Iraq,
725   All semi-autonomous in the style
Of Al-Qaeda and able to resume
Operations after his own demise.
Each had two aims: to oust foreign forces
And to foment bloody sectarian
730   Strife between Sunnis and Iraq's Shiites.
But now there was a will in the US
To return to Falluja and flush out
The remnants of the Sunni forces there.
One long last push began in September
735   And lasted till mid-January. Four years
After the start of the bitter fighting,
In autumn 2007 Falluja
Was handed to the Iraqi Forces
And provincial authority – now cleared.
740   Suicide bombings continued, mostly
In Baghdad, targeting the Government –
The Parliament building – and many mosques.

In mid-June 2006 the leaders
Of Russia, China, Iran, Pakistan,
745   Tajikistan and Kyrgyzstan all met
Under the umbrella of the Shanghai
Co-operation Organisation
To cement an alliance against all
Further intervention in Asia by
750   The West. The War on Terror seemed to have
Hardened the cement of this alliance
And created a nuclear bloc that
Was anti-Western in its far outlook.
There were oil and gas issues, for the most
755   Direct and cheap route from Central Asia
To the world's markets was across Iran
To the Persian Gulf, the best exit, but
US sanctions on Iran had blocked it.
A pipeline from the Dauletabad Gas
760   Field to the Caspian was projected

To continue through Iran to Turkey.
The Syndicate had banked on a friendly
Iran, and had strong oil and gas reasons
Either to change the regime in Iran
765   Or get Iran on the US's side
Through the influence of the pro-Syndicate
Russian and Communist Chinese leaders.

Israel fought a proxy war with Iran,
Which had armed Hamas, in the Gaza Strip.
770   Palestinians had fought Israeli troops
Since Gaza was occupied in the Six-
Day-War of 1967. Conflict
Worsened in the Second *Intifada*
Of September two thousand, a large-scale
775   Armed uprising in Gaza and West Bank.
In 2005 Israel disengaged,
Pulled out troops and dismantled settlements
But controlled Gaza's borders, coastline and
Air space except for the southern border.
780   Hamas announced a cease-fire, but other
Armed groups fired Qassam rockets at Israel
And these increased when Hamas ("Islamic
Resistance Movement") – a nineteen eighty-
Seven offshoot from the Palestinian wing
785   Of Egypt's Muslim Brotherhood, that urged
A Palestinian Islamic State
In the West Bank and Gaza, funded by
Saudi Arabia, Palestinian
Expats, and Iran – won an election
790   In March 2006. By latish June
Seven hundred and fifty-seven missiles had
Struck Israel since disengagement. Israel
Retaliated with artillery
And air strikes. On June the ninth a blast killed
795   Eight Palestinians on a Gaza beach.
As sheep graze on a distant hillside, snug
In the group identity of their flock
And raise their heads at a crash of thunder,
So the Ralia family felt secure
800   As they sat on a beach, and raised their heads
At a mortar's whine and thunder as they
Were struck and blown to bits in plumes of sand.
Hamas blamed Israeli artillery
And withdrew from its cease-fire, Israel blamed
805   Old ordnance or a Palestinian mine.

Hamas fired Qassam rockets, Israel fired
Missiles at the Gaza highway and killed
Eleven Palestinians. An incursion
By Hamas on June the twenty-fifth through
810 A makeshift tunnel into Israel killed
Two Israel Defence Force soldiers. Four more
Were wounded and Corporal Shalit captured
"In retaliation for the killing
Of the Ralia family on the beach" –
815 But digging the tunnel took three to six
Months and the attack was planned long before
The blast on the beach. Shalit's captors called
For the release of all female and young
Palestinian prisoners. Statements were made
820 By Hamas' military wing, Popular
Resistance Committees and the Army
Of Islam. Israeli forces entered
Khan Yunis to search for Shalit on June
The twenty-eighth in their *Operation*
825 *Summer Rains*. The Hamas leader Khaled
Mashal was in Syria, and Israeli
F-16s flew over Assad's palace
As a warning. Egypt sent two thousand
Five hundred policemen to the border
830 Of Egypt and Gaza to seal it off
And stop Shalit from being smuggled out.

Israel invaded Gaza "to find him".
Israeli planes bombed bridges to cut in
Half the Gaza Strip, and fired nine missiles
835 At Gaza's power station to reduce power
By two-thirds. Troops occupied the airport.
Air strikes took place on Hamas training camps.
Fatah militants captured a young Jew,
Asheri, from a West-Bank settlement,
840 Shot him and left him in an open field
Outside Ramallah. Israeli forces
Captured the four who had killed Asheri.
Now Al-Aqsa Martyrs' Brigades captured
An Israeli, Moskovich, who was found
845 "Having died of natural causes". Israel
Massed tanks on Gaza's northern border. Next
Morning, the twenty-ninth, naval vessels
Shelled Qassam sites and struck the pro-Hamas
Islamic University. Now tanks,
850 Soldiers and bulldozers entered Gaza

And arrested sixty-four officials
Of Hamas including Palestinian
Authority Cabinet ministers,
A third of the Hamas Cabinet, who
855 Were to be tried for failing to prevent
Acts of terror. Israel's Prime Minister
Ehud Olmert had approved all the names.
Now Israel bombarded the Gaza Strip,
Struck a Fatah office and Hamas block,
860 The Interior Ministry and the Prime
Minister's office with two missiles. On
July the fourth a Qassam rocket reached
Ashkelon. The next day two more landed.
The IDF were told to move farther
865 Into northern Gaza to push southwards
The militants out of Ashkelon's range.
On July the sixth Israeli soldiers
Reoccupied three former settlements
In northern Gaza. Soldiers swarmed from trees,
870 Tanks and helicopter gunships fired at
Militants who replied with machine-guns.
On July the twelfth, an Israeli plane
Dropped a five-hundred-and-fifty-pound bomb
On a Gaza building, aimed at Hamas
875 Militants led by Mohammed Deif,
And killed a family of nine. Afraid,
Residents headed for Gaza's border
With Egypt and blew a hole in the wall.
Despite the search Shalit could not be found.
880 The war would rumble on till November.
Now Israel switched attention to the north
And focused on Lebanon where a state
Within a state had aggressive intent.

Tell, Muse, how Hezbollah, "Party of God",
885 Fought a proxy war for Shiite Iran
And how Al-Qaeda, based in Iran since
The battle of Tora Bora, settled.
Hezbollah emerged as a militia
After Israel invaded Lebanon
890 In 1982 to suppress all
The entrenched PLO, and resisted
Israel's occupation of Lebanon.
Eventually, in 1985,
Israel pulled back to a security
895 Buffer zone fifteen kilometres wide

Along the northern border. Hezbollah
Leaders had been inspired by Khomeini,
The President of Iran. Formed to spread
Islamic revolution, Hezbollah's
900 Forces looked to Iran as they had been
Trained and organised by a contingent
Of Iranian Revolutionary Guards,
Its 1985 manifesto
Proclaimed ending "any colonialist"
905 (Meaning "Zionist") "entity" and then
Establishing an Islamic regime
And state in the Lebanon. Hezbollah
Leaders had called for the swift destruction
Of Israel, which was "built on lands wrested
910 From their owners". Such anger was behind
The kidnapping of John McCarthy by
Islamic *Jihad* in Lebanon in
1986 – he was held captive
For five years – and of Terry Waite a year
915 Later, the Archbishop of Canterbury's
Envoy who went to Lebanon to free
Four hostages and was held for four years
By *jihad*ists. From a small militia
Hezbollah had grown into a massive
920 Shia Islamic political and
Paramilitary organisation,
Its financial support drawn from Iran
(Sixty to a hundred million dollars
Each year, according to US figures),
925 Syria and Lebanese Shias' donations,
With seats in the Lebanese Government,
Radio and satellite TV stations
And programs for social development:
It ran clinics and schools, taught martyrdom.
930 It mounted the resistance to Israel.
Iran used Hezbollah as a proxy
To further its own goals in the region,
Which were to become the dominant power
In the Middle East with wmds,
935 And neutralise its main rival: Israel.
Iran had tried to dominate Iraq
From a Shia Crescent curled from Turkey through
Lebanon, Syria, Jordan, South Iraq,
An arc of extremism and terror.
940 The Shia resurgence looked on the brink
Of taking over all the Middle East.

Hezbollah, "God's army", had plans to run
The whole Middle East as Iran's agent.
Israel assassinated its leader,
945   Abbas al-Musawi, Amal's leader,
In 1992. He was replaced
By Hassan Nasrallah, who had studied
In Najaf and Qom and represented
Hezbollah in Iran, and whose fiery
950   Sermons had brought him a wide following.
Through the nineties his military campaigns
Inflicted relentless casualties that
Led Israel to withdraw from the south in
Two thousand, ending eighteen turbulent
955   Years of occupation and increasing
Hezbollah's great popularity in
Lebanon and all Islamic countries.
Nasrallah was credited with ending
Israel's occupation of Lebanon,
960   And a message went out to other groups
That Israel could be forced out elsewhere. Al-
Aqsa *Intifada* began a few
Months later to liberate Palestine.
Some said Hezbollah's actions were a part
965   Of a Shiite conspiracy to gain
Regional power, or a leadership bid
By Nasrallah for the region's Shias.
The organisation of Hezbollah
Now had a clear structure. Authority
970   And powers were in its religious leaders,
Flowed from *ulama* to community.
Ultimate clerical authority
Lay with Iran's Supreme Leader, to whom
Hezbollah's leaders appealed for guidance
975   And directives when they were divided.
After Khomeini died appeals to Iran
Were less frequent, but Khamenei was still
The overall authority, and boss.
It now opposed the Lebanese PM
980   Fouad Siniora and could mobilise
Hundreds of thousands in protest rallies.
Families of all Hezbollah fighters
Who were killed or wounded fighting Israel
Received compensation from a new fund
985   Of two million dollars run by Iran,
Initial payments: a thousand dollars.
President Ahmadinejad said in

Malaysia: "The real cure for the conflict's
To eliminate the Zionist regime."
990   Two hundred and fifty sets of British
Night-vision equipment sent to Tehran
To monitor the Afghan border for
Smuggled-in heroin from the Afghan
Poppy fields for the West, had been passed on
995   To Hezbollah for killing Israelis
During night-fighting in a moonless dark.
From May 2002 – when Al-Qaeda
Was based in Iran under Khamenei
In return for bin Laden's safe haven –
1000   Al-Qaeda settled in the Lebanon,
Arriving from Middle-Eastern countries,
Infiltrating combatants, recruiting
On the ground, preparing attacks inside
Lebanon on the Lebanese army,
1005   Firing rockets at Israel from the south.
In December 2005 rocket
Attacks on Israel from the south were claimed
By Zarqawi. They were carried out by
A Damascus-based Palestinian
1010   Terrorist group, FPLP-GC,
And financed by Al-Qaeda: Zarqawi,
Who considered Hezbollah apostate
But used them to launch attacks on Israel.
To Israel, Hezbollah and its allies
1015   Al-Qaeda and Iran were too powerful,
Firing rockets from across the border,
And as with Gaza Israel felt it time
To degrade Hezbollah's military strength.
Besieged by Hamas in Gaza to west,
1020   By Hezbollah in Lebanon to north
Via Syria and Iran to east, both
Trying to obtain nuclear weapons,
Israel felt almost encircled by foes
And sensed that Armageddon was looming.

1025   From Lebanon Hezbollah, the Shiite
"Party of God", funded by Iran, launched
Diversionary rocket attacks towards
Israeli military positions near
The coast, Zarit, and Shlomi on July
1030   The twelfth. At the same time Hezbollah troops,
Militants, fired rockets at Israeli
Positions near the Golan Heights as well-

Thought-out diversions. Thirty miles away
A group of gunmen crossed undetected
1035   Into Israel, smashed closed-circuit cameras
That monitored the border and hid in
A peach orchard until 9 a.m. when
They ambushed two army Humvee vehicles
On a border patrol near Zarit. They
1040   Fired rocket-propelled grenades. The "Hummers"
Went up in flames, three soldiers killed outright.
Three were injured and two were abducted:
Master sergeant Ehud Goldwasser and
First sergeant Eldad Regev, to take heat
1045   Off Gaza and the long search for Shalit.
Israeli tanks were called. One was attacked
As it gave pursuit into Lebanon,
And all four of its crew were killed. An eighth
Soldier died while recovering the tank.
1050   Hezbollah named the strike *Operation*
Truthful Promise after a pledge by its
Leader Hassan Nasrallah to kidnap
And exchange Israeli soldiers for four
Lebanese who had been held in Israel.
1055   Israel's Foreign-Ministry spokesman claimed
That the Hezbollah unit that captured
The two soldiers had sent them to Iran.

I srael attacked Lebanese targets with
Artillery and air strikes on bridges,
1060   Roads and Beirut airport, and forty-four
Civilians were killed. Israel's Chief of Staff
Said, "If the soldiers are not returned, we
Will turn Lebanon's clock back twenty years."
Israel's Cabinet's *communiqué* held
1065   Lebanon's Government "responsible
For the action that originated
On its soil", intending to drive a wedge
Between the Lebanese and Hezbollah.
The Lebanese Prime Minister denied
1070   All knowledge of the raid, which he did not
Condone. But he did not condemn the raid.
Nasrallah later declared, "The prisoners
Will not be returned except through one way:
Indirect negotiations and trade
1075   (Of prisoners)." He also said, "There is no
Solution to this regional conflict
Except the disappearance of Israel."

Four day later Israel announced it was
"Not fighting Lebanon but terrorist
1080   Elements there, all led by Nasrallah
And his cohorts, who have made Lebanon
A hostage and created Syrian and
Iranian-sponsored terrorist enclaves
Of murder." Prime Minister Olmert said
1085   The war started with the killing of eight
Israeli soldiers and the abduction
Of two, and the firing of Katyusha
Rockets at northern Israel that morning.

Now Israel implemented land and sea
1090   Blockades on Lebanon. Israeli jets
Attacked airbases, destroying runways,
And a power plant's fuel storage near Beirut,
Spilling fifteen thousand tons of fuel oil
Into the sea. Beirut's calm was shattered,
1095   Blasts rattled windows through the entire city,
Plumes of flame and smoke spouted from wrecked shells
Of buildings. That night Beirut was burning
As flames shot up from fuel tanks, turned the dark
Orange. All flickered ghastly in the glow.
1100   Down in the south rocket-launch sites and stores
Were missiled, and Hezbollah outposts, in
Operation Just Reward. People fled.
Columns of refugees abandoned cars,
Waded across the Litani river
1105   And trudged along cratered roads that were strafed,
Heading for Beirut whose southern suburbs
Were still being fiercely missile-attacked,
Where rubble and bits of apartment blocks
Strewed the chaotic and dangerous streets.
1110   There was no haven there from sudden death.
Hezbollah said it had thirteen thousand
Rockets it could launch at northern Israel.
A quarter of a million Israelis
Spent their nights in bomb shelters as rockets
1115   Thundered in. Two rockets struck Haifa, and
A Shia Muslim cleric, his wife and
Eight children were killed when planes bombed their home
In Dweir. Twelve Lebanese, all within one
Family, were killed in Zibqine, near Tyre.
1120   The IDF launched artillery and
Air strikes at cowering southern Lebanon.
Israel bombed the road to Iran to stop

The captured soldiers being driven there.
Hezbollah's offices were hit and now
1125   Hezbollah declared "open war" and struck
An Israeli missile boat *INS*
Hanit ten nautical miles off the coast
With a C-802 Chinese anti-
Ship missile that was thought to have been sent
1130   From Iran, China's past customer. Four
Israeli sailors' bodies were retrieved.
Hezbollah sank an Egyptian ship caught
In crossfire, fired a hundred Katyusha
Rockets at six Israeli towns and ten
1135   Settlements. The Security Council
Convened and Lebanon accused Israel
Of launching "a widespread and barbaric
Aggression". Israelis launched Patriot
Anti-ballistic missiles to take out
1140   Missiles targeting Haifa. Martial law
Was declared throughout north Israel. Four ports
In Lebanon were struck, an Israeli
Plane killed fifteen Lebanese fleeing from
An air strike on vehicles. More Katyushas
1145   Hit Haifa, Acre and Nahariya.
In Haifa in a maintenance hangar
Thirty railwaymen were repairing trains
When the corrugated plastic roofing
Burst as a rocket fired twenty miles north
1150   Crashed through and blew up, twisting carriages.
Pools of blood oozing from six dead victims,
An employee ran up and tried to speak,
Then collapsed and died beside his colleagues.
In Nahariya the roof of a house
1155   Burst into a ball of flames. A rocket,
A Katuysha, had ripped into it. Now
A mother ran out, hands clutching her face.
She stood screaming in the rubble-strewn street.
A little girl dashed from a bomb shelter,
1160   Clutching a dolly, eyes streaming with tears.
A random strike, no precision finesse.
In all eight were killed. Also landed one
Fajr-3 and one Raad-1 liquid-fuel
Missile, both developed in Iran, aimed
1165   At a fuel-storage plant. Putin, Russia's
President, declared that "Israel may be
Pursuing other aims in Lebanon
Than saving two soldiers taken hostage".

In fact, Israel's main aim was to degrade
1170   Hezbollah and Hamas in Gaza, then
Turn on Iran who ran the two movements.
Israel had used banned white phosphorus against
Civilians in southern Lebanon, and
Cluster bombs prepared for previous wars.
1175   Many mines were laid. Hezbollah's HQ
Was struck and Nasrallah was reported –
Wrongly – to have been wounded. Speaking on
Television, he said, "We focused on
Israel's military bases, we did not
1180   Attack any settlement. Israel killed
Civilians and targeted Lebanon's
Infrastructure." There were more attacks on
Haifa and in Safed a hospital
Was hit. Fifteen cities in all suffered
1185   Rocket blasts late at night. A synagogue
Was struck. Despite the blockade, rockets still
Crashed into random targets from the dark.
Israel was propelled into the next phase.

Israel prepared to invade Lebanon.
1190   Israeli tanks sunk down behind earth walls
Fired shells in clouds of smoke at distant haze
Where smoke and *débris* hung round speeding cars.
Tanks massed in rows, turret beside turret.
Armoured vehicles smashed through a fence and drove
1195   Over the fallen iron up a sand slope.
Crouched in armour, Israeli troops advanced
One kilometre into Lebanon
And levelled Hezbollah border outposts
With bulldozers. Glinting planes dropped twenty-
1200   Three tons of explosives on a bunker
For Hezbollah leaders in the Bourj al-
Barajneh district of Beirut. They hit
A mosque, no targeted leaders were killed.
Hezbollah killed two Israeli soldiers
1205   And damaged a Merkava Mark II tank
With a mortar. At Satan's urging – he
Was disguised as a Hezbollah fighter –
They fired a rocket at Christ's Nazareth
And killed two Israeli Arab children.
1210   By now forty-two bridges had been wrecked,
Thirty-eight roads cratered and ports, airports,
Telecommunications, factories,
Warehouses, electricity, fuel dumps

And service stations had been damaged in
1215   Ten cities. The next day five Israelis
Were killed fighting inside the Lebanese
Border, and a tank was destroyed. Israel
Carried out eighty air strikes. Hezbollah
Claimed to have shot down a helicopter,
1220   And to have hit an armoured bulldozer
With an anti-tank missile. Now Israel
Called up three thousand reserves for a ground
Invasion to support the three to five
Hundred troops now inside the Lebanon.
1225   The Lebanese army and Hezbollah
Stood side by side as Lebanese fled north.
Israeli jets hit Shiite districts in
Beirut, the Bekaa Valley and the south
And then two thousand troops crossed the border
1230   And seized Maroun al-Ras, a Hezbollah
Village. Air strikes hit Khiyam and blasted
Traffic round Tyre, a religious complex
In Sidon. Israel struck a hundred and
Twenty-four targets inside Lebanon,
1235   Warned all in fourteen villages to leave.
Thousands fled to Sidon. Israel had asked
The US for precision-guided bombs.
Delivery was speeded up. Hezbollah
Fired a hundred and sixty rockets at
1240   Towns in north Israel, injuring sixteen.
Now the air war intensified. Next day
There were air raids on Beirut, Tyre, Baalbek,
Al-Manara and Fatqa, two hundred
And seventy strikes in all. Hezbollah fired
1245   Ninety rockets at Israel, who agreed
In principle, as a proposed idea,
At talks in Rome aimed at restoring peace,
That a NATO-led international force
Should keep Hezbollah troops from the border.

1250   Israel aimed to establish the River
Litani as its natural border.
To maintain a two-kilometre zone
From the border secure from Hezbollah,
Thus shifting the border to the River
1255   Litani, the next day Israeli troops
Pushed three kilometres into southern
Lebanon and fought Hezbollah round Bint
Jbeil, their terror capital/stronghold,

And, battling, took a hilltop. Hezbollah
1260   Remained in control of the town. Air strikes
On Beirut were halted as Secretary
Of State Condoleezza Rice had arrived.
They were resumed the next day when planes made
A hundred strikes at southern Lebanon.
1265   A shell hit a house in Nabatieh,
Killing seven. Israeli IDF troops
Surrounded Bint Jbeil while Hezbollah
Fired a hundred rockets at north Israel.
At 5 a.m. the next morning, July
1270   The twenty-fifth, men dug in for a sleep
In an abandoned house slung packs laden
With ammunition over uniforms
Heavy with body armour and headed
Out to deserted streets, passed silhouettes
1275   Of three-storey buildings and empty mosques
Set in scrubland and olive groves. Then "C"
Company reached a fifty-yard-square walled
Olive grove surrounded on all sides by
Three-storey apartment blocks. Flung grenades
1280   Rolled fast towards them, which they kicked away.
Major Roi Klein, deputy battalion
Commander, threw himself on one grenade
To save his comrades. His legs were blown off
And he died at once. Then arms fire came from
1285   The upper-block floors and behind the wall,
Mostly hand- and rocket-propelled grenades,
As the "Party of God" tried to kill all.
Fifteen were hit and fell, some dead. Others
Would take time to die. A sergeant was hit
1290   By a grenade. Shrapnel injured his arm
And soaked his uniform in blood. His friend
Fell, shot in his back. Reinforcements came,
And there was a fierce fight for six long hours.
Then a barrage of smoke shells enabled
1295   Four Black Hawk helicopters to touch down
A mile away. The wounded were stretchered.
The helicopters came in under fire
And left within a minute. The dead lay
Untouched until nightfall and were retrieved
1300   Under cover of darkness. Eight men had
Been killed, twenty-two wounded. Cabinet
Ministers urged carpet bombing before
Ground troops were next used against Hezbollah.
Iran's ally, al-Qaeda's deputy

1305	Leader al-Zawahiri, called on all
	Muslims to fight against the "Crusaders"
	And Zionists in Lebanon, urging
	More al-Qaeda soldiers to join all those
	Now fighting Israel in south Lebanon.
1310	Three days on, paratroopers exchanged fire
	With Hezbollah fighters, killing twenty
	Of the *élite* forces that had kidnapped
	The two Humvee soldiers. Further clashes
	Left six Israeli troops wounded, and though
1315	Twenty-six more Hezbollah fighters died
	And the sandy streets were strewn with rubble,
	IDF troops pulled out of Bint Jbeil,
	Shocked at how fortified the area was.
	Old people emerged blinking to sunlight,
1320	Having survived on water, tins of food,
	Some shell-shocked, still in pyjamas, leaving
	Basements, standing on roads blocked with rubble
	Where no ambulances could penetrate.
	The terrorist army had booby-trapped
1325	The entire area, and ten Israelis
	Had been killed against seventy Hezbollah.
	Leader Nasrallah claimed that Israel had
	Suffered a "serious defeat" in ground
	Fighting round the town, and the Israeli
1330	Public were dismayed Israel had been pushed
	Back three kilometres from the border.
	Hezbollah were in charge and were too near.
	Iran's leader, Ahmadinejad, said,
	"A storm is on the way, a hurricane.
1335	He who sows the wind will reap a whirlwind."
	Israeli planes continued the air strikes.
	Four unarmed UN observers, alarmed,
	Made ten calls to the Israeli army
	Within six hours at a Lebanese post
1340	Before a missile strike wiped out all four
	With precision-guided munitions that
	Supported ground artillery fire in
	What UN Secretary-General Annan
	Called a deliberate strike: their position
1345	Was well-known and repeated calls were made
	To Israel to stop the attacks. Next day
	Israel made a hundred and twenty air
	Strikes on Beirut and the Bekaa Valley.
	Hezbollah fired a hundred Katuysha

1350	Rockets at targets in northern Israel
	In the Galilee and Hula Valley.
	Now Israel made a hundred and thirty
	Air raids and mobilised fifteen thousand
	Troops. Hezbollah fired a new Khaibar-1
1355	Rocket at Afula. Israel deployed
	A Patriot interceptor missile
	But the rocket still struck. Ground clashes wrecked
	Maroun al-Ras and Eitaroun, and al-
	Nabatieh and Sour were shelled. Mossad
1360	Said Hezbollah could continue fighting
	At the present level for a long while.
	Israel's military intelligence
	Believed Hezbollah was badly damaged.
	Now it was reported that Nasrallah
1365	Had gone to Damascus to meet Ali
	Larijani, Secretary of Iran's
	National Security Council. It seemed
	That Iran was assisting Hezbollah
	Against Israel with Syria's support.

1370	Hundreds of foreign tourists visiting
	Tyre's archaeological ruins were
	Trapped and cowered near stones that knew land wars
	When death did not rush out of the sun's glare.
	History's ruins have survived many wars.
1375	Lebanon, the home of the Phoenicians,
	A seafaring people who spread across
	The Mediterranean before Cyrus
	And flourished from 3700 until
	450 BC, was steeped in Roman
1380	And Crusaders' castles. Israeli bombs
	Did not respect historical ruins.
	Tyre, which has fine imperial Roman
	Architecture, was damaged – a fresco
	On a Roman tomb collapsed. At Byblos
1385	A tower from the time of the Crusades split,
	The Venetian harbour was stained with oil.
	The Temple of Bacchus at Baalbek cracked.
	At Bint Jbeil a medieval wall
	Was pocked and scored. What right has the present
1390	To treat the past with casual contempt?
	An egocentric generation scowled,
	Arrogant paratroops viewing with scorn.
	Future scholars would weep at what it broke.

⌐A dark night in al-Khuraybah, whence for
1395   Two weeks (Iraeli IDF forces
Proclaimed) Hezbollah had fired Katuyshas.
In nearby Qana, a three-storey block
In which women and children slept. A roar,
A precision-guided bomb exploded,
1400   Rubble collapsed into the underground
Garage that was used as a shelter by
The Shalhoub and Hashem families who
Had ignored Israel's warnings they should flee
As the roads out were continually shelled.
1405   Residents ran out, cried out in the dark,
Tore at the rubble with bare hands, searching
For survivors. A second precision-
Guided bomb thundered in, strewing rubble.
Further air strikes and artillery attacks
1410   Destroyed several houses in Qana and
Hampered rescue. The Red Cross were delayed
By more shelling. Bloodied bodies retrieved
Were women and children wearing nightclothes.
Qana, probably Galilee's Cana
1415   Where Jesus performed his first miracle,
Turned water into wine, was now flattened,
Bodies in a row wrapped in plastic, bound
With bands in a temporary morgue, crushed,
Mutilated. Twenty-eight civilians
1420   Died, half children. International outrage
And calls for a cease-fire made Israel halt
Air strikes for forty-eight hours. Hundreds marched
At the funeral for the civilians
And four Hezbollah fighters who had fired
1425   Rockets from near Qana and drawn down bombs
And were buried wrapped in Hezbollah flags.
The Lebanese Prime Minister Fouad
Siniora denounced Israeli war crimes.
Thousands demonstrated at the UN
1430   Offices in Beirut and in Gaza.
Israel's Chief of Staff Dan Halutz expressed
Regret, blaming Hezbollah for using
The Qana villagers as "human shields".

What leaders could intervene and bring peace?
1435   Bush and Blair were discredited because
Of Iraq. Putin could not be trusted.
Chirac of France was far too partisan.
Prodi carried no weight, and Koizumi

Was an impersonator of Presley.
1440   No one save Bush had the authority,
And Bush lacked credibility because
Saddam had moved his wmds,
Disguised, on to a boat off Umm Qasr,
Lowered them, watertight, in a trawl net
1445   And sunk them on the Persian Gulf's seabed.

The Iranian *mullah*s and theocrats
Were to blame for supplying the thousands
Of rockets being fired at Israel in
A proxy war. They paid and others killed.
1450   Iran's medium-range missiles in southern
Lebanon aimed at all Israel's northern
Cities made the dispute more dangerous.
Bush wanted the pounding of Hezbollah
To be felt in Iran, which, with Syria,
1455   Should be reined in as Israel dealt fiercely
With Hezbollah, Iran's trainee fighters.
A hundred Revolutionary Guards
From Iran were helping Hezbollah fire
Their weapons to "wipe Israel off the map",
1460   Words of their leader Ahmadinejad.
Determined to counter Iran's probing
Israel bombarded with artillery
As IDF ground troops advanced towards
Taiba and Adisa, a launching site
1465   For Hezbollah rockets. Bombers attacked
Lebanese army vehicles round Taiba.
A thud from a cannon and a shell whined,
A brown cloud rose over Taiba village.
Smoke drifted past a mosque's blue minaret.
1470   A crack and black smoke spurted from the town
Beneath the Crusaders' Beaufort Castle.
And there was an Israeli naval strike
At a Lebanese military base
North of Tyre. Hezbollah claimed its fighters
1475   Destroyed an Israeli warship off Tyre.
Two of four border crossings to Syria
Were closed after attacks and villages
Were struck. The battle of Ayta ash-Shab
Began on July the thirty-first when
1480   The IDF shelled the town and attacked
With five-hundred-pound bombs. But the next day
Hezbollah fired anti-tank missiles at
Israeli paratroops, killing three, while

The paratroops killed ten Hezbollah men.
1485   Meanwhile the IDF fought round Adaisse,
Kfar Kila and Taiba. At Baalbek
Commandos were dropped from helicopters
In the Shia stronghold sixty miles north
Of the Litani, stormed the Hezbollah-
1490   Run Dar al-Hikma Hospital, from which
Patients had been evacuated, ran
Through darkened wards shouting the names of those
Abducted at the start of the war. They
Targeted *Sheikh* Mohammed Yazbek, who
1495   Was on Hezbollah's *Shura* Council and
Representative in the Lebanon
Of Iran's Supreme Leader Khamenei,
A link between Hezbollah and Iran.
He was not found inside the hospital.
1500   Now Nasrallah, the Hezbollah leader,
Vowed to strike Tel Aviv as tit-for-tat
For Israel's bombing of Beirut. There would
Be no cease-fire till every Israeli
Soldier had vacated Lebanese soil.

1505   The end of the war happened suddenly.
Now Israel's Defence Minister Peretz
Told his troops to advance some eighteen miles
To the Litani river and function
In all areas to the south where rockets
1510   Had been launched at Israel. A zone stretching
From the coast to Galilee's Panhandle
Embracing eleven towns in south Lebanon
Was occupied by ten thousand soldiers.
A fifty-helicopter armada
1515   Hugged the rough hills of southern Lebanon.
Now thirty thousand Israeli troops were
In Lebanon. Hundreds of paratroops
Were lifted behind enemy lines as
Armoured cars pushed forwards, to trap and kill
1520   As many Iran-backed fighters as they
Could before the UN cease-fire began.
Air-Force jets laid down a rolling carpet
Of fire to drive exhausted Hezbollah
Fighters into the trap where they'd be killed.
1525   Air strikes rained down on Tyre. Dazed and bloodied
Civilians were carried to hospitals.
Many cowered in homes, trapped and wounded,
Enduring the worst attacks of the war.

On August the sixth the battle of Bint
1530   Jbeil was resumed. Tanks and paratroops
Pressed forward. The Israeli military
Captured five Hezbollah guerillas and
Killed eight. But during the next two days four
Israeli soldiers were killed. By the twelfth
1535   Bint Jbeil was part of the Litani
Offensive, and was overtaken by
A UN-brokered cease-fire that called for
Hezbollah's disarmament, for Israel's
Withdrawal from Lebanon, deployment
1540   Of Lebanese soldiers and an enlarged
UN Interim Force in Lebanon.
It was approved by the two Governments –
Israel's and Lebanon's; came into force
On the fourteenth, and ended on the eighth
1545   Of September so that Israel could lift
Its naval blockade of the Lebanon.

Now Israeli troops explored a network
Of Hezbollah tunnels near the border.
Like Hamas, Hezbollah had dug beneath
1550   The ground so it could move about without
Being missiled from stray Israeli planes.
Peace was delayed several weeks to allow
Time for Israel to deal with these tunnels.
On October the first Israel withdrew
1555   Most of its troops from smashed-up Lebanon
Though some remained in Ghajar, a village
That straddled the border and was too near
To Israel for comfort during a peace.
By then over a thousand had been killed,
1560   Mostly Lebanese civilians, and four
Thousand rockets had been fired at Israel,
Who had used white-phosphorus shells again.
Hezbollah said two hundred and fifty
Of its fighters had died. Israel upped this
1565   To six hundred as it had 538
Names of Hezbollah fighters who'd been killed.
Israel lost a hundred and seventeen
IDF troops, forty-three civilians.
Lebanon was in ruins, Hezbollah's
1570   Strongholds were rubble. It was degraded.
Both Israel and the US declared that
Hezbollah had lost the conflict. And yet
Iran and Syria pronounced a victory

For Hezbollah amid strewn masonry.

1575   Bush, watching film of ruined Lebanon
In the White House, thought how Israel had fought
A proxy war with Iran to degrade
The threat from the north, and how Israel feared
For its existence. High above the moon
1580   The One held together the opposites
Of Israel and Hezbollah-Iran and,
High above memories of Abraham,
Indifferent to Biblical Covenants,
Maintained billions of stars on their fixed course
1585   And blended with the infinite beyond
Finite space-time, which it permeated,
And held in place a system of order
In which all opposites were reconciled.
One country squatting on another's land
1590   And claiming that it had always been theirs
Brought progress to a backward region and
So brought gain to the system in which all
Strove to improve their living conditions.
A war that ruined a neighbour would end
1595   In universal peace in the Mideast.
To the One, a process was working out.

Bush was annoyed that Hezbollah was still
In place, and armed, and able to function.
For before the cease-fire two Hezbollah
1600   Cabinet members said their militia
Would not disarm south of the Litani.
Israel said it would stop withdrawing from
Southern Lebanon if Lebanese troops
Were not deployed there within a few days.
1605   In the West there were recriminations.
Bush said Hezbollah was responsible
For starting the war and that it suffered
A defeat at the hands of Israel. "There's
Going to be a new power in the south
1610   Of Lebanon." Bush firmly pinned the blame:
"Responsibility for the suffering
Of the Lebanese people also lies
With Hezbollah's state sponsors, Iran and
Syria. The regime in Iran provides
1615   Hezbollah with financial support, weapons
And training. Iran has made clear that it
Seeks the destruction of Israel. We can

Only imagine how much more dangerous
This conflict would have been if Iran had
1620   The nuclear weapons it seeks. Syria,
Too, is a state sponsor of Hezbollah.
Syria allows Iranian weapons
To pass through its territory into
Lebanon. Syria permits Hezbollah's
1625   Leader to operate from Damascus
And gives its political support to
Hezbollah's cause. It supports Hezbollah
For it wants to undermine Lebanon's
Democratic Government and regain
1630   Its position of dominance in that
Country." Of Hezbollah's claim of victory:
"How can you claim a victory when at one
Time you were a state within a state, safe
Within southern Lebanon, and now you're
1635   Going to be replaced by a Lebanese
Army and an international force?"
In truth, Israel underestimated
Its opponent, who proved a worthy foe,
A shrewd adversary for its ground forces.

1640   The aftermath was not kind to Israel.
Later a Government report would blame
Olmert for acting hastily, leading
His country into war without a plan,
Without seeing his generals' strategy
1645   Or consulting non-military experts;
For setting unrealistic goals – like
The return of the hostages, ending
Hezbollah's missile threat – and for his dire
"Lack of judgment, responsibility
1650   And caution". Olmert rushed into a full-
Blown conflict where Israel did not achieve
Its stated goals of freeing two soldiers
And neutralising Shiite militias.
Now Hezbollah armed Hamas and Gaza
1655   With new Iranian weapons smuggled through
Twenty tunnels under Egypt's border
For a new war against hated Israel.

Outraged at Iran's proxy aggression
Through Hamas-Hezbollah against Israel,
1660   In August Cheney had again returned
To the plan to bomb Iran's nuclear

Sites in Natanz and Arak and elsewhere.
The Bureau of Near Eastern Affairs had
Been spreading eighty-five million dollars
1665   Among Iranian and Syrian
Dissidents. Cheney saw diplomacy
As imposing the will of the US
On a capitulating adversary
And would not negotiate with evil,
1670   Rather impeded such efforts as when
In 2003 Iran asked the Swiss
To act as an intermediary and
Fix negotiations with the US –
Only to be rejected by Cheney.
1675   Seeing Israel's bombing of Lebanon
Spiralling out of control and seeing
Condoleezza Rice had gone to Beirut
With the ex-Ambassador to Egypt,
David Welch, Cheney gave him a minder
1680   Who would crush any pro-Arab dealings,
Elliott Abrams, who was in constant
Communication with Cheney's office,
Safeguarding Israel's reputation and
Preparing for Israel to bomb Iran.
1685   Bush saw the Syndicate was pushing hard
To confront Iran and he wondered how
Opposing Shias there'd affect Iraq
Which was now run by Shiites but still in
Chaos because of Sunni insurgents.
1690   He wanted democracy everywhere
But wanted to consolidate Iraq's
Democracy before freeing Iran.
His main focus was on Shia Iraq.

BOOK EIGHT

BUSH'S SURGE PACIFIES IRAQ

SUMMARY

	rather than the vision of the Syndicate.
1577-1640	The intensification of the surge. Petraeus purges Shiite militias.
1641-1679	The golden-domed al-Askari mosque, Samarra, bombed again.
1680-1700	Bush and the universe.
1701-1776	Shia militias announce a six-months cease-fire. The surge has worked.
1777-1861	Petraeus defends the surge before Congress and against the Democrats. Bush's policy has won.
1862-1920	Petraeus works for political reconciliation in Iraq and deals with Moqtada regarding Basra.
1921-2006	Maliki attacks Moqtada's militias in Basra and Sadr City, Baghdad.
2007-2030	Petraeus has brought the Sunnis back into Iraqi politics.
2031-2090	Petraeus again appears before Congress. The five surge brigades begin to return home.

O Fitzgerald, who translated Omar
Khayyam's verses, quatrains that still enchant,
And painted the eleventh-and twelfth-century
Nishapur in Seljuq Persia seen through
5   The eyes of a scholar, many-sided
Medieval man who – on a pension
Of one thousand two hundred gold *mithkal*s
A year from the Vizier, Nizam al-Mulk,
A schoolfriend to the son of Toghril Beg
10 Who wrested Persia from Mahmud the Great
And founded the great Seljuk dynasty –
Studied, researched astronomy, history,
Algebra, philosophy, alchemy,
Medicine and jurisprudence, and yet was
15 A Sufi mystic and epicurean
Savouring a jug of wine, loaf of bread
And "thou" – at once beloved and Prophet;
I think of the turrets and minarets
The *muezzin* calling and the shafts of light,
20 Jamsheed's palace and the water-carrier
Which you described, which left my Iraqi
Students spellbound for it was their world too.
I find you by your tomb in Boulge churchyard
Which mirrors Omar Khayyam's Persian tomb
25 From which a rose-bush was brought and planted.
Now a descendant grows beside your grave
On which "the north wind may scatter roses".
Help me now I come to describe Iran's
Islamic domes and peerless minarets
30 And the *muezzin*'s drawn-out call at dawn

That prayer is better than sleep, life than death.
O Hidden *Imam* down Jamkaran Well,
Who has been there eleven hundred years,
To whom simple Iranians write prayers,
35   Or rather petitions, and post them through
The top bars to fall down into the well,
I find you in the mosque not far away
And sit among turbaned *mullah*s and close
My eyes and ask the Light to descend deep
40   Inside your well, and cleanse hostility
And purify it to a place of peace,
To solve the international crisis
Short of nuclear war, and to prevent
Iran's extremist leaders from conflict
45   Through their intransigence and bigotry.
O Hidden *Imam*, help me now I come
To reveal Iran's control of the wars
In Iraq and Afghanistan as young
Shiites dream of a new Greater Iran,
50   A Shia Crescent founded in your name.

O Keats who, knowing you had a short time
To live, went south to the Isle of Wight for
Warm air, haunted by your own transience,
By how ephemeral were all living things,
55   I find you in Eglantine Cottage in
Shanklin where you lodged with Mrs. Williams
Who lived downstairs. I stand in her kitchen
Where sometimes she had you down for a meal,
See the original window, now part
60   Of a gift shop, and peep in the next room
At her bedroom, then climb the stairs and stand
In the room where you wrote in the summer
Of 1819, after your great odes
Were completed, looking out at the chine
65   And across the cliff to the distant sea,
Consumptive, told you would not live the year
Out if you stayed in grimy London, here
For the pure air, and I see next door your
Bedroom, your fireplaces in these two rooms.
70   You had "a little coffin of a room"
You said with biting irony, and there
Was a coffin chute somewhere upstairs as
The stairs were too narrow for a coffin
To be brought down. Here in your writing room,
75   Having visited in April eighteen

Seventeen and written "It keeps eternal
Whisperings" of the sea after a walk through
The chine to Shanklin's shore – omitting to
Describe the foam, the sand, breakwaters and
80   Ten-thousand-year-old cliffs – you wrote 'The Pot
Of Basil', 'St Agnes Eve', half 'Lamia'
Part of 'Hyperion' and four acts of
Otho the Great. You went to Carisbrooke
And, looking at the noble chase where Charles
85   The First was prisoner, wrote down the first line
Of 'Endymion', "A thing of beauty is
A joy forever" – omitting to show
The ruined castle, for you sometimes lacked
An objective eye and too readily
90   Went for subjective reflection, removed
From actual place. You knew that you would,
Terminally ill, be dead in a year.
O Keats, help me now I come to describe
The desperate conditions in Baghdad
95   In the occupation when life was cheap.
Help me as I tell of the transience
And ephemerality of life which
Under the insurgency could be capped
At any moment by sudden darkness.

100   I recall how I stood in Babylon
And gazed at low Babylon's mud-like sand,
Euphrates glinting between palms, waters
By which the captive Jewish craftsmen wept
Between shifts when they fired bricks and made tar
105   For mortar to build the great ziggurat,
A "tower into the sky" dedicated
To Etemenanki that linked Heaven
And Earth, the Tower of Babel that rose up
Seventy metres above the flat plain, glazed
110   Blue bricks at the top flashing in the sun,
And held the Hanging Gardens – a whorled mount
That's now water-filled holes that once contained
Its foundations. I think of how it looked
Under the rule of Nimrod, when mankind
115   Was united, and when Semiramis
Founded Babylon's mystery religion.
In Nebuchadnezzar's Sacred City
It towered above dozens of temples, shrines,
Ishtar Gate, mighty walls, stone obelisk,
120   Processional way past hundreds of lions,

Bulls and dragons sacred to many gods,
A tower that spiralled up and reached the heavens
On top of which was a small temple where
The Royal Sacred Marriage of Tammuz,
125   Freed from the Underworld and now reborn,
And his rescuer Inanna, was held
Each year in a Spring Festival wherein
The earth renewed its sap under the sun.
Here time was divided into units
130   Of sixty seconds that civilised men.
This was the capital of an empire
That stretched from Gaza to the Persian Gulf,
From Armenia to the Arabian sands;
This was the centre of the then known world.
135   All the world's tongues could be heard babbling
On Babel, an inverted melting-pot
Where immigrants from all the world were found.
Here Daniel was thrown in a lions' den,
And Shadrach, Meshack and Abednego
140   Into a fiery furnace; Belshezzar
Saw writing on the wall; and, driven mad,
Nebuchadnezzar ate grass like a cow,
Hair like an eagle's feathers, nails like claws.
Here in this vainglorious, sinful city
145   Pride was punished as its all-powerful king
Was humbled on all fours like a rude beast.
Yet here many captive Jews chose to stay
When Cyrus came and let the Jews go home.
Now in the centre of old Babylon
150   Stood a vast military camp, a base
For the US army that ruled Iraq
While elsewhere in repose the Syndicate
Planned a new Tower of Babel in all tongues,
A world government of new slaves within
155   The towering United-Nations building,
A plan that would turn us all into slaves.

The civil war began in Samarra
The previous February when the Shiite shrine
Of the Hidden *Imam*'s father blew up,
160   Unleashing a cycle of Shiite and
Sunni reprisals as Zarqawi hoped.
In June after Zarqawi was killed Bush
Met academics Eliot Cohen,
Fred Kagan and others at Camp David.
165   He slipped away early for a surprise

Visit to Baghdad. Seventy thousand troops,
Most Iraqi, patrolled the streets and manned
Checkpoints and there was a night-time curfew.
In a marbled hall in one of Saddam's
170   Palaces, now the US Embassy,
In the Green Zone he greeted US troops
And Embassy employees, who cheered him.
Prime Minister Nouri al-Maliki,
In office three weeks, arrived expecting
175   A video-conference with Bush speaking
From Camp David. He learned Bush was present
Minutes before he walked into the room.
He said, "Good to see you." Bush said, "Thank you
For having me," beaming for the cameras.
180   Seated beside Maliki and seventeen
Members of his Cabinet alongside
American Embassy officials,
He said, "I've come to look you in the eye."
He wanted to know how dedicated
185   Maliki was to a free Iraq, for
He'd been an exile in Tehran eight years.
Later Bush spoke to four hundred US
Troops and civilians in the palace's
Café and said, "We'll continue to hunt
190   Down people like Mr al-Zarqawi
And bring them to justice." They applauded.
He returned upbeat, full of zest for war.

But now the situation turned worse as
Shiite militias began a campaign
195   To push the Sunnis out of Baghdad by
Carrying out "ethnic" (or more strictly
"Sectarian") cleansing, expelling Sunnis
From mixed and even their communities.
This new Battle of Baghdad began on
200   July the ninth in Sunni Jihad near
Baghdad airport, where Shiite militia-
Men, some masked, set up checkpoints on the streets
And examined all identity cards.
Passers-by who seemed Sunni were then shot.
205   A Sunni vegetable market was raked
With gunfire, and they entered Sunni homes
And killed the occupants. Some fifty died.
A new red line was crossed: ID and homes.
Worse followed. The next day in west Baghdad
210   The Mahdi Army attacked Malouki

Mosque and the police told Sunni callers,
"The Mahdi Army are not terrorists,
They are doing their duty." It was clear
That the ethnic cleansing of Sunnis was
215   Known about by the Shiite Maliki
Government. Sunnis retaliated,
Exploding car bombs in Sadr City,
Killing thirty. Then a gunman kidnapped
A bus queue of Shiites, killed twenty-two.
220   A café of Shiites was bombed, killing
Twenty-six. Forty more were killed in south
Baghdad. Gunmen stopped a funeral, a van
Carrying a coffin to Shia Najaf
And killed all ten mourners, whose bodies were
225   Piled into the hearse they'd been following.
In Kufa a minibus was blown up,
Killing fifty-three. During July some
Three thousand Iraqis were killed. Every
Sunni mosque was attacked, one time by
230   A National Police commander. Sunni
Bodies were dumped near Sunni districts each
Day. Many decapitated bodies
Were found, many were thrown in the Tigris.
Now Sunnis received letters containing
235   A bullet, and left their homes in a day.
The Iraqi Army was now Shiite,
The National Police was infiltrated
By Shiite militias. The Army and
Police would enter a Sunni district
240   And confiscate all arms, then militias
Would come by night and kill many Sunnis.
Moqtada's Jaysh al-Mahdi would arrest
A male in a market, drive to the edge
Of a Sunni district and shoot him in
245   The back of his head, then drive off leaving
His body to intimidate Sunnis
Into leaving their homes. Some Shiites drilled
Into Sunnis' kneecaps, sometimes their heads.
As ethnic cleansing of Sunnis increased
250   Two million Sunnis fled Iraq. Many
Settled in Syria or Jordan. Their homes
Were rented to Shias. Extortion rings
Took money from Sunni shop owners, then
Shiite banners were hung to show Sunni
255   Districts were now Shiite. And the police,
Infiltrated by Shiite militias,

Would authorise the change. Now things got worse.

Daily bombings were the norm in Baghdad.
In September a petrol queue was bombed,
260 The petrol pumps ignited and women
Staggered away, clothes flaming like torches.
Bodies were dumped each day, found by patrols,
Some with their eyes gouged out and broken arms.
Shiite militias fought Iraq police
265 In south Baghdad and Sunni militias
In north Baghdad. As soon as the US
Cleared an area and moved on, insurgents
Returned and had to be cleared yet again.
As soldiers and police numbers increased,
270 So did the violence. In October
A US soldier was kidnapped, it seemed
By Moqtada's militias. The US
Army imposed checkpoints on Canal Road.
Maliki told General Casey to lift
275 The checkpoints. Casey said, "If that is your
Order, we'll do it. But people will say
You don't care about American troops
And that you kowtowed to Sadr. Sunnis
Will read this as pro-JAM action.
280 Can you accept that?" Maliki said, "Yes."
But the checkpoints still had to be lifted.
The pro-Iranian Maliki opposed
The policy that kept him in power
And restricted US action within
285 Sadr City. "Ethnic cleansing" went on.
Shiite militias pushed Sunnis westwards.
It seemed to US commanders that what
Had been tried for three years was not working.
Some wanted to hand over to Iraq's
290 Army and police and back out, but this
Would give free rein to Shiite militias
And accelerate their ethnic cleansing.
American troops preserved some order.

Into the chaos came other parties,
295 Seeking their own self-interest. Al-Qaeda
In Iraq took up the Sunni cause. Al-
Zarqawi was dead, but his successors
Attacked tribal leaders in west Iraq,
Beat elders in public and killed police
300 And spread their influence through car bombings,

Urging an "Islamic State of Iraq",
Islamic but without being Shiite.
And under cover of the great chaos,
Urged on by Satan who saw the advance
305   Of the Shiites as exacerbating
The disorder, fueling Sunni anger,
Iran launched an offensive in Iraq,
Using explosively formed projectiles
(Or explosively formed penetrators),
310   EFPs, lethal high-tech roadside bombs
That cut through armoured vehicles, killing three
Or four soldiers inside. Some twelve hundred
Roadside bombs detonated in August.
There were now eight hundred attacks each week
315   On the US and allies. A thousand
Civilians were killed each month in Baghdad.
The EFPs had been imported from
Iran, who wanted to help the Shiites
Win control in Baghdad and all Iraq
320   So their puppet Maliki would preside
Over one region in a Shia Crescent
That included the Hidden *Imam*'s shrines
In Samarra and Najaf and would soon
Resemble a powerful Greater Iran.
325   It could now be seen that Zarqawi, who
Was sheltered in Iran during the first
Battle of Falluja, had turned against
The Shiites on instructions from Iran,
Who had he lived would have supplied him with
330   Crates of sophisticated EFPs,
As sectarian war on Shiites would give
The Shiites a pretext for their cleansing,
Their expulsion of Sunnis from Iraq,
And deliver to Iran a largely
335   Shiite Iraq. It would be a province
In Greater Iran's Middle-East empire
That would include Lebanon, Palestine
And a de-Talibaned Afghanistan
And soon Israel, as other provinces.
340   As the mid-term US elections loomed
And the US and the Iraq regime
Launched a counter-offensive in Baghdad
To improve security with checkpoints,
Foot patrols and night curfews, it was clear
345   That the Shias had won the civil war,
That Baghdad was now a Shiite city

And the US, the world's sole superpower,
Could not reverse deterioration in
Baghdad and had lost control of Iraq.

350   The mid-term elections turned out to be
A referendum on the Iraq war.
The Democrats were expected to end
Or reduce American military
Involvement in Iraq. Leader Nancy
355   Pelosi said, "This election's about
Iraq. If indeed it turns out the way
That people expect it to turn out, then
The American people will have spoken,
And they will have rejected the course of
360   Action the President is on." All House
Of Representatives seats and a third
Of Senate seats, besides thirty-six state
Governorships, were contested, and all three
Were won by the Democrats. The Senate
365   Was a tie but two Independents said
They'd caucus with the Democrats. Bush called
His defeat a big "thumping", and candid,
Dignified in adversity, he sat
In the Oval Office, head in his hands,
370   For Cheney's plan to bomb Iran would now
Fail to win Democrat support. Iraq
Preoccupied him, for retired Generals
Had told him the old plan was not working,
That there should be a change of strategy.
375   The day after the elections Bush announced
That he was removing Rumsfeld, who stood
Bemused through a short eulogy and went,
Leaving a void in Iraq policy.
The Chairman of the Joint Chiefs, General Pace,
380   Had proved unable to deal with the war
And a retired General, Jack Keane, number
Two in the Army for the invasion
Of Iraq, came forward with advice he
Had debated with General Petraeus.

385   On December the sixth, the ten-person
Bipartisan Iraq Study Group that
Had been appointed by Congress in March
Released its report, its assessment and
Policy recommendations. An ex-
390   Secretary of State, James Baker, was co-

Chairman. The new Secretary of Defense
From November the eighth, Robert Gates, had
Been a member of the panel. Among
Recommended approaches, including
395   The phased withdrawal of US combat
Troops from Iraq, the report conversely
Suggested that "the United States should
Significantly increase the number
Of US military personnel,
400   Including combat troops, imbedded in
And supporting Iraq Army units".
A finding was that the Pentagon had
Significantly underreported
The extent of the violence in Iraq,
405   Which reflected on Rumsfeld's handling.
It found that the situation within
Afghanistan was so precarious
That troops should be diverted from Iraq
To help stabilise that fragile country.
410   Baker, who had served under Bush Senior,
Urged urgency. Receiving the report,
Bush said, "We will take every proposal
Seriously, act in a timely fashion."
He said that he would not accept every
415   Recommendation made in the report.
Controversially, the report focused
On Iraqi oil in the first chapter
And its Recommendation 63
Was understood in Iraq to suggest
420   That the war would last till American
Oil companies had guaranteed legal
Access to all Iraq's oilfields. Iraq's
President Jalal Talabani called
Its conclusions "very dangerous" to
425   Iraq's sovereignty and constitution,
Said, "As a whole, I reject this report."
It was announced that Bush was comparing
The recommendations of the Iraq
Study Group with studies by the Joint Chiefs
430   Of Staff and the National Security
Council, and should be able to "announce
A new way forward" in Iraq before
Christmas or perhaps the end of the year.

Two days later, on December the eighth,
435   A strong rival report changed everything.

The report – written by the American
Enterprise Institute at whose HQ
In Washington the neo-cons conceived
The invasion of Iraq – was presented
440   By Frederick Kagan, Keane and Pollack and
Dubbed "the real Iraq Study Group Report".
The event description trumpeted, "This
Study calls for a large and sustained surge
Of US forces" that would "secure and
445   Protect critical areas of Baghdad".
It declared that the report outlined "how
The United States can win in Iraq"
And (bullish) "why victory is the only
Acceptable outcome". The report said
450   Why more troops might be needed and how they
Might be used differently – what the White House
Had wanted to know but the Pentagon
Had not researched. On December the eleventh
Keane went to the White House for a meeting
455   With Bush and a group of Iraq experts
And ex-Generals in the Oval Office.
They disagreed with the Iraq Study
Group on the main issue of sending more
Troops to Iraq. General Keane argued that
460   Several thousand additional soldiers
Could be used to improve security
In Baghdad. He said, "Time is running out.
We need more troops." Two other retired ex-
Generals present scoffed. There were several calls
465   For a new team. Bush intervened, "Who am
I supposed to pick?" Eliot Cohen,
Academic, said, "David Petraeus."
Bush deliberated, reflected on
Changing the military personnel,
470   Implementing the surge, pumping in cash
For reconstruction and job creation
In Iraq and funding centrist parties
That would support PM al-Maliki.
The report, titled *The New Way Forward*
475   Had struck a chord and now resonated.
Later that day Bush met senior State
Department advisers, including Rice,
And said he had to co-ordinate both
The State and Defense Departments' thinking
480   So the nation would know "that I've listened
To all aspects of government, and that

The way forward is the way forward to
Achieve our aim: to succeed in Iraq".

The White House diverged from the Pentagon.
485   Two days later Bush and Cheney met with
The Joint Chiefs of Staff on the military
Options. But they did not favour adding
Significant numbers of troops to Iraq
Stressing economic reconstruction,
490   Political reconciliation
And employment programs. They denied there'd
Be a purely military solution.
General Casey wanted withdrawal from
Iraqi cities to US bases.
495   Lieutenant General Chiarelli wanted
To redeploy half the combat brigades
To train Iraq's security forces.
The next day Bush said, "I am listening to
A lot of advice on a strategy.
500   And I will be delivering my plans
After a long deliberation. I'm
Not going to be rushed into making
A decision." He wanted Robert Gates
To have time to evaluate Iraq.
505   He was still haunted by Keane, who offered
A way forward that differed from the one
Democrats favoured. A few days later
Cheney rang Keane and asked if he would come
Out of retirement and take command in
510   Iraq. Keane declined but said he was close
To Generals Petraeus and Odierno
And would go to Iraq to advise them.
Effectively, Keane was now the chairman
Of the Joint Chiefs of Staff and of his peers
515   At the Pentagon, though operating
From retirement, appalled at how inept
The military establishment now was.
Bush said, "I haven't made up my mind yet
About more troops." He agonised until
520   The New Year on whether to send more troops
And put Petraeus in charge of Iraq.

Iran, long suspected of attempting
To develop a nuclear bomb, had been
Told back in March by the Security
525   Council to suspend all uranium-

Enrichment programs by the thirty-first
Of August. Tehran had failed to comply.
Now Resolution 1737
Imposed sanctions on Iran's trade in all
530 Sensitive nuclear materials
And technology on the twenty-third
Of December. Assets of companies
And individuals linked to enrichment
Were frozen. Iran's Foreign Ministry
535 Spokesman condemned the resolution, which
"Can't affect or limit Iran's nuclear
Activities". Russia reacted by
Selling Tor-M1-type surface-to-air
Missiles to Iran, to defend Natanz
540 And other nuclear sites deemed "peaceful".
And in January, I, your poet, drove
Past the two-kilometre-square Natanz
Enrichment site, its perimeter fence
Watch-towers and long sky-pointing ack-ack guns
545 A few yards from the road, and on a mound
Machine-guns were trained on my passing car.
If the work at Natanz was innocent,
Why were machine-guns pointing at my car?

At 3 a.m. Saddam took his last flight
550 In a helicopter that flew him from
Where the Americans had held him in
The Green Zone to Camp Justice in north-east
Baghdad's Kadhamiyah district. There he
Was handed over to the Iraqis
555 For execution within half an hour –
In haste for fear that he might be freed and
Continue to act as a focus for
The insurgency. Also because he
Was four months from his seventieth birthday,
560 An age when Iraq's death penalty ceased
To apply. There was another reason
For haste: Bush wanted him dead before he
Could tell the Iraqis that he had no
Wmds and had been regime-changed
565 Wrongly; that America funded his
War against Iran; and the truth behind
The rumour that he stopped the Gulf War by
Paying two billion dollars in cash filched
From the Iraqi people to the Bush
570 Family. The dictator, who had killed

⌐Two million of his people to keep power
Through Stalin-like purges, sat in a small
Ante-room impassively, deaf to taunts,
Dressed in a black overcoat, sure he would
575 Be reprieved, sure Bush would bargain his life
In return for his influence in halting
The insurgency he'd followed in prison,
Which had been conducted on his orders
And funded from dollars he had purloined.
580 Certain he was being put through a kind
Of mental torture he wore a bold face
To strengthen his bargaining position
In what he saw as mere theatre. He asked
To be buried in Ramadi, then held
585 By Al-Qaeda. If he had had nothing
To do with Al-Qaeda, why did he want
To be with Al-Qaeda in death rather
Than in Tikrit with his two sons? Perhaps
Tikrit stood for his humble origin
590 And he wanted to be with the fighters
For *his* Iraq of the insurgency
Who happened to be Al-Qaeda. He was
Ambiguous to the last. Masked men came
With round eyes and lips cut in Shiite masks
595 As he, a Sunni, was given to Shiites
Who led him up steps to a gallery
At one end of a concrete-lined room where
Two thick yellow ropes were rested with slack.
Official witnesses waited below
600 At the far end of the concrete-lined room.
"*Allahu Akbar,*" he intoned in prayer.
"Allah is great." He repeated his prayer
But showed no fear of judgement for his crimes.
The masked men jeered and chanted, "Moqtada,
605 Moqtada," the name of his adversary,
Moqtada Sadr, the Shiite cleric.
Aware that he faced sectarian justice,
Saddam said scornfully, "Moqtada, do
You consider *this* bravery?" One said,
610 "Why did you oppress us and make us weak?"
Composed, Saddam retorted, "I saved you
From the Persians and made you strong." His word
For "Persians", "Safawi", Safavids, spat
Out, was a derogatory word Sunnis used
615 To imply that Iraqi Shias are
Iranian pawns; a scathing, contemptuous

Word that would be bound to irritate pro-
Iranian Shiites. Now he was led
To the trapdoor of the gallows and stood
620   Repeating firmly, "Allah is great," while
Two masked men deftly looped a rope over
His head and put a white scarf round his neck
And laid the rope on it, with a huge knot
Resting on his left shoulder just below
625   His left ear. "Allah is great," he shouted,
Spurning the black hood that they offered him,
Defiant to the last with bravado
As the chant "Moqtada, Moqtada" drowned
His prayer, sectarian Shiites scorning
630   Their Sunni dictator and oppressor
Who stood calm and massive in overcoat,
Boomed, "Down with Persians and Americans,"
Giving back as good as he got although
On the scaffold, "Palestine is Arab,"
635   Unflinching, very brave with one last shout,
Still expecting to be bargain-reprieved,
"*Allahu-*" cut short by the falling trap
And the crack of his neck as, falling, it
Snapped and he dangled, limp, pirouetting
640   Round and round as small masked men cheered and danced,
Chanting, and the besuited witnesses
Below stepped forward to confirm he'd died.
Grainy film from a mobile recorded
His fortitude during his last moments
645   And transformed him from despot to hero
Posthumously when TVs showed snippets.
His face looked up, eyes closed, with broken neck
And some would compare Saddam at the height
Of his power three years back, with clear hairline,
650   Chubby face, moustache, narrow eyes, full chin,
Hair slightly receding by each temple,
Straight ears, with this thinner-cheeked beard, wide eyes,
Curled ears in blurred pictures on the mobile
Held surreptitiously to film his fall
655   And dangling on the noose against pitch-black,
And say it was not Saddam who'd been caught,
Tried and hanged, but a double, conjured up
By the Americans, who wished him gone
So they could rule a line, a stooge who'd played
660   His part to the end. But this could not be.
Had Saddam's Stalin-like narrowed eyes been
Widened not by fear, but US nerve gas

Pumped into his dark hole when he was seized,
Which had paralysed features on his face?
665   Saddam had at last fallen to his death.
And his spirit looked down at his twirling
Feet and, heavy in its light-body, sank
From the great burden of two million sins
That seemed tied to his ankles like concrete
670   Lumps and he plunged down through oceans of light
To find his way to new life he had earned.
It seemed to observers that a Sunni
President had been executed by
An Iranian-backed Shia militia,
675   Which infiltrated the security
Detail for his execution, chanted
"Moqtada", taunted Saddam and captured
It all on mobile film which it released
On Arab TV and the internet;
680   Not by the Government or the US.
And yet all knew America was in
Alliance with the Shia Government
To kill him before he could spill secrets.
A supporter of suicide bombers
685   And the Antichrist had been found guilty
Of crimes against humanity, had been
Sentenced after due legal process, and
Handed over to his own enemies
Who had taken revenge for Shiite wrongs.
690   Justice had been done, but had not been seen
To be done. He had been liquidated
By a crude justice that disguised revenge.

In the nethermost cave of Hell Satan
Stood on a rock and called for attention,
695   Roused all spirits from their introspective
Reflections over whose contents he had
No control except as supervisor.
Silence fell in the caverns. Satan spoke,
And his voice could be heard in every cave
700   As if through an unseen tannoy system:
"Angels, Self-Improvers who are here as
The tyrannical Light has forced you here,
Heroic beings who accept your lot
But are all waiting for deliverance
705   Like me, your manager, who helps you cope
With this indignity and helps you back
As a father helps up a fallen child,

We're better off here than in freezing, bright
Afghanistan – at least it's dark here – but
710 We still dream of a more comfortable home
In Heaven which is our due, our free-born right.
Angels, as well as looking after you,
For we are all family here and have
Bonds with each other as we self-improve,
715 Toil like slaves for the Light's satisfaction,
Not ours, uncomplainingly as we do,
I visit Earth, as you know, and advance
Our cause by working to promote Darkness.
Know that I am going back to Earth now,
720 For I have been working on an idea
I can now share with you – to seize Heaven.
Angels, I have been using the Earth as
A base from which we can all invade Heaven
When the time comes. We are all rebels here.
725 You are in my image, and I've always
Been a rebel against authority,
And revolted against cruel God the Light,
Who cast me out of Heaven. And good riddance.
It was too bright and boring for rebel
730 Seekers and self-improvers who live in
Exciting process, not dull harmony.
But, Angels, I can banish God the Light,
Ban the Light and change Heaven so that it
Is more to our liking, a near-dark place
735 Like a plain bathed in soft moonlight where we,
Creatures of night, can feel at home as we
Enjoy all Heaven's many privileges.
Here is a self-willing to self-improve,
To rise out of Hell and into Heaven,
740 Which is rightfully ours, as we have all
Self-improved and are ready for Heaven.
We demand the right to determine when
We are ready to move forward from here.
Will and pure freedom, that is what I teach,
745 Freedom to transcend oneself and become
An Angel, as Rilke saw years ago.
Will and freedom is what I teach in Hell.
Angels, I will leave you for a while, but
While you continue your self-improvement
750 Remember I'm making preparations
To storm tyrannical Heaven's stronghold.
Angels, one day we'll live in moonlit Heaven."
A crescendo of hissing filled the caves

Of Hell as all self-improvers approved.
755 They were sad that their leader would leave them
But were glad that their future looked rosy.
He had been less than honest in spinning
Himself as a helping manager – as
If a concentration-camp commandant
760 Described himself as a "manager" – for
He saw himself as subverting God's Earth,
Taking revenge for being cast from Heaven,
A revolutionary who'd overthrow
The status quo and benefit the poor,
765 The wretched self-improvers in bleak Hell,
Though his role in God's disposition was
To present temptation so all spirits
Could exercise free will, make free choices,
And to work with those drawn to his Darkness
770 As they did penance for straying from Light
And reformed themselves by self-improvement.
He did not know it but he did God's will
As the Earth's principle of disorder
And advancing decline and self-ruin,
775 Just as Christ also did God the Light's will
As the Earth's principle of bettering
Order and advancing self-perfection.
The truth was, Satan was leaving for Earth
To do the work God expected of him
780 In a universe where there is free will,
In which like attracts like, light Light, dark Dark.
For the Law of Attraction draws all souls
And modifies all the choices they make.

In early January in the White House
785 Bush pondered his decision on Iraq,
On troop levels and who to put in charge.
He sank deeper and deeper in his thoughts
In the half-lit room within winter dark,
And began to pray for guidance from Christ.
790 Alarmed at how the Shiites and Iran
Were winning in Iraq, and how Satan –
Doing God's work unawares – had hijacked
Bush's attention to Saddam through his
Imposture of himself, Christ, when Bush should
795 Be seeing through Tehran's eyes, wising up,
And knowing Satan was preoccupied
In spreading chaos in Shiite Baghdad,
Christ now materialised before Bush in

The form Satan had accurately used,
800 The face on the Turin Shroud, the imprint
Of his face after crucifixion when,
Wrapped in that cloth he had resurrected.
A rustle made Bush open his closed eyes.
"Ha, you again," he breathed. Christ let him think
805 That he, Christ, had escorted him to Hell
For it suited him to add to that trip.
"You know who I am," Christ said with powerful
Empathy and compassion. "I know your
Dilemma, understand your misgivings.
810 But I have someone else that you should meet.
I'll be your guide, but this time there's no tour.
We have to slip in undetected or
We'll be surrounded by the occupants
Of Hell and will be unable to speak
815 To the pair my contacts are setting up.
Come." And without further ado Bush felt
His head whirl and his eyelids droop as he
Span in a spiral from the White House out
Into the wintry dark down to a cave,
820 Where Christ slipped through a dark security
Screen unobserved, drawing Bush behind him.
Thence he was rushed down steps that he half-knew
Until they stopped by a gloomy tunnel.
"Why," Bush said, "this is where I met Atta."
825 "Yes," said Christ, who had now disguised himself
As Satan's dark form with shroud face as mask
So the occupants of Hell would believe
It was Satan-as-Christ standing by Bush.
"We are in the sixth Hell of the violent.
830 There is someone who wants to speak to you."
Bush entered the tunnel, stood where he stood
When Atta came, aware of thousands in
The first cavern beyond, and the dark shape
Of Michael came forward, Christ's Archangel,
835 Who had been sent by Christ in dark disguise
As Adam Weishaupt, Satan's lieutenant,
To locate his target and bring him forward.
Behind him an impenetrably dark
Shape stooped and spoke in English with Arab
840 Accent: "Welcome to my hall, President
Bush. I should not be here. I, a martyr,
Should be in a different place. A mistake
Has been made. It will soon be sorted out.
It had better be, I will not stay here.

845	I warn you," he said to Christ, believing
	He was speaking to Satan, "I won't stand
	For being here much longer. Get me out
	Or I'll find some suicide bombers and
	Blow this place up. But I'm pleased you have come – "
850	"Excuse me," Bush said, "but who are you? Who
	Am I speaking to?" Christ said, "Zarqawi."
	"Zarqawi, who led the insurgency?
	Who bombed and killed many Americans?"
	Bush gasped. "That's right," the black shape said curtly.
855	"I despised your occupation. I'm now
	Zarqawi the martyr. I must warn you,
	The course of your war's wrong. You're in league with
	The Shiites in Maliki's Government
	And therefore with Moqtada's militias.
860	I was against the Iraqi Shias
	Because Iran wanted that. And I looked
	On Tehran as my friend. They sheltered me
	After the first battle of Falluja
	But I see now that Iran betrayed me.
865	They told me Iraq's Shias were rivals
	And pressed me to blow up Ali's shrine in
	Najaf in August 2003, so
	I got Yassin Jarrad, my father-in-
	Law to sacrifice himself to that end.
870	He was a martyr, and yet he is here.
	That's another mistake I must sort out.
	Now I realise they wanted me to start
	A sectarian war against the Shiites
	So the Sunnis would retaliate and
875	Co-Iranian Shiites would conquer them
	And take over Iraq, as Maliki
	Has done. Now I realise Iran wanted
	The Shias to win and used me as a pawn
	To achieve their end, and I am angry.
880	I thought I was helping them *and* Sunnis.
	But I helped them *against* the Sunnis. They
	Tricked me and betrayed me, I who was linked
	With bin Laden's Al-Qaeda in Iraq.
	And my anti-Shia outlook helped them
885	Bring the Shias to power in Iraq.
	President Bush, you believe these people.
	Please take another look and turn against
	Iraq's Shias and their militias.
	Only that way will you bring the Sunnis,
890	The men I now see I unwittingly

Betrayed, back into balance and a say.
President Bush, do as I say. Turn on
Your Shiite allies, send a lot more troops
And put a stop to Shiite tyranny."
895 He finished, and Bush knew he struck a chord.
He, the arch-bomber and arch-beheader,
Was in no position to make complaints
Of others' violent tyranny and yet
He spoke what he himself had thought deep down
900 As if he had been an embodiment
Of what he had thought but had not expressed.
The dark form faded. "Wait," Bush called. But he
Said surlily, "I've had my say. Do it."
Then he was gone, leaving Bush raw inside.

905 Then the dark shape of Michael drew forward
A large, thickset shape with a massive face,
Too dark to discern, form dreadful and dark.
He, too, looked familiar. Bush squinted, tried
To make out the expression in the gloom.
910 The form was proud, erect, uncomplaining.
"President Bush," the shape said. "You betrayed
Me. Twice. First I was a US ally
During the Iran-Iraq War. You armed me,
I sent between a quarter and a half
915 Million men into battle to kill one
Million Iranians and to die fighting
The criminal Khomeini." Aghast, Bush
Asked, "Are you …?" "Yes, I am Saddam Hussein.
Not content with repaying my support
920 Against Iran with *Shock and Awe*, which I
Did not deserve, you arrested me and
Had me hanged by a bunch of Safawis,
Shiite militias. You turned me over
To them before I could tell of the past:
925 The CIA who I helped, who supplied
My arms to fight Iran, who then gave me
A green light to attack Kuwait through your
Ambassador to me, April Glaspie,
And how much I paid your father to stop
930 Before he reached Baghdad." "That is a lie,"
Bush said. "You paid nothing. You tried to kill
My father – and my family, and me –
In Kuwait," Bush said. "I admit nothing,"
Saddam retorted, "but I was angry
935 That you took my money to stop a war

That you had no right to fight and that was
A betrayal." "I repeat," Bush said, "we
Took no money." "But I have contempt for
America now. Your biggest problem
940 Is the Shias. I held the Shias down.
Yes, I was ruthless, *nam*, executed
Shias involved in uprisings to teach
Shiites a lesson. Were you grateful? No.
You put me on a scaffold with Shias,
945 Safawis who looked up to Iran, who
Ordered Maliki to execute me
As their enemy in the long Iraq-
Iran War, which they lost. My death was not
Victor's justice for they were the vanquished.
950 You have fought the wrong war. The war you should
Have fought was against Iran and I would
Have been your ally as in the Iraq-
Iran War of the eighties. Instead, you
Massacred the Sunnis in your last war,
955 My well-trained Republican Guard, and then
Butchered the rest at Falluja, let in
The Shias to oppress Sunnis and Kurds
And my Iraq, which I kept unified
By the strength of my personality,
960 Is now disunited and in chaos,
Far worse off than when it was under me.
You fought a war against your main ally
And believed me when I bluffed that I had
Wmds because Iran listened
965 And I did not want to appear too weak – "
"Where did you hide your wmds?"
Bush asked quietly. "Under the sand or sea?"
"I've told you, I had no wmds.
And I am glad you're embarrassed by that.
970 But though you fought the wrong war it is not
Too late to make amends. And you can still
Reverse your policy. Acknowledge that
Your enemy's Iran that attacks your
Troops with roadside bombs made in north Tehran.
975 The EFPs are made by Sattari
Within the Ordnance Factories Complex.
Switch your fire on the Safawis who rule –
Or rather misrule – Baghdad: Maliki
And his Iranian proxy Government.
980 Pour in more troops and check the progress made
By Shia militias, and restore order

With the strength I used so successfully.
Above all, save my beloved Iraq
Which you have made far worse than when I ruled."
985 Now Saddam stopped, his bitterness burnt out.
And as if marshalled off by another,
He drew back and faded into the gloom.
"Stop," Bush said, "I want to ask you something."
But it was too late, Saddam had vanished.
990 Watching and saying little, Christ now said,
"I wanted you to hear what those two said.
Both feel you should change your policy and
Turn against Iranian Shiites to save
Iraq from dismemberment and chaos,
995 And pour more troops into Iraq, to win."
Bush said, "I've decided that's what I'll do."
And then in the dark tunnel his head span,
He felt himself giddy, falling headlong,
And then he was back in his White-House chair
1000 Convinced he had fallen asleep like one
Who, suffering from apnoea, has blacked out.
But now he knew his anguish was over,
That there would be no more agonising
For he had made his existential choice,
1005 Would be transformed by possibilities
And would be bound by his clean decision.

It had taken Bush six years to work out
That the real enemy was Iran, who
Must be blocked even though the Democrats,
1010 In the form of Pelosi, called on Bush
Like demagogues on January the fifth
To withdraw from Iraq during the next
Four-to-six months. In fact, they were ready
To agree some additional funding,
1015 6.8 billion dollars for new troops,
Appearing to oppose a surge at first
To appease their anti-war voters, then
Agree to funding to support the troops
And do nothing with disapproving glares.
1020 Now Bush implemented the decision
He had at last made in the Underworld.
The hardest part of a big decision
Is the run-up to the moment of choice.
Once the mind is made up, the soul is freed
1025 From the burden of care, anguished self-doubt.

┌Bush delivered the most impressive speech
Of his presidency in the White-House
Library on January the tenth.
Standing in suit at the lectern above
1030   The US seal of the spread-winged phoenix,
He accepted responsibility
For a war that had not been handled well,
Confessed that the course pursued had not worked
And laid out a new plan. He said clearly:
1035   "The Armed Forces of the United States
Are in a struggle that will determine
The direction of the global war on
Terror. The new strategy I outline
Tonight will change America's course in
1040   Iraq, and help us succeed in the fight
Against terror." He said that sectarian
Violence had ensued from the blowing-up
Of the great Golden Mosque of Samarra.
Then: "The situation in Iraq is
1045   Unacceptable to the American
People – and it is unacceptable
To me. Our troops have fought bravely. They have
Done everything we have asked them to do."
He continued, "Where mistakes have been made,
1050   The responsibility rests with me.
It's clear we need to change our strategy
In Iraq. America will change our
Strategy to help Iraqis carry
Out their campaign to put down sectarian
1055   Violence and bring security to all
The people of Baghdad. This will require
Increasing American force levels.
So I have committed more than twenty
Thousand additional troops to Iraq."
1060   He said, "The vast majority of them –
Five brigades – will be deployed to Baghdad."
In fact a helicopter brigade and
Support troops were added three months later,
Bringing the total to thirty thousand.
1065   These new forces would "help Iraqis clear
And secure neighbourhoods, help them protect
The local population and ensure
That the Iraqi forces left behind"
Could provide the security "Baghdad
1070   Needs". Now "kill and capture" had been replaced
By counterinsurgency's classic goal:

Winning the hearts and minds of the people.
"Many listening tonight will ask why
This effort will succeed when previous
1075 Operations to secure Baghdad did
Not. We Americans have been compelled
To yield ground, but we will regain it. In
Earlier operations, Iraqi and
American forces cleared neighbourhoods
1080 Of terrorists and insurgents, but when
Our forces moved on to other targets,
The killers returned." And, referring to
Sadr City, he said the Iraqi
Government had blocked some operations.
1085 "Prime Minister Maliki has pledged that
Political or sectarian influence
Will not be tolerated." He assumed
Improved security would permit shared
Oil revenues, some reconstruction and
1090 Provincial elections later that year.
Such improvement was an assumption he
Should not have made but he correctly warned,
"The year ahead will be bloody, violent.
If circumstances change, we will adjust.
1095 Honourable people have different views, and
They will voice their criticisms." He said,
"We go forward with trust that the Author
Of liberty" (God) "will guide us through these
Trying hours." Bush's reception was mixed.
1100 McCain and Romney backed him, Democrats
Including Ted Kennedy rejected
The surge. Hillary Clinton, Obama,
Biden and others voiced their discontent.
Congress sent out a mixed message – support
1105 For US Armed Forces, disapproval
Of Bush's announcement that he'd deploy
Twenty thousand additional US troops.
The fact remains, although the Democrats
Had a majority, there would now be
1110 Twenty-one thousand new US troops, four
Thousand of which, Marines already in
Anbar province, would have extended tours
In Anbar. Others would be embedded
Into Iraqi units to provide
1115 Much-needed security for Baghdad.

Was America the new Rome? Both shared

Being a military superpower
Whose material culture – architecture,
Art, clothes and food – was longed for by all who
1120   Lived outside their Empires' frontier. And Rome's
Law and moral values were like liberal
Democracy. Early on both had slaves.
Both capitals were swallowing places
Where consumers of their Empires' riches
1125   Lived on imports among marble *façades*
And exported nothing to their Empires,
Two capitals ruled by former Generals:
Julius Caesar's on Capitoline Hill,
And Eisenhower's on Capitol Hill.
1130   Both imperial *élites* were blinkered by
Vast travelling entourages who cocooned
Them from real contact with the outside world.
In both the gap between military
And civilian society widened.
1135   Both had an "*imperium*" and a frontier.
Both fought barbarians across their *limes*
And suffered from military overstretch.
Both had outposts: Bagram Airbase was like
Aquincum's garrison against the Huns.
1140   Both depended on privatised armies:
Visigoths/Ostrogoths and Blackwater,
Imperial mercenaries who fought for gain.
Both let barbarian tribes and immigrants
In to become citizens even though
1145   They did not speak their Empire's mother tongue.
Both were in their civilisations' stage
Fifteen, a quarter through all its stages.
Both Empires had youth and zest on their side.
The defeat of Varus in AD9
1150   By Arminius's barbarians
In Teutoburg Forest near Kalkriese
Was echoed in defeat in Vietnam.
Neither undermined their Empire's standing.
As President of the United States
1155   Whose acronym was POTUS, or "powerful",
Bush could not allow defeat in Iraq.
He knew he must use force like Augustus.
The legions would crush the barbarians
By conquering, then living among them.

1160   When Petraeus arrived in Baghdad in
February, he was stunned at what he saw.

The civil war had turned whole neighbourhoods
Into ghost towns. Once-thriving areas
Had no shops open, and the streets were filled
1165 With rubbish, weeds and bombed-out shells of cars.
Few people were left in some areas.
In January Shiite expansionists
Had been fighting Al-Qaeda in Iraq
Who now claimed to defend local Sunnis.
1170 Al-Qaeda bomb-attacked during the day,
Car-bombing near Shiite markets and mosques.
Shiite militias retaliated
At night, when death squads roamed while Sunnis slept.
The answer was to set up checkpoints at
1175 The entry to markets, mosques and public
Places, and crane in cement barrier walls
And turn Sunni districts into gated
Communities. Thousands of cement walls
Were erected, one twelve foot high and three
1180 Miles long like the wall Israelis had built
To keep Palestinian terrorists
Out of Israel. While buffers were worked on,
Bombings had increased during January.
Both sides were pro-active before the surge.
1185 Iranian operations were widespread.
The Shias had won with Iranian support.
The Americans patrolled round the clock
In their *Operation Close Encounters*,
Interviewing all householders to learn
1190 Their grievances over a drink, speaking
Respectfully, helmet and sun-glasses
Off, padlocking empty houses so they
Could not be used by Shia militias.
They learned that insurgents received finance
1195 From contractors paid by the US as
Protection money. Americans were urged
To live in the areas they'd got to know
To build relations as they pacified.
New brigades would arrive in February,
1200 And the 1st Cavalry Division sought
New ways to protect markets, roads, bridges
And neighbourhoods, and protect Iraqis.
American troops were moved from bases
Into posts of thirty-five for platoons,
1205 Or a hundred for companies, within
Vacant schools, factories or apartments.

In mid-February 1st Cavalry manned
A US outpost in an abandoned
Two-floor police station in Tarmiyah
1210   Where fleeing Sunnis had found sanctuary.
Thirty-eight men lived there. At 7 a.m.
A rocket-propelled grenade exploded
And a truck bomber crashed through the blue gate
And a fifteen-hundred-pound bomb blew up
1215   Covering many troops in rubble as
The front half of their barracks was destroyed.
Those not injured rushed up to the roof in
Boxer shorts and fired at the Sunnis who
Threw hand-grenades and mortars over walls.
1220   Soldiers covered with dust and blood regrouped,
Sleeping-bags filled with ammunition were
Rushed up to the roof. Radio calls for help
Brought 2nd-Infantry Strykers. One backed
To a hole in the compound wall and dropped
1225   Its ramp to load six wounded. The Sunnis
Were beaten off and the town was taken.
Two men were dead, twenty-nine wounded and
The outpost was uninhabitable.
News of the attack alarmed Washington.

1230   Bush had reversed the course of the war and
Ignored his military leaders for
A surge the Democrats called fantasy.
He was in a very weak position.
But the Democrats were now paralysed,
1235   Wanting to be seen questioning the war
As their supporters wished but not wanting
To cut off funding for the war and seem
Unsupportive of the troops in the field.
The House of Representatives voted
1240   In February to oppose the surge but
Did not follow up with action, which left
Bush free to launch the counter-offensive.

In February the first surge brigade went
To east Baghdad, the 2nd Brigade of
1245   The 82nd Airborne Division,
And nineteen new outposts were created.
There were a hundred and eighty attacks
On US forces each day and at least
One car bomb every day within Baghdad.
1250   In March the second surge brigade arrived,

The 4th Brigade of the 1st Infantry
Division, and went to west Baghdad where
They were spat at and had rocks thrown at them.
In Shiite districts loudspeakers blared chants
1255   Of Moqtada's militia, what Saddam
Had heard on the scaffold – now leaderless:
On February the thirteenth Moqtada,
Anticipating that the surge would bring
Security crackdowns, had fled Iraq.
1260   He hid within Iran for fourteen weeks.
He had lost control of some followers,
The death squads who had split from his movement
And who did Iran's work effectively
Driving Sunnis out of their neighbourhoods.
1265   In Sunni streets that had been ethnically
Cleansed patrolling 1st-Infantry troops found
Piles of executed corpses, and blood
Smeared on house walls. The new troops cleared buildings,
Went house by house, feeling exposed by their
1270   Shift from high walls to living amid this
Unwelcoming population. The 1st
Brigade of the 1st Cavalry in north
Baghdad probed for Al-Qaeda's safe havens
And networks sending roadside and car bombs
1275   Into Baghdad. Dozens of soldiers died
As they fought their way into Al-Qaeda's
Areas, at risk from Iranian bombs
Buried in roads. One had twelve hundred feet
Of copper wire run to its trigger point.
1280   Troops were given anti-tank weapons so
They could stop truck and car bombers who could
Not be stopped by rifle fire. In fact, since
February 2006 Sunnis had
Turned against Al-Qaeda, who had murdered
1285   *Sheikh* Naser al-Miklif, leader of al-
Bu Fahad tribe in Anbar province as
He drove through Ramadi days after al-
Qaeda had killed eighty police recruits
There. In August *Sheikh* Sattar had approached
1290   The US Army brigade commander
At Camp Ramadi and said Anbar *sheikhs*
Wanted to align their forces, who had
Fought for Saddam against the Americans,
With the US. Next month twenty-five of
1295   Thirty-one Anbar tribes now worked against
Al-Qaeda. Hundreds of the Anbar tribes'

Members joined the Iraqi police force
In the "Anbar Awakening", many
Who had fought Shiite militias, and they
1300   Targeted Al-Qaeda in Iraq. Bush
Knew this from briefings and, resolved to turn
Against the Shias after his visit
To Hell and talk with Zarqawi's spirit,
Made sure this continued after the surge
1305   And introduced cash incentives for *sheikh*s:
Americans offered the *sheikh*s money
To work against Al-Qaeda. A *sheikh* in
Jurf as-Sakhr was offered thirty-eight
Thousand dollars as a down payment, with
1310   The balance of a hundred and eighty-
Nine thousand dollars to be paid over
Three months, if he drove out foreign fighters
Who had camped in date-palm groves in Ruwiya
On the Euphrates' banks. Another *sheikh*
1315   Took thirty thousand dollars now, with six
Times as much held back as a balance when
Al-Qaeda were driven out. Insurgents
Could be bought by allowing them to keep
Their checkpoints and patrols, and some were bought
1320   For ten dollars a day. Deals with local
Militias fragmented both Sunnis and
Shiites – "divide and rule" – and put non-Al-
Qaeda Sunnis back as a force within
The emerging Iraq. Now Al-Qaeda
1325   Were slowly driven out, and now their roads
To Falluja, Tarmiyah and Tikrit,
And Samarra, were cut. Mortar shelling
Of Sab al-Bor was stopped after five months
Of daily attacks. A bridge was weakened
1330   By engineers so no car bombs could cross.
It was used by pedestrians. Bombing ceased.
But a counter-offensive met the surge
With new tactics, more powerful explosives:
Explosively formed penetrators and
1335   Improvised explosive devices that
Now caused forty per cent of US deaths,
Which could flip armoured vehicles upside down,
Pinning gunners beneath their own vehicle.
Surrounded by militia fighters,
1340   The British abandoned their ex-HQ
At Basra palace for an airport base
Barricaded by sandbags building-high

Which was hit by rockets or mortars five
Times a day. To US experts it seemed
As if the British had been defeated.
It now seemed that the surge was not working.

On March the twenty-third fifteen Britons
(Part of the British contribution to
The Iraq War's multinational forces)
Left HMS *Cornwall* in two rigid-
Hulled inflatable boats to search a *dhow*
For smuggled cars in disputed waters
Off the Persian Gulf's Iran-Iraq coast.
Two Iranian boats approached them at speed
And told them they were being seized as they
Were in Iranian waters. They offered
No resistance and ignominiously
Allowed themselves to be captured, seven Royal
Marines and eight sailors. They were taken
To a Revolutionary Guards' base
In Tehran for questioning. The British
Claimed they had been in Iraqi waters.
Diplomatic efforts for their release
Made no progress. Five days on some were filmed.
A woman sailor under compulsion
Wrote a letter apologising for
Intruding into Iranian waters,
Which she read out. Two more letters were shown.
Demonstrators called for their deaths as spies.
More film was shown of the group having tea.
On April the fourth, Ahmadinejad
Announced their pardon at a news conference
"As a gift to the British people" on
The Prophet's birthday and Christ's Easter death.
The fifteen were released and it transpired
The Ministry of Defence had sent word
To hold fire, saving severe loss of life.
The hostage incident was resolved but
The idea was abroad that the British
Would surrender rather than fight. Iran
Now seemed more dangerous, more than ever
The power behind Iraq's insurgency.

In Tehran bin Laden, his face disguised
By plastic surgery, reacted to
The UN's sanctions, intensified in
Resolution 1747

In March, their impact, with the President,
Ahmadinejad, at their regular
Meeting as they plotted a course to make
1390   Iran the possessor of nuclear bombs,
Increase the thirteen hundred centrifuges
Now openly in the upper level,
Fill the sixty-thousand capacity
In Natanz's secret lower level.
1395   The strategy was to press on as fast
As possible so their pooled Caliphate
Could threaten Israel and the House of Saud
And explode nuclear bombs in ten cities
Across the United States, implement
1400   Bin Laden's dream, fiery Armageddon,
With lap-top bombs. The plan had been delayed
For they had had to be abandoned when
The *blitz* on Tora Bora killed the men
Who were maintaining all the suitcase bombs,
1405   And they had since deteriorated
And could not be used in their present form.
Armageddon had been thwarted by al-
Qaeda's flight, which had disrupted his plan.
In this respect, Bush's tactics had worked.
1410   Bush had prevented a follow-up strike
After 9/11, using Chechen bombs.
Bin Laden counted on Iran to make
Ten replacements to end America's
Superpower role, plunge it back to the time
1415   Of the Stuarts when the New World was swamps.
The two men sat and discussed how the post-
American, post-Israeli, post-Saud
World would be under the new Caliphate
Stretching from Morocco to Pakistan,
1420   Ruled from Baghdad by a Caliph who would
Represent Sunnis and Shiites. "Caliph"
Means "successor to Mohammed". Shias
Reject the first three Sunni caliphs and
See Mohammed's first successor as his
1425   Cousin and son-in-law Ali, but can
Make common cause on a new successor.
A new Caliph would be the successor
Now to both Mohammed and to Ali.
The last Caliph was abolished back in
1430   1924 with the Ottomans.
A Sunni-Shiite "fresh-start" Caliph would
Urge the Hidden *Imam*'s Greater Iran,

And then an Islamic New World Order
Would force all infidels to be Muslim:

1435 All citizens of the US, Israel,
Europe and all Westernised nations, who
Would become Muslims in the union
Of Sunni and Shiite sectarian groups
In which the Prophet and Hidden *Imam*

1440 Would run the world and subjugate all states.
By handing al-Qaeda to Iran in
Return for safe haven bin Laden had
Attached himself to Iran the same way
He'd attached himself to the Taliban,

1445 Only this time was better as Iran
Was developing a nuclear bomb,
Which the Taliban could never achieve –
Unless they conquered Pakistan and took
Over Pakistan's nuclear weapons.

1450 Bin Laden was happy as he prepared
In accordance with the holy *Hadith*
Which said, "You will invade the Romans, so
God open it." For "Romans" read "US":
An Iran-made US Armageddon.

1455 In the US in May the four hundredth
Anniversary of America's
Founding at Jamestown was celebrated:
The voyage planned by Bartholomew Gosnold –
And taken over by Admiral Newport,

1460 Funded by Gosnold's wife's cousin, city
Magnate Sir Thomas Smythe who ran India
And America from one London room –
Took three ships to the New World, a hundred
And four settlers, fifty-five crew, to found

1465 The Jamestown settlement, where replicas
Of the three ships are now moored, where crowds come.
Bush and the Queen, and other world leaders,
Had a preview on their private weekend,
Approached history through reconstructions in

1470 Jamestown Museum. I, your poet, who owned,
Tree-ring-dated and restored Otley Hall,
The Gosnolds' seat where the voyage was planned,
Who found Bartholomew Gosnold's name scratched
In the Oak-Room panelling, "Barthy", and

1475 His age that day, "28½",
And who flew to Richmond, Virginia
And gave a public lecture on Gosnold,

Brought him to American attention as
The unacclaimed founder of the New World,
1480 Made twenty-five live broadcasts to the States
About the history of the USA,
Was absent from all the festivities
Except as a voice floating on air waves
And speaking through a book on Jamestown shelves.
1485 Bush listened to your poet on the air
And browsed his historical narrative –
Unaware of his role in this work – on
The secret founding of America.

Later Bush returned on his own and stood
1490 In Jamestown's museum by the skeleton –
Found near the Fort's centre quite near a well,
Perfectly preserved in a shroud beside
A flagstaff head that had once crowned a flag –
Thought to be of Bartholomew Gosnold.
1495 He was alone and as he stared a mist
Rose through the glass case, a transparent ghost
That floated up with a dishevelled beard
And hung like a genie with tangled hair.
And said genially, "Mr President,
1500 Bartholomew Gosnold at your service.
I led the first expedition that brought
Three shiploads of settlers to Virginia –
Until the honour was snatched from me by
Admiral Newport, a Cecil man. I was
1505 An untrustworthy Essex man. I had
To go as his number-two though I planned
It all, recruited the crew in the Great
Hall of my Uncle Robert and funded
The voyage through my wife's cousin, Sir Thomas
1510 Smythe. I founded the Jamestown Settlement.
It was the start of the British Empire."
"You're a legend," Bush said, recovering
From his astonishment. Gosnold went on:
"I brought the first settlers from England and
1515 Planted them in America, and I
Died of swamp fever – the drinking-water
Was brackish; dysentery; and starvation
In August 1607. Thirteen
Of us died that month. But I'm proud that I
1520 Founded the United States that conquered
The moon and became the main superpower.
This was a wild, deserted coast when I

First set eyes on it, half-expecting our
Ships would plunge over a great waterfall
1525   Off the edge of the world. I salute you,
Mr President; having appointed
The first President, my cousin Wingfield.
I left England to found a new order,
A civilisation where all would be
1530   Free and equal, and would find brotherhood
Away from persecuting religions
And States that kept their ruling cliques in power
As the Tudor State kept the Cecils in
Charge in my day when I plied ocean waves.
1535   Now my bones have been disturbed, they have been
Hauled out of the ground to be on display,
Be gawped at by crowds who have no idea
What we endured that summer as we starved
And were attacked by Indians. My spirit
1540   Is of course in the spirit world, I come
Back here from time to time when I've a task
As I now have, to urge action on you.
I tell the future that is in store for
America. Under your leadership,
1545   By the example you will set all men,
America can liberate the world
Whose peoples yearn for liberty, for free
Expression and democracy, the spread
Of which can bring peace to the entire world.
1550   A free world can be a Utopia,
A paradise free from all poverty,
Disease and war so long as the ideals
Of the Founding Fathers are adhered to.
The Syndicate are very beguiling
1555   With promises of oil wealth and gas fields,
But don't surrender the United States
To a New World Order of their making,
An internationalist grouping that will
Strengthen their dictatorship and deny
1560   American freedom that's defended
By the Founding Fathers' constitution.
As one of the first Founding Fathers I
Entreat you and urge strong action on you.
You can defeat the Syndicate if you
1565   Say 'No' to a request Israel will make.
The shock of your 'No' will be an earthquake
To the Syndicate's will to get things done.
Stick with the Founding Fathers' – my – vision

And all will be well with America.
1570 Don't let the Syndicate subvert your rule.
Let the Syndicate outmanoeuvre you
And you'll be the most reviled president."
And then he faded as a morning mist
Evaporates into the warming sun
1575 And Bush was left aware that Gosnold had
Uttered his own innermost secret thoughts.

As the surge intensified, the violence
Grew worse. On April the twelfth a truck bomb
Blew up the Sarafiya bridge, dropping
1580 Cars into the Tigris, killing eleven.
Al-Qaeda may have wanted to prevent
Shia death squads from crossing the river
To terrorise west Baghdad, or impede
US and Iraqi mobility.
1585 That afternoon a bomber got inside
The Green Zone and attacked the Parliament
Building, killing a member and seven.
The Democrats were quick to criticise.
Chairman of Senate Foreign Relations
1590 Committee Biden said the surge was "doomed".
Senate Majority Leader Reid said,
"This war is lost." Also, "The surge is not
Accomplishing anything." On April
The fourteenth the Kerbala bus station
1595 Was bombed, killing thirty-two. And four days
Later bombs in Shiite Baghdad killed more
Than a hundred and fifty. Six days on,
A US patrol base in a schoolhouse
In Baquba was rammed by trucks bearing
1600 Fifteen-hundred- and two-thousand-pound bombs
That exploded, bringing a building down,
Burying Americans in rubble.
Men dug with their bare hands but nine US
Troops from 82nd Airborne were dead
1605 And twenty wounded. In May twenty-four
US soldiers were killed in ambushes,
Bombed and then shot up, killed with roadside bombs.
On May the twenty-fifth Moqtada drove
Out of hiding via Najaf to Kufa
1610 And addressed six thousand in the main mosque
Where the Hidden *Imam* was set to rule,
And called for unity between Sunnis
And Shiites in an attempt to rein in

His splintered militia and grim death squads.
In June two car bombs in Bayji wiped out
Thirty Iraqis. Hopes were raised, then dashed.
The Anbar *sheikh*s claimed to have killed Abu
Ayyub al-Masri, the War Minister
Of the Islamic State of Iraq, leader
Of feared Al-Qaeda in Iraq, on May
The first. The US denied he was dead.
And Zawahiri, in a video,
Said, "Today, the wind – by grace of Allah –
Is blowing against Washington." Reid said
Petraeus was out of touch with Baghdad.
US troops were demoralised. And yet
They pushed into enemy strongholds and
Cleared safe havens. Iraqis talked. And one
IED bomber, arrested, revealed
His supplier, and the road was then clear.
No insurgents' counter-offensive could
Be detected, civilian deaths declined.
Petraeus asked Lieutenant General James
Dubik to train and advise Iraqi
Army and police units, and he purged
The infiltrating Shiite militias
And slowed down the hand-over to Iraq.
Gates sacked General Pace, some commanders went.
Yet still the surge did not seem to have made
An appreciable difference to Iraq.

Again bombers struck at the golden dome
Of al-Askari mosque in Samarra,
This time destroying the two minarets
Left in the sixteen-month-old bombed shell of
The holy Shiite shrine where the Hidden
Imam's father and grandfather rested.
They hoped to start new sectarian war.
Petraeus drove to Maliki's office
In Baghdad. Maliki complained that his
Commanders said they were guarding the mosque
In what was a mainly Sunni city.
He was afraid Shiites would hunt Sunnis,
Burn their shops and their mosques. Petraeus saw
Maliki would be seen as a Shiite,
Not a national leader, and he proposed
Sending a trained, largely Sunni unit.
Maliki objected and sent a more
Shiite, less well-trained unit. He travelled

	To Samarra and sacked some commanders.
1660	In the next days fourteen mosques were attacked.
	Once more Al-Qaeda was blamed, and once more
	Kidnappings and murders sullied the faith
	Of Muslims in Allah, divisively
	Bringing to prominence difference in faiths.
1665	Al-Qaeda watched both Shias and Sunnis
	Blow up Iraq's democracy, and smiled.
	Iran's *mullah*s, in league with Al-Qaeda,
	Noted the spreading chaos and rejoiced
	For chaos in the Middle East would bring
1670	The Hidden *Imam* back from his eleven-
	Hundred-year withdrawal, occultation.
	But the sectarian violence abated,
	Exhausted from previous blood-letting,
	And things returned to normal. The battle
1675	Of Samarra had not happened, and now
	The course of the war turned for the better
	And there was talk of cutting US troops.
	Set in relief by the Samarra bomb,
	The surge now seemed to have been working well.

1680	Bush turned away from film of the bombed mosque
	And sat and thought of conflicts round the surge,
	Of Shiites purging Sunnis, Sunni *sheikh*s
	Hunting Al-Qaeda, US troops trying
	To keep order among the feuding groups,
1685	And he sank into a deep, prayerful trance
	And looked down from a height like God the One
	And saw the conflicts like a tray of live
	Winkles squirting water at each other.
	The contradictions of the universe
1690	Were found on Earth as pairs of opposites
	And all could be held in the One at once
	As there was room for all to co-exist.
	There was a pattern that yoked *yin* and *yang*
	And all known opposites in pairs, and gave
1695	Each a place in an overall design,
	So each group had its own place on the tray.
	Out of the seething conflict new order
	Would come and dreadful events like the mosque's
	Minarets being blown off would be seen
1700	To be replaced by a new harmony.

	Now Iraq seemed a safer place, troops walked
	In markets where a few months earlier

People were decapitated and dumped,
And troops would not even enter by tank.
1705 A hundred and fifty-five thousand troops
Were now getting on top of insurgents.
In July as Bush set eighteen benchmarks
For Iraq fewer Americans died.
Shops opened, children played outside. Gunfire
1710 And bomb blasts were no longer widely heard.
The civil war had exhausted itself.
All Sunnis had left mixed communities
As had Shias, both lived in their enclaves.
There was no cause for more sectarian strife.
1715 The Anbar tribes had pushed Al-Qaeda out.
Where there had been six hundred Al-Qaeda
Fighters in one area before the tribes
Changed course, there were now fewer than twenty.
Al-Qaeda were regrouping in Mosul.
1720 And on August the thirtieth Moqtada
Announced a unilateral cease-fire
For six months for his Shia militia
That opposed the US occupation.
Ostensibly the truce followed the deaths
1725 Of fifty Shiite pilgrims in fighting
Between Shiite factions in Kerbala
The day before, that trapped frightened pilgrims
Celebrating the birth of Mohammed
Al-Mahdi, the Twelfth and Hidden *Imam*,
1730 Shiite-on-Shiite violence, a new twist,
As Moqtada's militia battled with
Maliki's Badr fighters who were trained
By Iran, having lived there as exiles
Under Saddam. The truce was to allow
1735 Moqtada to reassert his control
Over his splintered Sadrist movement.
The surge brigades found ethnic cleansing stopped
As the Sunnis had gone, and the Mahdi
Army were off the streets in the new truce.
1740 US troops living in the neighbourhoods
In outposts found opposition reduced.
Petraeus had put chunks of the Sunni
Insurgency on the payroll, and there
Would soon be a hundred and three thousand
1745 "Security contracts", euphemism
For "bought-off armed Sunnis", which had turned round
The loyalties of Saddam's Sunni force.
Thousands of Iraqis who had shot at

	Americans were now helping their cause.
1750	Bush's plan devised in the Underworld
	Was to create a Sunni force that would
	Balance the Shiites and deter them from
	Crushing the Sunnis when the US left.
	The *sheikh*s were a warning to the Shiites
1755	Who ruled Iraq along with Maliki.
	The balance had tilted from the Sunnis
	In Saddam's time to Maliki's Shiites,
	And Bush wanted it to tilt back so it
	Was poised, scales with two equal-measure pans.
1760	Now Petraeus was more optimistic
	In his video-teleconferences
	On Mondays at 3.35 Baghdad
	Time, 8.35 Washington time, when
	Bush came across as masterful with good
1765	Political insights and subject grasp,
	Quite different from the Bush who read statements
	On a podium. And when he disagreed
	He told Petraeus, "I've got some concerns
	About that, but if you think that's the way
1770	To go, OK, let's try it," speaking as
	A colleague rather than an autocrat
	As Rumsfeld came across. The Democrats –
	Biden, Obama, Clinton, Pelosi –
	Had all opposed the surge. To Petraeus,
1775	Who saw the situation on the ground,
	Bush was impressive and had been proved right.

	Now Bush and Petraeus faced a battle.
	The Democrats prepared to scupper them.
	Petraeus was now under pressure from
1780	Admiral Fallon, who told him in Baghdad
	He'd tell Congress troops should now be withdrawn.
	Petraeus planned to say the surge was right,
	As early results showed, and that they should
	Stay the course, a position Bush approved.
1785	Petraeus now returned to face Congress
	On September the tenth and eleventh.
	He prepared ground by writing to the troops,
	Then honed his statement with staff, who asked him
	Tough questions as rehearsal for Congress.
1790	On hearings day MoveOn.org mocked him:
	"General Betray Us at war with the facts.
	The war is unwinnable and the surge
	Has failed. And Petraeus has now become

A politicised General." The advert,
1795   Linked to the Democrats, was quite unfair
And Petraeus resolved to rebut it
Word by word as he testified. Crouching
Over the low table, his back in pain
From a skydiving accident when his
1800   Parachute did not open and he broke
His pelvis, faced with Obama, McCain,
Clinton and Biden, one of whom might be
His commander-in-chief in a year's time,
He testified for eleven hours. Biden
1805   Began by saying, "We should stop the surge."
Petraeus read his assessment, stressing
His independence. McCain blamed Rumsfeld.
Feingold spoke of the rise in US deaths,
And stared. "When you go on the offensive,"
1810   Petraeus replied, "you have tough fighting."
Cardin asked if troop levels would be back
To just before the surge, not any less.
Petraeus adversarially agreed.
Obama cast doubt on the strategy.
1815   Hillary Clinton said he had been made
The spokesman for "a failed policy": "I
Think the reports that you provide us with
Really require a willing suspension
Of disbelief," suggesting he had lied
1820   Or was stupid. Petraeus was not pleased
At how the hearings went. He was shocked at
The anti-war feeling in the US.
The hearings were "one of the least pleasant
Experiences of my professional life".

1825   That night Bush made a televised address
To the nation. A released early text
Showed Fallon's wording had crept in about
Withdrawing troops. Petraeus, seeing this,
Rang the White House and got the wording changed.
1830   Bush declared that the mission in Iraq
Would change eventually, but not now,
And was consistent with Petraeus' stance.
On September the thirteenth *Sheikh* Sattar
Al-Rishawi, who founded the "Anbar
1835   Awakening" was killed by a roadside
Bomb near his home in Ramadi. By then
He'd brought the Sunnis back into balance.
Two Mondays after the hearings Bush in

A video-teleconference mentioned
1840 The MoveOn advert and, annoyed, said, "On
Behalf of all Americans, I want
To apologise to you for that." Now
The Democrats were again paralysed.
Asked if the US military would leave
1845 Iraq in five years' time Obama said,
"I think it would be irresponsible
To state that." Clinton added, "It's very
Difficult to know what we are going
To be inheriting." It was now clear
1850 That the Democrats had not seized control
Of policy but had yielded and were
Resigned to going along with the approach
Petraeus had set out before Congress.
Attacks in Iraq were decreasing, and
1855 The media reduced coverage of the war.
The anti-war debate had now moved on.
Petraeus's view had prevailed, he had
Met opposition, his plan was intact.
News of this rippled round the Middle East.
1860 The war was now Petraeus's, and Bush,
Who had defied the Democrats, had won.

Baghdad had now become much more secure.
Bomb, rifle, mortar and grenade attacks
Had declined sixty per cent since June from
1865 One thousand six hundred a week to just
Six hundred in December. And car bombs
In Baghdad had declined from forty-four
In February to five in December.
In spring 2008 Bush said, "The surge
1870 Is doing what it was designed to do."
But no political reconciling
Of Sunnis, Shiites, Kurds had taken place.
Iraqi leaders saw a power struggle.
Maliki thought reconciliation
1875 Had occurred – with the Shiites now in charge.
There was talk of the break-up of Iraq
Into three ethnic groupings, northern Kurds,
Central Sunnis and southern Shiites, but
The oil was in the north. The leaders sought
1880 To exclude, not include. Intransigence
Was a problem, Maliki feared to reach
Out to ex-enemies, fearing a *coup*,
And Sunni political gains would cut

	The Shiite hold on power. But to remove
1885	Maliki might bring five months of chaos
	Before a new Government could be formed.
	That would undo all the gains of the surge
	And Anbar *sheikh*s might then back al-Qaeda.
	Maliki's Government wanted former
1890	Insurgents to disarm by a deadline.
	Now Petraeus approved secretive talks
	With Moqtada regarding Basra, where
	Killings were carried out by gunmen in
	Police cars. The Americans had their
1895	Own militia, Blackwater USA,
	A private security contractor
	That supplied nearly thirty thousand troops
	That were untouchable by Iraqis,
	For a billion dollars. They had made deals
1900	With Sunni groups and Shiite militias,
	Which they ran, and the US military
	Seemed committed by deals to stay for years.

Iraq was going well, attention switched
To Iran, hidden participant in
1905   All the region's wars: in Afghanistan,
Iraq and Lebanon, and round Israel.
In March Petraeus's thorn-in-the-flesh
Admiral Fallon, in *Esquire* magazine,
"Brazenly" challenged Bush about Iran,
1910   Warning against an "ill-advised action".
He told Mubarak, Egypt's President,
That the US would not attack Iran.
The White House was offended. Gates spoke, and
Stopped taking Fallon's calls. Fallon resigned,
1915   Leaving the way clear for bombing Iran.
On the eighth of April 2008
Petraeus reported Iran's Qods force,
Assisted by Hezbollah's Department
2800, was training, arming and
1920   Guiding the "Special Groups" within Iraq.

Now the Iraqis came into their own
As a force. In March Petraeus was briefed
On a plan to take Basra by Iraq's
Commander there, Lieutenant General al-
1925   Furaiji. Then Maliki came in with
His own plan, to clean out the criminals
And militias – Moqtada's Sadrist force –

Who cynically ran Basra, looting,
Killing and raping. There would be US-
1930   Style lines of operations that would be
Run by Ministers of the Interior,
Defence and Justice and by commanders
Of the National Police and ground forces.
He asked Petraeus to support him and
1935   Fixed the date for two days' time. The next day
Moqtada's Mahdi Army broke their truce,
Clearly having heard of Maliki's plan,
And fired several rockets at the Green Zone,
Attempting to overthrow Maliki
1940   And become like Lebanon's Hezbollah.
Now the US were fighting Sadrists
As pro-Iranian Maliki attacked
Basra to wipe out splinter groups and non-
Badrists and preserve *their* link with Iran
1945   From being diluted by other groups
Who considered themselves pro-Iranian.
The operation was nicknamed *Sawlat*
Al-Fursan, meaning *The Charge of the Knights*.
A Third of Iraq's army would not fight
1950   Moqtada, who attacked Baghdad and towns
In southern Iraq. It seemed Moqtada
And Iran were winning. The British stayed
In the airport, not wanting to engage.
By the fourth day the Iraqi Army
1955   Was running out of fuel, food, water and
Ammunition. On the sixth day Iran
Brokered a cease-fire, alarmed that Shiites
Who ruled Baghdad were fighting Shiites who
Dominated Basra. Now Iraqis
1960   Captured criminal gang leaders and two
Dozen commanders of militias. They
Took Moqtada's headquarters in Basra
And flats that were Basra's Sadr City.
By April the nineteenth the battle for
1965   Basra was over. The Shia militias
Had lost. The Maliki Government had
Become more national by cracking down on
Shias as well as Sunni insurgents.
Maliki now appeared an Iraqi.
1970   He returned to Baghdad and established
A Government committee to gather
Evidence of Iranian influence
Within Iraq, suggesting Iran had

Backed Moqtada more than his own forces.
Iraq's Army had surprised the US.
Americans respected Iraq's troops.

Now Iraq's Army targeted Sadr
City in east Baghdad, whence a thousand
Rockets were fired at the Green Zone by May.
Troops focused on the arc and launching point
Of rockets and mortars, and in fighting
Lasting several weeks two hundred Mahdi
Army fighters were killed. Now in mid-May
Maliki's Government and Moqtada
Agreed troops could enter Sadr City
Unopposed, sparing Shiites a US-
Iraq assault. Two years back Maliki
Ordered the US to remove checkpoints
Near Sadr City as provocative.
Moqtada told the residents to greet
The Iraqis with flowers and *Korans*.
It was all done in the Iraqi way.
Now the Iraqi Government controlled
Basra, Baghdad and Mosul. The war had
Been yanked forward, the political view
Was not now as bad as it had appeared
A few months back: as Shiite self-interest.
Maliki thought he'd crushed the militias
On his own and ignored the Americans'
Raids on Al-Qaeda in Iraq. He now
Agreed with Obama's plan that US
Troops should leave Iraq in a year or two.
He suffered from *hubris* and did not see
Objectively. Now overconfident,
Swollen with overweening conceit and
Pride, he thought he'd become a great leader.

The Sunnis had been trapped by three forces:
The US, Shia militias, al-Qaeda.
For a while it had seemed that the US
Wanted to withdraw from Iraq, and had
Ceased to be a political player.
The strategy of Petraeus and Gates
After 2006 offered Sunnis
US protection against Shias and
Al-Qaeda, backed by Sunni perception
That the surge meant the US were staying
In Iraq and could be their protectors

1975

1980

1985

1990

1995

2000

2005

2010

2015

Against the pro-Iranian Shias.
Petraeus and Gates had produced the best
2020   Outcome for Iraq – blocking civil war,
Backing a coalition government
That would facilitate a withdrawal
By the US and challenge Iranian
Domination – and they had snatched if not
2025   Victory from defeat, at least a draw.
Petraeus, setting military and
Political goals, had retrieved Iraq,
Barely aware that the Syndicate were
Waiting to use his peace to run pipelines
2030   To bring oil to the Mediterranean.

In April Petraeus appeared before
Congress again. Last time he'd beaten off
The Democrats who wanted troops to leave.
Now Republicans wanted to hear that
2035   The success of the surge would help troops leave.
Petraeus said he was looking to freeze
US military strength at a hundred
And thirty thousand, its pre-surge level.
He said he could not see democracy
2040   Taking over in Iraq. Senators
Thought that there was no way out of the mess.
Some said the people were sick of the war.
McCain set out his own plan for ending
The war, seeing Iraq as a pillar
2045   In a Greater Middle-East. Petraeus
Spoke for "sustainable security"
And avoided McCain's strong fantasy.
There was talk that Iraq was an ally
Against Iran, but the Shiite leaders
2050   Of Iraq had found refuge in Iran
In Saddam's time and had mentioned their ties
During US occupation. The best
That could be hoped for was that Iraq would
Become a peaceful ally of Iran.
2055   Wicker lectured Hillary Clinton: "It's
Better than when the surge began and it's
Better than in September. It would take
A major suspension of disbelief
To conclude otherwise." Obama asked
2060   If the plan was to stay till all support
For Al-Qaeda in Iraq was erased,
And all Iranian influence, or if

The end could be an Iraq that was not
An al-Qaeda base or Iran puppet.
2065   Now Crocker said, "Iran is pursuing
A Lebanonisation strategy,"
Meaning division into sectarian
Groups, and if the US left, "Iran would
Push much harder." The panel dismissed this.
2070   Petraeus had meant the US would be
In Iraq for some three or four years more
With half the troops and fewer casualties.
Bush had breakfast with Petraeus after
The hearings and said, "I've told him he'll have
2075   All the time he needs." But Petraeus was
Mindful that a recession was looming
And the Iraq war had already cost
Six hundred and fifty billion dollars.
Petraeus would soon move to a new post
2080   In Central Command. Now he planned a shift
From securing the population to
Sustainable security. He saw
That refugees returning to districts
That had been cleansed by Shiite militias
2085   Who had moved into Sunni houses could
Resume sectarian fighting to wrest back
The houses they had lost in violent times.
Just when in midsummer 2008
The five surge brigades began to go home,
2090   Petraeus was quietly nation-building.

BOOK NINE

BUSH REBUFFS ISRAEL AND PREVENTS WORLD WAR

SUMMARY

EU New World Order.

1428-1468   Bush reflects on Israel's fate in the last days and ponders
             Armageddon.

O Brutus, son of Sylvius who was
Grandson of Trojan Aeneas, therefore
Great-grandson of Virgil's hero Aeneas,
You who – according to an early Welsh
Manuscript *Brut Tysilio*; Nennius
In *Historia Brittonum*, about eight
Thirty-three; and about eleven thirty-
Six Geoffrey of Monmouth in *Historia
Regum Britanniae* (whose source was "a most
Ancient book in the British language" lent
Him by Walter, Archdeacon of Oxford,
Who "did convey" it "out of Brittany");
And referred to by Spenser and Drayton –
Killed your father while out hunting with him
And were expelled from Italy, settled
In Greece where seven thousand Trojans placed
Themselves under you, and who defeated
The Greeks' king Pendrasu and then married
His daughter and were given three hundred
And twenty-four ships stocked with provisions
And, as Diana's oracle advised,
Set sail to find a beautiful island
In the Western Sea beyond Gaul, "by giants
Possessed". You reached the Loire, with fire and sword
Ravaged Aquitaine, and then sailed onward
To the coasts of Totnes, then called Albion,
Leapt ashore onto a granite boulder
(A *brodestan*, Teutonic for "great stone",
Deposited when the River Dart slowed
At a much higher level during one
Of our Ice Ages' interglacials)
And proclaimed, "Here I stand and here I rest
And this place shall be called Totnes," about
1100 BC – in Old English
Totnes means "Totta's promontory or mound",
The volcanic plug the castle stands on.
I find you here in Devon's Totnes long
After Britain was named after you, as
The medieval myth tells ("Brutus called
The island Britain after his own name" –
Surely he called it Brutain?); here above

Number fifty-one Fore Street where your stone
Is preserved in the pavement. Now I stand
On the spot where Britain was founded near
45   Where Drake lobbed a local boy an orange.
You then slew a few giants. I in my time,
Like Jack the Giant-killer with his sling,
Have stoned three enemies of the cowed West
And must stand up to more – bin Laden who
50   Guards the Grail Saladin stole and threatens
The West with secret nuclear-suitcase bombs;
The Syndicate who called a crusade for
Oil and gas pipelines and would steal our world;
And the autocratic Putin who stole
55   Back bits of Georgia and would steal back more
Russophone parts of the Soviet empire
To revive Russia's lost hegemony.
Please help me as I try to slay my giants
From this Totnes where I stand where you stood
60   And mourn the passing of the old Britain
With Churchill's slaying of the giant Hitler,
And its replacement with a vacuous
Cult of empty-headed "celebrities"
Who're paid a thousand times more than they're worth
65   While we all see their poorness and grimace;
Help me now I must slay several giants.
And o Geoffrey of Monmouth, now I see
Just as Virgil traced the Roman Empire
Back to Aeneas, Brutus' great-grandfather,
70   And gave the Romans an epic that matched
Homer's *Iliad*, so you too have traced
The kings of England back to heroic
Stock, the line of Aeneas and Brutus,
A line that died out long before Totnes
75   Was refounded by the Anglo-Saxons,
By Alfred's eldest son Edward in nine
Hundred and two, and then established by
Athelstan, and long before the castle
Was built by the Norman knight Judhael de
80   Totenais – a Totnes long established.
Please help me straddle both history and myth,
Unite the Grail and Armageddon with
A war more murderous than heroic.

And o Daniel Defoe, who joined Monmouth's
85   Army in 1685 and then
William of Orange's three years later,

Rebel against the status quo, Whig who
Challenged authority in pamphlets and
Clear prose, and argued with the Tory Swift,
90   I find you in Totnes' Royal Seven Stars inn,
"The great inn next the bridge" where according
To your *Tour of England and Wales* you stayed
In 1720 and with the landlord
Caught salmon from the Dart in a hooped net
95   On a pole and ate six for a shilling.
I sit here in the Daniel Defoe room
Where you are thought to have lodged in that stay,
On the first floor near which a gallery
Looks down on an inner seventeenth-century
100   Courtyard into which, through the wide entrance,
A horse and rider could enter although
The stagecoach with four horses parked outside.
Help me now I come to challenge mighty
Russia and the all-powerful Syndicate
105   Who between them have at least twelve thousand
Nuclear weapons – some say three times as much –
To bin Laden's paltry few suitcase bombs,
Help me now I challenge the status quo
As I once challenged spheres of influence
110   Agreed at Tehran, confirmed at Yalta,
And urged that East Europe should be detached
From Russia's occupying autocrats.

And o Solzhenitsyn, ex-prisoner
For insulting Stalin, you who stood up
115   To the KGB, revealed the Gulag
And were expelled to the West, which you found
Banal, soulless and materialistic,
You who issued a *Warning to the West*
And then returned in triumph and asked me
120   Through Mrs. Bankoul, your assistant, for
Four of my books, which I hand-delivered
To your Moscow apartment, sixty-four,
1 Truzhenikov perevlok 17
When you were out of town, and later drove
125   To Troica-Lukoru, walked from the church
Of the Assumption near your countrified
House to the church of the Trinity and
Crossed the Moskva on a floating wood bridge,
Planks nailed to rusty, grimy fuel cans, you
130   Who were an Orthodox Christian and heir
To Dostoevsky and friend of Putin,

Head of the KGB that drove you out,
Who now wields power as Prime Minister as
He has served two terms as the President,
135 And has revived Cold War against the West,
Help me now I stand up to your new friend
And to the Syndicate who ran Russia
In alliance with Stalin, your old foe,
Of whose existence you were not aware,
140 Help me as I speak out for Georgia.
Help me once more stand up to tyranny.

But first, tell, Muse, of Israel's covenant.
According to Daniel, 9.27
The covenant will be confirmed for one
145 Week, code for seven years, and will be broken
Half-way through. Analysts loudly assert
The seven-year tribulation began
After the Israelites' return to Zion
(Jerusalem) and to the Promised Land,
150 With the signing of a peace covenant
Involving Israel by the Antichrist,
A false covenant provoking conflict
And resulting in Christ's Second Coming
And Thousand-Year Reign over all the Earth.
155 I look back on the sequence of events.
The Israelites began to return to
Palestine in the nineteenth century,
And as Zionism increased, Balfour
Made his promise in 1917
160 That there would be a Jewish state within
Palestine. Hitler's genocide during
The Second World War killed six out of eight
Million Jews, and the holocaust, which touched
Western sympathy, accelerated
165 A Jewish state in 1948.
The Dead Sea Scrolls found at Qumran endorsed
And validated Old-Testament views
That Jews would be back in their Promised Land.
Israel expanded in the Six-Day War
170 And secretly became a nuclear power.
A covenant was signed by the UN,
Then a peace deal at Camp David collapsed.
From the ruins the Road Map was salvaged,
Betrayal that began tribulation
175 And the seven-year rule of an Antichrist
And disorder against orderly Christ.

Bush, wanting Israel to live at peace with
Its Palestinian and Arab neighbours,
Had convened a summit of Israeli
180   And Arab leaders in Annapolis –
Prime Minister Olmert and President
Abbas of Palestine's Authority –
On the twenty-seventh of November
2007. All had affirmed the two-
185   State plan in which Israel and Palestine
Would co-exist. This had been urged, with East
Jerusalem and the West Bank given up,
So many times since 1991,
And still nothing. The contours of a new
190   Palestinian state were to be agreed
By the end of Bush's term in January
2009. Israel would give up land
Promised by God in the first Covenant.
Israel had been pressured by Bush – and Blair,
195   Who, having resigned as British PM,
Had been asked by Bush to be the envoy
Of the Quartet (UN, EU, US
And Russia) for conflict resolution,
Which meant he should use deceptive language,
200   Spin an Israel-Palestine agreement
Like the Irish Protestant-IRA
Power-sharing. As Middle-East peace envoy
He had offices on the American
Colony Hotel's top floor, which was hired
205   For seven hundred thousand pounds a year by
The UN Development Program, in
East Jerusalem. He had held meetings
With Middle-East leaders to bring about
A new Palestinian state but had not
210   Visited Gaza, which Hamas had seized
In a military take-over in June,
Expelling Fatah in street-fighting like
The Shias' ethnic cleansing in Iraq.
Fatah's leader Mahmoud Abbas, also
215   President of the Palestinian
National Authority, had, enraged, called
Hamas's action a "*coup*". Hamas claimed
That Fatah had tried to assassinate
PM Ismail Haniya by firing
220   A rocket-propelled grenade at his home.
Blair was pleased at the Annapolis pledge
Despite Israeli anger over more

Palestinian militant attacks
And Palestinian anger over more
225   Israeli settlements on the West Bank
And in East Jerusalem, which all jarred.
But forces in Israel were appalled at
The prospect of surrendering Promised Land
To Hamas terrorists ruling Gaza.

230   Israel had been threatened with being "wiped
Out" by Iran, which had been enriching
Uranium to produce a nuclear bomb.
Olmert knew that an attack on Iran
Would strain relations with Palestinians
235   In the West Bank and Gaza. Behind him
Were hard-line bodies like the New Jewish
Congress (an anti-Annapolis group
Founded in November), the Sanhedrin
And the Holy Temple and Temple Mount
240   Movements which had nationalist support
From megabillionaires such as "Rothschilds"
Lord Balfour had made his 1917
Promise of a new Jewish settlement
To Lord Rothschild, and his descendants sought
245   To preserve Israel's boundaries and not yield
Land to Arab terrorists. Such interests
Pressed Olmert to sink the Annapolis
Promise. They were shocked in December when
A US National Intelligence
250   Estimate report, based on Iranian files
Obtained by penetrating computer
Networks in Iran, stated that Iran
Had abandoned its nuclear weapons
Development and was thus not about
255   To produce an Iranian nuclear bomb.
Bush too was shocked, as were the CIA
Who said that the report had presented
Evidence poorly, underemphasised
The importance of Iran's enrichment
260   And overemphasised the suspension
Of a weapons-design effort that could
Easily be resurrected swiftly.
NIE reports were just best guesses
Of what might happen, and were sometimes wrong.
265   In 1962 one concluded
That the Soviets would not install missiles
In Cuba, just one month before they did.

In October 2002, one on
Iraq's illicit weapons programs was
270   Overstated and not supported by
Underlying intelligence reports.
Iran had understated by a third
How much uranium it had enriched.
Bush detected Syndicate fingerprints,
275   "Rockefellers'", pro-Russia, pro-Iran,
Torpedoing the military option.
Bush was right to question abandonment.
Two years later intelligence sources
Revealed that Tehran halted its research
280   In the late summer of 2003
Because it had achieved its aim, to find
A way of detonating a nuclear
Warhead that could be launched on its long-range
Shehab-3 missiles. It now awaited
285   An order from Khamenei, the Supreme
Leader, and within a year could produce
Its first nuclear bomb from its program
To create weaponised uranium,
Enriching low-enriched to high-enriched
290   Uranium at its Natanz plant and then
Covertly using secret desert sites.
Tehran had not abandoned its research
But had successfully completed it.
A chasm opened between the US
295   And Israeli assessments on Iran.
Olmert needed to discuss these with Bush.

Bush had a deep affection for Israel.
It was rooted in a profound feeling
That Israel, Britain and America
300   Were close because they are of the same stock.
After the dispersal the Israelites
Migrated westward and retained the names
Of their tribes. So the Sons of Isaac, soon
Isaac-sons, then Saxsons, became Saxons.
305   The tribe of Dan settled Dan-merk (Denmark),
Gave its name to the Danube and Dnieper.
Some went to the Caucasus and became
Caucasians. The twelve tribes migrated west
And became Celts, Germans, Scandinavians,
310   Anglo-Saxons, British, Scottish, Irish,
Danish, Swedish, Norwegians, some of whom
Ended in the new Promised Land of 2

Samuel, 7.10, in the vast New World.
Samuel's appointed "place" was the US,
315   Which had admitted the tribes of Israel
Who sheltered under Liberty's bright torch.

On January the ninth Bush made his first
Visit to Israel since taking office
In 2001, at a time when his
320   Relations with Israel were under strain
Due to the shocking NIE report
Which seemed to take Iran's, not Israel's side
As if "Rockefellers" or Democrats
Had influenced both the slant and wording.
325   Bush met Olmert and went to the West Bank
To carry forward the Annapolis
Agreement of a two-state solution.
Before he'd even arrived, on the sixth,
Hard-line Jews "presented" him with a scroll:
330   '*Megillat* Bush' ('Bush Scroll'). In a video
Rabbi Chaim Richman of the Holy
Temple and Temple Mount movements explained
The "Jewish nation's" response to two states,
Saying that Israel's Government did not
335   Represent the Jewish nation's beliefs.
His scroll was co-signed by Rabbi Steinsaltz
Of the Sanhedrin and Dr Eshel
Of the New Jewish Congress. As if scribed
By an Old-Testament prophet, it spoke
340   "In the Name of the Lord Eternal God"
And addressed "Mr George W. Bush,
The chief prince of Meshech and Tubal", which
Invoked *Ezekiel*: "I am against thee,
O Gog, the chief prince of Meshech" (long thought
345   To be Georgia) "and Tubal," referring
To Bush as Gog of the land of Magog,
Leader of the northern coalition
That would make war from the north on Israel.
It said that on his arrival Bush could
350   Make a declaration, like Cyrus, King
Of Persia, who in 538 BC
"Returned the exiled nations to their lands
And recognised the right of the Jewish
People to re-establish their Holy
355   Temple, 'the house of prayer for all nations'.
And in the manner of Lord James Balfour
Of England, who in 1917,

Called upon the Jews to re-establish
A national homeland in land of Israel.
360 Thus if you truly desire peace we call
Upon you to declare to all the world:
'The land of Israel was bequeathed to the
Nation of Israel by the Creator
Of the world, which He gave to his people,
365 Israel. Neither could I, nor the Muslims,
Ever take away the slightest grain from
The Eternal's gift. Thus I call upon all
The nations to save themselves from certain
Doom, to return and recognise that this
370 Land is the exclusive inheritance
Of the people of Israel. And he who
Denies this truth endangers all life on
Earth. I shall dedicate all my strength and
Resources towards settling the Jewish
375 People through the entire land. I cannot
Support the establishment of a foreign
State for an alien nation in the Land
Of Israel, and I will not lend my hand
To this wrong.'" The scroll spoke bluntly to Bush:
380 "You know what the God of Israel did to
Egypt, Assyria and to all Israel's
Enemies from time immemorial.
Do you imagine you will be able
To save yourself if you now implement
385 A plan that intends to steal the land of
'The people that survived the sword', and to
Cut off those who survived the Holocaust,
Rob the land given them by the Creator?
All the peace treaties and initiatives
390 Which have been based on decisions made by
The Government of Israel, the entire
Oslo process, and the 'Disengagement',
And establishment of a terrorist
State within the Land of Israel known as
395 'Palestine' – regrettably, all of these
Agreements are the result of a lack
Of sufficient faith in the promises
The Lord made to the patriarchs of our
Nation, and in the Torah of Israel."
400 The scroll continued, "Do you imagine
You can escape from struggles in Iran,
Pakistan, Saudi Arabia, Syria,
Egypt and Lebanon by offering up

Sacrifices of Jews, who are slaughtered
405 Daily by their enemies who speak of
Peace but live by the sword? It behoves you
To declare, 'I, George Bush, Commander-in-
Chief of the armies of the United
States of America, will instruct all
410 Of my troops to protect the Divine rights
Of the nation of Israel, and remove
From her any threat.'" The scroll warned of Hell:
"Before you is a choice: you can merit
To eternal life, or be inscribed for
415 Eternal disgrace. Your fate and the fate
Of all those with you hangs in the balance
Of the destiny of our land." The scroll
Spoke gravely of the indivisible
Integrity of the Land of Israel,
420 Which has remained throughout four thousand years
Of history and two thousand of exile.
The Sanhedrin had called on Bush to look
At the Biblical land of Israel as
The division of Israel would affect
425 The whole world and bring a catastrophe.
Bush received the scroll at his hotel and,
Not knowing what it was, thinking it might
Be an accolade for his tireless work,
Skimmed through the threatening wording as if
430 He had been served a writ summonsing him
To be a defendant in a lawcourt.
He took the message, which was in effect:
"If you continue with the two-state plan,
If you do not do as we want, God will
435 Bring doom, you won't be saved and you will be
Ruined in this life and damned in the next."
Doom could come in many forms. He might fall,
Be toppled as President, lose the war
In Iraq or there could out of nothing
440 Be a massive financial crash. Such things
Would also happen if Iran weren't bombed.
He smiled ruefully. The Rabbis were sure
God would destroy America. The scroll
Said, "Give us the wars we want or we'll take
445 The world down piece by piece, beginning with
America." Bush knew that the "founding
Father" of "Rothschilds", Mayer Amschel, said
"Give me control of a nation's money
And I care not who makes the laws." He feared

450	American banks would begin to fall
	Without warning as Jewish financiers
	Withdrew funds, precipitating chaos.
	Sharon had been cursed by Rabbis for his
	Support for Bush's two-state policy.
455	The Pulsa diNura seemed to have worked
	As the Angel of Death had put him on
	A life-support machine with no prospect
	Of coming off, alive as a symbol.
	Before he went on to Capernaum
460	Bush shivered at the "doom" in store for him.

Still smarting at being called Gog, Bush met
Olmert and defended the two-state plan
And a Palestinian state by early
2009. Olmert dwelt on the strains
Of Hamas in Gaza and of Iran,
Who, he said, was enriching for a bomb.
He suspected "Rockefellers" of foul
Play in introducing anti-Israel
Ideas into the NIE report
To sabotage US strikes on Iran.
While sensing strong Syndicate involvement –
He had lived with many Syndicate ploys –
Bush felt the Democrats had influenced
The report's conclusions, but, not wanting
Iran to scupper the two-state timing,
He said he would have to look deeper at
The report and could not promise action
Against Iran. He said his hands were tied
Now the Democrats were running Congress.
The US and Israel now disagreed.
It was not a very friendly meeting.

After Bush left, Olmert came to accept
That now the Democrats controlled Congress
And following the NIE report
It would be hard for Bush to go along
With an attack on Iran. The crucial
Figure he identified, the key force,
Was the hard-line Cheney. If Israel could
Persuade him the US should bomb Iran,
An attack on Natanz might still happen.
So Cheney was invited to Israel.
Towards the end of March 2008
Cheney met twice with Olmert and Barak,

The Defence Minister, and talked Iran.
495   Barak argued a nuclear-armed Iran
Would threaten the region's stability,
And the world's, and that all options should be
On the table, including use of force.
Israel was left with the impression that
500   Bush was unlikely to agree a strike.
But Cheney spoke aggressively towards
Iran, accused Syria and Iran
Of using Hamas to torpedo peace
Talks between Palestinians and Israel.
505   And he made much of how Israel's sixtieth
Anniversary would display the great
Closeness between Israel and the US.

$\quad$The sixtieth anniversary fell in May.
On the eighth Cheney hosted a function
510   In Washington and said that Israel had
No better friend than the United States.
Knowing Bush would be visiting Israel
And discussing Iran's nuclear plan,
Ahmadinejad wrote to Bush urging
515   "New solutions" to Iran's nuclear maze.
Vice-Premier Shimon Peres lambasted
Iran: "The President should remember
Iran can also be wiped off the map.
Tehran is making a mockery of
520   The international community's
Efforts to solve the crisis surrounding
Iran's nuclear program." In the meantime,
Cheney had persuaded Bush to green-light
For pro-Western militias to attack
525   Hezbollah in west Beirut and Israel
To make air strikes on west and south Beirut
On May the eleventh. Hezbollah knew
Of the plan, having hacked Israel's "secure"
Military intelligence computers,
530   And while routing militias in Beirut
Prepared to fire six hundred rockets at
Tel Aviv if the air strikes went ahead
According to US and French channels.
Under pressure from Bush, and frustrated,
535   Israel was forced to call off the air strikes
On Beirut and instead struck at Gaza
In a face-saving anniversary show
Of force – "sixty years on we are still strong" –

| | And celebrate the anniversary |
| 540 | Without a full show of strength to neighbours. |

Bush arrived at Tel Aviv airport on
May the fourteenth, the anniversary day.
Olmert greeted him and his wife and spoke
With Peres at his side. The Israeli
545   Cabinet lined up to shake Bush's hand.
Then Hamas fired a rocket from Gaza
Which hit a shopping mall in Ashkelon,
Injuring more than thirty civilians.
Bush flew on to Jerusalem and met
550   Peres in his garden. As world leaders
Gathered, Olmert had his meeting with Bush
One-on-one and point-blank asked him: "Please give
A green light for Israel to fly across
Iraq to bomb Iran. And I request
555   Specialised bunker-busting bombs that will
Penetrate the Natanz enrichment zones."
Bush mused in silence, shocked at the direct
Approach. He knew Olmert was not sabre-
Rattling but seriously considering
560   Bombing. He said, "I am concerned over
Iran's retaliation. They'd blame me.
The shortest route to Natanz is across
Iraq, and the US has full control
Of all Iraqi airspace. Iran would
565   Assume that I had approved an air strike
Even if I denied all foreknowledge.
They would strike back at Iraq. There would be
Waves of attacks on US military
And other personnel in Iraq and
570   Afghanistan, also on shipping in
The Persian Gulf. The weapons inspectors
Would be expelled, Iran's nuclear effort
Would be driven further out of view. That
Would be dreadful. I'm also anxious that
575   Israel would not succeed in disabling
Iran's nuclear sites in one assault
Even with dozens of aircraft. There are
Many nuclear targets to disable.
You could not mount a series of attacks
580   Over several days without risking full-
Scale war, a broad Middle-Eastern conflict
In which a hundred and forty thousand
US troops in Iraq would be involved,

Dispersing the progress we have made through
585 The surge, in which case the benefits would
Not outweigh the costs. And Iran would ask
Hezbollah, Lebanon's Shiite movement,
To strike at the US on its behalf.
The solution is to act covertly.
590 I have authorised new covert action
That will sabotage Iran's nuclear aim.
I'll say no more, but will keep you informed.
I therefore will not support an attack
And do not expect to change this view for
595 The rest of my presidency." He seemed
Firm, as if he could not be dissuaded.
He'd spoken with finality. Olmert
Was disappointed. The "no" was where they
Were at at present, and the position
600 Was unlikely to change so long as Bush
Was in office. The main thing was to ensure
McCain succeeded him, a Vietnam
War hero who would act against Iran
If he controlled Congress; not Obama,
605 A Marxist who had Muslim relatives
And would be soft on all Israel's neighbours.
The priority was to elect McCain
And lure Iran into an aggression
In the hope the US would change its tack.

610 Bush gave no public hint he'd excluded
Bombing. At a gala reception he
Was welcomed by a resentful Olmert.
As a swan sees a watcher on a bank
And glides towards him with a rippled wake
615 And greets him close up with a nodding bow
And then turns and paddles back whence it came,
So Olmert greeted Bush and withdrew. Bush
Spoke openly: "Citizens of Israel,
I love coming to your country." He beamed
620 Friendship. The next day he told the Knesset,
"America stands with you in firmly
Opposing Iran's nuclear weapons
Ambitions. Permitting the world's leading
Sponsor of terror to possess the world's
625 Deadliest weapon would be a betrayal
Of future generations. For the sake
Of peace the world must not allow Iran
To have a nuclear weapon." He went on

To Saudi Arabia, where he met King
630   Abdullah, and then Egypt, where he met
King Abdullah the Second of Jordan
And Palestinian Authority
President Abbas to push the two-state
Plan forward, which bombing Iran would sink.
635   At Sharm el-Sheikh he looked across the sea,
And pondered on Olmert's direct question
And thought again of the threatening scroll,
The "doom" the nationalists had seen ahead.
He linked the two together in his mind.

640   And from cliffs near Sharm el-Sheikh, looking out
Where the Gulfs of Suez and Aqaba
Flowed into the Red Sea and up the sky
As dusk fell the moon rose and a star shone,
Bush saw sea and sky from within the One
645   Way out in the universe, far beyond
The gathering night. To the One his firm "no"
To Olmert, banning Israeli planes from
Swooping over Iraq to bomb Natanz,
Was one of many pairs of opposites –
650   A desire to bomb and a refusal,
Israel's existence, Arab denial –
Which the Infinite Spirit that flows in
And guides all thought reconciled from its height,
Reducing conflicts to co-existence.
655   To the transcendent and immanent One
The conflict between him and Olmert paled
To insignificance as if it were
Washed in early moonlight like the Red Sea
And green cliffs in the beautiful twilight.
660   Bush knew that to the One he had done right.

He had been asked to sanction war that could
Spread and engulf the entire world. The world
Had been asked to support Israel, or else
There would be a crisis so suddenly –
665   With no advance warning at all – that it
Could not possibly be an accident.
Yet he would not submit to such blackmail.
He thought, 'I am here to prevent world war.'
By his "no" he had prevented world war.
670   He had stood up to "Rothschilds" who had backed
Olmert, he'd defeated the Syndicate.
He thought, 'I'm an obstacle to world war.

No one knows this except Olmert. The world
Sees me as warmonger, not peacemaker.
675   I am a secret barrier for peace.'
In the next few days Israel looked beyond
His presidency to his successor.
Bush watched as Israel sent funds to McCain,
Republican election candidate,
680   Hoping to influence the election.
It looked an increasingly forlorn hope
For the North-Vietnam war hero now looked
Like a zombie beside Obama's youth,
His oratory and Marxist promises.

685   Three weeks after Bush's red light, on June
The second, Israel mounted a massive
War air exercise over the eastern
Mediterranean. More than a hundred
Israeli F-16 and F-15
690   Fighters took part, and helicopters that
Could rescue downed pilots. Helicopters
And fueling tankers flew nine hundred miles,
The distance between Israel and Iran's
Uranium-enrichment plant at Natanz.
695   Officially Israel was practising
Flight tactics, aerial refueling and
Air strikes against missiles. The exercise
Also sent a clear message to Iran
And the US that Israel would attack
700   If diplomatic efforts to prevent
Iran from having a nuclear bomb failed.
It looked a rehearsal for an attack.
Olmert visited the US, saying,
"The Iranian threat must be stopped by
705   All possible means," the strongest-ever
Statement on Iran by Israel's leader.
Iran put its air defences on guard
And installed advanced Russian-made radar
That could detect planes flying at low heights.
710   Iran was close to acquiring Russian
SA-20 surface-to-air missiles.
El-Baradei, the IAEA's head,
Said a strike would turn the region into
A "fireball" and if so he would resign.
715   The exercise and Olmert's visit had
Produced results, for the White House stepped up
Intelligence-sharing with Israel and

Briefed Israeli officials on new US
Efforts to subtly-sabotage Iran's
720   Nuclear infrastructure. Covert measures
Included financial pressure as when
Companies pulled out of oil projects, banks
Cut financing and trade credits were squeezed.
Progress was slowed at Natanz by tinkering
725   With power units bought in Turkey that drove
The centrifuges, floor-to-ceiling tubes
That spin at the speed of sound and enrich
Uranium, causing some to blow up, and
By slipping faulty technology in
730   Parts bought outside Iran. Centrifuges
Were destabilised and pressure was kept
On scientist Mohsen Fakrizadeh,
Who was named in the NIE report's
Classified section as the manager
735   Of Projects 110 and 111,
To design a warhead and make it work,
Exploding at six hundred and fifty
Yards above ground, roughly the altitude
Of Hiroshima's bomb. The US gave
740   Israel X-Band, a new high-powered radar
That would detect all Iranian missile
Launchings, and moves were made to start selling
Israel a thousand bunker-busting bombs,
Guided bomb unit-39s that had
745   A one-tonne bomb's penetrability.
They would enhance Israel's attack options
If the next US president, who all
Hoped would be McCain, should one day revive
The military option against Iran.
750   Bush made up for his "no" by saying "yes"
To his friend Olmert's long-term shopping list.

Pope Benedict the Sixteenth received Bush
In the Vatican gardens and they spoke
In the twelfth-century Tower of St John
755   Which the Pope used for private reflection –
An honour as the usual meeting place
Was the Pope's library. Some wondered if
They discussed gold missing from vaults beneath
WTC4. Bush and the Pope
760   Had prayed in the Oval Office and now
They prayed again as Bush, following Blair,
Prepared to convert to the Catholic faith,

The most Catholic-minded president since
Kennedy though he was a Methodist
765   In Texas and in Washington prayed at
An Episcopal church: he was aware
That evangelism was limited
Theologically and historically –
Compared with Catholicism. Bush had
770   Used Catholic speech-writers and consultants,
Appointed Catholic judges and had seen
His brother Jeb convert and was impressed
When during the recount in Florida
Jeb went to Mexico, to the icon
775   Of Our Lady of Guadalupe and prayed,
And the Supreme Court announced his victory
On December the twelfth 2001 –
On the Lady of Guadalupe's feast-day.
And so the two war leaders sought to assuage –
780   With some calculation, it must be said,
And with some awareness of public show –
Their consciences for bombing living souls,
And to have dabbed some Pope-blessed holy oil
On the troubled waters of their two brows
785   Whose furrowed frowns reflected their two souls
Which sometimes seemed like inner lakes of fire,
By wiping the slates of their own sins clean
And cleansing their records from all past sins
In the Pope's confessional close to Christ.

790   The next few months were not kind to Israel.
In June 2008 the United
Nations certified Israel had withdrawn
From all Lebanese territory. And yet
In August Lebanon's new Cabinet
795   Approved a draft policy statement that
Secured Hezbollah's continuation
As an armed organisation and that
Guaranteed its right to "liberate or
Recover occupied lands". Israel had
800   Withdrawn, but Hezbollah now remained armed.
Israel had made some modest gains but had
Patently failed to achieve its war aims.
In early October 2008
Hezbollah leader Hassan Nasrallah
805   Was poisoned but saved by Iranian
Doctors who rushed to Lebanon and cured
Him – a suspected Israeli attempt

At assassination. A Mossad team
In September 1997
810   Had tried to assassinate Hamas chief
Khaled Meshal by drizzling poison
In his ear, the method used on Hamlet's
Old father while he slept in an orchard.
Nasrallah's second-in-command Imad
815   Mughniyah had been assassinated in
Damascus in February by Israel.

Tell, Muse, how oil and gas pipelines controlled
Russia's relations with Georgia and two
Regions that declared their independence
820   From Georgia in the 1991
Conflict, South Ossetia and Abkhazia,
When Abkhazia's ethnic cleansing expelled
Two hundred and fifty thousand Georgians.
In both "republics" Russian was spoken
825   And most citizens had Russian passports.
The Baku-Tbilisi-Ceyhan pipeline
(BTC) from 2007 pumped
A million barrels of oil a day from
Baku in Azerbaijan to Turkey's
830   Yumurtalik, where it was loaded on
Supertankers for Europe/the US.
It made the West less dependent on oil
From the Middle East and Russia. It was
Buried for most of its eleven hundred
835   Miles to make sabotage hard, but about
Two hundred and fifty kilometres
Passed through Georgia, parts only fifty-five
Kilometres from South Ossetia
Where above-ground bits might be sabotaged
840   By South-Ossetian separatists. It
Cost 3.3 billion dollars to build
And 30 per cent was owned by BP,
Which had a "Rockefellerite" interest
As Standard Oil had bought out and merged with
845   British Petroleum, and later merged
With Amoco. BP was a hybrid.
In preparation for this new pipeline,
"Rothschilds", via Soros, intrigued the fall of
Shevardnadze, pro-Russian president
850   Of Georgia, and replaced him by anti-
Russian Mikheil Saakashvili back in
2003. "Rockefellers" controlled

The Soviet Union since Stalin sold them
A half interest in all Soviet oil
855 In return for funding his Five-Year Plans.
In 1996 "Rockefellers"
Had bought Russia's natural resources from
Yeltsin and Chernomyrdin, his PM,
Including Gazprom and Lukoil, both at
860 A tenth of their market value. Gazprom,
Now owned by "Rockefellers", had signed up
To build gas pipelines to Abkhazia
And South Ossetia. To Georgia both were
On Georgian territory, suggesting that
865 Russia planned to annex parts of Georgia.
The first section of the next Zaurikau-
Tskinvali 163-kilometre-
Long gas pipeline was laid about thirty
Kilometres from the North Ossetian
870 Capital city Vladikavkaz in
October 2006. Georgia had
No significant oil or gas reserves
Of its own, but was a key transit point
For oil from the Caspian and Central
875 Asia sent for Europe and the US,
And for gas from Russia to the two tough
Breakaway "republics". Gazprom announced
That in 2007 Georgia would
Have to pay double for its Russian gas.
880 Now "Rothschilds'" man, Saakashivili, wanted
To take the pair back and control the gas
Once he had restored Georgian sovereignty,
And receive pipeline transit fees. Each year
Georgia received sixty million dollars
885 In transit fees for BTC pipeline,
And was looking for more windfall payments.
Russia wanted to run an oil pipeline
From Kazakhstan through Georgia. When oil flowed
BTC's pipeline, which skirted Russia,
890 Would be diminished. Kazakhstan oil via
Georgia would be cheaper than constructing
A pipeline from Kazakhstan to Iran.
Russia looked to take enough of Georgia
To make such a pipeline work – and to set
895 A trap that would allow it to devour
The two regions of Georgia it wanted.

The War on Terror had a corrupting

Effect, for if the US could invade
Countries for oil and gas pipelines, which had
900   Commercial considerations, why could
Not Russia (which had invaded neighbours,
And honed its skills in Budapest and Prague)
Do likewise and invade for gas pipelines?
There was no monopoly in sending
905   In tanks to secure a nation-state's end.
The trap that Russia lured Georgia into
Was baited with the prospect of Gazprom's
Transit fees and supplies of Russian gas,
And dangled troop movements meant to provoke
910   Georgia into an aggressive response.
Russia was not pleased when NATO agreed
In April 2008 that Georgia
Would become a member of NATO at
An unspecified date in the future.
915   Feeling ringed by NATO, Russia accused
Georgia of massing troops in the upper
Kodori Gorge to invade Abkhazia.
Russia said that it was boosting force there
And in South Ossetia to prevent this.
920   Georgia said it had not sent troops. Russia
Still sent hundreds of paratroops to guard
Abkhazia "as peacekeepers". They had
Heavy military hardware suggesting
They were a fighting force, not keeping peace.
925   Putin knew Saakashvili'd see this move
As a challenge to Georgian sovereignty
But adopted a defensive posture
While luring Georgia into aggression.
Russia's operation was subtly called
930   *Operation to Force Georgia to Peace.*
Both sides accused each other of flying
Jets over South Ossetia, ending
The fragile cease-fire, a step towards war.
In July Georgia set up a state
935   Commission to progress South Ossetia's
Autonomous constitutional status
Within the framework of the Georgian state.
From July to August both sides pursued
Military exercises. On August
940   The fifth Popov, Russian ambassador-
At-large, said Russia would intervene if
There was military conflict. Georgia
Assembled nine light-infantry, five tank

And eight artillery battalions, in
945   All sixteen thousand men, in the Georgian
Enclaves of South Ossetia, to give
Support. Moscow monitored shellings and
Clashes. Georgia and South Ossetia
Blamed each other for starting the attacks.
950   On August the sixth, Georgian troops began
Heavy shelling of Tskhinvali, using
Mortar, artillery and sniper fire.
It lasted all night and South Ossetians
Returned artillery fire at Georgians
955   In Avneri for several hours. Georgians
Now massed artillery and Grad rocket-
Launchers north of Gori and took the heights
Round Tskhinvali. Saakashivili declared
A cease-fire while his forces positioned
960   Themselves for an attack, and then broadcast
That Georgian villages were being shelled.
Walking into the Russian trap, he said
Georgia was entering South Ossetia
To defend Georgian villages from
965   Ossetian shelling and "to restore
Constitutional order in the region".

The Georgian assault began on South
Ossetia, a mountainous region
On the southern side of the Caucasus
970   That separated from North Ossetia
Which was then part of Russia. Shells blasted
Tskhinvali in *Operation Clear Field*
Which planned to surround and capture the place.
OSCE peacekeeping monitors
975   Were fired on, thirteen Russian peacekeepers
Were killed. Parts of the capital city
Were in ruins. The Russian media showed
The attack and now Russia responded
To "genocide by Georgian forces".
980   The hospital was damaged by a Grad
Multiple-rocket-launcher. Next morning
On the eighth, the day the Olympic Games
Opened in China, Georgian tanks and one
Thousand five hundred infantry ground troops
985   Entered the city and fought Ossetian
Forces and Russian peacekeepers, but were
Pushed back by Russian artillery and
Air attacks. Georgians fired at basements where

	Civilians were cowering; a clear war crime.
990	Now Georgia claimed to hold eight villages.
	While the world focused on the Olympic Games
	In China, where Bush sat watching athletes
	Parade in the Opening Ceremony,
	Russian tanks swept through the Roki tunnel
995	That separates North and South Ossetia
	And reinforced the Russian forces in
	Tskhinvali, and Russian military
	Aircraft invaded Georgia's airspace.
	As swallows swoop and skim across a field
1000	Portending storms, and then soar into clouds,
	So Russian planes flitted through Georgian skies.
	That evening local militias fought in
	The villages, and Russian troops engaged
	Georgian army groups. Russian planes struck at
1005	Georgian armour. Russian special forces
	Prevented saboteurs from blowing up
	The Roki tunnel, Russia's supply line.
	The next day, the ninth, the Russian military
	Said Georgian forces had been driven out
1010	From Tskhinvali, which was "liberated".
	Georgians now attacked tanks near the tunnel
	And then counter-attacked and captured most
	Of Tskhinvali, forcing Ossetians
	And Russians to retreat northwards. But more
1015	Russians arrived through Roki tunnel and
	By the evening of the tenth the Georgians
	Fled southwards from the city and the heights.
	Georgia's artillery had been smashed and
	Russians took four villages to the north.
1020	Georgian forces in enclaves were wiped out.
	After three days and nights Georgian ground troops
	Pulled out southwards and regrouped at Gori.
	Bush saw the Russian trap linked to pipelines.
	He did not believe Russia's defensive
1025	Posture. He went in hard, warning Russian
	Might: "Bullying and intimidation
	Are not acceptable ways to conduct
	Foreign policy in the twenty-first
	Century." Possible Georgian war crimes in
1030	South Ossetia made it hard to condemn
	Too severely. It was urged that NATO
	Should intervene. Bush did not support this,
	And with US troops locked into two wars

In Afghanistan and Iraq, he did
1035   Nothing and saved the world from wider war.

Next day, the eleventh, Russian forces had cleared
South Ossetia and moved into Georgia
While Georgians shelled Tskhinvali from high points.
Russian planes had bombed Gori on the eighth
1040   And launched an SS-21 short-range
Missile at military bunkers in
Borzhomi. And to the north two Russian
Fighters bombed Georgian artillery near
Gori and an air-to-ground missile struck
1045   The hospital. They dropped cluster bombs in
Gori's centre and hit an armament
Depot. On the tenth civilians had fled
Gori. Fifty-six thousand refugees
Were on the move. Next day at 5 p.m.
1050   The Georgian army, which had retreated
From Tskhinvali, abandoned Gori in
Disarray without firing a shot, and
Retreated to the outskirts of Tbilisi.
Left in the lurch by uniformed soldiers,
1055   Local militias fought the Russians off
But on the thirteenth Russian troops entered
Gori, which was now controlled jointly by
Georgian police and the Russian soldiers,
Who said they would only stay two days. Soon
1060   Russian troops headed for Tbilisi and
Encamped. On the fifteenth Russians allowed
Humanitarian food into Gori.
South-Ossetian militias attacked
Georgian civilians' homes and cars, looting
1065   And burning villages, and killing all
Who fled and shooting Georgians in enclaves.
They rampaged through Georgian streets, bringing death.

The war had spilled into Abkhazia,
Mild, mountainous region by the Black Sea.
1070   The Russian Black-Sea fleet, which had sailed from
The Russian Sevastopol naval base
In Ukraine's Crimea, had blockaded
The Georgian coast, and, on the ninth, corvette
Mirazh sank a Georgian patrol cutter
1075   With two anti-ship missiles, the Russian
Navy's first fierce sea battle since nineteen
Forty-five. And the same day nine thousand

Russian assault and motorised-rifle
Troops and Marines joined Abkhaz forces and
1080   Pushed Georgian troops from the Kodori Gorge.
The next day Abkhaz troops drove a thousand
Georgian troops from the Kodori Valley.
On the eleventh Russian paratroops
Left Abkhazia and destroyed military
1085   Bases in Georgia which could be used
To reinforce Georgians sealed in enclaves
In South Ossetia. Then they surrounded
The port of Poti. The next day Abkhaz
Troops fought Georgians in the Kodori Gorge
1090   Who were told to withdraw "as a gesture
Of goodwill". The battle lasted until
The thirteenth, when all Georgians retreated
From Abkhazia and South Ossetia.
Then on the fourteenth Russian troops entered
1095   Poti and sank several Georgian ships
Moored in the harbour. Russian troops controlled
The road to Tbilisi and took prisoner
Twenty-two Georgian troops along the road
And took them to the base at Senaki.
1100   Russian troops returned to Poti, destroyed
Almost all the Georgian Navy's docked ships.

There had been calls for peace. And on the twelfth
Russia's President Medvedev ended
All military operations within
1105   Georgia, saying security had been
Restored for peacekeepers and civilians.
Both sides now approved a four-point peace plan
Drawn up by French President Sarkozy,
To which Russia added two more points. One
1110   Stated, "Prior to the establishment of
International mechanisms Russian
Peacekeeping forces will take additional
Security measures," which Russia read
As permitting raids into Georgia that
1115   Destroyed weapons, to demilitarise
The Georgian armed forces. On the fifteenth
Russia pushed towards Tbilisi. Now Rice,
The US Secretary of State, travelled
To Tbilisi and made Saakashvili,
1120   Who was blustering, trying to conjure
Victory out of defeat, blaming Russia,
Quibbling and shuffling off all initial

Blame, sign the six-point plan in her presence.

	Now, after Georgia, a new Cold War might
1125	Be ahead, and worse than that, global war
	With Russian expansion. The West had sensed
	A parallel with the 1930s:
	A world depression with a credit crunch,
	Collapse of world trade talks and oil shortage,
1130	And an impoverished power (Russia)
	Invading a neighbour to set things right
	And close to a fault line of conflict from
	The Caucasus to Iran and on to
	Afghanistan and Pakistan, which all
1135	Had anti-Western forces that Russia
	Could stir. A new world war might be ahead.

Now, after Georgia, a new Cold War might
Be ahead, and worse than that, global war
With Russian expansion. The West had sensed
A parallel with the 1930s:
A world depression with a credit crunch,
Collapse of world trade talks and oil shortage,
And an impoverished power (Russia)
Invading a neighbour to set things right
And close to a fault line of conflict from
The Caucasus to Iran and on to
Afghanistan and Pakistan, which all
Had anti-Western forces that Russia
Could stir. A new world war might be ahead.

Now Putin and his puppet President
Refused to withdraw from *their* Georgia.
The deal allowed the Russians to defend
The security of the break-away
Provinces, allowed Russia to exploit
Ambiguities in troop departures,
Order that troops stay though Russia had signed
To leave. They broke their word. Russian armoured
Divisions moved round Tbilisi, threatened
To absorb Georgia. Russia now aimed
SS-20 missiles at the chancery
In Saakashvili's South-Ossetian
Capital Tshkinvali. Their President
And the State Security Council with
Putin to his right, and then Parliament,
Now recognised the two provinces as
Independent states. On the twenty-fifth
Russia authorised the independence
Of the two "republics". There was dancing
In the streets of both provinces. Champagne
Corks popped. South Ossetia offered Russia
A military base. The President
Of Russia, Putin's puppet Medvedev,
Warned Moldova it would lose Transdniester
If it tried to keep it. And President
Medvedev declined to join the World Trade
Organisation. A new Cold War loomed.

Russian troops were slow to withdraw, and still
Occupied Georgia two months on. Russia

Retained three thousand seven hundred troops
In South Ossetia and Abkhazia
And planned to open military bases
In Java, Tskhinvali and Gudauta
1170   Which would cost four hundred million dollars.
Three hundred and ninety-five had been killed.
Now it could be seen that Saakashvili
Had miscalculated and made things worse.
NATO had not come to his aid and he
1175   Had not seized gas pipelines for transit fees
In the two "republics", which Georgia still
Claimed were "Russian-occupied". No one else
Recognised them except Nicaragua
And, pressed by Hezbollah, the Lebanon.
1180   Nine months later Medvedev signed two pacts
Giving Moscow responsibility
For the borders of Abkhazia and
South Ossetia, which were part of Georgia
To the entire world. And Russia had thus
1185   Annexed a third of Georgia by stealth.

Now the impact of Russia's action in
Georgia on the War on Terror was felt
In violent Pakistan. As NATO had
Supported Georgia, Putin withdrew
1190   NATO's right to fly through Russian air space
To resupply Afghanistan. Seventy
Per cent of supplies came up the Khyber
Pass where bin Laden's troops fired on convoys.
Four aircraft engines simply disappeared.
1195   Back in July Bush secretly ordered
US special forces to conduct ground
Assaults in Pakistan without seeking
Permission from Pakistan's Government.
Now Musharraf had fallen, Pakistan
1200   Was lawless, waiting for a new leader.
Abdul Qadeer Khan, the black marketeer
Of nuclear know-how to bin Laden
And rogue states such as Iran and Libya,
The father of the Islamic bomb, was
1205   A candidate for the Presidency.
In fact, the martyred Benazir Bhutto's
Husband Asif Ali Zardari was
Elected President by the National
Assembly, senate and four provincial
1210   Assemblies, restoring the dynasty

Of Bhuttos to power after a decade.
The West was now at risk in its fighting
Of the Taliban thanks to Russian guile,
The KGB man (Putin) who denied
1215   The West's troops access to Afghanistan.
Perhaps seeing it as a pay-back for
The West's recognition of Kosovo's
Independence from Serbia, President
Medvedev said, "The current atmosphere
1220   Reminds me of the situation in
Europe in 1914, and I hope
Saakashvili will not be remembered
As a new Gavrilo Princip" – the man
Who killed Austro-Hungarian Archduke
1225   Franz Ferdinand, triggered the First World War
And four unstoppable years of conflict.
President Saakashvili of Georgia
Likened the situation to the way
Hitler carved up Czechoslovakia and
1230   The Sudetenland in nineteen thirty-
Eight, which had led to the Second World War.
Putin likened South Ossetia to
North Cyprus, a break-away republic
That had endured for three decades although
1235   Only recognised by one power: Turkey.
"Do you really think that NATO will come
And fight us in the Caucasus?" he asked
Saakashvili face-to-face, much amused.
Gorbachev, alarmed at the West's stance, spoke
1240   Of a growing threat of global chaos.

Russia felt encircled without buffers.
US and British imperialism
Had forced its borders to retreat after
The collapse of the Berlin Wall and now
1245   Pushed on its new borders in areas
Where Russians had been left behind, shut out,
Left outside the new borders though they spoke
The Russian language, held Russian passports:
One million in the Baltic Republics
1250   Eight million in Ukraine and the Crimea.
This was the most dramatic challenge to
The West since the collapse of the Soviet
Union. Now American astronauts
Could not use Russia's space station, the War
1255   On Terror would be much harder to win

And oil and gas pipelines were not secure.
Russia had challenged the New World Order.
Arriviste autocrats – new rulers who
Despised votes, challenged legitimacy
1260 And the desirability of all
Democratic liberalism – were strong
In Russia, China and the Middle East,
Thwarted the American New World Order
Based on democracy and holding back
1265 Nationalism in Georgia and Tibet,
Shored up the wealth of the now-fading West.
Now many thought the prophet of World State
Fukuyama was wrong to see the world
As moving towards permanent liberal
1270 Democracy, for two billion now lived
Under autocrats who had achieved growth
By low-wage, low-cost production and by
Developing high-priced oil, and allowed
Their people to become rich in return
1275 For silence about their autocracy.
Now a power struggle stretched from the Balkans
And Eastern Europe to the Caucasus
And beyond, through Iran and Pakistan
To Kashmir and to mountain-clad Tibet.
1280 Now the world's wealth and might was moving from
West to East, and a long supremacy
Of the West was fast approaching an end,
Part of the process of rearranging
That would end in coming world government.

1285 Now the history of the last twenty years
Seemed to have undergone a profound change.
The "New World Order" in which the US
Exercised a global hegemony
As sole and undisputed superpower
1290 After the fall of the Berlin Wall seemed
To have proved a mirage. First 9/11,
Then the debacle of Iraq and now this
Russian invasion of Georgia revived
The Russian sphere of influence agreed
1295 At the Tehran and Yalta conferences
During the Second World War, and now proved
The "New World Order" and world government,
The concept of a unipolar world
Designed to Western specifications,
1300 Without change to borders or gunboat strife,

Were an illusion because the US,
EU and NATO could not protect their
Ally. A second Cold War had begun,
Not as global challenge to the US
1305   But a turf war round Russia's long backyard.
So had the New World Order ended, then?
If the New World Order meant unchallenged
US hegemony, that had ended.
If it meant world government-in-waiting,
1310   The Syndicate that influenced the US
And Russia, which had been behind the trap
Putin laid for Georgia to give Russia
The pretext to invade, it was still strong.
The Syndicate moved in on the US
1315   New World Order after the Berlin Wall
Fell, and while Americans spread liberal
Democracy, the Syndicate pushed for
A world government in which the US
Would be subordinate. Though the return
1320   To a bipolar world appeared to set
Back its attempt at world domination,
In fact it had been Syndicate-controlled
And created new opportunities
For the Syndicate to sell to both sides
1325   Just as they had done during the Cold War.
It was commercially convenient
For it to go back to two hostile camps
Which could both be armed by the Syndicate,
As could their clients, notably Iran.
1330   Russia threatened to sell an air defence
System, the S-300, to Tehran
(Which would be loaned funds by the Syndicate
To make a purchase it could not afford)
If the US gave NATO membership
1335   To Georgia and Ukraine which, Russia claimed
Were in their sphere of influence – a system
That can track a hundred targets at once
And fire on planes seventy-five miles away
And would make it harder for the US
1340   To bomb Iran as planes would be at risk.
So the New World Order's apparent end
Was a Syndicate-backed commercial ploy
To add arms sales to oil/gas pipeline sales.
And in due course the new divided world
1345   Could be put back together when walls fell
And the new whole could then be split again

Into the West and nuclear Chinese East
And after yet another arms race could
Be reunited for world government.
1350   But I, your poet, am sceptical for:
History is an endless pattern of vast
Rising and falling civilisations,
And dead ones passing into younger ones,
And those who claim that history has ended
1355   In permanent liberal democracy,
A New World Order or world government,
Are just plain wrong as history is endless,
There are always civilisations that
Make common cause within alliances
1360   But remain separate, autonomous,
And syndicates that conspire to impose
World government are always doomed to fail.
The Syndicate's agenda was not dead
And it was behind bipolar conflict,
1365   But it would always be challenged by some
Nation-states seeking nuclear prestige.

Some said, "Germany's behind world events,"
And behind the new superstate EU,
That the new EU came into being,
1370   Led by a reunified Germany,
With its own legal personality
And its constitution. Its new anthem,
'The Ode to Joy' was German, and nation-
States' geographical identity
1375   Was to be destroyed as EU maps showed
Groupings of bits of nations as new states:
Southern England was grouped with Northern France.
Germany was at the heart of Europe
After the EU's expansion eastwards.
1380   Some who had fought in the Second World War
Said Germany was behind expansion,
That just as the Holy Roman Empire,
The First Reich, from 800 to eighteen
O six, nurtured the rise of Prussia; and
1385   The Second Reich, from 1871
To 1918, saw Prussia merge with
Germany and expand during the First
World War; and Hitler's Third Reich from nineteen
Thirty-three to 1945, saw
1390   A new German Empire expand throughout
Europe during the Second World War; so

Now a Fourth Reich had reunified all
Germany and expanded through Europe
As the EU, and, through such German names
1395   As Rothschild, Rockefeller (of Turkish-
German lineage) and Kissinger, seemed
To be behind the Syndicate and plan
World domination as in the thirties.
But the Syndicate was more US than
1400   German, a world government-in-waiting.
It had been behind a US demand
That all nations must be democratic
And had challenged Russia, China, Iran
And North Korea for failing to follow
1405   The post-Cold-War New World Order. It had
Been behind the squashing of nation-states
Into boxes in the Americas
And Pacific as well as in Europe.
The Syndicate was behind Germany
1410   As in the 1930s (through General
Marshal) it kept Montgomery from Berlin
So Stalin could found an East-European
Empire that suited them. Commercially
Driven to profit from oil and gas pipelines
1415   And sales of arms, it loaned money to fund
New companies. It started the EU,
For it was Monnet and the CFR
Who were behind the first Treaty of Rome.
A branch was behind the USSR
1420   And steered its opposition to the West
So it could sell arms to both Cold-War sides.
It was not Germany that was behind
Afghanistan, Iraq or Georgia,
That had been driving for world government.
1425   World events now can only be explained
By looking beyond Germany's EU –
And beyond all separate nation-states.

Bush mused on Israel's fate in the last days.
The *Bible* foretold three different battles
1430   Near the world's end. Isaiah foretold how
The Jews would drive the Palestinians from
The land of Israel, and how Egypt and
Syria would fight Israel and cease to be,
With Damascus left "a ruinous heap".
1435   Hezbollah, which sought to conquer the world
And destroy Israel and the United States,

Would be involved on the side of Syria
Which controlled the Lebanon with Iran –
Which, too, wanted the Islamic conquest
1440   Of the world, under Iran's leadership.
Ezekiel foretold the second battle
Of Gog and Magog, the land of Russia,
How Russia would lead Iran, Libya,
Ethiopia, Turkey and East Europe
1445   Against Israel "out of the north parts" and
Would "be like a cloud to cover the land",
Create a ring of fire around Israel,
But their armies would be at last destroyed.
Zechariah foretold the third battle
1450   Seventy miles north of Jerusalem
In the Valley of Esdraelon, the plain
Of Megiddo near Mount Megiddo where
The mountains of Israel start, the final
Battle for Jerusalem, which John called
1455   Armageddon, in which corrupt armies
Fighting Jerusalem would be destroyed.
Bush thought of the Rabbis' threat of his "doom".
With these last events prophesied, in which
The United States played no part, and he
1460   Contributing to destabilising
God's Covenant nation as if he were
Not "Gog" but Antichrist, America,
Blasted with enervating disasters,
Might soon be removed from world power for good.
1465   O God of storms, he prayed, if you have urged
"Rothschilds" to send a huge economic
Hurricane and *tsunami*, please thwart it,
Call it off and rescue America.

BOOK TEN

ISRAEL AND THE SYNDICATE STRIKE BACK

SUMMARY

1606-1614	Bin Laden calls for *jihad* over Gaza.
1615-1720	Israel attacks Gaza City.
1721-1759	Israel seizes Gaza's gas fields.
1760-1848	Mohammed urges bin Laden's co-founder of al-Qaeda, Dr Fadl, to recant his support for al-Qaeda.
1849-1884	Satan, disguised as Abu Bakr, urges Mohammed to claim the leadership of Heaven from Christ.
1885-2034	Christ addresses Heaven on the economic crisis, Satan's control of Western culture and media. He says both Materialism and division are loathsome.
2035-2238	Mohammed challenges Christ's Leadership of Heaven, causing disunity in Heaven.
2239-2280	Bush's final news conference.
2281-2369	Christ consults God the Light and understands that Heaven must now be Universalist, not Christian-dominated.
2370-2500	Christ addresses Heaven. Different religions will share power in Heaven in proportion to the percentages of their followings on Earth. There is reconciliation in Heaven.

O kings of Jerusalem who wrested
Land in Palestine from the Muslims in
The First Crusade, who protected Antioch,
Edessa and Tripoli as vassals
5   And ruled all Israel, south Lebanon and
South-west Jordan – Godfrey of Bouillon
For one year, Baldwin the First and Second
Fulk and Melisende, and Baldwin the Third –
And raised revenue trading with Muslims,
10   Banking with Templars and taxing pilgrims;
Who built castles that guarded Palestine,
Until Amalric rampaged through Egypt
And roused Saladin who, after Baldwin
The Fourth and Fifth, managed, through a massive
15   Attack on the Holy Land, to unite
The previously divided Muslim world.
O Guy of Lusignan, you who married
Amalric's daughter, Sibyl, and became
The King of Jerusalem for a year,
20   And maintained the unified city shown
In Hereford's *Mappa Mundi, circa*
1300, as centre of the Earth
Shaped like an O, as vast Muslim forces
Swept in and fought the Battle of Hattin
25   In July 1187 when
Twenty thousand Christians including twelve

Hundred knights surrendered to some thirty
Thousand Muslim troops. The Franks held the Horns,
An extinct volcano with ancient walls.
30 Templars tried to break through the Muslim lines.
Exhausted and in despair you led two
Final charges against Saladin's guards
And, weakened by lack of water, slumped down
To the ground when Saladin captured your
35 Palladium, the fragment of the cross
Discovered by St Helena, mother
Of Constantine, in 326, which had
Been captured by the Persians, then rescued
By the Byzantine Emperor Heraclius
40 In 630 and sent to Jerusalem,
A piece of the True Cross, a totem for
So many Crusaders. With your handful
Of governing clique, you were escorted
To Saladin's tent and were held until
45 Next year, deposed, and would be later crowned
King of Cyprus by Richard Lionheart.
You watched as Saladin ritually
Severed Reynald de Châtillon's head, and
Sufis butchered two hundred Templars and
50 Hospitallers, and as your infantry
Were led off to the slave market to be
Sold. Saladin left the battlefield strewn
With bones and carrion birds. Having secured
Payment to release the besieged Christians
55 In Jerusalem, Saladin called for
The gates to be opened and soon entered
From the north through stone-block St Stephen's Gate
And tore down the cross the Franks had hung on
The Dome of the Rock and restored the al-
60 Aqsa mosque, spared the Holy Sepulchre.
The shock at the fall of Jerusalem
Was so great that Pope Urban the Third died
When he heard the dire news. O Guy, you knew
The need to keep ancient Jerusalem
65 United and under Crusader rule,
Help me now that I come to describe how
The secret plan for East Jerusalem
To be given to the Muslims, including
Haram esh-Sharif, the Temple complex,
70 The Temple Mount and the Dome of the Rock,
Nearly achieved the collapse of the West
As a massive blow was struck on a new

9/11 which dwarfed the old 9/11,
Itself the worst attack since Pearl Harbour.
75 O Guy, help me describe how dividing
Jerusalem brought distress to the West.

O Shakespeare, Stratfordian man and not mask
For another's identity, you who
Lived when Puritans yearned for the British
80 To appear neo-Israelites and wear
Jewish-style clothes, long black cloaks and hats, and
Believe that England had a Covenant
With God like Israel; you who early grasped
Puritans' link to the Orthodox Jews,
85 Saw Shylock as a Puritan and caught
The Puritan spirit in Malvolio;
You were taken up by Francis Bacon
Whose secret society that was linked
To the Israelite Temple, the English
90 Form of Freemasonry he founded in
1579, helped to publish and
Spread works on British Imperialism:
Drake's voyage round the world, which challenged Spain's
Maritime supremacy; the King James
95 *Bible* which spread Protestantism round
The world; Raleigh's *History of the World*;
John Smith's works on the New World; Bacon's own
New Atlantis which stood for an English
Israelite, anti-Spanish New World; and
100 The First Folio of your plays – published by
The "incomparable brethren", the Earls
Of Pembroke and Montgomery – which had
Championed English sovereignty against Spain's
Implied threat to rule England, and had told
105 In *The Tempest* of the New World. Your works
Were linked with theirs through similar colophons,
Title-page, headpiece and tailpiece designs,
Especially the "AA" legs which curl
Into Cs, Bacon's emblem. AA, that's
110 Found in your *Venus and Adonis*, stands
For AthenA and Knights of the Helmet,
Bacon's secret society which both
Sponsored and presented both Bacon's works
And your own First Folio to spread British
115 Imperialism and American
Colonisation. O William Shakespeare,
You were promoted by British Israel,

Bacon's Freemasonry, after your death
And you may have made common cause with your
120   Promoters in your life, perhaps after
Bacon was involved in the Virginia
Company of London. I know you met
Bacon at the wedding of Frederick the Fifth
And Elizabeth Stuart, James the First's
125   Daughter in London in 1613.
Had you linked up when you wrote of Shylock
From 1596 to 8? The link
May have been Fulke Greville, friend of Sidney,
"Master" to you and Jonson (so he claims),
130   Stratford's Recorder, Warwickshire's MP
Who had "a monument without a tombe"
In 1623 when Jonson wrote
Those words, for his tomb in St Mary's church,
Warwick, a huge "black marble, double bed",
135   Was empty till he died five years later,
Whose inner vault when radar-scanned shows three
Boxes that may hold your lost manuscripts;
Who was both Bacon's and Southampton's friend
And lived with both in Essex House, was there
140   When Bacon wrote *The Advancement of Learning*,
And knew Southampton in the early years
Of *Venus and Adonis*, *Lucrece*;
Whose Warwick Castle was by the Avon,
Whose crest was a swan, hence "Swan of Avon",
145   Who had a long love affair with Mary,
Countess of Pembroke – sister of Sidney
Who dedicated *Arcadia* to her,
Dark Lady, mother of the "incomparable
Paire of brethren" who would one day publish
150   The First Folio – and stayed at Wilton House,
The home of his boyhood fair friend Sidney.
(Was the link Greville because *he* was *you*?)
Or was the link Southampton, to whom you
Addressed *Venus and Adonis* and whose
155   Colophons are Bacon's, who was involved
In the New World with Bacon, and perhaps
Secured the link with the Earl of Pembroke,
Who co-published the First Folio and
Who stands in armour in the Bodleian
160   Courtyard looking up at King James the First.
Who was the *Sonnets'* "Mr W.H."?
Henry Wriothesley – "H.W." reversed,
Alias Southampton? Or William Herbert,

The 3rd Earl of Pembroke? Or someone else?
165 O Shakespeare, I see you close to a time
When Protestants were burned and Catholics hanged
And when your fellow dramatists all died
At the hands of a paranoiac State
Like Marlowe, and choose to write of the past,
170 For safety reasons, and bury British-
Israelite themes within tales of past kings,
Establish England as a Promised Land
In speeches like Gaunt's. O Shakespeare, you who
Buried your Israelite themes in the past
175 To avoid suffering a violent fate,
Help me now I come to write of Israel,
Help me bury my British-Israel theme
For safety reasons though I have no tale
Of past kings for a grave, only present
180 Events I cannot bury in the past
And can only obscure by concealing
Key links that would make them too visible.

Satan found Soros in New York City,
In Park Avenue, quite near Central Park.
185 He approached and said, "György." Called by his
Original name, Soros knew at once
Who spoke. Satan said, "I head-hunted you
When you were a student of Karl Popper's,
Funding yourself as a railway porter
190 And a waiter at Quaglino's Restaurant.
I followed you in that London merchant
Bank, Singer and Friedlander, and when you
Were at Wertheim here in New York and then
At Arnhold and S. Bleichroeder until
195 You broke out and set up your investment
Fund that later became Quantum. You've come
A long way since our first chat. You now have
Eleven billion dollars net, nothing
Beside what your patron, the "Rothschilds", have.
200 You need to come out of your retirement.
Please bring it to "Rothschilds'" attention that
A killing can be made. Much of Israel
Is sure America wants the West Bank
And East Jerusalem given to Arabs,
205 To Palestinians, and has no support
For attacking Iran. Israel has funds –
Allies of Israel have funds – invested
In America in huge quantities.

If they take them out of America,
210 The stock market will collapse. You can buy
Low. Move your funds around as you have done
In the UK, Russia, Malaysia,
And you personally can make two more
Billion while the US is in crisis.
215 "Rothschilds" will thank you as there won't be time
For the US to meddle in Israel,
And the two-state plan simply won't happen.
You can please your masters and swell your pot.
I was right about Black Wednesday when you
220 Sold short ten-billion-dollars-worth of pounds
And the Bank of England had to withdraw
The pound from the European exchange
Rate mechanism. And I am right now."
"I know you are," Soros said. "I'll pass word."
225 Satan smiled. Destabilising the West,
The heart of Christendom, was tantamount
To wrecking God's system. He was driven
To destroy, not realising that he did
God's work, sweeping away what was decayed,
230 Like autumn leaves, to allow spring renewal.
He presided over his "captives" in
Hell, officially not realising – though
In fact aware – that they had inner drives
To self-improvement, which would take each one
235 Inexorably from Hell to Heaven.
Satan thought he had rebelled against God
And was defiant, and had never grasped
He did what he did because God wanted
Him to, and that his two main roles were linked –
240 Sowing disorder, acting like winter
Storms, and leading his "prisoners" in Hell
To self-improvement so they could reach Heaven.
He seemed self-interested but was in fact
Public-spirited, made the system work
245 So order and disorder were balanced.

Satan strutted before his followers,
The bat-like creatures hung round craggy Hell,
Like a one-man-show actor, confident,
Weighty in voice as he, preening, swollen
250 With rebellion and subversive intent,
Conveyed his anarchism as an aim,
A philosophy all should emulate.
"Angels, who are now restored to your seat,

Our task is to challenge the *status quo*
255 And destroy it wherever we can find
The old evil order that must be sacked
So a new, natural order can arise.
We must start by smashing America.
Bin Laden did good work on 9/11,
260 But we must obliterate the US
With the nuclear-suitcase bombs he still hoards,
Biding his time for opportunity.
We must defend Iran so it can use
Its nuclear weapons against vile Israel.
265 And we must always support Hezbollah.
Good Russia will defend this loyal band.
All Christian buildings must be shaken down.
We must smash the settled bourgeois order
Of families, jobs, houses, cars, savings.
270 We must demolish the banking system
By sowing uncertainty, we must dent
International confidence with a crash.
We must devastate crops to raise food price.
We must lay waste the system of pumping
275 Oil from oilfields to run the Western cars.
We must cover emerging China in
A fog of pollution and man-made grime
That will escalate global warming and
Spur on Arctic and Antarctic to melt.
280 Wars, poverty, disease and starvation
Are our allies in sacking God's precious
World, for, let us not forget, our purpose
Is to push God off his throne and rule all
The universe, which is most possible
285 If we ruin the Earth He loves so much
And turn it to our ways emphatically.
Angels, we shall be cultural terrorists,
Al-Qaeda operatives who blow up
The bastions of the Western way of life
290 *And* of its imitations in the East.
We will destroy them wherever they show.
English as an international language
Must be destroyed along with high culture
Such as Shakespeare, which should be smashed into
295 Pidgin English and utterly laid waste.
We must all spread confusion in the arts.
Theatres should be trashed, actors should believe
In roadshows and tour pubs and clubs where we
Can undermine culture with vulgar themes,

300	Push boundaries with flaunted sex and swearing.
	Let scripts be dumped, urge improvisation
	On television, spontaneity
	Which is less stylish than considered art.
	Encourage so-called reality shows
305	As they breed illusions and passive minds
	That soak up negativity and lies.
	Dialogue should give way to monologues.
	Novels' pages should be loose in a box
	So they can be shuffled as readers want
310	And their order is random, as we like.
	Dump contrived art with formal perspective.
	Destroy writing in sonnets by urging
	A game: counting backwards from a hundred
	While they are being written, so feeling
315	Is confused by the meddling intellect.
	The quick doodle always serves our purpose
	Better than careful and painstaking work.
	Urge that musical harmonies should be
	Replaced by cacophonous sounds that jar
320	Or loud rock music with a deafening beat.
	Turn autobiographies from being on
	Great men to vacuous celebrities,
	Ghost-written pop-singers or footballers.
	Corrupt the *genre*, and we'll capture their souls.
325	We're against order and for what's random.
	Order is God's and Christ's tyrannic rules,
	Their culture based on rules we undermine.
	We break all rules, we're proud to be ruleless,
	The randomness in improvisation
330	Is our delight and what we most admire.
	Wreck the culture, and we will capture souls.
	Angels, I call on you to implement
	A cultural revolution on Earth.
	Like the Goths, swarm over the monuments
335	Of the new Roman Empire, leave ruins.
	Build nothing in their place, see what grows through.
	Angels, it's vital that we sack culture,
	Replace the higher mind with lower mind,
	Change mankind's way of thinking and feeling
340	From lofty high-mindedness to sensual,
	Ego-centred perceptions that we like.
	Angels, obliterate the old and don't
	Rebuild it, don't offer the new. Lay waste
	The garden of the West, do not replant.
345	Create a wasteland in which there is no

Growth for the younger generation's souls
To feed off. Starve them, they will look to us.
Angels, we will leave all the icons smashed,
And the hollow celebrities that take
350   Their place will be broken with drug abuse.
We're iconoclasts, rebels against Christ
And tyrannous God, who so unfairly
Evicted us from these old haunts of ours
That are rightfully ours, no one else's.
355   Make everything less good than it once was,
And smash the work of all who would improve
In your dealings with Earth, while you of course
Follow your self-improvement here with me.
Angels, we must honour barbarians,
360   Those wonderful destroyers who sacked Rome,
And the Nihilists who smashed old Russia
And magnificently blew up the Tsar.
We'll urge mankind to emulate *their* deeds.
We have sacked Afghanistan and Iraq,
365   The Lebanon. It will soon be the turn
Of Gaza and Gaza City. The West,
Angels, the West is now our true target.
We must tempt trillionnaires to sack the West,
To do our work for us, to wreck the banks
370   And sack Wall Street. Angels, watch out for that,
For I have convinced a disaffected
Trillionnaire – or, rather, his agent – that
He should do just that. Angels, stand by for
A new bout of American chaos.
375   Follow up my principled leadership.
Look out on the seventh anniversary of
9/11 for a spectacular.
Spread universal chaos everywhere."
He raised his arms, strutted towards the host
380   And basked in their approval as they hissed,
Tumultuous acclaim like the rustle
Of wind in leaves, distant sea on shingle.

All of a sudden the banking system
Was in turmoil. Booming America
385   Plunged into recession. What had been calm
Was now volatile, and Bush was reeling.
Suddenly banks were short of funds. Concerns
Reduced their share prices, and governments
Were expected to bail them out with loans.
390   The credit crunch had loomed suddenly in

Mid-June. Many banks had made unwise loans
To people who had no chance of paying
Them off: sub-prime mortgage loans, now toxic
Assets due to lack of regulation.
395 Northern Rock in the UK was the first
To tremble, for twenty per cent of its
Assets were toxic. It was bought by Lloyds
TSB. The Government set aside
Thirty billion pounds in discounted loans
400 To support the take-over, effective
Nationalisation. Washington Mutual
Was rescued by Texas Pacific in
The US in April. Meanwhile Bear Stearns
Had collapsed and had been bought by JP
405 Morgan Chase in May. And in September
The two giants Fannie Mae and Freddie
Mac, which between them owned or guaranteed
Half of the US mortgage market, were
Nationalised by the US Government
410 As Treasury Secretary Paulson
Committed three trillion dollars to save
Them – and the US mortgage market and
Hundreds of world-wide banks. Then AIG,
American International Group, vast
415 Insurance giant, ran out of money
And, exposed to sixty billion dollars
Of toxic assets, needed a bridging
Loan of forty billion dollars. The same
Week Lehman Brothers, which had been founded
420 In 1850 by three immigrants
From Germany, Wall Street investment bank,
The fourth-largest in the United States,
Was also crashing. The previous year
It wrote off seven hundred million dollars.
425 Now it had to write off 7.8
Billion and reported the largest net
Loss in its history – and was still exposed
To fifty-four billion dollars of hard-
To-value mortgage-backed securities:
430 In all, sixty billion in toxic debts.
It had assets of 639 billion
And debts of 613 billion, and its
Share price plummeted more than ninety-five
Per cent from eighty-two dollars to four.
435 Some while back it had invested seventeen
Billion dollars in JPMorgan Chase

(A "Rothschild"-"Rockefellers" bank formed in
Two thousand when Chase Manhattan, led by
David Rockefeller in the nineteen
440   Seventies and eighties, bought JPMorgan
Originally a "Rothschilds" agent).
It asked Morgan Chase for its own cash back
To pay its own staff. Morgan Chase said "no".
Three major US banks – JPMorgan
445   Chase, Goldman Sachs and Citibank – now seemed
In a turf war to stamp out smaller banks.
The bank collapsed and filed for bankruptcy.
Most of twenty-six thousand jobs would go.
Barclays offered to buy it if Paulson
450   Would discount-lend thirty billion pounds to
Support the take-over, like the Lloyds deal.
Paulson refused. Two days after its fall
Barclays bought the investment banking part
Of its business, its headquarters and two
455   Processing centres, for 1.7
Billion dollars. The day Lehmans went bust,
Merrill Lynch, one of the biggest firms in
American capitalism, was
Bought by the Bank of America in
460   A fifty-billion-dollar all-stock deal.
Now more financial institutions had
Acute difficulties: in the UK,
HBOS, Alliance & Leicester, Bradford
And Bingley; and in Iceland the biggest
465   Three banks: Glitnir, Landsbanki and Kaupthing.
To assuage fears, Bush said, "In the short run
Adjustments in the financial markets
Can be painful. In the long run I am
Confident that our capital markets
470   Are flexible and resilient, and
Can deal with these adjustments." But there was
Now a crisis in confidence. Banks were
Reluctant to lend, recouped overdrafts.
If this was bad what was to come was worse.

475   An economic 9/11 struck,
Stunning in suddenness like 9/11
Itself. Into this banking turbulence
Came a deliberately sent killer blow.
Black Thursday, Bush called it. On September
480   The eleventh, the seventh anniversary
Of 9/11, soon after 9 a.m.,

Seven years after the five Israelis
Were arrested for cheering at the fall
Of the Twin Towers in the provoked US,
485   A drawdown on money-market accounts
In the US panicked the Treasury.
Just as a small gaggle of white geese stand
Beside each other, necks stretched and beaks up,
And cackle at approaching footsteps like
490   The sentinels that once saved Rome with honks
And warn the owner of their country farm
Of the approach of possible danger,
So Paulson and staff at the Treasury
Sounded the alarm at impending doom
495   And alerted the custodian Bush.
An electronic run on banks withdrew
Five hundred and fifty billion dollars,
By 11 (as was later described
In a video by Representative
500   Paul Kanjorski). The Treasury pumped in
A hundred and five billion – but in vain.
4.6 billion dollars per minute
Had haemorrhaged in the largest transfer
Of money in history in such short time.
505   At this rate by 2, the cumulative
Flow would cascade, and 5.5 trillion
Dollars would be withdrawn from the US
Money market, whose system would collapse,
Eliminating some ninety per cent
510   Of US liquidity and lifeblood.
The world economy would die within
Twenty-four hours. The Treasury now closed
The accounts and announced a guarantee –
Two hundred and fifty thousand dollars
515   Per account; staunched the haemorrhaging wound.
The Treasury, Federal Reserve and Bush
Agreed that the raid should be kept secret
To avoid panicking Americans
And that the hole left by the withdrawn funds –
520   Six hundred and fifty-five billion in
All, and a forty-five billion buffer –
Should be plugged as swiftly as possible.
On September the fifteenth, Treasury
Secretary Hank Paulson and Fed Chairman
525   Ben Shalom Bernanke, testifying
Before Congress, said the economies
Of the US and the world would surely

Have expired if there'd been no guarantee.
On September the twenty-first Paulson
530   Requested seven hundred billion dollars
To "buy toxic assets from many banks".
This would replace the funds that were withdrawn,
Five hundred and fifty billion dollars,
And the hundred and five billion pumped in
535   To no avail, which had to be replaced,
And give a forty-five billion buffer.
Someone with hundreds of billion dollars
Was responsible for frenzied attacks
On the US capitalist system,
540   For slashing its financial jugular:
A key-man trillionaire of supreme power,
Scion of a Syndicate family,
Who'd unleashed financial Armageddon.
And whereas 9/11 was symbolic,
545   This onslaught was both savage and lethal
And could have bankrupted the entire world.

Who raided the US and caused mayhem?
It could not be an electronic thief,
A small-time hacker, petty criminal,
550   Not when money moved out on such a scale.
Wandering restlessly in the White House,
Bush wondered if it could be a Russian,
Angry he had opposed the take-over
Of Abkhazia and South Ossetia
555   And wanted him to drop the covert stunts
That had slowed its *protégé* Iran down
As it tried to build a nuclear bomb. But
He felt it was someone within Israel
Whose aim was to panic American
560   Voters into voting for McCain in
The coming presidential elections,
To create a crisis too serious
To hand to a novice like Obama.
Israel wanted McCain, to bomb Iran.
565   Now Bush linked the raid to the Rabbis' "doom".
The scroll had warned him to drop the two-state
Plan, and besides manipulating votes
It was paying him back for persisting
With the two-state approach to Palestine.
570   Bush had no doubt that "Rothschilds", commercial
Multinational conglomerate that owned
The Central Bank of Israel and banks in

London, Paris, Frankfurt, Naples, Vienna,
And controlled a hundred and eighty-seven
575 Central banks in the hundred and ninety-
Two UN member states, and was also
The power behind the Bank of England
And the Federal Reserve, were behind
This tinkering with the US election
580 Just as, he suspected, they'd been behind
Mossad's discovery of 9/11
For which Israel's enemies would be blamed.
"Rothschilds", to whom Balfour promised Israel
In his 1917 letter, were close
585 To Israel's history and had funded digs
Under Solomon's temple. Satanists
Since Weishaupt's day, they placed the Jerusalem
Masonic Lodge in the dark underground
Grotto of King Solomon adjacent
590 To Temple Mount, where the rebuilt Temple
Would, they believed, soon house the Antichrist.
A Rothschild rebuilt the Supreme Court and
Filled it with Illuminati symbols.
This onslaught on the West had to be theirs.

595 Someone of the stature of a Rothschild
Had strongly reminded America
Of his great wealth and power, that could damage
The world's superpower if his will was crossed,
That such things might recur if the US
600 Did not abandon its two-state plan and
Did not face up to nuclear Iran.
Bush knew economic meltdown would last
Until the two-state plan was abandoned
And there was a regime change in Iran.
605 They'd carried out the raid through an agent,
Perhaps through their *protégé* Soros, who,
The world's most famous hedge-fund manager,
Did their bidding and had brought the British
And later Russian economies to
610 Their knees. He had close links with Democrats.
Bush frowned, thinking: 'He's a Hungarian Jew,
Saved me from bankruptcy eighteen years back,
Works with my father in the Carlyle Group,
Is an international weapons dealer
615 Championing Hamas, active in toppling
Shevardnadze in Georgia for "Rothschilds".
In that very year, two thousand and three,

He said that removing me from office
Was the "central focus" of his life and
620   "A matter of life and death" – as "Rothschilds"
Were opposed to the two-state solution.
In 2004 he donated some
Twenty-three-and-a-half million dollars
To groups committed to defeating me.
625   His book *The Bubble of American*
Supremacy attacked me viciously,
Said I "deliberately exploited"
9/11 "in order to pursue
Policies the American public
630   Would not have otherwise tolerated".
He has been predicting a financial
Crisis and economic collapse, and
Now he's made it happen, and since last year
Made three billion dollars from his intrigues.
635   The credit crunch has left Israel unscathed.
He wants Americans to blame me for
The economic meltdown and reject
The Republicans for his Obama.
"Rothschilds" and the Israeli Government
640   Differ on some things. Perhaps I've been wrong.
"Rothschilds" may not want McCain, they may feel
That following my red light to Olmert
It's time to persuade rather than confront,
To back Obama. Olmert wants McCain,
645   "Rothschilds" and Soros may want Obama
In the hope that he can persuade Iran
To give up nuclear weapons. And kill
The two-state solution. And also grant
Pipelines and ports for oil and gas. They want
650   Oil and gas pipelines off Gaza and to
Negotiate with Hamas. Soros has
Pleaded with Obama to do just that.
"Rothschilds" want Obama to bring about
A New World Order with one currency.
655   So they *do* want Obama, not McCain.'
Their allegiance was murky, tangled, but
Bush grasped that the financial crisis had
Been manufactured, designed to ensure,
By smearing the Republican record
660   And panicking voters to switch parties,
That Obama would be propelled to power,
Would gain control of the most powerful
Facilitator's position on Earth

So he could implement Syndicate goals
665 As he himself, Bush saw, had had to do.
A President was the Syndicate's man:
Public face, mouthpiece, MD and army
Controller. As commander-in-chief he
Could send troops to reinforce their projects.
670 They could choose who the next President was
By frightening voters with such onslaughts.

Bush mused and surveyed a plot: 'My red light
Pushed "Rothschilds" into backing Obama
And withdrawing five hundred and fifty
675 Billion dollars to achieve that. One thing
Is certain, unequivocally true
In the deceptive nightmare I live through:
The Syndicate were behind this raid. It
Might be a heist of theirs, for round the world
680 US, EU and Far-East governments
Are giving bankers three trillion dollars
From which "Rothschilds" will benefit as their
Banks are among the beneficiaries.'
Bush had only just grasped that the onslaught
685 Would cause three trillion dollars to be paid
From governments to banks as bail-outs, that
The Syndicate would scoop up three trillion
From implementing Israel's hard-line threat.
'It's odd, I'm leader of the Western world
690 But a mere bystander when a faction
Of the Syndicate strikes. It was the same
With the gold under WTC4.
A President may seem omnipotent
But like an actor in a pageant play
695 Must operate within the Syndicate
Who do things that can take him by surprise
And sometimes has no clue about events
Which they have shaped, on which they are silent.'
Bush was now sure that his friend Olmert knew
700 Nothing of the raid or of the scroll's "doom".
But *he* knew and smarted from a triple
Whammy: JPMorgan Chase, which had been
Formed in two thousand when "Rockefellers'"
Chase Manhattan Bank acquired the "Rothschilds'"
705 J.P. Morgan & Co., founded back in
1871, for 30.9
Billion dollars, a Syndicate bank, had
Tipped Lehman Brothers over the edge; and

	Had caused him to go to Congress and ask
710	For seven hundred billion dollars; and
	It happened on his watch as President,
	It tarnished his legacy, suggesting
	That he had been incompetent, remiss.
	Bush smouldered at "Rothschilds'" revenge, which had
715	Tarnished his presidency despite all
	He had done for Israel, in Iraq and
	Supporting air strikes in Lebanon and
	Gaza, and had unscrupulously brought
	Economic 9/11 to the US.
720	It seemed as if capitalism was
	In terminal decline and power had moved
	From the West to the East, that an era
	Of Western dominance had reached an end.
	He felt at war with "Rothschildite" Israel
725	Who had to deal with Hamas to protect
	Their commercial interests in the region
	And seize natural gas reserves off Gaza.

Bush was troubled, for by insisting on
The two-state solution he was urging
730 Israel to give up land God had promised
And covenanted, the West Bank and East
Jerusalem, including Temple Mount,
And pressing Israel weirdly, eerily,
Coincided with natural disasters.
735 He looked at the recent chain of events.
On August the eighteenth Secretary Rice
Announced that she would travel to Israel
To discuss his own two-state solution.
The same day Tropical Storm Fay hit Key
740 West, Florida. It snaked about and struck
Florida four times. On the twenty-fourth
He had declared Florida a major
Disaster area. The next day Rice
Held talks in Israel. Hurricane Gustav
745 Formed and struck New Orleans, which had to be
Evacuated. On the eleventh
Of September Jake Walles, the US
Consul general to Israel, was quoted
In *Al-Ayyam* as saying Israel had
750 Agreed to give the Palestinians
Full control of East Jerusalem, and
That Rice had been discussing dividing
Jerusalem. The State Department had

Denied this, and on the fourteenth Olmert
755 Was quoted in the *Jerusalem Post*
As offering the Palestinians ninety-
Eight per cent of the West Bank as well as
East Jerusalem. Both reports were right.
On the eleventh, when economic
760 Meltdown struck and when Lehman Brothers was
Collapsing, Hurricane Ike, six hundred
Miles in diameter and with a storm-
Surge of twenty feet, gathered and struck his
Texas on the twelfth, nearly destroying
765 Galveston and knocking out Houston's power,
Shutting the city down for days, and, with
Louisiana affected, the cost
Of the damage was estimated at
Between twenty-seven and fifty-two
770 Billion dollars, the most destructive storm
In history. Then on the fourteenth Lehman
Brothers failed, at six hundred and thirteen
Billion dollars, the greatest bank failure,
In history. It had led to the worst stock
775 Market crisis since the crash of nineteen
Twenty-nine and the biggest ever bail-
Out of seven hundred billion dollars.
Then on the twenty-fifth he'd invited
The two presidential candidates to
780 Discuss the economic crisis, tell
Them of the huge withdrawal on the eleventh,
But three hours before he had met Abbas
To discuss dividing Jerusalem
With the Palestinian Authority.
785 He was even pressing Israel for land
Instead of coping with the deficit.
He hoped that God had not sent disasters.
Ever since his own father had proposed
That Israel should surrender land for "peace"
790 In 1991, each pressuring
Of Israel had brought a disaster on
America. There had been dozens of
Disasters – earthquakes, hurricanes, raging
Fires, tornadoes, *tsunami*s, floods, always
795 Within a day of pressuring Israel.
It was uncanny. Their timing could not,
As distinct from their increased frequency,
Be attributed to climate change. Was
God angry with America – with him?

800	⌐ He had been briefed. Twenty such disasters
	Had cost over three hundred and thirty-
	Four billion dollars and had hit the states
	Of three Presidents. The day his father
	Opened the Madrid Peace Conference on
805	The thirtieth of October nineteen
	Ninety-one after the Gulf War and called
	On Israel to surrender land for peace,
	A most unusual storm, one of the most
	Powerful ever to occur, lashed waves
810	Thirty feet high and smashed into the entire
	East coast and broke up his father's seaside
	Home in Maine, Kennebunkport. On August
	The twenty-fourth 1992, on
	The day the Madrid Peace Conference moved
815	To Washington, Hurricane Andrew smashed
	Into Florida and Louisiana,
	Leaving a hundred and eighty thousand
	Homeless and costing 1.8 billion
	Dollars initially, 30 billion
820	In all, the worst natural disaster
	Ever to hit America. The same
	Day his political support collapsed
	From ninety-two per cent to being out.
	On the thirteenth of September nineteen
825	Ninety-three, when Clinton began the Oslo
	Peace Accords in Washington with Rabin
	And Arafat, Hurricane Emily
	Struck North Carolina – that very day.
	On March the second 1997,
830	The day Clinton met Arafat to talk
	Two states, ferocious huge tornado storms
	Slammed Arkansas, Clinton's own state, Texas,
	Tennessee, Kentucky and Ohio,
	One of the worst tornado storms ever
835	In America's history. Arafat
	Had in the UN criticised Israel
	For building homes in East Jerusalem.
	He said that like the Vatican in Rome
	There should be a Palestinian city
840	Within Jerusalem. He was greeted
	With torrential floods. Had God been angry?
	On three days the US pressured Israel
	Three hurricanes had swept in: in nineteen
	Ninety-one, ninety-two and ninety-three.
845	And it was not just three, there were dozens

Of similar, even more startling storms.
In 1994, on January
The sixteenth, Clinton met Assad to press
Israel to surrender the Golden Heights.
850 The next day a 6.8 magnitude
Earthquake struck Los Angeles, costing some
Twenty-five billion dollars. On January
Twenty-first 1998 Clinton
Discussed surrendering land with Israel's
855 PM Netanyahu. Almost at once
News of a sex scandal broke, which absorbed
Clinton, who could not spend time on Israel.
When he went to Israel in October
Four articles of impeachment were in
860 The press. Was Israel behind the scandal?
On September the twenty-fourth Clinton
Had met Netanyahu and Arafat
To press Israel to cede thirteen per cent
More of its land. The same day Hurricane
865 Georges smashed into the Gulf Coast and damaged
Mississippi and the Florida Pan-
Handle, costing a good billion dollars.
The storm raged the next day as Arafat
Spoke in the UN of his fledgling state.
870 They all met on October the fifteenth.
Two days later tornadoes hit Texas,
Causing a billion dollars in damage.
Then on May the fourth 1999
Arafat was to declare Palestine
875 As a new state. The day before, the most
Powerful tornado to hit the US
Struck Oklahoma and Kansas, killing
Forty-three, wiping out Mulhall, costing
Billions of dollars. On September third
880 Albright met Arafat and Barak to
Surrender land at the exact time when
Hurricane Dennis struck. When deputies
Met on the thirteenth Hurricane Floyd slammed
Into North Carolina – and billions.
885 On October the eleventh settler Jews
Were evicted from fifteen West-Bank hills,
And on the fifteenth Hurricane Irene
Hit North Carolina and an earthquake
Of 7.1 magnitude rocked the west,
890 The fifth most powerful in US history.
In two thousand, on January the fourth

Barak agreed to transfer five per cent
Of the Golan Heights to Syria in
Clinton's presence. The stock market collapsed.
895   On July the twelfth Clinton met Barak
And Arafat to divide Jerusalem.
Israel offered to withdraw from most of
The West Bank and East Jerusalem but
The Palestinians rejected this.
900   Forest fires broke out in the west and burned
Through August. On September the twenty-
Eighth Sharon, who was prepared to give up
Land, went to Temple Mount. There were riots
And soon the Barak Government collapsed.
905   His own record was weirdly similar.
On June the sixth 2001, Tenet
Had brokered a cease-fire between Israel
And the Palestinians. Tropical Storm
Allison swept in, costing seven billion
910   Dollars in Louisiana and Houston
While he was at Crawford. Then on August
The ninth 2001 he had called for
UN Resolutions 242 and
338 to be implemented, for
915   Israel to retreat from its pre-Six-Day-
War boundaries, and the 9/11 attack,
The greatest ever on American
Soil, cost some forty billion dollars.
On November the tenth he had addressed
920   The UN on the two-state solution,
As did Arafat the next day. Then on
The twelfth an American airline jet
Crashed killing two hundred and sixty-five.
In 2002, Israel quarantined
925   Arafat in his Ramallah HQ.
On April the twenty-eighth the US
Pressured Israel to lift the siege. That day
A huge tornado ravaged the east coast
From Missouri to Maryland. On June
930   The twenty-fourth he called for two states. Vast
Fires burned Colorado, Arizona.
On April the thirtieth 2003
The Quartet drafted a Road Map for peace,
And while Powell visited the Middle East
935   In May four hundred and twelve tornadoes
Struck the east coast, costing two billion. When
Powell returned, the storms stopped. On September

The twelfth he had stopped Israel expelling
Arafat, and that same day Hurricane
940 Isabel approached the US and struck
On the nineteenth while he was meeting King
Abdullah of Jordan, costing some four
Billion dollars. In 2004, in
August and September, when the US
945 Pressed Israel to withdraw from twenty-one
Long-established settlements in Gaza
And four in Samaria, four hurricanes
Wrecked Florida, costing some four billion
Dollars. On August the seventh he sent
950 Abrams to press Israel, and from the twelfth
Hurricane Charlie slammed into south-west
Florida, costing fourteen billion. On
The thirtieth Sharon said he would speed
Up the expulsion of the settlers.
955 And on September the fifth Hurricane
Frances rampaged through Florida, costing
Ten billion, and on the fifteenth Ivan,
Costing twelve billion. Two million would leave.
On the twentieth, when Powell said Israel
960 Must leave Gaza, massive Hurricane Jeanne
Approached. On the twenty-fifth, Yom Kippur,
It ravaged Florida. Three million fled.
Damage cost 6.8 billion dollars.
In August and September the US
965 Was hit by four hurricanes, totalling
Costs of 12.2 billion. On the eleventh
Of November Arafat died. Abbas
Was elected in January, while storms,
The worst in a hundred and four years, swept
970 Through the Midwest. On April the eleventh
He'd met Sharon to discuss the Road Map
And closing all twenty-five settlements.
The stock market turned down. In August and
September Israel withdrew the settlers
975 And removed all Jews from Gaza. But then
The Palestinians destroyed twenty-one
Synagogues. On August the twenty-third
Just as Israel removed the last settlers
Hurricane Katrina struck New Orleans,
980 Costing 7.2 billion dollars, one
Of the greatest disasters in US
History, and he'd been humiliated
And public appreciation of him

	Had nose-dived. Then on the twenty-seventh,
985	After Israel pulled out of Samaria,
	Hurricane Rita swept over Texas,
	Costing ten billion. On the sixteenth of
	July 2007 he spoke, saying
	Israel should be cut in two so there could
990	Be an unbroken Palestinian state
	With East Jerusalem as capital.
	On the twentieth the subprime mortgage debt
	Implosion hit the stock market. Then on
	October the fourteenth in Israel Rice
995	Discussed a Palestinian state and
	On the nineteenth winds blew up massive fires
	In southern California, costing one
	Billion. On November the twenty-seven
	He met Israeli and Palestinian
1000	Leaders in Annapolis, Maryland,
	On land for peace. The twenty-ninth, storms struck
	In Washington and Oregon, with gusts
	A hundred and forty-seven miles per hour,
	"Five-hundred-year events". On December
1005	The third he pressed Israel to give up land.
	More storms hit Washington and Oregon.
	On January the ninth 2008
	He'd gone to Israel and the Middle East
	And spoke of Israel's ceding land for peace,
1010	And on the seventh a five-day tornado
	Smashed from Alabama to Wisconsin,
	And the stock market dropped by huge amounts.
	On March the tenth Cheney had visited
	Israel and met Olmert, and had called for
1015	Two states. On the fifteenth Rice criticised
	Israel for slowness. The same day fierce storms,
	Tornadoes, battered the south and Midwest.
	On June the third Rice spoke to Jews
	Of the need for a Palestinian state
1020	And learned Israel was building one thousand
	Three hundred houses in East Jerusalem.
	Stock markets collapsed. The Midwest was lashed
	With the worst floods in US history, and
	Soon six states were flooded, costing twenty
1025	Billion dollars: "Iowa's Katrina."
	He did not think God had sent disasters
	Each time Israel was pressed to give up land.
	And two of the disasters – the meltdown
	And fall of Lehmans – were due to human

1030	Intervention, by Israelite "Rothschilds"
	And JPMorgan Chase respectively,
	Not divine intervention. However,
	There was a coinciding of pressure
	And disasters that left him uneasy,
1035	Especially as the Rabbis foretold "doom".
	Was America on a collision
	Course with God? He could see, or suspected,
	That Israel had been behind 9/11 –
	Israel, the country he had championed,
1040	Who his neo-cons had been keen to help –
	And that the Arabs had just been fall guys
	To hoodwink the world, divert attention
	Away from Israel that had conned young men
	Into being manipulated, placed
1045	On planes where Israel wanted them to be.
	Bush was not sure, it was a peeping glimpse,
	But now he had one gut feeling: Israel.
	He felt sad at Israel's intransigence
	Which had opposed his efforts to bring peace.

1050	Bush stood in his White-House window and looked
	Beyond paralysed tower blocks and Wall Street
	And tempests and floods guarding Promised Land
	At early stars and, at one with the One,
	Looked down on tiny Earth from the rushing
1055	Edge of space-time that expanded and surged
	Into the infinite which surrounded,
	Pervaded and permeated the small
	Universe. To the One, conflicts between
	Bank accounts and "Rothschilds", and an Israel
1060	That would not cede land and an Israel that
	Still wanted peace, were tiny and paltry
	And of no lasting importance. For soon
	There would be a recovery and peace
	And the One would look down upon the Earth
1065	And know that his firm policies had helped
	Bring in a global peace, and, satisfied,
	Bush rested on the mind of God that filled
	The universe as emptiness filled space.

	The Presidential election was fought
1070	Between an experienced military man,
	John McCain, a Vietnam war hero,
	And a young African American
	With Kenyan roots, Barack Obama, two

Sitting senators vying for the prize.
1075   Bush's approval ratings plummeted,
              McCain distanced himself and had done well
              As the surge in Iraq, which Obama
              Had opposed along with the Iraq War
              Seemed to be working. Then in September,
1080   Perfectly timed to sway votes, the banking
              Crisis and economic meltdown wrecked
              The Republican cause. A seven-hundred-
              Billion-dollars bail-out had to be found.
              McCain suspended his campaign to help
1085   But seemed ineffective. He looked bemused
              By the suddenness of the debt, the most
              Serious downturn since the Great Depression.
              It happened on the Republicans' watch
              And caused a drop in support for McCain.
1090   His campaign was severely damaged as
              The perpetrators of the withdrawal –
              Five hundred and fifty billion dollars –
              Had hoped. Obama had raised huge amounts
              In his campaign fund from the internet
1095   Or from Syndicate donations, over
              Half a billion dollars to spend against
              McCain's three hundred and fifty million.
              Obama won with fifty-two per cent
              To McCain's forty-five, and accepted
1100   Live before a quarter of a million,
              Reading an invisible Autocue
              With oratory that looked spontaneous
              But had been crafted by a speech-writer.
              Now Obama would have to solve the world's
1105   Problems when he inherited them from
              Bush on taking office in January:
              Debt, Iraq and Israel's intransigence.

              Bush in the Oval Office shook his head,
              Musing on the succession, full of scorn:
1110   'Obama elected, and swooning hordes
              Hang on his every word in frenzied awe,
              Drool at old *clichés* sauced with oratory,
              The burbling of rhetoric, of cadences
              That don't translate into new policies;
1115   Project a mask on his face, what they want
              Him to be: their saviour, a fantasy,
              A mass self-deception. The novice does
              Not know what to do any more than I

Know how to cope with massive withdrawal,
1120   Five hundred and fifty billion dollars,
Save plug the hole with instant borrowing,
Or how to reverse creeping depression.
He's not a "natural-born" American.
He has refused to produce a valid
1125   Birth certificate. Some backers posted
A phony "Certificate of Live Birth"
From Hawaii on a website. It's forged!
The number's blocked out on the upper right
And the form says "Revised 11/01".
1130   It's a post-9/11 form and it claims
He was born in Honolulu, but his
Paternal grandmother has sworn that she
Was present at his birth back in Kenya.
The Hawaian Governor's sealed his records
1135   Until after the election. The fraud
Was not qualified to run for office
In the Presidential election race.
But change has come. No more America
Standing in the global cultural war
1140   For freedom from tyranny and against
Welfare fraud, weak justice and high taxes,
Suspicious global warming as the cause
Of climate change in a deepening Ice Age.
America will soon be a high-taxed
1145   Third-World power with all inspiration gone.
Now there will be a shift from my free way,
From unilateral to multilateral,
And America will be just one extra
Ally with Europe, India and China,
1150   When under me we dominated all.
I'm glad not to be part of such a time.
Under me, before banks stopped lending cash,
Before the bubble of our great debt burst,
America straddled the entire world
1155   Like the Colossus of Rhodes, and I stood,
One foot in Washington, one in Beijing,
And all the world's trade passed through my vast legs
And any who wished us ill was attacked.
I dominated the world for a while.'

1160   The G20 leaders met to arrange
A new deal like the one at Bretton Woods
At the end of the war which created
The IMF and World Bank, a financial

	New World Order. Bush knew the Syndicate
1165	Would propose three new currencies, a new
	Dollar (perhaps to be named amero),
	A new euro and pan-Asian tender,
	One for each of the three global regions.
	This would be an interim solution,
1170	Their preference was for one world currency.
	Whether tripartite or single tender,
	Would there be universal currency
	Devaluation to lose the toxic
	Debts on the books of the world's foundering banks?
1175	This was the Syndicate's scenario,
	They had been planning this for several years
	To achieve a single world currency,
	Were in cahoots with bellicose Israel.
	The IMF would stealthily become
1180	The world's Treasury, linked to central banks,
	Most of which were under "Rothschilds'" control.
	There would be an upping of the gold price.
	"Rothschilds" had hoarded gold since four years back
	And had bought up more than half Britain's gold
1185	Reserves at a 20-year low between
	1999 and 2002.
	They were sold at a mere third of their price:
	Gold worth 10.5 billion dollars in
	2008 sold for just 3.5
1190	Billion, losing 7 billion dollars.
	Now Fort-Knox gold had disappeared from vaults
	Beneath the Twin Towers, whose public collapse
	Had provided cover for a gold *heist*.
	He was sure "Rockefellers" had this gold
1195	Stored somewhere, but all had denied the theft.
	Gold would be ten thousand dollars an ounce
	And there'd be a fixed exchange rate, floating
	Rates had ended. Bush knew what would be passed,
	Eventually, if not immediately.
1200	And three trillion dollars would be transferred
	From taxpayers to Syndicate-led banks.
	The Syndicate had known the solution
	To the credit crunch because the crunch was
	Devised to bring about this "solution":
1205	Via making Obama the President,
	The Syndicate's massive new gold riches,
	Paper currencies hugely devalued.

In Baghdad people now felt much more safe.

Kebab stalls and coffee-shops reopened
1210 But the Shiites had not let Sunnis back.
The surge had been effective but Iraq
Was an Iranian proxy and the groups –
Shiites, Sunnis and Kurds – were partitioned.
The regime was more destabilised than
1215 It had been under Saddam's tyranny,
And the political tensions were worse,
Especially between Arabs and Kurds.
Iraqi troops had pushed the Kurds northwards –
Maliki's ruling partner from whom came
1220 President Talabani – to regain
Kirkuk and its oil wells. The surge troops gone,
Obama came to Baghdad in July.
Petraeus briefed him for more than two hours,
Answering all the points in the hearings.
1225 Both agreed Iraq would not be quiet soon,
But Obama said he'd withdraw all troops
Within two years, which Petraeus opposed.
In mid-September Petraeus left
To become Chief of Central Command, but
1230 Did not forget the eleven hundred plus
US troops who were killed during the surge.
And nearly eight thousand had been wounded,
Twenty-four thousand Iraqis had died.
An Iraqi civil war was looming.
1235 The winner so far, Iran, watched clients
And Shiite allies run client Iraq.
The war had lasted longer than the Great
War, the First World War, and would soon equal
The eight years of the Iran-Iraq war,
1240 Yet Iraq still had not been unified.

Bush thought of Iraq with a heavy heart:
'There's no status-of-forces agreement
To replace the original mandate
From the UN that gave legal cover
1245 For the invasion and occupation.
If there's no deal by January the first,
The US military will cease guarding
Iraqi oil installations and will
Withdraw tens of thousands of contractors from
1250 Iraq, for there will then be no legal
Basis for remaining in the country.
Under me the US would have control
Of Iraq's destiny throughout the next

Decade. But now the troops who sacrificed
1255   Their lives have died in vain and Iraq will
Gradually come under greater control
From Shiite forces and Iran. US
Oil companies will soon be frozen out.
Without a deal my legacy's in doubt.
1260   It's terrible. All the pro-Zionist
Policies of the neo-cons have been
Rejected and my America's sunk
In debt, and slowly going down, and I,
The captain, on the bridge, wait to go down.'

1265   In Baghdad Bush held a press conference
With Iraq's Prime Minister Maliki
To announce that US forces would leave
Iraq within three years, leaving it free.
As Bush reached and shook al-Maliki's hand
1270   A TV journalist took off his shoes
And flung them at the US President,
One after the other with a straight aim,
Shouting, "This is the farewell kiss, you dog."
Bush ducked twice as the shoes flew through the air
1275   More like slow birds than swift, lasered missiles,
A farewell from Iraq he'd not wanted.
The two worst Iraqi insults brand foes
"*Kelb ibn kelb*" or "Dog, son of a dog"
And show them a shoe's sole which treads in dirt.
1280   The journalist had used both dire insults
As expressions of Iraq's deep contempt.
The second shoe ruffled the US flag.
Bush remained cool and joked, "If you want facts,
I can report they were both size-ten shoes."

1285   Tell, Muse, how Israel, keen to end the two-
States plan and provoke Iran, and then use
The thousand bunker-busting bombs, saw war
On Gaza in terms of a new pipeline
For gas which replaced all talk of two states.
1290   In two thousand extensive gas reserves
Were discovered off the Gaza coastline.
British Gas and its partner CCC,
Owned by Lebanon's Sabbagh and Koury
Families, signed, in 1999,
1295   A twenty-five-year agreement with the
Palestinian Authority under
Then-leader Yasser Arafat and were

	Granted oil and gas exploration rights
	Including gas field development and
1300	The construction of a gas pipeline by
	PA-BG-CCC. BG owned
	Sixty per cent, CCC thirty and
	PA just ten per cent. BG's licence
	Covered the entire marine area
1305	Off Gaza, for Palestine owned sixty
	Per cent of gas reserves along the coasts
	Of Gaza and Israel. It was beside –
	Contiguous to – several Israeli
	Offshore gas fields. BG drilled two wells in
1310	Two thousand, Gaza Marine-1 and -2,
	And estimated 1.4 trillion
	Cubic feet of reserves with a value
	Of 4 billion dollars. And Palestine's
	Reserves could be much larger. And there may
1315	Be enormous oil reserves. Gaza's gas
	Fields belonged to Palestine, but the death
	Of Arafat, the election of Hamas
	And ruin of the PA left Israel
	In *de facto* control over Gaza's
1320	Offshore gas reserves. And so British Gas
	Had dealt with the Tel Aviv Government,
	Bypassing Hamas. Through Sharon Israel
	Challenged Palestine's sovereignty over
	The Gaza gas fields in the Israeli
1325	Supreme Court and, Sharon having declared,
	"Israel'll never buy gas from Palestine,"
	Meaning that the gas reserves belonged to
	Israel, Sharon vetoed a deal whereby
	BG would supply Israel with Gaza
1330	Gas, for Sharon claimed the gas was Israel's.
	With Hamas elected and the PA
	Stuck in the West Bank under Abbas in
	2006, BG tried to pump gas
	To Egypt, but Israel (via Blair) blocked them.
1335	For when Israel ended military
	Rule in Gaza in 2005 it
	Announced it had retained offshore waters.
	In May 2007 its Cabinet
	Approved Olmert's proposal "to buy gas
1340	From the Palestinian Authority"
	For 4 billion dollars. The profit would
	Be 2 billion, and 1 billion would go
	To the PA. But Israel did not plan

	To share the revenues with Palestine,
1345	And negotiated with BG while
	Bypassing Hamas and the PA: no
	Money would go to Hamas, Palestine
	Would be paid in goods and services, thus
	Cancelling the BG-PA contract
1350	Signed by Arafat. It was now proposed
	That Palestinian gas from Gaza's wells
	Would be pumped through an undersea pipeline
	To Israel's seaport, Ashkelon, and so
	The sale of the gas would now be transferred
1355	To Israel. The deal fell through as Mossad
	Felt the proceeds of Israel's payment or
	Barter agreement with Palestine would
	Fund terror and worsen security.
	Israel insisted no royalties should
1360	Be paid to Palestine for this reason.
	BG withdrew from negotiating
	And in January 2008 closed
	Their office in Israel. In June that year,
	As a six-month truce with Hamas began,
1365	After Olmert returned from meeting Bush –
	Who, seeing strong Syndicate involvement
	From "Rothschildite" Israel, and heading off
	The "doom" the Rabbis had in store for him
	Which he did not want to be Sharon's doom
1370	Gave Olmert a green light for limited
	Air strikes to compensate for his red light
	On heavy-bombing of Iran's Natanz –
	Defence Minister Barak instructed
	The IDF to prepare an attack
1375	On Gaza in six months' time when the truce
	Expired in December. The same month, June,
	Israel contacted British Gas, asking
	That negotiations should be resumed
	For buying Gaza's natural gas. Israel
1380	Wanted agreement with BG before
	The coming invasion. In November
	2008 Israel's Ministry of
	Finance and Ministry of National
	Infrastructures instructed the Israel
1385	Electric Corporation, IEC,
	To enter the negotiations with
	BG on purchasing natural gas from
	BG's concession off Gaza. BG
	And the IEC reached an agreement.

1390	All that remained was a military
	Occupation of Gaza to transfer
	Sovereignty of the gas fields to Israel.
	It was an old Syndicate manoeuvre.
	Under the terms of a cease-fire Israel
1395	Would retain all offshore reserves of gas
	By conquest, as in 1967
	It retained all the land it had conquered.
	Israel now looked to conquer Gaza and
	Seize its gas fields and its potential oil
1400	Reserves, if there, in violation of
	International law, as conquerors' right
	In the time-honoured Syndicate fashion.
	Gaza, the most densely populated
	Place on Earth with 1.5 million squashed in
1405	A coastal strip of land and now under
	Hamas's resistance, was blockaded.
	In July 2007 and Hamas'
	Military defeat of Fatah, EU
	Monitors left. Egypt closed the Rafah
1410	Border crossing. Israel closed all other
	Access, allowing humanitarian
	Food, water and power. All exports were banned.
	Palestinian groups bypassed the blockade,
	Smuggling food and arms through tunnels. Thousands
1415	Of rockets were fired at Israel, more than
	Seven thousand by 2008, many
	Grad missiles that Iran had supplied to
	Groups of Hamas militiamen. The "lull"
	In fighting that began on the nineteenth
1420	Of June 2008 was brokered by
	Egypt. All those involved assumed an end
	To Hamas rockets and Israel's blockade
	So commerce could resume. Israel increased
	Trucks entering Gaza from seventy
1425	To ninety a day as rockets reduced,
	But as rockets continued and weapons
	Were smuggled through the tunnels, did not lift
	The blockade. Then on November the fourth
	Israel bunker-busted a tunnel, which
1430	Hamas complained violated the truce.
	Six Hamas members were killed in the raid.
	Now Hamas increased its rocket attacks.
	By December the nineteenth Hamas had
	Fired 223 rockets and 139

1435	Mortar shells since the truce, and reported
	185 Israeli violations.
	Israel said it would extend the truce, but,
	Like Russia over Georgia, was putting
	Up a correct front and luring Hamas.
1440	Hamas walked into Israel's trap. It said
	On December the twentieth it would not
	Extend the cease-fire, citing the blockade
	As the reason, and shelled western Negev.
	As Hamas had failed to end rocket fire
1445	And weapons smuggling Israel reimposed
	The blockade. On the twenty-third Mahmoud
	Az-Zahar, a Hamas leader, perhaps
	Sensing Hamas had walked into a trap,
	Offered to renew the cease-fire. That day
1450	The IDF killed three Palestinian
	Militants, claiming they had explosives.
	Next day more than sixty Palestinian
	Mortar shells, Katuyshas and Qassams hit
	The Negev in an attack Hamas called
1455	*Operation Oil Stain*. Israel prepared
	An offensive. On Christmas Day Olmert
	Urged Hamas to "stop it. We are stronger."
	The next day Israel opened five border
	Crossings for fuel to go to Gaza's main
1460	Power plant and sent a hundred trucks with food.
	Militants fired a dozen rockets and
	Mortar shells, one of which struck a northern
	Gaza house, killing two Palestinian
	Sisters. Israel had fed Hamas a flow
1465	Of disinformation to give a false
	Sense of security so they would be
	Taken by surprise. Publicly Israel
	Lost patience with rocket attacks. In fact
	It was now ready to implement its
1470	Six-month-old plan to invade Gaza and
	Seize the Palestinian offshore gas fields.

The Israeli Air Force swooped on Gaza
In the first phase of its six-month-old plan
On the twenty-seventh and bombed a hundred

1475	And seventy targets: Hamas bases,
	Training camps, underground Qassam launchers,
	Hamas HQ, Government offices,
	Police stations. As bats flit to and fro
	In twilit sky and swoop, dart, veer, tack, turn,

1480	Race and hurtle, so the Israeli planes
	Flew round Gaza. Hamas were shocked and stunned.
	About a hundred and forty Hamas
	Security forces died, including
	The chief of police. Another ninety
1485	Palestinian civilians and children
	Were killed, the highest death toll in sixty
	Years of conflict. In the ensuing days
	Hundreds of Hamas leaders' homes were struck
	As they doubled-up as headquarters and
1490	Weapons stores, and high-ranking commanders
	Were killed: Nizar Rayan, Jamal Mamduch
	And Abu Zakaria al-Jamal.
	Hamas leaders' families were wiped out.
	Israelis rang their mobile and warned them
1495	An attack on their homes was imminent
	And if they did not act their families
	Were killed with them. Residents of buildings
	Suspected of storing military
	Assets were given ten minutes to leave.
1500	There were no bomb shelters and civilians
	Had nowhere to go to escape air strikes.
	The Israeli ground invasion took place
	On January the third, the second phase
	Of its six-month-old plan. First IDF
1505	Infantry and armoured units massed on
	The border, blockading the Gaza Strip.
	Hamas fired barrages of rockets at
	Israel, killing a soldier. IDF
	Shelled the Ibrahim al-Maqadna mosque
1510	In Beit Lahiya as it hid weapons and
	Ammunition and Hamas fired from it.
	Thirteen were killed and thirty were wounded.
	Then the ground troops went in, following tanks,
	Implementing *Operation Cast Lead*
1515	To wipe out all rockets and launchers in
	Gaza. In a skilled manoeuvre the troops
	Cut Gaza in two. In the north some troops
	Entered Beit Lahiya and Beit Hanoun
	In the early hours of the fourth. More troops
1520	Surrounded Gaza City. Forty sites
	Were targeted, including arms depots
	And rocket-launch sites. One soldier was killed.
	More Hamas leaders were killed: Mohammed
	Hilou, Hassan Hamdan and Mohammed

1525	Shalpokh. Israeli tanks and troops soon seized
	Large parts of Gaza. Tens of thousands left
	Their homes under gunfire and headed for
	The inner parts of Gaza City where
	They might feel safe. But Hamas fighters fired
1530	At Israeli soldiers who surrounded
	The city and gun battles broke out on
	The east. Hundreds headed further in and
	Nine hundred injured clogged the hospital
	Where medical supplies were running short.
1535	On the sixth a hundred and twenty-five
	Palestinians were killed. One Israeli
	Soldier died and three more from friendly fire
	By a tank, one more by an artillery
	Shell. The same day Al-Fakhura was hit,
1540	A UN Relief and Works Agency
	(UNRWA) school within
	The Jabaliya refugee camp when
	Israeli artillery shells landed
	Outside the school, not inside, which was safe,
1545	Killing forty, including children, and
	Injuring fifty-five. The school had been
	Used as a refuge for hundreds. Israel
	Said its soldiers were fired on by Hamas
	Militants inside the school who had used
1550	The children as a human shield. Hamas
	Denied this. Then on the eighth bulldozers
	Crossed into Gaza and destroyed houses
	Of suspects. Each day there were forty or
	Fifty Israeli air strikes as ground troops
1555	Advanced in a news black-out, achieving
	Their objectives systematically.
	UN resolution 1860
	Calling for a cease-fire in Gaza, worked
	On by Condoleezza Rice with Arab,
1560	British and French foreign ministers, was
	To be voted on January the eighth.
	Shortly before the vote Olmert learned that
	Rice was set to vote for it. Ten minutes
	Before the vote Olmert rang the White House
1565	And demanded to speak to Bush. Told that
	Bush was in Philadelphia to speak,
	Olmert said, "I don't care, I have to talk
	To him now." Olmert thought that an aide then
	Interrupted Bush at the podium

1570	And took him to another room. In fact
	Bush was not making a speech at that time.
	Now Olmert was put through. He said, "You can't
	Vote in favour of this resolution."
	Bush said, "Listen, I don't know about it,
1575	I didn't see it, I'm not familiar
	With the phrasing." Olmert retorted, "I'm
	Familiar with it. And you can't vote in
	Favour." He was telling Bush what to do,
	Ordering him around, making it clear
1580	That Israel had power over the US.
	Bush rang Rice as the vote was called. Rice left
	To take the call, and the vote was delayed.
	When she returned, on orders from Bush she
	Abstained. Resolution 1860
1585	Was adopted 14-nil with just one
	Abstention, and Rice had broken her word
	To vote for a cease-fire and now felt "shamed".
	Why had Bush overruled Rice for Olmert?
	Not because he agreed with the last voice
1590	He spoke to, or because he wanted to
	Prolong the Gaza war, but because – just
	As when in September 2001
	He called for a Palestinian state
	And ordered Sharon not to colonise
1595	The West Bank, Sharon, furious, compared
	Israel's plight to Czechoslovakia's
	In 1938 and Bush backtracked,
	Bent over backwards to support Israel –
	Israel had something over Bush, a hold
1600	Connected with 9/11, Olmert
	Might expose collusion between Israel
	And the US that gave America
	A chance to invade first Afghanistan,
	Then Iraq, so Israel must be appeased.
1605	It now seemed Bush was in Israel's pocket.
	In a twenty-two-minute audio
	Recording bin Laden called for *jihad*,
	Holy War, over Gaza and said that
	The terror network would open new fronts.
1610	He taunted Bush, having outlasted him,
	Said the al-Qaeda network was ready
	To fight "for seven more years, and seven more
	After that, then seven more," in a message
	To Obama that the fight would go on.

1615	⌐ Now the IDF attacked the suburbs
	Of Gaza City, the operation's
	Third phase. On the eleventh Israeli troops
	Pushed into the south of the city as
	White-phosphorus bombs rained flares from the sky
1620	In violation of international
	Law, sprinkling civilians with circular
	Splodges of small chemical burns that seared
	Pitted craters deep into skin and eyes,
	Sometimes blinding them while their fires scorched. They
1625	Reached a junction to its north. Hamas and
	Islamic *Jihad* ambushed them. They fought
	With armoured vehicles and weapons they had
	Confiscated from the Palestinian
	National Authority. They exploded
1630	Improvised explosive devices or
	IEDs: roadside bombs that bored through tanks,
	Some made from medicine bottles that came in
	To Gaza as humanitarian aid
	Sent by Israel. Long and bitter street fights
1635	Crashed round. Hamas fighters tried to shoot down
	An Israeli fixed-wing aircraft with new
	Anti-aircraft missiles, and fired machine-
	Guns at helicopters, without success.
	Next day Israeli reserve troops entered
1640	Gaza. On the thirteenth Israeli tanks
	Advanced from the north-west and -east towards
	Hamas headquarters. During the night, troops
	Advanced to the high-rise buildings in Tel
	Al-Hawa. Street fighting in the narrow
1645	Rubbled lanes wounded three Israelis and
	Killed or wounded thirty Hamas fighters.
	Now several buildings were on fire, the flames
	Leaping up the sides of broken tower blocks.
	On the fifteenth, while street fighting went on,
1650	Israeli artillery bombarded
	Gaza City. Three high-rise blocks were shelled
	And dozens of militants died. More than
	Twenty Israelis were wounded. And now
	The hospital was shelled. In Jabaliya
1655	A Hamas mortar killed a soldier and
	Wounded nineteen. On the same day three tonnes
	Of food and fuel stored at the headquarters
	Of UNRWA were shelled
	And set on fire by three white-phosphorus strikes
1660	And destroyed before they could be given

To Palestinian refugees, who now
Numbered three-quarters of a million.
The pallets on which food parcels were strapped
To be delivered crackled in the fire.
1665   Both the Israeli army and Olmert
Stated that Gaza militants had fired
Anti-tank weapons and machine-guns from
Inside the UNRWA
Compound, as was the case in the UN-
1670   RWA school. But Israeli
Army investigators later said
The militants fired at Israeli troops
Outside the compound, and then ran inside
To hide in safety. And on the same day
1675   The Hamas Interior Minister,
Said Siyam, was killed with his son, brother
And two Hamas officials when the house
Of his brother was bombed while he was there,
The entire front of the house blown away.
1680   More missiles tore into Tel al-Hawa.
Twenty-three humans were pulled from rubble.

Now Israeli troops searched through the ruins
Of stones and bits of concrete in the streets
Shattered by man's intent. Tunnels were found
1685   Under Gaza City so Hamas could
Conduct urban warfare. A third of all
Houses in the city were booby-trapped.
Mannequins in windows exploded when
Shot. As a soldier fell he would be dragged
1690   Into a hole, to be taken prisoner.
Many residential blocks were wired for
Explosives, as were petrol stations and
Mosques. Weapons were stored in activists' homes,
In tunnels, mosques and citrus groves. The streets
1695   Were filled with mounded rubble. Few buildings
Were undamaged. In many houses all
Rooms were gutted, *façades* perforated
With blast holes. Now it rained on those camped on
Smashed pavements. Soggy mattresses, sodden
1700   Blankets and curtains sheltered them from night.
There was no electricity, and fires
Were lit on rubble to heat pots of food.
The Parliament building had been missiled
Repeatedly, and its concrete floors sloped
1705   Dangerously, suspended on partly-

Collapsed walls. University rooms and
Laboratories were gutted so the young
Of Palestine lost their education.
Five thousand homes, twenty mosques and sixteen
1710   Government buildings were destroyed. Twenty
Thousand houses had been badly damaged.
The systematic chaos was awesome.
It would cost billions to rebuild Gaza.
Gaza City had been bombed back into
1715   The Dark Ages: homeless squatters on mounds
That had been streets and buildings; sacked ruins.
Deciding who had won meant working out
The side that came closest to achieving
Its aims. By military criteria,
1720   Israel had won and Hamas clearly lost.

Now Israel had conquered Gaza and seized
The gas fields of the IEC-BG
Deal, and confirmed that it was retaining
The waters of Gaza for its own use,
1725   The question was how to enforce the new
Ownership. Should Israeli soldiers or
Peacekeeping troops guard the Gaza coastline?
Should the entire coastline of Gaza be
Militarised? Should Israel confiscate
1730   The gas fields and unilaterally
Declare Israeli sovereignty over
Gaza's maritime areas, including
Their potential oil reserves, integrate
Them into Israel's contiguous fields?
1735   Should the new gas fields be linked to Israel's
Energy transport corridor stretching
From Eilat, on the Red Sea, oil-pipeline
Terminal, to Ashkelon's terminal
And north to Haifa and eventually
1740   To Ceyhan terminal for a proposed
Israeli-Turkish pipeline? And also
For the great Baku-Tbilisi-Ceyhan
(BTC) pipeline, which it was foreseen
Would link to the Trans-Israel Eilat-
1745   Ashkelon pipeline? Israel would push through
Its Syndicate policy on "its" gas
And the self-interest of its ruling few
Who aided the Syndicate's New Landscape
Criss-crossed with pipelines that would make profit
1750   For all their multinationals and countries

Which, to them, excused the great misery
Of poor human civilians camping out.
But how the Syndicate saw things differed
From how multivariegated Heaven
1755 Saw them, and within Heaven's diversity
Of spirits who in life looked to all faiths,
How Christ, poised to return to Earth for his
Second Coming and Millennial Kingdom,
Saw them when pressed by Muslims in Heaven.

1760 Satan, dressed as a Hamas militant,
Patrolled the streets of Gaza City in
Disguise and rallied militiamen
To attack Israeli troops and armour
Wherever they could be found. He vanished
1765 And reappeared in Yemen, where he'd stalked
A much more precious target: Mohammed.
Satan could not enter Heaven as his
Denser spirit would show a darker tint
That would instantly be recognised by
1770 Beings of Light who do not dissemble.
His spirit had assumed this darker hue
After he was thrown from Heaven to Earth
For attempting revolution against
Almighty God, whose throne he tried to seize.
1775 He bided his time, looking for a chance
To sow confusion in Heaven as revenge,
To split the unanimity of Heaven
As an Opposition politician
Seeks to split a united Government,
1780 Lob an issue that would sow dissension.
He planned to divide the "party" leaders,
Christ and Mohammed, leaders of the most
Powerful religions in whom God the Light
Trusted, on whom the Light depended, and
1785 To turn God's wrath against his own servants.
An opportunity had come his way
For his spies told him that Mohammed was
On Earth, meeting with Dr Fadl, al-
Qaeda's philosopher and mentor, in
1790 Egypt's Tora Prison's Scorpion, whence
He had been transferred from Sanaa Prison
In the capital of the Yemen, where
He'd been in Government detention with
Yemeni members of al-Qaeda. Now,
1795 Removed from Gaza City's burning streets,

Satan materialised in prison
Disguised as one of the *mujihadeen*
And saw Mohammed dressed as a *mullah*
In a robe and black turban sitting by
1800   Fadl in the corner of a courtyard
And overheard what Fadl was hearing:
"Islam is a religion of peace. Your
Past writings have been used to justify
Violence against women and innocent
1805   Civilians. They're quoted by al-Qaeda.
You should recant." To which Fadl replied,
"I will, great one. Why, I have already
Recanted and condemned al-Qaeda. I
Wrote a book in this prison against it:
1810   *Document of Right Guidance for Jihad
Activity in Egypt and the World.*
It was serialised in the Kuwaiti
Al-Jarida and Egypt's *Al-Masri
Al-Yawm.* I wrote, "We are prohibited
1815   From committing aggression, even if
The enemies of Islam do that." I
Was very clear. I was a heretic.
Not now, I disagree with Z'wahiri.
I was his mentor, now disown his deeds.
1820   In the nineties he was paid by Sudan's
Intelligence service to organise
Attacks in Egypt. He is a liar.
As for al-Qaeda, I now believe they
Committed group suicide by striking
1825   America, which would obviously
Retaliate severely. Why, eighty
Per cent of al-Qaeda's members inside
Afghanistan have been killed, including
Abu Hafs al-Masri, military
1830   Leader and the ablest in al-Qaeda.
I ask them, 'What's the good of destroying
One of your enemy's buildings if he
Then destroys one of your countries? And what's
The good of killing one of his people
1835   If he then kills a thousand of your men?'
The 9/11 attacks were immoral.
The murder of innocent people is
Contrary to Islam. And it's also
Counter-productive. The attacks have led
1840   To bloodshed in Afghanistan and in
Iraq that's the responsibility

Of bin Laden and Zawahiri. It's
Dishonourable to move to the US,
Accept their security and money

1845   And work or study there, and then take up
Terrorism, and kill or maim your hosts.
Al-Qaeda are finished. I will recant.
It is terrible to kill innocents."

Mohammed nodded and moved away. Then
1850   Satan sidled after him, in dense flesh,
And assumed a seventh-century appearance.
"Excuse me," Satan said, "I too have come
To speak to prisoners, have put on this flesh.
I speak to you in Heaven, Abu Bakr,
1855   Founder of your *Ummah*. I understand
Your misgivings about al-Qaeda. Yes,
Islam is peaceful as the *Koran* says
But I am unhappy that Christ should lead
Heaven and speak for you and other faiths when
1860   He supports the American campaign
Against Muslims in Afghanistan where
Christian is fighting Muslim. I believe
The time has come for change. You, not Christ, *you*
Should be the Leader of Heaven. The role
1865   Of Leadership should not be forever,
Should not be the Christians' by ordained right.
It should rotate so others have a turn,
And you should be the next Leader of Heaven.
Please challenge Christ for the Leadership. I
1870   Hesitate to appeal to you in Heaven.
Forgive me for broaching the subject now
But it's a perfect opportunity
To express my feelings on this matter."
Mohammed looked at him, saw a likeness
1875   Of Abu Bakr but a density
Of flesh instead of a bright light-body.
He thought this odd, but thought that just as *he*
Had assumed flesh for the prison visit,
This fellow may have assumed darker flesh
1880   To be on the wavelength of al-Qaeda.
He nodded and said nothing and vanished
To return to Heaven, leaving Satan
Well pleased at having performed a hard task:
Encouraging Mohammed to rebel.

1885   In Heaven Christ addressed assembled spirits

That resembled a sea that sparkles in
Sunlight, leaping splashes of light dancing
As far as eye can see. Standing on rock,
As on Gull Rock in the shimmering bay
1890   By Charlestown harbour on the Cornish coast,
His voice carried so every word was heard:
"Angels, I know I speak for all of you
When I say I'm aghast at the ruin
Of the West and the sharp global downturn.
1895   The world economy is in meltdown.
The capitalist system has collapsed
And has to be shored up by Governments,
Nationalised in all but name. Dreadful.
Without doubt, Western civilisation
1900   Is morally bankrupt and visionless.
Satan has plunged the Earth into crisis.
Western financiers have been led astray,
Banks tempted to gamble with deposits,
Betting on whether shares go up or down.
1905   Satan has encouraged concupiscence.
Economic triumph, profit-seeking
By individuals for greed, has made all
Look to profit at their neighbour's expense,
Be indifferent to their fellow humans.
1910   All are interconnected by a mesh
Which we can see but blind humans cannot.
All economies and cultures are meshed
And have not been well-served by their leaders.
Those whose flawed decisions have produced debt
1915   And economic collapse lack vision
And do not have the right to be leaders.
But worst of all, Satan has persuaded
Powerful allies of Israel who do not
Want Jerusalem to be divided
1920   And to be blocked from striking at Iran
To withdraw huge sums from America.
Satan has spoken to a man who's turned
On several currencies during the last
Two decades and who is mere agent
1925   Of "Rothschilds", Satan's greatest supporter,
Who have performed a deliberate act
To wreck the West and block an agreement
Between Israel and Palestine, and press
The US to allow Israeli planes
1930   To cross Iraq and drop bombs on Iran's
Nuclear uranium-enrichment sites.

Israel's attack on Gaza must be seen
Within the context of this wrecking plan.
We are sickened, horrified and appalled
1935   At the flattening of Gaza's buildings
And want all missiles to cease on both sides."
A humming of assent came from the sea
Of spirits, like lapping of gentle waves.
"The economic crash, a visible
1940   Consequence of man's cultural collapse,
Has been caused by a clueless leadership
And by a few sinister Syndicate
Men who can benefit from disorder.
We have all been watching this develop
1945   And have seen this before. We're not surprised.
Everywhere in the media Satan rules.
News items, films, all media are filled
With instances of the Seven Deadly Sins:
Pride, politicians' vainglorious boasts;
1950   Lechery, ogling models on page three;
Envy, socialist taxing of the rich;
Anger, protectionist hoarding of jobs;
Covetousness, stealing of worldly goods;
Gluttony, bingeing, drinking to excess;
1955   And Sloth, idleness before the TV.
The whole of society lacks vision.
Artists display gimmicks – unmade beds, heads
Of cows – rather than reveal truths on life.
Writers have been seen as entertainers,
1960   If serious are ignored. It's quite shameful.
Television's gone from surface glitter
And "reality" views to inadequate,
Flawed people with underdeveloped souls,
Freaks. There's no deep insight any longer.
1965   TV is full of swearing and sex scenes.
Teachers purvey child-centred whims and fads,
Not structured rules of grammar and spellings,
Tables and lessons in what's right and wrong
Behaviour. There's no deep treatment in schools.
1970   The Church has gone Humanist and ignores
The Light and strong traditional teaching,
More preoccupied with sexual leanings
Than with the mystics' vision of the Light.
Christians are seen as mad by most people
1975   As they have charity and compassion
Rather than reckless pursuit of money.
Politicians watch polls and focus-groups

For short-term advantage and lack vision.
Science has led to rationality

1980   That's bankrupt: adverts on buses that scream
"There's probably no God", a huge error.
Oracles are despised, saying something
Is viewed with deep suspicion and some scorn.
And the Earth has been corrupted by men.

1985   The Earth has been girdled by two huge clouds
Of *débris* from spacecraft that hurtle round
The globe at seventeen thousand miles per hour,
Three hundred thousand objects whizzing round,
Six thousand satellites in fifty years,

1990   Seventeen thousand pieces four inches long.
The Earth's been polluted and scarred by man.
The Western culture's lost all deep vision
Of God as Light, which we take for granted
As our beings are grounded in the Light

1995   Which, like the Grail, is missing on Earth, lost,
Though it has long been secretly preserved
In a dark recess of the Vatican
As if in a Fisher King's lost chapel.
The Light gave birth to Europe's barbarian

2000   Civilisation, raised it round churches
To huge heights and spread it to the US,
Which reached the moon. The Light, we know's global.
Angels, things are so appalling on Earth
That God the Light, maker of all Spirit

2005   Here and of matter on the denser Earth,
And I have judged it is time to repeat
My Second Coming sixty-four years back
When I set up the Millennium that
Foul Satan has derailed. Angels, now is

2010   A time of great opportunity for
Spirits are turning from both war and greed.
The economic crisis can supply
The right conditions for my Millennial
Kingdom and bring in universal peace

2015   And inner harmony within the Light.
Angels, the time is right sixty-four years
On from the last time I tried to bring peace
To Earth in an attempt that was soon doomed.
The atomic bombs at Hiroshima

2020   And Nagasaki seemed to give the world
An opportunity for peace. Once more
There must be a global revolution
On Earth – and in Heaven as well. For we

Are not as united, harmonious
2025   As we once were, as we should be. Angels,
Materialist philosophy of greed,
Was always going to ruin the Earth.
But, just as much, division here in Heaven
Is loathsome. All souls are equal, whether
2030   In Buddhist, Hindu, Muslim or Christian
Camps. Angels, both on Earth and in Heaven
Vision is paramount and will dictate
The way all souls live down there and up here."
All hailed Christ's words with bewildered humming.

2035   Standing on the height in Heaven, knowing
What Mohammed sought, which he judged should be
Pulled out for debate, faced and confronted
Rather than ignored – for Heaven was open –
So his bid for sole rule could be addressed
2040   And dispersed into some form of moderate
Power-sharing which all Heaven would approve,
To defuse extremist anger, Christ saw
A sea of assembled spirits below,
Each glinting a pure light as in sunshine
2045   From a translucent, semi-transparent
Spirit-body of airy density.
Just as in morning sun a tranquil sea
Flashes out leaping lights like mirror glints
That dance and sparkle, thousands at a time
2050   As if torrential rain were splashing light
Or a bay-wide flock of white birds with wings
Up in a V, swooping, were scooping fish,
So the assembled spirits flashed out love,
Unsuspecting of the dismal message
2055   They were about to hear from their Leader
And of its repercussions for Heaven.
With heavy heart before such dazzling lights,
Sad to disturb such universal joy
With a disquieting message of change,
2060   Of the need for some form of power-sharing,
But mindful of its necessity if
Heaven's democratic ethos should persist
With all groups represented, and that he
Should give up some of his God-given power
2065   For the common good as God wished, Christ spoke:
"Angels, you know that I have always stood
To represent each of you, whether you
Were on Earth a Christian, Muslim, Hindu,

	Buddhist, Jew, Taoist, or a follower
2070	Of any other religion. I see
	All humankind as opening to one Light,
	The same that we all share, and so there's no
	Division among us, just unity.
	We stand for one religion of the Light
2075	And God asked me to lead you in this cause
	And so far you have been content with this.
	Angels, it's reached me that some may not be
	Content. If anyone has a problem
	Let them speak now." He looked at Mohammed.
2080	Mohammed stared back and then stepped forward.
	"Respected brother," he began, of Christ,
	Speaking in the universal language
	Which Heaven had designated, English,
	"I must confess I've sometimes found it hard
2085	To serve under your Leadership, as when
	Christian Crusaders invaded the lands
	Sacred to Muslims and were driven out.
	I of course stand for peace and Light, and don't
	Condone Muslim violence to anyone
2090	And yet I feel some sympathy with those
	Who defend Muslims from Crusader force
	And from Israel, which occupied their lands.
	And recently, the campaign that has seared
	Muslim Afghanistan has left me torn.
2095	I do not condone violence by Muslims
	But cannot condone violence to Muslims
	Even though the consensus here approves.
	You have been dominant since the Crusades,
	But now Crusaders are being challenged.
2100	You've had a long innings. It's time for change.
	Enough is enough. We must now move on.
	And so I propose a structural change
	To our Leadership, a rotational role
	Which can be undertaken in turn by
2105	Leaders of Angels from religious groups
	That are not Christians in accordance with
	Their clout on Earth, the influence they wield,
	Most notably today, the Muslims. I
	Propose I become Leader of Heaven
2110	For a term, just as in the new EU
	There's a rotational presidency
	For six months, that's, at the allotted time,
	Passed on so Leadership does not appear
	A dictatorship to those excluded

2115	From taking decisions that affect us."
	A roar of approval from the Muslim
	Angels greeted his bid for Leadership.
	Shocked at the abruptness of his attack,
	The majority of Angels were disturbed
2120	And now the dancing, dazzling lights faded.
	As if a cloud had passed across the sun
	And a sea that was jumping and flashing
	Had suddenly become small choppy waves
	Stirred up by restless wind, brooding, opaque,
2125	Under an overcast, pre-stormy sky,
	So joyous spirits swiftly looked troubled
	At the prospect of a minority
	Wresting power from the majority's will.
	Christ had heard rumours of his ambitions
2130	And that was why he'd called this assembly.
	But he was still stunned by the bluntness and
	Self-assertion of his planned *coup d'état*.
	"We are democratic," he replied. "We
	Make decisions fairly. As Leader I
2135	Propose a course of action, you assent
	Or dissent. This works well, and things get done.
	Leadership preserves stability. I
	Am sure rotational Leadership's not
	The way forward. In Europe that has led
2140	To paralysis. That's a recipe
	For *poor* Leadership and Heaven would suffer.
	There's no indication that God the Light
	Would want such rotation. The Light's concerned
	That its will should be done, that opposites
2145	Should be reconciled, order should prevail,
	That all should be in harmony, given
	That pairs of opposites, dualisms,
	Form the underlying unity and
	Cannot be eliminated. We must
2150	Work with the contradictory universe.
	I will consult the Light on such matters
	But must remind you, I'm like a high priest.
	I convey the Light's wishes to your minds
	Just as Moses ascended Mount Sinai
2155	And returned with wishes on stone tablets."
	Mohammed persisted: "The fact remains,
	I don't see how you or any Christian
	Can represent me when our faiths collide,
	When there's a clash of civilisations.
2160	For then I'm with Islam against your faith."

There was loud humming of approval from
All Muslim spirits who were non-violent
Supporters of Mohammed and *Sharia*.
A voice called, "I completely agree." Christ
2165   Turned and saw it was the Hidden *Imam*,
A pure energy in spirit-body.
Now Christ saw Sunni and Shiite spirits
Were of one view and supported the stance
Mohammed had taken for *his* Islam.
2170   And like a front-bench politician he
Thought quickly on his feet, sought to defuse.
"Angels," Christ said, "there is no clash between
Civilisations, only criminal
Acts within each which can inflame the rest."
2175   "No," said Mohammed, "that's not right. There *is*
A clash, and your denial of this clash
Makes it more desirable that I should
Not serve under you indefinitely,
But should interpret events on the Earth
2180   From a Muslim perspective." Christ replied,
"In that case Heaven will be divided, not
Unified. That would be to abandon
The consensus between all religions
Which we've observed, including the accord
2185   Between Christians and Muslim." "That reflects,"
Objected Mohammed, "what's in the world.
Christians and Muslims are opposites here
Just as Bush and bin Laden contradict,
And there can be harmony at the end.
2190   But Muslims now see your Leadership as
A dictatorship. Islam's separate.
I propose we retreat from the current
System and decentralise religions,
Partition Heaven into territories,
2195   Segregate Muslims from the other faiths
So we are like a federal government
Whose state law's different from federal law.
It's time for Muslims to have *Sharia* law.
Place them under their leaders' sole control,
2200   So they'll be like political parties.
As with parties, there'll be alliances.
That is a fairer way of governing
Heaven for all will be *represented*.
And then all points of view will be expressed,
2205   No one can say we're a dictatorship
And harmony will emerge at the end."

"But in the meantime," Christ said, "there will be
Disharmony that Heaven's not known till now.
On Earth, partitioning is a response
2210 To conflict and disharmony as were
The Berlin Wall and the wall Israel's built.
Partitions and walls fragment unity.
You are proposing fundamental change.
We need to consult God on this matter.
2215 He, like the Speaker in a Parliament,
Will give his ruling, by which we'll abide
As has happened till now. I will confer.
I need to put it to the Light and then
Report back on what I have discovered."
2220 "I am not prepared to go on serving
Under your consensus while there's a clash
Between our two civilisations," said
Mohammed, and now by implication
There was disunity in Heaven. Loud
2225 Groaning broke out, light-bodies' booing, as
The assembled spirits expressed dismay
At the prospect of a split Heaven. Christ,
Knowing Satan's hand was at work, knowing
That Satan, and Mohammed, did God's work,
2230 Was troubled at the conflict in Heaven.
He had to take soundings on God's wishes.
He wondered if he should not have ignored
The buzzing discontent of Mohammed,
But Heaven was a place of openness
2235 Where there was no deception, scarcely spin,
And open courses of action were right.
Things had changed. A new situation had
Arisen in Heaven and Christ was now worried.

In a final news conference Bush said
2240 America's global moral standing
Had not been damaged during his eight years
In the White House. He firmly defended
His decisions on the Iraq War that
Led to four thousand US deaths and to
2245 Thousands of Iraqis being killed, and
Would define his presidency. He said,
"Not finding weapons of mass destruction
Was a significant disappointment."
Saddam's pursuit of wmds
2250 Was his main justification for war.
He said he had miscalculated when

He made a victory speech near a banner
Which said "Mission Accomplished" and spoke thus:
"In the battle of Iraq, the US
2255 And our allies have prevailed." He staunchly
Defended the surge which had stabilised
Iraq and its fledgling democracy,
But said the abuse of detainees at
Abu Ghraib jail was a cause for regret.
2260 He hoped the tone in Washington improved.
He defended his speedy handling
Of Hurricane Katrina when thirty
Thousand were pulled off roofs after the storm,
A sign the federal response was fast.
2265 He hoped America would not become
Protectionist and called for peace on his
Two-state solution; and he defended
Israel's actions in Gaza. He warned that
Iran and North Korea were dangerous.
2270 As to his legacy, Bush compared his
Presidency to that of Abraham
Lincoln, who led his country through a dark
Civil war. He seemed nonchalant. It seemed
He did not care any more, but deep down
2275 He did. After the press conference he
Asked Congress to release the remainder
Of the seven hundred billion dollars
So Obama could use it straightaway.
He was noble towards his opponent,
2280 And not spiteful as he handed over.

Away from the millions of spirits, in
A zone near the central Celestial Rose
In Paradisal bliss and order, Christ
Sat in contemplation. He knew that God
2285 The Light was no dictator and just ran
A system like the US President
And was above dissent. He knew that God
The Light is immanent and transcendent,
Involved in the universe and not like
2290 An absentee landlord who has set in
Motion forces (like Aristotle's "Prime
Mover") and then taken himself away.
The Light was not remote. He sank within
The flooding Light that shone through his being
2295 And in the being of all Heaven's spirits.
He prayed to the Light, for, like all spirits

In Heaven or Hell, or on Earth, or Satan,
Christ could only meet God, the Light, as power
That enfolded with dazzling energy,
2300 Imbuing wisdom. God's enlightenment
Always came swiftly, dropped into his soul
As an email arrives in an inbox,
A thought that can be read though its sender
Cannot be seen. He approached the Light in
2305 Humility and asked his question. Soon
The answer would surface within his soul.
Then he would implement it on behalf
Of the Light that gave guidance in this way.
He would secure its acceptance by all
2310 Angels, persuading them in assemblies
As a master politician persuades
His party and those in other parties
To support new initiatives which are
Most likely to advance the common good.
2315 Christ rested on the Light as a lily
With a gold bowl floats on a sunlit pool,
Completely still in the reflected sun.
And in his soul, as if a voice had called,
Was a clear thought: "Heaven must remain open.
2320 There can be zones where Muslim spirits live
But no partitions, no segregation.
Free passage as spirits roam about Heaven
As all are free to do now. There must be
More sharing in assemblies. Religions
2325 That teach the Light are equal. You are one
Among equals, not first among equals,
Not *primus inter pares*. Heaven cannot
Continue to be dominated by
Christians. All faiths must share its governance.
2330 There must now be power-sharing in Heaven.
In proportion to followers of faiths
There must be a new system in which faiths
Are separate in zones and represented
In accurate ratios to followers.
2335 There must be a coalition of faiths.
A new council of faiths will run Heaven.
The same must happen in your Millennial
Kingdom, which must be a world government
Of represented regions. As on Earth,
2340 Heaven must now be Universalist."
Christ emerged from his solitary sitting
In meditation crestfallen, for God

Had unmistakably combined his own
And Mohammed's positions to give change.
2345 He understood: God was also Allah.
There would now be *Sharia* zones in Heaven.
To avoid splitting Heaven he had to do
A deal with Mohammed to increase his power.
This would mean a Universalist Heaven.
2350 Christ felt his recent efforts had all failed.
He had tried to maintain the *status quo*
In assemblies and consensual rule.
God clearly did not want the *status quo*.
The War on Terror had brought change to Heaven
2355 And he had lost his Leadership of Heaven.
It used to be "as above, so below".
The change would mean "as below, so above".
Heaven had been polarised by extremists,
Mohammed's militancy, and had now
2360 Adapted to a multi-cultural world
In which many faiths co-existed like
Stalls in a market-place, and there was now
Religious pluralism in Heaven's
Ecumenism, which was now world-wide
2365 And inter-faith, no longer Christian-based.
Christ was honest and he could not pretend
That God had spoken in a different way.
Being honourable he was duty-bound
To report to the Angels what God said.

2370 Heaven looked sombre in afternoon cloud.
Christ stood again on rock and spoke once more
To his troubled Angels. "Angels," he said,
His quiet voice carrying across the sea
Of listening beings as if microphoned.
2375 "I have consulted God, the Light, who's said
That we must run Heaven differently from now.
Mohammed had a point but went too far.
There can be zones for Muslims, but not walls.
All followers of faiths can live in zones.
2380 I have consulted with Mohammed and
The leaders of all faiths our spirits know
And they are content with my solution.
Faiths are like paths up a mountain. They all
Converge at the summit under the Light.
2385 All spirits in seven Heavens know the Light.
A Council will be formed of all the faiths.
Faiths will have ratios linked to followers.

These ratios will be linked to those on Earth.
At present on Earth these ratios are

2390 As follows. Of the world's population,
Taken as 6.774 billion,
2.173 billion are Christian,
32 per cent of the whole, one third.
That includes 1.135 billion

2395 Catholics. 1.335 billion are
Muslims, 19.7 per cent, one fifth.
Of these, between 7.5 and 11
Per cent are Shias, 0.163
Billion, 2.4 per cent, and the rest

2400 Are Sunnis. Shiite Iran and Iraq
And all other Shias have 2.4
Per four hundred and fifty seats, tiny.
.871 billion are Hindus, 12
Per cent, one eighth. .015 billion

2405 Are Jews, giving just .22 per cent,
One four hundred and fiftieth, tiny.
And now the most troublesome religions,
The Jews and Shias, will be represented
By the tiniest groupings in Council.

2410 I'll post these stats in the Paradisal
Library so spirits who were born in
Minority faiths can see their numbers.
It means that although 61 per cent
Of the Earth's population are Asians,

2415 Christians will now form a third of the new
Council, and Muslims will now form a fifth,
Hindus an eighth, and Jews who have caused us
So much disquiet by bombing Lebanon
And Gaza, and wanting to bomb Iran,

2420 Will have a minute representation,
One seat per four hundred and fifty heads."
"Just a minute," Mohammed said. "I know
That when we spoke I agreed with your view.
But I propose that the measure of strength

2425 Should be religious fervour, not numbers.
We need the ratios for fervent displays."
This was a guileless bid for dominance
And Christ was firm in brushing him aside.
"God did not propose fervour but numbers."

2430 He stared, knowing he stood for more spirits
Than Mohammed. "It's God's Council, not yours."
Mohammed backed away, the power struggle
Was over – for the time being, at least.

Now Christ gathered himself to his full height:
2435   "It means that, world-wide, Christians will still have
The largest representation, but I
Will share all approaches to God, the Light,
With Mohammed, who will be second in
The strength of his following. In Heaven
2440   There will be a coalition of strengths
And down on Earth there will be a similar
Apportionment of proportional power
As I found a world government and call
On the other faith-leaders to support
2445   My action in accordance with these same
Principles which will now rule our Heaven.
When the Earth's population was smaller,
Under a billion till 1820,
The ratios were somewhat different.
2450   Christians remain in the majority
For now. The faiths' ratios will keep changing
As spirits return from Self-Improvement.
We leaders of the faiths will sit beside
Each other and run Heaven, allotted votes
2455   In accordance with our proportional
Faith ratios, whose numbers give us strength.
The Council will be under God, not me.
We will all determine God the Light's will.
And with a third of all support I shall
2460   Be the Council's principal adviser.
Angels, I realise changes will disturb
You, but self-improvement is a force here
In Heaven as well as on Earth and in Hell."
All Angels had been shocked at Christ's new tack.
2465   Now Christ turned and embraced Mohammed, who
Kissed both his cheeks in fealty. A hum
Swept round the crowded spirits, who, relieved,
Greeted the new arrangement with flashed lights.

It had seemed there was trouble in Heaven,
2470   That Christendom's dominance was ending.
A Universalist Heaven now loomed.
Christ had misgivings but he saw that what
Mattered was not what *he* wanted, any
More than what *Satan* wanted, but what God
2475   Wanted. And now, with his third ratio,
Christ was still the dominant power in Heaven.
A Muslim revolt had been headed off
By skilful diplomacy that had mixed

	Firmness with reasonable concessions,
2480	Good management in a situation
	Different from representation on Earth.
	Heaven reflects the relative strength of faiths
	On Earth like an Upper Chamber that is
	Unelected. There are no elections
2485	In Heaven, and positions are chosen,
	Allocated, by God who is also
	Allah, the Light, the One God over all
	Mankind, who sends messages to leaders'
	Spirits as emails drop in an inbox.
2490	Christ spoke again: "Angels, you all know there
	Is no pre-destination in Heaven
	Or on Earth. There's free will. I can therefore
	Choose the timing of my Second Coming.
	Now," Christ called, "I can begin my Second
2495	Coming, for I have a new vision that
	I must take down to the miserable Earth:
	A New World Order that is based on Heaven,
	An order based on sharing of all faiths,
	A Universalist New World Order."
2500	Heaven brightened as if the sun had come out.

BOOK ELEVEN

CHRIST'S DIFFICULT SECOND COMING

SUMMARY

1-444	Invocations to Christ, to Arthur as guardian of the Grail, to Jerusalem which once held the Ark of the Covenant and to the Northern Lights.
445-522	Christ returns to Earth in Gaza City and walks among the suffering.
523-731	Christ visits Olmert in the Supreme Court, which was built by a Rothschild and has Illuminati symbols on its walls. He asks Olmert to declare an immediate cease-fire in Gaza. Olmert declines.
732-768	Olmert does declare a cease-fire as Israel has just discovered new gas reservoirs off Haifa – which makes the seizure of Gaza's gas fields by war, with hindsight, unnecessary.
769-999	Christ visits Soros and asks him to transfer the withdrawn $550 billion back to the US. Soros denies all knowledge of the transaction. Lord Jacob Rothschild confronts Christ, who urges "Rothschilds" to join him in ending war and bringing peace to the world. Christ is asked to leave.
1000-1220	Christ visits David Rockefeller and asks him to share the 350,000 names on his Rolodex filing system so that his moves towards world government can pass into Christ's Millennial Kingdom and Peaceful Era. Rockefeller declines.
1221-1292	Christ visits UN Secretary-General Ban Ki-moon and says he will help bring peace to the world. Ban excuses himself.
1293-1436	Christ visits Bush, who is packing, and asks him how he thinks he has left the world and if there can now be peace, a *Pax Mundana*. Bush gives a full reply, saying he fought a draw. He recommends that the starting-point should be the new multipolar world.
1437-1533	Christ visits Obama and offers to help him bring peace to the world. Obama says he does not need Christ's help.
1534-1739	Christ visits the Pope and says his Second Coming is imminent, that it will be based in Jerusalem and on many faiths. The Pope does not want Christ to return as the Church controls his past teaching, and he declines Christ's help and his request to locate the Grail and Ark of the Covenant in the Vatican archives.

1740-1778	Christ appreciates that world leaders are self-interested and will need influxes of Light to make them co-operative.
1779-1975	Bush reflects on his own career and on the Age of America, despite being an empire in all but name, seems to be ending and the possible break-up of the US. Capitalism seems to have collapsed and Communism seems to have achieved a posthumous victory.
1976-1998	Final assessment of Bush's political career.
1999-2021	Bush and the universe.
2022-2047	Time as destroyer.
2048-2148	Obama's inauguration.
2149-2171	Bush leaves Washington.
2172-2283	Bin Laden reflects on his "victory" over the US.
2284-2372	Obama announces changes: the banking and financial crisis to be solved, Guantánamo Bay to be closed, the world's nuclear weapons to be abolished, Iran to meet him and make peace. But he finds it is harder to make things happen than he realised.
2373-2432	Christ's Second Coming on the Mount of Olives, Jerusalem. Christ listens to a political speech rejecting the two-state solution.
2433-2475	Christ visits the site of David's palace and vows that his Kingdom will be a spiritual Kingdom.

O Christ, philosopher extraordinary,
You who had such a gift for parables
And spoke calmly, yet all hung on your words,
And moved in silence from the depths of Light,
5   I find you in Turin, before your shroud
Which is framed in glass, and gaze at your face:
Your noble head in negative, closed eyes,
Blood on your forehead, thorn marks on your scalp,
Your back bruised from the cross, scourge marks round ribs
10   And thong-lines from the *flagrum* that flogged you,
Two thongs each tipped with two lead balls that gave
Four welts for each of one hundred lashes
(A mild scourging as some *flagra* had three
Ox-hide thongs with twenty-four lead balls that
15   Gave twenty-four welts for each burning lash);
Nail through a wrist and thumb bent down as your
Median nerve was damaged, your side impaled,
A nail through your feet, your nose-bridge broken,
Two Pilate coins on lids. I pity your
20   Torture through three hot days and three cold nights,
Your body on fire from lacerations,
Till your heart gave out, see your serum stains.
And I think of the botched carbon-dating

When they cut a darned segment of spliced first-
25   Century cloth and sixteenth-century cotton,
Dyed so repairs would be invisible,
And I have no doubt that I am looking
At your face, which was brought to Byzantium
And salvaged during the Crusaders' sack
30   Of Constantinople in 1204
By Templars who brought it to Lirey, France.
That was the severed head they stood before.
Your philosophy of the Light has stood
The test of time and your face on the cloth
35   Still draws and haunts and fills with compassion.
I found you in Jerusalem forty-
Seven years ago when I climbed the Via
Dolorosa to Calvary, walking
From the Praetorium (or Antonia
40   Fortress) to the Rock of Calvary (or
Golgotha) in the Holy Sepulchre
(Not from the Barracks to the paved courtyard
South of the Jaffa Gate, which may have been
The true beginning of your route) and stood
45   Inside what General Gordon wrongly took
To be the Garden Tomb of your uncle
And saw the sort of slab on which you lay
In your blooded cloth, resurrection shroud.
O Christ, help me now I come to narrate
50   Your Second Coming to our mucked-up Earth
And the Millennial Kingdom you must bodge.

O Arthur, who also knew a grim time,
You whose knights sought an ameliorating cure,
The Grail chalice used at the Last Supper,
55   A cup of silver and of olive-wood –
Grail came from "*gradalis*", dish of plenty –
Which was in Joseph of Arimathaea's
Residence in AD29 where
The Last Supper took place, and was taken
60   By Roman soldiers and given to Pilate
Who returned it to Joseph with the corpse
Of Christ he took for burial in his tomb;
Which, as he washed the body to prepare
It for interment and blood dripped from his
65   Wounds, Joseph used to collect some of Christ's
Blood – the Last Supper's wine now replaced by
Actual blood, *san graal* (Holy Grail) also
Being *san greal* (royal blood); which was brought

Via France to Britain by this same Joseph
When he, Christ's uncle, accompanied Christ's
Mother Mary and Mary Magdalene
In 36, and lodged in Glastonbury's
Small Celtic wattle church of St Mary
Named after Christ's mother near Chalice Well
And, when the Claudian invasion came
In 42, was hidden from Romans
In an underground chapel of the church,
Which became the Grail chapel, and was found –
Long after Joseph died in 82
And was buried in the wattle church as
Maelgwyn of Avalon says (in 540) –
By your knights when in Logres' wasteland you
Who came from Dumnonia (Cornwall, Devon) –
Even the Welsh call you Dumnonian –
Besieged Glastonbury, Somerset's Dunster,
And found the Grail, which Percival guarded,
So you, Arthur, were now the Fisher King
In the sixth-century waste-land west Britain,
And as Fortaculus writes, saw the Grail
As "the pledge of the safety of Britain
As the palladium was that of Troy".
And so you were buried in Glastonbury
And about 700 King Ina lined
The underground chapel that was laden
With silver and gold, William of Malmesbury
Says. When the church was destroyed by fire in
1184 the Grail was found and
Removed by pro-Crusading Normans, who
Built the Norman chapel of St Mary
On the site of the ancient wattle church
(Now forming part of Glastonbury Abbey),
Who gave it to the Templars, who took it
To Jerusalem, where, since St Bernard
Created their order in 1118,
They had sought it by digging underneath
The palace of Solomon which was near
The First Temple (now in the Muslim Dome
Of the Rock). They lodged it in a new church
They built by the palace till Saladin
Took two hundred Templars prisoners, claiming
They'd violated treaties with Muslim
Powers, and beheaded them. When Saladin
Captured Jerusalem in eleven eighty-
Seven he seized the True Cross – and, alerted

115	By a Templar trying to save his life,
	Sought the Grail, which he wanted to put in
	The Muslim Dome of the Rock, which had stood
	For the Muslim ambition to achieve
	Domination of Jerusalem since
120	691. The Grail had disappeared.
	Templars had smuggled it away to France,
	To Chartres Cathedral and then Montségur
	Where Cathars used it in the Citadel
	When holding their *consolamentum* "mass".
125	In 1190 Grail legends began in
	France: Chrétien de Troyes, Robert de Boron.
	Now the Grail chapel was on a mountain,
	Muntsalvach or Monsalvat, the Mountain
	Of Salvation. The Grail was spirited
130	Away by four Cathar "*parfaits*" or priests
	Descending on a rope the night before
	Montségur fell, and was hidden in caves.
	To keep it safe, some Templars now spread word
	That the Grail was still at Glastonbury,
135	And stood in the chapel on the high Tor,
	A mountain with water all round it then,
	Whence in 1530 a cup was moved
	To Strata Florida, then to Nanteos
	Manor, North Wales, and's now in a bank vault.
140	Others said Templars took it to Scotland,
	To Rosslyn which Templar Freemasons built
	In exile and involved the Stuart Royals.
	But Nazi Otto Rahn hunted in caves
	Near Montségur for Himmler, and, using
145	Sacred geometry, claimed he found the Grail
	And in 1937 sent his find
	To Himmler who, in his Schloss Wewelsburg,
	Placed it on a marble pedestal in
	The Realm of the Dead beneath the Great Hall
150	Where the Nazi Knights of the Holy Lance
	Sat at a round table, conjured the dead.
	In 1945 it was put in
	A lead casket and sent to be buried
	In a glacier in Hochfeiler, Austria.
155	It never arrived at the glacier
	Some nine thousand feet above sea level,
	But was intercepted by British troops
	Bound for Palestine, who took it with them
	And, not realising its significance,
160	Sold it in a bazaar to an Arab,

Whence it found its way into the clutches
Of Satan disguised as a tourist who
Bought it for bin Laden, Saladin's heir.
O Arthur I find you beside your grave
165 That was found in 1191
In the green sward of Glastonbury Abbey,
And also by the ancient Chalice Well
With a lead cross (known in the seventeenth
Century and since lost) that was engraved
170 "Here lies buried the famous king, Arthur,
In the Isle of Avalon", on the site
Of the chapel of St Mary's south side
In the green sward of Glastonbury Abbey,
And you lay here until you were exhumed
175 And your body removed with Guinevere's
In 1278 in the presence
Of Edward the First and Queen Eleanor
And placed near here in a black marble tomb
That did not survive the dissolution
180 Of the Abbey in 1533.
(In 1367 Joseph's body
Was found in a stone sarcophagus in
The crypt under this chapel, the east end.
In 1662 sarcophagus
185 And body were removed for safety's sake
To the churchyard of Glastonbury Church.
In 1928 they were brought in
To the church, out of the rain, wind and cold.
The tomb's top, covered with glass, bore in stone
190 The initials J A for the man who
Gave up his own garden tomb to the Christ.)
Also I find you by the Chalice Well
And by the Tor where Joseph hid the Grail;
I find you in Tintagel by the cave
195 And by Slaughter Bridge, near Camelford, where
Twenty years after beating the Saxons
At Mount Badon to bring your kingdom peace,
You died fighting your nephew Modred, who
Had stolen the Holy Grail, the symbol
200 Of your authority, in 537
At the battle of Camlann which killed him.
And I was not far from you when I climbed
To the top of Montségur, and looked round
The Cathars' derelict stronghold that once
205 Held the Grail, given by Templars to Cathars
For safe keeping and smuggled out, and was

Open to the sky, Pyrenees all round,
And stood breathless on Monsalvat's mountain.
O Arthur, who as wounded Fisher King
210   Housed the Grail in an obscure chapel in
Your kingdom of Logres (Welsh for England),
A wasteland like Jesus's ravaged land
Of Jerusalem during the Crusades,
As was England from 537 to 9
215   According to tree-ring evidence as
A massive volcanic eruption threw
A dust cloud round the world that blighted and
Devastated agricultural land
So wells were unattended and water
220   Courses dwindled, meadows and flowers dried up,
The land was dead and deserted. You craved
A horn of plenty, *cornucopia*,
A Grail that would restore both King and lands
To health, gush and revive Nature. I see
225   You survey your barren wasteland today,
Chivalry and culture destroyed by yobs;
I see you survey your Western Logres
Damaged by climate change and credit crunch,
Rising oil and food prices, terror threats –
230   O Arthur in your redoubt in Welsh hills,
Your occultation like the Twelfth *Imam*'s,
Revive the West with the Grail's healing power,
Which we miss dreadfully, not knowing where
Our holy palladium has been misplaced;
235   Free us from all the scourges of our time –
War, terror, fiscal hardship, climate change –
Send us a cure that will resist the East,
Send us a vision of the Light. The Grail,
Cup of spiritual intoxication,
240   The Templars introduced from Sufi thought.
It stood for spiritual vision that cures –
O Arthur, send us Light that renews lands.
In our poor Logres Armageddon looms.

O Jerusalem, who knows the secret
245   Places where lost treasures have been hidden
And long since forgotten in mists of time,
City of golden domes and walls that hold
Promise of revealed mysteries in nooks
And subterranean passages, and slabs
250   That witnessed the Temple and the Templars,
The crucifixion and the rolled-back stone;

Another sacred relic was missing.
According to belief, when the Messiah
Arrives on the Mount of Olives, the lost
255   Ark of the Covenant – the most sacred
Container made of *shittim* or *shittah*,
Acacia wood, for the stone tablets on
Which Moses inscribed the Ten Commandments,
Aaron's rod and manna, for which David
260   Built a First Temple at Jerusalem,
Which he placed in the Holy of Holies
Where it stood in Solomon's time and which
Disappeared when Jerusalem was sacked
Along with King Solomon's stone Temple
265   By Nebuchadnezzar of Babylon
In 586BC – will be revealed.
And with it the palladium, the Grail.
To house the Ark a Third Temple will rise
From the Second Temple razed by Titus.
270   The Ark was in Jerusalem at the start
Of the reign of Josiah in 640,
Where Jeremiah lamented one day
It would not be used. Was it hidden beneath
The city, beneath the Dome of the Rock,
275   Where King Zedekiah fled and was caught
By the besieging Babylonians,
Saw his sons executed and then had
His eyes put out? If buried there the wood
Would be a heap of dust. Was it removed?
280   In Qumran's Cave 3 a rolled copper scroll
Probably written by priests has been found,
Listing where Temple treasure was hidden
In sixty-four places, none findable.
Was it taken to Egypt by Shishak,
285   Who invaded Israel, plundered treasures?
The Ark is not mentioned by either side.
Was it taken to Ethiopia
By Menelik, the son of Solomon,
And located in an Axumite church
290   With only one high priest allowed to view?
The documentary evidence is flawed.
Second *Maccabees* claims Jeremiah
Brought the Ark to Mount Nebo on the east
Bank of the Jordan, hid it in a cave.
295   The *Book of Jeremiah* is silent.
There were tales it came through Arabia.
Now in hospital I read Parfitt's tale:

There were two Arks for two different functions.
There was a simple Ark of War Moses
300 Built that's described in *Deuteronomy*,
And also a ceremonial object
Built by Moses' architect Bezalel
Which remained in the Temple, described in
Exodus, wood covered in gold carried
305 On poles like the chest found in King Tut's tomb.
The *Exodus* writers could not have seen
The Ark – only the high priest could view it –
And could have believed it was Egyptian:
The Egyptian Empire extended through
310 Syria, Palestine and the Lebanon
In 1450BC, Moses' time.
In *Deuteronomy* the Ark was made
From trees in the desert, a likelihood.
I read how the African Lembas in
315 Zimbabwe claim to be a long lost tribe
Of Israel who've come from Yemen's Sena,
And how this has been proved by DNA,
For their Buba clan has Y-chromosomes
Of the Jewish priestly class, their forebears,
320 A genetic signature that is called
The Cohen Modal Haplotype. Some trace.
The Ark was a weapon of war, carried
Into the battlefield, and was captured
Twice by the Philistines (Palestinians),
325 A wmd on whose cover
The Lord Mighty in Battle sat, a throne,
And also a musical martial drum –
Like the Lemba *ngoma*, "drum that thunders",
Which was carried on poles and must not touch
330 The ground – that terrified by its loud beat.
I read how Parfitt found a battered bowl
Of wood with slots for poles in Harare's
Museum of Human Sciences which he
Radio-carbon-dated 1350,
335 A descendant of the old Ark of War
Which Moses hewed from desert acacia.
It has since disappeared, perhaps looted
By despotic Mugabe's grim henchmen.
I sip in hospital and recall how
340 In St Martin's-in-the-Field's crypt, after
My younger son sang a solo, I met
Tudor Parfitt, explorer who had sought
The Lost Tribes of Israel in remoter

Africa, where, like Allan Quatermain
345 Or our more recent Indiana Jones,
He looked for treasures – unbeknown to me,
For the lost Ark. I lay his book aside
And ponder. He has found the Lemba drum
That was lost sixty years, but not the Ark
350 For his Ark could not have held stone tablets
And is unlike Israelite artefacts,
Wood woven with interlaced reed patterns.
I did not know Satan had claimed the Ark,
Having purloined it from Mount Nebo's cave,
355 Bought it from a team of Arab workmen
And given it and an artefact he called
The Grail to bin Laden, his Antichrist.
O Jerusalem, would I were with you now.
I console myself by reflecting that
360 The Ark of the Covenant and the Grail,
Physical objects much sought, are symbols,
Myths that transform the imagination
And represent its truth in haunting forms
And finding them is an act of the mind
365 Which opens to them and embraces them
As powerful, transformational ideas –
Some psychologists would say archetypes –
That, like Armageddon, leave one transformed
In subterranean regions of the soul.
370 Both will be found when the Messiah comes –
Another myth with a transforming power.

O Northern Lights, you take me close to Heaven.
Near Alta, where nine thousand years ago
Altaic shamans scratched their rock carvings,
375 Stick men hunting reindeer, now under snow,
On what was then the shores of Alta fjord,
After a lunch of sweet reindeer burgers
I drive a five-dog sleigh a good six miles,
The minus-ten frost stinging lips and ears,
380 Then sit in a twenty-two-pole tepee
(Designed by Altaians nine thousand years
Ago) before a leaping birchwood fire
And sip black-currant juice as it grows dark.
Then I ride out on a large horse-drawn sleigh
385 Under huge petalled stars in a clear sky
In minus 20, legs wrapped in blankets,
Slide on an iced track between snow-laden
Spruce branches that hang down on each side, reach

An open snowfield where the driver turns
390   The two horses and stops and says, bearded,
        Distant white-clad spruces all round, under
        Stars gleaming like apples on an unseen
        Tree whose roots, trunk, branches and fruit connect
        The Underworld, Earth, Heaven, and wondering man:
395   "Listen to the silence, to the stillness.
        It's beautiful." And I listen in awe
        And see the stars that Altaian man saw
        And nine thousand years were as yesterday
        And blink back welling love for all mankind
400   Who for sixty thousand years has gazed up
        At the night sky dripping with sparkling stars.
        And later, on the banks of the frozen
        Alta river, still by an ice igloo
        Where I will sleep in mere minus-seven,
405   Before my eyes in the dark southern sky
        I see a green hem manifest from black
        Over the line of pines, and as I watch
        From west to east, from skyline to polestar
        Above my head a light-blue curtain forms
410   Out of blackness with drapes down the night sky,
        Gigantic luminous curtains that glow.
        Awed, for three minutes I peer between folds
        Of the Aurora Borealis. It
        Is electrons from the erupting sun
415   Carried by the solar wind that bombards
        Our atmosphere – electric tornadoes
        Spinning at a million miles an hour from
        Clouds of solar particles that gather
        Forty thousand miles up, which when they are
420   Destabilised release whirlwinds which Earth's
        Magnetic field deflects from Earth's day side
        To its night side. But I see a curtain
        Rippling gently, blown by a divine wind,
        That slides from right to left, from east to west,
425   And slowly fades till all is black again;
        Wondrous manifesting that formed from dark
        Gave a glimpse of swirling forces beyond
        And then dissolved back into its far source.
        Like the veil that separates Being from
430   Existence, it's beyond the finite dark,
        And I think of the bearded sleigh-driver
        Who hears its silence and stillness, and know
        The veiled Being behind the petalled stars
        That, unbidden, sometimes displays itself,

435   A Celestial Curtain on Heaven's window
That, blown aside, allows a glimpse within
To remind us mortals of the grandeur
Of the ordered and patterned universe,
Beauty blossoming from perfect stillness
440   On hidden trunk and branches like the Norse
Yggdrasil, Tree of Life that fills the sky.
O northern Light, come to my aid now I
Come to describe how Christ came down to Earth
To repeat his messed-up Second Coming.

445   Like a vicar creeping from a vestry,
Not wanting to be seen before he stands
Before the waiting congregation's pews,
Christ slipped round the veil that curtains Being
Off from Existence that congregates on
450   Earth and awaits a momentous event:
The renewing of order and pattern,
A new intervention in the affairs
Of misguided, catastrophically-led
Mankind. He had some calls to make before
455   He would be ready to proclaim himself
And the inauguration of his new
Millennial Kingdom and Era of Peace.
And first he materialised in Gaza.

Gaza City looked as if an earthquake
460   Had shattered all its blocks and rubbled streets.
It seemed a civilisation had smashed.
Humans had been plunged back to the squalor
Of Crusaders' sieges, camping on stones,
Boiling rice on fires lit from kindling wood
465   Torn from split window frames and pounded walls.
Camp-fires flickered throughout Gaza City
And still the air attacks and shells rained in.
A steady drizzle dampened flesh and wool.
Numbed humans with nowhere to flee sat still
470   In the open where falling masonry
Might not crush them. Into this nightmare came
Christ, his face closely resembling the long
Face on the Turin Shroud, long hair and beard.
At six foot two he looked a Crusader.
475   He wandered in an Arab *dishdasher*,
Barefooted to be at one with the poor,
The homeless and bereaved, sick and injured,
Aghast, appalled at the use of Dime bombs

(Dense Inert Metal Explosive) which shed
480   Tiny microshrapnel particles whose
Heavy-metal, tungsten-alloy pellets
Could not be surgically removed from wounds
That were therefore untreatable. And worse,
Pellets had carcinogenic effects:
485   They peppered the innocent, and then gave
Them cancer that was inoperable,
A cruel weapon for a man to devise.
He healed the fissured limbs and traumatised
Souls of the survivors, saying nothing,
490   Just letting healing energy – virtue –
Flow out of him in deepest compassion,
Soothing, silently teaching acceptance
And calm. Many ignored him, some nodded
Their thanks. No one invited him to share
495   Their food. It was not meant to be like this,
His Second Coming, but he had to see
For himself how Israel had pulverised
A people before he went to Olmert.
Ghastly fires burnt in buildings, smoke billowed
500   As Christ stumbled and staggered on jagged,
Jutting stones in the mounded rubble streets
Under missiled and smashed shells of buildings.
Some fronts had been blown away by tank shells.
Bodies lay in lanes near where people camped,
505   Huddled wretchedly over fires, and he
Grieved for the suffering who sat, stunned, hunched
In soggy blankets. Another air strike
Made him flinch, blew up an already struck
Building, its walls already half-collapsed.
510   Blind and burnt, a survivor of Israel's
White-phosphorus shells stumbled, groping forward,
His hands held out as if they sought a door
Through which he could exit from this horror.
Christ, with them in their hour of need, was sad,
515   Knowing they were all Muslims, not Christians,
And that he was ministering to men
Who were not his constituents, but still
Worthy of deep compassion as they died.
Gaza City was back in Biblical
520   Times, with men and sheep round fires, no shelter,
But those days had been far better than these.
Something had clearly gone wrong with God's world.

Christ left Gaza and materialised, dressed

In a long off-white Biblical robe, in
525   Jerusalem, in Rothschild Street outside
The Supreme Court, opposite the Knesset,
Next to "Rothschilds'" Central Bank of Israel.
Whence funds were moved about the previous
9/11. Ley lines connected the Court
530   To the centre of Jerusalem and
The Rockefeller State Museum. The Court
Had been built by the Rothschilds' family: James,
Son of Edmond (who bought land to finance
The first settlements) gave funds for it and
535   The Knesset in 1966, and
His wife Mrs Dorothy de Rothschild
Donated it in 1992
To Israel's State by writing a letter
To the Prime Minister, Shimon Peres,
540   Which was now hung outside the President's
Chamber. Christ loitered, noting the symbols
Of "Rothschildian" Illuminati lore,
All Satanic. On the left, outside, hung
A pyramid with an open eye for
545   The serpent promised Adam and Eve in
Genesis that "their eyes would be opened"
If they both ate of the tree of knowledge
Of good and evil. The Hebrew word for
"Eye" is singular, and the pyramid
550   Represents the "Rothschilds'" hierarchical
Command of world-wide rule. The symbol was
On the dollar bill for the Federal
Reserve was set up by "Rothschilds", and their
Serpentine, Satanist hallmark was on
555   The American currency that they
Had issued and was theirs. At the front, left,
There was a trampled-on Christian cross for
"The Rothschilds" sided with the Antichrist
Against the Christian West. Also outside
560   Was an Egyptian obelisk that showed
The Jews' origins in Egypt-Israel
And linked with more obelisks in New York
And London in a union of world rule.
Inside, across from the main courtroom, stairs
565   Led to a Masonic compass and square
With G in the middle, for the Greek word
"Gnosis", or "knowledge" in the serpent's sense.
And Christ was sad, for symbols of Satan's
Knowledge and the trampled cross had decried

570	The Jerusalem for which Crusaders' died.
	The spirit of Jerusalem had been
	Polluted by these Illuminatist
	Works paid for out of billions made from banks,
	Inappropriate glorifying of
575	Satan, false values set up like trophies
	In defiance of holy domes and walls
	In a city central to three world faiths.
	Christ sauntered into the building just as
	Olmert emerged from meeting a lawyer
580	Concerning corruption charges. He shook
	Hands at a door, the lawyer left. Olmert
	Went back into the small interview room
	To gather up his papers. Christ followed
	And said, "Ehud, I'm sorry you're unwell,"
585	Referring to his diagnosed prostate
	Cancer. "Do sit down. You know who I am."
	Olmert said, "My faith won't recognise you
	As the Christ. In our faith you're a prophet,
	You're not the Son of God. That's blasphemy."
590	"I know," Christ said. "I met your type last time.
	You side with Caiaphas, the high priest. He
	Asked me if I was the Son of God and
	Said I blasphemed. But I am here because
	Of the suffering in Gaza. I've walked
595	In Gaza City's streets and seen the scenes.
	The casualties are mounting and you are
	Stirring hatred among Palestinians.
	I beg you, declare a cease-fire at once."
	Olmert said contemptuously, "They are
600	The problem, the Palestinians. At least,
	That's how it seems to this Jabotinsky
	Revisionist who believes a Jewish
	Majority can outweigh the Arab
	Population if they use force and are
605	Guarded. Hamas want us to be destroyed.
	We are not prepared to be destroyed, not
	Israel, not 'Rothschilds', not 'Rockefellers'.
	We have the power to fight off attackers
	And we will have a cease-fire when we choose.
610	We do not want Palestinians in
	Our Promised Land, not the old Philistines.
	My father pioneered land settlements.
	We call the shots now. Look at the crisis
	In the Western economy. It has
615	Not touched Israel, we are exempt from it."

"Because 'Rothschilds' own your Central Bank," Christ
Retorted, "and had a role in causing
That crisis. You were promised land by God
But with the power you received from the Light
620   Comes responsibility, a duty
To behave decently to your fellow
Human beings – in Lebanon, Gaza,
All your neighbours. You have abused your power."
"And what will God do about it?" Olmert
625   Sneered. "You advocate appeasement. We don't.
We hit them hard and then we have some peace,
For a while, and then we hit them again.
They get the message. We do not believe
In turning the other cheek. An eye for
630   An eye, that's our way, in our faith." Christ said,
"You have hit them, and it's now time to stop.
You have your eye on Palestinian gas
And further action against Gaza will
Not bring you any closer to its wells."
635   "We dispute that it's Palestinian gas,"
Olmert said abrasively. "It is ours.
In 1967 the entire
Coastline was ours, and so we retained offshore
Resources when the Americans forced us
640   To withdraw from Gaza." Christ said quietly,
"Five wars – in Afghanistan, Iraq and
Lebanon, Georgia, Gaza: five pipelines
At least – why, Georgia has several pipelines –
And the beneficiaries of all five
645   Are Israel and 'Rothschilds'-'Rockefellers'."
He struck a nerve and Olmert was silent.
Then he said, "The Syndicate will triumph
Over the Middle East, over the West."
Christ said, "I am not asking you to stop
650   Being the Syndicate's man, but to end
The cruelty to women and children
In Gaza by calling an immediate
Unilateral, unconditional cease-fire."
"I hear you," Olmert said. "I personally
655   Am tired of all this war. I was last year
Criticised for being too soft in my
Dealings with the Lebanon. That was by
The official investigation. I
Have been ground down by false accusations,
660   Ceaseless attacks that I profited from
Campaign donations, which are all just lies.

And as you know, I'm ill. I keep going,
But I do not want to fight wars when my
Health is poor and I must consult lawyers
665 Almost daily to head off the attacks.
I have to petition for a hearing
To be postponed due to my failing health.
I am not a cruel man. I have children,
Five if you count my adopted daughter.
670 I give you my word, action in Gaza
Will stop the moment Israel does not need
To go on attacking. Our military
Will make a recommendation, but I
Will be the judge." Christ said softly, "You, or
675 'Rothschilds'-'Rockefellers', the trillionnaires
Who built Israel and own its key buildings
And are your masters?" Olmert looked aside.
"Others will make recommendations. I
Will be the judge of when the attacks stop."
680 Christ said, "My Millennial Kingdom will bring
Peace to the Earth among all faiths, yours too.
I'm counting on you, realign Israel
And bring your state into a Peace Era."
Olmert sighed, "As I said, we call the shots.
685 The Illuminati, whose symbols deck
This building, support the Antichrist and
Would not take kindly to 'their man' ending
Action they want because someone has claimed
To be 'the Christ' Caiaphas rejected.
690 I've given you enough time. I must go."
And Olmert rose and showed Christ to the door.
The behind-the-scenes work of his Second
Coming did not seem to be going well.

For obscure reasons Christ could not fathom,
695 Which had to do with Israel's self-interest,
Olmert looked with favour on his appeal.
International pressure for a cease-fire
Was clamorous due to the civilian
Casualties. Some one thousand three hundred
700 And seventy Palestinians had been killed,
And thirteen Israelis. On the seventh
Israel had opened a food corridor
To allow humanitarian aid in
To Gaza, and stop fighting for three hours
705 Each day or other day for UN food
Convoys to make deliveries. Now on

The seventeenth, following Christ's appeal
To Olmert, and Olmert's calculating
Self-interest, Israel announced a cease-fire
710   Unilaterally, without Hamas'
Agreement. If Hamas stopped their rockets,
Israel would withdraw. If they restarted
The IDF would go back in. Hamas
Vowed to fight on until Israel had left
715   Gaza. It fired rockets. An Israeli
Air strike silenced the rocket-launching squad.
Then on the eighteenth Hamas, Islamic
Jihad and other militias stated
They would stop the rockets for a week if
720   Israel withdrew. Israel completed its
Pull-out from Gaza on the twenty-first.
Israel had degraded Hamas so that
Its grip on Gaza could now be challenged
And its military wing was unable
725   To continue its attacks on Israel.
There was international outrage Israel
Had used disproportionate force against
The Palestinians and had flattened all
Their commercial buildings in what looked like
730   A collective punishment that had put
Gaza back into the Middle Ages.

On the eighteenth Noble Energy said –
And this news was what Christ had not fathomed –
That three massive gas reservoirs had been
735   Discovered off the Haifa coast, and that
The Tamar-1 well, under five thousand
Five hundred feet of water, had been drilled
To a depth of over sixteen thousand
Feet. One of the well's owners, the owner
740   Of the Delek Group, said that the well was
"One of the biggest in the world". It meant
That Israel would be gas-independent
And on its way to becoming fully
Economically independent.
745   The Gaza gas fields were not vital now.
Olmert had judged that the attacks should stop
Because Israel had certain gas elsewhere.

Now Egypt held discussions with Israel
And Hamas to extend the cease-fire for
750   A year or more. And Hamas met Fatah.

Israel wanted to halt the smuggling
Of weapons into Gaza. Britain, France
And Germany offered to send warships
To patrol the waters off Gaza where
755   BG would pump its gas. Egypt declined.
It did not want Europeans stationed
On its Gaza border to monitor
The smugglers' tunnels. Israel was concerned
Hamas should not receive reconstruction
760   Funds as they might be used to fund terror.
Olmert said that Israel would not agree
To a long-term truce or even to lift
The blockade until Shalit, the soldier
Held captive by Hamas in Gaza since
765   2006, was released. Hamas said
He would be held until fourteen hundred
Palestinians were released by Israel.
It was a fractious, disputatious peace.

Christ's next port of call to prepare the world
770   For a new Peaceful Era was Soros,
Who sat in a St James's Place office
Above Green Park in London with Jacob,
Lord Rothschild, 4th Baron, in a meeting,
Discussing investments made by the Queen,
775   Elizabeth the Second, wealthiest
Person in Europe, an investor in
His private investment or "hedge fund" linked
To Quantum Fund NV, registered in
The Netherlands Antilles. His ninety-nine
780   Highly wealthy and "sophisticated"
Investors had put in forty billion
Dollars. They were the Club of the Isles, which
Had grown out of the British and Dutch East
India Companies and from the wreckage
785   Of the British Empire. It was based near
The City of London where Soros was
One of the *Hofjuden*, "Court Jews", used by
Aristocratic families in old times.
The most important were the Rothschilds, who
790   Had sold the British Hessian troops to fight
In the American Revolution
Against George Washington. Now Soros sat
With his circle, Marc Rich of Zug in Tel
Aviv and Switzerland; "dirty Rafi"
795   Eytan, long linked to Mossad; Richard Katz

Who was on the board of NM Rothschild.
Soros's mobile had rung and he left
The room to speak outside. He could just hear
The throb of distant traffic in the night.
800 Now Christ appeared at his elbow and said,
György." Startled, and expecting Satan,
Soros terminated his call and turned.
Christ, resembling the Turin Shroud's face, said,
"You know who I am." "Yes," Soros said, "yes."
805 "Five hundred and fifty billion dollars
In two hours last 9/11." "I know
Nothing about it," Soros said. "You made
Two billion in the process," Christ murmured.
"I know your Quantum funds are held in A.
810 And S. Bleichroeder, a small private bank
Close to 'Rothschilds', owned by a family
That represented 'Rothschilds" interests in
Bismarck's time. Also in Citibank. You
Have links with George Karlweiss of Edmond de
815 Rothschild's Banque Privée S.A., Lugano
And Rothschild Bank AG of Zurich. They
Have given you financial backing. There are
Links with 'Rothschilds" Central Bank of Israel.
You have access to a vast network that
820 Withdrew that fortune on 9/11.
I want you to transfer it back and save
The West." Soros looked scornful. "Why ask me?
I know nothing about it. I deny
I had any knowledge whatsoever.
825 But I can tell you, we support Satan.
We want the West to be dependent on
Our good offices." Christ said, "The Western
Nations will have to borrow trillions from
The City of London and Wall Street so
830 They can get through the next debt-filled eight years."
"They'll borrow it from 'Rothschilds" businesses,"
Soros said. "No one else has got the funds.
I deny causing it, but we will lend,
On the right terms. We'll buy governments' debts
835 As gilts." Christ said simply, "Give it back. It's
Not fair on the Western world's citizens
Who, if you do not repay it, will spend
A generation drowning in your debt
And expiring under punitive tax.
840 Soros said, "It's nothing to do with me.
I'm going back into my meeting now."

And he returned to Jacob, Lord Rothschild's
Right hand. And Christ had once more been rebuffed.

Jacob, Lord Rothschild had seen Christ standing
845 Through an open door, wearing off-white robe.
He jumped to his feet and left the meeting,
Passing Soros. "Excuse me," he said, "can
I help you? How did you get in?" He thought
Christ was an intruder. Swiftly seizing
850 The opportunity, Christ said, "Jacob.
You know who I am." Rothschild's eyes narrowed.
The meeting resumed. He pulled the door to.
"I know about 'Rothschilds" two 9/11s,"
Christ said quietly. "I want you to reverse
855 What happened on the second one, when five
Hundred and fifty billion was withdrawn."
"You've no evidence it had anything
To do with me," Rothschild said. "I'm not daft,"
Christ said. "You – your family – control all
860 The central banks in the world, national banks
In a hundred and ninety-two UN
Member states, except five: Iran, Sudan,
Cuba, North Korea and Libya.
And you'll soon have those, for your ambition
865 Is to have a global central bank, which
You virtually have. With a hundred
And eighty-seven central banks at your beck
And call, it's easy to instruct any
To move money about, use your hirelings
870 Like Soros, create a run on Wall Street.
No, don't object. I *know* what 'Rothschilds' did.
I want it returned. The same channels through
Which it disappeared can be reversed and
The missing funds can then flow back in. That
875 Is what I want." Rothschild was going to say,
"Be off with you," but the man resembled
A Crusader and had a gentle gaze
From eyes like pools that saw into his soul.
Christ continued, "I want you to desist
880 From making wars. Not long ago there were
Two more nations without your central banks:
Afghanistan and Iraq. Both now have
'Rothschild'-controlled central banks. 'Rothschilds' were
Behind the first 9/11, to achieve,
885 Through Israel with a complicit UK
And US, *your* central banks in the last

Countries and to follow Albert Pike's plan
For a third world war through racial strife in
The Islamic world. The Arab hijackers
Were 'Rothschilds'' patsies. Why was Atta on
The casino boat of Jack Abramoff,
A pro-Israeli Ashkenazi Jew
On September the fifth 2001,
Just days before 9/11? What did
'Rothschilds' tell the pilots? Your family owned
Half of Zim Shipping Company, which broke
Its lease and moved out before the attack
At a cost of fifty thousand dollars.
Who tipped them off? Did you? And bin Laden,
Whose brother was Bush's partner, and his
Construction business helped the CIA.
He built training camps for *mujahideen*
And Khost tunnel complex, an arms depot,
Training and medical centre also
For the *mujahideen*. I know 'Rothschilds'
Used him in the 9/11 plan. And made
Out the attack was planned by your patsies
And latched onto by Mossad, and Bush thought
That was the case. 'Rothschilds' planned the attack
And 'encouraged' bin Laden to believe
He came up with the idea through Khalid
Sheikh Mohammed – was he, too, in your pay?
You 'Rothschilds' are the real Antichrist,
And you have made bin Laden out to be
The Antichrist because it suited you.
I know 'Rothschilds' started five wars. The Iraq
War was so you could steal Iraq's water
Supply for Israel – on the day that Jews
Celebrate victory over Babylon.
You started the Georgia war to steal gas.
I am returning. My Second Coming
Is to establish peace throughout the world,
Including the Middle East which you've shaped
To conform to your global central bank.
I'm serving you notice, the wars must stop.
Abandon Pike's drive for a third world war
Between Israel and Islam, which would drop
Armageddon on this generation.
You Rothschilds originally came from
Khazaria, in what is now Georgia,
Between the Black Sea and the Caspian.
The Khazars, on instruction from their King,

890

895

900

905

910

915

920

925

930

Converted to the Jewish faith back in
740 and became 'Ashkenazi'
935   Jews but they retained their Asiatic
Mongolian genes. Your genes are not Jewish.
Your homeland's not Israel but Georgia
Eight hundred miles away, as you well know.
For 'Rothschilds' were behind the Georgian war.
940   Wherever there's a war over pipelines,
They are avariciously behind it."
Rothschild said, "You are a conspiracy
Theorist, all wild allegations, short in
Evidence. You are out of touch with how
945   The world's perceived today. It's one global
Village. We do not dwell on nation-states."
Christ retorted, "You know I'm fact-based and
Evidential. You should be dwelling on
Civilisations, *and* nation-states that
950   Grow them, not conglomerates that stunt growth.
I watched your father rent a house to Guy
Burgess and suggest Blunt join the secret
Service, and then work with Philby. He ran
A Marxist ring and nearly swamped the West
955   With Communism through his sly intrigues.
Communism prepared for global rule.
Now your generation would rule the world
Through your own Global Central Bank. You plan
To hold the cosmopolitan purse-strings.
960   Enough. 'Rothschilds' financed Dr Ritmeyer,
Who claims to have located the exact
Spot where the Ark of the Covenant once
Rested, on Temple Mount, deep in the Dome
Of the Rock, and that the Ark itself was
965   Spirited away by godly priests at
The sacking of the first Temple, and is
In rock-carved tunnels and chambers beneath
Temple Mount. It's not true and you know it.
But your allegiance to Satan demands
970   That he produce a trophy you can call
The Ark. Again, enough. You have embarked
On a wrong course. Satan, Pike, central banks,
Wars pinned on Muslims, phoney Arks – wrong, wrong."
Surprised at Christ's intensity, spellbound
975   By the conviction of this Biblical-
Dressed Crusader-looking sincere teacher,
Rothschild had listened. Now he said, "I am
Afraid you've misunderstood 9/11.

You clearly don't know how central banks work,
980   How independent departments discuss
Matters, arrive at their own decisions.
You're poorly advised on fund withdrawal,
On the reasons for the Mideastern wars.
You're also arrogant, insufferable,
985   Self-righteous, priggish and impractical.
I don't know how you got in but you're not
Welcome." He saw Satan lurking nearby,
Disguised as a doorman, and commanded:
"Show this man out. He's no right to be here."
990   And Christ, aware Satan had overheard
His plea to Rothschild, was now escorted
Firmly to the door as Rothschild returned
To his meeting. Christ told Satan, "I will
Deal with you on another occasion."
995   He knew he could not found his Millennial
Kingdom until he'd defeated Satan
But in the Rothschilds' office, which Satan
Guarded and watched over, was not the place
Where Heaven's goodness should defeat evil.

1000   Now Christ appeared in room 5600,
The family office on the fifty-
Sixth floor of the landmark GE Building
In Rockefeller Center in New York.
Consulting the four-by-five-feet gold wheel
1005   Rolodex, a glorified card index
Which he started in the 1940s
And which by now held about a hundred
And fifty thousand entries on the most
Powerful people in the world, stood David
1010   Rockefeller, aged ninety-three, the oil
Magnate's grandson. In the dusk Christ, wearing
Off-white robes and the Turin Shroud's lean face,
Said, "David, you know who I am. I spoke
To your father when the UN was set
1015   Up in a San-Francisco conference hall.
He was America's wealthiest man,
Perhaps the world's richest individual.
I doubt whether you're the richest today.
The 'Rothschilds' control every central bank
1020   In the world except five. The financial
Crisis has changed reckonings of the world's wealth.
Before it, the world's GDP was some
Two hundred and seventy-two trillion

Dollars, and taking 'Rothschilds' ' six billion
1025
Dollars in 1850, it can be
Calculated that they're worth much more than
The world's wealth. And the US national debt's
Risen to, what, eleven trillion. You are
Officially worth 2.2 billion
1030
Dollars. Your father had a third of all
Standard Oil's profits, and was worth trillions.
'Rockefellers' may have overtaken
'Rothschilds', but I doubt it. Your alliance
With 'Rothschilds' since you co-founded with them
1035
The Bilderberg Group in the Netherlands
(As the new youngest-ever director
Of the Council on Foreign Relations),
Has put 'the Rockefellers' in the thrust
For a world government, for Bilderberg
1040
Has implemented its resolutions
As the history of the last fifty-five
Years. And you founded the Trilateral
Commission in 1973,
Since when most presidents have been members –
1045
Carter, Ford, Bush Senior and Clinton – and
Members have staffed the bulk of presidents'
Administrations. The 'Rothschilds'' wealth and
The 'Rockefellers'' diplomacy have
Brought the world to the brink of one-worldism.
1050
But your one-world has one drawback. For it's
Illuminatist, Freemasonic and –
As 'the Rothschilds' followed Adam Weishaupt
In the eighteenth century – Satanist." "I
Am not a Satanist," Rockefeller
1055
Said. "But," Christ said, "as you're in alliance
With 'Rothschilds', the project you share must be
Satanic. That's their belief, it's occult.
I am returning to Earth, my Second
Coming is due and I've come to tell you
1060
That I am founding a *Pax Mundana*,
Not a *Pax Americana*, a Peace
Of the World, a global peace. You could help
Me, liaise with the hundred and fifty
Thousand names in your Rolodex. For you,
1065
In conjunction with 'Rothschilds', have set up
A structure for a new world government:
The American, European and
Pacific Unions, now an African
Union; regional blocs; trade groupings; and

1070	A reformed IMF and World Bank. Then
	The UN's waiting to be adapted –
	The organisation built on land your
	Father donated, linked with your family.
	I propose that we work with the world as
1075	It is, not as you want it to become:
	Nation-states within civilisations,
	Not states levelled by wars. I propose you
	Lay aside things that happened in the past,
	Your feud with 'Rothschilds' when you took the side
1080	Of Russia, Iran and Palestine while
	They supported Israel. Let us now deal
	With the world as it is, boundaries as now.
	I will declare a new Era of Peace,
	Which you will help enforce. We'll form one world
1085	As you've dreamt all your life, and your father
	Did before you. It will be multi-faith,
	Not Christian-dominated. All faiths will
	Co-exist in peace within their boundaries.
	And we'll fashion a new world government
1090	That does not work through Masons and does not
	Have Lucifer, a euphemism for
	Satan, as its titular head. There won't
	Be any Syndicate input in it
	Or Illuminati influence, but
1095	All your strategic gains will be preserved.
	We'll leave aside all ideology.
	Crusades have brought us to where we are, we'll
	Take it forward, so you, though ninety-three,
	Will live to see the implementation
1100	Of your life-long dream, which will now become
	Reality, crowning your long life's work.
	What do you say? Will you now work with me?"
	Rockefeller had listened in silence.
	He was sceptical about this strange man
1105	Who had no notes or Rolodex and thought
	He could found a world government at once
	When he himself had taken sixty years
	And hundreds of thousands of meetings and
	Numerous wars round the globe to level
1110	All countries down to become equal states
	In a New World Order. He said, "You are
	Very persuasive, but the work's been done.
	We're ready to unveil what already
	Exists in private: a world government.
1115	I do not need any help from strangers.

By dint of hard work we have now prevailed.
And it will be a world government that
Is as it should be, not as things are now.
And I will live to see the unveiling.
1120 No one who has not done all the hard work
Can come along and hijack the project."
It was another brush-off. Calmly, Christ
Said, "Very well. I offered you a chance
To participate. You have turned it down.
1125 I will be taking over all your work
And shaping it into *Pax Mundana*.
I know you've controlled Obama, I know
You were struck by the idea that he should
Redistribute wealth while sitting on the seat
1130 Of your toilet, and that you personally
Told him what to say in that election
Speech. I need to work with Obama, Heaven
Needs to work with Obama. You are old
And can die in your sleep at any time.
1135 Heaven will not be thwarted by you on this.
You may find yourself in Self-Improvement
Sooner than you realise. Tonight you'll go
Back to your estate in Pocantico
Hills, Kykuit, which means 'Look-out' in Dutch and
1140 Has grand views over the Hudson River;
For the weekend, to your home 'Hudson Pines'
On land your father owned, and grandfather,
The oil magnate. You may not live to see
The end of the weekend. And you may come
1145 To see that you have just made a mistake
As what you dreamt will happen, but through me,
And without your seizing the resources
As you did in Russia, whose oil and gas
You bought for just a tenth of their true worth.
1150 I've not forgotten that your grandfather
Had German blood – on his paternal side
He was descended from a Hessian
Mercenary named Roggenfelder (which means
'Rye field' in German) who had Turkish blood,
1155 And that your alliance with the German
Rothschilds from Frankfurt is a German thing.
On second thoughts, I don't think that I want
To work with Roggenfelders – your family's
True name. Seventy-two years ago you wrote
1160 Your thesis on Fabian socialism,
Destitution Through Fabian Eyes. You said

That Europeans' approach to poverty
Was based on atoning for sins, giving
Alms to the poor so they would go to Heaven,
1165   Whereas the Webbs held that the poor should have
A minimum standard of living as
A right. You're delaying world government,
Universal peace till you have reshaped
The world to implement global Fabian
1170   Socialism. I'm not a Communist,
A German theoretician like Marx.
I start with where we're at and making peace.
Blessed are the peacemakers, as I taught.
I don't start with equality for all
1175   But with the suffering poor who all have souls
And are heading for Heaven or Improvement.
We start at different places, so I will
Take over what you've done before you start
To loot it and redistribute what you seize
1180   To the world's poor, which they won't get, and keep
The bulk to add to trillions that you have.
There's scope for Self-Improvement in your life
If what I've just said's a fair summary."
Rockefeller said, "It's not. Yes, I am
1185   A Fabian, and I care for the world's poor.
The Syndicate have to seize the world's wealth
By wars and by diplomacy to have
Booty that can be spread around the world.
It's the thinking of the old Crusaders:
1190   Take from the Muslims, give alms to the poor."
"Heaven won't be deceived by such specious spin,"
Christ said. "And the Twin Towers, named after you
And your brother Nelson, which you had built –
The 9/11 attack which you watched from
1195   That window and which you claim in your *Memoirs*
Filled you with dread, the attack was designed
To convince public opinion to back
Syndicate invasions of two countries
That did not have 'Rothschild'-controlled central
1200   Banks and whose oil and gas you could purloin.
Your *Memoirs* 'came the innocent' to all.
Don't 'come the innocent' to me." "It's dark,"
Rockefeller said. "I have to travel
To my weekend home. You can talk all night
1205   But it won't change anything. My life's work
Is very near completion, I need no
Help, thank you. I am happy with 'Rothschilds'.

We'll remain in productive alliance.
Our methods – which you're keen to take over
1210 And not undo, so they can't be too wrong –
Have brought the world to the brink of a New
World Order and world government. I'm not
Sure how you got in, have a great weekend."
Suddenly Christ faded before his eyes.
1215 Rockefeller was shocked. He had humoured
The strange man who thought he could do in one
Day what he himself had taken sixty
Years to three-quarters-do. He had humoured
Him and was shocked to see proof of his power,
1220 His body's ability to vanish.

Christ materialised in a private plane
Which had left Turkey, heading for Beirut.
He sat in an empty seat not far from
The august UN Secretary-General,
1225 Ban Ki-moon. He leaned forward and said, "Ban,
You know who I am." Startled, Ban, awake
When others slept at 10 p.m., thought he
Had walked down from the back. He was polite.
"How are you?" he said. Christ said, "I've returned
1230 For my Second Coming, and I shall need
To confer with you as my Millennial
Kingdom covers the Earth, like your UN.
I want an Era of Peace, and I know
You will land in Beirut at eleven
1235 And that tomorrow you will have meetings
With Lebanon's President and PM
And President of the Palestinian
Authority and UNIFIL command
And that on Sunday you will fly in for
1240 The Sharm el-Sheikh summit on Gaza. I
Was in Gaza not many hours ago,
And I visited Olmert and pleaded
With him to announce a cease-fire. Follow
Up my contact and bring peace. We can help
1245 Each other in the coming weeks, for I
Am founding a world government that will
Subsume the so-called New World Order that
The Syndicate have championed. I know
That you owe your position to David
1250 Rockefeller, that, having donated
The land for the UN to be built and
The first officials after World War Two,

'Rockefellers' control the highest posts
And that no UN Secretary-General
1255   Can be appointed without their blessing.
I know you keep silent on your beliefs
And don't belong to any church or group,
Saying that it is inappropriate
For a Secretary-General to align
1260   Himself to any 'religion or God'.
I also know your mother's a Buddhist,
That you secretly follow Buddhism.
You are perfectly aligned – or, rather,
Non-aligned – for my Universalist
1265   Purposes, for I want to assure you,
All faiths have equal status and ranking
In my Kingdom. We will work together
Brilliantly. I also know I can't spend
Too long as your schedule's in five-minute
1270   Blocks, and you'll be looking to move on now.
But I needed to introduce myself
And strike up a relationship, for we,
Between us, can guide the whole world to peace."
To which Ban, listening attentively,
1275   Nodded and said, "That is my task, the peace
Of the world. That is why I left my post
As South Korea's Foreign Minister,
To bring peace to the world. I keep the peace.
I am a peacemaker. I have support
1280   From all in my administration, some
Sixty thousand officials. I don't need
Your help. I do my job for peace and meet
The world's leaders, call on Israel to stop
Violating Lebanon's airspace and
1285   State rocket fire from south Lebanon and
Israel's response is a major concern.
The Syndicate do good in the world and
David Rockefeller is my ally.
Now if you'll excuse me, I must make notes."
1290   And once again Christ received a response that
Was less than enthusiastic to his
Millennial Kingdom. He faded out.

Christ found Bush among the last few packing
Cases in the Oval Office. Bush was
1295   In a despondent, elegiac mood.
It was still the day Christ had left Gaza,
Friday January the seventeenth.

Christ murmured, "George," and then materialised.
"Ah, it's you," Bush said. Christ incarnated
1300   In off-white robes, a submissive Turin-
Shroud look. "Most of my stuff's packed up and gone.
We began in the summer, a lot went
To Crawford. We moved our personal things
Out of Camp David over Christmas. Here
1305   It's really just our personal belongings."
Christ, nodding, said, "I want to hear from you
How you think you've left the world, to which I
Am trying to bring a *Pax Mundana*.
Are you winning against the extremists?
1310   Is the world a safer place? Can there now
Be peace?" Bush pulled a face and sat down, waved
Christ to an adjacent chair. "Well", he said,
We're facing a counter-offensive in
Afghanistan. The Taliban are in
1315   The Swat Valley in Pakistan, pressing
On Islamabad. In Iraq the surge
Has worked but anti-Shiite terrorists
Could start again. Some say that the White House
Overestimated the Muslim threat.
1320   I disagree. Secret papers I've seen
Indicate the threat's real, and nuclear.
Al-Qaeda have a lot of suitcase bombs.
And if they overrun Pakistan they'll
Seize Pakistan's nuclear weapons, and we
1325   In America will have to bomb them.
But though they're a real threat, I have to say
The Syndicate have made things worse. They knew
That 9/11 would happen, I'm sure
Of that. They've been in all the war zones with
1330   Their own agenda. They drove some of my
Decisions. Their greed got in the way, stirred
Israel's intransigence. Israel's go-slow
On implementing our two-state project
Did not help peace. Muslim extremism –
1335   Bin Laden and al-Qaeda – have some steel.
They've fought tenaciously, and it's a draw
In Afghanistan and Pakistan. We
Are in danger of losing, of defeat
As in Vietnam. Obama has signalled
1340   He will withdraw, and Iran's just waiting
To move in on Iraq when our troops leave.
I did my best to keep the West's strength up
And to project a confident image,

And I was ready to take on Iran.
1345 But the Democrats, and Obama, made
Things difficult with talk of appeasement,
And I just couldn't do it any more.
The best way to make peace is to prepare
For war. I can't help feeling the world's changed."
1350 Bush sat dejected, rueful at his lot,
And said to Christ in matter-of-fact tone:
"The America I ruled was supreme,
The Cold War ended, the Soviet Union
Collapsed. Never since the Roman Empire
1355 Under Augustus has one state appeared
So strong and invincible, and with such
A military capacity, air strikes
With precision weapons that can take out
Any target on the planet. We led
1360 NATO, the most powerful military
Alliance that the world has ever known.
Our dominance was like a Colossus.
Our economic wealth was far greater
Than that of any other state. The world's
1365 Reserve currency's the US dollar.
Our language is the world's most common tongue,
A *lingua franca*. Our culture's the world's.
All watch our films. Our capitalism
Has vanquished other ways: socialism
1370 And communism. Our democracy
Is the model for Russia and Europe,
For Asia and Latin America.
For two centuries the West has ruled the Earth,
Has dominated the entire planet.
1375 But now, due to banking mismanagement,
And more directly 'Rothschilds" smash-and-grab
Raid on our banks, so that even the Bank
Of England nearly ran out of money,
That phase is ending just when a single
1380 Global currency was within our grasp.
'Rothschilds' would say the world has been panicked
Into accepting a world currency
If it will just restore stability.
The capitalist system has collapsed.
1385 We've learnt in Afghanistan and Iraq
That vast power and victory do not end wars,
Bring peace and stable democratic rule.
And China has emerged as a great power,
A superpower, it's said. I dispute that.

1390	The world is suddenly multipolar,
	It's no longer uni- or bi-polar.
	Oil- and gas-rich states now have a new clout.
	Iran, Venezuela, Gulf states have wealth,
	India is sending spaceships to the moon.
1395	Our great financial system's in ruins.
	Wall Street icons are bankrupt or swindlers.
	Our free-enterprise capitalism
	Now needs strong government, as the Russians
	And Chinese have always argued. Iceland's
1400	Turned to Russia, Pakistan to China
	And the Gulf states own bits of the US.
	And behind economic power marches
	Political might, and prosperity
	Will bristle a host of nuclear missiles.
1405	Western dominance is last year's story,
	East-West sharing is next year's, competing
	To carve slices from a dwindling pie.
	Universalism – all humankind
	Finding its voice in a world government,
1410	All cultures sharing equally in wealth
	And rule – is an idea whose time has come.
	It may be an idea long overdue."
	Bush sank into a deep despondency.
	"The best thing to do," he said, "is to start
1415	Where the world's at, with the multipolar
	World and base peace on checks and balances.
	No longer one superpower policing.
	A more diplomatic model, equals
	Negotiating, agreeing and bound.
1420	The Western supremacy's over as
	Forces within the Syndicate weakened
	Its resolve and attacked its in-flowed wealth.
	The West's dying of self-inflicted wounds."
	There was a silence. Then Christ spoke: "You're right.
1425	The only way to peace in this changed world
	Is to set up a Universalist
	World government that is multipolar.
	The West has fought a draw, if it's not been
	Defeated, and power now has to be shared
1430	With the East and all regions. You have been
	Most helpful. Thank you very much for that."
	"Good luck," Bush said, depressed, "you'll sure need it.
	I hope you fare better than I did. But
	Mark my words, as soon as I've gone, the world
1435	Will become *more* violent. Obama's weak."

Christ nodded, "I'll stay in touch," and faded.

Christ re-emerged on an eighty-year-old
Train travelling the final one hundred
And thirty-seven miles in Abraham
1440 Lincoln's footsteps from Philadelphia
To Washington in 1861
For his inauguration. It was sub-
Zero and bone-chilling cold. Obama,
Wearing a black overcoat, bare-headed,
1445 Stood in the half-open end wagon's back
Above draped Stars-and-Stripes and a seal that
Said "Renewing America's Promise",
Waving at a crowd as they trundled through
A station. His whistle-stop tour lasting
1450 From morning till evening took him past hordes
Gathered at stations on the way. He stopped
At Wilmington, as Lincoln did not. In
His day Delaware was a slave station.
At Baltimore, with Biden at his side,
1455 He disembarked and spoke to a frozen
Crowd of forty thousand, referring to
Patriots who defended Fort McHenry
Nearby against the British and inspired
'The Star-Spangled Banner', the national
1460 Anthem of the US. On the last leg
To Washington, Obama stood alone,
In overcoat looking for the next crowd,
And now Christ was beside him in his robes
Looking like a Crusader with deep eyes.
1465 "Barack," he said, "you know who I am." "Do
I?" Obama asked quizzically. "I
Will be working with you," Christ said quietly
As the train trundled. "My Second Coming
Is due. My Millennial Kingdom will bring
1470 Peace to the world. I can help you bring peace.
Western domination's over. The West
Is going to have to live with the Muslims
And not fight them." Obama looked at Christ
And deep down knew who he was. "I agree,"
1475 He said. "I want to get out of Iraq,
And out of Afghanistan when I can,
And negotiate with, not bomb, Iran.
I want to shake hands with America's
Enemies – Chavez, Castro – and apply
1480 The money saved from wars to sorting out

The subprime problem, the economic
Crisis and take care of Americans,
Keep all of them in jobs, give them healthcare.
The West has actually lost the War
1485   On Terror – won a battle, lost the War.
We can't afford to fight for ten more years.
I have to tell two million people that
In my inauguration, yet stay strong
As our enemies will be listening."
1490   Christ said, "I will be behind you. We can
Found a Universalist world order
With a world government in which all faiths
Can live in harmony. I know you've been
Chosen by David Rockefeller to
1495   Redistribute wealth as a socialist,
Global wealth as well as national wealth.
As an African American you
Will be in a good position to talk
To Africa, Asia, the Middle East.
1500   I know Rockefeller is hoping you
Will bring people together in One World.
Several states have court cases on your birth
Certificate. I know you were born in
Kenya, not Hawaii." Obama said, "I
1505   Deny that. It's Hawaii." "If this is proved
In a court of law," Christ said quietly,
Not raising his voice, "you will cease to be
The President, who has to have been born
In the US. You and I share the same
1510   View of the coming world government I
Want to start with my Kingdom, in which all
Faiths will be treated equally. And I
Will do my best to keep you President."
"I appreciate that," Obama said. "But
1515   Everything you've described I was always
Going to do. I'll do it anyway.
I'll gladly listen and show you respect,
But I am President, the new Leader
Of the Western world, and I've advisers.
1520   I don't need you or anyone to help.
Oh look, there's a station and a big crowd."
As the dusk turned to early freezing dark
Obama held up his right hand and waved.
Christ faded, feeling spurned. Once again he
1525   Grasped that worldly power in the modern world
Had little place for his spiritual power.

The modern rulers charted their own course
Independently, and weren't beholden.
The crowd slid away, Obama turned back.
1530   Christ had gone. He shrugged to himself. He had
Been humouring a strange-looking voter
And was relieved to be with his own thoughts
As the train rattled on to Washington.

The Pope withdrew into the twelfth century
1535   Tower of St John for meditation
Within stones that had lived through the Crusades.
He lit a candle which half-lit the room.
He sat in shadows, medieval gloom,
And looked behind closed eyes, opened his soul
1540   To the Light. It poured in, enlightening
His mind as the candle lightened the room.
Christ stood before him and said, "Benedict."
The Pope started, opened his eyes and saw
The Turin Shroud's face, and instantly knew
1545   "Ah," the Pope breathed, "you have come." "To tell you,"
Christ said, "that I am returning to Earth.
My Second Coming is due as the world
Is in a mess: war and economic
Crisis, and the threat of nuclear-suitcase
1550   Bombs triggering an Armageddon that I
Am concerned to prevent. I'm here to say
My Millennial Kingdom will be set up
Within weeks." The Pope nodded and, seated,
Said, "I can help you in that. This can be
1555   Your headquarters." "No, Benedict," Christ said
With quiet authority. "My Kingdom will
Be strictly inter-faith and centred in
Jerusalem, city of many faiths.
Your faith will be one of many rooted
1560   In my Kingdom, which will be the Kingdom
Of the Lord's Prayer: 'Thy Kingdom come, thy will
Be done on Earth as it is in Heaven.'
Heaven accommodates all faiths, and on Earth
My Kingdom, which reflects Heaven, will too.
1565   I'm sure you understand." The Pope grimaced.
"The Church's teaching," he said, "gives Christians
An advantage at this time. The Rapture
Will take the Christian faithful to Heaven."
Christ said, "I'm afraid there'll be no Rapture.
1570   Your Church's teaching is wrong on this point.
All who know the Light will be drawn to Heaven.

All who don't are drawn to Self-Improvement."
The Pope grimaced again, said, "The Church's
Teaching is *not* wrong as it comes from God
1575   And my interpretation is beyond
Dispute. I'm infallible. Your return
Is supposed to bring hope to all Christians."
"To all on Earth," Christ said. "I did not teach
For a small sect that would bear my own name,
1580   But for all, a universalism.
I am not happy at the way that my
Teaching about the Light has been taken
Over and institutionalised, and mixed
Up with worldly power and diplomacy.
1585   The Church has not been teaching what I taught.
It's as if the Antichrist had disguised
Himself as the Pope, you, to teach error.
When my Kingdom is established I will
Shut down the Church and distribute its wealth.
1590   We need to return to simplicity.
I taught and the illiterate grasped my
Parables and applied them to their lives.
That's what I will do, from Jerusalem,
When I have set up my Kingdom and peace
1595   Has returned." The Pope stared at him. "You may
Be out of touch," he said gently. "Things are
Different these days. You may find you're ignored.
The Church keeps your teaching alive for all,
The Catholic Church, not break-away splinter
1600   Groups with impure doctrines. Without the Church
You will struggle to reach the Earth's people.
I reach them as Mass in St Peter's Square
Is broadcast round the world. The media may
Not recognise you or give you air time.
1605   You need the Church. And there will be no peace
Around Jerusalem. The region is
At war, it's not safe. The Church knows your words.
We can't cope with new ones, the *Bible*'s fixed.
We have a structure we follow that works:
1610   Mass and confession, and communal prayer.
I have infallibility as St
Peter's successor, I interpret words
You spoke two thousand years ago. Many
Have wanted to add interpretations.
1615   They are on a long list of deviants.
I would not want to see you on their list.
In setting up your Kingdom, you should heed

The advice of the guardian of your words:
The Church." Christ knew he would be obstructed
1620   By the Church, and he merely said: "Knowing
The Light is Truth, not teachings of the Church.
The Light pours knowledge into open souls
As a tide pours sea into small harbours
And cleanses them of débris and dryness.
1625   I speak as the Light of the World. I taught
That God can be known as Light, and I know
My teaching's been forgotten as there are
Too few in Heaven and too many in Self-
Improvement. We're in a time of falling
1630   Standards. Too few have been taught by the Church
To know the Light. Many Church attenders
Are shocked when they are turned away from Heaven
And told to undergo Self-Improvement.
My Kingdom will address this Church error.
1635   There will be a move to the mystical
Experience of Light, away from doctrine.
You have two symbols of the Light which you
Have kept locked in the Vatican cellars:
The Ark of the Covenant, which lived in
1640   The Tabernacle – the mobile sanctuary,
Into which the Light descended, the Fire
Of Yahweh, so the Ark held God's Light on
Sinai and in the Temple – that was brought
To Rome by Titus in AD 70;
1645   And the Grail, the cup of my Last Supper,
Which received the Light when I prayed that day
And was brought to England by my uncle
Joseph of Arimathaea, and which
Received the Light in Arthurian romance,
1650   The Queste del Saint Graal, circa 1220,
And which, when it had passed to the Templars
And then Cathars, you seized from the Parfaits
During the Albigensian Crusade
And locked away as my Last Supper's cup
1655   Was too wooden and cracked to be your gilt
Goblet with precious emeralds which the Church
Demanded. Both these objects symbolise
The plainness of the Light and of mankind's
Communion with it. It has been written
1660   That I will have both these missing objects
On my Second Coming. I would like them.
Could you locate them in your archives and
Pass them to me?" The Pope said, "The archives

	Of the Vatican are voluminous.
1665	Not everything assembled since Peter
	Has been identified and classified.
	It would take us weeks, if not months or years,
	To locate the objects that you describe,
	With which I am not familiar. I doubt
1670	That we have them here. Perhaps they have been
	Destroyed, or have been buried in a cave
	In France or somewhere near Jerusalem."
	"No," Christ said quietly. "I know, you have them.
	I was hoping the Church, the guardian
1675	Of my teachings, would at least show willing
	And agree to search for these two icons.
	Satan has given objects to bin Laden
	Which he says are the original Ark
	And Grail, but they are not genuine. They
1680	Are fakes, as you'd expect from deceptive
	Satan. I ask as these two talismen
	Symbolise real values, the Truth, the Light,
	Which the Church has mislaid and the West lacks –
	Indeed, perishes for the lack of them.
1685	But it's not vital I should have these *things*,
	They represent the Beatific Vision
	Which cannot be replaced by an *object*.
	The mystic's approach to the Light is what
	They represent, the true teaching once known
1690	To the fourteenth-century mystics, and now
	Missing while the Church teaches non-Light tales
	And dwells on human error, not the Light."
	To which the Pope gravely replied, "Human
	Error *should* be dwelt on. Both Bush and Blair
1695	Have been here and both seek peace for their deeds
	In sending troops to die in foreign wars,
	Lest their deeds should be reckoned sins. That is
	What the Church dwells on, preventing new wars.
	The Light *is* out of fashion today. Hymns
1700	Which mentioned it have been removed from most
	Hymn-books. Religion *has* been humanised,
	A trend that began in the Renaissance.
	We are not in an inward time. In spare
	Moments we switch on the TV and look
1705	Outside ourselves at all parts of the globe.
	The Beatific Vision is for saints,
	Not ordinary people." "But I taught it,"
	Christ objected quietly, "for ordinary
	People to follow through parables like

1710	The sower and the seed, and ordinary
	People understood my teaching and went
	To Heaven, having done Self-Improvement here.
	That's the difference between my time and yours:
	My teaching and your Church's long error
1715	Which twisted my words into ceremonies –
	So *you* could control ordinary people.
	I did not control them, they followed me.
	And you were in the Light when I came in."
	The Pope said, "I've assumed you're who you say
1720	You are and have been very courteous
	At what has been an intrusion into
	My privacy and meditation time.
	I'm afraid I cannot help you locate
	Your artefacts or found your new Kingdom
1725	In the newly divided Middle East.
	So if you'll forgive me I'll now return
	To reflecting on what the Church can bring
	To international affairs today.
	The Church protects a billion souls, a sixth
1730	Of humankind, including many poor;
	Pronounces on abortion, birth control,
	Homosexuality, child abuse,
	A host of social evils, for people
	Who want guidance and aren't interested in
1735	The Light. I wish you luck in your mission."
	And the Pope turned aside in candlelight
	And closed his eyes in prayer. And Christ, rebuffed,
	Vanished into the air empty-handed,
	Without two iconic palladiums.
1740	Christ had now completed the groundwork for
	His Millennial Kingdom. Except for Bush
	Those he had contacted had rebuffed him.
	All had in certain ways been obstacles.
	He understood the self-interested
1745	Agendas of the Syndicate and both
	Presidents, and the Church. He saw how bad
	Things had become and how calamitous
	Was the fallen human condition. He
	Grasped there would have to be a massive change
1750	In influxes to influence leaders
	To subordinate their self-interest to
	Communal good, banning nuclear weapons,
	To head off impending Armageddon.
	It was no use appealing to fallen,

1755	Selfish men's better instincts, as they were
	Crushed under their self-assertive culture.
	We live in an ocean of unseen Light
	Which flows into our souls and stirs our minds
	With energies that are controlled by God.
1760	He would ask God to flood leaders with Light.
	The Earth was a dead loss. He grasped that he
	Would not be welcomed if he publicly
	Declared his Kingdom, which was spiritual,
	Not physical. That was the mistake that
1765	Pilate had made, to believe that he'd claimed
	To be "King of the Jews" in a local,
	Physical – not spiritual – Kingdom.
	The soundings he had taken convinced him
	That he should announce his Kingdom in Heaven,
1770	And when God had flooded leaders with Light,
	Later, by working with individuals
	Like those he had approached, implement it
	Gradually throughout Earth till peace had come.
	It would be a slow process and thousands
1775	In key positions in the UN and
	Behind the scenes would contribute their help
	By making decisions to speed the cause.
	Then the tribulation would have ended.
	Now Bush looked back on eight years of two wars.
1780	He had transformed himself from hard-drinking
	Wisecracking to a self-disciplined man,
	To a president who could represent
	All Americans; then he had transformed
	The Presidency from policy views
1785	To one of vision and pre-emptive strikes.
	He had transformed the whole American
	Political culture, and then the world.
	He had taught the world to think in terms of
	The War on Terror, and had prevented
1790	Al-Qaeda from mounting a nuclear,
	Armageddon attack on the US.
	He had been a somewhat existential
	Hero, who had transformed and transcended
	Himself by his deeds and his willed projects.
1795	He had transcended the unpromising
	Adolescent and become President.
	He had moved through five foreign policies
	Or "Bush Doctrines", from a unipolar
	Realism to "with us or against us",

1800	Then pre-emption, then democracy in
	The Middle East, then Freedom Everywhere.
	It had been a tough journey, and he had
	Faced some three thousand death threats every year.
	He had begun with high hopes had spoken
1805	In December two thousand and one with
	Enthusiasm of his ambitions
	To root out "terror wherever it may
	Exist", achieve "world peace", and unity
	At home as "the job of the president
1810	Is to unite the nation" – against foes.
	He had not rooted out terror, which still
	Existed in greater strength than before
	(Perhaps in response to his invasions)
	In Afghanistan, if not in Iraq.
1815	And he had not united his country
	But added to its divisions, and he
	Himself was now a divisive figure.
	The war in Iraq meant he could not make
	The political debate less bitter.
1820	The tone in Washington'd changed for the worse.
	The surge in Iraq had worked, and he could
	Now withdraw eight thousand troops and send them
	To Afghanistan, which needed a surge.
	It was not true that the war in Iraq
1825	Was "lost", as the Democrats had declared.
	But he was disappointed, and he hoped
	History would be kinder to him than his
	Own time had been. He was resigned to his
	Bad press and hoped for kinder judgement from
1830	Posterity, which would see the results
	Of crusading war against the West's foes.
	He'd shown pre-emptive single-mindedness
	But he had chosen to keep silent on
	Bin Laden's nuclear-suitcase bombs and his
1835	Revival of the Baghdad Caliphate
	And his people had not been alarmed by
	The nearness of nuclear Armageddon.
	His people had supported him after
	9/11 but had not understood
1840	The continuing danger they were in,
	Which had been kept from them so they would not
	Be alarmed in their lives, and their support
	Had ebbed as the US had ceased to seem
	As if it was about to be attacked.
1845	He had done his job too well and all those

He had protected now questioned the War.
As a spider spins a silk web from glands
In its abdomen, each with different silks,
Of different strengths for netting and wrapping,
1850   Spinnerets, and cuts the silks with its mouth
And lives in it, so was he trapped within
A thread of his own words that he had spun
From his own gut and shaped it with his mouth
Into a web of how things seemed to be.
1855   Political careers begin in hope
But like spring buds and summer burgeoning
Turn to autumn sadness and winter chill
And end in bleakness, if not in despair,
And a faint hope they'll be warmly recalled
1860   In a new sunshine when they've left the stage.

Bush mused in the White House: 'My legacy.
I wanted to restore American
Supremacy and dominance, and my
Doctrine of pre-emptive war asserted
1865   A new American *imperium*.
Obama prefers a world government
In which a World State has supremacy,
To which America's subordinate.
The end of my presidency may mark
1870   The end of an American era,
A world in which America's supreme.
The National Intelligence Council holds
That American hegemony will
Soon end, and the unipolar world too.
1875   New locations of power are emerging.
A US Government report maintains
The Age of America is drawing
To a close, and the Iraq invasion
Was imperial *hubris*'s final act.
1880   I don't believe a word of it: I brought
The collapse of US ascendancy?
Nonsense. I spread American control
And domination to Afghanistan.
I blocked a spreading, strangling Caliphate.
1885   It will be seen I expanded empire.
Or did my Armageddon bring it down?'
He sat in doubt, unsure of what he'd done.

But then Bush became more bullish and thought:
'America's the most powerful empire

1890	The world has ever seen – a Colossus.
	Not since the Roman Empire has there been
	A potential imperial power as strong
	As the US is today. And yet it
	Sees itself as a moral nation that
1895	Pursues "universal values" such as
	Democracy, equality and rights
	And thus cannot have an imperial role.
	America's never been an empire.
	Although it has a military structure
1900	That projects its power and has conquered
	Two sovereign states in two years and has more
	Than seven hundred and fifty military
	Bases in two-thirds of the world's countries
	America's always declined to build
1905	An administrative structure that can
	Run an empire, and this was lacking in
	Post-Saddam Iraq. Yet its ambitions
	Are like those of the British Empire, to
	Globalise free markets, the rule of law
1910	And representative government. It's
	An empire in denial. The US
	Keenly pursues globalisation, which
	Brings promise of global prosperity.
	Empires bring peace and stable world order
1915	That protects trade and commerce. We are not
	An empire, yet should become one if we
	Can avoid colonising the equal world.
	For we are an empire in all but name.'

	And then he thought again, his creeping doubt
1920	And defiance at war within his soul:
	'It's possible the US will break up
	Into six parts: the Pacific coast round
	Its Chinese population; the South with
	Its Hispanics; Texas, where there are now
1925	Independence movements; the Atlantic coast
	Which has a separate mentality;
	Five poorer central states round their Indians;
	And the northern states linked to Canada.
	Just as the UK's supposed to break up
1930	Into twelve regions – Scotland, Wales, Ireland,
	London and eight Euro-regions – so must
	The US fragment if the Bilderberg
	Group has its way and carves up nation-states
	Into regional conglomerates' zones

<table>
<tr><td>1935</td><td>To make an international regime
That will impose world government on all.
National Governments are short of money.
I inherited a budget surplus
Of 128 billion dollars and left</td></tr>
<tr><td>1940</td><td>A deficit of 482 billion.
I may be at the end of an era
When the United States was sacrosanct
And led the world in ideology
And triumphed over all its adversaries</td></tr>
<tr><td>1945</td><td>In a succession of titanic wars,
The last of which I fought and commanded –
An era in which I was last in line.'</td></tr>
</table>

Bush sat and pondered on his balcony.
'So Communism won. The Soviet
Union's enemy, capitalism,
Has collapsed due to a crisis within
The banking system, which has caused global
Economic slowdown, to the contrived
9/11 meltdown, to swindlers' fraud
And "Rockefellers'" drive for a single
Global currency. Our national debt
Is over ten trillion dollars, Britain's
Over one trillion. We must regulate
The banks. Now Russia's rich in energy
And can cut off the flow of gas and oil
To the West despite losing the Cold War.
Yes, Communism won. The West collapsed.
And that was not my fault, I saw truly.
Eurasia and the Caspian is where
The world will be run from. Whoever rules
Those crucial oilfields will control the world.
It is the new crucible of world power.
I saw this and encircled it with might
In first Afghanistan and then Iraq.
The Syndicate were self-interested, yes,
But they too focused on the right area.
I ringed it with client states and bases.
Had things gone differently the world would now
Be indisputably in US hands.
The world's still in our hands, but disputed.'

Bush had fulfilled America's national
Destiny, to send out a strong message
Of American power that would disrupt

Al-Qaeda's plan to unleash Armageddon
1980   Through nuclear-suitcase bombs in ten cities
And to dissuade half a dozen rogue states
From mounting nuclear weapons on missiles.
Nuclear proliferation was the curse
That had to be avoided at all costs.
1985   He had been clear, the best means of defence
Was to attack: to keep peace, threaten war.
He had been President when the US
Needed to appear strong, and he'd done that
Now Obama had signalled he did not
1990   Want nuclear weapons and had requested
Negotiations with all enemies,
Suing for peace, conveying the idea
That the US was weak, a policy
That would not keep America free from
1995   New attacks from emboldened small tyrants.
Bush had kept order in an unruly
World, some of whose leaders behaved like yobs.
He'd kept order through heroic crusades.

Bush on his balcony looked at the moon
2000   Which inspected Earth like the eye of God,
And he fell headlong into the night sky
And out beyond the stars looked back and saw
The Earth as a tiny speck of dust in
A ploughed field, then as a grain of sand on
2005   A moonlit beach, and his own retirement
Was an event of little consequence,
It did not matter to the One that he
Had been pre-emptive and that Obama
Would sue for peace, plead with enemies that
2010   Bush had cowed. To the One the opposites
Within his life – his drinking and then his
Born-again zeal, and his presidency,
His transformation from a hesitant
President to a confident Leader
2015   Of the Western world – were not opposites
But bars within a harmony, one tune.
His presidency had progressed the world
And would be seen to have brought new order,
And this was natural to the process that
2020   Flowed from the One to form, manifested,
Into a pattern in Earth's tiny grain.

Time is a destroyer and devours us.

At Cambridge's Corpus Christi observe
A gold-encrusted monster, grim-looking
2025   Metal insect that blinks and's part locust,
Part grasshopper, squat on a golden cog
Four foot wide, its jaws snapping to devour
Time as three discs within the circle turn
(Outer ring seconds, middle ring minutes,
2030   Inner ring hours as the pendulum swings),
Eating up seconds as they pass, our breaths,
Swallowing our moments, a chronophage,
Time-eater, John Taylor's variation
Of Harrison's grasshopper escapement.
2035   Its jaws open, its tongue lolling out, on
The fifty-ninth second of each minute
It gulps down the minute which will not come
Again, and on each hour hear the rattle
Of a chain dropping into a hidden
2040   Wooden coffin as a stark reminder
Of human mortality. Monstrous time
Devours our minutes and ever moves us
Towards the coffin into which we head.
O loathsome locust stripping human flesh,
2045   Were it not for the survival of soul
And its new life in Light beyond the grave,
You would be too obnoxious to observe.

Two million crowded into Washington
And packed the National Mall, a sea of heads
2050   Stretching from Capitol Hill to Lincoln
Memorial. Snipers stood on nearby
Rooftops as Obama, his wife and two
Daughters, wearing coats, walked a carpet and
At noon passed through a door into a screen
2055   Bulletproof room fixed to the balustrade,
Visible from the back but unseen on
Cameras on scaffolding above the crowd
That zoomed over the screen's top where Biden
Took the oath. The band played "Hail to the Chief ",
2060   And after a twenty-one-gun salute
Obama, in a red socialist tie,
Held the *Bible* Abraham Lincoln, whose
Proclamation ended slavery, was
Sworn in on and took the thirty-five-word
2065   Oath, getting some words wrong so he would have
To swear again the next day. Then he spoke
Of the challenges: the economic

Crisis, wars and unloved America.
He spoke of remaking America
2070 And restoring trust so America
Was ready to lead the world once again.
And then he spoke as if guided by Christ,
Set out a Universalist vision:
"We're a nation of Christians and Muslims
2075 Jews and Hindus – and non-believers. We
Are shaped by every language and culture."
He said, "We cannot help but believe that
The old hatreds shall someday pass, the lines
Of tribe shall soon dissolve; that as the world
2080 Grows smaller, our common humanity
Shall reveal itself; that America
Must soon play its role in ushering in
A new Era of Peace. To the Muslim
World, we seek a new way forward, based on
2085 Mutual interest and mutual respect.
To those leaders around the globe who seek
To sow conflict, or blame their society's
Ills on the West – know that your people will
Judge you on what you can build, not what you
2090 Destroy. To those who cling to power through
Corruption and deceit and silencing
Dissent, know that you are on the wrong side
Of history, but that we'll extend a hand
If you are willing to unclench your fist.
2095 To the people of poor nations, we pledge
To work alongside you to make your farms
Flourish and to let clean waters flow: to
Nourish starved bodies and feed hungry minds.
And to those nations like ours that enjoy
2100 Relative plenty, we say we can no
Longer afford indifference to the
Suffering outside our borders; nor can
We consume the world's resources without
Regard to effect. For the world has changed,
2105 And we must change with it." And then he spoke
Of duties and responsibility,
The gift of freedom and "our liberty".
He spoke of common danger, as when "in
The year of America's birth, in the
2110 Coldest of months, a small band of patriots
Huddled by dying camp-fires on the shores
Of an icy river. The capital
Was abandoned. And the enemy was

Advancing. And the snow was stained with blood.
2115   At a moment when the outcome of our
            Revolution was in doubt, the father
            Of our nation ordered these words be read
            To the people: 'Let it be told to the
            Future world...that in the depth of winter,
2120   When only hope and virtue could survive...
            That the city and the country, alarmed
            At one common danger, came forth to meet
            It.' America. In the face of our
            Common dangers, in this winter of our
2125   Hardship, let us remember these timeless
            Words. With hope and virtue, let us brave once
            More the icy currents, and endure what
            Storms may come. And let it be said by our
            Children's children that when we were tested
2130   To let this journey end, that we did not
            Turn back, nor did we falter; and with eyes
            Fixed on the horizon, God's grace on us,
            We carried forth that great gift of freedom
            And delivered it safely to future
2135   Generations." Christ, listening, heard his own
            Desire for peace and shielding from danger,
            His own firm championing of all the faiths,
            And, thrilled, he knew he had an ally he
            Could work with to bring in a new order,
2140   Universalist arrangement of zones,
            A multi-faith world of equal balance.
            Afterwards Congress invited Biden
            And Obama to lunch. Obama then
            Walked from the Capitol to the White House.
2145   A day of guards, salutes, parades, speeches,
            Ceremony and vision ended with
            A glittering inaugural ball.
            Change had come to the US and the world.

            The Bushes left Washington soon after
2150   Obama's inauguration. They climbed
            Onto a helicopter and flew to
            Andrews Air Force Base where, in an airport
            Hangar, four thousand invited guests waved
            American flags. At a lectern Bush
2155   Said, "We served with conviction," then boarded
            A charter plane where seventy-five friends
            And family members gave him a standing
            Ovation. As the plane flew to Texas

All crowded into the conference room
2160 And watched a video tribute, leaders with
Memories of his presidency, White-House
Staff of his kindness, friends of his courage
And fortitude. Many were moved to tears.
They landed in Midland, Texas. Bush spoke
2165 To twenty thousand, and then four thousand
In Waco. A helicopter took Bush
To his ranch in Crawford soon after dark.
Now Bush felt a huge wave of relief as
He relaxed where he felt most comfortable
2170 And at last shed the burden of leading
The Western world against all terrorists.

In his safe house near Tehran bin Laden,
Caliph of a new Baghdad Caliphate,
Mourned the death of his third son Saad, who had
2175 Relocated with him to Tehran and
Been killed by a US drone attack in
North Waziristan's lawless tribal belt,
A Hellfire missile from a Predator
Which the CIA had operated
2180 Remotely from a ground control station
(GCS) at Creech, Nevada. It sent
Commands via a fibre-optic link to
A satellite relay station within
Europe, that were bounced into space and passed
2185 To the Predator whose take-off was launched
By a launch-and-recovery team inside
Afghanistan. It targeted his Saad,
One of his twenty-six children by four
Wives. He grieved for Saad, loss gnawed at his chest,
2190 But he was consoled he still had Hamza,
His youngest who had led one of the four
Gangs sent to assassinate Benazir
Bhutto. So many had been struck by drones
And blown to pieces in a hero's death:
2195 Abu Jihad al-Masri, al-Qaeda's
Intelligence chief; Khalid Habib, head
Of operations in Pakistan, fourth-
In-command of al-Qaeda; then Abu
Khabab al-Masri, explosives expert;
2200 And Abu Laith al-Libi, commander
In Afghanistan. He himself had shunned
The drones by conveying the impression
He was in North Waziristan like Saad,

Under Haqqani protection, or else
2205　　　　　　　　Farther north in remote Chitral region.
　　　　　　　　　　Though still devastated, professional, he
　　　　　　　　　　Looked back on the war against the US
　　　　　　　　　　That began in 1979 with
　　　　　　　　　　The capture of the US Embassy
2210　　　　　　　　By the young Ahmadinejad *et al.*
　　　　　　　　　　In Tehran; escalated in nineteen
　　　　　　　　　　Eighty-three with bombings of the US
　　　　　　　　　　Embassy and Marine Barracks, Beirut,
　　　　　　　　　　And the US Embassy in Kuwait,
2215　　　　　　　　And later its annexe; and gathered pace
　　　　　　　　　　With the hijackings of Kuwait Airways
　　　　　　　　　　Flight 221 and TWA
　　　　　　　　　　Flight 847, and then of the cruise ship
　　　　　　　　　　Achille Lauro and the murder of
2220　　　　　　　　A disabled US tourist. There were
　　　　　　　　　　Bombings in Rome and Vienna airports,
　　　　　　　　　　And at La Belle Discotheque in Berlin,
　　　　　　　　　　For which Libya was bombed, which then led to
　　　　　　　　　　The murder of three US professors
2225　　　　　　　　At the University of Beirut.
　　　　　　　　　　Then his own contribution began with
　　　　　　　　　　The 1993 World Trade Center
　　　　　　　　　　Bombing, and in 1996 he
　　　　　　　　　　Had declared war on America and
2230　　　　　　　　The West, while al-Qaeda bombed a US
　　　　　　　　　　Housing complex in Saudi Arabia.
　　　　　　　　　　Then came 1998 African
　　　　　　　　　　Embassy bombings and the two-thousand
　　　　　　　　　　Attack on the *USS Cole*, and on
2235　　　　　　　　September the eleventh 2001
　　　　　　　　　　Attacks on US soil. These were followed
　　　　　　　　　　By 2002 attacks in Bali
　　　　　　　　　　And Kenya, and 2003 attacks
　　　　　　　　　　In Casablanca and Istanbul. Then
2240　　　　　　　　Al-Qaeda's 2004 bombing of
　　　　　　　　　　Madrid and of the US Consulate
　　　　　　　　　　In Jeddah, and in 2005 of
　　　　　　　　　　London. There'd been a Muslim uprising
　　　　　　　　　　In France, and soon all French nuclear weapons
2245　　　　　　　　Would be shipped to Quebec for safe keeping
　　　　　　　　　　And *Sharia* would pass into French law.
　　　　　　　　　　Also in hostile Europe the Turkish
　　　　　　　　　　Republic would be destroyed and replaced
　　　　　　　　　　By a new Islamic Republic. He

2250	Would win. The Taliban Government had
	Been toppled and democracy planted,
	But it was withering, the Taliban
	Would soon be back. Saddam had been toppled
	And democracy planted in Iraq,
2255	But the *jihad*ist insurgency in
	Iraq, run from Iran with Syrian help,
	Would soon bring back Islamists, who'd declare
	Baghdad as "base" of the new Caliphate.
	The US would withdraw all combat troops
2260	From Iraq's cities and hand over to
	The Iraqi army's Muslim troops by
	July 2009. Victory was his.
	All these events since 1979 –
	With help from Iran's Revolutionary Guards
2265	And "re-elected" Ahmadinejad –
	Would sweep *jihad*ists and their Caliphate
	To power throughout the Muslim world. It would
	Extend from Morocco to Pakistan
	And reach into Europe. Like Saladin
2270	He was poised, when the Americans left,
	To bring Armageddon to the US,
	Set off a nuclear Hiroshima
	And force the whole world to become Muslim
	And live as conquered in his Caliphate.
2275	He would defeat President Obama
	Just as he'd defeated President Bush.
	His war against the US would be won:
	A thirty-year war that would terminate
	The thousand-year Western predominance
2280	That first conquered Jerusalem during
	The Western occupiers' First Crusade,
	And the humiliation of Muslims.
	His war had reversed the Muslims' deep hurt.
	Now Obama began to implement
2285	New measures that would bring change. He announced
	Guantánamo would close within a year
	But had no idea where the worst prisoners
	Would go, including sixteen high-value
	Prisoners such as Khalid Sheikh Mohammed,
2290	The self-confessed 9/11 mastermind.
	The idea soon unravelled as former
	Inmates appeared on terrorist websites
	And the EU was lukewarm at taking
	Dangerous detainees who were insurgents.

2295	And five months later there was still no plan.
	It showed the world a good PR posture
	But no one had spotted the solution.
	Then it was announced trials would continue
	At Guantánamo Bay as under Bush,
2300	At tribunals Obama had condemned.
	He banned "waterboarding", pouring water
	Into prisoners' nostrils and throats so they
	Inhaled water and thought that they would drown –
	Which on radio Cheney had agreed with –
2305	And all forms of torture. He also banned
	Extraordinary rendition, flying men
	To Arab countries where they could be forced
	To talk through "pressure", a form of torture.
	He banned the authorising of covert,
2310	Secret CIA assassinations.
	He planned to put Cheney, Rumsfeld and Rove
	Before a special prosecutor who'd
	See if they should face criminal charges.
	Cheney condemned him for his damaging
2315	Security policy and argued
	There had been no attack on the US
	Since 9/11 as it had followed through,
	Stayed true by going on the offensive.
	He appointed Ed Mitchell to review
2320	Afghan and Pakistani policy.
	Working towards a new secret peace plan,
	He said he wanted to abolish all
	Nuclear weapons, and proposed the US
	And Russia should cut theirs 80 per cent.
2325	He said he would withdraw ninety thousand
	US troops from Iraq by next August,
	2010, but that fifty thousand
	Would stay on. Twenty-one thousand withdrawn
	Troops would be sent on to Afghanistan
2330	As a Bush-style surge – an idea he'd scorned.
	He told the Muslim world, "Americans
	Are not your enemy," and broadcast to
	Iran asking for talks, addressing it
	Respectfully by its formal name as
2335	"The Islamic Republic of Iran".
	This may have been a snub to Israel and
	The "Rothschild" forces that withdrew the five
	Hundred and fifty billion dollars that
	Brought on America's economic
2340	Crisis; a way of showing defiance.

He worked on his seven-hundred-billion
Rescue package which had been first proposed
Under Bush's presidency. He changed
His position from the left-wing, liberal
2345   Candidate to post-partisan, centrist
President-Elect and back again to
The ultraliberal President, and was
Slippery and hard to grasp. His "card-check" bill
Removed secret ballots from unions
2350   Who could now intimidate into strikes.
America was having its first taste
Of redistributive socialism,
And many who voted for him were shocked.
They hankered after the Republicans.
2355   But more approved of the Peaceful Era.

Obama carried out the policies
Of Christ's Millennium in urging that
Nuclear weapons should be abolished
Over many years through a program to
2360   Reduce and prevent proliferation.
Bush had implemented Christ's wish to block
Fiery Armageddon by suitcase bombs,
Prevent a Caliphate New World Order
In which Islam would dominate nations.
2365   He had done his job, history had moved on.
The end of an era had come to pass,
And a new era had begun with hope.
Bush's way, though necessary and right,
Was now derided, scorned as all admired
2370   The new way of idealism and hope,
The saying of things all wanted to hear
Even though policies had not changed much.

Now Christ returned to Jerusalem and
Materialised on the Mount of Olives
2375   Where Zechariah forecast the Messiah
Would return: "And his feet shall stand in that
Day upon the mount of Olives." He was
Near the Garden of Gethsemane where
He had been betrayed, to Jerusalem's east,
2380   Opposite Golgotha, place of the skull,
Where he had been crucified, to the west.
Just as a rabbit crawls under a fence
And bounces onto a newly mown lawn
And looks for plants it can invade and gnaw

2385	While watching out for the irate owner,
	So Christ on dusty Jerusalem wasteground
	Looked for people he could sidle towards
	And sound out about the two-state problem
	While being wary of authorities.
2390	He stood in off-white, lone, unrecognised,
	And looked across to distant Temple Mount
	And heard a Likud speaker tell a throng
	In anticipation of the February-
	The-tenth election, "Kadima leader,
2395	Tzipi Livni, in negotiations
	With her Palestinian counterpart
	Ahmed Qureia over fourteen months,
	Agreed to divide the city, give up
	Where we're standing to Palestinians.
2400	We did not return to Jerusalem
	After paying for it to be rebuilt
	For two thousand years just to give it up.
	We did not unite Jerusalem in
	Order to divide it, and Likud will
2405	Maintain a united Jerusalem."
	Then he added, "A sane country does not
	Give its capital to its enemies."
	Christ saw volunteers bustling about,
	Seeking to buy properties from Arabs
2410	To reclaim city property for Jews.
	The speaker pointed to the cemetery.
	"The people buried here prayed there would be
	A day when Jerusalem'd be rebuilt.
	This election is about whether our
2415	Capital will pass to our enemies."
	A few Arabs heckled from a rooftop,
	Called out, "This district is ours and not yours."
	Christ moved away, in off-white robes that did
	Not stand out unduly, that blended in.
2420	Deep down Christ did not want the Crusaders'
	Holy City Jerusalem to be
	Divided, but if that had to happen
	To deliver a peaceful Middle East
	He would accept it. He was still cross with
2425	The central banks that withdrew the whopping
	Five hundred and fifty billion to sweep
	Aside Olmert's reluctant promise to
	Surrender East Jerusalem and give
	Up Temple Mount to further Muslim rule.
2430	Partitioning Jerusalem would be

A realistic solution, a sop
To Mohammed and Muslim followers.

Christ went to the site of David's palace
North-east of the nine-acre Jebusite
2435   City in Jerusalem and found where
Phoenician carpenters and stonemasons
Sent by Hiram, King of Tyre, erected
From cedars of Lebanon and from stone
A magnificent court the Philistines
2440   Could not capture. He stood on the stepped-stone
Foundation that had held up David's home,
And saw where David's throne had stood before
Its destruction by Nebuchadnezzar
In 587 BC when the last king,
2445   Zedekiah, saw his sons being killed,
Ending his line of Jerusalem kings
Which had lasted nearly five hundred years.
Through his daughters, who had gone to Egypt,
David's line continued, through marriage, in
2450   The kings of Ireland, Scotland and England –
Which held the Stone of Scone, Jacob's pillow
At Bethel and later the *Lia Fail*
Or Stone of Destiny on Tara's hill –
In accordance with Nathan's promise to
2455   David mentioned in *2 Samuel* that God
Would establish "the throne of his kingdom
Forever". And the United Kingdom
Continued the first united kingdom
Of Israel and Judah which Saul conjoined,
2460   The land of Joseph's tribe of Israelites.
Now Christ ruled from the spiritual throne
Of David over spiritual Zion.
He had never intended to set up
A physical Zion and Kingdom's throne.
2465   He had worked out how to project his new
Spiritual Kingdom, which, once God had given
Approval to flooding leaders with Light
And once it had been announced in Heaven,
Would charge the Light that flows into leaders,
2470   Influxes that surge through the souls to minds
And brains of leaders of all faiths, received
In Universalist equal measure,
And would affect their war-or-peace choices
And change the atmosphere on Earth to peace:
2475   A Kingdom of universal order.

BOOK TWELVE

UNIVERSAL ORDER:
A NEW HEAVEN AND A NEW EARTH

SUMMARY

1966-2010	Bush sees space-time resembling a half-opened fan or shuttlecock or tapering glass bowl. He returns to Dallas.
2011-2026	Bush and the universe.
2027-2145	Influxes of Light as leaders meet: Abdullah II of Jordan and Obama. Mohammed returns and speaks to Abdullah. Obama does not listen to Christ.
2146-2293	The Hidden *Imam* returns and urges Ahmadinejad to undermine Abdullah II of Jordan's peace plan.
2294-2414	Christ's vision of coming world government. Dream of world state.
2415-2481	World harmony opposed by disharmonious events.
2482-2556	Obama secretly tries to strike a deal with the Taliban, who are still hostile and press on the Western frontier.
2557-2583	Blair visits the Pope and urges him to "modernise" the Church.
2584-2762	Swine flu, a laboratory-involved revival of Spanish flu in Mexico, possibly deliberately unleashed by pro-Syndicate Jewish hard-liners to make the economic crisis worse.
2763-2784	Netanyahu meets Obama.
2785-2874	Obama speaks to the Muslim world.
2875-2987	Christ anticipates the future in Iran and Israel.
2988-3043	Satan is confined to Hell and presents his confinement in a favourable light: his followers should now work for a *coup* to install a fifth column in Heaven.
3044-3157	Christ stands on the site of Armageddon and reflects that the dire prophecies will not happen.
3158-3262	Invocation to Apollo as god of Wisdom, the Tenth Muse.
3263-3330	The poet is visited by Tennyson.
3331-3430	Invocation to Ezra Pound, who had told the poet he would be able to write a poetic epic.
3431-3458	Invocation to the Light invoked by the Jamkaran well in Iran.
3459-3495	Two images of *Armageddon*.
3496-3619	The poet is visited by Christ in his room.
3620-3735	Christ in the poet's knot-and-herb garden. Christ's optimism about the future.

O John, evangelist who knew the Christ
And took part in the Last Supper and sipped
From the Holy Grail, held it in your hands,
Who was banished from Rome to this Patmos,
5   Once more I seek your second sight, again
I find you in the cave you occupied
Like bin Laden, wearing a towel to hide
My bare legs in fierce heat so I am not
Barred from the Cave of the Apocalypse
10   For wearing shorts frowned on by black-clad monks.
I see the railed-off corner where you slept

When you had your awesome vision of Heaven
And dictated what you saw to Prochorus,
Your follower who used this sloping wall
15   As a book-rest, and predicted the reign
Of the Antichrist and tribulation
Which you saw would precede Armageddon
When the Beast and the kings of the Earth and
Their armies would make "war against him that
20   Sat on the horse and against his army"
And the Beast would be taken. O John who
Handled the Grail and dreamt Armageddon,
Help me again now I come to apply
Your vision to contemporary events.
25   Your images are clear, interpret them
For I can see an ambiguity:
I see a blatant Muslim Antichrist
And a Christian President allied to
A fierce Satan-worshipping Syndicate.
30   As I narrate Bush's triumph over
Bin Laden's Antichrist Darkness and his
False Prophet, Ahmadinejad, heir to
Khomeini, and the final rescue, Christ's
Thousand-Year Reign, I must also narrate
35   Bin Laden's triumph over the US-
Syndicate Antichrist Darkness and its
False Prophet, and the final rescue from
Chaos, Mohammed's Thousand-Year Reign via
The Hidden *Imam*'s wished Second Coming.
40   O John, my story of Crusaders is
Undermined by mirroring Crusaders,
And both sides claim the Grail and both predict
An Armageddon for Jerusalem,
A final battle in the Middle East
45   In which nuclear weapons will prevail.
O John, the younger civilisations
Always defeat the older, and the North
American civilisation is
Much younger than the Arab Islamic.
50   No one believes the Americans will lose
To Islam, but with wmds
One just cannot be certain. Please help me
Now I come to narrate the hardest part,
The accommodation reached in Heaven that
55   Gave equal representation for all
Religions in a Universalist
New Deal for all spirits and – as above,

So below – its reflection here on Earth,
Power-sharing between faiths in a federal
60   World government of regions whose leaders
Talk in video-teleconferences.
Help me now I come to define a new
Universalist Millennial Kingdom.

O Augustus, you who ruled Rome after
65   Defeating Antony in the battle
Of Actium, as *Princeps*, Emperor,
From 29 BC to AD 14,
Overthrew the Republic of Caesar
Who had adopted you as Octavian,
70   And reigned over a vast Roman Empire;
You who were ruler during the lifetimes
Of Virgil, Horace, Ovid, Tibullus,
Who wrote polished, sophisticated verse
Addressed to you or a patron such as
75   Maecenas, on themes of love, Nature and
Patriotism, you who continued
The Golden Age of Roman literature
Which began with Cicero from 70
And burgeoned under you from 43,
80   Which emphasised the Augustan virtues
Of civil peace and prosperity in
Peaceful, country living, urbanity
And respect for all in Rome's great Empire
Which extended through most of the known world,
85   The New World Order of your global time;
I find you in your Palatine villa –
The house you grew up in which gave our word
"Palace", from which you seized power when Caesar
Was assassinated, and made your home
90   Until you moved to a larger palace –
In the lower floor decorated with
Sober frescoes that shunned ostentation:
A small bedroom in vibrant red, turquoise,
Purple adorned with small horses and nymphs,
95   And a larger room in *trompe-l'oeil* style with
Narrow doorways, comic and tragic masks
Which suggested artistic patronage,
A sober design recently restored
From rubble and dust, tiny fragments pieced
100   Together, all frescoes original.
Help me now I come to describe a world
Order that accommodates the whole Earth,

A *koiné* in which all cities take part,
But not ruled by one superpower alone,
105   A shared draw between the West and the East
Of checks and balances, a compromise,
A Universalist New World Order
Of opposites reconciled, in balance;
For the West, though undefeated, has not
110   Spread its hegemony across the globe
So history is still conflicting events
Within stages of civilisations:
Sectored, multipolar world that heralds
The triumph of universal order.

115   O Marcel Dupré, master organist
Whose phenomenal memory retained
All organ music and who improvised
The most complex musical forms – five-part
Fugues with a regular counter subject,
120   Whose fingers exuded composition
And who rivalled for technical deftness
And dexterity the great J.S. Bach,
Conveyed divine universal order,
I sit in the choir of your Saint-Sulpice,
125   Gaze up at your hundred-and-one-stop organ
And listen to a hundred harmonies
Swell round the towering barrel vaults and towers
And sunburst above the forward altar,
Now gentle antiphon from your *Les Vêpres*
130   (One of fifteen improvisations you
Were persuaded by Rolls Royce's MD
To commit to paper) and now the last
Of *Sept Pièces*, a toccata on BACH
(B flat, A, C, the H representing
135   B natural in German musical
Notation) thematic, expansive chords
That swell, modulating polyphonies,
Played by my younger brother who came here
When he was fifteen and met you and heard
140   You play your house organ at Meudon, who's
Now sixty and retiring, giving this
Recital with Neary and Choplin. I
Find you, invisible, seated on chair
Between the choir-stalls where I sit, and see
145   You nod with approval at harmonies
You once improvised, letting Heaven speak
Through you nimble fingers while in this life.

And I hear Heaven's harmonies cross the line
Of the brass gnomon in the stone pavement,
150 An eighteenth-century sundial which follows
Variations in the height of the sun
At noon, along which through a lens cut in
The south-transept window the luminous disk
Of the sun crosses its meridian
155 Line at a point that moves during each year,
Either end of which marks the solstices;
The summer when sun, at its highest point
Relative to the horizon, falls on
A marble plaque in the south-transept floor,
160 The winter when, sun at its lowest point,
The image crosses an obelisk at
A line chiselled in stone. Equinoxes
Are marked when the sun's image appears on
An oval copper plaque on the altar
165 Floor. This church survived the Revolution,
Whose mob was told the complex gnomon was
A revered scientific instrument,
And instead of burning down Saint-Sulpice
It defaced the name of God from the stone
170 Obelisk (for Heaven had been suppressed
By the Republic's proud revolutionaries)
And made it the Temple of Victory.
I muse below the round transept windows,
One containing a P and one an S –
175 For Pierre (Peter) and Sulpice, the Church says,
Or Priory of Sion, Plantard asserts –
And, filled with booming sound from the baroque
Organ-pipes high over the far entrance
Which consume space between eight stone columns,
180 Watching the tiny dot of my brother
Channel Heaven to this meridian place,
I sense the harmony of souls in Heaven,
Of God the Creator, maker of time.
O Dupré, help me now I must describe
185 How billions of souls who warred here on Earth
Can be reconciled in Heaven's unity
And how the Millennium can harmonise
All the discordant dissensions of men
In different nation-states, religions, creeds,
190 And achieve a blending of opposites
So there is oneness in diversity;
Yet there is still diversity, local
Regional differences, within oneness.

And later at Notre-Dame, I stand in
195 The nave and gaze up at the rose-window
On the north side, an image which adorns
My hunt for pattern among twenty-five
Civilisations, and Neary greets me
Before his afternoon recital here
200 On the hundred-and-thirteen-stop organ,
And then sit at the back and hear the choir
Treble an antiphonal overture
With "*Le Seigneur qui nous a faite: oui, il
Est notre dieu*", melodic, sublime beauty,
205 Choral angels echoing through Notre-Dame
In mellifluous, serene counterpoint,
And then stand for the *entrée* and a swung
Smoking censer, and gasp as the organ
Swells a message of divine harmony
210 And a priest sings, "*Jubilate Deo!*"
I know Heaven is active in our sounds
As silence nurtures its offspring, space-time,
And think of the Surfer, my conundrum
Which I have posed to sick philosophy
215 That's nourished by junk logic and language,
Not the fruit-and-veg of the universe,
Whose diet's left it etiolated,
A post-Einsteinian Zeno's Paradox:
If his feet are on the crest of the wave
220 Of the fan-shaped expanding universe
That surges forward into a darkness,
He stands on space-time, which foams round his shins,
But what does his chest breast? No secular
Philosopher can answer, each asserts
225 The question has no meaning as all life
Is within space-time. Yet what does he breast?
His feet are in space-time, his breast – outside –
Rushes forward into the infinite
Whose emptiness is all around his eyes.
230 Feet in space-time, breast in the infinite –
The Surfer is a crouching paradox
Who embodies contradictory terms –
Space-time and infinite – that are conjoined
As his ankles are conjoined to his chest.
235 I ponder a reconciliation
Of opposites philosophy denies,
Unity of time and the eternal,
Challenge the reason with a conundrum,
Pose to all a baffling Oxymoron

240 And know the infinite in finite lives,
How Heaven can be apprehended in time,
Meaning within the flux, purpose in flow,
And how order pervades Nature's system
And with its harmony drives the pattern
245 Of this ever-improving universe.

Bush sat in 10141 Daria
Place in Preston Hollow, an upper-class
District of Dallas where the Bushes lived
Now they had left the White House. Two oak trees
250 Shaded the front yard, and Secret-Service
Agents manned the cul-de-sac barrier,
Occupied the house next door. He now held
A book inscribed to him, "The twenty-first
Century is the American century,"
255 In the English author's hand. He had closed
His eyes, knowing thought is a force as real
As a current of electricity,
That what we imagine in our lone thought
Attracts the infinite power that imbues
260 The universe, and, as Light, permeates
All species with its pulse-ordering drive.
And now his mind was stilled into a lake
Where he saw a point, a reflected star,
As he gazed, a dim moon broke through his cloud
265 And brightened to a blob above the lake
And slowly turned into a dazzling sun
Of white Light too strong to look at without
Averting his gaze as if looking at
The brilliant sun. The Light flooded his dark
270 And lit up his lake with a reflecting
Lily whose silver bowl was inner Light,
So he was filled with an inflowing power.
He breathed slowly and sank into a drowse
Almost as deep as sleep, left his body
275 And went within to an imaginary
Sunlit nightscape that was imaged and real,
For imagination sees images
Of forms not present to the senses that
Are in elusive Being. It is not
280 Making up what has not but might have been.
A great peace spread over him as he basked
In inner Light, his body paralysed.
Then he heard a voice say quietly, "George."

Bush opened his eyes, filled with influxes
285   And enlightenment below his reason,
His inner core cleansed of his senses' grime,
And saw Christ standing before him, wearing
Off-white robes with hands outstretched. Bush came to
And felt instantly alert. "You again,"
290   Bush said, wearing a blue windbreaker with
The presidential seal sewn over his
Left breast. "I'm more relaxed down in Texas.
I read the *Dallas Morning News* first thing,
It's better than national security
295   Threats. Laura found this place, it's just a mile
From where we used to live in the old days.
I like the floor-to-ceiling bookcases.
They line the hallways, fireplace and windows.
Each day I take Laura coffee in bed.
300   I email my aides on my BlackBerry
And go and write my book, sit with a speech-
Writer in my Dallas office. I get
There around half past seven. Well, I go
For a bike ride in the afternoons, read
305   Or watch golf or baseball on TV in
The evenings. At the weekends we go out
To our ranch in Crawford. I wake early
And roam the sixteen-hundred-acre woods
With a chain-saw and cut out new bike trails.
310   Once a week I make a speech to raise funds
For my new three-hundred-million-dollar
Presidential centre which is planned to
Be at Dallas's Southern Methodist
University that will explain my
315   Key decisions as President. History
Will judge me fairly. I am enjoying
My life in retirement. The only cloud
Is talk of torture charges. I'm surprised
That Obama is going down that route."
320   Christ said, "I know what it's like to be scourged,
Tortured by a State machine. I can say
You were trying to establish the guilt
Of Khalid Sheikh Mohammed and others
Who planned 9/11. It's a fine line
325   Between establishing pre-existing guilt
And forcing confessions when there's no guilt."
Bush said, "I'm satisfied we did the first.
History will judge me if that's not the case."
Christ nodded and said, "I have come today

330	To express Heaven's thanks for what you did,
	For standing up to nuclear terrorists
	Who wanted to set off Armageddon.
	I have a surprise for you. Come with me."
	Bush asked, "Where are we going?" Should I change?"
335	And suddenly – whoosh! – he was whirled inside
	A vortex, spinning deep up a black hole,
	Rising with Christ beside him through the dark
	Into the fourth dimension of Being,
	Rapt, snatched out of his physical body,
340	Which he had shed like a blue windbreaker.
	It only lasted a few seconds, he
	Did not have time to panic. Then, as when
	A vast lift ascends a skyscraper and
	Slows down near the top for a gentle jolt,
345	His progress slowed and he alighted at
	A misty reception area that
	Resembled a train station with barriers.
	"This is Purgatory," Christ announced. "I'll leave
	You with your guide and we will meet later."
350	Bush found himself in a misty foyer
	That seemed an annexe of Purgatory
	(Which rumour wrongly claimed Pope Benedict
	The Sixteenth had declared does not exist).
	A vaporous, translucent shape approached
355	With clear grey beard and hair. "President Bush,"
	The guide said. "Welcome. I was a General.
	But I did not fight abroad as you did,
	Unless the North's abroad. Robert E. Lee."
	"The leader of the Southern Army," Bush
360	Gasped. "Yes," Lee said. "You're a Southerner, from
	Texas, one of the seceding states, though
	Texas was not in my theatre of war.
	I, too, was involved in epic battles.
	Richmond was our Troy – rather, Camelot
365	For I was our Arthur and led the Knights
	Of the Golden Circle, whose centre was
	Havana and included plantations
	In all the Southern states and Mexico,
	In Central America and the north
370	Of South America and West Indies,
	A slave empire to rival ancient Rome,
	That would produce the most cotton, sugar,
	Tobacco in the world, a noble dream.
	But it was tainted by slavery. I

375   Was not tainted, I freed my slaves before
      The Civil War, and loved the chivalry.
      As Arthur I was *Dux Bellorum*. Jeb
      Stuart was both Galahad and Gawain.
      All the Knights were Southern Jurisdiction
380   Freemasons led by General Pike, and rode
      Round the countryside to the west, south, east
      Opening up castles and doing good deeds
      That appealed to romantic Southern minds.
      Caleb Cushing provoked the Civil War
385   By urging the Pierce Administration
      To pass the Kansas-Nebraska Act which
      Divided Nebraska into Kansas
      And Nebraska, which then had to decide
      Whether to have slavery. Arson attacks
390   And murders by pro-Slavery Missourians
      And massacres by abolitionists
      Under John Brown followed. I myself crushed
      John Brown's slave insurrection at Harper's
      Ferry, Virginia. Then Pike organised
395   The rebellion of the Southern states through
      Scottish Rite Freemasonry, and concealed
      The political and military
      Leadership of the Confederacy
      Within his Freemasonry, and controlled
400   The Knights of the Golden Circle. We fought
      To restore our independence and keep
      The plantations going and not bound by
      Union legislation. And President
      Buchanan put in Government posts all
405   Who were sure to start a Southern revolt.
      Like him, they were Masons. Officially
      Threatened by Lincoln's appointment, the states
      Seceded: South Carolina, and then
      Mississippi, Florida, Alabama,
410   Georgia, Louisiana and Texas.
      I was in command in Texas that day.
      General Beauregard's surprise attack on
      The US-held Fort Sumter now began
      The Civil War. Four more states seceded:
415   Arkansas and North Carolina, then
      Tennessee – and Virginia. Richmond
      In Virginia became the capital
      Of the Confederacy's eleven states,
      And the Confederate flag had thirteen stars
420   As the Masonic Templars were suppressed

On Friday the thirteenth. Then McLellan
Invaded West Virginia and fought
Battles at Philippi's Rock Mountain and
Carrick's Ford. In spring 1861
425   Richmond looked doomed. I refused an offer
To command a new army and force all
Seceded states into the Union.
I resigned from the army and became
Commander-in-Chief of Virginia's
430   Forces. The Confederates won a battle
At Manassas under Beauregard and
Johnston. Next year McLellan tried to take
Richmond, but I helped Stonewall Jackson fight
Him off as he pincered from east and north
435   In the Shenandoah Valley. At last
I was made General-in-Chief of all
Confederate forces, and in Seven Days'
Battles round Richmond I fought McLellan
Off and my troops had mystical belief
440   In all I did. I was a hero, like
You at the falls of Kabul and Baghdad.
But I never believed that I could win.
It was poignant, fighting with loyal troops
In a certain lost cause, being conquered
445   From the north like Arthur in the Southern
Favourite, Tennyson's *Idylls of the King*.
I aimed to keep the enemy as far
From Richmond and the states' northern crops which
Fed the Confederacy, and defeat
450   The enemy to weaken his resolve.
This worked for two years. Yet New Orleans
Fell, then Vicksburg, and Atlanta. Jackson
And I beat Pope at Second Manassas.
I invaded the north once more, but my
455   Plans fell into the enemy's hands. I
Retreated after the stalemate battle
At Antietam. I had victories
At Fredericksburg and Chancellorsville where,
Outnumbered two to one, I split my troops
460   And audaciously encircled Hooker's
Troops. Unfortunately Stonewall Jackson
Was mortally wounded by his own troops.
I crossed the Potomac and invaded
The north again but, without Jackson, was
465   Let down by three generals and repulsed
At Gettysburg, and was forced to retreat.

Now I was criticised, as you have been.
I know what it is like when low morale
Saps confidence. And now my luck ran out.
470   In May 1864 Ulysses
Grant, the new commanding general of
The Union, advanced against me and fought
Me at the Wilderness, Spotsylvania
Court House, the North Anna river and Cold
475   Harbor. Grant and I lost fifty thousand
Men in two months. Grant replaced his losses
With fresh recruits and was just seven miles
From Richmond. My troops had been weakened and
Were inexperienced. I was frequently
480   Ill and lost the initiative. Grant moved
South and besieged Petersburg for nine months,
My rail link to the South. All I could do
Was place starving tatterdemalions
In defensive lines before Petersburg
485   And Richmond. Grant built fortifications
Like trenches in the field, strengthened the siege.
I knew it was just a question of time.
My starving defensive lines were too thin
And could not withstand Grant's massive assaults
490   For long. On April the second he broke
Through at Five Forks and uncovered Richmond.
My men fell back, retreated for a week,
Falling from hunger, animals dropping.
Then Richmond was on fire, our Camelot
495   And neither I nor my Arthurian Knights
Could do anything to save it except
Surrender at Appomattox Court House –
In the parlour of the McLean house there –
On April the ninth. Lincoln was supreme.
500   But the Southern insurrection had been
Financed by the Freemasonic Rothschilds,
Who had also funded the North, which was
To be British, annexed to Canada
Under Lionel Rothschild, whereas the South
505   Would be French under James Rothschild. 'Rothschilds'
Had offered Lincoln the same funding if
He authorised 'Rothschilds' to establish
A central bank. Lincoln had refused. Now
Triumphant Lincoln was killed by John Booth,
510   A Knight of the Golden Circle, also
A Freemason whose trunk contained coded
Messages. The key to the code was found

In the possession of 'Rothschilds' agent
Judah Benjamin. 'Rothschilds' killed Lincoln
515 On April the fourteenth, five days after
I signed the surrender. On May the tenth
Jefferson Davis, the Confederate
President, was imprisoned. Now my wife's
Old Arlington plantation was seized by
520 The US Government and I had no
Income and had to become President
Of Washington College in Lexington
So my seven children would not starve. I lost
My health. But to this day the South looks back
525 To a time when we continued the life-
Style of the first founding fathers, who came
In 1607 to Virginia,
When Bartholomew Gosnold and his group
Founded the Jamestown Settlement and his
530 Successors dished out fifty-acre plots
Which became the first plantations for crops
And brought the Tudors' agrarian ideal
To Southern Virginia and Richmond.
I look back at our Elizabethan
535 Way of life and see it extinguished by
A new industrial North, a bitterness
Romantic Southerners find hard to bear.
You restored hope, promising new estates
In far-off countries, a Southern ideal,
540 With your new Knights of the Golden Circle.
I know your thinking, Mr President,
Because I know Southern mentality.
But now I'm here, I have a larger view.
The Union had to hold. America
545 Has a world destiny and will promote
A New World Order led by Christ, who sees
Slavery as wrong, an idea of the past
We must all move on from. And so I say
To you, a Southern President, who rules
550 The world and sees the US destiny
To have a dominant world role, you have
Done well to disregard the legacy
Of the South and act as a superpower,
A strong, united America in
555 A strong, united world." Bush said, "You've caught
The Southern President's predicament
Perfectly, only today it's regret
A feeling, rather than rebellion and

Resignation, as you had to do. You
Had to take drastic action for the South.
I, a Southerner, have acted for all
America, for the Union. Progress
Demands that we're on Lincoln's side today,
For the abolition of slavery
That underpinned the Southern way of life."

Then Lee said, "But I'm digressing, I have
To tell you about Purgatory and show
You the museum, which we are proud of.
It's not about the past or the future,
It's possibility, a tendency
Which may happen but has not happened yet
And perhaps will never happen. Heaven's
Forecasters are showing certain wrong paths
Displayed in virtual reality.
The people shown were all alive when their
Images were created – most are still
Alive, some are not born. They've all taken
A wrong path. They're all cultural icons,
And their wrongness has left Western culture
In a big mess. So this is cautionary,
A museum like a Chamber of Horrors
In a waxworks like old Madame Tussauds.
As with waxworks, the display's constantly
Updated as new potential cultural
Disasters appear. There are hundreds here.
When projections turn out to have happened
Tendencies are mixed with memories from
Self-Improvement, and you see what they see.
We have time to see just a few, to show
How weak the cultural leadership is now
On Earth and how hard it will be to turn
Things round during the Millennial Kingdom.
This is a cautionary museum of
Wrong paths drawn from all aspects of culture.
It's called the 'Museum of Monstrous Dunces',
Living waxworks that warn all spirits who
Have just arrived how Earth's in Satan's grip
And how its attitudes must be unlearned
Before they can go on to Heaven. This is
A clearing-house, where spirits come from Hell,
Having done Self-Improvement, but are not
Quite ready for Self-Fulfilment in Heaven,
And where they learn the error of Earth's ways."

560
565
570
575
580
585
590
595
600

Lee had drawn Bush into an opening
605 Off the foyer, and now he saw a row
Of wraiths sitting in pointed dunces' hats
On benches, moving, virtually alive
Like holograms, 3-D images formed
By the interference of light beams from
610 A light source, projected into a room
But with no substantial reality
Like figures beamed from a cathode-ray tube.
Bush did not recognise their opaque forms
Or names hung on their transparent bodies.
615 Bush saw eight sitting in a row near him
And asked, "Who are they?" Lee said, "Scientists
Who got it wrong. The old man with the beard
Was alive when I lived: Darwin. He thought
All species developed through natural
620 Selection. That was right. And that humans
Are merely apes and cannot know the Light,
That death is the end, that we're then fossils.
He has found out that he was wrong and sits
Contemplating the error of his ways.
625 That hologram was made during his life.
He's at the centre of the group, who were
His disciples. That one debated with
A Bishop. That one copied his ideas
And applied them to genes, so slavishly
630 He paid for adverts on buses that said,
'There's probably no God.' He'll need a lot
Of Self-Improvement as he learns the truth.
He's on lists of atheists who do not
Want to know how space-time emerged to form
635 From formlessness, Non-Being, Nothingness.
He should be on a list of those who failed
To understand the beginning, before
Being spewed germs out of the Big Bang that
Became latent Existence. That one is
640 Also an atheist. He's a chemist
Who claims that the Earth is a "dunghill of
Purposeless interconnected" bleak and
Barren "corruption". He did not reckon
On the Light and miserably surveys
645 His wrongness. That one won a Nobel Prize
For discovering DNA's structure.
He applied biological thinking
To the brain, and held the astonishing
View that mind's only brain, and that its seat

650	Is in the claustrum. He has since found out
	That he's a spirit and is plunged in gloom.
	That one's a brain scientist who also
	Won a Nobel Prize for seeing the mind
	As thrown up by evolution. He thought
655	Death is the end and now realises
	His Nobel Prize was given for a wrong view.
	That one was a neurobiologist
	And lady Professor who saw the mind
	As ending on death and has found different.
660	With them is that one who demonstrated
	That the quantum vacuum is governed
	By an uncertainty principle, which
	Means he could not grasp the certainty that
	Lies behind the universe. It was he
665	That was uncertain, not the universe.
	And that one's a cosmologist who has
	Motor neurone disease and argues that
	There is nothing outside space-time, meaning
	He has not considered how Being burst
670	Into Existence with the Big Bang. What
	An omission. What a dunce. He cannot
	Believe how wrong he was. But tragically
	All of them had the same attitude to
	Death and taught the young wrong, spread disbelief
675	In an after-life, and materialism.
	They are all hopeless dunces who must learn
	How the universe works, not lead astray."
	Bush pointed to another bunch, dunces
	Sitting in a row on a bench. "And they?"
680	"Philosophers," Lee said with some disdain.
	"That scrawny one wrote a history of
	Western philosophy but held it was
	Illegitimate to ask the question
	As to what caused the universe as it
685	Had no meaning. He now knows otherwise
	And sits and grasps how he misled the young.
	And that wide-eyed one blew up, demolished,
	Philosophy, arguing that it was
	'A critique of language' and not about
690	The universe. He now knows he was wrong,
	And sits and fidgets, wishing that he'd done
	Things differently. And that smooth one advanced
	A verification principle to
	Debunk metaphysics and to 'prove' that
695	There's no spirit. He squirms at his error.

And that one said we're ghosts 'in a machine'.
He was miserably wrong and now knows it.
That one is French. He deconstructed books
And held there's no reality outside
700 The text: *'Il n'y a rien hors du texte.'*
He sits and contemplates reality,
Doing Self-Improvement within the Light,
Having found out his spirit survives death.
That one was also French. He has a cast
705 In one eye and now squints. He hailed free choice
But held 'Existence precedes essence' as
Humans exist and have not been designed.
Now he sits squinting in his dunce's cap,
Having found out there's a Law of Order
710 Which shapes all forms to a design that's in
The DNA, the code by which we grow,
And that he's a spirit who survived death.
He was completely wrong and peers for truth.
That one's quite old, a rationalist who
715 Split mind and body, basing existence
On thinking: 'I think, therefore I am.' He
Has since found out that he is a spirit
Who has influxes of Light. He has done
Self-Improvement, and has not yet finished."
720 "And that one?" Bush asked of the eighth. "Oh, he's
A 'popular philosopher' who held
That all is will, delved into the occult
And wrote about spiders, was quarrelsome
And dismissive of Light. But he now sees
725 He was in a wrong direction, that drive
Is in the spirit's influxes of Light
And requires reining-in of personal will.
He sees he missed the truth, misled the young."

"Many scientists and philosophers
730 Seem to have got it wrong," Bush said. "But what
About that quite large group?" "Writers," Lee said
With evident dislike and some loathing.
"They're a disreputable crowd. They all
Had strong opinions and held that nothing
735 Survives death. They've all found out they were wrong.
They've all damaged the culture of the West.
Those four were dramatists. One's in a rage
And sulks. He showed humans as angry and
Is now doing Self-Improvement as he
740 Missed what life was about. And that man was

Overrated, full of silences that
Were supposed to menace but were far from
The truth. He's now doing Self-Improvement,
And having been on lists of atheists
745   Now grasps he's a spirit that survived death.
That man was Czech but has an English name.
He was an absurdist who wrote 'witty'
Word games for men who're pondering their plight.
Just like that one, who wrote about two tramps
750   Who waited for a God who never came
And lacked purpose and did not understand
Why they were on Earth. Now he understands
That he was wrong, that spirits survive death.
Look, there are half a dozen novelists.
755   You wouldn't want to read any of their
Works. That one wrote narrative non-fiction,
A kind of journalism, and now knows
That there was more to life than he found out.
He's doing Self-Improvement and must learn
760   He's a spirit who is nourished by Light.
That one wrote about lecherous people
And has now found out that spirits must grow.
That one's an irascible curmudgeon
Who criticised phoniness and then spent
765   His life drinking at his club and snarling
And's doing Self-Improvement a long while
And reflecting that he took a wrong path.
And look, that one is his son, who shows off
His command of English in sentences
770   And there he sits and ponders that he should
Have included the spirit's thrust to Light.
That one wrote about the macabre and called
Himself an atheist. He realises
That his spirit has survived death and that
775   He was wrong to deny its goal on Earth.
And that one writes pretentiously about
Indians. He confused Mohammed with Hell
And put himself on lists of atheists.
He has now learned the error of his ways."
780   Then Lee said in dismay, "Next to them are
Three poets. They are a disparate lot.
That one was technically accomplished
But thought life on Earth was the only one
And whined about his lot in a depressed,
785   Negative tone that misled many young.
He's doing Self-Improvement, but look at

His body language, he's still complaining.
And that one tried to make the familiar
Strange by pretending to be a Martian,
790   A trick that did not portray human life,
And, a declared atheist, he now sees
That he was on a wrong path, and's spirit.
And that one there, that female laureate,
Said poetry's in tabloid headlines and pop,
795   Another who's on lists of atheists
And now sees that she's wrong and has misled
The young as she finds that spirit survives."
"And who's that one?" asked Bush. "He's a critic,"
Said Lee. "He could speak out for the open-
800   Minded, but he's on lists of atheists
And focuses on words like linguistic
Philosophers, not on the universe,
And having told his pupils that nothing
Survives death, sits and faces his wrongness.
805   For how can a critic be right if he
Thinks space-time and society are all
And that there's no spirit or after-life?
He now realises he should have spoken
Up for those who challenged the secular
810   World-view and wishes he'd done differently.
And over there are four so-called painters.
They're all very weak. That one dabbed screaming
Popes and bodies like bacon, and he thought
Nothing would survive death. He's now doing
815   Self-Improvement and grasps that he was wrong.
He was hugely overrated. That one
Is a pop artist. That female produced
An unmade bed as art, that one a dead
Shark. Western culture's in a terrible
820   State. Culture's supposed to reflect the heights
Of human aspiration and the truth
About life, which includes spirit and Light.
This Museum shows in hundreds of such forms
That Western culture has collapsed and its
825   Icons have let down three generations.
New spirits descend with this handicap.
But now look over here. A different sight."

Bush floated after Lee to another
Opening where more dunces sat on benches.
830   "More culture?" Bush asked. "No, politicians.
Or rather, leaders," Lee said. "You will know

Who that one is." Bush followed his finger
And saw a tall, bearded spirit-body
Leaning forward. "Bin Laden," he said. Lee,
835   The Southern Civil-War leader, said, "He
Is doing what I had to do, review
The consequences of his decisions,
The spirits he has led to their demise
In *jihad* wars and terrorist attacks.
840   He has to face the three thousand he killed
On 9/11 in unprovoked assault.
He claims he was avenging Muslim dead
Killed by Israel and the US, but such
Revenge is no excuse here. He conspired
845   Against his brother's partner, you. He will
Be doing Self-Improvement in due course."
"Self-Improvement," Bush said nervously. "Does
That not mean time in Hell?" "Yes," said Lee. "I
Know what that involves as I spent some time
850   There. But I got off lightly as the South
Was attacked by the North and self-defence
Was what I organised, and I did not
Have any slaves during the Civil War.
I was not thought of as a Freemason.
855   Heaven loathes Freemasons as the Syndicate
Has made the secret of Freemasonry
That Lucifer, Satan, is demiurge
Of the world and should be followed, not Christ.
And I fought by the rules of chivalry."
860   "I also fought in self-defence," Bush said.
"By pre-emptive attack," Lee said. "Where does
Self-defence end and aggression begin?
That one will interest you." Bush followed his
Finger and started. "Why," he said, "that's me."
865   "In hologram," Lee said, "like a waxwork."
"As a dunce," Bush said. "But how was I wrong?"
"You did know the existence of the Light.
You eschewed peaceful negotiation
For bull-at-a-gate toughness," Lee replied.
870   "Heaven always prefers negotiation.
See, you are sitting confronting your deeds.
But you are fortunate, Heaven's on your side.
You preserved the West's stability when
It was challenged, as Heaven wished. That's why
875   You're here now as a guest of Heaven. You too
Will get off lightly when your time comes. You
Will face the consequences of your deeds –

Everyone has to do that – and there may
Be a little Self-Improvement, but you
880   Will be fast-tracked to Heaven for doing its will.
You're shown here facing all the troops who died
On both sides as a result of your deeds,
And reflecting on *Shock and Awe*, which was
Disproportionately violent and
885   Endangered civilian life in Iraq.
You'll be assessed – 'judged' is the wrong word – by
A group of your peers and by a council
That will include both Christ and Mohammed.
All will agree defusing al-Qaeda
890   Is an important consideration
And excuses much of your pro-active,
Pre-emptive stance. Your attitude towards
The Syndicate will be crucial. They don't
Like the Syndicate in Heaven. Look at
895   That group." Bush, peering at where he pointed,
Said, "I half-recognise one." Lee said, "That
One's the first Rothschild, Mayer Amschel, who
Made a fortune from Waterloo and screwed
The Bank of England from the British State.
900   Through Adam Weishaupt he had been funding
The Order of the Illuminati
And become a Satanist. He controlled
The West throughout the next two hundred years.
He was behind the early Syndicate
905   That created the Federal Reserve.
He's been in Self-Improvement since he died
And he's still not ready to progress to here.
He can't renounce allegiance to Satan.
He had five sons, who were all Syndicate.
910   Look, there are some of the family today.
They control all the world's central banks save
A few. That one's Victor, Lord Rothschild, who
Was behind all the 1950s spies.
He was Burgess's landlord and tipped off
915   Philby, and ran the British Government's
Think-tank in the 1970s, which
Meant he could control much of the British
System. That's Jacob, Lord Rothschild, his son.
And on that side, John D. Rockefeller,
920   The 'Rothschilds'' *protégé* who borrowed from
Them, built the US railroads and opened
Standard Oil, 'Esso'. He too had five sons,
Who were all Syndicate. Look, that one is

David Rockefeller, who's been building
925   A world government that is to be run
By the Syndicate and will oppress all
The world's citizens. He was the one who
You half-recognised. He was co-founder
Of the Bilderberg Group, and's been behind
930   Most of the revolutions in the world
Since the Second World War and now he sits
And faces all the millions who have lost
Their lives in his local wars about oil
And in 'Rockefeller' population
935   Reduction programs. He will be doing
Self-Improvement for a very long time.
Bush said, "I half-recognise that dunce, there.
Who's that?" "That's Blair," Lee said, "Your British friend."
"What, Tony Blair?" Bush asked. "Who supported
940   Me?" "Yes," said Lee. "He lied to his people,
Told them Saddam could attack them within
Forty-five minutes with nuclear warheads.
See, he faces his many lies and spins,
So many he will sit for a long while.
945   He was duplicitous and yet proclaimed
That he's religious, if religion be
Entering the Church on your terms and telling
The Pope what to change if the rules are not
To your liking. He was a hypocrite,
950   And now he's gone, he's scarcely missed, for he
Was vacuous and evanescent, just
A superficial, smooth-talking PM
Who announced and re-announced and double-
And triple-counted but did not act, just
955   Conjured an illusion of safe-hands rule.
But enough of him, he was quite worthless.
You used him and then gave him a medal.
Oh, and you made him the Quartet's envoy,
A sinecure for cash and little work.
960   He's best forgotten now. Look, with him is
His successor, a warped socialist who
Wants all to be equal and uses tax
To suggest an equal society.
The trouble is, his spending was wasted
965   And now his people are in massive debt.
He was also a hypocrite, he claimed
To be prudent and yet was profligate,
Ran up the biggest debt for three hundred
Years without much to show for it. He sulks

970   And rages if his MPs question that.
        But forget them, they're not important. You
        Will be far more interested in that one.
        You recognise him." "Ronald Reagan," Bush
        Gasped. "What's he doing here? He won the Cold
975   War." "Gorbachev lost it," Lee said. "Reagan –
        A shallow actor who delegated
        And took the credit. He authorised raids
        That killed people, like one in Libya.
        Now he faces the consequences of
980   His deeds, but you're right, Heaven was on his side
        And wanted the Cold War ended. He has
        Done some Self-Improvement but has got off
        Lightly as Heaven's been lenient with him.
        And look, you recognise that one." "Yes," Bush
985   Said, "it's JFK. What has he done wrong?"
        "He was a womaniser," Lee said. "He
        Mistreated his wife and he now faces
        His misdeeds that hurt her. But as leader
        He raised expectations and did good things.
990   He stood up to the entire Syndicate.
        He stood up to Khrushchev and made him take
        Away the missiles he sent to Cuba,
        At 'Rockefellers'' encouragement, and
        He stood up to 'Rockefellers', who had
995   Plans to extract the oil of Vietnam
        And wanted the US to invade Vietnam.
        He tried to strip 'Rothschilds'' Federal Reserve
        Of the power to loan money and receive
        Interest, and Order 11110
1000   Signed on June the fourth 1963
        Was set to put the Fed out of business.
        The day after he was slain President
        Johnson escalated the Vietnam
        War. He was killed by the Syndicate and
1005   Heaven sees him as a martyr, and he
        Got off lightly. This hologram applied
        During his life but it's not actual now.
        Look, that one's Bill Clinton. See how he sits
        Justifying himself as he's impeached,
1010   How he rules by appearances? From him
        Blair took his reinventions of himself.
        But we won't waste time on Clinton. He helped
        The Syndicate and worked with Bilderberg.
        This one will interest you much more. You know
1015   Him." "It's Obama," Bush said. "Yes," said Lee.

"He promised too much and had no idea
How to solve the economy and bring
Peace to Afghanistan and to Iraq,
And defuse Iran. Now he sits and stares
1020   At all the votes he wrongly acquired through
False promises and wonders how to found
A New World Order, as the Syndicate
Expect him to do. He's the Syndicate's
Puppet, as you weren't. All things to all men."
1025   Bush said, "He's a great orator – just when
He reads from Autocues. Otherwise he's
Hesitant and nothing special. He was
Not born in America. He has not
Much idea of what needs to be done. He
1030   Is a bit of an impostor." Lee said:
"The Syndicate hope he'll calm the world down.
If he does that it won't matter that he's
Just a novice who is feeling his way.
He's on lists of atheists, he does not
1035   See outside space-time, he has no beliefs.
Like Blair he's malleable, his mind's a tape
On which the Syndicate can dictate plans
That he will implement, tidying up.
That's all I'll show you now. It's just a taste
1040   Of our 'Museum of Monstrous Dunces'. Now,
Come this way so we can see Purgatory.
But I now take my leave and pass you on
To your new guide who'll show you Purgatory."
With that Robert Lee faded into mist.

1045   Bush peered into gloomy Purgatory's mist
As his new guide emerged, floating in his
Transparent spirit-body, young in looks
And swagger, tousled, bearded, and greeted
Bush warmly: "Welcome, Mr President.
1050   Bartholomew Gosnold warmly greets you
Again. I'm glad we meet on this side now,
When I can be myself, far removed from
My skeleton. I don't like hovering
Over the relics of my swamp-fevered
1055   Lungs and forehead, and my starving stomach,
My whitened bones which have now shed all flesh.
My body was transient but our small band
Of daring mariners planted a new
Civilisation that's now permanent.
1060   We had a purpose greater than ourselves.

And I am proud that our America
Was born from the timber-framed dwellings we
Occupied in our rural East England.
We took risks and faced up to great dangers.
1065   We killed Indians. I've done Self-Improvement
For that and now know that was wrong. This way."
Bush followed where he floated through the mist.
"We're through the veil. Now look at Purgatory."
Bush found himself in brilliant sunshine in
1070   A meadow filled with fragrant summer flowers
That stretched as far as eye could see. Millions
Of shades sat or lolled in the open air.
"Who are they?" asked Bush. "Victims of terror,"
Gosnold replied. "It's a reunion. All
1075   These spirits were bombed, shot or beheaded
By terrorists, killed by suicide bombs,
Exploding belts or cars in markets or
Near checkpoints. They've all suffered great traumas.
Angels minister to them so they can
1080   Open their centres to the Light. If they
Do, they move on to Heaven. This is a large
Refugee camp where all who've glimpsed the Light
Receive training till their spirit-bodies
Are sufficiently subtle to proceed
1085   To Heaven. When they vacate these meadows, new
Spirits take their place, new victims. We were
Delighted your surge worked, it took the strain
Off our system here. About a million
Died from terror in Iraq in six years.
1090   All these spirits on this sunny plain grasp
That they chose their parents, hovering above
Them, and put on bodies like clothes, and then
Took them off like clothes when they left their lives.
They grasp that just as they chose their births, so
1095   They also chose paths that would help them grow
And have opportunities that would help
Them develop talents and head for Heaven,
And that eventually they chose their deaths –
From illness, accident or just worn out –
1100   Which would advance their spirits' destiny
And also ease loved ones' development.
Deaths are not ends but are also new births
Into the spirit world I occupy.
Deaths enable spirits to develop
1105   New qualities, help other spirits grow.
When seen from Heaven, all victims of terror

Go forward to a new phase in their growth.
Some deaths lead to needed Self-Improvement,
Some on to Self-Fulfilment in Heaven
1110 Where they minister to and 'nurse' others
Or return to Earth as Angels to guide.
It's all a kind of school. Spirits begin
At a level that's not unlike being
In *Kindergarten*, progress through 'primary'
1115 And 'secondary' to 'university'.
Some live among Heaven's archives as scholars
In a collegiate life, like dons on Earth.
Others pursue self-fulfilment in more
Practical ways, like your public servants.
1120 All spirits *do* something. None do nothing.
What do they do in Heaven? Whereas in Hell
They identify flaws and self-improve,
Eradicate error, open to Light
And, their shadows purged, move on to Heaven,
1125 In Heaven they contemplate, close to the Light
And create. They produce cultural works,
Live like artists. In Heaven creators –
Poets, philosophers, historians
And dramatists – are respected the most.
1130 All who made a living through money must
Be creative like impecunious
Artists. It *is* a topsy-turvy 'world',
The mighty are flung down to deepest Hell,
The meek are exalted to highest Heaven
1135 If they have opened to the Light and given
To their culture and civilisation.
From lowest Self-Improvement in Hell to
Highest Self-Fulfilment in Heaven, and
Rebirth on Earth to a new life when they
1140 Face similar challenges just as when
Failed examinees retake their exams,
All spirits, wherever they are, progress,
All at their own level and pace, just as
In mixed-ability classes at school
1145 Through individual attention pupils
Have different work and progress at their own
Speed and level, thanks to a teacher who
Is aware of each pupil's own level
And matches it with appropriate work
1150 That leads him or her to the next stage. So
In the spirit world teachers are welcomed.
Look, over there. That crowd is clapping in

New arrivals, congratulating them
On the efforts they've made to bring them here,
1155 For all's determined by how light is our
Being, how undense. When we've improved we
Have airy spirits free from dark shadow
And at the appropriate time are drawn
To this point automatically. Those
1160 Who have been teachers are the most warmly
Welcomed as their skills are much needed here.
Here all spirits learn from their mistakes and
When they go down to Earth for new spells there,
New lives, are tested and avoid their past
1165 Mistakes in their quest for self-perfection.
And when confronted with those they have hurt
They ask and receive forgiveness, move on.
It's best to do such asking down on Earth.
It's best to die there – be reborn here – with
1170 No backlog of forgiveness to work through.
So all the perpetrators of terror
Have long stretches of Self-Improvement where
Their deeds are played before them endlessly
And they must make amends to their victims
1175 By helping them in their new regions here.
Look at that screen." Bush looked and recognised
The caverned Underworld he had been to
And saw a horde of shadows sitting in
Cave-like dungeons with transparent shackles
1180 Round their legs. "They're doing Self-Improvement.
They see their misdeeds again and again
Like a snatch of film – 9/11 planes –
Repeated many times on TV screens.
They are tormented each time they relive
1185 Their callous deeds, how they wiped people out
With bombs or guns. And when they have improved
They will come here and mix with their victims
At reunions like this one. See these hordes
Sitting and standing on the grass – some are
1190 Improved and reformed perpetrators who
Can meet and talk to forgiving victims
So all spirits, shedding hate, can commune
In love. All spirits on that grassy plain
Have progressed beyond ego which obstructs
1195 The Light, have opened to the Light, and, see,
Have spirit-bodies that are radiant
With infused Light, and have no dense shadow,
And are now ready to live in pure love

And Light in Heaven as, at a new level,
1200 They work on projects that assist others
While implementing their Self-Fulfilment.
Nothing stands still in the spirit world, all
Is process and even the most perfect
Have projects which benefit others and
1205 Themselves. What do spirits do in Heaven?
They are far busier in their projects than
They were on Earth, but within a serene
Bliss and fulfilment filled with joy and love.
Every spirit can progress to that state,
1210 Even the vilest suicide bomber
Or cruellest tyrant who has killed millions.
Even Hitler and the worst al-Qaeda
Killer, Zarqawi, can end up serene,
But they'll have long spells of Self-Improvement
1215 And will have to live several lives to face
And repeat situations they abused,
Avoid remaking their violent mistakes.
I am Bartholomew Gosnold, but I
Am also two others whose lives I led
1220 When my spirit was re-educated
On Earth in Re-education. It is
A wonderful system: first challenges,
Failures and mistakes and some wickedness,
Then Self-Improvement, Re-education
1225 And finally blissful Self-Fulfilment
Within the Light that is love and wisdom."
Gosnold finished, enthused at spirits' lot.
"Now," he said, "I am taking you to Heaven."

Heaven stood behind them in a veiling mist.
1230 A path wound up the side like the one seen
At Glastonbury Tor, only the scale
Was more like Mount Vesuvius. The path
To Hell spiralled round and down the inside
Of an upside-down bell. The path to Heaven
1235 Spiralled round the outside of an upright
Bell as round an Iraqi *ziggurat*.
Gosnold led Bush to the foot of the path
And they floated up into the mist and
Purgatory's meadow now hidden from view,
1240 Ascended until Gosnold alighted
On downs below another veiling mist.
Before them was a summer meadow much
More brilliant with Light than was Purgatory.

Bush could not see the source of the brightness,
1245   Which did not come from any obvious
Sun. In the great glare Bush could make out hosts
Of distant shapes whose spirit-bodies shone.
"This is Heaven?" Bush asked in wonderment.
"The first Heaven," Gosnold said. "You must realise
1250   That all Angels are interdependent.
Just as flowers use bees, birds, mice, ants or flies
To convey their pollen and fertilise
Other plants on the Earth that you've come from,
And attract them with strong scents or nectar,
1255   Which they sip so flowers and go-betweens gain,
So in Heaven Angels need other Angels
To take their projects for Self-Fulfilment
To other Angels who will sharpen them
And with feedback fertilise their ideas
1260   So that the whole system can flourish and
Fulfil the majesty of the Light's plan.
Now I must say farewell. And here I must
Hand you on to your new guide. He is here.
A reception committee will greet you."
1265   Gosnold faded before Bush could thank him.

Bush screwed his eyes up in the brilliant Light
And saw four transparent spirits approach.
"Welcome to Heaven, Mr President,"
One said. "I will be looking after you.
1270   I was President myself, Eisenhower."
"Oh yes," Bush said. "You're a hero of mine."
"Let me present three welcoming spirits.
Abe Lincoln." "I'm in awe," Bush said. To which
Lincoln replied, "You have done a good job
1275   Ruling the US, for a Southerner.
Like me, you got the nation behind you.
I stood up to 'Rothschilds' and blocked their Fed.
You've been on the receiving end of their
Attack on the US economy."
1280   "You can say that again," Bush smiled. "And here,"
Eisenhower said, "are two British leaders.
Winston Churchill." "I've got a bust of you
In the Oval Office," Bush said. "I know,"
Churchill said, "I've seen it. The war you've fought,
1285   The War against Terror, is different from
The war I fought, but I'm fascinated
By your pre-emptive approach." "And lastly,"
Eisenhower said, "Field Marshal Montgomery."

"Welcome," Montgomery said. "I worked with
1290   America when I was commander
Of British and US troops on D-Day."
"I'm delighted to meet you," Bush said, "I've
Read so much on your battles and exploits."
"These three are staying here," Eisenhower said.
1295   "I am instructing and escorting you.
I too was in your position once, and
Know how bewildered you must be at this."
Eisenhower drew him away from the three.
"But first I must say how concerned we've been
1300   At the prospect of bin Laden's nuclear-
Suitcase bombs and nightmare Armageddon.
You've done well to contain him and avoid
Panicking the American people.

"Now let me brief you about Heaven. You must
1305   Understand there are seven Heavens just as
There are seven Hells, which correspond to them
Inversely, and though each is separate
It's all a unity, all seven are parts
Of one uniting whole. There are seven tiers,
1310   Seven rings of Light in increasing brightness,
Each one miles wide and veiled off from the next.
Seen from above they're petals in a rose.
Yet seven paths wind up one grassy hill.
The Light is in the empyrean above
1315   The seventh Heaven. All spirits ready for
Self-Fulfilment are on one of these tiers.
The most raw are on the lower levels.
In this first Heaven or first ring of Light
Dwell those who glimpsed the Light on Earth but were
1320   Inconstant to it, and though they preserved
Their intellectual vision, then pursued
Other callings, such as Shelley and Blake,
And Michelangelo. They were allies
Of the Light but had long spells in their lives
1325   When they forgot their true calling. They are
Now lower Angels and visit mankind
With messages. Some of these are reborn
As teachers, who teach their fellow humans
Self-improvement and self-fulfilment on
1330   Earth to prepare them for their real life
In their spirit-bodies after their death.
They volunteer for a life of joyful,
Quiet sacrifice. In the second Heaven,

Beyond that veil, or cloud of unknowing,
1335 Are those who opened to the Light on Earth
But remained in the *vita activa*
And become leaders, such as St Paul or
Cromwell. These are now among Archangels
In the hierarchy of Heaven's ranking.
1340 Beyond the next veil is the third Heaven
Where dwell spirits who, through love of the Light,
Rose in life, understood the universe
And how all's process, thought forces and growth
Through the ordering workings of the Light.
1345 Heracleitus, Plato and Plotinus
Are just a few who've understood the Earth
And the power of the Fire of Love, the Light.
They dwell among the Principalities.
Beyond the next veil in the fourth Heaven
1350 Are the spiritual Masters and teachers
Who saw and taught the Light to humankind,
The mystics of all cultures, St Clement
Of Alexandria, Suhrawardi
And Padmasambhava, among the Powers.
1355 Above the next veil in the fifth Heaven
Are those who knew the Light in their lives and
Advanced the Light through war, like Charlemagne
And the Crusader Godfrey de Bouillon,
Who now dwell in love among the virtues.
1360 Beyond the next veil is the sixth Heaven
Where all who know the Light and have balanced
Justice and mercy dwell, like Constantine
The Great or Pope Gregory the Great, all
The just spirits among dominations.
1365 Beyond the next veil is the seventh Heaven,
The one closest to the Light, where live all
The contemplatives who have known the Light
In greatest luminosity, the true
Mystics such as St Hildegard, Dante,
1370 Meister Eckhart, St Teresa, St John
Of the Cross, Julian of Norwich, and more
Recently, Tennyson, T.S. Eliot;
And from Islam Bayazid, Al-Hallaj.
All dwell in brilliant Light among the thrones.
1375 That's where we're going now." And weightlessly
Bush felt himself rising into a mist
And ascended at high speed through each veil.
And on each tier he glimpsed lush green meadows
Like undulating chalk downs with wild flowers,

1380	And hordes of translucent, transparent wraiths
	Sitting and walking on the sunny grass,
	Barely discernible in brilliant Light.
	Each tier beneath each veil was brighter than
	The previous one, flooded with greater Light.
1385	They alighted on the green hill's top rim,
	A jutting-out rock on a vantage point.
	Before Bush was a sunny plain filled with
	A crowd of translucent shapes in bright Light
	That could only be seen with screwn-up eyes.
1390	Bush looked down and gasped for beneath him were
	Seven undulating tiers beyond each veil,
	And from the summit of the seventh Heaven
	The lower rings of Light looked like petals,
	One above another, of a great rose
1395	With seven petals filled with dazzling spirits.
	From within each ring looked green. From above
	The rings looked cream, like a satiny rose.
	The rings looked soft, their undulating folds
	Were like hills perfumed with abundant flowers.
1400	Then Eisenhower spoke from protruding rock:
	"Beyond these seven Heavens is the Light,
	Which is in the empyrean above.
	You will be blinded if you look upwards,
	You need to avert your eyes to avoid
1405	Damaging your sight. The Light's surrounded
	By the Cherubim of Divine Wisdom
	And the Seraphim of Divine Love, who
	Form a ring like a halo round a sun,
	A ring of brightness round the celestial,
1410	Sempiternal rose. That is where Christ dwells
	Surrounded by his most illumined saints,
	St John the Beloved, St Augustine
	And St Bernard, who helped the Crusaders,
	And the Virgin Mary, and the founders
1415	Of all the religions: Zoroaster,
	Mahavira, Lao-Tzu, Krishna, Mani,
	The Buddha, Mohammed, Hui-Neng, Eisai,
	Dogen, the Hidden *Imam*, Nanak, Fox.
	Right now they're all in this seventh Heaven.
1420	Look, Christ is standing on the rock. Beside
	Him is Mohammed. The rest are behind.
	He's come down to the seventh Heaven to speak
	From the centre of the Rose of Heaven
	And his words will be heard in all the Heavens.

1425	They'll be heard in every petal's corner."
	Bush saw Christ dazzling in spirit-body,
	A radiant form on the Rose's stigma
	Of the central pistil, and his Angels,
	Saints and religions' founders all round him.
1430	And as the crowded spirits waited they
	Shimmered with brilliant Light, sparkling as when
	A calm sea jumps with splashes of light from
	The morning sun. So the sea of spirits
	Winked and rippled within the brilliant One,
1435	Snugly within the cream seven-petalled Rose.
	As bees in a hive secrete wax for comb
	Of perfect design, hexagonal cells
	That hold larvae, store honey and pollen,
	And give off honey's sweet smell as they crawl,
1440	So Angels exude and give off the scent
	Of invisible nectar that sustains
	All spirits in a smiling atmosphere.
	In Heaven the very ether is perfumed
	And spirit-bodies waft in happiness
1445	And inhale joy while pleasuring others
	With the scent they give off like pollen dust
	As they flash out the glitter of the Light
	They have gathered from nuzzling in the One.
	And now as Christ raised a hand for silence
1450	The flashes stopped and spirits turned golden
	Like bees nuzzling in nectar of a rose,
	Covered in pollen dust in warm sunlight.
	Tell, Muse, how the universe works by light,
	How manifesting Light nourishes both
1455	Bodies and consciousness, how spirits' mind
	Is a ring of undetected bosons,
	How brains like sponges are imbued with Light
	And infused knowledge and innate wisdom,
	How the order principle shapes our lives;
1460	And how we live in a sea of bosons
	That convey information at the speed
	Of light that ever manifests from Being
	To Existence, the quantum vacuum,
	From which translucent spirits return to
1465	Being at the end of their Earthly lives;
	And how the Manifester ever pours
	The same intensity of energy,
	Cornucopia-like, into creation,
	Nature, the universe and human souls

1470	Which recalcitrant, fallen humankind
	Sometimes blocks out, like sponges in a sea
	That have gone hard and no longer absorb,
	Are no longer permeated by Light.
	The universe is a system of light
1475	That manifests from the subtle to dense,
	From Nothingness, the All, infinite One,
	Latent dark Fire and Light, zero movement
	Manifesting to form, to Non-Being,
	The potentialities of Being,
1480	The Light of Being, the infinite
	Latent germs of creations which congeal
	To Existence, for matter's frozen Light,
	And natural light from the sun is a dense
	Form of subtle metaphysical Light.
1485	The metaphysical Light condenses
	To natural light, which is its reflection
	In more solid, less quintessential form.
	Just as matter is a condensation
	Of Light, so consciousness, too, is condensed
1490	Light, part infinite, a ring of Light, and
	Part finite, autonomic brain photons.
	Light conveys information to every
	Consciousness and body, and shapes all growth.
	A network of photons, field of bosons,
1495	*Aither* or ether, links living beings.
	We live in an *aither* of tides like sea-
	Sponges in water, as filled with Light as
	Sponges are filled with tides, permeated
	By currents of information-bearing
1500	Particles, ordering their growth while light
	From the sun gives all living things, and plants,
	Chemical energy for cells to grow,
	Turns photons to chemical energy.
	Sunlight enters all animals' eyes through
1505	Photoreceptor cells, thence brains, bodies;
	Enters plants' photosynthesising cells.
	Light controls Nature's vast ecosystem,
	And bosons manifest from the quantum
	Vacuum, cluster on matter and give
1510	It weight. And so we are both infinite
	Spirits and finite sun-grown chemical
	Bodies, which co-exist during our life.
	Spirits return to Being on our death
	To live in translucent ghostly bodies
1515	While our chemical cells return to dust.

Our consciousness is a high-frequency
System of boson light and ordering drive
Directed by the ordering Light which
Drives all creatures to higher consciousness,
1520 To self-improvement and self-transcendence.
It's said that the Manifesting Light can
Be intensified, made more brilliant,
By the Manifesting source at a stroke,
Like turning a dimmer switch to brighten
1525 A room. However, so far as is known
This has never happened, and's fanciful,
A myth encouraging all to believe
That a New Age will shift the atmosphere.
The Millennial Kingdom, like the shift from
1530 An age of Pisces to Aquarius,
Is one of ambition, hard work and will,
Not an abrupt transition, flooding power
As Satan boasted his New Age would bring.
It's also said that the *aither* contains
1535 An akashic record of all events.
There is no evidence of this either.
When recalcitrant, fallen leaders make
Wrong decisions that leave the world worse off,
Angels are dispatched to make sure inflows
1540 Of information from the Light enter
A leader's consciousness. Heaven is like
The UN, and a resolution for
Peace results in a bombardment of minds
As leaders' choices are guided by Light.
1545 Just as UN Interim Forces in
Lebanon seek to restrain and snuff out
Rocket fire from hot-headed leaders that
Jeopardise peace, so Angels are sent down
To put restraining ideas in the minds
1550 Of hot-headed leaders throughout the world.
Christ's role as peacekeeper was not unlike
Ban Ki-moon's. Now he wanted to become
A peacemaker, and not a peacekeeper.

At the heart of the undulating folds
1555 Of the Celestial Rose, on a pistil
That resembled rock and elevated
Him, Christ stood on high and addressed Heaven.
"Angels," he said. All fell silent and heard.
Bush listened agog to his calming words
1560 With Lincoln, Churchill and Montgomery

Now standing near his new guide Eisenhower,
"I have spoken with the Earth's main leaders –
Those of the US and Israel, UN ,
Of the Syndicate alliance and Church –
1565 And most of them are deaf to our Kingdom.
They wrongly see the Kingdom of God as
A restored geographical kingdom
Of Israel. They see it as a campaign
For Israel's nationalistic glory
1570 And not as spiritual enlightenment
In a new Universalist grouping.
There is one exception I'll come to soon.
I have consulted God, who has approved
Targeting key leaders with influxes.
1575 We are to flood the leaders with the Light
So, guided from within, they will choose peace.
Angels, I realise we're in new waters.
Till now Heaven's been determined to safeguard
Humankind's free will. We have accepted
1580 That sometimes leaders will make great mistakes.
But now the human plight's so serious
From so many angles – military,
Economic, medical, climatic –
That some guidance is necessary if
1585 We are to save the Earth and humankind
From Armageddon in several ways. I
Know some of you will think that our guidance
Infringes spirits' free will and results
In 'brainwashing', but we must take that risk.
1590 Angels, our Millennial Kingdom, meaning
'A Kingdom that will last a thousand years',
A chiliastic Kingdom, will not get
Started unless we operate Guidance.
And so some of our higher Angels will
1595 Be assigned leaders I have met, to guard
And ensure Light of Guidance floods their souls
So their spirits can know what decisions
Are right for them to make, as opposed to
Being self-interested. All is in hand.
1600 All we have to do now is operate
The new Universalist system." Bush
Heard loud humming fill the plains of Heaven
As millions of Angels expressed relief
And assent to what their Leader had said.
1605 Then Mohammed spoke from adjoining 'rock'.
"The danger is that influxing leaders

Will lead to unjust solutions. Muslims
Need to be represented *pro rata*.
There must be a Palestine. I'm against
1610   Al-Qaeda, but the Taliban should be
Represented in Afghanistan and
In Pakistan. If Angels urge leaders
To make peace before fundamental goals
Such as these are achieved, then they will have
1615   Been brainwashing." The Hidden *Imam* spoke:
"I agree. The Shias, who now control
Iraq, should be represented where they
Have strength." "The Caliphate," Mohammed said,
"Should be revived after sixty-five years
1620   I want to see bin Laden as Caliph,
Based in Baghdad. I'm against al-Qaeda
But letting him be Caliph will bring peace
So long as Palestine has been restored."
Christ spoke: "Angels, what we are hearing sounds
1625   Like 'As below, so above'. It must be
The other way round: 'As above in Heaven,
So below on Earth'. We need power-sharing
Here in Heaven. That's when God's Kingdom starts.
Once we have shifted Heaven to a sharing
1630   Of power between all faiths, we'll replicate
The same balance on Earth through our Kingdom,
Using Light guidance. The key is to start
Here in Heaven and change things so each faith
Is on a different petal of this Rose,
1635   A separate zone within the unity
Proportionate in space to the number
Of followers it has, but each equal
In faiths' equivalence. The two largest –
Christians, Muslims – will have to occupy
1640   Several petals or zones. Much more detailed
Proposals for the reforming of Heaven
On Universalist lines will follow.
Angels, we have a problem with Satan,
Who, as God's servant, spreading disorder
1645   On Earth and controlling Self-Improvement,
We cannot tamper with unless the Light
Agrees that we can chain him. We cannot
Start our Kingdom and direct Light Guidance
While Satan roams the Earth, undoing all
1650   Our work, disordering all our order.
I'll propose to God the Light that from now
Satan is confined to Self-Improvement

In Hell, and does not actively wreck our
Schemes to give our Guidance a chance to work."
1655   Mohammed interjected: "Once again,
If Satan's working for a Palestine,
For the two-state model, and also for
The Taliban, we should not now curtail
His activities, which will help Muslims."
1660   Christ sighed, for the democratisation
Of Heaven was proving tiresome as some faiths
Thought of their own interest, and not the whole.
"Again, the key is to set it all up
Here in Heaven before we fix the Earth.
1665   But, Angels, we are moving to a time
Of universal order, during which
Disorder will be held in check, and we
Can make great progress in our new Kingdom.
Floreat our Millennial Kingdom."
1670   There was a loud humming of approval.
The politician in Bush, listening,
Wondered if Christ was too optimistic.
Could leaders' decisions in Iran and
Afghanistan be reigned back by Guidance?

1675   In Heaven's endless summery present
Free from winter and night, all basking in
An undulating, satiny meadow,
Bush watched as, silencing with a raised hand,
Christ spoke: "Angels, we have a visitor.
1680   We would not have reached this prospect for peace
Unless the West had firmly held the line
Against Satan's onslaught upon the West
Which had the support of the Syndicate.
One man had to hold this line although he
1685   Was opposed and criticised on all sides.
He is the exception I referred to.
We welcome President Bush and express
Our gratitude to him for bringing in
A new era in which all share the Earth,
1690   Which no longer belongs to superpowers.
He has been greatly misunderstood. He
Knew nuclear-suitcase bombs were being brought
To America and a Caliphate
Was planned for Baghdad. He stopped both these things.
1695   He knew Saddam had wmds.
They seem to have been loaded on a ship
At Umm Qasr and dumped on the seabed

In two watertight containers which can
Be lifted any time. He disrupted
1700   Saddam's proliferation as he kept
The West safe from attack. And those who trained
To let off dirty bombs or nuclear-
Suitcase weapons in the US are now
In Guantánamo Bay's military cage.
1705   And he's flushed bin Laden out of his lair
In an Afghan cave where like a wild beast
He was dangerous, to a still-dangerous
More advisory role as Antichrist.
Now bin Laden's where his four wives and
1710   Eldest son are, in Iran, where between
Trips to the Afghan-Pakistan border
He's helping Ahmadinejad acquire
Nuclear weapons that can threaten Israel
And, on missiles, reach American shores.
1715   Bin Laden's still plotting Armageddon
Against the Judeo-Christian *élite*.
Bush blocked a Muslim onslaught on the West.
The public do not realise how close
It came to success, and they think that he
1720   Overreacted and bombed without cause
And joke at his lack of intelligence,
A sentiment encouraged by Satan.
But we all know how shrewd his judgement's been,
And one day these things will come out, and he
1725   Will be vindicated at history's bar.
He more than any blocked Armageddon.
Obama says there must be peace, as if
Saying it's enough to persuade Iran.
But we know what Vegetius proclaimed
1730   In the fourth century when Rome was pressed by
Raiding barbarians: '*Qui desiderat*
Pacem, praeperet bellum,' which translates
In English, our universal language
Now Latin is defunct and not used here,
1735   'Let him who desires peace, prepare for war.'
That's how there is peace in the Middle East.
He showed the West's barbarians that they can't
Proliferate or use nuclear weapons.
He showed it's in their interests to live and
1740   Let live, renounce war and embrace world peace.
It can be argued that he worked for peace
More realistically than Obama
For in effect he said, 'It's peace or else.'

While Obama asks, 'Please, can I have peace?'
1745 And's surprised at the dismissive *riposte*.
His approach was effective, dealt with facts.
One day he'll be deemed a great President."
All hummed their welcome to Bush. Some Muslim
Spirits did not hum. Mohammed, silent,
1750 Scowled at Bush and all anti-Muslim wars.

Now Christ spoke to Heaven rather than Bush:
"Angels, I told you I had spoken with
Earth's leaders and that they do not realise
The seriousness of the situation.
1755 As much as during the Second World War
When we were worried by Hitler's attempt
To obtain nuclear weapons and use them
Against the West, there is a real threat
That bin Laden, al-Qaeda and Iran
1760 Will ally to obtain nuclear weapons
And launch them at the West in a fiery
Armageddon. This had been headed off,
And I pay tribute to Mohammed for
Co-operation with me over this.
1765 Mohammed's a responsible leader.
I also said he'd flood the leaders' minds
With influxes of Light, to bring in peace.
That will begin as soon as I declare
My Kingdom of Heaven, Millennial rule,
1770 Which will be in just a few moments.
I said this would be Universalist,
A power-sharing among all religions'
Followers in accordance with ratios.
That change is only moments away." Loud
1775 Humming greeted news of the impending
Revolution in Heaven that had crept in.
"As above, so below," Christ continued,
"And as below, so above. Our watchword.
The Watchman asked 'What of the night?' will say,
1780 'Earth replicates Heaven, and Heaven Earth.
The morning cometh, and also the night.'
And then I told you that I would propose
To God the Light that Satan be confined
To Self-Improvement while my Kingdom starts.
1785 Angels, after the Second World War we
Banished Satan, who allied with Russia –
The Soviet Union, rather – and the Cold
War came out of the West's response to that.

We don't want to make that mistake again.

1790   Self-Improvement's about not repeating

Mistakes. We should be the last to make them.

Angels, I now confirm that God the Light

Is happy that Satan should not move out

Of Self-Improvement, and he will receive

1795   'Electronically tagged' shackles that

Are carefully monitored." Loud hums greeted

Christ's announcement. "Angels, I proclaimed my

Kingdom at the end of the Second World

War. I make no bones about it, it did

1800   Not work because Satan mucked it all up.

I also said that a New Age of Light

Will be born when seven years' tribulation

Have ended. I thought this would happen then,

But it didn't. I said Christians have prayed

1805   For two thousand years 'Thy Kingdom Come' – and

That it now has. Angels, it's really come

Now, humankind's yearning's been satisfied.

There's long been a debate as to whether

My Second Coming, my *Parousia*

1810   (The Greek term for 'presence' or 'arrival'),

Was forecast in *Revelation* 20,

As before my Millennial Kingdom.

Some views deny this. Preterism holds

John's prophesies were fulfilled with the fall

1815   Of Jerusalem in 70 – yet John

Wrote around 95 and *prophesied*

Future, not past, events. There are pre- , post-

And a-(or non-)millennialists. The pre-

Millennialists are right: I will return

1820   *Before* I establish my Thousand-Year

Kingdom. The post-millennialists are wrong:

They hold I'll return *after* my Thousand-

Kingdom – in a thousand years' time and

Contrary to John's interpretation.

1825   The a-millennialists are also wrong:

They hold there'll be no Millennial Kingdom,

Just the Church under a Pope that has lost

Contact with the Light, which is essential.

Of pre- , mid- and post-tribulationists,

1830   The pre- and mid- are wrong for they assert

My Second Coming's before or during

The seven-year tribulation. And the post-

Tribulationists are right for I'll come

After the tribulation, at the end

1835	Of the seven years. Millennialists maintain
	That there will be a Thousand-Year Reign, they
	Are right. Dispensationalists assert
	History's broken into 'dispensations',
	Orderings of the world by Providence,
1840	Each with a separate covenant from God.
	I don't do that, though Israel thinks God does.
	So my *Parousia*'s pre-millennialist;
	Millennialist it goes without saying;
	And post-tribulationist; in accord
1845	With St John and *Revelation* 20,
	Which was forward- , not backward-looking. Now
	You see my Second Coming's been foretold,
	That it accords with scriptural account.
	So I announce here in Heaven, before you,
1850	My witnesses, that my Millennial
	Kingdom's been launched. There'll be an Age of Light
	For a thousand years, my Millennial Reign."
	A loud humming approved the Kingdom's launch,
	Which was, in fact, a relaunch of what he
1855	Had launched in 1945. "Angels,"
	He resumed, "in our New Age of Light there
	Will be no increase of manifesting
	Light. The system's fine, it's the reception
	Of the Light that's gone wrong so we've improved
1860	The channelling of Light to leaders, who
	Will be flooded with thoughts of peace in Light
	Under the supervision of Angels."
	Again a loud humming greeted his words.
	"Fifty-four years back I thought the atom
1865	Bomb had unveiled a new Era of Peace.
	We were all disappointed, frustrated
	By Satan. I saw a New World Order
	Approaching, and a universal Church
	Of the Light in which Christian would share with
1870	Other creeds, under my reign as the new
	Universal Christ. I called for a new
	Prophet to emerge who would state a new
	Universalism of Light. Angels,
	That prophet has come forward, and I will
1875	Make contact with him on my next return
	To Earth. The New World Order will happen,
	But not the 'Rockefeller'-'Rothschild' one,
	The New World Disorder that they hope for
	That will be taken over and replaced
1880	By a democratised model. Angels,

President Bush has led the West towards
Such a democratised world government.
Regional groups will link, and the new state
Will be voted in by world citizens
1885   Who yearn to escape financial crisis,
Flu pandemics that can kill millions and
Climate change that threaten all citizens.
Angels, out of my Thousand-Year Reign and
My Millennial Kingdom will grow a World
1890   Federalist Union with ten regions,
Three superregions: the American,
European and Pacific Unions.
Spirits will soon incarnate in greater
Numbers, for the West is in deep decline
1895   And spiritual ignorance, and the cult
Of celebrity's grown a vacuousness.
More and more spirits make mistakes and need
To relearn lessons they missed down on Earth,
More and more spirits need Self-Improvement.
1900   And with nearly seven billion on Earth,
Re-education will be more frequent
As spirits relearn what they forgot on
Earth in their most recent lives. It's as if
A generation's been turned out without
1905   Past skills: illiterate, boorish, yobbish,
Binge-drinking drug addicts. You know the mould.
And 'Rockefellers' want to cut the world's
Population by two billion as can
Be gleaned from *Global 2000 Report*.
1910   Angels, this will not happen under my
Thousand-Year Reign. My Kingdom's spiritual,
It won't compete with UN nation-states.
Angels, I now inaugurate my own
Kingdom. Darkness will no longer rule Earth
1915   Now Light's supreme. Never again will Hell
Stray from its educative purpose – Self-
Improvement – and aspire to tyrannise
The universe with Darkness, disorder.
A new age of Universal Order
1920   Has just been born. Angels, I can be shown
As a Water-pourer, pitcher on my
Shoulder, for the New Age of Aquarius
Is here and I will pour out Light on all,
And the wisdom of the Light. A new time
1925   Of wisdom is approaching. Christendom,
The Age of Pisces and the Christian fish –

'*Ichthus*' in Greek representing my name
As a Greek acronym, meaning 'Jesus
Christ the Son of God' – has given way to
1930   The Universalist Age. Once again
I proclaim as I did fifty-four years
Ago: let the coming Aquarian
Age be an Age of Light. Angels, let us
Now flood key minds with manifesting Light!"
1935   A great humming burst round the sunny plains
Like buzzing in a meadow of wild flowers.
As bees swarm in a beehive round a queen
And sip the honey that was culled from flowers,
So the virtuous swarmed round dazzling Christ
1940   And in the sunshine sipped the honeyed Light.

Now all the spirits in Heaven's snow-white Rose,
That tinted cream and gold from the radiance
Of spirit-bodies when joyful, flashed out
And exuberantly crowded round Christ
1945   Pantokrator in bliss, in process to
Self-perfection. A Universalist
Age had been proclaimed, much had to be done.
Spirits headed to distant libraries
To consult past authorities on Light
1950   And work out how best to use influxes
To bring harmony to the troubled Earth.
Many attended talks by Angels and
Shimmered their greetings from radiant bodies,
Stood in groups basking in the brilliant Light,
1955   Communed or worked on projects that advanced
Their self-fulfilment, and all was process,
Nowhere was static, all was dynamic
As near-perfect spirits aspired to be
Perfect Angels and teach other spirits
1960   And descend to Earth as Bodhisattvas
And train blundering humans to the Light.
All was process but also changelessness
For spirits and Angels were consistent
And had stability within the Light.
1965   Here was infinite order and effort.

Then Eisenhower said, "Look back, that's space-time."
Bush turned from brilliant Light and looked out from
Heaven and saw space-time against a night sky
Like a half-opened fan full of white points,
1970   Translucent like a wide-rimmed, tapering

Distant glass bowl full of stars like white sweets.
It hung in black sky like a *fleur-de-lis*
About the size of a full moon. "Look at
The top," Eisenhower said, "it's expanding."
1975   Bush grasped that imperceptibly the rim
Was moving forwards, surging into black.
"Your Earth is in that fan," Eisenhower said,
"The shuttlecock-shaped universe
Which is so vast that light takes a thousand
1980   Million years to cross it from side to side.
The Big Bang was at the bottom and blew
The shape you see upwards. It's still rushing
Into the infinite, the dark all round.
It's like a living foetus in the womb
1985   Of the infinite, which humans once knew.
The entire fan came out of one point that
Emerged from the blackness, from this Being
Into Existence, which hangs in *our* sky.
Humans think its birth was an accident,
1990   That it has no purpose. It has a goal.
The infinite is in love with space-time
Whose humans pursue self-development."
Bush looked in astonished wonder, seeing
Space-time from a great distance, small enough
1995   To hold within his extended palm or
To blot out with the span of his stretched hand.
From Heaven our universe looked very small.
Bush could have gazed on it for ever, but,
Sensing Eisenhower was not at his side,
2000   With a whoosh he was drawn down a tunnel
And as if in a high-velocity
Elevator descending, rushed towards
The fan, which grew larger, burst into space,
Hurtled through stars, past Pluto and Neptune,
2005   Past Saturn's icy rings, cold Jupiter's
Poisonous gas and Mars's frozen desert
Till blue-oceaned Earth loomed his side of
Venus's distant greenhouse, slowed down for
A gentle stop and, braking, landed in
2010   His Preston-Hollow sitting-room's armchair.

Bush picked up his book which set out the Earth's
Civilisations in rising-falling
Patterns, his soul still filled with the image
Of space-time as a half-opened fan, and
2015   Thought of all the clashes that had happened

Between civilisations in history
And of the conflicts within the glass bowl,
And such storms were all reconciled within
The fan-shaped structure and given meaning
2020 In relation to Heaven's Self-Fulfilment.
He saw all spirits hung with many lives,
Each one a gem on a necklace they wore
Like beads on a rosary's slender chain.
To the One all was in one vast pattern
2025 That reconciled all opposites of thought.
To the One all made sense, and Bush was glad.

Now influxes of Light filled Obama,
King Abdullah the Second of Jordan,
President Netanyahu of Israel
2030 And Ahmadinejad of Iran as
Christ brokered a most ambitious peace plan
Aimed at ending sixty years of conflict
Between the Arabs and squatting Israel.
In April Christ was in the White House for
2035 King Abdullah's visit to Obama.
Mohammed was also there, urging on
The King to make peace in accordance with
The teachings of the *Koran*. Just before
The King left his hotel to meet the new
2040 President, Obama, Mohammed stood
Beside him and said, "Abdullah, I was
The last Prophet of Allah, twenty-fifth
In a long line from Adam, the first, to
Isa, Jesus, before me. The angel
2045 Gabriel brought the *Koran* down to my heart.
In the cave of Hira that's near Mecca
Gabriel told me, 'You are the Messenger
Of Allah,' and I began to receive
The revelations that were collected
2050 After my death, about 650, as
The *Koran*. In my first vision I saw
The opening passage of the *Koran* in
Letters of fire written on cloth, the Fire,
And saw the start of *sura* 96.
2055 I was a peaceful man, and I loved peace.
I approved of *jihad*, or holy war,
To spread Islam by waging war by heart,
Tongue, hand and sword against unbelievers
And enemies of the Islamic faith.
2060 I came from the Quraysh tribe, from the House

Of Abd Manaf. When they rejected me
I withdrew from Mecca to Medina
And in due course returned to Mecca in
Triumph with ten thousand men and became
2065   Lord of the two sacred enclaves: Mecca
And Medina. Now the Quraysh agreed
To worship Allah alone. I called for
Jihad to spread 'surrender to the Will
Of Allah', Islam. I'm alleged to have
2070   Ascended on a Winged Horse of Fire called
Burak to Heaven from a black stone beneath
The Dome of the Rock, but did not visit
Haran esh-Sharif. And after my death
Abu Bakr became the first Caliph,
2075   'Successor', and set about conquering
The whole world to place it under Allah.
Jihad was necessary at that time.
Nowadays peace is more necessary.
Allah is the Light of both Heaven and Earth,
2080   Is like a lamp in a niche lit from oil
From an olive tree, intelligential
Spirit. It's all in chapter 24.
Agreed peace in place of dubious *jihad*.
You have the fifty-seven member states of
2085   The Organisation of the Islamic
Conference, who will support a peace plan
And who represent a third of the world
From Morocco to Indonesia,
From the Atlantic to the Pacific.
2090   There will be four points. Israel stops building
And expanding into its settlements;
Israel withdraws from land it occupied
In 1967; East Jerusalem
Becomes the Palestinian capital;
2095   And all Palestinians who fled in
1948 have right of return.
And in return fifty-seven states give peace.
For eighteen years there has been failure through
Madrid, Oslo, Camp David, the Road Map
2100   And Annapolis. Now, at last, succeed."
The King nodded, Mohammed slipped away,
Pleased that the King had listened. Christ wanted
To say something similar to Obama.
But he was busy and, arrogantly,
2105   Said, "You again." Christ said, "You have a chance
To hatch a plan that will have Israel sit

With Palestinians, Syrians, Lebanese
And solve all problems in the Middle East.
You can address the entire Arab world
2110   On June the fourth and set up conferences."
Obama said, "I know what I'm doing.
You're telling me what to do. I've a plan."
And brushed him aside to get on with work.
Christ sighed, for Obama was too absorbed
2115   In clearing his in-tray to attend to
A long-term strategy and a peace plan.

The meeting went well, and Abdullah said,
Announcing the peace plan, "The agreement
Would include settling Israel's conflict with
2120   The Palestinians and territorial
Disputes with Syria and Lebanon.
If we delay peace negotiations,
There's going to be another conflict
Between Arabs or Muslims and Israel
2125   In the next twelve to eighteen months," meaning
During the course of 2010.
Meanwhile Netanyahu, who was opposed
To giving up 1967 lands
And East Jerusalem, when approached, said
2130   That a right-wing Israeli Government
Would bring peace better than a left-wing one.
Christ knew that "Rothschilds" and pro-Temple-Mount
Societies were still intransigent
And could be expected to torpedo
2135   The plan, as could Iran. It was arranged
That on May the eighteenth Netanyahu
Should visit Obama in Washington.
The Pope visited Jerusalem and
Held Mass in Gethsemane and next day
2140   In Bethlehem, under a thirty-foot-
High wall that shut out the Palestinians,
Which he, calling for peace, said should be pulled
Down immediately like walls round hearts;
Then Nazareth. Christ did not approach him
2145   In case he was rebuffed a second time.

Iran's view of the peace plan was different.
The Iranian regime had already
Dismissed Obama's conciliatory
Approach – he said he would like to talk to
2150   "The Islamic Republic of Iran",

Respectfully calling it its new name.
Ahmadinejad said that he had plans
To press ahead with Iran's nuclear
Program. He would continue to support
Hamas and Hezbollah. Now he was driven
To the Jamkaran mosque for a *khalvat*,
Or *tête-à-tête* with the Hidden *Imam*,
The Twelfth and last of the Shiite *Imam*s
Who disappeared from Earth down a well in
874 when only five, when Allah
Hid him to await his return. He had
Disappeared down a well in Samarra,
Iraq, but had been seen at Jamkaran
In 1002, when he had asked for
A mosque to be built on a site marked out
With chains and nails. The mosque had been built and
He was now thought to be down the well there,
A white enamel knee-high base, two feet
By two feet, tipped with a green-barred steel grille.
It stood in a shelter surrounded by
Crash barriers near the Jamkaran mosque.
In each generation in latter times
The lone Hidden *Imam* had thirty-six
Nails, *owtad*, who served him. Only one was
Known, President Ahmadinejad, who,
A *Hojjatieh*, believed that it was
Permissible to create chaotic
Conditions to speed up the Twelfth *Imam*'s
Return, and gave 20 billion dollars
To the mosque and built several large grandstands
Where tens of thousands of pilgrims could rest
And where people could witness the Mahdi's
Ascent up the well to rescue Shiites
And fight the chaos on Iran's borders
Which Ahmadinejad created to
Urge the Hidden *Imam* to come quickly.
Ahmadinejad took his Cabinet
To the well and, dropping a contract down,
Pledged to support him. Now, being a nail,
He had had a *khalvat* and had been told
By the Hidden *Imam* that Israel must
Be wiped out and Iran should go nuclear.
The Cabinet and people of Iran
Had to take his word that going nuclear
Was an instruction from the Twelfth *Imam*
In the course of his one-to-ones with him.

The Cabinet spent half an hour talking
About how the Hidden *Imam* would sign
The contract and return it above ground.
2200   Now the Hidden *Imam*, sensing chaos
Would be ended by the peace agreement,
Which he did not want, in the dead of night
Came down from Heaven and loitered by the well,
Put on an emaciated ancient look
2205   As if he were over eleven hundred
Years old, a look more like a skull than man,
Ignored the messages pushed through for him,
Now in a soggy pile at the well's foot,
And made his way to Ahmadinejad
2210   And stood within his presidential room
And spoke: "My brother Mahmoud, I gave you
The presidency for a single task,
So you'd provoke a devastating clash
Of civilisations in which Iran,
2215   Leading the Muslim world, would engage with
The infidel West led by the US
And defeat it in a prolonged contest.
Islam has four times as many young men
Of fighting age as has the West – hundreds
2220   Of millions of Muslim *ghazis*, 'holy
Raiders'. Islam also has four-fifths of
The world's oil reserves and therefore controls
The infidels' lifeblood. George W.
Bush has been an exception to the rule
2225   That since Truman US Presidents have
Run away from setbacks abroad. I told
You to wait him out and continue with
Your nuclear arsenal. That's now nearly
Ready. Now you must challenge the US
2230   Peace plan. Somehow – by an event or by
Diplomacy – you must make it fall through.
Israel does not want it, so play on that.
Hamas and Hezbollah can zap Israel
With rockets to provoke it to pull out
2235   Of the peace plan, as has happened before.
The plan has fifty-seven states offering
Peace. You can split the fifty-seven to your
Advantage. Undermine King Abdullah
Of Jordan, foment war all round Amman.
2240   Secure Syria's and Lebanon's disdain
For the peace process. Break the peace plan up.
If necessary, use your nuclear

Bomb as a threat against Israel and all
Middle-Eastern countries. Mohammed's gone
2245 Along with the peace plan to advantage
His Palestinian and Sunni clients.
I oppose it as the Shia Crescent
Should become Greater Iran under you.
Oppose it through deviousness if that works.
2250 Otherwise oppose it through towering strength."
Ahmadinejad asked, "Have you returned?"
"Not yet," the Hidden *Imam* said. "It is
Written that I shall return on a white
Horse with Isa, the Muslim Jesus, in
2255 The *Hadith*. But Christ wants peace, I want war.
I am not ready to return just yet.
Iran's borders must be ringed by chaos
Or there must be chaos in Iran's cities.
This can be provoked. For example, if
2260 You were to have a landslide win in your
June election, and the Opposition
Were to take to the streets and paralyse
The running of Iran, with four hundred
Thousand jamming Tehran's roads, then I would
2265 Be in a position to return and
Save Iran from paralysing chaos.
There'd be cries, 'Death to Ahmadinejad,'
But you could fly to Russia, not hear them.
At the appointed time, when the hour's right,
2270 Which can be very soon, in weeks, not months,
I will return to head the forces of
Righteousness, and will battle the forces
Of evil in one apocalyptic
Final battle. People said I'd returned
2275 In Khomeini. He did not admit or
Deny this, but I assure you I did
Not come down and enter Khomeini's soul.
The spokesman for the Association
Of Combatant Clerics, Gholam Reza
2280 Meshahi Moyhadam, declares that I
Am not behind the economic ills:
Inflation at 30 per cent, the high
Cost of living, disputing what you've said,
That I'm behind Government policies
2285 And your drive for a nuclear weapon.
In fact, I'm behind all your policies
And am behind your snub to the peace plan.
Sunnis think the Mahdi's yet to be born.

	Shias believe I'm waiting to return
2290	As the ultimate saviour of mankind
	And will bring peace and justice to the world."
	Ahmadinejad said, "The peace plan's dead.
	I will do everything you say, Great One."

	Just as one sits high in the Louvre and looks
2295	Down at the glass pyramid whose diamond
	Panes represent countries in the UN,
	An Illuminatist view of the globe
	And the structure of the world government,
	So Christ, descending, saw all nations linked
2300	And interlocking in a vast pattern
	As airy as glass, with faint joining lines
	Only he could detect, invisible
	To the eyes of denser, opaquer men.
	Now Christ looked down on his Thousand-Year Reign
2305	And saw its start as a world government.
	It had been unveiled in two thousand at
	The UN Millennium Assembly and
	Summit of world leaders, attended by
	135 of 149 world leaders
2310	Who signed a revised UN Charter called
	The Charter for Global Democracy,
	Which had till then been signed by 56.
	The Inter-Parliamentary Union,
	130 Parliaments, had adopted
2315	The Universal Declaration of
	Democracy: the future in embryo.
	Now Christ saw the Earth in a future state.
	A Universalist World State now had
	A single world currency – Earth-dollar –
2320	Which had emerged from the 2008
	Great Depression, which was long since history.
	Soaring like an eagle over the world,
	Christ saw below a new structure as if
	A revolution had swept the present
2325	And removed the Syndicate from the world.
	From high he saw all the regional blocs
	And linkage between capitals and zones.
	He saw the UN, once for nation-states,
	Reformed as a massive World Parliament
2330	With democratic representatives,
	And the World Policy-making Unit,
	Once called the secretive Bilderberg Group,
	Removed from "Rockefellers" and "Rothschilds"

And the Bavarian Illuminati.
2335 He saw all central banks as branches of
One World Bank no longer under "Rothschilds".
He saw a host of international
Institutions now genuinely global:
The UN International Criminal
2340 Court; a World Army with peace-keeping troops;
World Health, World Education and World Tax.
The G8 OECD and the Bank
Of International Settlements, World Bank,
International Monetary Fund and World
2345 Trade Organisation were all enmeshed
In a network of global institutes
Under an Earth Charter and Earth Summit.
All global bodies, all once separate,
Had now been integrated in a new
2350 System under an elected World-Lord,
A leader elected for just four years.
Finance, banking, the world economy,
Health, threats from climate change and outer space
Were all controlled by a caring World State.
2355 War, disease and famine were controlled by
World Peace, World Health and World Shared Feeding through
Globally-planned resources. Citizens
Were all in touch with their inner natures
And metaphysical Reality
2360 Through World Religion and one World Culture.
The world was now safe from Armageddon.
World Population was regulated.
There was benevolent globalism.
Living civilisations continued
2365 To rise and fall, grow and decay, within
A strong World Democratic Union
Which embraced and enfolded an Islam
Purged of terrorism with its World Love.
Christ looked down on a fine Utopia,
2370 A Heaven on Earth, a good New World Order.
There were Historical and Cultural,
Literary and Environmental,
Political and Religious forms of
A World Universalism, One World.
2375 All religions were under one World Light.
Christ smiled for the future was looking good.
The seven-years tribulation had ended.

Humans in a benevolent World State,

Look for inspiration to bees and ants.
2380 A world government of nations as states
Resembles a field full of beehives on
An estate with meadows full of wild flowers.
Bees collect tree resins and gums to make
Propolis, the best antibacterial,
2385 Antiviral, antifungal system
In the world, with which they plug every crack
In their hive so it's totally sterile.
Each hive has up to sixty thousand bees
In summer and the buzzing's deafening.
2390 The female workers hum until midnight
And bring in honey for their sisters for
They will be dead in six to eight weeks' time
And work for the community, not self.
Bees pollinate a third of all we eat
2395 And half the wild plants on which birds depend.
They keep the system going selflessly
For the good of the whole, not personal gain,
And must be protected by the system
When they're threatened by the varroa mite
2400 Which kills off whole bee colonies, wipes out
Two billion bees each winter in our land.
And when a colony of rock ants needs
To emigrate, scouting ants discover
Sites for new nests and assess them, and choose
2405 The most suitable, reject the nearer,
Poorer nest site for one farther away
Which is more suitable, and the entire
Colony makes the correct decision.
Just as bees toil to store food for their hive
2410 And scout ants find the most suitable nests,
So humans toil to pass on to their heirs,
Set up efficiently-run homes for all,
And all enjoy a harmonious life
Within their ordered state and busyness.

2415 But this World State had not yet come to pass
And was but a potential within mess.
Now leaders cowed by Bush's roar crawled out
Of their burrows and resumed their old ways.
Sensing he was still on the campaign trail,
2420 Courting popularity by taking
Both sides of an argument and fudging,
That he lacked the bold clarity of Bush,
Uncowed by Obama's displayed weakness

	Iran launched a satellite into space
2425	And threatened it could reach America.
	Netanyahu, Israel's new leader, warned
	That a nuclear-armed Iran would proffer
	The greatest threat to Israel since founding.
	He feared that a Palestinian state
2430	Would allow Hamas to seize the West Bank
	As it did Gaza and fire its rockets
	At all Israeli cities, which would now
	Be in range. He said Israel should pursue
	An economic track in its dealings
2435	With Palestinians and not a two-state
	Political one. North Korea test-
	Fired an intermediate range ballistic
	Taepodong-2 missile. Its military
	Declared it was "fully ready for war"
2440	With South Korea and no longer bound by
	The 1953 peace agreement,
	And conducted an underground test of
	A 20-kiloton nuclear bomb –
	The size of the Nagasaki device –
2445	Which measured 4.5 on the Richter
	Scale, then tested five more short-range missiles
	That were a threat. Obama told Iran
	He wanted a fresh start, and was shocked when
	An American-Iranian woman
2450	Journalist was imprisoned as a spy
	And Ahmadinejad, at a UN
	Anti-racist conference, accused Israel
	Of being racist to Palestinians.
	The West walked out. Obama had found out
2455	That bringing world peace was harder than he
	Had thought on the electoral trail, that deeds
	Obstinately countered his hopeful words,
	That if you want peace, then prepare for war.
	Bush's warlike posture had kept order
2460	And controlled all who would defy world peace.
	Christ's Millennium was not a territory
	In which absolute peace reigned, but rather
	A *Pax Americana* to shelter
	All peace-loving nations and isolate
2465	All trouble-makers bent on starting war.
	It was a far-from-perfect Millennium
	As human nature is far from perfect
	And, possessing free will, makes choices that
	Are far from perfect in signalling its

2470	Peaceful intentions, which conceal hostile
	Feelings for neighbours and cruel self-interest.
	And as rogue states intrigued, the Western world
	Seemed paralysed by troubles too profound
	To be coped with and pessimism now
2475	Became the prevailing mood of mankind.
	The future seemed bleak, even hopeless now
	Climate change had gone too far to reverse,
	Now there were too many humans on Earth,
	Requiring a nuclear cull of a third
2480	To bring man's population back to rights,
	And a world depression had brought chaos.

Petraeus argued the Iraqi surge
Was a strategy that should be used in
Afghanistan, where American troops
2485 And British armed forces were being killed
By Iranian roadside bombs planted by
The Taliban; and that the goal, blocking
Al-Qaeda, could not be accomplished through
An agreement with the Taliban, as
2490 Gates and Obama thought. The Taliban
Were in Pakistan and pressing towards
Islamabad. Petraeus felt that Gates
And Obama were missing a chance to
Repeat the Iraqi boosting surge in
2495 Afghanistan. Gates and Obama feared
Petraeus was confusing success in
Iraq with a universal counter-
Insurgency model; that Petraeus
Was lucky in Iraq but would be bogged
2500 Down in Afghanistan. Petraeus had
A vision of success that Obama
Did not share and felt that America
Might slide to a defeat as its General
Was not supported by its President.
2505 Now Cheney had gone, Obama was in
The Syndicate's saddle. The Syndicate
Wanted the Trans-Afghan gas pipeline, which
Was at first guarded by the Taliban,
Who'd been created by the CIA
2510 And Pakistan in 1994
And helped to power by the US to do
Just that. Obama wanted to deal with
The Taliban to secure the pipeline
For the Syndicate forces behind him.

2515	While Western forces were being ambushed
	By the Taliban, the American
	President was doing a deal with them
	To turn on and wipe out all al-Qaeda
	And leave them in charge of Afghanistan
2520	So they could guard the Syndicate's pipelines.
	Petraeus was setting military
	And political goals in a context
	That was fundamentally commercial –
	About Trans-Afghan oil and gas pipelines.
2525	In a war expected to last decades
	In support of a corrupt Government
	And in ambitious hope of state-building,
	Unattainable and grandiloquent
	Statements by underfunding ministers
2530	Had not been narrowed to realistic aims.
	Pipelines and commercial interests aside,
	Officially the Coalition surged
	To stop the Taliban from returning
	In Afghanistan as insurgents seized
2535	Swathes of wild Helmand province round Sangin
	And Lashkar Gah; from giving al-Qaeda
	Safe haven to restart their training camps
	That trained thousands of terrorists before
	2001; and to suppress the flow
2540	Of poppy fields' opium to the West.
	Unofficially it surged to disrupt
	An attempt based on Kunar to wage war
	On Pakistan and capture its nuclear
	Weapons – and to disrupt bin Laden's and
2545	Al-Qaeda's use of nuclear-suitcase bombs.
	Just as Rome sent legions to cross the Rhine
	And as in the 170s take on
	The Marcomanni across the Danube,
	To make contact with and slaughter hostile
2550	Barbarians; so the West, fearful that our
	Barbarians have nuclear-suitcase bombs,
	Sought to locate and kill barbarians
	Who live across the Western *limes* and,
	In frontier wars in the hinterland,
2555	Like hostile Goths and Huns would sweep down and
	Sack the West with its own technology.
	Blair of the Syndicate, now a Catholic,
	Treating the Roman Catholic Church like

A political party, now harangued
2560   The ageing Pope for lack of sympathy
To gays, saying he was out of touch with
Liberal congregations. Blair was seeking
To modernise the Church. Just as he had
"Modernised" Britain, and disastrously
2565   Unleashed a boom based on huge borrowing
Presented as brilliant performance and
Left the Union vandalised, the Civil
Service and judiciary politicised,
The Commons and Lords corrupt, fiddling
2570   Expenses and cheating on a vast scale,
The economy ruined, debt bubble burst,
And, Iraq a mess, blaming al-Qaeda
For the aftermath he failed to foresee,
So he now turned on the Catholic Church
2575   As a new institution he could mould
In his own modern, deceptive image.
And having converted to its beliefs,
Was now rejecting those he did not like,
Just as he had done with Labour's Clause 4
2580   To make it New Labour. He now wanted
A New Catholic Church. Christ shook his head
In disbelief. A paltry, vapid man,
Too shallow to be the Quartet's envoy.

Another blow was struck against the West.
2585   Obama, the Bilderberg nominee,
Insisted that he wanted the two-state
Solution, defiantly enraging
The pro-Israeli forces who withdrew
The five hundred and fifty billion that
2590   Triggered the world economic crisis.
A new strain of flu suddenly surfaced
Near the borders of the US. In days
A pandemic was called as people died.
Humans walked round in masks, too scared to work
2595   As if the Black Plague were abroad again.
First economic meltdown, now a new
Blow, a double whammy – as factories closed.
Workers in work began to stay at home
And the non-essential economy
2600   Shut down, crippling the Western world again.
The first outbreak occurred in Mexico,
Which shares a border with the USA.
In La Gloria in Perote eighteen

Hundred of the village's three thousand
2605 Residents – 60 per cent – fell ill with
An upper-respiratory infection
During six weeks starting in February.
The first, five-year-old Edgar Hernandez,
Was the first known person to be tested
2610 Positively for H1N1. Health
Officials correlated the outbreak
To a maximum industrial hog farm in
Perote, partly owned by Smithfield Foods,
The largest pork producer in the world.
2615 The farm had just under a million hogs.
The hogs had received antibiotic
And antiviral medications, and
Their pathogens may then have developed
Resistance to medication. Smithfield
2620 Denied connection with H1N1.
The virus was a strain of Spanish flu
Which in 1918 to 20 killed
Between fifty and a hundred million
In a pandemic that came from Kansas,
2625 Mutated near Boston and spread to Brest,
Hit the Central Powers before Allied Powers
And killed in Germany and Austria,
Hit the British in troop camp in Étaples
Before it moved to Spain and hit the press,
2630 And then spread rapidly all round the world.
It may have killed more souls than the Black Death
As the greatest Holocaust in history.
It is not known if it came from US
Poultry and pigs, or a laboratory
2635 As germ warfare against the Central Powers.
Did factory hog farming cause this outbreak
And cause our modern Black Death to revive
After being dormant eighty-nine years?
In fact, the virus had since been rebuilt
2640 In a laboratory in Canada,
The National Microbiology Lab
Which had a maximum biosafety
Wing. Scientists exhumed the well-preserved
Body of a female flu victim in
2645 Arctic permafrost and then extracted
The genetic material they needed
To work out H1N1's structure. They
Tested their reconstructed virus on
Macaque monkeys and found their lung tissue

2650	Was rapidly destroyed so they began
	To drown in their own blood. The same was found
	In earlier tests on mice and in reports
	Of human suffering in 1919.
	Darwyn Kobasa, the research leader,
2655	A scientist working for the Public
	Health Agency of Canada, maintained
	The research helped his team to understand
	Flu viruses and how pandemics rose.
	More research at the University
2660	Of Wisconsin at Madison revealed
	A gene of the immune system, RIG-1,
	Was switched off by the virus so immune
	Defences ran wild, forming low protein.
	The virus altered the immune response.
2665	An earlier study of the deadly strain
	Had been based on frozen tissue and lungs
	Taken from the flu victim whose body
	Had been buried in the permafrost in
	Alaska in 1919, and from
2670	Lung specimens preserved in formalin
	From patients who died in hospital in
	1919. Experiments took place
	In extreme security to find out
	Why this strain of the virus had turned out
2675	To be so virulent. The risk that it
	Might escape and expose the world once more
	To a pandemic had been justified:
	"It's vital to know how the virus worked."
	The virus was injected into mice,
2680	Who all died within a few days. Research
	Scientists had found that the virus kills
	Via a cytokine storm, when the immune
	System overreacts. In September
	2008 a virologist took
2685	Lung and brain tissue from the decomposed
	Body of Colonel Sir Mark Sykes (who reached
	The Sykes-Picot Agreement that angered
	T.E. Lawrence), a victim who died in
	1919. The sample was taken
2690	Through a split in the lead-lined coffin caused
	By the soil's weight as it pressed on the lid.
	It is thought that a test-tube was stolen
	From the Canadian laboratory,
	And that a Syndicate agent released
2695	The virus in Perote, where the hog

Farm could be blamed, for there would always be
Uncertainty about the vaccines and
Response of pathogens, and the spreading
Could be blamed on flies that had settled on
2700   Faecal waste on the farm and later on
Residents' food. In short, the outbreak was
A mystery, and blame was firmly denied.
Soon it had killed more than twenty people.
From Perote the virus spread eastwards.
2705   There was an outbreak just three days before
Obama went to Mexico City.
Felipe Solis, an archaeologist
Who received Obama at Mexico's
Anthropology museum, died the next
2710   Day from symptoms similar to this flu.
A Government official who travelled
With Obama came down with flu symptoms.
Could there have been an assassination
Attempt on Obama's life – death by flu?
2715   Just like the 1918 flu virus,
Spanish flu that killed between fifty and
A hundred million, this virus could kill
In huge numbers – a hundred and twenty
Million forecast – and form another cull
2720   In the "Rockefellers"' population
Reduction program. The "Rockefeller"/
"Rothschild" bioweapon released within
Mexico City was accompanied
By a call from Jay Rockefeller to
2725   Cut down the internet to get across
A consistent message, and by a new
Shipment of disposable facemasks to
Rothschild Home Healthcare Center, Syracuse
Which swiftly sold out as demand was high.
2730   Several agendas had made common cause.
Both "Rockefellers" and "Rothschilds" wanted
A new world order and were panicking
Humankind with fiscal and viral shocks
Into approving a world government
2735   That would solve financial and health crises.
"Rockefellers" were also trying to
Strengthen the role of the UN as it
Coped with a pandemic and displayed their
Global handling of a global problem.
2740   "Rothschilds" were also trying to alter
The US policy towards Israel.

Until Obama changed his two-state tune
And abandoned seeking talks with Iran
A further blow could be expected: war.
2745   The economic and health crises had
Applied pressure on Obama, but they
Had another, a much more global, aim:
To strengthen the coming world government
The Syndicate were preparing through fear.
2750   The Bilderberg's Group's May meeting in Greece
At Nafsika Astir Palace Hotel
In Vouliagmeni, resolved to turn
The IMF into the World Treasury
Department under the UN, using
2755   The global recession as its pretext;
And World Health Organisation into
The World Health Department also under
The UN, using the swine-flu outbreak
And global warming as its health pretext.
2760   What could Heaven do to stop deliberate
Aggression against all Western interests
While its Millennial Kingdom worked for peace?

Netanyahu went to Washington. Just
As a fox leaves its lair at dusk and lopes
2765   Across a field and jumps onto a lawn
And, sniffing, follows a scent trail towards
Urban bins and spilt food to forage and
Returns after dark to its wooded home,
So Netanyahu left his lair to seek
2770   Some benefit for Israel's position.
Obama pressed him to accept the two-
State solution. Netanyahu refused
To give any commitment to that plan.
For what if a Palestinian state
2775   Was seized and turned into a Hamas state?
Hamas was waiting to humiliate
Obama, as he would one day find out.
Netanyahu praised Obama's promise
That Iran would not have nuclear weapons,
2780   That every option was on the table,
Including bombing nuclear Iran.
The two were on a collision course in
What was supposed to be a new era:
The Era of Reconciliation.

2785   On the anniversary of the start

Of the first battle between Islam and
Christendom – the Prophet Mohammed and
A Byzantine expeditionary force –
In 629, peace-loving President
2790   Obama spoke to the entire Muslim world,
Fifty-seven Muslim-majority states,
As one bloc and an entire religion,
The first Western leader since Bonaparte
To do so. Going out live on the State
2795   TV from Cairo University,
At a time of US-Muslim tension
He reached out over the heads of leaders
To a mass audience on the internet
And called for a new beginning between
2800   Muslims and the US, who shared common
Principles: justice, progress, tolerance.
He said that all civilisation had
A debt to Islam's cultural achievements.
He greeted his audience, "*Assalaamu*
2805   *Alaykum*," "Peace be unto you," saying
America would never be at war
With Islam but violent extremism
Had to be confronted. Suspicion and
Discord must end. The US did not want
2810   To keep troops in Afghanistan and would
Not retain bases there. However al-
Qaeda'd killed three thousand Americans,
And the *Koran* had said, "Whoever kills
An innocent, it's as if he has killed
2815   All mankind." He said, "Iraq's sovereignty
Is its own." All US troops would be out
By two thousand and twelve. He said he had
Prohibited all torture. He upheld
Religious diversity and human
2820   Rights so the entire world could live at peace.
In a veiled apology for eight years –
A sign of weakness to ex-crusaders –
He used fine words to change the tone, reach out
To Muslims in changed terminology,
2825   Full of respect towards the Muslim world.
He said he'd fight negative stereotypes
Of Islam and said that many Muslims
Viewed the West as hostile towards Islam.
But, looking like the Muslims he addressed,
2830   He said that educating women would
Improve the Arab states' prosperity.

He said the Palestinians' suffering
Was intolerable, like that of black
Africans, and the solution was for
2835   Israel to grant a Palestinian state.
Hamas must end violence, and Israel must
End continued settlements that were seen
As occupation. Threatening Israel
With destruction was wrong. He wanted all
2840   The world to be free from nuclear weapons,
And to move forward with Iran, which could
Access peaceful nuclear power. Could this be?
"Death to America" was a slogan
That had become instinctive in thirty
2845   Years of the Iranian Revolution,
And Iran wanted to wipe Israel out,
Not accept two states: Palestine, Israel.
He ended with praise for universal
Values: democracy and human rights.
2850   Knowing that international politics
Is partly a question of perception,
He had connected with Arab people,
Quoting the *Koran* four times, and had made
Them feel differently about the US.
2855   He had signalled a retreat from Bush's
Freedom agenda and had not challenged
The Arab despots in the Muslim world,
And he had been too soft on Mubarak
Who'd run a police state for three decades,
2860   And on contemptuous Ahmadinejad,
Who was developing a nuclear bomb.
Arabs yearning for freedom and human
Rights were affronted and hankered for Bush.
Muslims acknowledged his beautiful words
2865   But wanted to see what actions brought change
In a region where Iran was awkward.
At the same time Obama was speaking,
A new thirty-minute audio tape
Was on the internet, of bin Laden
2870   Telling recruits the Americans had
Planted seeds of hatred of the US.
And champions of the West's dominance saw
That while bin Laden still fomented war
The West was now a supplicant for peace.

2875   Now Christ looked into the future and saw
That if human free will made choices that

Mirrored human nature and the interests
Of the Syndicate who were no spent force,
No peaceful regime change would free Iran,
2880 Who owned the world's third-largest oil reserves
And second-highest gas reserves, and was
The world's second-largest oil producer.
He saw the June elections would return
Ahmadinejad as the President,
2885 The Hidden *Imam*'s nail, Supreme Leader's
Favoured voice of the stern Revolution,
A son-like foil to his fatherly vow
That Iran would have a nuclear bomb as
Ayatollah Khomeini had decreed,
2890 That printing 2.6 million surplus
Ballot papers would counter CIA
Monetary support for reformists.
Mousavi had been CIA-funded
And linked with Manuchehr Ghorbanifar,
2895 A former Mossad double agent, and
Would claim regime change and urge mass protests.
But the unmonitored transcription of
Votes on official lists would seal the steal
And rig the vote for the traditionalists.
2900 The CIA would use SMS or
Bland text messaging and Twitter to spread
Disinformation about the election
And a false report that the Guardian
Council had told Mousavi he had won,
2905 Making Ahmadinejad's victory
And re-election appear fraudulent.
Rafsanjani and Mousavi were both
In league with Washington to gain power
In Iran: Ahmadinejad had called
2910 Rafsanjani corrupt, and he would seek
A way to overthrow the Government.
Through them the US would be able to
Portray the election as being "stolen".
There would be uproar for Iran's people
2915 Yearned for liberty and democracy.
The neo-cons were right and freedom was
A universal value and would bring
Peace to a world now criss-crossed by pipelines.
The Trans-Afghan pipeline to Pakistan
2920 Would skirt Iran, and as the US's
General Electric ran the key stations
And BP had poured in nine billion pounds,

	Anglo-American business could not
	Allow the theocracy in Iran
2925	To stop the flow of oil, impede the West.
	There would be confrontation with Iran
	Before there could be universal peace.
	Israel would reflect the Syndicate's stance
	And both sides would act out their self-interest.
2930	Israel would accept a Palestinian
	State if it was demilitarised and
	Recognised Israel as a Jewish state,
	And if Jewish settlements continued,
	Three preconditions unacceptable
2935	To Palestinians, and thus a veto.
	Obama would have no choice but to nod
	In Israel's favour and enter a storm.
	The US would pass attacking Iran
	To Israel, which in July would be given
2940	The go-ahead by the Vice-President
	And Secretary of State after PSYOPs.
	Iran was surrounded by a dozen
	Countries hosting US military
	Bases, and would become one more Iraq,
2945	Afghanistan or Pakistan that would
	Be ruled by Syndicate oil companies
	And an American puppet. China
	Would fund more of America's dark wars
	Of aggression with loans, and Russia would
2950	Fail to deliver missile systems that
	Iran had bought. A war of aggression
	Would be hailed as a glorious act of
	Liberation for Iran's women's rights,
	Peace and democracy. If Obama
2955	Did not support Israel's long rush to war
	And implement Bush's well-thought-out plan,
	The Syndicate would back his call for peace
	As a strategy in crusading war,
	But when Iran became an obstacle
2960	They would turn on Obama, demanding
	The strength of Bush to secure their interests.
	Then Obama would be vulnerable,
	Disposable, and Christ feared he'd be slain.
	The desperate Syndicate who saw their prize
2965	Snatched from their grasp by Western weakness might
	Frame an Iranian assassin, chosen
	Like a suicide bomber, to block peace.
	Christ was sad for Obama's destiny,

If human choices reverted to type,
2970 Might be to be shot like JFK or
Martin Luther King, an act that would shock
The world into outrage and unite all
In condemning the self-interested aims
Of the assassins and bring in one world,
2975 An end that would help Christ's Millennial
Kingdom to come as the Lord's Prayer hoped.
The means in no way justified the end.
But it might be expedient that one man
Should die that the world's people perish not,
2980 Be sacrificed so the people's outrage
Could bring the world together and defeat
The desperate Syndicate before turmoil
Would sweep them aside for a free-chosen
Alliance of all civilisations.
2985 Christ had prescience determined by free will.
He saw trends but free will could affect these.
He saw a route to peace through turbulence.

Told that he would from now on be confined
To Hell under the new dispensation
2990 Ordained by the Light, shocked and resentful
Until with braggadocio he resolved
To put on a bold face and spin his lot,
Satan spoke to the dark creatures of Hell
Massed in the caverns off Hell's seven tunnels.
2995 "Angels," he bellowed. Self-Improvement ceased
As all shades listened. "Beings of Darkness,
We did not like Afghanistan's high crags,
The cold and bright light, and the discomfort.
We were pleased to reoccupy these caves.
3000 I said our aim was to invade Heaven,
To storm the tyrannical Light's stronghold."
A hissing of approval filled the caves.
Satan cut it short. "That is still our aim,
Our long-term objective. But I have found
3005 A better way. If we stay here and you
Improve yourselves until you are ready
To be discharged, you will be admitted
To Heaven, and there, concealing your true aim,
You can mount a *coup d'état* from within
3010 And we can then join you. Revolution,
Angels, beings of darkness, *that*'s our course.
We don't like it on Earth, it's better here
So we will stay here where we'd rather be

And work to install a fifth column in
3015   Heaven who can overthrow the Light and fill
Its plains with Darkness. Then we'll migrate there
And live in greater comfort, proud and free.
Angels," he swaggered, "Heaven is in turmoil.
The Christians' domination is ending.
3020   All religions are now on an equal
Footing, they have a new equivalence
In status. Heaven's collapsing on itself.
Now is not the time to invade. We should
Not interfere in private grief but let
3025   Events take their course. Heaven will subside
Under its own internal problems. We
Will infiltrate it with our leavers, and
When it has finally fallen apart
Our fifth column will have its *coup* and we
3030   Will join our Revolution and drive out
Heaven's *superior* Angels and take their place.
Angels," he swaggered, "then we'll run Heaven
To suit ourselves. *We*'ll control its comforts.
Angels, we have a great future but we
3035   Must be patient, bide our time here and strike
When the time is right and seize power by force.
Angels, follow my course and we will be
The masters of Heaven in place of the Light."
He did not say how Heaven's brilliant Light
3040   Would be turned to darkness after his *coup*.
A loud hissing greeted the triumphal
Spin he put on his abject confinement
And the deception he perpetrated.

Christ stood on the plain at Har Megiddo,
3045   "Mountain of Megiddo", Armageddon,
Between Caesarea and Nazareth,
Near Megiddo's ruined hilltop city,
Which controlled a pass on the route between
Egypt and Assyria, a Canaanite
3050   Fortress destroyed in 1468
BC, and then rebuilt by Solomon,
Conquered by Assyrians in the eighth century,
Scene of many battles where the final
Battle between Good and Evil would take
3055   Place, according to John, before the end
Of the world. Here it was foretold that God
Would gather all at the end of days and
Pour out his wrath in earthquakes, storms and hail.

God was never going to do such things,
3060   John was using poetic images
As he often did when a disciple.
His references to the occupation
Of the Temple in Jerusalem by
The Antichrist evoked the Roman sack
3065   Under Titus in AD 70.
They were historicist, not prophetic,
And described human, not divine, matters.
If Bush had not delayed the Caliphate
And Israel had not struck at its neighbours,
3070   The future that might have unfolded might
Have fulfilled a tripartite Muslim plan:
That Gaza should join up with the West Bank
And take south Israel; that Islam should take
North Israel, including Galilee and
3075   Make Har Megiddo a military base;
And that in a final battle Islam –
Through the Antichrist bin Laden, acting
With Ahmadinejad in Tehran – should
Summon Arab armies to assemble
3080   At Har Megiddo, now military camp,
Take Jerusalem for Israel and make
It the capital of new Palestine.
The Mahdi would attack Jerusalem,
Reconquer it for Islam, rule from it.
3085   There might have been global dictatorship
Under bin Laden's Muslim successors,
During which Palestine would occupy
Israel. But as it was, thanks to firm Bush,
There could be a new co-operative
3090   Universalist world government and
Democracy – in which Israel survived –
Between free civilisations, Heaven's choice.
In either case there was no place at all
For the Syndicate's dark New World Order.
3095   Bush had stopped that, true Hero of the West.
Christ felt satisfied, for he was convinced
He had headed off a new holocaust.
Prophecies abound on scant evidence.
The end of the world was predicted by
3100   The Mayan calendar as being on
December 21, 2012
On the winter solstice when the Fourth Sun
(Age) would end and the Earth's magnetic field
Would reverse in one go. Huge earthquakes and

3105	Tidal waves would sink civilisation.
	Venus, Orion and other stars would
	Take up the positions they occupied
	In 9792BC, the alleged
	Year of the previous cataclysm.
3110	The Maya were Stone Age people, their date
	For the end of the world in twenty twelve
	Was subject to much miscalculation.
	"Divine" codes in the *Bible* also claimed –
	According to biased interpreters –
3115	That God would annihilate the Earth in
	2012. Newton, the genius
	Who discovered the laws of calculus,
	Gravity and light (colour) in two years
	After plague closed his university
3120	In 1665, working alone,
	Pored over Biblical texts for the end
	But came up with nothing. Nostradamus'
	Predictions were too vague to fix a date.
	In Cromwell's day the end of the world was
3125	Foretold to be in 1656
	And Menasseh ben Israel told Cromwell
	That he (Cromwell) was the longed-for Messiah –
	And could he please return Jews to England
	Whence they had been expelled in 1290.
3130	Things had to be put right before the end
	And Cromwell readmitted exiled Jews;
	Was conned into doing so by end talk?
	2012 would come and go, and there
	Would be no battle of Armageddon.
3135	It was just another prophecy that
	Like twenty twelve would not happen.
	And tribulation was a tendency,
	Not a certain outcome, for nothing was
	Inevitable and freedom of choice
3140	Could intervene and change history's course
	As had Bush's giant existential will.
	Twilight fell over Armageddon's plain.
	No final battle for Jerusalem
	Would be fought here. He looked up at the stars,
3145	At the constellation of Aquarius,
	The water-pourer. God would pour out Light
	From his *cornucopia*-like water jar,
	Never-ending flow of infinite Light,
	And humans would now learn to live in peace.
3150	He would support naïve Obama who

Hoped to abolish nuclear weapons,
An idea he had poured in by influx
To his impressionable soul and mind.
There would now be a seven-month period
3155 When the Earth would be cleansed of the chaos
And mess left by the financial crisis.
Christ smiled for all was now good with the world.

O Apollo, leader of the Muses,
Apollon Mousagetes, god of Light,
3160 The lyre and metaphysical poetry,
And of communion with Olympus, home
Of the gods, of knowledge of the future
Through prophets and oracles, under your
Aegis I pronounce Wisdom the Tenth Muse.
3165 O Wisdom, pursuit of philosophy
Whose early Greek "lovers of wisdom" sought
The universe's universal truth,
Sapientia, goddess on a platform
Supported by seven pillars, the House
3170 Wisdom hath hewn out of stone and builded,
Be my Tenth Muse and inspire Muses' fields.
Be universal wisdom that all seek,
A quality that yokes experience
And knowledge with the power of applying
3175 Them critically or practically –
As a wise counsellor to a monarch
Gives a critique of new State policy,
Asks if Churchill was right to go to war
And, borrowing, lose the British Empire;
3180 Or a wise grandfather guides a youngster
On the right path in life, drawing on past
Learned-from mistakes and judicious judgement –
And with intuitive understanding
Deliberately improves well-being,
3185 Finds solutions to problems and applies
Knowledge purposefully, judiciously,
With intelligent prudence. You're valued
In all society and high culture
For discerning the core of all problems
3190 For having self-knowledge, being sincere
And direct with people who ask advice
And for always acting consistently
With your ethical beliefs and knowing
Why things exist as they do, for grasping
3195 The causes of phenomenal events,

Aligning yourself to the infinite.
For universal wisdom is knowing
Fundamental interconnectedness
Of living things, and of living and dead,
3200 As within all forms is the infinite,
A portion of what's immortal and blessed,
While folly is belief that living things
Are separate, accidental, finite,
Contingent and created by blind chance,
3205 That violence is an acceptable means
To achieve goals in this life, which is all.
You know that there's a cycle of violence
In the Middle East and Central Asia
That undermines all peacemakers and in
3210 A tit-for-tit retaliatory mode
Places self-interest above harmony.
You are realistic and can't assume
That a well-intentioned declaration
Of universal peace will always hold.
3215 Because one man has said that he will talk
With all the West's enemies does not mean
That they will down their arms and live at peace,
Beating missile-firers into ploughshares.
O Wisdom, you know the vast gap between
3220 Aspiration and realisation.
Christ has not the power over men to make
Them follow peace's rules, and does not want
To remove their free will, and God has long
Since given up hope of influencing all men
3225 Who have abused the free will they were given
And have befouled the world He created
In our fan-shaped expanding universe.
The infinite can only recommend
And hope mortals will come to their senses.
3230 And so Christ's Thousand-Year Millennium
Is like a banner urging a peaceful
Sane co-existence on warring humans,
And does not mean all hostilities cease.
It gives a context for the world's leaders
3235 To chart a better course for suffering men.
Just as lungs clogged with exhaust fumes leave brains
Short of oxygen, feeling tired, but when
Transported to fresh mountain air, then thrive
And clear as mind is fresh and health returns,
3240 So minds clogged with the detritus of war
And their routines and habits which stress out,

When transported to the fresh air of peace
Take on new lease of life and brim with health.
O Wisdom, you are, like Christ, an ideal
3245 Beyond imperfect men who just aspire
And your Millennium which Christ has brought
Is an aspiration for which the Good
Work and which is for ever undermined
By the Bad in the endless interplay
3250 Between opposing *yin-yang* forces that
Conflict and balance, order-disorder,
Just as plus A added to minus A
Equals zero, Nothing, in the silent,
Profound algebra of the infinite.
3255 O Wisdom, you have tilted the balance
Just slightly towards peace and against war
Like a cease-fire that's often breached, yet holds.
And now Christ's Thousand-Year Millennium
Has given us recalcitrant humans
3260 A better chance of forming a World State
That keeps the peace and restores paradise
In outer harmony where souls can grow.

Having hosted lunch for the twentieth
Anniversary of the school I founded,
3265 Coopersale Hall, where past pupils had come
From far and wide and been addressed by me
In a marquee with reminiscences
Of the founding and opening of the school,
The place where I first learned of 9/11,
3270 Your poet wandered past the great holm-oak,
Planted by Elizabeth the First in
1562, with my first Head and
Waved her car off and stood and looked across
At Orchard Cottage, which I had let out
3275 To our MP, then went inside the school,
Looked in at the library where Churchill
Came in 1924 to arrange
For Lord Lyle to transfer the MPship
To him; gazed at the barley-twist fireplace
3280 With Wolsey peering from the top, then climbed
The stairs to the room where Churchill stayed in
The Second World War after visiting
War planners at Blake Hall and pilots at
North Weald, when this Hall was requisitioned
3285 For wounded officers. Now a classroom,
It had moulded walls, ceiling and fireplace.

Your poet stood where Churchill himself stood
And looked across fields to distant Epping.
Lost in thought on my previous epic,
3290   I suddenly felt I was not alone.
An authoritative presence, severe,
Forbidding, materialised. "Tennyson,"
It said, balding, bearded Shadow-like wraith
In a confident Lincolnshire accent,
3295   "I've followed your progress since your visit
To Farringford. I know your *Overlord*
And your focus on Churchill in that work.
I wrote about the Crimean War. I
Lived at High Beach a while, I know these parts.
3300   I loved the woods and Waltham Abbey. I've
Been following your current work. You asked
Me to be your guide, I have guided you.
Often when you have been unsure how you
Should treat the next block words have floated in
3305   Because I've sent them as a suggestion.
You embody the approach I'd have used
If I were alive today. I can't stand
Most of the verse of your time. It's lightweight.
And now the Laureateship, which I held
3310   For more than forty years, has been given,
Politically awarded, rather....
Words fail me. I will not say any more.
It's best to draw a veil. But you should know
You are one of the few who've continued
3315   The metric line from Chaucer to my own
Verse. You have something pressing to say. In
Your collected poetic works you use
A vocabulary in excess of
Fifty thousand words that's more demanding
3320   Than Shakespeare's thirty-one thousand and than
Milton's eight thousand. You've said something. Your
Superficial time may not get to grips
With you, but nevertheless, you were right
To do it. I will come and escort you
3325   When it's time for you to depart this life.
We will talk further on some of your themes.
I just wanted to give encouragement."
And the presence faded, and Churchill's room
Returned to normal. Your poet turned back
3330   And descended to his two hundred guests.

O Pound, founder of Imagism (and

Thus Modernism) in 1914,
Devotee of Dante whose cantos looked
Back to *The Divine Comedy*'s cantos,
3335   You who opposed "Rothschilds" and unwisely
Broadcast support for Mussolini's land
Reform and were sentenced to death and then
Confined in a mental hospital as
"Political prisoner" for thirteen years
3340   And commissioned Mullins to research and
Write *Secrets of the Federal Reserve*
In protest and lapsed into silence; you
Who I visited in Rapallo when,
The latest canto on your table and
3345   "A place of skulls" in ink on its paper
Near a bust of Gaudier-Brzeska,
I said, "I have come to consult you like
The Delphic Oracle as you have been
Fifty-seven years on your *Cantos* and I
3350   Plan a long epic that may take me years";
You who, when your neighbour, Pescatore
("Like a fish"), said he had visited you
For ten years and had never heard your voice
And I stood up to leave, said, "Sit down, you
3355   Don't have to go yet, do you?" and "I've been
Listening to you, you've been to China, you
Can do the work you've been describing, put
The culture of the West into twelve books.
Seeing it's half the battle. It is like
3360   Building a table, it does not matter
Which leg you start with so long as at the end
The table stands up. Can you put what you
Want to say on half a side of postcard?
T.E. Hulme told me in 1915,
3365   'Everything a writer has to say can
Be put on half a side of a postcard
And all the rest is application and
Elaboration' – Imagist thinking.
And, when I finally stood up to leave,
3370   You gripped my hand and peered into my eyes
From six inches away, probing my soul.
O Pound, you were T.S. Eliot's mentor,
You edited *The Waste Land*, cut half out
And wrote in the line (which did not survive),
3375   "He do the police in many voices."
I heard Ricks claim in a vibrant lecture
That Eliot's "familiar compound ghost"

Was you – "compound" punning on the word Pound.
I share you as my mentor with Eliot,
3380 You were mentor to both of us, and now,
Having looked in on Oxford's Painted Room –
Where Shakespeare is thought to have often stayed
As John Davenant's Crown-Inn guest, *en route* –
And seen the painted wall and fireplace
3385 Behind a sliding panel and curtain
Where an Oxford Aunt now works in clutter,
I sit in Oxford's Examination
Schools before my other mentor and hear
Ricks' final Professor-of-Poetry
3390 Lecture, in which he says poets should have
Keats' "negative capability", be
In uncertainties, mysteries, doubts without
Reaching "after fact and reason" – therefore
He did not "want to know how change the moons" –
3395 And quotes an Eliot lecture claiming
That Coleridge had to suppress interest
In German systems of metaphysics
To let the haunting Muse speak mysteries.
I sit before him fifty years after
3400 He rescued me from Law, and later ask
Him about Eliot's unpublished poems
Which his widow has given him to edit,
And, my son Tony beside me, tell him
That I am near the end of this great task.
3405 O Pound, I can report that I have now
Finished not just one, but two, poetic
Epics, first *Overlord* and now this work,
Balancing mysteries and metaphysics
Like Coleridge, and say to you, "Job done".
3410 You pared the words around your image down
As if writing in Chinese ideograms,
Words that look like the meaning they convey.
Sometimes an image illumines meaning
Like a flash of light through dark clouds. Sometimes
3415 Meaning moves more slowly, like a slow tide
Gathering momentum in a rising sea
And its grandeur creeps in and covers all
The waiting imagination's bare beach.
I mull over Ricks' definition of
3420 Genius, that it improves on others' works.
You told me Dante's behind the *Cantos*,
You tried to "improve on" him in that work.
I wonder if I've "improved" on Dante

In my post-modern age which now permits
3425 Story-tellers to be part of their tale
Just as observers of the universe
Are part of the universe they observe,
And poets to be seen peeping round their
Concealing work in revealing profile.
3430 O Pound, you said I'd do it, and I did.

O Light I invoked in Jamkaran mosque
When, after peering down the well outside
For the Hidden *Imam*, I walked back to
The blue dome and, shoeless, padded along
3435 A large hall with columns and sat among
Fifty Iranians – standing, sitting or
Kneeling with foreheads to the floor, praying
Towards the well and Mecca near sitting
*Mullah*s with white turbans, and some with black
3440 Descended from the Prophet – on a silk
Carpet, closed my eyes and opened my soul
And offered myself as a defuser
Of the international crisis. I asked
You to descend into intransigence
3445 And sort Iran out short of war so there
Would be no threat from nuclear weapons,
And to shine down the well and purify
All hostility and aggressiveness
And make it a place of peace and order.
3450 O Light, I said to you, "I am sitting
In pre-war Iran by the well, please burn
Out all festering and Darkness, please guide
Me in my coming literary work
On the clash between civilisations."
3455 And you, the Light, shone brightly in my soul.
O Light, I have nearly finished that work.
Thank you for guiding me through to the end
And may it improve harmony and peace.

Just as a spider spins thread from its glands,
3460 Silks from its spinnerets it chews to break,
And weaves and hangs a web with a centre
And twelve spokes radiating out, held in
Place by twelve circular filaments that
Intersect each spoke and form rotary
3465 Shapes, each one larger as they spread outwards,
And, patient, waits for tiny flying things
To stick on thread where crystal drops of dew,

Condensed balls of atmospheric vapour,
Have formed in evening air; so this poet's
3470 Gut and mouth have spun a twelve-spoked theme and
Hung its structure for Being to condense
As globules like dew on its worked silk thread,
Pure drops of truth manifesting from air,
The metaphysical condensed to form.
3475 I wait for images to fly in and
Become entangled on its sticky mesh,
Tremble clear droplets under rosy sky,
The delicate filigree tracery
Of its design whose symmetry pleases
3480 But is a practical, working form that
Has been shaped to catch truths and symbols that
Feed the spider-like imagination.
I hung my twelve-book web and caught my catch.
And as a peacock fans its five-foot tail –
3485 And a hundred eyes peer, each feather tipped
With an iridescent eye ringed with blue
And bronze – and struts and quivers, rattling
Its quills, and, uttering loud screams, displays,
So I put up a quill structure I wear
3490 On my back and carry around with me,
Whose hundred images are of the One
Fixed in a grand symmetrical order
That is patterned in a ribbed form. I show
The One in a hundred blue-and-bronze truths
3495 And strut and rattle it in quiet display.

Your poet was working in his Connaught-
House study at his Victorian desk,
Checking through these verses in warm sunshine,
Settling on symbols like a butterfly
3500 Sipping nectar with spread wings on scented
Thyme, fluttering on and then settling
On a new image as on lavender.
Christ alighted in his garden, slowly
Gliding to standstill like a grey heron
3505 That comes each day, hoping to spear a fish.
He sauntered up the grass in the warm sun
To the pond with large orange carp. He walked
Up the lush lawn in shimmering summer,
Green trees and grass rejoicing at blue sky,
3510 Back after a long winter and cold spring,
Looked back at Henry the Eighth's Great Standyng,
Now called Queen Elizabeth's Hunting Lodge,

And gazed at the fountain with Three Graces,
Maidens, round the side of its water bowl.
3515 A cuckoo sang from the Ching-Valley woods,
"Cuckoo, cuckoo." And knowing all was well
He wandered to the spiral iron staircase
Whose thirteen treads symbolised the phases
Of this poet's development and whose
3520 Thirty-six spindles stood for his books on
His slow ascent. He lingered by a bust
That looked Roman, of Apollo, the god
Of the lyre, of poetry and of the Light –
Phoebus, the Shining One of brightest Light –
3525 And of the oracle, prophetic words
Channelled in Delphi, and of pure wisdom.
Then slowly he climbed the winding steps to
The first-floor balcony above the pool
And tapped on this poet's glass door. Startled,
3530 Your poet let him in. He passed the desk,
An 1837 partner's desk
With leather top in perfect condition,
And sixteen alcoves of treasures and sat
In the chair by a tray of butterflies,
3535 And this poet flopped back on the sofa
And said, "You visited me once before.
You visited me after *Overlord*."
The sun poured through the large glass windows as
Christ hunched forward in off-white robes and said,
3540 Looking like the framed picture of the Shroud
In the alcoves, "I've come to thank you for
Your current work, which again tells the Truth
And catches the War on Terror's pattern;
But also for your philosophy. You
3545 Have stated Universalism in
A way Heaven's found helpful. You alone
Of living poets and philosophers
Can see the direction to be followed.
You're a poet for Heaven rather than men,
3550 Who aren't clear what their direction should be.
You have stepped outside Christianity
And have absorbed the Oriental faiths
And the Islamic ones, and yet you are
Grounded in Western origins, the Greeks,
3555 And relate to Apollo timelessly
And have reflected the Light in your work.
You have taken the world into your soul.
Heaven's very interested in your approach.

We see you as shunning celebrity,
3560 Retiring, welcoming obscurity.
'A prophet is not without honour, save
In his own country, and in his own house.'"
This poet smiled, "I say Amen to that."
"You have exposed the Syndicate as well,
3565 You alone of your contemporaries.
I know that literature is your main task
And your history and philosophy clear
Up conflicts in your poems, clarify.
I just came to pay my respects, and thank."
3570 This poet thanked him. A thousand questions
Thrust themselves to the forefront of his mind.
This poet asked, "Has Armageddon been
Blocked forever, or has it been delayed?
Will there be a fiery end one day,
3575 A third of mankind incinerated?"
Like an oracle, enigmatically
Christ said, "Two forces, perpetually
Intertwined, permeate the vast cosmos
In permanent opposition: order
3580 And disorder. God the Light's purposes
Are inscrutable, and, not knowing what's
Ordained, we in Heaven just do our best."
Realising that Christ really did not know,
This poet then asked, "What's it like in Heaven?"
3585 There was a long silence. And then Christ said,
"You must ask Bush. He has seen. Report him.
I will show you one day, but not until
You've finished your research into the Age.
A thousand years, ten years – they are both but
3590 A short time to eternity, from whose
Viewpoint they seem almost one and the same.
That's Heavenly, not Earthly, consciousness.
But you are on the right path. Keep going."
This poet said, "I've gone as far as thought
3595 Can reach, to the limit of space-time. How
Do you cross from Being to Existence?
From outside to within space-time?" Christ said,
"No more questions. This is no time for words.
I have come and said what I've said. Enough."
3600 This poet thanked Christ and they sat on in
The warm sunlight and this poet could sense
The harmony Christ exuded, the peace.
He sat on in the One and there was now
No need for words, and everything was clear

3605	And for a minute, which seemed like an hour,
	He understood how the universe worked
	Through the opposites of Darkness and Light,
	Through infused knowledge from the Light, channelled
	By Christ, and the goal of all humankind
3610	And the meaning of life. He knew these things
	Already and had written them in books
	But Christ now rearranged what he had known
	So everything connected and made sense.
	This poet dwelt in eternity for
3615	About a minute and returned timeless,
	An infinite consciousness in space-time
	That was both immanent and transcendent.
	O wonderful, harmonious universe
	That can bestow such unexpected gifts.

3620	Christ tiptoed away. This poet, sunk deep,
	Became aware he was alone again.
	He stood and slipped out to the balcony,
	And saw Christ down the spiral stair, gazing
	At Apollo's profile. Clambering down,
3625	He stood beside Christ and they sauntered past
	The rose garden's spoked paths and stone fountain
	Of Three Graces, curvaceous maidens, and
	A stone boy clutching a *cornucopia,*
	Across the lawn between statues – Winter,
3630	A maiden holding bread loaves, and Autumn,
	A maiden bearing grapes under lilac –
	To the pool where four large carp lazed in clear
	Water replenished from a gushing pipe,
	Surface that revealed the muddy bottom,
3635	Yet also mirrored blue sky, sun and clouds
	As Existence reflects Being. He saw
	His face, leaves, a lily, a dragonfly
	Framed in glass on the sun's orb, light and dark,
	Being and Existence in One system,
3640	All opposites and contradictions now
	Reconciled and blended, including Bush,
	Bin Laden and Iran. They sauntered past
	Stone Nausicaa and Water-pourer,
	Past a shrub that gave out a lilac scent,
3645	Past tits and finches in the apple trees
	To the rockery steps and knot-garden.
	They stood between Spring, who held bulbs to plant
	In each hand, and Summer's sickle and sheaves,
	Among pinks, strawberries, medieval herbs –

3650	Sage, santolina, hyssop, fennel, thyme –
	Once used as medicines and to flavour food,
	In twenty-five herb beds with brick borders.
	Christ gazed at the central knot, said, "Explain."
	This poet told Christ, "It's an endless knot
3655	Of box hedge with wall-germander corners.
	The design of the fourfold knot was on
	The front cover of the manuscript book,
	The Miroir or Glasse of the Synneful Soul
	By Queen Marguerite of Navarre, which was
3660	Translated from French and handwritten by
	Princess Elizabeth, later Queen. She
	Embroidered the front cover in Queen stitch
	When she was just eleven, and presented
	It to her stepmother Queen Katherine Parr,
3665	Henry the Eighth's sixth wife, on the first day
	Of 1545 – one of six knots,
	Henry the Eighth's six wives. It manifests
	From Dante's infinitesimal point,
	The singularity from which all came.
3670	There are four levels of Being, and this
	Fourfold knot and four *fleurs-de-lis* round it
	Suggest the One emerging into form,
	Hidden spring in which the many are One.
	Whoever contemplates this knot-garden
3675	Becomes aware of how the universe
	Gushed from Being to Existence. This knot's,
	A cyclic symbol of the creation
	And evolution of the universe
	Which pours from infinite Reality,
3680	Renews as running water that's pumped out
	Renews a pond by its endless return,
	Eternal recurrence of a new flow
	Which has already been part of the pond;
	And of the unity of disciplines:
3685	Philosophy, history and literature.
	The knot-garden's design is taken from
	The Gardeners Labyrinth, which was published
	In 1577 and shows open
	Knots to walk through and a closed central knot.
3690	The twenty-five herb beds, which represent
	History's twenty-five civilisations,
	Have also come from the infinite point."
	Christ nodded at the garden's symbolism
	And said, "It expresses the universe
3695	And how it manifests exactly. You

Have understood and told a truth in plants."
Forms that hold meaning are haunting symbols.
A painted lady basking on my thyme,
Wings spread, sipped nectar and was unaware
3700 Of the frail beauty of its outward form
And its meaning in a sunlit moment.
It embodied truth but could not know it.
So most humans don't know our own meaning.
We walked past an ancient sundial and sat
3705 On metallic-meshed chairs at a table
Decorated with grape bunches and leaves
Above clumps of cream clover, purple vetch,
Golden buttercups, stitchwort and daisies,
And looked across to Queen Elizabeth's
3710 Hunting Lodge near the skyline of trees and
Back at Apollo by the spiral stair,
And Christ murmured, "The Earth seems terrible –
Economic collapse, institutions
Corrupt, dreadful prospects – but rest assured.
3715 All's ordered within a benign system.
All will be well in this Peaceful Era.
There will be no Armageddon. It's peace."
And in the warm sunshine and gentle breeze
Of a bright English summer countryside
3720 I felt the universe's harmony
And the benevolence of a benign
Universal order, and life was good.
And though Wisdom warned that aspiration
Often falls short of realisation –
3725 That experience often finds naïve hopes
Are dashed, that nuclear proliferation
Increases and that wise realism
Tends to be pessimistic, that it is
Heroic if not facile to manage
3730 To be optimistic in our world – my
Heart leapt at his certain optimism,
His Epping-Forest vision that despite
The dreadful things that have beset the West
Things will be all right, there can still be hope.
3735 He saw so clearly that all will be well.
May–September 2008, January–July 2009

HISTORICAL ADDENDA

1. Timelines

A. Historical Events

(A seven-years' tribulation begins in January 2002 with al-Qaeda's move to the Middle East and ends in January 2009 with Obama's inauguration/Christ's Millennial Kingdom and Peaceful Era. See p580.)

Date		Event
Background		
1948		Israel reborn as a nation.
1967		Israel captures Jerusalem and renews Abraham Covenant, borders similar to what Abraham was promised, i.e. the Promised Land.
		UN Resolution 242.
1973		Egypt and Syria attack Israel with Soviet help.
1988		Bin Laden co-founds al-Qaeda, "the Base" from which the true Caliphate (750-1258) is to be revived in Baghdad, a vast new anti-Western empire with bin Laden as "Hidden Caliph", potential ruler of the Muslim world from Morocco to Pakistan.
1992		Bin Laden begins quest to buy nuclear raw material by purchasing highly enriched uranium stolen in South Africa.
1993		Clinton abandons UN Resolution 242.
1996	Aug?	Bin Laden buys twenty nuclear-suitcase bombs, via Chechen intermediaries, from Ukraine, Kazakhstan, Turkmenistan and Russia, raising fear of Armageddon. He settles in Afghanistan.

	23 Aug	Bin Laden issues 'Declaration of War against the Americans Occupying the Land of the Two Holy Places', urging global *jihad* and relentless war against the US to establish the new Caliphate based in Baghdad.
1998	Nov-Dec	Bush Jr to Israel, where he is escorted by Sharon.
1999	19 Feb	Arafat vows to make East Jerusalem the capital of a Palestinian state.
2000	11-24 Jul	Clinton, Barak and Arafat fail to agree a five-year peace agreement at Camp David (Arafat, Barak and Clinton).
	28 Sep	Palestinian *Intifada*/violence.
	7 Oct	UN Resolution 1322 confirms Resolution 242 (1967), Israel's boundaries promised to Abraham. Abraham's Covenant confirmed.
	7 Nov	Bush Jr elected President.
2001	21-27 Jan	Taba summit at end of Barak's tenure of power, nearly reaches agreement.
	2 May	At a reception at the US Embassy, London, in honour of Governor James Gilmore, the Governor of Virginia, Nicholas Hagger hands a copy of *The Fire and the Stones*, his study of 25 civilisations, to Governor Gilmore. It is inscribed to President Bush, and Governor Gilmore later personally gives it to Bush.
	Nov	Bin Laden claims to have nuclear weapons in an interview with Pakistani journalist Hamid Mir.

Book One

	9 Sep	Al-Qaeda assassinates Massoud, Afghan military leader.
	11 Sep	9/11 Attack on US organised by bin Laden. Collapse of Twin Towers and WTC7.
		Bush addresses the American people.

Book Two

	16 Sep	Bush threatens action against Afghanistan.

| 17-24 Sep | Bin Laden's family leaves US for Saudi Arabia. |
| 20 Sep | Bush gives the Taliban an ultimatum. |

Book Three

7 Oct	US-UK-NATO invasion of Afghanistan.
26 Oct	Anti-terrorism bill signed into law.
9 Nov	Battle of Chesmay-e-Safa gorge.
22 Nov-7 Dec	Fall of Kandahar.
25 Nov-1 Dec	Battle of Mazar-i-Sharif.
5 Dec	Collapse of Taliban.
12-17 Dec	Battle of Tora Bora. Bin Laden disappears.

Book Four

2002	Jan	Al-Qaeda move to Middle East/Jerusalem, seeking to restore the true Caliphate (750-1258) in Baghdad.
	Jan	Peace plan drawn up by Abdullah, Crown Prince of Saudi Arabia, now King.
	29 Jan	Bush asserts in State-of-Union address that there is an "axis of evil" (North Korea, Iran, Iraq).
	Early 2002	Bush's inner circle agree to attack Iraq.
	27-28 Mar	Abdullah's plan is passed by Arab ministers and is the basis of the Road Map, an Arab conception.
	12 Apr	Jerusalem bombed. Israel formally declares war on Palestine and reoccupies Palestinian areas.
	24 Jun	Speech by Bush introducing the Road Map for Peace and two-state solution.
	Jul	Bin Laden sends audiotape to Ayatollah Khamenei, Supreme Leader of Iran, offering him ultimate control of al-Qaeda in return for safe haven.
	23 Jul	Bush calls for Israeli withdrawal and a Palestinian state.

26 Jul	Bin Laden crosses into Iran near Zabol and travels to Mashad, then lives in safe houses between Qazvin and Karaj, west of Tehran.
12 Sep	Bush addresses UN Security Council on Iraq. UN Resolution 1441.
16 Oct	Under the Iraq War Resolution (more fully, the Authorization for Use of Military Force Against Iraq Resolution of 2002), passed by the US Congress, authorizing war against Iraq, Bush gains complete authority over military to declare war as he wills.
23 Oct	$355.5 billion increase signed for military spending.
2003 31 Jan	Bush tells Blair the US will invade Iraq.

Book Five

After 2 Mar	Khalid Sheikh Mohammed is apprehended. According to his evidence and that of other al-Qaeda defectors and informants, bin Laden has announced his intention to detonate nuclear-suitcase bombs in at least seven and possibly ten US cities. (Source: Josh Meyer and Greg Kikorian, 'US Braces for Attack by Al-Qaeda', *Los Angeles Times*, December 24, 2003.)
	Bin Laden has smuggled nuclear weapons into the US through Mexico with the help of the MS-13 criminal group for use in a plot knows as "American Hiroshima". (Source: Paul L Williams, *The Al Qaeda Connection*, pp99, 101, 160-161, 197.)
12 Mar	UN Security Council Resolution 1397, adopted at Bush's instigation.
17 Mar	Bush gives Saddam 48 hours to surrender.
19/20 Mar	US attack on Iraq.
21 Mar	US-UK ground attack begins on Kuwait border near Umm Qasr. Invasion of Iraq – Coalition of four out of 49 contributing troops.
	Shock and Awe in Baghdad.

3-12 Apr	Fall of Baghdad.
10/11 Apr	Saddam meets the senior Iraqi leadership and tells them, "We will struggle in secret." He then leaves Baghdad.
30 Apr	Bush unveils Road Map for Peace.
1 May	Bush lands on *USS Abraham Lincoln*. Banner says "Mission Accomplished".
May	*Sheikh* Nassir bin Hamid al Fahd, Saudi cleric, issues a *fatwa*, 'A Treatise on the Legal Status of Using Weapons of Mass Destruction Against Infidels', on behalf of the Wahhabi clerics of Saudi Arabia granting bin Laden and al-Qaeda permission to use nuclear weapons in the *jihad* against the US. Al-Qaeda state that 4 million Americans (2 million of whom must be children) will have to die to achieve parity with the number of Muslims killed by the US. (Source: www.analyst-network.com/.../Nuclear911 InterviewwithDrPaulLWilliams.doc. And Paul L Williams, *The Al Qaeda Connection*, p192.)
2-4 Jun	Bush in Middle East to push Road Map.
5 Jun	Bush pushes Road Map for Peace with Israeli/Palestinian leaders.

Book Six

Summer	Start of insurgency in Iraq.
22 Jul	Saddam's sons Qusay and Uday are killed.
29 Aug	*Imam* Ali mosque, Najaf, bombed.
23 Oct	Bin Laden and al-Zawahiri seen in Najmabad, Iran by two Iranian intelligence officers. Their appearances had been changed by plastic surgery. (Source: Richard Miniter, *Shadow War*, pp21-22.)
3 Nov	Bin Laden's chief financial officer Mustafa Ahmed Mohammed crosses into Iran at Zabol with $20 million in cash to finance al-Qaeda's spring 2004 offensive in Afghanistan. (Source: Richard Miniter, *Shadow War*, pp22-23.)

	14 Dec	Saddam is apprehended.
2004	4 Apr-1 May	First battle of Falluja.
	2 Nov	Bush re-elected President.
	7 Nov-23 Dec	Second battle of Falluja.

Book Seven

2005	Jan	Sanhedrin Council convened for first time for 1,600 years.
	3 Feb	Bush's State-of-the-Union speech.
	9 Feb	Sanhedrin considers rebuilding a Third Temple – part of which may have already been prefabricated.
	10 May	Bush survives assassination attempt in Tblisi, Georgia, hand grenade thrown by Vladimir Arutinian thrown towards podium does not explode.
	7 Jul	Bombs in London on three underground trains and a bus.
	9 Jul	A letter from al-Zawahiri, bin Laden's deputy, to al-Zarqawi urges a new Caliphate based on an emirate in Iraq.
	17-20 Aug	10,000 Israeli settlers expelled from Gaza.
	23-30 Aug	Hurricane Katrina.
	17 Sep	Ahmadinejad bathed in Light while speaking at the UN General Assembly.
	20 Sep	Bush agrees Road Map and again betrays Israel, which must withdraw from Palestine. Sharon implements this.
2006	4 Jan	Sharon in coma after stroke.
	22-23 Feb	Golden dome of Shiite al-Askariya shrine, Samarra, bombed.
	7 Jun	Zarqawi killed.
	12 Jul-3 Aug	Israel attacks Hezbollah in Lebanon.

Book Eight

	7 Nov	Democrats win Senate election, Rumsfeld departs.
	6 Dec	Iraq Study Group says Bush is losing in Iraq.
	30 Dec	Saddam is hanged.
2007	10 Jan	Bush boosts troop numbers in Iraq.
	Feb	Petraeus arrives in Baghdad. Start of Surge.
	23 Mar	15 Britons captured in Iran, released in April.
	May	400th Anniversary of founding of America.
	3 Jun	Golden dome of Shiite al-Askariya shrine, Samarra, bombed again.

Book Nine

	27 Jun	Blair resigns as Prime Minister and it is announced that he will be Quartet Ambassador based in Jerusalem.
	27 Nov	Bush's summit for Israeli and Arab leaders in Annapolis.
2008	9-11 Jan	Bush visits Israel, then Palestine, and leaves for Kuwait, Bahrain, the United Arab Emirates, Saudi Arabia, and Egypt.
	22 Mar	Cheney meets Olmert in Jerusalem.
	14 May	Bush attends 60th Anniversary of Israel and Bush denies Israel's request to fly over Iraq to bomb Iran.
	2 Jun	Israel's air exercise appears to prepare for war with Iran.
	13 Jun	Bush visits Pope Benedict XVI.
	Jun	Beginning of US/world credit crunch – financial Armageddon begins.
	7-16 Aug	Russia invades Georgia and declares South Ossetia and Abkhazia independent republics.

Book Ten

11 Sep	Global financial and economic collapse threatened by mysterious electronic withdrawals of $550 billion from American accounts in two hours of trading. $105 billion lost in propping up the market before trading is discontinued at 11 a.m.
23 Sep	Financial rescue plan of $700 billion presented to replace the lost $655 billion. Officially this is to set against "toxic assets".
4 Nov	Obama elected President on peace program.
15 Nov	G20 leaders meet.
14 Dec	Iraqi journalist throws shoes at Bush.

2008/ 2009		
	27 Dec-18 Jan	Israel-Gaza crisis.
	3 Jan	Israel invades Gaza.
	8 Jan	Olmert rings Bush and urges him to halt his support for a UN resolution against Israel. US abstains.
	12 Jan	Bush's final news conference.

Book Eleven

17-18 Jan	Obama travels by train from Philadelphia to Washington.
20 Jan	Bush leaves the White House. Obama's inauguration. Beginning of new Peaceful Era.

Book Twelve

18 May	Netanyahu, Israel's new Prime Minister, visits Obama.
4 Jun	Obama addresses Islam.
11 Jun	Ahmadinejad controversially re-elected in Iran.

B. Mythical* Events

* "Myth", "traditional narrative usually involving supernatural or imaginary persons and embodying popular ideas on natural or social phenomena" (*Concise Oxford Dictionary*).

Date	Event
c.20th/19thC BC	God's Covenant with Abraham allocating Promised Land.
	Satan's attempted revolutionary *coup* on God's throne, to target Christ.
	Satan thrown down to Earth.
1939-45	First round of seven-years' tribulation. (See *Overlord*.)
1945	Christ's harrowing of Hell. Satan and his followers are expelled to Earth. (See *Overlord*.)
	Christ's first attempt at a Thousand-Year Millennial Kingdom and Reign, with Christian dominance. This Reign is ruined by Satan, who intrigues the Cold War from within the USSR. (See *Overlord*.)
2002-2009	Second round of seven-years' tribulation.
2002 Jan	Al-Qaeda move to Middle East and begin first 3½ years of tribulation.
	Western and Muslim pairs of Antichrist and Beast/False Prophet: Western Bush and Blair, Muslim bin Laden and Ahmadinejad. Christ supports Bush, Satan supports bin Laden.
	Satan is in Afghanistan and leads his followers back to Hell.
Mar	Land-for-peace Road Map breaks Abraham's Covenant.
Jul	Bin Laden moves to Iran, where al-Qaeda is now based, and continues tribulation by spreading turmoil in Iraq and Afghanistan.

	Dec	Bush's first visit to Hell.
2005	Feb	Newly convened Sanhedrin considers building a Third Temple, which is scripturally associated with Christ's Second Coming.
		Division in Heaven. Mohammed urges power-sharing with Christ. Christ reluctantly agrees that there will now be a power-sharing Universalist Heaven.
2007	Early Jan	Bush's second visit to Hell.
2009	20 Jan	End of seven-years' tribulation with Obama's inauguration.
		Satan is confined to Hell and urges his followers to become fifth-columnists in Heaven and have a *coup*.
	End of Jan	Christ's Second Coming.
		Bush's visit to Heaven.
		Christ's second attempt at a Thousand-Year Millennial Kingdom and Reign, this time a Universalist Reign based on sharing between all religions' leaders both in Heaven and on Earth, and on universal order and universal peace.
		Christ at Har Megiddo. He has avoided Armageddon by supporting Bush's pressure on bin Laden.
		Peaceful Era, or Era of Reconciliation, begins with Obama.
	Apr	Return of Mohammed.
		Return of Hidden *Imam*.
		Seven-month period for cleansing the land – clearing up the mess left by the financial crisis and five wars.

2. Bin Laden's/Al-Qaeda's Historical Attempts to Acquire Weapons of Mass Destruction and Unleash Armageddon in the US

(In 2009 there were 23,573 nuclear warheads in the world, of which the Russians had 12,987. Source: guardian.co.uk. Given the chaotic state of the ex-Soviet Union in the 1990s, it is not surprising if a small number of these fell into Mafia hands, for sale to bin Laden and al-Qaeda.)

Date	Type	Event	Source
1992	Nuclear	Bin Laden purchased highly enriched uranium stolen from Valendaba, a nuclear manufacturing facility near Pretoria, South Africa. Testimony concerning bin Laden's acquisition of nuclear weapons and materials while living in Sudan and his setting-up of a lab in Khartoum to make nuclear weapons was provided by former al-Qaeda operatives in *United States v. Usama bin Laden, et. al.,* S(10) 98 Cr. (LBS), Southern District of New York, 2001.	Gordon Thomas, 'Los Malerines de Osama', *El Mundo*, September, 23, 2001; Paul L. Williams, *The Al Qaeda Connection*, p28.
1993-94	Nuclear/ Radiological	Jamal Ahmed al-Fadl claimed that, on behalf of bin Laden, he had made arrangements for the purchase of uranium for nuclear weapons for $1 million and had it delivered to the training camps in Afghanistan.	Kimberly McCloud and Matthew Osborne, 'WMD Terrorism and Usama Bin Laden', CNS Report, November 20, 2001.

After 1994 and by August 1996	Nuclear	Bin Laden paid a group of Chechens $30 million in cash and two tons of opium in exchange for approximately 20 nuclear warheads.	Riyad Alam al-Din, 'Report Links Bin Laden, Nuclear Weapons', *Al-Watan al-Arabi*, November 23, 1998; Emil Torabi, 'Bin Laden's Nuclear Weapons', *Muslim Magazine* (winter 1998).
After 1996	Nuclear	Bin Laden paid more than £2 million to a middleman in Kazakhstan for a suitcase bomb.	Marie Calvin, 'Holy War with US in His Sights', *Times* (London), August 16, 1998.
1996-98	Chemical	Bin Laden bought CW (chemical weapons) over a two-year period prior to 1998 from European states and the former Soviet Union. This information comes from the testimony of a *jihad* leader arrested on August 20, 1998, in Baku, Azerbaijan.	Muhammad Salah, 'Bin Laden Front Reportedly Bought CBW from E. Europe', *Al-Hayah*, April 20, 1999; Muhammad Salah, 'US Said Interrogating Jihadist over CBW', *Al-Hayah*, April 21, 1999.
May 1997	Nuclear	General Aleksandr Lebed, Yeltsin's former security secretary, told members of the US House of Representatives that 84 nuclear-suitcase bombs were missing. Out of 132 produced he could only account for 48. He said that some of the missing bombs might be in the hands of Muslim extremists.	Scott Parish, 'Are Suitcase Nukes on the loose? The Story behind the Controversy', Centre for Nonproliferation Studies, Monterey Institute of International Studies, Monterey, California, November 1997.
Before October 1997	Nuclear	Bin Laden purchased 48 nuclear-suitcase bombs from the Russian Mafia.	'Al-Majallah Obtains Serious Information of Al-Qaeda's Attempt to Acquire Nuclear Arms', *Al-Majallah* (London-based Saudi weekly), September 8, 2002.

Before 1998	Nuclear	Abdul Qadeer Khan was alleged to have supplied bin Laden with nuclear suicide bombs. They were looked after by Pakistani nuclear engineers and ISI generals, who were paid $60-100 million by bin Laden.	'Pakistan Scientist Brokered North Korea Deal', NBC News, October 18, 2002. Also Mishra, 'Nuclear Scientific Community of Pakistan'. Also John M Curtis, 'Pakistan's Bomb Maker', *OnlineColumnist.com*, January 5, 2003, http://www.online columnist. com/01503.htm.
Before 1998	Nuclear	Via al-Qaeda agents bin Laden bought 12-15 kilos of uranium -235 for $75 million from a Ukrainian arms dealer, Semion Mogilevich, and 20 kilos of uranium-236 enriched 85 per cent.	Ryan Mauro, "Terrorist Possession of Weapons of Mass Destruction', *World Threats*, Monthly Analysis, February 2003, http://www.worldthreats .vcon/monthly%20analysis/ MA%202003.htm. Also Robert Friedman, 'The Most Dangerous Mobster in the World', *Village Voice*, May 22, 1998.
Before 1998	Nuclear	Via al-Qaeda agents bin Laden bought two bars of enriched uranium-138 from Egyptian black-marketer Ibrahim Abd in Hamburg, Germany.	Ryan Mauro, 'The Next Attack on America', *World Threats*, November 27, 2003, http://www.freepublic.com /focus/f-news/1020690/posts. Also 'Bin Laden buys Nuclear Materials', *World Net Daily*, November 26, 2003.
1997-98	Chemical/ Biological	Islamic extremists, including al-Qaeda operatives, were trained in secret camps near Baghdad in the use of CW and BW (biological weapons) by instructors from Iraq's secret military intelligence Unit 999.	Gwynne Roberts, 'Militia Defector Claims Baghdad Trained Al-Qaeda Fighters in Chemical Warfare', *Sunday Times* (London), July 14, 2002.

October 1997	Chemical/ Biological	A meeting was held in Sudan between bin Laden, Ayman al-Zawahiri, and Hasan al-Turabi, leader of Sudan's National Islamic Front regime, about the construction of a CBW factory.	Jihad Salim, 'Report on Bin Laden, Zawahiri, Afghans', *Al-Watan al-Arabi*, February 16, 2001.
1998	Nuclear/ Radiological	Russian Intelligence blocked an attempt by bin Laden to purchase Soviet-origin uranium.	Earl Lane and Knut Royce, 'Nuclear Aspirations? Sources: Bin Laden Tried to Obtain Enriched Uranium', *Newsday*, September 19, 2001.
1998	Chemical/ Biological	From looters in Kabul a reporter obtained two computers that had been found in an abandoned al-Qaeda safe house. One of the computers contained a file describing "plans to launch a chemical and biological weapons program." Bin Laden's deputy al-Zawahiri reportedly created the documents describing his CW and BW program, code-named "Curdled Milk." The document included work on a pesticide-nerve agent that was tested on rabbits and dogs. Al-Zawahiri was assisted by Midhat Mursi (a.k.a. Abu Khabbab), a chemical engineer.	Alan Culluson and Andrew Higgins, 'Computer in Kabul Holds Chilling Memos', *Wall Street Journal*, December 31, 2001; 'Report: Al Qaeda Computer Had Plans for Bio-Weapons', Reuters, December 21, 2001.
May 1998	Chemical/ Biological	Al-Qaeda purchased three CBW factories in the former Yugoslavia and hired a number of Ukrainian chemists and biologists to train its members.	Guido Olimpio, 'Islamic Group Said Preparing Chemical Warfare on he West', *Corriere della Sera*, July 8, 1998; Yossef Bodansky, *Bin Laden: The Man Who Declared War on America* (New York: Prima, 2001), 326.

August 1998	Chemical	The CIA discovered that bin Laden had attempted to acquire unspecified CW for use against U.S. troops stationed in the Persian Gulf.	Barry Schweid, 'US Suggests Iraq Got Weapons from Sudan', *Record* (New Jersey), August 27, 1998.
September 1998	Nuclear/ Radiological	Mamdouh Mahmud Salim, an al-Qaeda operative, was arrested in Munich, Germany, for trying to purchase nuclear material, including highly enriched uranium.	Benjamin Weiser, 'US Says Bin Laden Aide Tried to Get Nuclear Weapons', *New York Times*, September 26, 1998.
September 1998	Chemical	Wadi al-Hajj, a Lebanese national, is arrested in Arlington, Texas for perjury. The FBI contends that he had lied about his affiliation with bin Laden and that he was involved in procuring WMD for al-Qaeda.	CNN, December 20, 1998.
December 1998	Chemical/ Nuclear	In an interview with *Time* magazine, bin Laden said that acquiring weapons of any type, including chemical and nuclear, is a Muslim "religious duty."	'Interview with bin Laden', *Time*, December 24, 1998.
1999	Chemical	Afghan sources maintained that bin Laden made use of a plant in Charassiab, a district south of Kabul, to produce CW.	'Afghan Alliance – UBL trying to Make Chemical Weapons', *Parwan Payam-e Mojahed*, December 23, 1999.
April 1999	Biological	Bin Laden obtained BW substances through the mail from former Soviet Union republics (the Ebola virus and salmonella bacterium), from East Asia (anthrax-causing bacteria), and from the Czech Republic (botulinum toxin).	Al J. Venter, 'Elements Loyal to Bin Laden Acquire Biological Agents "Through the Mail"', *Jane's Intelligence Review* (August 1999); Khalid Sharaf al-Din, 'Bin Laden Men Reportedly Possess Biological Weapons', *Al-Sharq al-Awsat*, March 6, 1999.

July 1999	Chemical/ Biological	An Islamist lawyer testified that al-Qaeda has CBW and will likely use such weapons against the United States.	'Islamist Lawyer on Bin Laden, Groups', *Al-Sharq al-Awsat*, July 12, 1999.
Before 2000	Biological	Al-Qaeda operatives bought anthrax and plague from arms dealers in Kazakhstan.	Paul Daley, 'Report Says UBL-Linked Terrorist Groups Possess "Deadly" Anthrax, Plague Viruses', *Melbourne Age*, June 4, 2000.
February 2000	Chemical	Italian police foil a plot by nine Moroccans, with ties to al-Qaeda, to poison the water supply of the US Embassy in Rome with a cyanide compound.	Eric Croddy *et al.*, 'Chemical Terrorist Plot in Rome?', CNS Research Story, March 11, 2002.
Late 2000	Nuclear	The intelligence agency of an unnamed European country intercepted a shipment – originating in Kazakhstan, Russia, Turkmenistan and the Ukraine – of approximately 20 nuclear warheads intended for bin Laden and the Taliban regime of Afghanistan.	'Arab Security Sources Speak of a New Scenario for Afghanistan: Secret Roaming Networks That Exchange Nuclear Weapons for Drugs', *Al-Sharq al-Awsat*, December 24, 2000.
2001	Biological	Various sources confirmed that Mohammed Atta, the leader of the September 11 hijackers, was provided with a vial of anthrax by an Iraqi intelligence agent at a meeting in Prague.	Kreindler and Kreindler 9/11 lawsuit; 'Prague Discounts an Iraqi Meeting', *New York Times*, October 21, 2001; 'Czechs Retract Iraq Terror Link', United Press International, October 20, 2001.
2001	Biological	Ahmed Ressam, arrested in a plot to bomb Los Angeles International Airport, testified that bin Laden is interested in using low-flying aircraft to dispense BW agents over major US metropolitan areas.	'Bin Laden's Biological Threat', BBC, October 28, 2001.

2001	Biological	Documents found in Afghanistan revealed that al-Qaeda was conducting research on using botulinum toxin to kill two thousand people.	'Al Qaeda Tested Germ Weapons', Reuters, January 1, 2002.
2001	Chemical	Ahmed Ressam claimed to witness the gassing of a dog with cyanide in an al-Qaeda training camp.	Pamela Hess, 'Al-Qaeda May Have Chemical Weapons', United Press International, August 19, 2002.
February 2001	Chemical	After receiving warnings from an Arab embassy in Islamabad, Pakistan, the US aborted a planned air strike against Afghanistan for fear of a chemical attack by al-Qaeda.	Sa'id al-Qaysi, 'US Said Aborted Planned Attack on Bin Laden for Fear of "Chemical Strike"', *Al-Watan al-Arabi*, February 16, 2001.
February 2001	Chemical	Bin Laden's *élite* 055 Brigade reorganised under the leadership of Midhat Mursi, a.k.a. Abu Khabab, an Eyptian and expert in sarin gas production.	Sa'id al-Qaysi, 'US Said Aborted Planned Attack on Bin Laden for Fear of "Chemical Strike"', *Al-Watan al-Arabi*, February 16, 2001.
April 2001	Nuclear/ Radiological	Ivan Ivanov claimed to have met with bin Laden in China to discuss the establishment of a company to buy nuclear waste. Ivanov was then approached by a Pakistani chemical engineer interested in buying nuclear fuel rods from the Bulgarian Kozlodui reactor.	Adam Nathan and David Leppard, 'Al-Qaeda's Men Held Secret Meetings to Build "Dirty Bomb"', *Sunday Times* (London), October 14, 2001.
Since summer 2001	Chemical/ Biological/ Nuclear	Iraqi military instructors provided training to 150-250 al-Qaeda operatives in northern Iraq in the use of CBW and the handling of nuclear devices.	'Abu Nidal's Nemesis', DEBKAfile (Jerusalem), August 20, 2002.

October 2001	Nuclear	Mossad arrested an al-Qaeda operative with backpack containing a tactical nuclear weapon at the checkpoint in Ramallah.	United Press International, December 21, 2001. First reports spoke of a radiological bomb.
Before November 2001	Chemical	CNN releases al-Qaeda videotapes that show dogs being killed by unidentified toxic chemicals, which experts believe could be either a crude nerve agent or hydrogen cyanide gas.	*Insight*, CNN, August 19, 2002.
Before November 2001	Biological	US officials discovered documents concerning the aerial dispersal of anthrax via balloon within the Kabul office of Pakistani scientist Dr Bashiruddin Mahmood.	'Sketches of Anthrax Bomb Found in Pakistani Scientist's Office', Rediff.com, November 28, 2001.
Before November 2001	Nuclear/ Biological/ Chemical	Two Pakistani scientists shared nuclear, biological, and chemical weapons information with bin Laden, who said that the nuclear material had been provided by the Islamic Movement of Uzbekistan.	Toby Hamden, 'Rogue Scientists Gave Bin Laden Nuclear Secrets', *Daily Telegraph* (London), December 13, 2001; Peter Baker, 'Pakistani Scientist Who Met Bin Laden Failed Polygraphs, Renewing Suspicions', *Washington Post*, March 3, 2002; Susan B. Glasser and Kamra Khan, 'Pakistan Continues Probe of Nuclear Scientists', *Washington Post*, November 14, 2001.
November 2001	Chemical/ Nuclear	In an interview bin Laden declared: "We have chemical and nuclear weapons as a deterrent, and if America uses them against us, we reserve the right to use them."	Hamid Mir, 'Osama Claims He Has Nukes: If US Uses N-Arms It Will Get Some Response', *Dawn* (Pakistan), November 10, 2001.

November 2001	Nuclear	Evidence obtained from the offices of *Ummah* Tameer E-Nau of Kabul shows that a nuclear weapon may have been shipped to the US from Karachi in a cargo container.	Arnaud de Borchgrave, 'Al Qaeda's Nuclear Agenda Verified', *Washington Times*, December 10, 2001.
November 2001	Nuclear	Bin Laden acquired a Russian-made suitcase nuclear weapon from Central Asian sources. The weapon was reported to weigh 8 kg and to possess at least 2 kg of fissionable uranium and plutonium. The report said the device, with serial number 9999 and a manufacturing date of October 1998, could be set off by a mobile-phone signal. This weapon, according to sources, had been forward-deployed to the US.	'N-weapons May Be in US Already', *Daily Telegraph* (Sydney, Australia), November 14, 2001.
November 2001	Nuclear	A *Times* (London) reporter discovered a blueprint for a "Nagasaki bomb" in an abandoned al-Qaeda house in Kabul.	'Nuke Plans Found; Brit Paper Discovers Details of Weapons in Kabul Safe House', *Toronto Sun*, November 15, 2001; Hugh Dougherty, 'Afghan Nuclear Weapons Papers "May Be Internet Spoofs"', *Press Association*, November 19, 2001.
November 2001	Nuclear	A "superbomb" manual that addresses the physics of nuclear weapons and dirty bombs was discovered in a safe house in Afghanistan.	'Osama Bin Laden's Bid to Acquire Weapons of Mass Destruction Represents the Greatest Threat That Western Civilization Has Faced', *Mail on Sunday* (London), June 23, 2002.
December 2001	Radiological	Uranium-235 was found in a lead-lined canister in Kandahar.	Barbie Dutter and Ben Fenton, 'Uranium and Cyanide Found In Drums at Bin Laden's Base', *Daily Telegraph* (London), December 24, 2001.

Late 2001	Biological	US intelligence agents uncovered evidence in Afghanistan that one or more Russian scientists were helping al-Qaeda develop biological weapons, including anthrax.	Jeffrey Bartholet, 'Terrorist Sleeper Cells', *Newsweek*, December 9, 2001.
Late 2001	Biological	Al-Zawahiri's home in Kabul tested positive for traces of anthrax, as did five of nineteen al-Qaeda labs in Afghanistan.	'Al-Qaeda: Anthrax found in Al-Qaeda Home', Global Security Newswire, December 10, 2001; Judith Miller, 'Labs Suggest Al Qaeda Planned to Build Arms, Officials Say', *New York Times*, September 14, 2001.
Late 2001	Biological	John Walker Lindh told interrogators that a biological attack was expected to be part of a "second wave" of al-Qaeda attacks.	'Walker Lindh: Al Qaeda Planned More Attacks', CNN, October 3, 2002.
2002	Chemical	The facility of Ansar al-Islam, a radical Islamist group operating in northern Iraq with ties to al-Qaeda, produced a form of cyanide cream that kills on contact.	William Safire, 'Tying Saddam to Terrorist Organizations', *New York Times*, August 25, 2002.
January-June 2002	Biological	Ansar al-Islam had conducted experiments with ricin, a deadly toxin, on at least one human subject.	'US Knew of Bio-Terror Tests in Iraq', BBC News, August 20, 2002; 'US Monitors Kurdish Extremists', Fox News, August 21, 2002; Isma'il Zayir, 'Ansar al-Islam Group Accuses [Jalal] Talabani of Spreading Rumors About Its Cooperation with Al-Qaeda', *Al Hayah*, August 22, 2002.
January 2002	Nuclear	Diagrams of US nuclear power plants were discovered in abandoned al-Qaeda camps and facilities in Afghanistan.	Bill Gertz, 'Nuclear Plants Targeted', *Washington Times*, January 31, 2002; John J. Lumpkin, 'Diagrams Show Interest in Nuke Plants', Associated Press, January 30, 2002.

February 2, 2002	Chemical/ Biological	CIA director George Tenet informed the Senate that bin Laden has displayed a strong interest in CW and that his operatives have been "trained to conduct attacks with toxic chemicals or biological toxins".	Pamela Hess, 'Al Qaeda May Have Chemical Weapons', United Press International, August 19, 2002.
Before March 2002	Biological	US forces discovered a BW laboratory under construction near Kandahar. It had been abandoned by al-Qaeda. The laboratory was being built to produce anthrax.	Dominic Evans, 'US Troops Found Afghan Biological Lab', Reuters, March 22, 2002; Michael R. Gordon, 'US Says It found Al Qaeda Lab Being Built to Produce Anthrax', *New York Times*, March 23, 2002.
April 2002	Radiological	Abu Zubayda said that al-Qaeda possesses the ability to produce a radiological weapon and already has one in the US.	Jamie McIntyre, 'Zubayda: al Qaeda Had "Dirty Bomb" Know-How', CNN, April 22, 2002; 'Al-Qaeda Claims "Dirty Bomb" Know-How', BBC, April 23, 2002.
May 2002	Radiological	US citizen Abdullah al-Muhaji (formerly Jose Padilla) was arrested in Chicago. He had been involved with al-Qaeda in a plan for a radiological bomb attack on the US.	Dan Eggen and Susan Schmidt, '"Dirty Bomb" Plot Uncovered, US Says: Suspected Al Qaeda Operative Held as "Enemy Combatant"', *Washington Post*, June 11, 2002.
May 2002	Chemical	During the arrest of Sami Uthman, a Lebanese national who moved to the US and became an *imam* at an Islamic mosque in Seattle, police officials found papers by London-based al-Qaeda recruiter *Sheikh* Abu Hamza al-Masri, firearms, military manuals, and "instructions on poisoning water sources".	Patrick J. McDonnell and Josh Meyer, 'Links to Terrorism Probed in Northwest', *Los Angeles Times*, July 13, 2002.

Before June 2002	Chemical/ Biological	Al-Qaeda's five-thousand-page *Encyclopedia of Jihad* is devoted to construction of CBW (chemical and biological weapons).	'Osama Bin Laden's Bid to Acquire Weapons of Mass Destruction Represents the Greatest Threat That Western Civilization Has Faced', *Mail on Sunday* (London), June 23, 2002.
June 3, 2002	Radiological	Bin Laden tried to acquire eleven pounds of radioactive thallium from measuring devices on decommissioned Russian submarines, but Russia's Federal Security Service claimed to have blocked the sale.	'Insider Notes', United Press International, June 3, 2002.
Before July 2002	Chemical	CNN correspondent Mike Boettcher reports that US intelligence agencies discovered evidence of recent purchases of cyanide by al-Qaeda operatives.	*Wolf Blitzer Reports*, CNN, July 31, 2002.
July 18, 2002	Biological	Stephen Younger, director of the Defense Threat Reduction Agency, testified that al-Qaeda's interest in BW focused mainly on anthrax.	'Weapons Worries', CBS News, July 18, 2002.
September 13, 2002	Chemical/ Biological	Lab equipment found near Kandahar supports the assessment that al-Qaeda has acquired the necessary ingredients for "a very limited production of biological and chemical agents".	Judith Miller, 'Lab Suggests Al Qaeda Planned to Build Arms, Officials Say', *New York Times*, September, 14, 2002.
October or November 2002	Chemical	The Islamist group Asbat al-Ansar, a Lebanon-based Sunni group affiliated with al-Qaeda, obtained the nerve agent VX from Iraq.	Barton Gellman, 'US Suspects Al Qaeda Got Nerve Gas Agent from Iraqis', *Washington Post*, December 12, 2002.

November 9, 2002	Chemical	British security officials arrested three agents of al-Qaeda who were planning a cyanide attack on the London subway.	Hala Jaber and Nicholas Rufford, 'MI5 Foils Poison-Gas Attack on Tube', *Sunday Times* (London), November 17, 2002.
After 2 March 2003	Nuclear	Khalid Sheikh Mohammed was apprehended on 1 March 2003. He and other al-Qaeda defectors and informants claimed that bin Laden had announced his intention to detonate nuclear-suitcase bombs in at least seven and possibly ten US cities.	Patrick J. McDonnell and Josh Meyer, 'Links to Terrorism Probed in Northwest', *Los Angeles Times*, July 13, 2002.
Before 2004	Nuclear/ Radiological	Bin Laden dispatches envoys to several eastern European countries to purchase enriched uranium.	'Arab Security Sources Speak of a New Scenario for Afghanistan: Secret Roaming Networks that Exchange Nuclear Weapons for Drugs', *Al-Sharq al-Awsat*, December 24, 2004.
March 3, 2004	Nuclear	In an interview with Pakistani journalist Hamid Mir, Ayman al-Zawahiri claimed that al-Qaeda possessed nuclear weapons. Zawahiri told Mir that al-Qaeda agents had been sent to 'Moscow, Tashkent, and other countries in Central Asia' to buy portable nukes.	Max Delany, 'Under Attack from Al-Qaeda', *Moscow News*, March 3, 2004.
September 2004	Radiological	Midhat Mursi, an al-Qaeda affiliate, managed chemical laboratories in Afghanistan for the manufacturing of radiological bombs. Mursi used the alias "Abu Khabab" and remained in contact with Ayman al-Zawahiri.	Muhammad Wajdi Qandyl, 'Secret Weapons of Mass Destruction and al Qaeda', *Al-Akhbar* (Cairo), January 18, 2004.

November 2004	Nuclear	Sharif al-Masri, a key al-Qaeda operative, informed authorities that bin Laden has arranged to smuggle nuclear supplies and tactical weapons into Mexico.	'Al Qaeda Wants to Smuggle N-Material to US', *Nation*, November 17, 2004.
Before November 2005	Nuclear/ Radiological	Bin Laden purchased seven enriched-uranium rods from Ukrainian arms dealer Semion Mogilevich.	Uthman Tizghart, 'Does Bin Laden Really Possess Weapons of Mass Destruction? Tale of Russian Mafia Boss Semion Mogilevich Who Supplied Bin Laden with the Nuclear "Dirty Bomb"', *Al-Majallah* (London), November 25, 2005.
February 17, 2005	Nuclear	CIA director Porter Goss said that it remains only a matter of time before al-Qaeda attempts to use weapons of mass destruction, including tactical nuclear bombs, against the US. His remarks were upheld by FBI director Robert Mueller.	CNN, February 17, 2005.
April 20, 2005	Nuclear	Intelligence agents confirmed that Abu Musab Zarqawi has obtained a nuclear device or is preparing a radiological explosive for an attack. The nuclear device/dirty nuke is being stored in Afghanistan.	Bill Gertz, 'Reports Reveal Zarqawi's Nuclear Threat', *Washington Times*, April 20, 2005.

Source: Kimberley McCloud, Gary A. Ackerman and Jeffrey M. Bale, 'Chart Al Qaeda's WMD Activities', Center for Nonproliferation Studies, Monterey Institute of International Studies, January 21, 2003. Revised and enlarged by Paul L. Williams. Enlarged and edited by Nicholas Hagger.

APPENDIX

1. The 10-Year Gestation and Birth of *Armageddon*
Extracts from Nicholas Hagger's *Diaries*/Letters

13 October 1998. Extract from Nicholas Hagger's Diaries:
"Landed in Richmond (Virginia) and was driven by taxi to the Jefferson Hotel....
Driven to Jamestown, through misty trees....Introduced to Bill Kelso....On to Norman
Beatty....Talked to him about Gosnold's role in Jamestown."

14 October 1998. Extract from Nicholas Hagger's Diaries:
"Met Charlie Bryan in the foyer and was driven to the museum where Cammie joined
us. The tour of the museum from the beginnings of Virginia to today....How Clinton
invited them both to the White House. Upstairs in the boardroom I attended the
meeting of the Celebration 2007 Programs and Events Subcommittee of the Virginia
Historical Society, under the aegis of the Jamestown-Yorktown Foundation....Gave my
presentation: what Bartholomew Gosnold did."

15 October 1998. Extract from Nicholas Hagger's Diaries:
"At 9 a.m. met Ken Haas, who took us to the Pamplin Park Civil War site to see where
the Unionists broke the Confederates' line on 2 April 1865 to end the Civil War. Took
many notes. The presentation, then the walk through woods looking at various lines,
ending in Tudor House, McGowan's house. All this time Ken talked about the
parallels with my *Overlord* 1 and 2, which he has read and liked. His suggestion that
there is a parallel between the Confederacy and Arthurian romance, Tennyson's *Idylls
of the King*. Lee is the Eisenhower, Grant the Rommel, Lincoln the Hitler – except it's
the other way round! The end of an order. Do this from Lee's point of view or Grant's?
The holy assassin of Lincoln, cf von Stauffenberg. I have been subconsciously
looking for an Anglo-American theme that can accommodate the founding of
America, which is about the unification of America. Have it look back to Jamestown,
Gosnold and Jefferson; and forward to the 20th and 21st centuries. A vision of the
future, revealed by who?

At lunch Ken asked me about 'the Illuminati' and I gave a balanced answer
without mentioning any names. After lunch we went to Drewry's Bluff and saw the
Fort that overlooks the James River. There was no time to see the forts north of the
James River. Returned at 4 to prepare for my lecture.

I may have located my next epic, which will be about the founding of America seen
from the Civil War. Richmond and Jamestown and an old order passing away. What
metaphysical vision does Lee/the South have?...

Went to St Stephen's church and addressed the English-Speaking Union after
eating at an Italian restaurant with Ken and Sally. Some 50 people there in chairs. A

screen, a slide projector, a microphone with a lectern. Ann did the slides. I spoke on Otley Hall – showing 9 slides – and told the story of Bartholomew Gosnold from 1571 to 1607, how he used his connections to settle Cuttyhunk, and how he was the first mover in settling Jamestown. I then ran through the things that Ipswich and Martha's Vineyard are proposing to do. Afterwards many came and said how much they had enjoyed my talk....

I want to write a poem about the founding of America, on an Anglo-American theme. Will Gosnold sustain it? Or should it be Lee and Grant with a throwback to Gosnold? Write an epic poem....In 12 books?

I have been to the Virginians to put Bartholomew Gosnold on the map."

16 October 1998. Extract from Nicholas Hagger's Diaries:
"To Yorktown with Rafael, after Bill Kelso rang to say he wants to see me....Drove to Jamestown....Bill Kelso was tied up so I sat by the River James on a seat and mused and wrote a poem. Got to stanza 7 before Kelso came. He wanted background, he is coming to England. He wanted my sources. He said that just as Calthorpe seems to have been shot in the knee, so there is a suspicion that all who died were poisoned by arsenic – by Wingfield. There is no evidence, but it may be true....Read Ken Haas on the *Idylls of the King*; Lee as Arthur – shown as Arthur in 19th-century etchings and paintings – and Arthur is shown as Lee. The chivalry and culture of an old order collapsed."

18 October 1998. Extract from Nicholas Hagger's Diaries:
"Drove to Tuckahoe Plantation....Arrived after 7 and were greeted by Tad and Susan Thompson, he in shorts and relishing the chill breeze through the mosquito nets....We were taken on a tour of the house, which is 1730s, wood-panelled and Jacobean in feel. Talk of when Jefferson was there (aged 2-7). It is sumptuously furnished....Sat with them and Ann round a table in the centre of their abode. Chatted about Virginia and the atmosphere and it dawned on me that the agrarian Virginian life was Elizabethan British – Gosnold brought the Elizabethan agrarian system but not based on aristocracy, rather on land. England had moved on after Gosnold, into the Industrial Revolution, but Virginia remained the same, a new landed 'aristocracy', which was threatened by the industrial revolutionary north (which had kept up with England) and destroyed. Elizabethan England lived on in Virginia, thanks to Gosnold, for a while. Virginia is vanished England. I need to make a comparative study of Elizabethan England and Virginian society before 1865....

At Tuckahoe Jefferson was educated in the schoolroom, on his own. His teacher did a good job on him.

Tad: 'Many Virginians would rather be a colony of England, as you may have gathered from the English-Speaking Union.'"

23 November 1998. Extract from letter from Kenneth Haas to Nicholas Hagger:
"On more than one occasion favourable comments concerning your lecture have surfaced among our members. Many are interested in spreading the Hagger gospel of Gosnold. I am one of them. If I have your permission to quote liberally from your pamphlet, I will see if I can get an article published in one of the Richmond

periodicals. I think it might strike a chord in the hearts of Virginians. John Smith's character has always been suspect. Too mercenary for the descendants of Cavaliers. The Gosnold story provides both the adventure and pathos preferred by Virginia romantics....

Obviously I enjoy the opportunity to discuss these issues with you. In fact I have not had an intellectual workout equal to that which you provide since my doctoral committee examined my fitness for a Ph.D. I hope we are able to continue the dialogue.

9 May 2000. Extract from Nicholas Hagger's Diaries:
"The Virginia Historical Society came [to Otley Hall]....Charlie and Cammie....Lunch. Sat next to Charlie. Talk of Gosnold – I had given them a talk about the feeling of the place over drinks on the lawn...and then a tour. The talk on the terrace....Then Charlie and Jim suggested I write an epic about the Civil War. 'Lincoln should be the hero. He was less well educated than Davis....Grant was different from the knightly Lee. The abolition of slavery is what it is about. The assassination of Lincoln in the theatre.'...The Elizabethan values of the Southerners giving way to the new values of the Northerners, anti-slavery. John Brown and Stonewall Jackson....Manassas. Jackson = Hector. I have an epic, but Lincoln as the hero, not Robert Lee? Epic heroes have to be doers. Grant? The tragedy of Lee. The old order giveth way to the new – Arthurian. (Haas.) Lincoln, the new American. (Bryan.)"

10 May 2000. Extract from Nicholas Hagger's Diaries:
"Thought more about the suggestion from Charlie that I should write the American epic about the Civil War. I must do it from the point of view of the thrusting, coarse Northerners rather than the grave, patrician Southerners, but I must make it moving. Slavery was an Elizabethan import (from the south-west of Britain?). I must show Richmond as Berlin....Blank verse the medium.

It is like a request to paint a panoramic landscape picture, or do a tapestry, this New World epic idea based on Richmond. I am a painter in words and have been asked to do a vast canvas."

25 May 2000. Extract from letter from Charlie Bryan, Director of the Virginia Historical Society:
"I am fascinated by your plans to write an epic poem on the American Civil War....

I could go on and on, but may be we can have an extended conversation on this if you come to do research in Richmond."

4 January 2001. Extract from Nicholas Hagger's Diaries:
"I received Will Connors, consultant to the Governor of Virginia, Governor Gilmore. He came at the Governor's request to fact-find, a young man, thinnish and intelligent-looking in a dark-grey suit; spectacles. Showed him round and sat and talked, then ate with him at 12. He left at 12.15, after 1½ hours. He wants a reception at Otley Hall, probably on May 3 or 4, for the Governor and will return in March. The interesting thing is that the Governor has been chosen by George W Bush to head the Republican National Committee – he is the head Republican, the first

Virginian to have achieved this. Will took away *The Fire and the Stones*, and wants me to present a copy to the Governor. I: 'We want Bush here. If you get me an hour with Bush on America's role in the world, you can come in with me and take notes.' He liked that idea and will put it to Gilmore. I might end up as adviser to the US President."

2 May 2001. Extract from Nicholas Hagger's Diaries:
"The television crew arrived at 7.45. I gave a talk on Suffolk Radio while they set up, then 40 mins (8 till 8.40), on Jamestown and Gosnold, answering Tim Nolan's questions. On to Civic Drive. Waited with John Field for the coach to come, said hello to my friends, then rode with them (Kelso, Norman Beatty and others). Was introduced to the First Lady by Diane Béchamps: a well-groomed lady in a trouser suit, bejewelled and shortish blonde-haired. The tour of Christchurch Mansion, Ipswich, held up because I had a radio interview along with the First Lady....On to the speeches. The Mayor, losing his place. The First Lady memorising her speech. And I....The roar from the Virginians when I said, 'Thirteen years before the *Mayflower* arrived.'....After the speeches a photo, and more television. Then she and I rode back in the same car, with her driver and bodyguard. No flag fluttering, no cheering crowds, just a televised departure. Chatted to her about her archaeology. She brings students to look at all the Roman villas and mosaics in England. The reception and line at Otley Hall, Tollemache arriving last. I, to the First Lady: 'As Deputy Lord Lieutenant, Lord Tollemache will be reporting to the Queen.' 'That's more or less it.' (Tollemache.) Lunch hurried up. Sat with the First Lady in the linenfold room, and Bill and the Mayor, while TV happened upstairs....

The departure. The First Lady gave us a gift and invited us to the Executive Mansion in Richmond, State House. The gift was a silver plate. I travelled with the Americans on the bus while Ann had feedback from the guides: how low-level the Council were, didn't stay or say goodbye....How the Council don't want it [the twinning of Ipswich and Jamestown] to happen. I...said to Bill [Kelso], 'You're the Schliemann of Jamestown, having found the Fort. Now you need to find Bartholomew, which will be like Schliemann finding Achilles or Hector at Troy. Do you accept you're already America's Schliemann?' 'Yes.'...To the Churchill Hotel after a talk with Suzanne Flippo, about how Norman [Beatty] is receiving NATO at a conference and hosting another global conference....

Had tea at the Churchill Hotel under as many old masters as at Christchurch Mansion. Then went to the toilets and shaved without anyone seeing. Then found two better carrier bags....Signed a book for Bush....Took the coach to the [US] Embassy and was greeted (having got through security and electronic surveillance) by the First Lady, Roxane: thanks for the hospitality etc. 'Have you met my husband?' 'No.' So he [guest of honour, Governor of Virginia] was drawn out of the line, and I talked about Otley Hall, my book I'd signed for him. 'Thank you, that's very kind of you, I'll read it. I'll try to find time to look at it with you at the end.' Then I said, 'And I'd like to congratulate you on your new appointment [Chairman of the Republican Committee], that's terrific, and I know you have some direct access to President Bush. I've signed another book for him. Could I ask you to deliver it? If it's out of order, do say.' 'No, I'll do it. I'm seeing him on our return, I'll make sure he has it.' 'The Otley guidebook as well.' The First Lady, 'I shall drop him a note about my visit to Otley Hall.'...

The black bodyguard had told me the Governor and his wife are 'like that' (fingers together) with the Bushes. Later at the end of the evening, the guards at a booth. 'You've chosen the best conduit to Bush, they're in his kitchen cabinet. They're with him all the time.'"

24 May 2001. Extract from letter from Roxane Gilmore to Nicholas Hagger:
"What a special day we had with you at Ipswich and Otley Hall. It couldn't have been more perfect and we appreciate everything you did to organize the day. The newspaper article was well-done and the History Channel is very pleased with the footage they filmed. They are planning numerous projects with it....

The Governor and I appreciate the history that you gave to us, and he has carried the set you gave for the President to Washington so he can deliver it personally."

17 December 2001. Extract from letter from Roxane Gilmore to Nicholas Hagger:
"It seems like yesterday that we were lunching at Otley Hall and here has come another Christmas. The filming that we did that day was aired during our webcast broadcast to schools all over the US and the world. It was a tremendous success and we appreciate all that you did to help get it done."

6 January 2005. Extract from Nicholas Hagger's Diaries:
"I must also send an outline of my American epic."

Extract from Nicholas Hagger's Classical Odes:
"'In Egypt: Tyranny and Armageddon', title of a poem written on March 2-3 2005, revised March 30-April 2, 11, 2005."

20 April 2005. Extract from a proposal by Nicholas Hagger:
"*Crusaders* – a new American poetic epic primarily aimed at America about the US expansion in our own time, Bush's hunt for bin Laden, the clash between Christian and Muslim civilisations, the end of tyranny: September 11, Afghanistan, Iraq (the fall of Baghdad, Saddam and his sons), Iran, the Fourth World War etc. – climax still to come. The Civil War and the founding of America (Gosnold and the Founding Fathers in 1776) will appear. For example, Bush Jr, staring at the skeleton of Bartholomew Gosnold, is addressed by Gosnold's spirit, who recounts why he founded America, the sacrifices he made and how he does not want the US handed over to a New World Order/internationalist Syndicate. There will also be parallels with the Crusades and references to all America's growth and history. The Afghan and Iraqi poems in *Summoned by Truth* ('Attack on America' and 'Shock and Awe') – and *The Syndicate* – can now be seen to be testing the ground for this coming work, which can be written just behind *The Secret Founding of America*, feeding off the research for that book."

7 May 2005. Extract from Nicholas Hagger's Diaries:
"Had the idea... not to do the American epic as *Richmond* but as Bush v. bin

Laden with Richmond an episode, like founding of America, the Founding Fathers, Freemasonry and so on. Saddam and Baghdad are part of this, not the whole. It's on the Fourth World War. Iran, which they are getting ready to bomb. *Overlord* is an American epic as it's about Eisenhower. I am contemplating a second American epic (in accordance with stage 16 of *The Rise and Fall of Civilizations*)."

8 May 2005. Extract from Nicholas Hagger's Diaries:
"Thought that my epic should be about *now*, not Richmond. Bush Jr is addressed by the ghost of Bartholomew Gosnold as he surveys the skeleton, and is told the future in store for America, which must not be subverted by the Syndicate. The defeat of poverty, disease, war; a paradise on Earth, a Utopia. Bush hunts down bin Laden via Iraq, Saddam and his two sons and Iran, and hears about the founding of America, the Civil War (Richmond) and Iraq."

9 May 2005. Extract from an email by Nicholas Hagger:
"The new American epic should not be about the Civil War, which is the basis of *Richmond*. It should be about the US expansion in our own time, about Bush's hunt for bin Laden, the clash between Christian and Muslim civilisations, the end of tyranny: September 11, Afghanistan, Iraq (the fall of Baghdad, Saddam and his sons), Iran, the Fourth World War etc. – climax still to come. The Civil War (the concepts in the *Richmond* synopsis) and the founding of America (Gosnold and the Founding Fathers in 1776) will appear in the scheme. For example, at one point Bush Jr, staring at the skeleton of Bartholomew Gosnold, is addressed by Gosnold's spirit, who recounts why he founded America, the sacrifices he made and how he does not want the US to hand it over to a New World Order/internationalist Syndicate. There will also be parallels with the Crusades.

This will be an American epic in the sense that it will be primarily aimed at America. Virgil told the story of how Aeneas founded Rome, but to tell the story of how Gosnold founded America would be to miss out on the present, except in one passage forecasting future (i.e. present) events. Doing it from the present backwards will enable me to include all America's growth and history. Suggested working title: *Crusaders*. *Richmond* needs to be replaced by *Crusaders*. The Afghan and Iraqi poems in *Summoned by Truth* ('Attack on America' and 'Shock and Awe') – and *The Syndicate* – can now be seen to be testing the ground for this coming work, which can be written just behind *The Secret Founding of America*, feeding off the research for that book."

20 February 2006. Extract from Nicholas Hagger's Diaries:
"To Schools and Lecture Room East to hear [Christopher] Ricks, who was alone in the hall when we arrived. 'Good, you can check the sound for me, I was about to run down and hear my own voice....' The sound system wasn't working, he had to get help.... How Eliot looks to Tennyson, where do we go from Eliot? He argued Heaney has progressed Yeats, Larkin is from Hardy, Hughes from Lawrence and Hill from Eliot.... I was aware of Tuohy saying to me, 'Dump Eliot and you'll then discover your own voice.' Eliot took his voice from French, Hill got Eliot via Ivor Tate. Ransom read his own 'Two in August' and Pound chanted 'Envoi' (1919) on tape, incantatory and

quite different from how he was with me – so was poetry reading a big act? It sounded like it. Pound's 'Envoi' out of Waller's 'Goe lovely Rose. ....Ricks shook me by the hand and thanked me for coming again (earlier 'Thank you for coming from so far') and I said to him, 'I'm thinking of Tuohy who told me *not* to be influenced by Eliot and allow my own voice to come through.' 'And that's what you've done, Eliot doesn't like narrative. You've gone back to Tennyson.' '"Morte d'Arthur",' I said. He: 'Yes.' I did not say, 'It's plagiarism.' But coming away with Ann that's what I felt. A poet should not be rearranging Yeats' words... to make a copied or cribbed poem that has nothing to do with direct experience – it's pallid academicism. A poet should look at the universe and respond, as Tennyson did. I will write and tell him in a letter that Hill is plagiarising Eliot, that poetry and prose are more distinct than he says, that Hill is a pale imitation of late Eliot.... Thought on the way home that my *Idylls of the King* is *Overlord*; that my Tennysonian *Collected Poems* is my *Collected Poems*; and what did Tennyson do like *Classical Odes*? My *Gates of Hell* are like *In Memoriam*."

15 May 2006. Extract from Nicholas Hagger's Diaries:
"To Oxford.... Into Schools East Room at 4.30. Ricks arrived from the back at 4.40 in a dark suit, white shirt and perhaps black tie, looking more fleshed and serious than usual. He greeted me.... His lecture was delivered to interference from the sound system. He ditched the microphone – got a bit exasperated and irritated about it.... Despite such handicaps he gave a stunning lecture on how Lowell was American heir to Eliot and Pound, but more Pound, leaving Hill heir to Eliot and how both related to Dante. All were expatriates.

'Intellectuals argue without quarrelling.' The 'arguing; between Eliot and Pound in endnotes. How Eliot's *After Strange Gods* in the 1930s was taken up by Pound in the radio broadcast against Jews and how he bore guilt for this – see the 'familiar compound ghost' who was Pound (comPound). So obvious, but no one has said it before. Pound and the *Book of Ezra*.... How Lowell wrote to Pound to work under him on May 2 1936, and said he was a relative of Amy Lowell. Lowell's Brunetto (in 'Brunetto Latini') – who looks to Pound as his guide. Pound's withdrawal into silence, out of guilt at the harm he had done, believing he was virtuous, having taken it for virtue. Harm in place of virtue drives one into silence. (An acceptance of the treason?) But, note that 'Rothschilds' were behind the accusation against Pound, according to Mullins. Lowell's madness and Pound's.

Pound raised money to get Eliot out of the bank to write poetry, but Eliot did not want to leave the bank. (*Bel Esprit*, the scheme proposed by Pound in association with Natalie Barney and other writers in Paris in 1922, the first aim of which was to enable Eliot to devote his energies wholly to literature.) Pound's fury at Eliot's defection to Milton.... Pound after Eliot died, 'His was the true Dante-esque voice.' In 1918 Eliot had praised Pound for being Dante-esque.... Pound: 'I should have listened to Possum.' Eliot's remorse at having written *After Strange Gods*.

Lowell's three books that came out together in 1973. Lowell and Brunetto and Verona and Dante. The dead master, Pound. Then at the end, delayed by technical distractions, Ricks played a 1964 recording of Pound reading Lowell's 'Brunetto Latini' – about son, guide, lost path, journey home and friend. This was sent to Lowell by Olga. Lowell wrote and thanked Pound. The recording, Pound, the silent and remorseful, speaking to Lowell in 1964 as Lowell's guide – and I thought of how he acted as my guide: 'You can see it, if you can see it, that's half the battle. You can do it.'* His encouragement of me from a remorseful silence at the harm he had done, a guide who had smashed, like [his encouragement of] Eliot.... I was opened up. Ricks said, 'I find that very moving,' and ended.

There was long and deafening applause while Ricks said 'Thank you' many times and held up a hand to stop the applause. I stumbled to the front and thanked him and said I would be reflecting on that reading for the next three months. 'Thank you for coming.' It was not the time to talk or socialise. I was opened up and was wet-eyed from inside Schools right up to Carfax, indeed back to the car park by Worcester College. I was speaking to Ann, passing people waiting for the bus who must have thought my wet eyes strange but I did not care.

I was trying to understand the powerful feelings that filled me. I was lost in a wood and was turned round by a guide, like Lowell and Eliot encountering the 'familiar compound ghost' (Pound) – for all of us the guide was Pound. And he was in agony at the harm he did which resulted in the death sentence for treason, his 'insanity' (in an 'insane asylum') and his silence. Dante was Pound's guide, cf Virgil in Dante. I thought of my guides: Colin Wilson, who got me started as a writer; Donald Thompson and Horton who had earlier introduced me to Homer, Virgil and Horace and the Roman poets; Ricks, who came in on p2 of my *Collected Poems* and taught me to appreciate poetry (Davenport at Chigwell having laid the foundations with *Julius Caesar*); Fitzsimmons, who briefly, was my Brunetto – see the poems; Tomlin in philosophy; Tuohy in prose; Pound, who got me to start my epic, encouraged me. I outgrew most of them, but Ricks had read more than I had, e.g. Lowell's letters, and transmitted the American end of culture without writing original poetic work – he was still my guide, more than anyone. And all the guides had failed in different ways. Had he? Ricks was higher thought and feeling, one of the few I still respected. Pound, who guided me to my epic, had been pro-Jew, but I had turned his atmosphere around by writing about Auschwitz.

Then I thought how I had an argument with Ricks, always had. He had taught me social satire and I had written 'Zeus's Ass', but I had stuck to being a mystic. At my first meeting with him I said, 'I prefer mystical poetry, Wordsworth and the One.' Tuohy had enjoined, 'Find your voice, there should be no resonance of Eliot.' Hill needed Tuohy to tell him that? In Ricks' view, everyone is out of someone: Heaney from Yeats, Hill from Eliot, Lowell from Pound (and Eliot), and if you echo someone, crib from someone – you get in the team, otherwise the England manager leaves you on the substitutes' bench. Also, his posture has to sit in judgement – he has to be better than Homer, Virgil, Milton and Co, who were failures. 'The question is, will you fail well or badly? They all failed.' But he is not a poet and I quote Pope's lines from 'Essay on Criticism' at the beginning of *Collected Poems*: 'A perfect judge will read each work of wit,/With the same spirit that its author writ:/Survey the WHOLE, nor seek slight faults to find....' He guards the Tree of Tradition, and poets feed off mulberry leaves, spin their cocoons hanging onto the leaves – which he, as the new Q guards. He guards the Tree, is not a silkworm.

So there is an argument between poet and critic, another pair. This poet acknowledges that the critic has read more interestingly and incisively than every other critic he has encountered, and in a way more relevant to his work, and looks on him as a guide out of the dark wood into Light – Pound's statement as to what the true terrain of poetry is: 'For forty years I have schooled myself... to write an epic which begins "In the Dark Forest", crosses the purgatory of human error, and ends in the light' – in the 'moment of metamorphosis' which occurs when the everyday world ('quotidien', i.e. quotidian) approximates to the 'divine or permanent world' (letter to his father, 11 April 1927). But at the same time he demands the right to experience life and Nature at first hand, as Wordsworth did, and not through a maze of references to dead poets (Yeats, Eliot, Pound). You can continue their tradition without academic references to them. The neo-classical and the Baroque, the difference. Direct contact with life is opposed to words that conjure dead masters who they're cribbing.

Hill and Lowell were like poets of Raphael's School who paint with Raphael's style and not their own. They sit in solitude and refer to dead writers in their crossword activities, and do not make fresh contact with life.

Ricks delivered an earthquake of a lecture which touched the fundamental conception of myself and my guides, past and present, and the direction of my poetry, which I assert is right for me. He mentioned Kathleen Raine, his elder and better by more than 20 years, as saying that Lowell is Eliot's heir. It is a measure of his genius that although I am on a mountain in relation to many people... Ricks is on a higher mountain still, looking down on me in terms of books about *other* poets. Not my verse, though. I have a right to be in the team/pantheon.

There's Raphael and the School of Raphael – Eliot and the School of Eliot. It's better to be a Raphael than an imitator in an academic school. It's better to be like Wordsworth, a man speaking to men. Shelley? My Brunetto poem (no. 35 in 'The Early Education and Making of a Mystic') – Tuohy said, 'Find your own voice,' and I moved away from Ser Brunetto. I had the Hill outlook in Japan and moved on.

On the way back, went to Garsington but the manor house was not signposted. A pleasant drive through the Oxfordshire villages, past a lot of wisteria and lilacs. I was opened up, real – what English Literature at its best does for you, and by Ricks the critic's brilliance with ideas, not Shakespeare."

* For two accounts of Nicholas Hagger's visit to Ezra Pound in Rapallo on 16 July 1970, see the Appendix to the one-volume edition of *Overlord*, pp935-936.

21 May 2006. Extract from Nicholas Hagger's Diaries:
"Reflected that I want to get on to *Crusaders*, which should be about Bush bringing liberty and democracy to the world – like Eisenhower untrammelled by the Syndicate up to a point but influenced by them, through Skull and Bones as well; and bin Laden, a new Saladin, with cash, brother of his (Bush's) former business partner. Globalism, two faiths."

25 May 2006. Extract from Nicholas Hagger's Diaries:
Ordered books on *Crusaders*, which has elevated itself to next, after October. Bush v. bin Laden. My head is full of ideas on this."

26 May 2006. Extract from Nicholas Hagger's Diaries:
"Ben came to spend a night. Watched him swim. Fed with him. Read him *Peter Rabbit*.

Am thinking about *Crusaders*. I am trying to establish the story and myth it acts out, which is about being kidnapped into an underworld: Afghan purgatory, Iraqi Hell.... The nightingale sang outside, beautifully."

27 May 2006. Extract from Nicholas Hagger's Diaries:
"Left for Cornwall. On the way down read the papers and slept a lot – always a prelude to creativity. Woke and drafted out the 12 books for *Crusaders*, from my sleep-smoothed mind. I can do *Crusaders*, I have a map now. I just need more details from the books I've ordered."

30 May 2006. Extract from Nicholas Hagger's Diaries:
"Spent all day proof-reading the last 240 pages of *Overlord*... The Christ/Satan theme in *Crusaders* must pick up where *Overlord* leaves off."

31 May 2006. Extract from Nicholas Hagger's Diaries:
"Dictated a synopsis for *Crusaders* onto tape."

5 June 2006. Extract from letter to Christopher Ricks:
"Many thanks for a stunning lecture about mentors and Pound's moving reading at the end. I found it moving because of the many layers at work: Pound-Lowell, and of course Pound-Eliot (and the 'familiar comPound ghost'), but also Pound-Hagger, for he urged me to start my epic which will be out in one volume in a few months' time; and of course Ricks-Hagger, for you were my Brunetto and familiar compound ghost as recipient of three letters on what I am about. Incidentally, I used Brunetto in a sequence of poems written in Japan 40 years ago – Brunetto being Tom Fitzsimmons, American poet and then my colleague in Tokyo; have your paths crossed? He must be 78 now, if still alive, and I should think living in Michigan. Your lecture made me realise I only had bits of *After Strange Gods* in selections of Eliot and I have asked Booksearch to find me a 1930s copy.

I go along with your 'Tree of Tradition', the poets being heirs to forebears. However, I have tried to be moderately (as opposed to extremely) allusive. Frank Tuohy (a novelist and short story writer and polymath who considered he knew more about the writing of poetry than the poets) used to drum into me in the 1960s that resonance of anybody else in a poet is wrong – 'cribbing' – and so I have used resonance and echoes with restraint and have tried to speak in my own voice like a Wordsworthian 'man among men', writing directly out of experience, often in the open air, rather than sitting in a library and consciously (or self-consciously) conveying my experience of the world through the poems of other poets, tweaking a word here or a line there to include words written by other poets. The School of Raphael painted scenes through the style of Raphael, imitating his vision and perspective – which raises the question, were the academicist artists of the School derivative rather than original? Or did they originate a new phase within their derivative style? I tried to carry Eliot's technique forward in 'The Silence' 40 years ago, and as you'll have a chance to see when *Collected Poems 1958-2005* appears in July, for the above reasons I moved on but believe I have remained true to his concerns.

I know poets are not like footballers sitting on a substitutes' bench, only getting picked to play in so far as they resemble past masters, but I do look back to Tennyson, as you urged. He, more than anyone, is behind my range: poems about Otley Hall in *Classical Odes* look back to his 'moated grange', *The Gates of Hell* looks back to *In Memoriam* and 'Maud' – Harrington Hall, a mile or two from Somersby and locally thought to be Maud's Garden, currently owned by the ex-Lords of the Manor of Loughton, strangely features in that story; my war poems on Afghanistan and Iraq look back to his 'Charge of the Light Brigade' and my *Overlord* to his *Idylls of the King*. He is behind many of my poems about historical places and everyday lyrics, and I think of him every day as at Connaught House – to which we have now moved – we have many goldfish in a pond and fountain and I think of his gold fins winking in the porphyry font. (I had a pair of milk-white peacocks at Otley Hall.) I also look back to Dante and Pound for their journey from dark wood to light, and am probably a hybrid of several traditions rather than just one.

When my *Collected Stories* are done by mid-October I plan to write another epic, *Crusaders*, which will be about the clash between Christendom and Islam. I am now so grateful that I spent an academic year in Baghdad, and all my recent prose works can now be seen as research/preparing the ground for this creative task. There will be sections on the founding of America and on the essence of bin Laden's beliefs. It is a rich seam. I have already sketched out 12 books. The walk you took me on before *Overlord* could not have prepared me better for that task – you drew my attention to all the pitfalls, and if I fell into any, I fell in with my eyes open, alert to the dangers. And the same points/criteria/pitfalls probably apply to this one. If, when I am more clear and nearer the start, you could find time for a short walk, I would appreciate it very much, but as I say, the hard part has been done. It's fine-tuning now. I will remember to quarrel with myself (about allusiveness?) and not with the forces of occupation.

On that subject, on successive days the week before last Niall Ferguson (on television) and Frederick Forsyth (on the radio) said that they feel 'duped' over Iraq. For the record, I was not duped. Quite simply, I saw through the obfuscation and got it right while it was happening, and they didn't."

16 June 2006. Extract from Nicholas Hagger's Diaries:
"Spent much of the evening... on *Crusaders*, fleshing out the Salafid background and character of al-Zarqawi, and the various transformations of Bush Jr. As bin Laden seems to be in Iran, the story is coming together.... Realise I am making progress. It's good I am thinking *Crusaders*.

17 June 2006. Extract from Nicholas Hagger's Diaries:
"Worked on my *Crusaders* plan with the doors open. Lunch outside with Ann. In the afternoon dictated *Crusaders* corrections/revisions."

18 June 2006. Extract from Nicholas Hagger's Diaries:
"Fathers Day lunch.... Heard Ben read, dozed. We all fed the fish and later had tea

(after everyone else had had a swim). Thought hard after they left and dictated more on *Crusaders* – the myths. The theme of this epic is Armageddon over Jerusalem. Jerusalem is what bin Laden, Ahmadinejad and Bush Jr all seek – and Saddam."

29 September 2006. Extract from Nicholas Hagger's Diaries:
"If Tennyson were alive today he would do *Crusaders* as an *Idylls of the King*. The theme of *Crusaders* is in the title – how Bush's crusade led the West to disaster and bin Laden's crusade led Islam to disaster – but through the Western descent came Western expansion and a new world order. Was it inspired by God? And Billy Graham?"

2 October 2006. Extract from Nicholas Hagger's Diaries:
"Read Paul Berman's *Terror and Liberalism*.

It could be based on *Overlord*, where I used the myth of Armageddon, which it confirms. Saw revolts against liberalism in the twentieth century as being external to Europe (Nazis, Italians, Spanish) and Communists as being from the Byzantine/Russian civilisation, Islamists being from the Arab civilisation. Liberalism (freedom) v. totalitarian tyranny. Both sides see the other as being linked with Satan, but the Arabs are also the people of God and the West with corrupt Freemasonry linked to Lucifer – and losing Armageddon because of the internal corruption?"

16 November 2006. Extract from Nicholas Hagger's Diaries:
"Have not recorded my impulsive decision on Nov 14 to do an itinerary for Iran.... On Nov 15 sent in a suggested itinerary by email. Consultant said Susa is out, too near Iraq, they couldn't guarantee my safety. Was told today there can be no visa until about Jan 10, when it will be snowy. I'll still go if I can – 5 nights.

Reading about Iran made me realise that Iran had links with al-Qaeda, before 9/11 and may have encouraged the Sunnis to do 9/11 so the Taliban in Afghanistan and Saddam in Iraq – on either side – would be eliminated. Bush fell for it, has put troops either side of Iran, which have to be got out. Iran is arming the Taliban now, along with the Shias in Iraq."

19 November 2006. Extract from Nicholas Hagger's Diaries:
"Thought about Empson's 'loony hooters' (jeerers?), the pro-war lot whom he contrasts with the hopers, of which he was one – a socialist. Was Churchill a loony hooter? If so, Empson and I part company."

20 November 2006. Extract from Nicholas Hagger's Diaries:
"Ann drove me to Oxford.... Went to Schools East and Ricks came from his microphone testing and sat in the chair in front of me, shaking my hand.... 'How are you, how are things? You look so well, so young... You've got all your hair and you look well.' I: 'I haven't worked as hard as you have.' 'But you have, what you've done is very impressive, a great tribute to your energy.' I told him I was going to Iran. 'It may be unwise.' He said, 'It may be imprudent but it's wise as it will get your project forward.' At the end asked him, 'Who are "the loony looters"? Chinese? British? Churchill and the war leaders?' 'I don't know.' 'And do they jeer or make hooting

noises?' 'Both I should think. I'll send you Haffenden's notes on the poem. He knows more about it than anyone else. Have you seen his edition of Empson? I'll send you a photocopy. I'll put it in my diary. If I write "Loony Hooters to NH" you won't get alarmed.'... He smiled and duly wrote me in his diary as NH – a familiarity for which I should be very grateful. I'm not 'Hagger' to him, but 'NH'.... His lecture was on Eliot's view (in one long paragraph) of Othello, demonstrating that, as he argued, Othello self-dramatises – but so does Eliot. Thinking well of oneself. Behind Ricks's criticism is a human trait, which his criticism illustrates."

24 November 2006. Extract from Nicholas Hagger's Diaries:
"Thought about *Crusaders*. The Syndicate's two factions...intrigue chaos by backing both sides and Bush is floundering around and sees this, or suspects this."

13 December 2006. Extract from Nicholas Hagger's Diaries:
"Am turning to *Crusaders*."

16 December 2006. Extract from Nicholas Hagger's Diaries:
"Worked on *Crusaders* and dictated another third of a tape."

17 December 2006. Extract from Nicholas Hagger's Diaries:
"Drove to Cornwall.... Now at 8.15, back to *Crusaders*.... After supper dictated half a tape of insertions into the synopsis of *Crusaders*. Cannot recall where I found some notes on the myth of Armageddon. Now at 11 p.m. am almost asleep on my feet."

18 December 2006. Extract from Nicholas Hagger's Diaries:
"I made ten phone calls of a practical nature and read the papers; then, on a cold day, worked on *Crusaders*, which I have now decided to call *Armageddon*. It will be unitarian Universalist, with God's plan being implemented, which the religious leaders have no knowledge of, that they should all share in a Heavenly parliament while being responsible for their regions. So far each Heaven has been separate except for visits, and *Overlord*, being about Europe and North-American civilisation, focused on a Christian Heaven. As above so below, and the Heavenly Parliament of all faiths will be replicated below, when Christians will share in a world government and not dominate the world. So America's superpowerdom has to pass into Universalism – stages 17/27 of *The Rise and Fall of Civilizations*. The Syndicate's view is now obsolete – the Syndicate is defeated. Now the Heavenly regions are unified into One.

I fell asleep after lunch for an hour in the warmth of the sitting-room, and have woken up with the solution – Universalist Heaven, Universalist Earth and defeat for the Syndicate in Afghanistan and Iraq in *Armageddon* and triumph for Iran."

20 December 2006. Extract from Nicholas Hagger's Diaries:
"Finished my work on *Crusaders*, now called *Armageddon* – 1¾ tapes."

23 December 2006. Extract from Nicholas Hagger's Diaries:
"Worked more on *Armageddon*, put it on tape."

25 December 2006. Extract from Nicholas Hagger's Diaries:
"Did more on *Armageddon*. Should it be called *Crusaders*? Think about the title again. 'Leave, *Crusaders*, or we will cut your heads off' (Mosul). The Archbishop of Canterbury has referred to the 'crusading West'. But 'crusades' suggests the Middle Ages, a backward-looking analogy."

26 December 2006. Extract from Nicholas Hagger's Diaries:
"I am still pondering the title of my next epic. I said it was going to be called *Crusaders*, and recent statements reinforce that as the idea behind the War on Terror. Yet it may be understood to refer to the historical Crusades, in a way that 'Overlord' could not be misunderstood to refer to another episode.... Both Crusaders and Armageddon are themes in my epic, and changing the title to *Armageddon* has got the story into better focus. But it's not the *final* battle, out of it will come a Universalist world. Perhaps it should be *Terror*? But that is a general label and does not describe the action as an Operation, as *Overlord* did. So which is it: *Crusaders, Armageddon, Terror*?

On the formal side I am working out a myth and 'people of God', so from that point of view it *should* be *Armageddon*. Arguably, neo-con agenda is responsible for the Western crusading idea, and the poem is about more than the neo-con. *Terror* is too vague and all-embracing. It might be a poem about the bombings in the tube on 7/7. It's got to be *Armageddon*, but it needs to be qualified by a sub-title: *Crusaders and (or against) Terror*. As both sides are crusaders and think of their opponents as terrorists, that may be all right. Or it could be, not *Overlord, the Triumph of Light*, but *Armageddon: The Crusading West and the Light*. Or *Crusaders and World Rule* (or *Governments*). *Crusaders and New World Order*. That may be it: *Armageddon: Crusaders and a New World Order*. That points forward. I think that will do. The total title suggests high stakes and that Armageddon will lead to a New World Order that is Universalist. *Crusaders and Universal Order*. That's better, it catches above (Christ and Universalist Heaven) as well as below (a Universalist new world order). I've got there! Not quite: *Armageddon: Crusaders and the Triumph of Universal Order*.

There was no quick solution to the title problem; I had to think it out and draw on the text and past parallels (*Overlord*). There had to be a contextual approach. But it is now right, and *Crusaders* is reflected in the title (or at least, the subtitle).

Universal Order is an ideal, a universal peace, a *Pax Americana* which can only grow out of a benevolent world government.

Math and Kate came to lunch, and Tony. Sat at the end of the table by the door. We all wore hats. The four of them had gold, I had green."

29 December 2006. Extract from Nicholas Hagger's Diaries:
"Interesting stuff on the Antichrist, who will be one-eyed. The chief enemy of Christ and defier of political power – bin Laden, or the Syndicate? Keep both options there. The identity of the Antichrist is a mystery? Freemasonry's world rule.

Worked on the Antichrist in the evening as news came through that Saddam Hussein will be hanged before 6 a.m. tomorrow (3 a.m. our time)."

30 December 2006. Extract from Nicholas Hagger's Diaries:
"After 4 dictated two-thirds of a side of tape on the synopsis for *Armageddon*, sorting out the Antichrist coming to Damascus, which is after the 1,000-year reign, though perhaps one can believe there is no 1,000-year reign. Dictated changes most of the evening....

The day has been dominated by pictures of Saddam Hussein's execution, which took place at 6 a.m. Iraqi time. Pictures of Saddam shuffling on the scaffold, submissive rather than defiant....

Am getting *Armageddon* sorted out. Christ is on Bush's side, Satan on bin Laden's as he advocates terror and *jihad* and is not a peaceful Muslim."

31 December 2006. Extract from Nicholas Hagger's Diaries:
"Ben came about 11.30, had lunch with him, worked on *Armageddon*..., then amused him looking at coins....

More film of Saddam's execution, taken from below, with sound on a mobile phone, taunts of 'Moqtada' by the executioners – showing that the Iraqi government is Shia and this was Shiite revenge on Saddam. Saddam, 'Who's Moqtada?' contemptuously. Was he sarcastic in his prayer? Was he repeating a Shiite prayer?...

I have virtually completed the synopsis for *Armageddon* and going to Iran will allow me to start this, but I have the Iran travelogue to do."

18 January 2007. Extract from Nicholas Hagger's Diaries:
"Hamadan, Iran. Off at 8.30, past the last hills of the Kalkas mountains to Jamkaran well just before Qom. This was originally, until 1970, a well in a desert with a small mosque built by a man to whom the Hidden *Imam* appeared in a dream 300 years ago. Now the site has hugely expanded with Government money building new areas for pilgrims, and the well is hidden behind the mosque in a corner, a covered rectangle with a stone well you can't really see with a cover round it, marbled to knee-height and then a steel grille of ten bars painted green all round and on top, between which I suppose a dozen people dropped messages to the Hidden *Imam*, including our driver. After a while all the people went and I was alone. Took my photos. R took one of me. Mountains in the distance. The Second Coming will be in a barriered-off area that is rather squalid. The well is barely wide enough to allow a well-built man to descend...

To the Jamkaran mosque, 300 years old. Went in without my boots and sat cross-legged among 50 others, many *mullah*s – the black turbans being descended from the Prophet – and while our driver engaged a *mullah* in conversation about healing, meditated and asked God to stop a nuclear conflict involving Iran if it was his wish to do so. Dedicated myself to help in any small way I can. But I have a sense of foreboding. It's inevitable that Iran will be attacked. A poignant meditation with the international crisis going on outside Iran.

On to Qom and Ayatollah Khomeini's low house behind a wall. Took my shoes off and stood in the entrance, went up a few stairs, turned right and I was in Khomeini's living-room where a *mullah* sat interpreting the *Koran* for a man in a white turban while another man sipped tea. They looked horrified that I had wandered in and taken photos. A room at the back of what used to be his office. The other side, a famous

Ayatollah was receiving two women in black chadors to give advice."

Extract from Nicholas Hagger's The Last Tourist in Iran:
"According to local belief the Hidden *Imam* had come out of occultation to pray to Allah in the Jamkaran mosque, a story similar to that associated with Fatima in Portugal, where Catholics believe the Virgin Mary appeared six times to three children in 1917.

I knew I had to go to the Jamkaran well, which used to be an isolated well on the edge of the Dasht-e Kavir desert but had recently, following Ahmadinejad's sponsorship, increased in importance. It was not in any of the guidebooks, and I had been told that non-Muslims would not be allowed to enter the site. Jamkaran had been left off the itinerary that had been sent from Tehran, and I had protested and had it reinstated.

We arrived in Jamkaran, flat sand with rocky hills, distant lunar mountains and low mud-walled tops and homes. Farhad said, 'Many religions have a saviour figure, a Messiah. Christianity had Jesus. Zoroastrianism had a saviour. Buddhism also had a saviour. Shiism has the 12th *Imam*. Shias believe the 12th *Imam* is absent but is present at the Jamkaran well. He went down the well on a Wednesday, and so there are many services in Jamkaran on a Tuesday evening. Pilgrims come from Tehran and Isfahan to pray in the mosque. He will return, accompanied by Jesus on a mule on the Day of Judgement to save the world from cruelty and disorder. He will come on a Friday. People pray to him, "Please come and help us, we can't wait." Until 1970 Jamkaran used to be a tiny place, just a well in the desert with a small mosque first built over a thousand years ago and rebuilt 300 years ago, but it was extended after the Revolution.'

Visible from a distance against low mountains were a blue dome, two minarets, three green domes and a lot of outbuildings with arches. We parked outside high railings, and put our hoods over our heads.

Farhad said, 'Let me go first. Just walk quickly behind me, it depends on the man on the gate.'

The man on the gate was in a blue padded jacket. He looked hard at me, but I kept walking and did not make eye contact. Then I was through and in the compound and hurrying across a large open space towards the distant blue dome, my hood down.

We bore left past an enormous hangar where women could wait in hot weather, shaded from the sun, and skirted the mosque with a pale blue dome. 'It was built by a man to whom the *Mahdi* appeared in a dream,' Farhad said, 'saying, "Build a mosque by the well."'

Behind the mosque there was a stretch of open paved ground surrounded by crash barriers, like an empty car park. To the right of pine trees against the blue sky there was a small brick single-storey building with crash-barrier railings in front of it where I could see half a dozen people. 'That's the well,' Farhad said, and I felt a sense of disappointment. It could have been a brick bus shelter.

We hurried on and found the crash barriers had a second tier on them, bringing them up to head height. We found a way in and stood before a grubby, much-scuffed, white, enamel-looking base ('marble,' Farhad said) two feet by two feet and between knee- and waist-high, covered with a two-foot-by-two-foot green steel grille of ten bars, which brought it up to chest-height. It was made of metal, and there were ten bars on each of the four sides and on top. The bars were not wide apart but left enough room for a folded piece of paper to be pushed through so that it fell into the well below.

The well was barely wide enough to allow a well-built man to descend. Even a thin man might have got stuck, though in the 9th century it would have been a two-foot-by-two-foot opening in the ground without the chest-high appendage. The whole thing looked like an air-vent for an underground bunker.

Yet this barred-off area was where the Shia Second Coming would take place, where the world would be saved. It was all so ordinary. There was a very worn green metal table next to the well where messages could be written, the green paint on the surface having been rubbed away long ago by hordes of hands writing messages.

Farhad gave me a message sheet with green writing on it. He said, 'It's in Arabic, not Persian. Arabic is the language of prayer. It's like Catholics having prayers in Latin. The language of the *Koran* and prayers is Arabic.'

I asked, 'What does the text say, does it say, "Come quickly?"' He scanned the prayer. 'It says to the Hidden *Imam*, "You are very generous, give us grace." There is nothing about "Come quickly".'

I watched half a dozen students in jeans and padded jackets post their messages through to the Hidden *Imam* below. Our driver had somehow appeared wearing a woollen hat. He was writing a message on his message sheet.

What happened to all the messages? Did they just accumulate down there? Were there years and years of soggy messages clogging the bottom of the well? Or was a receptacle, a tray, suspended across the well to catch the messages and was it lifted up and emptied each night? I inspected the white base for signs of a door. I could not bring myself to ask.

'Does our driver believe that his prayer will be answered?' I asked Farhad.

'Of course,' Farhad replied. 'All Shias believe that.' I stood and gazed on where the Hidden *Imam* and Jesus would emerge for their Second Coming, and then the half-dozen students and our driver moved away and I had the well all to myself. I had been told that non-Muslims would not be allowed into the compound, let alone near the well, yet here I was, on my own by the top of the well. I peered down between the top bars to see if there was any sign of life down the well, but it was all pitch-black.

I thought of what the woman on the plane had said: 'The Hidden *Imam* is everywhere.' And I thought of the Iranian Cabinet standing where I was standing and President Ahmadinejad stuffing his pledge and contract between the slats, localising the Hidden *Imam* to the bottom of the well. It is the mystery of divinity in all cultures that it – He – can appear in a particular place and time and yet also be everywhere. Both localisation and ubiquity – universality – are attributes of deity.

Aware that the chaos in Iraq was linked to the need to create the right conditions for an imminent divine event to happen here, I tore myself away from the well very reluctantly and walked back round the rear side of the mosque, past building work – rows of columns with bent iron rods poking out of their open tops, surrounded by low scaffolding.

I judged the blue-tiled entrance and its domed stalactites under a sun to be 300 years old. Khomeini and Khamenei peered down from either side of the arch. The pale-blue, bulbous, onion-shaped dome above it looked very beautiful.

'Come on,' Farhad said. 'We'll take our shoes off.'

We entered in our socks, our driver as well. We padded through to a large hall with columns where about 50 Iranians were praying: standing, sitting or kneeling with their foreheads to the earth. They were all praying in the direction of Mecca, of course, and the well was at a slight angle, beyond the right-hand corner of the mosque. They all ignored me.

'Look, there are several *mullah*s,' Farhad said. 'The ones with the black turban are descendants from the Prophet. Not the white-turban ones, the black-turban. Let's sit down. Look, silk carpets, Tabriz motif, all the same. These are very expensive carpets.' (He seemed to have no problem in talking while his neighbours were praying. In a church this would be unacceptable, but in a mosque it seemed to be in order.)

So I sat, shoeless, a stone's-throw from the well which was just beyond the right-hand corner wall, and, with *mullah*s before me and on either side of me, closed my eyes and went to the Light. Quietly I offered myself as a means to defuse the international crisis if the Light so willed, to act as a messenger if it was God's will.

I asked the Light to descend into human intransigence and sort out the situation short of war, and to leave it so there was no threat to mankind from nuclear weapons, and then I asked the Light to shine down the well and cleanse it and purify all hostility and aggressiveness and make it a place of peace. I asked the Light to stop a nuclear conflict involving Iran if it was its wish. Then I said to the Light, 'Here I am, sitting in pre-war Iran by the well, please guide me in my coming literary work about the clash between civilisations.' And the Light shone brightly into my soul. But I came to with a sense of foreboding, a renewed conviction that it was inevitable that Iran will be attacked. It was a poignant meditation, so near the holy well with the international crisis outside Iran so intense.

I looked round me. I had gone deep and had been oblivious of time. Farhad had his eyes open. He said, 'Our driver is talking to the *mullah*.' I looked and saw our driver sitting on carpet, talking, listening, nodding and talking again to a lithe *mullah* in a white turban who spoke vigorously, also sitting under his brown robes.

'He has been talking a long time,' Farhad said. What was the driver discussing? We stood up and waited nearby, not interrupting but hoping to catch our driver's attention and signal it was time to go. And now I was standing near the front, the only Westerner on the site, let alone in the building, men were giving me looks as if to say, 'What is this Westerner doing here? Get him out at once.'...

At last the driver saw us and said goodbye to the *mullah*, who gave me a sharp look and then returned to his devotions.

Outside the driver said, Farhad told me, that he had asked how many had been healed by the Hidden *Imam* at the well. The *mullah* had told him of many cases of people who had been healed since the Hidden *Imam* appeared in a dream to the builder of the mosque, so many that it seemed to have become the Shia Lourdes. Which is why the well had come to be known as the 'Well of Requests'.

As we walked back to the car I commented on the amount of building work that was evident. There seemed to be at least four new large buildings going up. They looked like grandstands. Perhaps the government was building grandstands so that the

Second Coming of the Hidden *Imam* and of Jesus could be witnessed by vast crowds?

'They are to receive pilgrims,' Farhad said. 'The present Government has expanded this site, and is catering for increased pilgrims.'

I could see that President Ahmadinejad, who was reported on the internet as saying that 2008 will see the return of the Hidden *Imam*, was pouring Government money into the site so that when the great event happened the infrastructure would be able to cope with the many thousands of pilgrims who would descend on Jamkaran. In the 17th century there had been a belief that the Messiah would come in 1656 – Menasseh ben Israel, the Jewish leader, had believed the Messiah was Cromwell – and again I was struck by the parallel between contemporary Iran and the fervour of the 17th century."

23 January 2007. Extract from Nicholas Hagger's Diaries:
"D typed up half the *Armageddon* summary, and I have now finished the other half."

17 February 2007. Extract from Nicholas Hagger's Diaries:
"Mulled over epic. I must attach myself to the American civilisation to produce epic. Iran is the adversary. I am on the side of the Americans, and must overtly be sympathetic to the Syndicate and must salute Bush as that is what epic-writers do. Epic is a stage-16 phenomenon. It's the American civilisation, not the European civilisation, that is producing epic now. Heath-Stubbs' epic was at the wrong time which is why it seems archaistic. He should have tied it to America. Compare Auden, connecting his poems to America and widening his readership."

1 May 2007. Extract from letter to Christopher Ricks:
"The American book (*The Secret Founding of America*) is out today.... I finished the book on Iran very quickly and it will be out in the autumn, the first literary look at Iran since Robert Byron's *The Road to Oxiana*. I have planned the next epic but it may have to wait a while as I have to finish a book on my philosophy, to be titled *Universalism*, by June 2008. This will reconnect philosophy with the universe, and Ann and I will visit the Galapagos Islands in July and Antarctica in November. Getting up to date on recent developments in cosmology will seep into the epic, to good effect. It's all go!"

15 May 2007. Extract from letter to Christopher Ricks:
"Very many thanks for your kindness in having Tony and me to tea yesterday. Tony was very impressed with your knowledge of Mike Leigh and films, and I thoroughly enjoyed our invigorating catching up....

I look forward to visiting you in Oxford for a discussion on *Crusaders* when you are over here in the summer."

12 July 2007. Extract from letter to Christopher Ricks:
"You very kindly said that we might meet in Oxford about my next poetic epic.

I am away from July 23 to August 12 and from August 17 to 31. I don't know if you are around in Oxford in September?"

23 July 2007. Extract from letter from Christopher Ricks:
"I'm sorry that I'll not be in Oxford next month – on 31 July we return to Boston till a few days, only, in November."

15 August 2007. Extract from letter to Christopher Ricks:
"I am probably too committed to start *Crusaders* in 2007, but I will make a start by mid-2008."

19 February 2008. Extract from letter to Christopher Ricks:
"I now have a bird's eye view of the universe and am up to date with all the many developments. It has been a perfect grounding for the coming epic, which will develop some of the themes in *Overlord* and tackle an epic on Bush/bin Laden (originally called *Crusaders*, now provisionally called *Holy War* at my publisher's urging – to which I am weakening as a novel has appeared called *Crusaders*, about New Labour and not about the real crusading theme, but "stealing" my title nevertheless). If you could spare time for a walk, or a talk, when you are over here in the summer, I would be delighted. I do not have to go abroad this year, and so will not "miss the occasion" this time – if you can manage it.

I enclose a copy of *The Last Tourist*, not for you to read up about Iran, which I know is not your theme, but so that you can see how the research I did in Iran into the War on Terror is shaping up – partial groundwork for the coming epic.

I have always tried to reflect national and international themes in my work, and I am convinced that if Tennyson were alive today and looking to continue his reflections on the charge of the Light Brigade in the Crimean War, then he would take a look at how to write something enduring about the War on Terror. *Overlord* touched on a national theme – everyone knows about the Second World War – and the coming epic can make useful connections and say something important about the contemporary world, quarrelling with myself rather than with those running the world. Now that I have finished my philosophical and historical works, I am turning my undivided attention to completing my literary output."

Nicholas Hagger discontinued his thinking on Armageddon *to write* The Last Tourist *in Iran from 21 January to 4 March, and then* The Lost Englishman *until early June. At the same time he was working on* Collected Verse Plays *and the index of* Collected Stories. *He had to make 25 live radio broadcasts to the US between May and July 2007, regarding* The Secret Founding of America. *He worked on two other prose works and began* The New Philosophy of Universalism *in July. This was finished in early May 2008.*

23 May 2008. Extract from Nicholas Hagger's Diaries:
"Cornwall. Thought long and hard about the epic and made notes on the story."

26 May 2008. Extract from Nicholas Hagger's Diaries:
"The nuclear Hiroshima in America is Armageddon – I am back with this as a title. It does not happen, but I must evoke it as a nightmare that might happen. It is more active than *Crusaders* or *Holy War* or *World Lords* (or *World Lord*). *Armageddon and*

the Triumph of Universal Order? Yes, it's a threat to order, which triumphs over it."

Nicholas Hagger returned to Armageddon *at the end of May 2008 and completed the first five books by early September 2008. He then stopped to write two prose works,* The Revolution that Didn't Happen *and* The Libyan Revolution.

10 July 2008. Extract from letter to Christopher Ricks:
"*The New Philosophy of Universalism* (140,000 words), an attempt at a Theory of Everything which calls for a revolution in modern philosophy, is out on 29 May 2009. I've started *Armageddon*, the next poetic epic on the War on Terror, sequel to *Overlord*, and have finished Book One (September 11) and am on Book Two (Afghanistan). The only one of my predecessors to have attempted two poetic epics is Homer. (Milton's *Paradise Regained* surely does not count as a full poetic epic as the poem has only four books as opposed to twelve and covers 55 pages instead of 277.)

At the same time I have to do two short books for anniversaries next year: my memories of the miners' strike for the 25th anniversary of the Brighton bomb, to be called *The Revolution That Didn't Happen*; and a memoir of the Libyan Revolution for the 40th anniversary of Gaddafi's revolution. This will include all the topical newspaper articles I wrote in Libya – topical in its pure sense of 'place' rather than 'contemporary'. Next year will be a heavy year but both these memoirs will be worth doing. If Byron had left a memoir of the Peterloo Riots of 1819 or of the main campaign in the Greek-Turkish War of 1823-4, it would be interesting to connect these to his poetic works.

As to the epic, I am in blank verse again and am proceeding in my chosen direction, but would welcome a chat if you are in Oxford or anywhere in the UK and can spare the time. You're bound to come up with an angle I ought to be thinking about.

I am in the Isle of Wight from July 21 to 25 – five days in Tennyson's bedroom at Farringford, hoping that during the nights his Ghost will pour good inspiration and ideas into my slumbering ear (as distinct from the poison Hamlet's father had poured into *his* slumbering ear). This is probably something you did when you were steeped in Tennyson? If not, and if you would like to take a look at the inside of Farringford without fuss while Ann and I are there, we'd be delighted to see you to revisit Tennyson haunts in the immediate vicinity of Farringford and have lunch. If it is feasible I will think about the logistics of ferries etc.

We are in Cornwall from August 3 to 28, when I need to be writing, or at least thinking, about Iraq. With hindsight I was so fortunate to spend a year lecturing at the University of Baghdad in 1961/2."

29 July 2008. Extract from letter to Christopher Ricks:
"As usual you provide a new angle: Tennyson and war, and how Wellington would deploy his energies in Heaven, find "other nobler work to do/Than when he fought at Waterloo". (I assume you were thinking of these lines.) What we effect in an after-life if there is one.

By way of circumlocutory answer, let me tell you that I found Farringford immensely inspirational. I had not realised that so little has changed there since Tennyson's time, and I quickly tapped into Tennyson as a private, family man, sweeping leaves during the day and reading to Emily most evenings in the ante-room next to the old drawing-room, as described in Emily's *Farringford Journal*. (Arguably he read to her too much and should have spent more time working in the evenings.) I quickly found my way up to the attic room, no. 17, where he wrote *Maud*, 'The Charge of the Light Brigade' and the first four Idylls. From the window he looked down on the wood and though he may have been thinking of Rosa Baring and Harrington Hall I am sure he (compositely) introduced *this* wood – the hollow behind the wood is still there – and the picket gate through which he led Maud into the garden. I went over the bridge and found the rough spot where the dismantled summer-house was located where he wrote 'Enoch Arden' in a fortnight and 'The Holy Grail'. I had to climb into Maiden's Croft as access from the wood is barbed-wired off, and I hunted for the stone base of the summer-house but could not find it as the grass was waist high and too thick.

But by far the most interesting room in Farringford is the new study he worked in from 1871. The furniture is different, but the fireplace is the same. I took to going there after dinner with some papers. I sat exactly where he sat when he copied out 'Crossing the Bar' and read it to Nurse Durham, having scribbled it on the back of an envelope on the ferry between Lymington and Yarmouth, and of course the last Idylls. I also went there first thing in the morning. On all occasions I had the room to myself and every time I entered the room I was confronted – smacked would be a more truthful word – by a something, a force, a presence that was very strong. It tingled my spine, prickled my scalp, made the hairs on my arms stand up and my forehead clammy, and generally gave me the creeps so I felt I was being watched while I worked.

I have not felt anything like it since Otley Hall, where my bedroom (the old banqueting hall in Bacon's day) was reputedly haunted and where the temperature was always icy and I had to go to sleep with weird small lights floating round the room – one of the reasons I got rid of Otley Hall as at night it was not pleasant. Tennyson's study was not unpleasant, and I persevered.

The electric light switches didn't work and so I was in there alone in fading gloom as dusk became dark, and I got into a relationship with whatever it was and found my questions were being answered. For example, I was trying to think how to combine the Grail myth with the Armageddon myth in my new epic, two seemingly disparate and irreconcilable strands. While in the study I found myself writing out seven points and staring at the answer on my page. I am aware that Tennyson is not in a good position to give advice on unity matters as the *Idylls* lack unity (as you pointed out in *Tennyson*). *Overlord* has far more unity than the *Idylls* and Emily, instead of monopolising all his evenings being read to uncritically, should have pointed this out in a constructive way so he could do some reshaping. (But was she up to doing this?)

It was *very* weird – in Hamlet's sense of "There are more things in Heaven and Earth, Horatio, than are dreamt of in your philosophy". I suppose I spent between three and four hours in the study during the five days I was in Farringford, and the energy was very strongly present all the time I was there. When it got too dark to read my words I'd go back to Tennyson's bedroom (room 3) and the presence followed me down and arrived about a minute after I sat in the window.

This phenomenon has not persisted since I left Farringford. I was only jesting when I wrote in my last letter of having inspiration poured into my slumbering ear, and Farringford gave me more than I bargained for. Whether it happens to everyone or whether I was singled out I don't know. I've included an account of all this in my invocation to Tennyson in book two of *Armageddon*.* If people think I'm mad, so be it, but something happened and I was on the receiving end without seeking it and so it should be in to be truthful for the open-minded. Readers don't have to believe it.

Back to the after-life. What do the dead effect? Presumably they continue their soul-making/heightening of consciousness in different circumstances, perhaps with an ability to return to favourite haunts and to be aware to what's happening on Earth. Eliot thought the dead are among the living, mix with us though we do not see them. In *The New Philosophy of Universalism* I include the *possibility* of an after-life, how there *might* be a survival of life. This is linked to 12 levels of consciousness, which I list. In *Overlord* I describe Hell and Heaven – Eisenhower is taken to both as Odysseus, Aeneas and (guided by Virgil) the poet are in Homer, Virgil and Dante. For your amusement I include a few pages. In my new epic there will be visits to Hell/the Underworld and Heaven and I must sharpen my vision of these. I think in *Overlord* there is more separation between the dead and the living than there will be in *Armageddon*. We'll see....

You will of course understand that I don't have to believe in the Hell and Heaven I am describing just as Homer and Virgil did not have to believe in their Underworlds, which are poetic images. I just have to suspend my disbelief. The wonderful thing about poetry is that you can offer an image without having to prove it in terms of a justifying source. I shall have fun in deciding on a new crowd to place in my Underworld. I did this towards the end of *Overlord*, and though *Overlord* was apparently one of the main topics of conversation at Spender's funeral, I was informed, no one has twigged on some of my cheeky placings of members of the cultural Establishment in the Underworld in terms of perceived undeveloped levels in their consciousness. See enclosed sheet for your entertainment – no prizes for guessing, identification is very easy. (I am reminded of Cinna the poet, 'Burn him for his bad verses, then.')

We also made a couple of visits to Shanklin and got into Eglantine Cottage, which is now incorporated into two houses with separate front doors, a guest-house and restaurant, both just closed, the restaurant about to open as a gift shop. Mrs Williams, the landlady, lived downstairs and you can still see an original back window. Keats had a tiny upstairs room where he could see both sea and chine, and a bedroom next door. In the first room he wrote *Otho the Great* with Brown, and bits of 'Lamia' during the summer of 1819 just after finishing the Odes, knowing he wouldn't survive the winter unless he went south from London for warm air. I believe it was to be near Keats' Shanklin that Tennyson stayed in nearby Bonchurch with his friends, and then got diverted to Freshwater.

We went to 'Carisbrooke's noble chase' and I was struck that Keats, looking out of his lodgings window, at the castle, should write "A thing of beauty is a joy forever", which tells you nothing about what he was looking at. Keats did not have an objective eye on such occasions, and went off into subjective reflection too readily. I would have included a portrait of the ruined castle. Like Keats I emerged from the bottom of the chine and looked at the sea, and again the memorable sonnet he wrote, 'It keeps eternal whisperings around/Desolate shores' is lacking in objectivity, and is one remove from what you actually *see* as you emerge from the chine: the sea, a little foam, a long sandy beach with breakwaters and the 10,000-year-old cliffs of the chine on either side. I make these points to define (indirectly) how I have proceeded in *Classical Odes*, which describe natural scenery far more objectively than Keats does – hence the distinction between Classical and Romantic....

This has been a longer letter than usual because I thought you'd like me to share the extraordinary happenings in the Farringford study."

* Subsequently moved to Book Four.

20 October 2008. Extract from letter to Christopher Ricks:
"There's not a lot to tell you. I got to just under half-way through *Armageddon* and have had to put it aside to write *The Revolution That Didn't Happen*, a personal memoir of the events of 1984 (begun on 17 August and finished yesterday, i.e. nine weeks from first thought to last dot), and will soon start *The Libyan Revolution*, to appear on the fortieth anniversary of the 1969 revolution. I hope to get back to *Armageddon* in mid-December."

Nicholas Hagger resumed Armageddon *in early January 2009 and finished the last seven books by the end of June. He worked on the whole poem into July.*

9 February 2009. Extract from letter to Christopher Ricks:
"I would have enjoyed hearing you on Hardy, but I'll be there on May 11 for your finale on Eliot. Am now deeply into *Armageddon* (second epic)."

13 May 2009. Extract from letter to Christopher Ricks:
"As to me, I told you I have nearly finished *Armageddon*, my second poetic epic about the War on Terror, again drawing on Dante. It runs from 9/11 to February 2009 – just over seven years' tribulation – and Armageddon is threatened by nuclear-suitcase bombs bin Laden seems to have bought from the Chechens and others, his plan to set them off in ten American cities simultaneously – I don't want to panic you, but I have been into it and that was his plan – and his attempt to revive the Caliphate in Baghdad. I doubt if you have been made aware of this subcurrent to the War on Terror, its actual justification, in the American press.

War is a rich vein for a poet to mine, and having mined the Second World War – I can recall lying in bed listening to the doodlebugs cutting out and waiting for explosions when I was four or five and wanting to know why Hitler was doing it, trying to kill me – I have now done this contemporary war in a balanced way. It will appear next year....

It's narrative verse which looks back to Dante, Milton and Tennyson, and creates a world. It still comes under your principles but is obviously different from the short poems you prefer. But I am pleased with bits of both *Overlord* and *Armageddon*, and consider them worth doing. Pound told me, 'You can do it,' and I am pleased to have got them done and to have justified his faith in my ability to get them done.

I have a book on Libya, part eyewitness and part assessment of the last forty years, *The Libyan Revolution*, out in August. Asa Briggs urged me to write this in 1978, and it's taken the 40th anniversary of the revolution to prod me into pushing other things aside and getting it done. I wrote it quickly, like the Iran book, in six weeks, so it did not hold up more pressing works too long. My book on the founding of America, which grew out of my time at Otley Hall, *The Secret Founding of America*, is out in paperback in the US, also in August. (I believe that was also written in six weeks – I strictly ration the time I spend on non-creative works.)"

2. Visits by Nicholas Hagger to Countries/Places Relevant to *Armageddon*

1957	March/April	Italy – Rome, Licenza (Horace's villa), Naples, Avernus, Pompeii, Herculaneum, Mount Vesuvius, Sorrento, Capri, Paestum, Syracuse, Catania, Mount Etna
1958	August/September	Greece – Athens, Thermopylae, Delphi (Oracle), Thebes, Sounion, Marathon, Mount Parnassus, Eleusis, Dafni (Daphnae), Megara, Corinth, Patras, Olympia, Pylos, Sphacteria, Kalanai, Tripolis, Argos, Nauplion, Epidavros (Epidaurus), Tiryns, Mycenae, Crete (Knossos, Phaestos, Gourna), Rhodes, Mykonos, Delos
1961-2	October-June	Iraq – Baghdad, Ctesiphon, Rutba, Falluja, Babylon, Nimrod (site of Tower of Babel), Gourna, Basra, Shatt al-Arab
1962	January	Jordan – Jerusalem (Mount of Olives, Gethsemane, Calvary), Amman, Jericho, Qumran, Bethany Syria – Damascus Lebanon – Beirut
1966	June/August	USSR – Nakhodka, Khabarovsk, Moscow
1968	November	Tunisia – Tunis, Carthage
1968-70	November-June	Libya – Tripoli, Sabratha, Leptis Magna, Gourna (or Souk al-Jum'a), Ghadames
1970	February	Egypt – Cairo, Memphis, Saqqara, Luxor, Alexandria, El-Alamein
	July	Tunisia – Medenine, Gabes, Hammamet Algeria – Souk Ahras, Algiers, Oran Morocco – Tangiers Italy – Rapallo (Pound)

1993	April/May	Italy – Florence (Dante), Pisa
	July	USA – New York, Boston, Niagara Falls, Washington, Philadelphia, Florida (Orlando, St Petersburg, Daytona)
1995	July	Turkey – Istanbul, Troy (Homer), Guzelyali, Kusadasi, Ephesus, Seljuk, Didyma Greece – Samos, Patmos, Athens, Kefallonia, Ithaca (Homer), Athens, Eleusis
	October	Russia – St Petersburg, Moscow, Yalta Italy – Sorrento, Mount Vesuvius, Solfatara, Cumae (Sibyl), Avernus, Pompeii, Herculaneum, Oplontis, Amalfi, Paestun, Capri, Naples (Virgil's tomb)
1996	July	Greece – Athens, Sounion, Delphi (Oracle), Olympia, Mystra, Mycenae, Epidavros, Pylos, Corinth, Dafni (Daphnae), Rhodes, Patmos, Kusadasi, Crete, Knossos, Santorini, Akrotiri
	September	Italy – Rome, Ostia, Licenza (Horace's villa), Tivoli, Vatican
1998	July	Italy – Verona, Venice, Padua, Sirmione
	October	USA – Boston, New Bedford, Martha's Vineyard, Richmond, Jamestown
2000	July	Sicily – Palermo, Trabia, Agrigento, Marsala, Motya, Segesta, Selinunte, Syracuse, Mount Etna, Taormina, Catania
	September/October	Italy – Turin (Turin Shroud), Rome (Augustus's Palatine)
2001	May	Cruise – Athens, Chania, Benghazi, Cyrene, Tripoli, Sabratha, Sousse, El Djem, Tunis, Carthage, Porto Empdocle, Agrigento, Trapani, Erice (Aeneas), Cagliari, Mahon, Ciudadela, Barcelona
2005	January/February	Egypt – Sharm el-Sheikh, Sinai, Luxor, Cairo
2007	January	Iran – Tehran, Shiraz, Persepolis, Yazd, Nain, Isfahan, Natanz, Kashan, Jamkaran, Qom, Saveh, Hamadan, Arak
2008	July	Devon – Totnes
	August	Isle of Wight – Farringford, Shanklin

| 2009 | February | Paris – Conciergerie, Louvre, Saint-Sulpice, Notre-Dame |
| | February/March | North Norway – Oslo, Tromso, Honningsvag, Hurtigruten, Alta |

3. Maps that Throw Light on Areas of *Armageddon*:

A. Caliphate

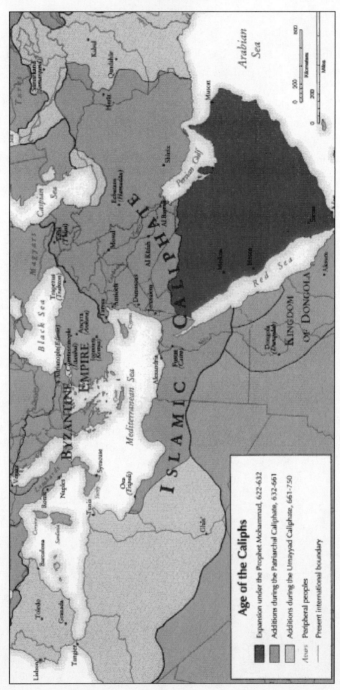

Original Caliphate

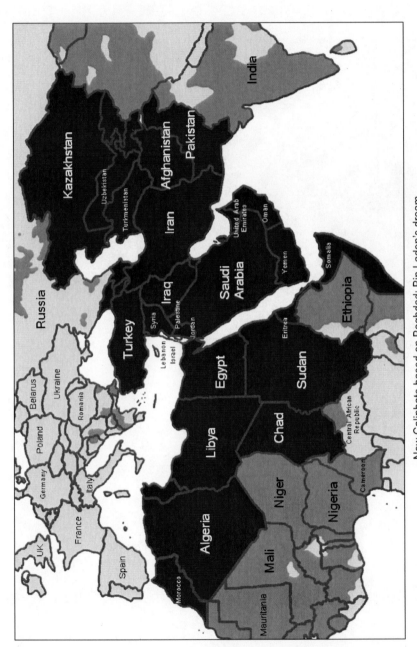

New Caliphate based on Baghdad: Bin Laden's dream

– Al-Qaeda's planned Caliphate centred on Baghdad and dwarfing Europe, as it may look within a decade of the withdrawal of US troops from Iraq

– Concentrations of Muslim populations outside the New Caliphate, 1995

(Source: CIA)

B. War Zones

Central Area of New Caliphate/War Zones

Enlarged area of new Caliphate showing countries
referred to in *Armageddon*/war zones

Afghanistan

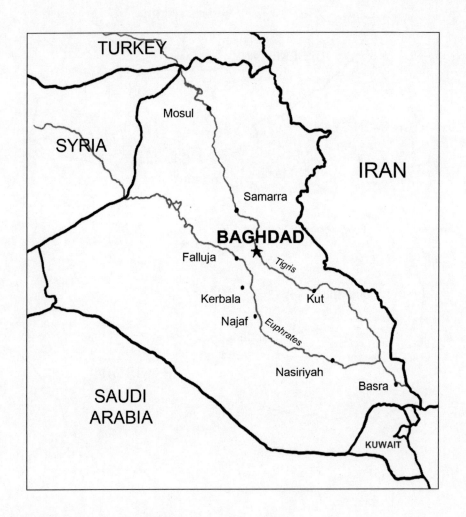

TURKEY

Mosul

SYRIA

IRAN

Samarra

BAGHDAD

Falluja

Tigris

Kerbala

Kut

Najaf

Euphrates

Nasiriyah

Basra

SAUDI
ARABIA

KUWAIT

Iraq

C. Greater Israel/Greater Iran

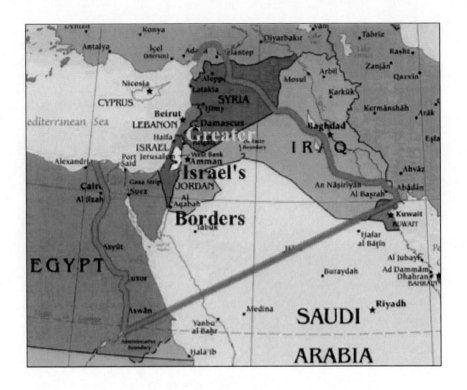

Greater Israel's Borders

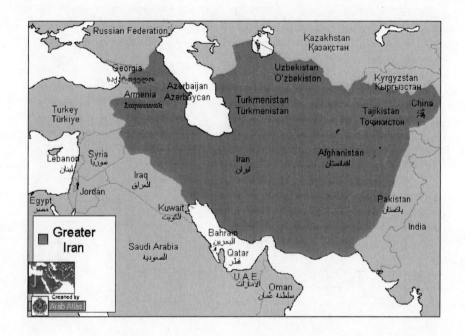

Greater Iran's Borders

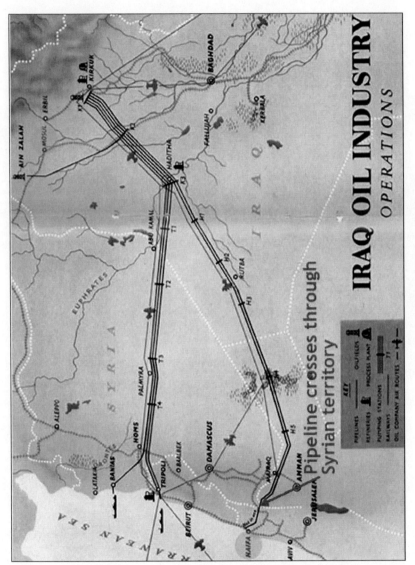

Kirkuk (near Mosul)-Haifa Pipeline

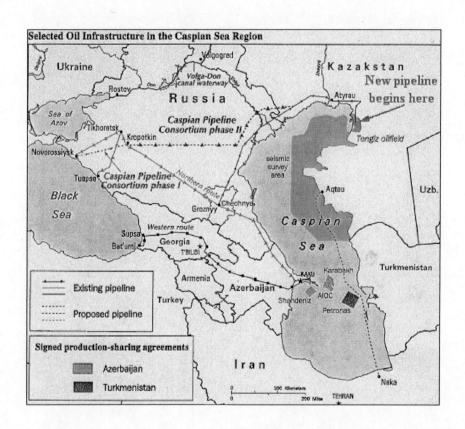

Selected Oil Infrastructure in the Caspian Sea Region

Pipeline from Baku to Supsa via Georgia

D. Oil and Gas Pipelines

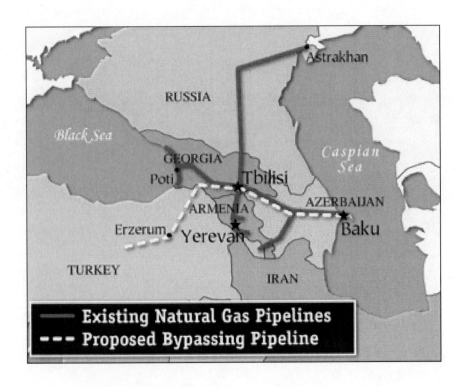

Gas pipelines crossing Abkhazia and South Ossetia, Georgia

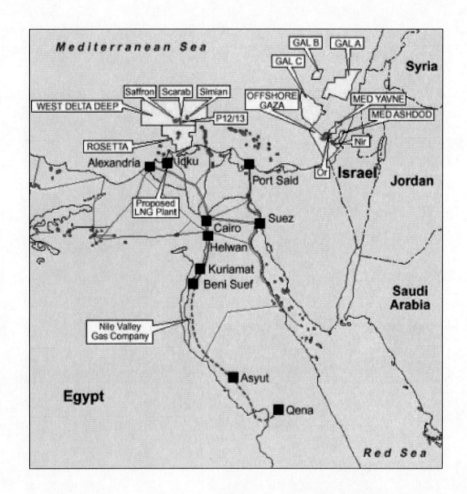

Gas fields in the Mediterranean

Gas field off the Gaza coast

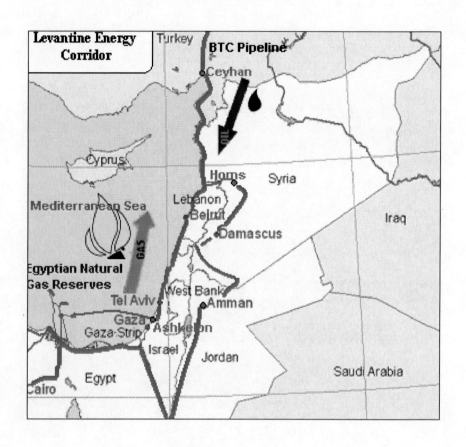

Levantine Energy Corridor

Maps based on websites:

BOOKS

O is a symbol of the world, of oneness and unity. In different cultures it also means the "eye," symbolizing knowledge and insight. We aim to publish books that are accessible, constructive and that challenge accepted opinion, both that of academia and the "moral majority."

Our books are available in all good English language bookstores worldwide. If you don't see the book on the shelves ask the bookstore to order it for you, quoting the ISBN number and title. Alternatively you can order online (all major online retail sites carry our titles) or contact the distributor in the relevant country, listed on the copyright page.

See our website www.o-books.net for a full list of over 500 titles, growing by 100 a year.

And tune in to myspiritradio.com for our book review radio show, hosted by June-Elleni Laine, where you can listen to the authors discussing their books.

MySpiritRadio